D1460444

INTERNATIONAL HANDBOOK OF
ORGANIZATIONAL TEAMWORK AND COOPERATIVE WORKING

INTERNATIONAL HANDBOOK OF **ORGANIZATIONAL TEAMWORK AND COOPERATIVE WORKING**

Edited by

Michael A. West
Professor of Organizational Psychology and Director of Research, Aston Business School, UK

Dean Tjosvold
Chair Professor of Management, Lingnan University, Hong Kong

and

Ken G. Smith
Dean's Chaired Professor of Business Strategy, Robert H. Smith School of Business, University of Maryland, USA

WILEY

Telephone (+44) 1243 779777

Email (for orders and customer service enquiries): cs-books@wiley.co.uk
Visit our Home Page on www.wileyeurope.com or www.wiley.com

Other Wiley Editorial Offices

John Wiley & Sons Inc., 111 River Street, Hoboken, NJ 07030, USA

Jossey-Bass, 989 Market Street, San Francisco, CA 94103-1741, USA

Wiley-VCH Verlag GmbH, Boschstr. 12, D-69469 Weinheim, Germany

John Wiley & Sons Australia Ltd, 33 Park Road, Milton, Queensland 4064, Australia

John Wiley & Sons (Asia) Pte Ltd, 2 Clementi Loop #02-01, Jin Xing Distripark, Singapore 129809

John Wiley & Sons Canada Ltd, 22 Worcester Road, Etobicoke, Ontario, Canada M9W 1L1

Wiley also publishes its books in a variety of electronic formats. Some content that appears in print may not be available in electronic books.

Library of Congress Cataloging-in-Publication Data

International handbook of organizational teamwork and cooperative working / edited by
Michael A. West, Dean Tjosvold, and Ken G. Smith.
p. cm.
Includes bibliographical references and index.
ISBN 0-471-48539-X (alk. paper)
1. Teams in the workplace—Handbooks, manuals, etc. I. West, Michael
A., 1951– II. Tjosvold, Dean. III. Smith, Ken G.
HD66 .I584 2003
658.4′02—dc21 2002152545

British Library Cataloguing in Publication Data

A catalogue record for this book is available from the British Library

ISBN 0-471-48539-X

Typeset in 10/12pt Times and Helvetica by TechBooks Electronic Services, New Delhi, India
Printed and bound in Great Britain by Biddles Ltd, Guildford and King's Lynn
This book is printed on acid-free paper responsibly manufactured from sustainable forestry
in which at least two trees are planted for each one used for paper production.

CONTENTS

ABOUT THE EDITORS

Michael A. West is Director of Research and Professor of Organizational Psychology at Aston Business School, Aston University. He has been a member of the Corporate Performance Programme of the Centre for Economic Performance at the London School of Economics since 1991. He is a member of the Council of the British Psychological Society, and Chair of the Society's Journals Committee.

He has authored, edited, or co-edited 12 books, including *Developing Creativity in Organizations* (1997, BPS) and the *Handbook of Workgroup Psychology* (1996, Wiley). He has also written more than 120 articles for scientific and practitioner publications, and chapters in scholarly books. He is a member of the editorial boards of several international journals, including *Applied Psychology: An International Review* and the *Journal of Organizational Behavior*. He is a past editor of the *Journal of Occupational and Organizational Psychology*.

He is a Fellow of the British Psychological Society, the American Psychological Association, the APA Society for Industrial/Organizational Psychology and the Royal Society for Arts, Manufacture, and Commerce. His areas of research interest are team and organizational innovation and effectiveness, and the well-being of people at work.

Dean Tjosvold is Chair Professor of Management, Lingnan University in Hong Kong. After graduating from Princeton University, he earned his Master's Degree in History and his Ph.D. in the social psychology of organizations at the University of Minnesota, both in 1972. He has taught at Pennsylvania State University, Simon Fraser University, and was visiting professor at the National University of Singapore in 1983–84, the State University of Groningen in The Netherlands, 1991–92, Hong Kong University of Science and Technology, 1994–95, and the City University of Hong Kong, 1995–96.

In 1992, Simon Fraser University awarded him a University Professorship for his research contributions. He received the American Education Research Association's Outstanding Contribution to Cooperative Learning Award in 1998. His review of cooperative and competitive conflict was recognized as the best article in *Applied Psychology: An International Review* for 1998. He is past president of the International Association of Conflict Management. He has published over 200 articles on managing conflict, cooperation and competition, decision making, power, and other management issues. He has served on several editorial boards, including the *Academy of Management Review*, *Journal of Organizational Behavior*, *Journal of Management*, and *Small Group Research*.

He has written 15 books which have been selected by *Fortune*, *Business Week*, Newbridge, and Executive Book Clubs and translated into Chinese and Spanish. These include: *Conflict Management in the Pacific Rim: Perspectives on International Business* (Wiley, 1998) (edited with Kwok Leung); *Psychology for Leaders: Using Motivation, Power, and Conflict to Manage More Effectively* (Wiley, 1995; Chinese Translation, Business Weekly Publication, 1999) (with Mary M. Tjosvold); *The Emerging Leader: Ways to a Stronger Team* (Lexington Books, 1993) (with Mary M. Tjosvold); *Learning to Manage Conflict: Getting People to Work Together Productively* (Lexington Books, 1993); *Teamwork for Customers: Building an Organization that Takes Pride in Serving* (Jossey-Bass, 1993); *Leading a Team Organization: How to Create an Enduring Competitive Advantage* (Lexington Books, 1991) (with Mary M. Tjosvold); *Team Organization: An Enduring Competitive Advantage* (Wiley, 1991); *The Conflict Positive Organization: Stimulate Diversity and Create Unity* (Addison-Wesley's OD series, 1991); *Working Together to Get Things Done: Managing for Organizational Productivity* (Lexington, 1986).

He has given invited seminars at universities in the US, Canada, Europe, and East Asia. He has consulted with large US banks, hotels in Asia Pacific, Canadian, US, and Hong Kong government agencies, family businesses, and organizations in other industries. He is a partner in his family health care business, which has 600 employees and is based in Minnesota.

Ken G. Smith is the Dean's Chaired Professor of Business Strategy in the Robert H. Smith School of Business at the University of Maryland at College Park, where he is also the Chair of the Management, Organization and Entrepreneurship Department. Dr Smith received his MBA in Organizational Behavior from the University of Rhode Island in 1972 and his Ph.D. from the University of Washington in Seattle in 1983. From 1972 to 1980 he was an entrepreneur and chief executive officer in the pump and marine products industries where he developed three separate and successful corporations.

The former editor of the *Academy of Management Review*, Dr Smith has served on a number of editorial boards, including *Academy of Management Journal* and *Academy of Management Executive*. He has published over 50 articles, in such journals as the *Academy of Management Journal*, *Administrative Science Quarterly*, *Strategic Management Journal*, *Management Science*, *Organization Science*, and *Organizational Behavior and Human Decision Processes*, and he has presented numerous papers at national and international meetings, and at many different universities around the world. In addition, he has also published two books: *The Dynamics of Competitive Strategy* (with Grimm and Gannon) (Sage Publishing, 1992); and *Strategy as Action: Industry Competition vs Cooperation* (with Grimm) (West Publishing, 1997).

Dr Smith's research interests in strategic management include strategic positioning, competitive advantage, and the dynamics of competitive and cooperative strategy. He is also a leader in the field of entrepreneurship where his research on the relationship between entrepreneurs and organizational innovation and growth is well known. His research has been supported by grants from the University of Maryland General Research, the National Science Foundation and the Small Business Administration.

In 1991 Dr Smith was a Fulbright Fellow in Strategic Management at the University of Limerick, Plassey, Ireland, and in Spring 2000 was Visiting Professor of Strategy, INSEAD, France. He was elected Fellow to the Academy of Management in 1998.

Professor Smith has participated in a wide variety of executive development programmes, and in 1987, 1990, and 1997 was awarded the Alan Krowe Award from the University of Maryland for teaching excellence. In 1996, Dr Smith was granted the University of Maryland Distinguished Scholar Teacher Award. Dr Smith has been a consultant to a variety of organizations, and is a member of the Academy of Management, the Strategic Management Society, and the Decision Sciences Institute.

LIST OF CONTRIBUTORS

Ritu Agarwal, *University of Maryland, Robert H. Smith School of Business, Decision and Information Technologies, Van Munching Hall, College Park, MD 20742-1815, USA*

James G. Barnes, *Faculty of Business Administration, Memorial University of Newfoundland, St John's, NF A1B 3X5, Canada*

Pamela S. Barr, *Robinson College of Business, Georgia State University, 35 Broad Street, Atlanta, GA 30303, USA*

Michael M. Beyerlein, *Department of Psychology, University of North Texas, PO Box 311277, Denton, TX 76203, USA*

Maureen Blyler, *Department of Sociology, Emory University, 1300 Clifton Road, Atlanta, GA 30322, USA*

Susan E. Brodt, *Fuqua School of Business, Duke University, Box 90120, Durham, NC 27708, USA*

Kevin D. Clark, *Assistant Professor of Strategic Management, College of Commerce and Finance, Villanova University, 80 Lancaster Avenue, Villanova, PA 19085, USA*

Dana R. Clyman, *The Darden School, University of Virginia, 100 Darden Boulevard, Charlottesville, VA 22903, USA*

Russell W. Coff, *Emory University, Goizueta Business School, 1300 Clifton Road, Atlanta, GA 30322-2710, USA*

Peter T. Coleman, *Teachers College, Columbia University, 525 West 120th St, New York 10027, USA*

Steven C. Currall, *Jones Graduate School of Management, Rice University, PO Box 1892, Houston, TX 77251-892, USA*

Carsten K. W. De Dreu, *University of Amsterdam, Department of Psychology, Raetesstraat 15, 1018 WB, Amsterdam, The Netherlands*

Morton Deutsch, *Teachers College, Columbia University, 525 West 120th St, New York 10027, USA*

Robert Drazin, *Goizueta Business School, Emory University, 1300 Clifton Road, Atlanta, GA 30322, USA*

Peter A. Dunne, *Memorial University of Newfoundland, St John's, NF A1B 3X5, Canada*

Amy C. Edmondson, *Associate Professor, Morgan Hall T-93, Harvard Business School, Boston, MA 02163, USA*

Martin Evans, *Professor of Organizational Behavior, Rotman School of Management, University of Toronto, 105 St George Street, Toronto, M5S 3E6, Canada*

Catherine Fieschi, *Director, Centre for the Study of European Governance, School of Politics, University of Nottingham, University Park, Nottingham NG7 2RD, UK*

Mary Ann Glynn, *Goizueta Business School, Emory University, 1300 Clifton Road, Atlanta, GA 30322-2710, USA*

Barbara Gray, *Center for Research in Conflict and Negotiation, 408 Beam Business Administration Bldg, Pennsylvania State University, University Park, PA 16802, USA*

Cheryl L. Harris, *Department of Psychology, University of North Texas, PO Box 311277, Denton, TX 76203, USA*

Giles Hirst, *Aston University, Aston Business School, Birmingham B4 7ET, UK*

Andrew C. Inkpen, *Thunderbird, The American Graduate School of International Management, 15249 N 59th Avenue, Glendale, AZ 85306-6000, USA*

Susan E. Jackson, *94 Rockefeller Road, Room 216, Department of Human Resource Management, School of Management and Labor Relations, Rutgers University, Piscataway, NJ 08854-8054, USA*

David W. Johnson, *Cooperative Learning Center, University of Minnesota, 60 Peik Hall, Minneapolis, MN 55455, USA*

Roger T. Johnson, *Cooperative Learning Center, University of Minnesota, 60 Peik Hall, Minneapolis, MN 55455, USA*

Aparna Joshi, *University of Illinois at Urbana-Champaign, 1401 West Green Street, Urbana, IL 61801, USA*

Robert K. Kazanjian, *Goizueta Business School, Emory University, 1300 Clifton Road, Atlanta, GA 30322, USA*

M. Audrey Korsgaard, *Associate Professor of Management, University of South Carolina, Moore School of Business, Columbia, SC 29208, USA*

Janice Langan-Fox, *Department of Psychology, University of Melbourne, Parkville 3052, Victoria, Australia*

Kwok Leung, *Department of Management, City University of Hong Kong, Tat Chee Avenue, Hong Kong, China*

Xiangfen Liang, *Department of Management, City University of Hong Kong, Tat Chee Avenue, Hong Kong, China*

Lin Lu, *Department of Management, City University of Hong Kong, Tat Chee Avenue, Hong Kong, China*

Joan R. Rentsch, *Associate Professor, Industrial/Organizational Psychology Program, Department of Management, 408 Stokely Management Center, The University of Tennessee, Knoxville, TN 37996-0545, USA*

Christel G. Rutte, *Eindhoven University of Technology, Department of Technology Management, PO Box 513, 5600 MB Eindhoven, The Netherlands*

Harry J. Sapienza, *University of Minnesota, Carlson School of Management, 321 19th Avenue South, Minneapolis, MN 55455, USA*

Ken G. Smith, *Robert H. Smith School of Business, University of Maryland at College Park, College Park, MD 20742, USA*

Cynthia Kay Stevens, *Robert H. Smith School of Business, University of Maryland, Van Munching Hall, College Park, MD 20742, USA*

Dean Tjosvold, *Department of Management, Lingnan University, Tuen Mun, Hong Kong, China*

Daan van Knippenberg, *Erasmus University Rotterdam, Rotterdam School of Management, PO Box 1738, 3000 DR Rotterdam, The Netherlands*

Maxim Voronov, *Teachers College, Columbia University, 525 West 120th St, New York 10027, USA*

Laurie R. Weingart, *Graduate School of Industrial Administration, Carnegie Mellon University, 236A Posner Hall, Pittsburgh, PA 15213, USA*

Michael A. West, *Aston University, Aston Business School, Birmingham B4 7ET, UK*

Greg Young, *Associate Professor, North Carolina State University, College of Management, Department of Business Management, 1326 Nelson, Raleigh, NC 27695-7229, USA*

Jacqueline A. Zelno, *Associate Professor, Industrial/Organizational Psychology Program, Department of Management, 408 Stokely Management Center, The University of Tennessee, Knoxville, TN 37996-0545, USA*

PREFACE

To live, work, and play is to cooperate with others. We express both our collective identity and our individuality in groups and organizations. Our common experiences of living and working together bind us with each other and with our predecessors.

We are also students of cooperation. As we navigate our relationships and reflect on them, we develop our own theories and perspectives. We have values about how people should relate to each other, assumptions about how they do, and we devise complex strategies to guide our communication and conflict management.

Today we face new demands that make cooperative work more vital and more challenging. To meet the pressures of the global marketplace, organizations are moving away from rigid, hierarchical structures to more organic, flexible forms. Groups are developing and marketing products, solving production problems, and creating corporate strategy. Managers are experimenting with participation, high-commitment organizations, self-managing work teams, labour–management cooperation, and gainsharing programmes. These innovations, though they have different backgrounds, all involve the explicit use of teams to accomplish central organizational tasks. The team rather than the individual is increasingly considered the basic building block of organizations.

Teamwork is spilling out across organizational and national boundaries. Many manufacturers form teams with suppliers to boost quality, reduce costs, and assure continuous improvement. International alliances are becoming the accepted way to participate in the global marketplace. American and Japanese automakers and other traditional competitors have developed a wide variety of cooperative strategies. Increasingly, people with different organizational and national loyalties from diverse cultural backgrounds and unequal status are asked to work together.

This handbook provides a comprehensive and critical synthesis of knowledge of cooperative working, with a clear focus on the psychological and social processes and emerging relationships that can facilitate and obstruct successful teamwork. The editors have brought together established and emerging perspectives from the world's leading authorities on collaboration within and between organizations. Professionals and researchers can turn to the following chapters for guidance on best practices, methods, successful and problematic experiences, and concepts and agendas for future research. This handbook assists students, professionals, and researchers to appreciate that interdependence pervades organizational life, understand the critical effects of collaboration on productivity and people, learn frameworks for analysing and strengthening teamwork, and stimulate behavioural research that will extend our knowledge base of cooperation in organizations.

THE BOOK'S ORGANIZATION

The book has five sections with ascending micro to macro scale and complexity. However, we do not, for example, take the boundary between work groups and integrated organizations literally because collaboration cuts across levels. Concepts used to investigate interdependence within a team can help analyse interdependence between groups and organizations. Dynamics within teams affect and are affected by organizational-wide characteristics.

I. Introduction. This section connects the reader and the book, provides an overview, and identifies common concepts and contingencies. Collaboration and interaction are generic terms and refer to the exchange, communication, and mutual influence between individuals, groups, and organizations and are used interchangeably in the book.

II. The Psychology of Individuals in Groups. Although individuals and groups are often considered opposing choices, teams depend upon the drive and competence of individuals and individuals find meaning and support in teams. These chapters examine individuals' psychological orientations and predispositions, needs and aspirations, and cognitive capacities that affect and are affected by teamwork. Chapters also identify conditions under which independent and competitive work may be more useful than cooperation.

III. Work Groups. Organizations are experimenting with self-managing teams, temporary task forces, national sales forces, and work improvement teams. These chapters also investigate central issues in teams, such as team leadership, training for and within teams, and using conflict constructively.

IV. Integrated Organizations. Developing strong intergroup relations is perhaps the most difficult challenge in building a viable team organization. Participative management, alignment of principals and agents, and positive power can help unite organizations. An important part of this section is to focus on the types of organizational structures, processes, and incentives that promote "organizational collaboration". Of special interest is the role of information systems and social networks. Significantly, this section also examines the role of virtual teams and Internet systems for managing teamwork in today's dispersed "netcentric" organizations.

V. Alliances between Organizations. Organizations are seeking competitive advantage by teaming and collaborating with suppliers, customers, stockholders, and even competitors. Such teamwork is made more complex and difficult in the global economy where teams and organizations are connected across cultures and national boundaries. This section explores how firms can use teamwork as a source of competitive advantage. Of special interest is the network organization and how firms use social and intellectual capital developed from teamwork to effectively compete in complex, changing environments. This section also identifies the critical contingencies for effectively using teamwork in supply chain management, relational marketing, and research consortiums.

The issues explored here are fundamental to our understanding of the journey of our species. It is through teamwork and cooperation that we have progressed so far in our understanding of our existence and of this universe and our shaping, for good or ill, of our world. Reading the handbook therefore is an opportunity to deepen our understanding of cooperative work. However, our extensive experience with cooperative work and our own elaborate, largely implicit theories can make it difficult to confront our own biases and consider new theory, ideas, and research open-mindedly. For the editors, it has been a stimulating and challenging intellectual exchange with each other, with the authors who come from many countries and disciplines, and with much inevitably new theoretical and philosophical content. We hope that the readers of this handbook will have a similar challenging and enriching experience.

MAW
DT
KGS
August, 2002

ACKNOWLEDGEMENTS

The editors express their grateful appreciation to all of the contributors to this handbook for their enactment of teamwork and cooperation. From 4 continents and 27 institutions, the 45 contributors cooperated helpfully, positively, and swiftly to all our requests. We also wish to thank Angie Harris of Aston Business School, who was the central hub in this vast communication network. Her patience, good humour, attention to detail, and perseverance were key elements in the production of the handbook. We acknowledge all these unseen contributions with thanks.

MAW
DT
KGS

To my wife Jenny and to our children: Jason, Wesley, Lena, and Colleen, a wonderful team.

DT

To my partner Gillian and our children Ellie, Nik, Tom, and Rosa. You have taught me that kindness is the heart of cooperation.

MAW

To my family Laurie, Cassidy, Conor, Amy, Jason, and Myles; cooperation and love mean a happy life!

KGS

Section I

INTRODUCTION AND CONTEXT OF COOPERATION

1

TEAMWORK AND COOPERATION

FUNDAMENTALS OF ORGANIZATIONAL EFFECTIVENESS

Dean Tjosvold, Michael A. West, and Ken G. Smith

UNDERSTANDING COOPERATION

A straightforward way to consider cooperation is in terms of its outcomes: cooperation occurs when people have strong relationships where they work together well so that they succeed at their tasks. They are not simply a group but have become an effective team. Their cooperation is clear from the results of their collaboration. The issue then is to identify the antecedents and conditions that give rise to this productive teamwork. Researchers often focus on the interaction that collaborators develop. The essence of cooperation is thought to be constructive, pro-social interactions. Cooperation involves helpful, supportive, and integrative actions that in turn help the team succeed at its task and strengthen interpersonal relationships.

In the 1940s, Morton Deutsch (1949, 1973, Chapter 2 this volume) defined cooperation in terms of how individuals and groups believed they were interdependent with each other. Considerable research has developed this perspective and shown how goal interdependence, interaction, and outcomes are related. Deutsch proposed that individuals self-interestedly pursue their goals, but how they believe their goals are related determines how they interact, and their interaction determines outcomes. Individuals may conclude that their goals are structured so that as they move toward achieving their own goals they promote the success, obstruct, or have no impact on the success of others. Deutsch identified these alternatives as cooperation, competition, and independence.

In cooperation, people believe their goals are positively related. They understand their own goal attainment helps others reach their goals; as one succeeds, others succeed. They then share information, exchange resources, and in other ways support each other to act effectively. Mutual expectations of trust and gain through cooperation promote ongoing efforts to support and assist each other (Deutsch, 1962). This promotive interaction results in relationships characterized by positive regard, openness, and productivity.

International Handbook of Organizational Teamwork and Cooperative Working. Edited by M. A. West, D. Tjosvold, and K. G. Smith.

In contrast, people may believe that their goals are competitive, that is, one's goal attainment precludes, or at least makes less likely, the goal attainment of others. People with competitive goals conclude that they are better off when others act ineffectively. This atmosphere of mistrust restricts information and resource exchange. They withhold information and ideas to increase their chances of winning the competition and may even actively obstruct the other's effective actions. These interaction patterns result in mutual hostility, restricted communication, and mutual goal independence occurs when people believe their goals are unrelated. The goal attainment of one neither helps nor hinders the goal attainment of others. Success by one means neither failure nor success for others. People conclude that it means little to them if others act effectively or ineffectively. Independent work creates disinterest and indifference.

In most situations, all three goal interdependencies exist but it is the one that people emphasize that is expected to affect their interaction and outcomes most significantly. People have a choice of whether to emphasize cooperative, competitive, or independent goals (Evans, Chapter 3 this volume).

This theorizing suggests the potential of cooperation but also the demands in developing cooperative work. Competition and independence are viable alternatives that can be highly attractive to individual team members. Moreover, team members must also interact in ways that promote cooperation in order that the team can progress toward the success that reinforces mutual commitment to cooperative work. The next sections discuss the potential for, and challenges to, developing sustained cooperation.

COOPERATION FOR PRODUCTIVITY AND INDIVIDUALITY

Cooperation has been theorized to have a wide range of beneficial effects. Indeed, it provides the basic rationale for an organization and can bridge its two major interfaces: the organization with the environment and the individual with the organization (Fieschi, Chapter 4 this volume). By combining resources and ideas, cooperative work can help an organization innovate and produce value so that it can continue to gain necessary support from customers, governments, and other stakeholders (Dunne & Barnes, Chapter 25 this volume). By providing a rich and rewarding social environment, cooperative work can also integrate organizational members and gain their commitment. For example, specific benefits of cooperation are thought to include mutual assistance and support, division of labor, specialization of effort, accurate communication, open discussion of diverse views, identification of problems and shortcomings, creation of new alternatives, confidence in new ideas, effective risk-taking, and commitment to implementation (West & Hirst, Chapter 15 this volume).

Cooperative teams are practical mediums within which we can foster communication between diverse people and build coalitions that result in innovation. Teams help employees and managers share hunches, doubts, and misgivings and discuss emerging ideas and practices to solve and even find problems. Their mutual support encourages them to consider these problems as opportunities to exploit. They exchange ideas and suggestions that give them a fresh perspective, together withstand frustration, and integrate ideas in unique, effective ways. They share the work of collecting data on their solution, and together debate the virtues and pitfalls. Because they have challenged the idea from several perspectives they have the confidence they can be successful and believe they have the resources and strength to see the idea through. Teams can involve and gain the commitment of representatives from the groups and departments who must implement the innovation.

Organizational members are also thought to gain a great deal through cooperation. They are fulfilled by superior achievement, feel supported, receive feedback, strengthen their self-esteem, and see themselves as part of a larger effort. They develop their individuality as they take on different roles and perform specialized duties. They express and defend their own perspectives and negotiate agreements that promote their self-interests. Rewarding interaction, individual fulfillment, and team success strengthen people's commitment to cooperative goals and form a mutually beneficial cycle.

However, cooperation has been thought to involve costly and potentially inefficient coordination. These costs may distract and nullify any benefits. Group members may only reinforce each other's biases and inadequate reasoning (Coff, Chapter 23 this volume). Cooperative work can also result in significant obstacles and frustrations such as "groupthink" pressures to conform, lowered motivation, social loafing, a willingness to "free-ride," and shirking one's own duties (Rutte, Chapter 17 this volume).

Deutsch (1962) argued that cooperation's effects, even those that are generally useful, may prove counterproductive in the long term. Strong relationships can result in favoritism that discriminates against outsiders and resists necessary change. Cooperators can become overspecialized and unable to adapt to new roles and demands. They may be too open to influence and become vulnerable to exploitation. Cooperation creates dynamics that undermine as well as reinforce it. Moreover, competition has been theorized to promote motivation as people seek to be the best and to pose challenges that strengthen people's resolve and confidence. Studies have shown that competition as well as independence can be constructive and promote productivity under certain conditions.

Recent meta-analyses of hundreds of empirical studies have clarified that over the situations and tasks investigated, cooperation is much more facilitative of productivity and achievement than competition and independence (Johnson & Johnson, Chapter 9 this volume; Johnson & Johnson, 1989; Johnson et al., 1981; Stanne, Johnson, & Johnson, 1999). This general finding holds between groups as well as within them, though cooperation's superiority appears to be less for simple compared to complex tasks. These meta-analyses also indicate that cooperation promotes social support, strong relationships, and self-confidence much more than competition and independence. These results reinforce the practice of relying on teams to accomplish vital organizational tasks.

Although the meta-analyses of the research do not support the claim that competition and independence are widely useful in organizations, they do not imply that cooperative work is always superior. We need much more research to identify the conditions under which competition and independence have important, constructive roles within and between organizations. For example, it may be that competition between groups and organizations is useful when it occurs within a more general cooperative framework (Stanne, Johnson, & Johnson, 1999).

Nor do the strong meta-analyses results imply that cooperation is a quick-fix solution that easily integrates individuals into the organization and the organization with its environment. In addition to identifying the conditions when cooperation is appropriate, teamwork must be well structured before its potential is realized. Cooperation's beneficial cycle should be strengthened and its undermining effects dealt with. Managing cooperation so that it continues to promote individuals and the organization may be the most demanding challenge facing organizations.

THE MANAGEMENT IMPERATIVE

Cooperation between two individuals each with his or her agenda and unique style is often emotionally and intellectually challenging. They must coordinate so that they both choose to cooperate, together develop practical and fair ways to assist each other, and manage their inevitable conflicts. Promoting cooperation within a group of diverse people under pressure to perform is usually significantly more challenging. Leading various departments, teams, and business units each with its own identity to work as a cooperative organization team to meet present demands and prepare for the future can be a most daunting goal (van Knippenberg, Chapter 18 this volume).

Managing cooperation is not getting easier. As chapters in this handbook attest, managers and employees are increasingly asked to work together across disciplinary, organizational, national, and cultural boundaries (Leung, Lu, & Liang, Chapter 27 this volume). They are often geographically dispersed where they must rely on technology to communicate and coordinate (Agarwal, Chapter 21 this volume). Multifunctional teams must coordinate with each other and deal with their discipline differences to develop new products quickly and efficiently (Drazin, Kazanjian, & Blyler, Chapter 22 this volume; Harris & Beyerlein, Chapter 10).

Ongoing trust in strategic alliances typically requires the commitment of both organizations and the individuals who must actually work together, as mistrust at one level can undermine trust at another (Currall & Inkpen, Chapter 26 this volume). Gray and Clyman (Chapter 9 this volume) identify and categorize the many significant obstacles and hurdles to developing integrative consensus with multiple parties. Power and status can be corrupting and invite exploitation (Coleman & Voronov, Chapter 12 this volume).

Research, though it does not specify plans for how managers and employees can manage cooperation, does suggest major ways to proceed. Positively related goals, mutually supportive and open interaction, and team and individual success are the reinforcing ingredients that managers and employees can develop. All participants, not just the leader, must choose to work cooperatively. They feel their destinies are mutually bonded together and that they "are in this together." They trust that other team members will reciprocate. Cooperation involves interaction and procedures, but it also involves the internal, psychological commitment of individuals who also believe their goals are positively related (Young, Chapter 5 this volume). The organization's structure, reward system, culture, and leadership style should reinforce this internal commitment.

Chapter authors have summarized research that can be used to develop the different components of cooperation. Organizational structures such as corporate governance and human resource management practices of recruitment, retention, and compensation are potentially powerful tools to strengthen cooperative interdependence and interaction (Stevens, Chapter 24 this volume). Organizations can develop compensation programs such as profit sharing that motivate teams to continue to make their contributions (Coff, Chapter 23 this volume). Task structures should also foster the interaction that promotes teams (Young, Chapter 5 this volume). Diversity within and between groups can make cooperative teamwork more productive but they must be aligned with the organization's context and in other ways managed effectively (Joshi & Jackson, Chapter 14 this volume).

Interventions can also focus on promotive interaction among team members. Group identity and attachment foster effective teamwork (Korsgaard, Brodt, & Sapienza, Chapter 6 this volume). Aligning members' thinking can help develop the team cognition that facilitates decision making (Glynn & Barr, Chapter 12 this volume). Team mental models can help members operate on the same basis so that they can communicate successfully (Langan-Fox, Chapter 16 this volume). Team identity is important to the organization and individual but it should reinforce rather than oppose the identity of other groups (van Knippenberg, Chapter 18 this volume). Focusing on quality customer service and effective customer relationships can bind organizational groups together (Dunne & Barnes, Chapter 25 this volume).

Learning to become a successful team can be a vital cooperative goal that binds people together for the long term. However, learning is risky so that people need considerable psychological safety to experiment and receive feedback (Edmondson, Chapter 13 this volume). Training can also be useful by helping team members understand how such elements as individual accountability and group reflective processing strengthen cooperative teamwork (Johnson & Johnson, Chapter 9 this volume).

Misunderstandings, disputes, and other conflicts provide a critical test that, if handled well, can strengthen cooperative teamwork but, if handled poorly, undermine it (Deutsch, Chapter 2 this volume). Team members must understand the types of conflicts and their choices of how to approach them (De Dreu & Weingart, Chapter 8 this volume). Accurate, shared schemas about the value of open, cooperative approaches facilitate the productive use of task conflict and reduce interpersonal misunderstandings (Rentsch & Zelno, Chapter 7 this volume).

Power and cultural differences must also be faced. Making power positive and avoiding the oppressive effects of power differences are important team skills (Coleman & Voronov, Chapter 12 this volume). People with diverse cultures can develop a framework for collaboration through understanding of each other's ways and together learning how to develop common methods (Leung, Lu, & Liang, Chapter 27 this volume).

Managers and employees then have powerful methods that they can use to strengthen their cooperative work. However, structures and interaction patterns can undermine as well as strengthen cooperative teamwork (Clark, Chapter 20 this volume). Ineffective communication and conflict management threaten to reinforce competitive elements. Developing cooperative work requires persistence as well as skill.

INTEGRATION

Trade-off, "either-or" thinking, has dominated organizational theorizing. Societies and organizations value either the collective group or the individual: what is good for the organization costs individuals. Organizations prosper through discipline and conformity whereas individuals thrive on self-expression and relationships. But cooperation research summarized in the following chapters reveals the limits of this theorizing. Although there may be some trade-offs, the individual flourishes and the organization delivers value to stakeholders through open, spirited cooperative work.

The choice is usually posed as to be for the self or for the team, to act selfishly or altruistically. Although some situations require such a choice, many situations in organizations allow and promote working for mutual benefit. In cooperation, people have a vested interest in each other's success and encourage each other to act effectively. When they exchange their abilities and discuss their differences cooperatively, they all benefit by working together to reach goals. Cooperative work melds the value of individuality with the power of group action. By combining their opposing ideas and perspectives, people in cooperation take effective action. Within a strong cooperative team, individuality and freedom of expression very much contribute to the quality of group life and the productivity of the organization.

Leaders often believe that they have to choose between "tough" productivity-oriented or "soft," people-oriented approaches. But cooperative work points to a contemporary style of leading and changing organizations. Cooperative teamwork is soft in that it requires people to be respectful and sensitive to each other and develop strong, trusting relationships, but it is also tough in its demands on completing common tasks and confronting problems and struggling to work through conflict. In this way, leaders empower individuals to get vital organizational tasks done.

Cooperative work can also integrate traditional rivals. Organizations that compete in the same market are learning how they can work together to strengthen their industry and together participate in other markets. Suppliers and manufacturers are forging long-term relationships that improve quality and reduce costs.

A most pressing need is to channel our organizations to help integrate diverse people so that they value their differences and learn from each other. Our global world has opened up great potential for new cooperative work. Indonesians are joining forces with European and Indian people to develop global products and solve global problems. Editors from England, the United States, and China, along with authors from around the world, together developed this book published in England and distributed worldwide. But our global world has also made direct warfare and terrorism to revenge ancient and emerging injustices more possible.

Will we have the long-term vision, the insight, and discipline to put cooperation into place to realize these integrations? Confidence may not be warranted but hope is essential. Although we need much more research on fundamental cooperative processes as well as professional practice and documented procedures, researchers and practitioners have worked hard to develop a knowledge base for cooperative work. We believe the ideas and research summarized in the following chapters provide a realistic basis for hope.

> Because we are traveling on the same ship, we will either sail or sink together.
> (Chinese proverb)

REFERENCES

Deutsch, M. (1949). A theory of cooperation and competition. *Human Relations, 2*, 129–152.

Deutsch, M. (1962). Cooperation and trust: some theoretical notes. In M. R. Jones (ed.), *Nebraska Symposium on Motivation* (pp. 275–319). Lincoln: University of Nebraska Press.

Deutsch, M. (1973). *The Resolution of Conflict*. New Haven, Conn.: Yale University Press.

Johnson, D. W. & Johnson, R. T. (1989). *Cooperation and Competition: Theory and Research*. Edina, Minn.: Interaction Books.

Johnson, D. W., Maruyama, G., Johnson, R. T., Nelson, D., & Skon, L. (1981). Effects of cooperative, competitive and individualistic goal structures on achievement: a meta-analysis. *Psychological Bulletin, 89*, 47–62.

Stanne, M. B., Johnson, D. W., & Johnson, R. T. (1999). Does competition enhance or inhibit motor performance: a meta-analysis. *Psychological Bulletin, 125*, 133–154.

2

COOPERATION AND CONFLICT

A PERSONAL PERSPECTIVE ON THE HISTORY OF THE SOCIAL PSYCHOLOGICAL STUDY OF CONFLICT RESOLUTION

Morton Deutsch

INTRODUCTION

Conflict is an inevitable and pervasive aspect of organizational life. It occurs within and between individuals, within and between teams and groups, within and between different levels of an organization, within and between organizations. Conflict has been given a bad name by its association with psychopathology, disruption, violence, civil disorder, and war. These are some of the harmful potentials of conflict when it takes a destructive course. When it takes a constructive course, conflict is potentially of considerable personal and social value. It prevents stagnation, it stimulates interest and curiosity, it is the medium through which problems can be aired and creative solutions developed, it is the motor of personal and social change.

It is sometimes assumed that conflicts within teams in organizations should be suppressed, that conflict impairs cooperation and productivity among the members of a team. This may be true when conflict takes a destructive course as in a bitter quarrel. However, it is apt to strengthen the relations among team members and to enhance productivity when it takes the form of a lively controversy.

In this chapter, I present an overview of the major research questions addressed in the literature related to conflict resolution, as well as a historical perspective to see what progress has been made in this area. My premise is that anyone interested in understanding teamwork and cooperative working should be familiar with the field of conflict resolution. As I stated above, conflict is inevitable in teamwork; how the conflict is managed can lead either to the enhancement or disruption of cooperation and team productivity.

International Handbook of Organizational Teamwork and Cooperative Working. Edited by M. A. West, D. Tjosvold, and K. G. Smith.

Some Definitions

Throughout my many years of empirical and theoretical work in the field of conflict studies, I have thought of conflict in the context of competition and cooperation. I have viewed these latter as idealized psychological processes which are rarely found in their "pure" form in nature, but, instead, are found more typically mixed together. I have also thought that most forms of conflict could be viewed as mixtures of competitive and cooperative processes and, further, that the course of a conflict and its consequences would be heavily dependent upon the nature of the cooperative–competitive mix. These views of conflict lead me to emphasize the link between the social psychological studies of cooperation and competition and the studies of conflict in my assessment of this latter area.

I have defined conflict in the following way (Deutsch, 1973, p. 10): "A *conflict* occurs whenever incompatible activities occur.... An action that is incompatible with another action prevents, obstructs, interferes, injures, or in some way makes the latter less likely or less effective." Conflicts may arise between two or more parties from their opposing interests, goals, values, beliefs, preferences, or their misunderstandings about any of the foregoing. These are *potential* sources of conflict which may give rise to actions by the parties which are incompatible with one another; if they do not give rise to incompatible actions, a conflict does not exist: it is only potential.

The terms "competition" and "conflict" are often used synonymously or interchangeably. This reflects a basic confusion. Although competition produces conflict, not all instances of conflict reflect competition. Competition implies an opposition in the goals of the interdependent parties such that the probability of goal attainment for one decreases as the probability for the other increases. In conflict that is derived from competition, the incompatible action reflects incompatible goals. However, conflict may occur even when there is no perceived or actual incompatibility of goals. Thus if two team members of a sales group are in conflict about the best way to increase sales or if a husband and wife are in conflict about how to treat their son's mosquito bites, it is not necessarily because they have mutually exclusive goals; here, their goals may be concordant. My distinction between conflict and competition is not made merely to split hairs. It is important and basic to a theme that underlies much of my work. Namely, conflict can occur in a cooperative or a competitive context, and the processes of conflict resolution that are likely to be displayed will be strongly influenced by the context within which the conflict occurs.

AT THE BEGINNING...

The writings of three intellectual giants—Darwin, Marx, and Freud—dominated the intellectual atmosphere during social psychology's infancy. Each of these major theorists significantly influenced the writings of the early social psychologists on conflict as well as in many other areas. All three theorists appeared—on a *superficial* reading—to emphasize the competitive, destructive aspects of conflict. Darwin stressed "the competitive struggle for existence" and "the survival of the fittest." He wrote (quoted in Hyman, 1966, p. 29): "...all nature is at war, one organism with another, or with external nature. Seeing the contented face of nature, this may at first be well doubted; but reflection will inevitably prove it is too true." Marx emphasized "class struggle," and as the struggle proceeds, "the whole society breaks up more and more into two great hostile camps, two great, directly antagonistic classes: bourgeoisie and proletariat." He ends *The Communist Manifesto* with a ringing call to class struggle: "The proletarians have nothing to lose but their chains. They have a world to win. Working men of all countries, unite." Freud's view of psychosexual development was largely that of constant struggle between the biologically rooted infantile id and the socially determined, internalized parental surrogate, the superego. As Schachtel (1959, p. 10) has noted:

> The concepts and language used by Freud to describe the great metamorphosis from life in the womb to life in the world abound with images of war, coercion, reluctant compromise, unwelcome necessity, imposed sacrifices, uneasy truce under pressure, enforced detours and roundabout ways to return to the original peaceful state of absence of consciousness and stimulation. . . .

Thus, the intellectual atmosphere prevalent during the period when social psychology began to emerge contributed to viewing conflict from the perspective of "competitive struggle." Social conditions too—the intense competition among businesses and among nations, the devastation of World War I, the economic depression of the 1920s and 1930s, the rise of Nazism and other totalitarian systems—reinforced this perspective.

The vulgarization of Darwin's ideas in the form of "social Darwinism" provided an intellectual rationale for racism, sexism, class superiority, and war. Such ideas as "survival of the fittest," "hereditary determinism," and "stages of evolution" were eagerly *mis*applied to the relations between different human social groups—classes and nations as well as social races—to rationalize imperialist policies. The influence of evolutionary thinking was so strong that, as a critic suggested, it gave rise to a new imperialist beatitude: "Blessed are the strong, for they shall prey upon the weak" (Banton, 1967, p. 48). The rich and powerful were biologically superior; they had achieved their positions as a result of natural selection. It would be against nature to interfere with the inequality and suffering of the poor and weak.

Social Darwinism and the mode of explaining behavior in terms of innate, evolutionary derived instincts were in retreat by the mid-1920s. The prestige of the empirical methods in the physical sciences, the point of view of social determinism advanced by Karl Marx and various sociological theorists, and the findings of cultural anthropologists all contributed to their decline.[1] Since the decline of the instinctual mode of explaining such conflict phenomena as war, intergroup hostility, and human exploitation, two others have been dominant: the "psychological" and the "socio-political–economic." The "psychological" mode attempts to explain such phenomena in terms of "what goes on in the minds of men" (Klineberg, 1964) or "tensions that cause war" (Cantril, 1950); in other words, in terms of the perceptions, beliefs, values, ideology, motivations, and other psychological states and characteristics that individual men and women have acquired as a result of their experiences and as these characteristics are activated by the particular situation and role in which people are located. The "socio-political–economic" mode, in contrast, seeks an explanation in terms of such social, economic, and political factors as levels of armaments, objective conflicts in economic and political interests, and the like. Although these modes of explanation are not mutually exclusive, there is a tendency for partisans of the psychological mode to consider that the causal arrow points from psychological conditions to socio-political–economic

[1] This is a decline, not a disappearance. The explanation of social phenomena in terms of innate factors justifies the status quo by arguing for its immutability; such justification will always be sought by those who fear change.

conditions and for partisans of the latter to believe the reverse is true. In any case, much of the social psychological writing in the 1930s, 1940s, and early 1950s on the topics of war, intergroup conflict, and industrial strife was largely nonempirical, and in one vein or the other. The psychologically trained social psychologist tended to favor the psychological mode; the Marxist-oriented or sociologically trained social psychologist more often favored the other mode.

The decline of social Darwinism and the instinctivist doctrines was hastened by the development and employment of empirical methods in social psychology. This early empirical orientation to social psychology focused on the socialization of the individual; this focus was, in part, a reaction to the instinctivist doctrine. It led to a great variety of studies, including a number investigating cooperation and competition. These latter studies are, in my view, the precursors to the empirical, social psychological study of conflict.

EARLY STUDIES OF COOPERATION AND COMPETITION

Two outstanding summaries of the then existing research on cooperation and competition were published in 1937. One was in the volume of Murphy, Murphy, and Newcomb, *Experimental Social Psychology*; the other was in the monograph *Competition and Cooperation*, by May and Doob. It is not my intention here to repeat these summaries but rather to give you my sense of the state of the research and theorizing on cooperation–competition in the 1920s and 1930s.

My impression is that practically none of the earlier research on cooperation and competition would be acceptable in current social psychological journals because of methodological flaws in the studies. Almost all of them suffer from serious deficiencies in their research designs. In addition, there is little conceptual clarity about some of the basic concepts—"competition," "cooperation," "self-orientation"—that are used in the studies. As a result, the operational definitions used to create the differing experimental conditions have no consistency from one study to another or even within a given study.

Further, the early studies of cooperation and competition suffered from a narrowness of scope. They focused almost exclusively on the effects of "competition" versus "cooperation" on individual task output. There was no investigation of social interaction, communication processes, problem-solving methods, interpersonal attitudes, attitudes toward self, attitudes toward work, attitudes toward the group, or the like in these early investigations of cooperation–competition. The focus was narrowly limited to work output. The simplistic assumption was made that output would be an uncomplicated function of the degree of motivation induced by competition as compared with cooperation. The purposes of most of these early investigations appeared to be to support or reject a thesis inherent in the American ideology; namely, that competition fosters greater motivation to be productive than other forms of social organization.

FIELD THEORY, CONFLICT, AND COOPERATION–COMPETITION

During the 1920s, 1930s, and 1940s, quite independently of the work being conducted in the United States on cooperation–competition, Kurt Lewin and his students were theorizing and conducting research which profoundly affected later work in many areas of social psychology. Lewin's field theory—with its dynamic concepts of tension systems, "driving" and "restraining" forces, "own" and "induced" forces, valences, level of aspiration, power fields, interdependence, overlapping situations, and so on—created a new vocabulary for thinking about conflict and cooperation–competition.

As early as 1931, employing his analysis of force fields, Lewin (1931, 1935) presented a penetrating theoretical discussion of three basic types of psychological conflict: *approach–approach*—the individual stands between two positive valences of approximately equal strength; *avoidance–avoidance*—the individual stands between two negative valences of approximately equal strength; and *approach–avoidance*—the individual is exposed to opposing forces deriving from a positive and a negative valence. Hull (1938) translated Lewin's analysis into the terminology of the goal gradient, and Miller (1937, 1944) elaborated and did research upon it. Numerous experimental studies supported the theoretical analysis.

My own initial theorizing on cooperation–competition (Deutsch, 1949a) was influenced by the Lewinian thinking on tension systems which was reflected in a series of brilliant experiments on the recall of interrupted activities (Zeigarnik, 1927), the resumption of interrupted activities (Ovsiankina, 1928), substitutability (Mahler, 1933), and the role of ego in cooperative work (Lewis & Franklin, 1944). But even more of my thinking was indebted to the ideas which were "in the air" at the MIT Research Center for Group Dynamics. Ways of characterizing and explaining group processes and group functioning, employing the language of Lewinian theorizing, were under constant discussion among the students and faculty at the MIT Center. Thus, it was quite natural that when I settled on cooperation–competition as the topic of my doctoral dissertation, I should employ the Lewinian dynamic emphasis on goals and how they are interrelated as my key theoretical wedge into this topic. Even more importantly, the preoccupation with understanding group processes at the Center pressed me to formulate my ideas about cooperation and competition so that they would be relevant to the psychological and interpersonal processes occurring within and between groups. This pressure forced my theory and research (Deutsch, 1949a, b) to go considerably beyond the prior social psychological work on cooperation–competition. My theorizing and research were concerned not only with the individual and group outcomes of cooperation and competition but also with the social psychological processes which would give rise to these outcomes.

My theorizing and research have been published and widely referred to, so there is little need here for more than a brief summary of some of the theory's predictions, which have been validated by extensive research. Assuming that the individual actions in a group are more frequently effective than bungling, among the predictions that follow from the theory are that *cooperative relations* (those in which the goals of the parties involved are predominantly positively interdependent), as compared with competitive ones, show more of these positive characteristics:

1. *Effective communication* is exhibited. Ideas are verbalized, and group members are attentive to one another, accepting of the ideas of other members, and influenced by them. They have fewer difficulties in communicating with or understanding others.
2. *Friendliness, helpfulness, and less obstructiveness* are expressed in the discussions. Members are more satisfied with the group and its solutions and favorably impressed by

the contributions of the other group members. In addition, members of the cooperative groups rate themselves high in desire to win the respect of their colleagues and in obligation to the other members.

3. *Coordination of effort, divisions of labor, orientation to task achievement, orderliness in discussion, and high productivity* are manifested in the cooperative groups (if the group task requires effective communication, coordination of effort, division of labor, or sharing of resources).
4. *Feeling of agreement with the ideas of others and a sense of basic similarity in beliefs and values, as well as confidence in one's own ideas and in the value that other members attach to those ideas*, are obtained in the cooperative groups.
5. *Willingness to enhance the other's power* (for example, the other's knowledge, skills, resources) to accomplish the other's goals increases. As the other's capabilities are strengthened, you are strengthened, they are of value to you as well as to the other. Similarly, the other is enhanced from your enhancement and benefits from your growing capabilities and power.
6. *Defining conflicting interests as a mutual problem to be solved by collaborative effort* facilitates recognizing the legitimacy of each other's interests and the necessity to search for a solution responsive to the needs of all. It tends to limit rather than expand the scope of conflicting interests. Attempts to influence the other tend to be confined to processes of persuasion.

In contrast, a competitive *process* has the opposite effects:

1. Communication is impaired as the conflicting parties seek to gain advantage by misleading the other through use of false promises, ingratiation tactics, and disinformation. It is reduced and seen as futile as they recognize that they cannot trust one another's communications to be honest or informative.
2. Obstructiveness and lack of helpfulness lead to mutual negative attitudes and suspicion of one another's intentions. One's perceptions of the other tend to focus on the person's negative qualities and ignore the positive.
3. The parties to the process are unable to divide their work, duplicating one another's efforts such that they become mirror images; if they do divide the work, they feel the need to check what the other is doing continuously.
4. The repeated experience of disagreement and critical rejection of ideas reduces confidence in oneself as well as the other.
5. The conflicting parties seek to enhance their own power and to reduce the power of the other. Any increase in the power of the other is seen as threatening to oneself.

The competitive process stimulates the view that the solution of a conflict can only be imposed by one side on the other, which in turn leads to using coercive tactics such as psychological as well as physical threats and violence. It tends to expand the scope of the issues in conflict as each side seeks superiority in power and legitimacy. The conflict becomes a power struggle or a matter of moral principle and is no longer confined to a specific issue at a given time and place. Escalating the conflict increases its motivational significance to the participants and may make a limited defeat less acceptable and more humiliating than a mutual disaster.

As Johnson and Johnson (1989) have detailed, these ideas have given rise to a large number of research studies indicating that a cooperative process (as compared to a competitive one) leads to greater productivity, more favorable interpersonal and intergroup relations, better psychological health and higher self-esteem as well as more constructive resolution of conflict.

GAME THEORY AND GAMES

In 1944, von Neumann and Morgenstern published their now classic work, *Theory of Games and Economic Behavior*. Game theory has made a major contribution to social scientists by formulating in mathematical terms the problem of conflict of interest. However, it has not been either its mathematics or its normative prescriptions for minimizing losses when facing an intelligent adversary that has made game theory of considerable value to social psychologists. Rather, it has been its core emphasis that the parties in conflict have interdependent interests, that their fates are woven together. Although the mathematical and normative development of game theory has been most successful in connection with pure competitive conflict ("zero-sum" games), game theory has also recognized that cooperative as well as competitive interests may be intertwined in conflict (as in "coalition" games or "non-zero-sum" games).

The game theory recognition of the intertwining of cooperative and competitive interests in situations of conflict (or in Schelling's (1960) useful term, the "mixed-motive" nature of conflict) has had a productive impact on the social psychological study of conflict, theoretically as well as methodologically. Theoretically, at least for me, it helped buttress a viewpoint that I had developed prior to my acquaintance with game theory—namely, that conflicts were typically mixtures of cooperative and competitive processes and that the course of conflict would be determined by the nature of the mixture. This emphasis on the cooperative elements involved in conflict ran counter to the then dominant view of conflict as a competitive struggle. Methodologically, game theory had an impact on an even larger group of psychologists. The mathematical formulations of game theory had the indirect but extremely valuable consequence of laying bare some fascinating paradoxical situations in such a way that they were highly suggestive of experimental work.

Game matrices as an experimental device are popular because they facilitate a precise definition of the reward structure encountered by the subjects, and hence of the way they are dependent upon one another. Partly stimulated by and partly in reaction to the research using game matrices, other research games for the study of conflict have been developed. Siegel and Fouraker (1960) developed a bilateral monopoly, "buyer–seller" negotiation game; Vinacke and Arkoff (1957) invented a three-person coalition game; Deutsch and Krauss (1960) constructed a "trucking game"; Deutsch (1973) employed an "allocation" game; and many other investigators have developed variants of these games or new ones. Pruitt and Kimmel in 1977 estimated that well over 1000 studies had been published based on experimental games. Much of this research, as is true in other areas of science, was mindless—being done because a convenient experimental format was readily available. Some of it, however, has, I believe, helped to develop more systematic understanding of conflict processes and conflict resolution. Fortunately, in recent years, experimental gaming has been supplemented by other experimental procedures and by field studies which have overcome some of the inherent limitations of experimental gaming.

THEMES IN CONTEMPORARY SOCIAL PSYCHOLOGICAL RESEARCH ON CONFLICT

Social psychological research on conflict, during the past 35 years or so, has primarily addressed the following major questions:

(1) *What are the conditions which give rise to a constructive or destructive process of conflict resolution?* In terms of bargaining and negotiation, the emphasis here is on determining the circumstances which enable the conflicting parties to arrive at a mutually satisfactory agreement which maximizes their joint outcomes. In a sense, this first question arises from a focus on the cooperative potential inherent in conflict.
(2) *What are the circumstances, strategies, and tactics which lead one party to do better than another in a conflict situation?* The stress here is on how one can wage conflict, or bargain, so as to win or at least do better than one's adversary. This second question emerges from a focus on the competitive features of a conflict situation.
(3) *What determines the nature of the agreement between conflicting parties, if they are able to reach an agreement?* Here the concern is with the cognitive and normative factors that lead people to conceive a possible agreement and to perceive it as a salient possibility for reaching a stable agreement: an agreement which each of the conflicting parties will see as "just" under the circumstances. This third question is a more recent one and has been addressed under the heading of research on the social psychology of equity and justice.
(4) *How can third parties be used to prevent conflicts from becoming destructive or to help deadlocked or embittered negotiators move toward a more constructive management of their conflicts?* This fourth question has been reflected in studies of mediation and in strategies of de-escalating conflicts.
(5) *How can people be educated to manage their conflicts more constructively?* This has been a concern of consultants working with leaders in industry and government and also with those who have responsibility for educating the children in our schools.
(6) *How and when to intervene in prolonged, intractable conflicts?* Much of the literature in conflict resolution has been preventive rather than remedial in its emphasis. It is concerned with understanding the conditions that foster productive rather than destructive conflict (as in question (1)) or developing knowledge about the circumstances that lead to intractable, destructive conflict, in the hope of preventing such conflict. More recently, the reality that many protracted, destructive conflicts exist in the world has induced some scholars to focus their attention on this problem.
(7) *How are we to understand why ethnic, religious, and identity conflicts frequently take an intractable, destructive course?* With the end of the Cold War, there appears to be a proliferation of such conflicts. In the past 10 years, interest in such conflicts has been renewed. Attention has been addressed to what causes such conflict but also what can be done after the typical atrocities of such conflict to bring about reconciliation and reconstruction.
(8) *How applicable in other cultural contexts are the theories related to conflict that have largely been developed in the United States and Western Europe?* In recent years, there has been much discussion in the literature of the differences that exist in how people from varying cultural backgrounds deal with negotiations and, more generally, manage conflict.

In the next section, I shall attempt to describe tentative answers which social psychological research has given the foregoing questions.

What Are the Conditions which Give Rise to a Constructive or Destructive Process of Conflict Resolution?

In social psychology this question has been most directly addressed in the work of my students and myself and summarized in my book, *The Resolution of Conflict: Constructive and Destructive Processes* (1973). Our research started off with the assumption that if the parties involved in a conflict situation had a cooperative rather than competitive orientation toward one another, they would be more likely to engage in a constructive process of conflict resolution. In my earlier research on the effects of cooperation and competition upon group process, I had demonstrated that a cooperative process was more productive in dealing with a problem that a group faces than a competitive process. I reasoned that the same would be true in a mixed-motive situation of conflict: a conflict could be viewed as a mutual problem facing the conflicting parties. Our initial research on trust and suspicion employing the prisoners' dilemma game strongly supported my reasoning, as did subsequent research employing other experimental formats. I believe that this is a very important result which has considerable theoretical and practical significance.

At a theoretical level, it enabled me to link my prior characterization of cooperation and competitive social processes to the nature of the processes of conflict resolution which would typically give rise to constructive or destructive outcomes. That is, I had found a way to characterize the central features of constructive and destructive *processes* of conflict resolution; doing so represented a major advance beyond the characterization of *outcomes* as constructive or destructive. This was not only important in itself but it also opened up a new possibility. At both the theoretical and practical level, the characterization of constructive and destructive processes of conflict created the very significant possibility that we would be able to develop insight into the conditions which initiated or stimulated the development of cooperative–constructive versus competitive–destructive processes of conflict. Much of the research of my students and myself has been addressed to developing this insight.

Much of our early research on the conditions affecting the course of conflict was done on an ad hoc basis. We selected independent variables to manipulate based on our intuitive sense of what would give rise to a cooperative or competitive process. We did experiments with quite a number of variables: motivational orientation, communication facilities, perceived similarity of opinions and beliefs, size of conflict, availability of threats and weapons, power differences, third-party interventions, strategies and tactics of game playing by experimental stooges, the payoff structure of the game, personality characteristics, and so on. The results of these studies fell into a pattern which I slowly began to grasp.

All of these studies seemed explainable by the assumption, which I have labeled "Deutsch's crude law of social relations," that *the characteristic processes and effects elicited by a given type of social relationship (cooperative or competitive) also tend to elicit that type of social relationship*. Thus, cooperation induces and is induced by a perceived similarity in beliefs and attitudes; a readiness to be helpful; openness in communication; trusting and friendly attitudes; sensitivity to common interests and de-emphasis of opposed interests; an orientation toward enhancing mutual power rather than power differences; and so on. Similarly, competition induces and is induced by the use of tactics of coercion, threat, or deception; attempts to enhance the power differences between oneself and the other; poor communication; minimization of the awareness of similarities in values and increased sensitivity to opposed interests; suspicious and hostile attitudes; the importance, rigidity, and size of the issues in conflict; and so on.

In other words, if one has systematic knowledge of the effects of cooperative and competitive processes, one will have systematic knowledge of the conditions which typically give rise to such processes and, by extension, to the conditions which affect whether a conflict will take a constructive or destructive course. My early theory of cooperation and competition is a theory of the *effects* of cooperative and competitive processes (see earlier section "Field theory, conflict, and cooperation–competition" (p. 12) and Deutsch & Coleman, 2000, Chapter 1 for a summary). Hence, from the crude law of social relations stated earlier, it follows that this theory provides insight into the conditions which give rise to cooperative and competitive processes.

The crude law is *crude*. It expresses surface similarities between "effects" and "causes"; the basic relationships are genotypical rather than phenotypical. The crude law is crude, but it can be improved. Its improvement requires a linkage with other areas in social psychology, particularly social cognition and social perception. Such a linkage would enable us to view phenotypes in their social environments in such a way as to lead us to perceive correctly the underlying genotypes. We would then be able to know under what conditions "perceived similarity" or "threat" will be experienced as having an underlying genotype different from the one that is usually associated with its phenotype.

What Are the Circumstances, Strategies, and Tactics which Lead One Party to Do Better than Another in a Conflict Situation?

Most of the important theoretical work by social scientists in relation to this question has been done not by social psychologists but by economists, political scientists, and those concerned with collective bargaining. Some of the most notable contributions have been made by Chamberlain (1951), Schelling (1960, 1966), Stevens (1963), Walton and McKersie (1965), Kahn (1965), Jervis (1970, 1976), and Snyder and Diesing (1977). Machiavelli (1950) earlier had described useful strategies and tactics for winning conflicts: Machiavelli's emphasis was on how to use one's power most effectively so as to intimidate or overwhelm one's adversary; Potter's (1965) on how to play upon the good will, cooperativeness, and politeness of one's opponent so as to upset him and make him lose his "cool." More recently, Alinsky (1971) has described a "jujitsu" strategy that the "have-nots" can employ against the "haves" and described various tactics of harassing and ensnaring the "haves" in their own red tape by pressuring them to live up to their own formally stated rules and procedures.

Social psychologists have just barely begun to tap and test the rich array of ideas about strategies and tactics for winning conflicts or for increasing one's bargaining power and effectiveness that exist in the common folklore as well as in the social and political science literature. This research has provided some support and qualification of preexisting ideas about bargaining strategy and tactics. I shall briefly discuss research relating to "being ignorant," "being tough," "being belligerent," and "bargaining power."

"BEING IGNORANT"

Common sense suggests that one is better off if one is informed rather than ignorant. Schelling (1960) has, however, advanced the interesting idea that in bargaining it is sometimes advantageous to be in a position where you are or appear to be ignorant of your opponent's preferences; similarly, it may give you an edge to be in a situation where you could inform your opponent of your preferences but the other hand could not so inform you. Research (Cummings & Harnett, 1969; Harnett & Cummings, 1968; Harnett, Cummings, & Hughes, 1968) provides experimental support for Schelling's idea. In several different bargaining situations it was demonstrated that a bargainer who did not have complete information about the bargaining schedule of his opponent began bargaining with higher initial bids, made fewer concessions, and earned higher profits than bargainers with complete information. Being ignorant of what the other wants, or appearing so, may justify to oneself and to the other a relative neglect of the other's interests in one's proposals; neglecting the other's interests when they are known is a more obvious and flagrant affront.

The bargaining tactic of "ignorance," as well as other tactics such as "brinkmanship" and "appearing to be irrational," can be characterized in terms of the bargaining doctrine of "the last clear chance." The basic notion here is that a bargainer will gain an advantage if he can appear to commit himself irrevocably so that the last clear chance of avoiding mutual disaster rests with his opponent. A child who works himself up to the point that he will have a temper tantrum if his parents refuse to let him sit where he wants in the restaurant is employing this doctrine. So is the driver who cuts in front of someone on a highway while appearing to be deaf to the insistent blasts of the other's horn. Such tactics do not always work. They seem most apt to do so when the situation is asymmetrical (you can use the tactic but your opponent cannot) and when your opponent does not have a strong need to improve or uphold his reputation for "resolve" or "toughness."

"BEING TOUGH"

"Bargaining toughness" has been defined experimentally in terms of setting a high level of aspiration, making high demands, and offering fewer concessions or smaller concessions than one's opponent. It is a widely held view, to quote the late Leo Durocher, that "nice guys finish last." The results of many experiments (see Magenau & Pruitt, 1978) support a more complex conclusion, stated by Bartos (1970, p. 62): "Toughness plays a dual role and has contradictory consequences. On the one hand, toughness *decreases* the likelihood of an agreement, while on the other hand, it increases the payoffs of those who survive this possibility of a failure." A relentlessly tough approach throughout bargaining appears to result in worse outcomes than a more conciliatory approach (Hamner & Baird, 1978; Harnett & Vincelette, 1978). There is, however, some evidence to suggest that initial toughness in terms of high opening demands, combined with a readiness to reciprocate concessions, may facilitate a fuller exploration of the alternative possibilities of agreement and lead to the discovery of an agreement which maximizes payoffs to the bargainers (Kelley & Schenitzki, 1972); premature tendencies to reach an agreement without full exploration of the possibilities may be prevented by tough, initial positions (Deutsch, 1973).

"BEING BELLIGERENT"

Since the initial research of Deutsch and Krauss (1960) demonstrated the deleterious effects of threat upon bargaining, there has been a deluge of bargaining experiments bearing upon the use of weapons, threats, fines, punishments, rewards, promises, and the like. Tedeschi, Schlenker, and Bonoma (1973, p. 141) have summarized the results of this research as follows: "Threats seldom improve and almost always decrease a bargainer's outcomes if his adversary is similarly armed and the values are important to both parties. Yet when threats are available, bargainers are tempted to use them." Research (see Deutsch, 1973) also demonstrates that threats have considerable reputational costs: a "threatener" as compared to a "promiser" is viewed much more negatively and is much less likely to get compliance.

Although belligerent, coercive tactics usually impair negotiation, it is evident that one is apt to yield to an adversary when there is a gun pressed against one's head. Coercion can be successful, especially when the power of the conflicting parties is unequal. Although coercion can be successful, its success is usually limited to immediate compliance; the long-term consequences of the use of such tactics are usually counterproductive.

"BARGAINING POWER"

Common sense would suggest that a bargainer is likely to be better off if he has more power than the adversary. The results of social psychological research indicate that the situation is more complex than it first seems. Experimentally, bargaining power is sometimes defined as the relative power of each of the bargainers to inflict harm upon one another; the relative desirability of the alternatives to bargaining that are available to each of the bargainers; the relative time pressure on each bargainer to reach an agreement; and so forth. The research evidence (Magenau & Pruitt, 1978; Rubin & Brown, 1975) indicates that when bargaining power is equal, agreement is relatively easy to reach and the outcomes to the parties are high. When bargaining power is somewhat unequal, a power struggle often ensues as the bargainer with more power tries to assert superior claims and as these are resisted by the bargainer with lesser power; the result of this struggle is that the agreement is difficult to reach and the bargainers have low outcomes. When bargaining power is markedly unequal, the differences in power are more likely to be accepted as legitimate and lead to quick agreement, with the advantage going to the more powerful bargainer. However, if the differences in power are not viewed as providing a legitimization of relatively low outcomes to the low-power bargainer, he will resist what he considers to be greed and exploitation; agreement here also will be difficult, and outcomes will be low. Differences in bargaining power may lead the bargainer with greater power to make claims which he feels are legitimate but which he cannot force the other to accept; the bargainer with lesser power may resist the claims as being exploitative and illegitimate and as a way of asserting his equal status as a person. His resistance causes the low-power bargainer to suffer relatively more than the high-power bargainer, but the high-power bargainer also suffers. In essence, the bargaining research demonstrates that having higher power than one's bargaining opponent may be less advantageous than having equal power if your fellow bargainer is apt to resist any greater claims that you might make as a result of your greater power.

From this brief and very incomplete survey of some of the experimental research bearing on the strategy and tactics of waging conflict, it is evident that social psychological research has given some support for surprising tactics ("being ignorant") and has raised some doubts about common assumptions relating to the advantages to be obtained from "toughness" as a strategy, from "coercive tactics," and from "superior bargaining power."

The extensive research literature on negotiation (summarized in such books as Bazerman & Neal, 1992; Breslin & Rubin, 1991; Deutsch, 1973; Deutsch & Coleman, 2000; Kritter, 1994; Lewicki & Letterer, 1985a, b; Lewiki, Sanders, & Minton, 1999; Pruitt, 1981; Pruitt & Carnevale, 1993; Rubin, Pruitt, & Kim, 1994; Thompson, 1998) has investigated many of the strategies and tactics that relate to both "integrative" or "win–win" bargaining (those related to the first listed question above) and "distributive" bargaining (those related to the second listed question): only some of which have been discussed here. For a fuller discussion of such topics as "concession making," "the use of time pressure," "promises and threats," "establishing credibility," "enhancing bargaining power," "building rapport," etc., the books listed above should be consulted.

What Determines the Nature of the Agreement between Conflicting Parties if they Are Able to Reach an Agreement?

A bargain is defined in *Webster's Unabridged Dictionary* as "an agreement between parties settling what each shall give and receive in a transaction between them." The definition of "bargain" fits under common social science definitions of the term "social norm." What determines the agreement or social norm for settling the issues in conflict? Two compatible ideas have been advanced in answer to this question, one related to "perceptual prominence" and the other to "distributive justice."

Schelling (1960) has suggested that perceptually prominent alternatives serve a key function in permitting bargainers to come to an agreement. Research has provided some support for Schelling's idea (see Magenau & Pruitt, 1978, for a summary).

Homans (1961, 1974) has suggested that the principle of distributive justice would play a role in determining how people would decide to allocate the awards and costs to be distributed between them. Although Homans was not primarily concerned with conflict or bargaining, it is evident that his conception of distributive justice does not exclude them. In his discussion, Homans has emphasized one particular canon or rule of distributive justice, that of "proportionality" or "equity": in a just distribution, rewards will be distributed among individuals in proportion to their contributions. "Equity theorists" such as Adams (1963, 1965), Adams and Freedman (1976), and Walster, Walster, and Berscheid (1978) have continued Homans' emphasis on the rule of proportionality and have elaborated a theory and stimulated much research to support the view that psychological resistance and emotional distress will be encountered if the rule of proportionality is violated. In recent years, other social psychologists—Lerner (1975), Leventhal (1976), Sampson (1969), and myself (Deutsch, 1974, 1975)—have stressed that proportionality is only one of many common canons of distributive justice. We know very little about what makes a given rule of justice stand out as saliently appropriate in a given situation of conflict. However, a number of us (Deutsch, 1975; Lamm & Kayser, 1978a, b; Lerner, 1975; Leventhal, 1976; Mikula & Schwinger, 1978; Sampson, 1975) have articulated hypotheses about factors favoring the selection of one or another rule and done related experiments. It seems evident that if a conflict is experienced as having been resolved unjustly, it is not likely that the conflict has been adequately resolved; similarly, a bargaining agreement that is viewed as unjust is not apt to be a stable one. "Justice" and "conflict" are intimately intertwined; the sense of injustice can give rise to conflict, and conflict can produce injustice.

Social psychological research on justice and conflict is too new to have led to definitive results. However, let me note the direction of my thinking in this area. I have applied and elaborated my crude hypothesis of social relations (the typical consequences of a given type of social relation tends to elicit that relation) so as to be relevant to the question of what rule of justice will predominate in a group or social system. I (Deutsch, 1975, 1985) have developed rationales to explain the tendency for economically oriented groups to use the principle of equity; for solidarity-oriented groups to use the principle of equality; and for caring-oriented groups to use the principle of need. I have then characterized typical effects of economically oriented relations, solidarity-oriented relations, and caring relations and have hypothesized that these different kinds of typical effects will elicit different principles of distributive justice.

Thus, among the typical consequences of an economic orientation (Diesing, 1962) are:

(1) the development of a set of values which includes maximization, a means–end schema, neutrality or impartiality with regard to means, and competition;
(2) the turning of man and everything associated with him into commodities—including labor, time, land, capital, personality, social relations, ideas, art, and enjoyment;
(3) the development of measurement procedures which enable the value of different amounts and types of commodities to be compared; and
(4) the tendency for economic activities to expand in scope and size.

The crude hypothesis advanced above would imply that an economic orientation and the principle of equity are likely to be dominant in a group or social system if its situation is characterized by impersonality, competition, maximization, an emphasis on comparability rather than uniqueness, largeness in size or scope, and so on. Specific experimental hypotheses could readily be elaborated: the more competitive the people are in a group, the more likely they are to use equity rather than equality or need as the principle of distributive justice; the more impersonal the relations of the members of a group are, the more likely they are to use equity; and so forth.

Results in my laboratory, as well as in the laboratories of other investigators, are consistent with my crude hypothesis. It seems likely that the reason "equity" has been the central principle of distributive justice to social psychologists is that there has been an unwitting acceptance of the view that the dominant orientation of American society, a competitive–economic orientation, is a universally valid orientation. This is too parochial a perspective. Equity is only one of many principles of distributive justice. It is evident that questions of justice may arise in noneconomic social relations and may be decided in terms that are unrelated to input–output ratios. For a fuller discussion of "justice and conflict," see Deutsch and Coleman (2000, Chapter 2) and for a comprehensive discussion of the social psychology of justice see Tyler et al. (1997).

How Can Third Parties Be Used to Prevent Conflicts from Becoming Destructive or to Help Deadlocked or Embittered Negotiators Move toward a More Constructive Management of their Conflicts?

Kenneth Kressel and Dean Pruitt have edited an issue of the *Journal of Social Issues* (1985) and published a book (1989) on mediation research which provide a definitive review of the work being done in this area. As they point out, informal mediation is one of the oldest forms of conflict resolution, and formal mediation has been practiced in international and labor–management conflicts for many years. More recently, formal mediation has been increasingly applied to an ever-widening array of disputes in such areas as divorcing, small-claims cases, neighborhood feuds, landlord–tenant relations, environmental and public-resource controversies, industrial disputes, school conflicts, and civil cases. Following in the wake of the explosion of the practice of mediation (and of the proliferation of textbooks and "how-to-do-it" books on mediation), there has been important but modest growth in research and theorizing on this topic. Most of the research and theorizing has occurred in the past two decades.

Here, I shall highlight some of the main points which emerge from the cogent summary by Kressel and Pruitt of the work in this area.

There is considerable evidence of user satisfaction with mediation and some evidence that the agreements reached through mediation are both less costly to the conflicting parties and more robust than traditional adjudication (Kressel, 2000). However, there is strong evidence to suggest that mediation has dim prospects of being successful under adverse circumstances. As Kressel and Pruitt (1989, p. 405) have succinctly expressed it: "Intensely conflicted disputes involving parties of widely disparate power, with low motivation to settle, fighting about matters of principle, suffering from discord or ambivalence within their own camps, and negotiating over scarce resources are likely to defeat even the most adroit mediators."

Kressel and Pruitt, in characterizing the research describing what mediators do, indicate that their diverse actions can be grouped under four major headings: (1) establishing a working alliance with the parties; (2) improving the climate between them; (3) addressing the issues; and (4) applying pressure for settlement. As Kressel (2000, pp. 525–526) points out:

> Mediation should be helpful in any conflict in which the basic framework for negotiation is present (Moore, 1996). The framework includes these elements:
>
> - The parties can be identified.
> - They are interdependent.
> - They have the basic cognitive, interpersonal, and emotional capabilities to represent themselves.
> - They have interests that are not entirely incompatible.
> - They face alternatives to consensual agreement that are undesirable (for example, a costly trial).
>
> Mediation is especially likely to prove useful whenever there are additional obstacles that would make unassisted negotiations likely to fail:
>
> - Interpersonal barriers (intense negative feelings, a dysfunctional pattern of communicating).

- Substantive barriers (strong disagreement over the issues, perceived incompatibility of interests, serious differences about the "facts" or circumstances).
- Procedural barriers (existence of impasse, absence of forum for negotiating).

Although many disputes meet these formal criteria, getting mediation started turns out to be something of a challenge. In interpersonal disputes of all kinds, one-third to two-thirds of those given the opportunity to use formal mediation decline it. It is also apparent that in work settings where informal mediation could be used (as by a manager), the would-be mediator declines to intervene, looks the other way, or chooses to employ power and authority rather than the skills of facilitation. Characteristics of the social environment, the disputing parties, and the potential mediator are among the variables that determine whether or not mediation occurs.

I have, from my theoretical perspective, expressed similar ideas, somewhat differently in answer to the question: *What framework can guide a third person who seeks to intervene therapeutically if negotiations are deadlocked or unproductive because of misunderstandings, faulty communications, the development of hostile attitudes, or the inability to discover a mutually satisfying solution?* I suggest that such a framework is implicit in the ideas that I have described earlier. The third party seeks to produce a cooperative problem-solving orientation to the conflict by creating the conditions which characterize an effective cooperative problem-solving process: these conditions are the typical effects of a successful cooperative process. Helping the conflicting parties to develop a cooperative, problem-solving orientation to their conflict may be sufficient when the conflicting parties have reasonably well-developed group problem-solving and decision-making skills. Often they do not, and, hence, they need tutelage in these skills if they are to deal with their problem successfully. And, often, conflicting parties do not have sufficient substantive knowledge concerning the issues in conflict to manage them constructively. Here, too, they may need tutelage by a third party if their conflict is to be resolved sensibly.

Third parties (mediators, conciliators, process consultants, therapists, counselors, etc.) who are called upon to provide assistance in a conflict require four kinds of skills if they are to have the flexibility required to deal with the diverse situations mediators face. The *first* set of skills are those related to the third party's establishing an effective working relationship with each of the conflicting parties so that they will trust the third party, communicate freely with her, and be responsive to her suggestions regarding an orderly process for negotiations. The *second* are those related to establishing a cooperative problem-solving attitude among the conflicting parties toward their conflict. Much of the earlier discussion of my theoretical work on conflict resolution focuses on this area. *Third* are the skills involved in developing a creative group process and group decision making. Such a process clarifies the nature of the problems that the conflicting parties are confronting (reframing their conflicting positions into a joint problem to be solved), helps to expand the range of alternatives that are perceived to be available, facilitates realistic assessment of their feasibility as well as desirability, and facilitates the implementation of agreed-upon solutions. And, *fourth*, it is often helpful for the third party to have considerable substantive knowledge about the issues around which the conflict centers. Substantive knowledge could enable the mediator to see possible solutions that might not occur to the conflicting parties and it would permit her to help them assess proposed solutions more realistically.

It seems reasonable to assume that the diverse situations facing mediators will emphasize one or another of the four skills just described. When the conflicting parties have suspicions about mediation, the skills involved in establishing a good working relationship with the conflicting parties are especially important; when the relationship between the conflicting parties is a poor one, the skills involved in establishing a cooperative problem-solving attitude between the parties is crucial; when the conflicting parties have inadequate techniques for solving problems and making effective joint decisions, then the mediator needs skills related to facilitating creative group decision making; and when the conflicting parties have little knowledge of the substantive issues they are describing, the knowledgeable mediator can be a very helpful resource person on such issues.

It seems reasonable to assume that mediators will differ in the kinds of skills they have mastered and, thus, one can expect that the effectiveness of mediation will be considerably dependent upon how well matched the mediator's skills are with the needs of the case being mediated. There are undoubtedly some "universally competent" mediators who can be successful across a wide variety of cases, but it is safe to say that they are probably rare. Research has indicated that mediators differ in their styles and skills and also in their effectiveness in particular settings. However, not enough research has been done to make definitive statements about the conditions under which different styles and approaches to mediation are most effective.

Kressel (2000) classifies mediator style into two major types, each of which has two subtypes: *task-oriented* and *social–emotional*. The first subtype of the task-oriented style is the *settlement-oriented* mediator who is primarily interested in reaching agreements on any terms acceptable to the conflicting parties. By contrast, the *problem-solving* subtype attaches greater importance to sound problem solving than to settlement per se. Both subtypes, Kressel indicates, are able to resolve low-level conflicts, but the problem-solving style is more effective in providing durable settlements when there is a high conflict.

Mediators with social–emotional styles focus less on the issues and more on opening lines of communication and clarifying underlying feelings and emotions, with the view that once this is accomplished, the conflicting parties should and will be able to work through the issues to their own solution.

Transformational mediation (elaborated by Bush & Folger, 1994; Folger & Bush, 1996) is considered to be a social–emotional subtype. It focuses not only on the relationship between the conflicting parties through emphasizing *recognition* (which refers to improving the capacity of the disputants to become responsive to the needs and perspectives of the other), but also on *empowerment* (which refers to strengthening each party's ability to analyze its respective needs in the conflict and to make effective decisions). The optimistic hope of the advocates of transformative mediation is that the conflicting parties who are subjected to such mediation will be personally transformed whether or not they are able to reach a settlement. Its advocates are critical of settlement or problem-solving orientations to mediation. They believe that such orientations narrow the parties' opportunity to become self-reflective and autonomous as well as aware of the other's separate reflective and distinctive reality.[2]

As Kressel states (2000, p. 536): "Polemical claims not withstanding, there is no empirical evidence for preferring one mediation style over another." And, I add, it seems likely that

[2] See Robert Kegan (1994) for his theory of development of different orders of consciousness which suggests that the transformation that Bush and Folger seek is a desirable movement from the third stage of development where one is socially determined by one's loyalties, group membership, and cultural assumptions, to a fourth stage of development where one is self-knowledgeable, self-reflecting, and self-determining in relation to others and is able to recognize this potential in others. Kegan's research indicates that such a transformation is often difficult and slow to achieve.

the different mediation styles are apt to be differently suitable for different types of issues, parties, circumstances, and social contexts.

To sum up, research on mediation is in its early stages. The research has already demonstrated a high level of user satisfaction in a number of different contexts and it has also suggested that the robustness of agreements and the economy of the process are greater than in traditional methods. But there is as yet insufficient understanding of how to mediate difficult conflicts in adverse circumstances or how to make the most effective match between mediator characteristics and the characteristics of the case to be mediated.

How Can People Be Educated to Manage their Conflicts More Constructively?

During the past two decades, there has been a rapid proliferation of training in conflict resolution—for industry, for government, for families, and for schools—and the publication of many textbooks and how-to-do-it manuals in this area. Unfortunately, there has been very little research to assess the effectiveness and consequences of such training. Most of the existing research has been immediate "consumer satisfaction" studies in which the participants in the training program evaluate their training and indicate how useful the training has been for them. The good news is that these studies indicate a high level of immediate consumer satisfaction; the bad news is that there have been only a few studies which have examined the more enduring consequences of such training. "More enduring" in these instances refers to effects that last for six months or a year (see Bodine & Crawford, 1998; Deutsch & Coleman, 2000, Chapter 27; Johnson & Johnson, 2000, and Jones & Kmitter, 2000, for reviews of the existing research).

There are many different conflict resolution programs which vary as a function of the age, occupation, and types of conflicts on which they focus. I have examined many of them and believe that there are some common elements running through them. These common elements, I believe, derive from the recognition that a constructive process of conflict resolution is similar to an effective, cooperative problem-solving process (where the conflict is perceived as the mutual problem to be solved), while a destructive process is similar to a win–lose, competitive struggle (Deutsch, 1973). In effect, most conflict resolution training programs seek to instill the attitudes, knowledge, and skills which are conducive to effective, cooperative problem solving and to discourage the attitudes and habitual responses which give rise to win–lose struggles. Below I list the central elements which are included in many training programs, but I do not have the space to describe the ingenious techniques that are employed in teaching them. The sequence in which they are taught varies as a function of the nature of the group being taught. Below, I describe what my students have labeled as "Deutsch's Twelve Commandments of Conflict Resolution."

1. *Know what type of conflict you are involved in.* There are three major types: the zero-sum conflict (a pure win–lose conflict), the mixed-motive (both can win, both can lose, one can win and the other can lose), and the pure cooperative (both can win or both can lose). It is important to know what kind of conflict you are in because the different types require different types of strategies and tactics. The common tendency is for inexperienced parties to define their conflict as "win–lose" even though it is a mixed-motive conflict.

In a zero-sum conflict one seeks to amass, mobilize, and utilize the various resources of power in such a way that one can bring to bear in the conflict more effective, relevant power than one's adversary; or if this is not possible in the initial area of conflict, one seeks to transform the arena of conflict into one in which one's effective power is greater than one's adversary. Thus, if a bully challenges you to a fight because you will not "lend" him money and he is stronger than you, you might arrange to change the conflict from a physical to a legal confrontation by involving the police or other legal authority. Other strategies and tactics in win–lose conflicts involve outwitting, misleading, seducing, blackmailing, and the various forms of the black arts which have been discussed by Machiavelli, Potter, Schelling, and Alinsky, among others. The strategy and tactics of the resolution of cooperative conflicts involve primarily cooperative fact-finding and research as well as rational persuasion. The strategy and tactics involved in mixed-motive conflicts are mainly what are discussed below.

2. *Become aware of the causes and consequences of violence and of the alternatives to violence, even when one is very angry.* Become aware of what makes you very angry; learn the healthy and unhealthy ways you have of expressing anger. Learn how to actively channel your anger in ways that are not violent and are not likely to provoke violence from the other. Understand that violence begets violence and that if you "win" an argument by violence, the other will try to get even in some other way. Learn alternatives to violence in dealing with conflict.

3. *Face conflict rather than avoid it.* Recognize that conflict may make you anxious and that you may try to avoid it. Learn the typical defenses you employ to evade conflict, e.g. denial, suppression, becoming overly agreeable, rationalization, postponement, premature conflict resolution. Become aware of the negative consequences of evading a conflict—irritability, tension, persistence of the problem, etc. Learn what kinds of conflicts are best avoided rather than confronted, e.g. conflicts that will evaporate shortly, those that are inherently unresolvable, win–lose conflicts which you are unlikely to win.

4. *Respect yourself and your interests, respect the other and his or her interests.* Personal insecurity and the sense of vulnerability often lead people to define conflicts as "life and death," win–lose struggles even when they are relatively minor, mixed-motive conflicts, and this definition may lead to "conflict avoidance," "premature conflict resolution," or "obsessive involvement in the conflict." Helping people to develop a respect for themselves and their interests enables them to see their conflicts in reasonable proportion and facilitates their constructive confrontation. Helping people to learn to respect the other and the other's interests inhibits the use of competitive tactics of power, coercion, deprecation, and deception which commonly escalate the issues in conflict and often lead to violence.

5. *Distinguish clearly between "interests" and "positions."* Positions may be opposed but interests may not be. Often when conflicting parties reveal the interests underlying their positions, it is possible to find a solution which suits them both.

6. *Explore your interests and the other's interests to identify the common and compatible interests that you both share.* Identifying shared interests makes it easier to deal constructively with the interests that you perceive as being opposed. A full exploration of one another's interests increases empathy and facilitates subsequent problem solving.

7. *Define the conflicting interests between oneself and the other as a mutual problem to be solved cooperatively.* Define the conflict in the smallest terms possible, as a "here-now-this" conflict rather than as a conflict between personalities or general principles, e.g. as a conflict about a specific behavior rather than about who is a better person. Diagnose the problem clearly and then creatively seek new options for dealing with the conflict that lead to mutual gain. If no option for mutual gain can be discovered, seek to agree upon a fair rule or procedure for deciding how the conflict will be resolved.

8. *In communicating with the other, listen attentively and speak so as to be understood: this requires the active attempt to take the perspective of the other and to check continually one's success in doing so.* One should listen to the other's meaning and emotion in such a way that the other *feels* understood as well as is understood. Similarly, you want to communicate to the other one's thoughts and feelings in such a way that you have good evidence that he or she understands the way you think and feel. The feeling of being understood, as well as effective communication, enormously facilitates constructive resolution.

Skills in taking the perspective of others and in obtaining feedback about the effectiveness of one's communications are important. Role reversal seems to be helpful in developing an understanding of the perspective of the other and in providing checks on how effective the communication process has been.

9. *Be alert to the natural tendencies to bias, misperceptions, misjudgments, and stereotyped thinking that commonly occur in oneself as well as the other during heated conflict.* These errors in perception and thought interfere with communication, make empathy difficult, and impair problem solving. Psychologists can provide a checklist of the common forms of misperception and misjudgment occurring during intense conflict. These include black–white thinking, demonizing the other, shortening of one's time perspective, narrowing of one's range of perceived options, and the fundamental attribution error. The fundamental attribution error is illustrated in the tendency to attribute the aggressive actions of the other to the other's personality while attributing one's own aggressive actions to external circumstances (such as the other's hostile actions). The ability to recognize and admit one's misperceptions and misjudgments clears the air and facilitates similar acknowledgment by the other.

10. *Develop skills for dealing with difficult conflicts so that one is not helpless nor hopeless when confronting those who are more powerful, those who do not want to engage in constructive conflict resolution, or those who use dirty tricks.* It is important to recognize that one becomes less vulnerable to intimidation by a more powerful other, to someone who refuses to cooperate except on his or her terms, or to someone who plays dirty tricks (deceives, welches on an agreement, personally attacks you, etc.) if you realize that you usually have a choice: you do not have to stay in the relationship with the other. The alternative may not be great but it may be better than staying in the relationship. The freedom to choose prevents the other, if he or she benefits from the relationship, from making the relationship unacceptable to you. Second, it is useful to be open and explicit to the other about what he or she is doing that is upsetting you and to indicate the effects that these actions are having on you. Third, it is wise to avoid reciprocating the other's noxious behavior and to avoid attacking the other personally for his behavior (i.e. criticize the behavior and not the person); doing so often leads to an escalating vicious spiral.

A phrase that I have found useful in characterizing the stance one should take in difficult (as well as easy) conflicts is to be "firm, fair, and friendly." *Firm* in resisting intimidation, exploitation, and dirty tricks; *fair* in holding to one's moral principles and not reciprocating the other's immoral behavior despite his or her provocations; and *friendly* in the sense that one is willing to initiate and reciprocate cooperation.

11. *Know oneself and how one typically responds in different sorts of conflict situations.* As I have suggested earlier, conflict frequently evokes anxiety. In clinical work, I have found that the anxiety is often based upon unconscious fantasies of being overwhelmed and helpless in the face of the other's aggression or of being so angry and aggressive oneself that one will destroy the other. Different people deal with their anxieties about conflict

in different ways. I have found it useful to emphasize six different dimensions of dealing with conflict which can be used to characterize a person's predispositions to respond to conflict. Being aware of one's predispositions may allow one to modify them when they are inappropriate in a given conflict.

(a) *Conflict avoidance–excessive involvement in conflict.* Conflict avoidance is expressed in denial, repression, suppression, avoidance, and continuing postponement of facing the conflict. Excessive involvement in conflict is sometimes expressed in a preoccupation with conflict, a chip on one's shoulder, a tendency to seek out conflict to demonstrate that one is not afraid of conflict.

(b) *Hard–soft.* Some people are prone to take a tough, aggressive, dominating, unyielding response to conflict, fearing that otherwise they will be taken advantage of and be considered soft. Others are afraid that they will be considered to be mean, hostile, or presumptuous, and as a consequence, they are excessively gentle and unassertive. They often expect the other to "read their minds" and know what they want even though they are not open in expressing their interests.

(c) *Rigid–loose.* Some people immediately seek to organize and to control the situation by setting the agenda, defining the rules, etc. They feel anxious if things threaten to get out of control and feel threatened by the unexpected. As a consequence, they are apt to push for rigid arrangements and rules and get upset by even minor deviations. At the other extreme, there are some people who are aversive to anything that seems formal, limiting, controlling, or constricting.

(d) *Intellectual–emotional.* At one extreme, emotion is repressed, controlled, or isolated so that no relevant emotion is felt or expressed as one communicates one's thoughts. The lack of appropriate emotional expressiveness may seriously impair communication: the other may take your lack of emotion as an indicator that you have no real commitment to your interests and that you lack genuine concern for the other's interests. At the other extreme, there are some people who believe that only feelings are real and that words and ideas are not to be taken seriously unless they are thoroughly soaked in emotion. Their emotional extravagance impairs the ability to mutually explore ideas and to develop creative solutions to impasses; it also makes it difficult to differentiate the significant from the insignificant, if even the trivial is accompanied with intense emotion.

(e) *Escalating versus minimizing.* At one extreme, there are some people who tend to experience any given conflict in the largest possible terms. The issues are cast so that what is at stake involves one's self, one's family, one's ethnic group, precedence for all time, or the like. The specifics of the conflict get lost as it escalates along the various dimensions of conflict: the size and number of the immediate issues involved; the number of motives and participants implicated on each side of the issue; the size and number of the principles and precedents that are perceived to be at stake; the cost that the participants are willing to bear in relation to the conflict; the number of norms of moral conduct from which behavior toward the other side is exempted; and the intensity of negative attitudes toward the other side. Escalation of the conflict makes the conflict more difficult to resolve constructively except when the escalation proceeds so rapidly that its absurdity even becomes self-apparent. At the other extreme, there are people who tend to minimize their conflicts. They are similar to the conflict avoiders but, unlike the avoiders, they do recognize the existence of the conflict. However, by minimizing the seriousness of the differences between self and other, by not recognizing how important the matter is to self and to other, one can produce serious misunderstandings. One may also restrict the effort and work that one may need to devote to the conflict in order to resolve it constructively.

(f) *Compulsively revealing versus compulsively concealing*. At one extreme there are people who feel a compulsion to reveal whatever they think and feel about the other and their suspicions, hostilities, and fears—in the most blunt, unrationalized, and unmodulated manner. Or they may feel they have to communicate every doubt, sense of inadequacy, or weakness they have about themselves. At the other extreme, there are people who feel that they cannot reveal any of their feelings or thoughts without seriously damaging their relationship to the other. Either extreme can impair the development of a constructive relationship. One, in effect, should be open and honest in communication but, appropriately so, taking into account realistically the consequences of what one says or does not say and the current state of the relationship.

12. *Finally, throughout conflict, one should remain a moral person, i.e. a person who is caring and just, and should consider the other as a member of one's moral community, i.e. as someone who is entitled to care and justice*. In the heat of conflict, there is often the tendency to shrink one's moral community and to exclude the other from it: this permits behavior toward the other which one would otherwise consider morally reprehensible. Such behavior escalates conflict and turns it in the direction of violence and destruction.

How and When to Intervene in Protracted, Intractable Conflicts?

Coleman (2000, p. 429) has characterized an intractable conflict as "one that is recalcitrant, intense, deadlocked, and extremely difficult to resolve." Such conflicts persist over time, they usually escalate (Fisher, 2000), and tend to take on a life of their own. I have termed the social process involved in such conflicts, a malignant social process (Deutsch, 1983).

Perfectly sane and intelligent people, groups, and nations—once caught up in such a malignant process—enmesh themselves in a web of interactions and aggressive–defensive maneuvers which instead of improving their situation, make both sides feel less secure and more burdened. They trap themselves in a vicious process that leads to outcomes of mutual loss and harm. In such a social process both sides come to be right in believing that the other side is hostile, malevolent, and intent on inflicting harm. Their interactions provide ample justification for such beliefs. Typically, in such a conflict, the participants see no way of extricating themselves without becoming vulnerable to an unacceptable loss in a value central to their self-identities, self-esteems, or security.

A number of key elements contribute to the development and perpetuation of such a process. They include:

1. *An anarchic social situation*, which provides no basis for mutual trust, in which an attempt by one party to increase its own security or welfare—without regard to the security or welfare of others—is experienced as a threat by the others.
2. *A win–lose or competitive orientation* to the conflict.
3. *Inner conflict* within each of the parties, that are displaced, suppressed, or channeled into the external conflict.
4. *Cognitive rigidity*, which limits the ability to search out or create mutually satisfactory agreements.
5. *Misjudgments and misperceptions* which enhance negativity toward the other and toward possible solutions.

6. *The development and investment* in the skills, attitudes, and institutions involved in waging and perpetuating the conflict.
7. *Self-fulfilling prophecies*, in which one's hostile behavior toward the other elicits a negative response from the other which confirms one's negative view of the other.
8. *Vicious escalating spirals*, which often result from the biased tendency of each side to see their own aggressive–defensive behaviors as justified and the other side's as unjustified.
9. *A gamesmanship orientation* which turns the conflict away from issues of what in real life is being won or lost to an abstract conflict over images of power.

In the social science literature, there has been extended discussion of the question of when an intractable conflict is "ripe" for resolution. Zartman (Touval & Zartman, 1985; Zartman & Berman, 1982; Zartman, 1985), Pruitt and Olzack (1995), and Coleman (1997) have provided important discussions of the concept of ripeness and how it can be fostered. Zartman's (2000, pp. 228–229) definition of the concept is widely used: "If the (two) parties to a conflict (a) perceive themselves to be in a hurting stalemate and (b) perceive the possibility of a negotiated solution (a way out), the conflict is ripe for resolution (i.e., for negotiations toward resolution to begin)." However, as Zartman himself points out; increased pain may, under certain conditions, strengthen the determination to achieve one's objectives. Or to paraphrase one of Festinger's (1957, 1961) quotes illustrating his theory of cognitive dissonance, rats and men come to love and be committed to the things (and to the principles) for which they have suffered.

I shall not summarize here the valuable discussion of Zartman, Pruitt and Olzack, and Coleman (referred to above) about the conditions which foster ripeness. Here, I wish to consider the therapeutic principles involved in helping a married couple who were involved in a bitter stalemate conflict over issues which they considered nonnegotiable to negotiate these issues constructively (Deutsch, 1988). The couple, who were in a "mutually hurting stalemate," sought help for several reasons. On the one hand, their conflicts were becoming physically violent: this frightened them and it also ran counter to their strong constraints making it difficult for them to separate. They felt they would be considerably worse off economically, their child would suffer, and they had mutually congenial intellectual, esthetic, sexual, and recreational interests which would be difficult for them to engage in together if separated.

Let me briefly discuss the steps involved in getting the couple to the point where they were ready to negotiate. There were two major interrelated steps, each of which involved many substeps. The first entailed helping each spouse to recognize that the present situation of a bitter, stalemated conflict no longer served his or her real interests. The second step involved aiding the couple to become aware of the possibility that each of them could be better off than they currently were if they recognized their conflict as a joint problem, which required creative, joint effort in order to improve their individual situations. The two steps do not follow one another in neat order: progress in either step facilitates progress in the other.

It should be recognized that, in many instances, the external conflicts between two parties may be generated or sustained by internal conflicts within each party, e.g. as a way of blaming the other for one's own inadequacies, difficulties, and problems so that one can avoid confronting the necessity of changing oneself. Thus, in the couple I treated, the wife perceived herself to be a victim, and felt that her failure to achieve her professional goals was due to her husband's unfair treatment of her as exemplified by his unwillingness to share responsibilities for the household and child care. Blaming her husband provided her with a means of avoiding her own apprehensions about whether she personally had the abilities and courage to fulfill her aspirations. Similarly, the husband who provoked continuous criticism from his wife for his domineering, imperial behavior employed her criticism to justify his emotional withdrawal, thus enabling him to avoid dealing with his anxieties about personal intimacy and emotional closeness. Even though the wife's accusations concerning her husband's behavior were largely correct, as were the husband's toward her, each had an investment in maintaining the other's noxious behavior because of the defensive self-justifications such behavior provided.

How does a therapist help the conflicting parties overcome such internal deterrents to recognizing that their bitter, stalemated conflict no longer serves their real interests? The general answer, which is quite often difficult to implement in practice, is to help each of the conflicting parties change in such a way that the conflict no longer is maintained by conditions in the parties that are extrinsic to the conflict. In essence, this entails helping each of the conflicting parties to achieve the self-esteem and self-image that would make them no longer need the destructive conflict process as a defense against their sense of personal inadequacy, their fear of taking on new and unfamiliar roles, their feeling of purposelessness and boredom, and their fears of rejection and attack if they act independently of others.

What are the conditions that are likely to help conflicting parties become aware of the possibility that each of them could be better off than they currently are if they recognize that their conflict is a joint problem that requires creative, joint efforts in order to improve the individual situations? A number of such conditions are listed below:

1. Critical to this awareness is the recognition that one cannot impose a solution which may be acceptable or satisfactory to oneself upon the other. In other words, there is recognition that a satisfactory solution for oneself requires the other's agreement, and this is unlikely unless the other is also satisfied with the solution. Such recognition implies an awareness that a mutually acceptable agreement will require at least a minimal degree of cooperation.
2. To believe that the other is ready to engage in a joint problem-solving effort, one must believe that the other has also recognized that he or she cannot impose a solution—that is, the other has also recognized that a solution has to be mutually acceptable.
3. The conflicting parties must have some hope that a mutually acceptable agreement can be found. This hope may rest upon their own perception of the outlines of a possible fair settlement or it may be based on their confidence in the expertise of third parties, or even on a generalized optimism.
4. The conflicting parties must have confidence that if a mutually acceptable agreement is concluded, both will abide by it or that violations will be detected before the losses to the self and the gains to the other become intolerable. If the other is viewed as unstable, lacking self-control, or untrustworthy, it will be difficult to have confidence in the viability of an agreement unless one has confidence in third parties who are willing and able to guarantee the integrity of the agreement.

Issues that seem vitally important to a person, such as one's identity, security, self-esteem, or reputation, often are experienced as nonnegotiable. Thus, consider the husband and wife who viewed themselves in a conflict over a nonnegotiable issue. The wife who worked (and wanted to do so) wanted the husband to share equally in the household and child-care responsibilities: she considered equality between the genders to be one of her core personal values. The husband wanted a traditional marriage with a traditional division of responsibilities, in which he would have primary responsibility for income-producing work outside the home while his wife would have primary responsibility for the work related to the household and child care. The husband considered household work and child care as inconsistent with his deeply rooted image of adult masculinity. The conflict seemed nonnegotiable to the couple—for the wife it would be a betrayal of her feminist values to accept her husband's terms; for the husband, it would be a violation of his sense of adult masculinity to become deeply involved in housework or child care.

However, this nonnegotiable conflict became negotiable when, with the help of the therapist, the husband and wife were able to listen and really understand each other's feelings and the ways in which their respective life experiences had led them to the views they each held. Understanding the other's position fully and the feeling and experiences which were behind them made them each feel less hurt and humiliated by the other's position and more ready to seek solutions that would accommodate the interests of both. They realized that with their joint incomes they could afford to pay for household and child-care help, which would enable the wife to be considerably less burdened by these responsibilities without increasing the husband's chores in these areas: of course, doing so lessened the amount of money they had available for other purposes.

This solution was not a perfect one for either party. The wife and husband each would have preferred that the other share their own view of what a marriage should be like. However, their deeper understanding of the other's position made them feel less humiliated and threatened by it and less defensive toward the other. It also enabled them to negotiate a mutually acceptable agreement that lessened the tensions between them despite their continuing differences in basic perspectives.

The general conclusions that I draw from this and other experiences with a "nonnegotiable" issue is that most such issues are negotiable even though the underlying basic differences between the conflicting parties are not resolved when they learn to listen, understand, and empathize with the other party's position, interests, and feelings, providing they are also able to communicate to the other their understanding and empathy. Even though understanding and empathy do not imply agreement with the other's views, they indicate an openness and responsiveness which reduce hostility and defensiveness and which also allow the other to be more open and responsive. Such understanding and empathy help the conflicting parties to reduce their feelings that their self-esteem, security, or identity will be threatened and endangered by recognizing that the other's feelings and interests, as well as one's own, deserve consideration in dealing with the issues in conflict.

The positions of the conflicting parties may be irreconcilable, but their interests may be concordant. Helping parties in conflict to be fully in touch with their long-term interests may enable them to see beyond their nonnegotiable positions to their congruent interests. An atmosphere of mutual understanding and empathy fosters the conditions that permit conflicting parties to get beyond their initial rigid, nonnegotiable position to their underlying interests (for a comprehensive discussion of various methods of "interactive conflict resolution" that have been employed in intractable intergroup conflicts, see Fisher, 1997).

How Are we to Understand Why Ethnic, Religious, and Identity Conflicts Frequently Take an Intractable, Destructive Course?

It is not uncommon for scholars concerned with intergroup or interethnic relations to assume, implicitly, that all or most intergroup relations are characterized by destructive conflict. However, as Ronald Fisher (2000, p. 166) points out: "In most ongoing intergroup relations in countless settings, cooperative relations exist and conflict is handled more or less constructively, to the satisfaction of the parties involved." Similarly, Gurr (1993, pp. 290–291), in his global survey of ethnopolitical conflicts, writes:

> Some observers have concluded that ethnopolitical conflicts are intractable. The evidence suggests otherwise. . . . Our images of intractable communal conflicts are largely shaped by ethnonationalist wars in the Middle East, Asia, and Africa. Yet for each example of protracted communal conflict in these regions, one can point to neighboring states where similar conflicts have been managed more effectively. . . . In central and West Africa more than a dozen states straddle the cultural and religious divide between the Muslim, Arab-influenced peoples of the savannah and the Christian, European-influenced peoples of the forest and coastal regions. Only in Sudan and Chad have protracted civil wars been fought across this divide.

In light of the foregoing, the question above should be reformulated into several questions:

1. What are the factors which lead to a constructive rather than a destructive resolution of communal or ethnic conflict?
2. Is there anything distinctive about ethnic conflict which may predispose it to a destructive resolution?
3. If such a conflict takes a destructive course, how can reconciliation be fostered after each side has inflicted indignities and grievous harm on the other?

Gurr (1993), in his global study of ehtnopolitical conflicts, provides research on 233 ethnic groups involved in communal conflicts of one sort or another which bears upon (1) above. He concludes (p. 213):

> there are two keys to the constructive management of ethnopolitical conflict. One is to search out politically and socially creative policies that bridge the gaps between the interests of minorities and states. All parties, including outside observers, can contribute to this process. The second is to begin the process of creative conflict management in the early stages of open conflict. . . . States and their leaders . . . should be able to respond creatively to political mobilization and protest by communal groups before the groups cross the threshold of sustained violence.

Gurr (1993, p. 313) discusses four types of state policies that are used to accommodate the interests of ethnopolitical minorities: regional autonomy, assimilation, pluralism, and power sharing:

> The conclusion for states is one of caution: public efforts to manage ethnopolitical conflicts have risks as well as potential gains. If policies of accommodation are to be effective they must be pursued cautiously but persistently over the long term, slowly enough not to stimulate a crippling reaction from other groups, persistently enough so that minorities do not defect or rebel. The conclusion for communal groups is that persistence in the nonviolent pursuit of group interests is a strategic virtue, and so is a willingness to compromise about the specifics of accommodation. . . . Violent means in the pursuit of communal interests usually are politically more effective as threats than in actuality.

The answer to the second question (what is distinctive about ethnic conflicts which may predispose them to a destructive resolution?) lies in *the importance of one's membership in an ethnic group to one's self-identity* (see Tajfel, 1978, 1981, and Turner, 1987, who have developed "Social Identity Theory" which articulates in detail the links among group membership, social identity, and self-concept). Among the strongest membership bonds are those arising out of certain ascribed statuses such as family, sex, racial, and national group membership, all of which one acquires by birth rather than by choice. Such statuses can rarely be changed. It is the combination of their unalterability and their social significance that gives these ascribed statuses their personal importance. One's handedness, left or right, may be as difficult to alter as one's race, but it is by no means as socially significant. Membership in a family, racial, sexual, ethnic, or national group affects one's thoughts and actions in many situations; these effects are pervasive. In addition, by common definition, membership in such groups typically excludes membership in other groups of a similar type. That is, if you are black, you are not also white; if you are male, you are not also female; if you are Jewish, you are not also Christian. Thus being a member is thought to be more or less distinctive, and since membership is linked to experiences from early on in one's life, it is not unusual for one to get emotionally attached to such groups, with the result that these memberships play an important positive role in determining one's sense of identity.

Suppose that one is emotionally attached to one's identity as a Jew, woman, or black, but that it results in systematic oppression and discrimination and places one at a distinct disadvantage in obtaining many kinds of opportunities and rewards. How one copes with this situation will be largely determined by whether one views the disadvantages to be just or unjust. If those who are disadvantaged by their group identity accept their disadvantages as being warranted, they are unlikely to challenge and conflict with those who are profiting from their relatively advantaged positions. The sense of being treated unjustly because of one's membership in a group to which one is strongly attached and bound is the energizer for much intergroup conflict. The sense of injustice is felt particularly intensely in interracial, interethnic, and intersex conflicts because of the centrality of these group identities to the individual's self-esteem. When women or blacks or Jews are devalued as a group, those who are identified and identify with the groups also are personally devalued.

There is considerable evidence from the anthropological literature (see LeVine & Campbell, 1972, for a summary and references) that the pyramidal–segmentary social structure is more conducive to destructive intergroup strife within a society than the cross-cutting type. The reason for this is easy to see. If, for example, in a society which has a pyramidal–segmentary social structure a conflict arises between two ethnic groups in the society (e.g. about which group's language shall be paramount in the total society), then the individual's membership in all the groups that are nested within his ethnic group (his neighborhood, his recreation group, his kinship group, etc.) will strengthen his loyalty to his ethnic group's position. But this will happen on both sides, making it more difficult to resolve the differences between the two groups. On the other hand, in a cross-cutting social structure, members of the conflicting ethnic groups are likely to be members of common work groups, common neighborhood groups, and so on. Their common membership will make it difficult to polarize individual attitudes about the ethnic conflict. Doing so would place the individual in the dilemma of choosing between loyalty to his ethnic group and loyalty to his other groups that cut across ethnic lines. Thus cross-cutting membership and loyalties tend to function as a moderating influence in resolving any particular intergroup conflict within a society. However, if the ethnic conflict becomes sufficiently intense even cross-cutting ties may be torn, resulting in an even greater bitterness and violence as one experiences a sense of betrayal of trust.[3]

[3] There are excellent discussions of relevant theory and of specific ethnic and other intergroup conflicts in Staub (1989), Gurr (1993), Ross and Rothman (1999), and Christie, Wagner, and Winter (2001). For a recent, excellent symposium on the concept of "Social Identity," see *Political Psychology, 22*(1), 2001, 111–198.

The third question, which focuses on how to achieve forgiveness and reconciliation after bitter conflict, has been of increasing interest to students of conflict. There have been outstanding discussions in Lederach (1997), Shriver (1995), Minow (1998), and in various chapters in Christie, Wagner, and Winter (2001). I have also discussed these matters in Deutsch and Coleman (2000, Chapter 2).

Wessels and Monteiro (2001, p. 263) have articulated very well the scope of the task and challenges involved in reconstruction of civil society after bitter, destructive, dehumanizing ethnic conflict. It involves interrelated tasks of economic, political, and social reconstruction as well as psychosocial intervention. As they point out, "In all of these tasks, a high priority is the establishment of *social justice*, transforming patterns of exclusion, inequity, and oppression that fuel tension and fighting."

In my discussion of reconciliation (Deutsch & Coleman, 2000, pp. 58–62), I have articulated some basic principles for establishing cooperative relations after a bitter conflict. They are:

1. *Mutual security*. After a bitter conflict, each side tends to be concerned with its own security, without adequate recognition that neither side can attain security unless the other side also feels secure. Real security requires that both sides have as their goal *mutual* security. If weapons have been involved in the prior conflict, mutually verifiable disarmament and arms control are important components of mutual security.

2. *Mutual respect*. Just as true security from physical danger requires mutual cooperation, so does security from psychological harm and humiliation. Each side must treat the other side with the respect, courtesy, politeness, and consideration normatively expected in civil society. Insult, humiliation, and inconsiderateness by one side usually leads to reciprocation by the other and decreased physical and psychological security.

3. *Humanization of the other*. During bitter conflict, each side tends to dehumanize the other and develop images of the other as an evil enemy. There is much need for both sides to experience one another in everyday contexts as parents, homemakers, schoolchildren, teachers, and merchants, which enables them to see one another as human beings who are more like themselves than not. Problem-solving workshops, along the lines developed by Burton (1969, 1987) and Kelman (1972), are also valuable in overcoming dehumanization of one another.

4. *Fair rules for managing conflict*. Even if a tentative reconciliation has begun, new conflicts inevitably occur—over the distribution of scarce resources, procedures, values, etc. It is important to anticipate that conflicts will occur and to develop beforehand the fair rules, experts, institutions, and other resources for managing such conflicts constructively and justly.

5. *Curbing the extremists on both sides*. During a protracted and bitter conflict, each side tends to produce extremists committed to the processes of the destructive conflict as well as to its continuation. Attaining some of their initial goals may be less satisfying than continuing to inflict damage on the other. It is well to recognize that extremists stimulate extremism on both sides. The parties need to cooperate in curbing extremism on their own side and restraining actions that stimulate and justify extremist elements on the other side.

6. *Gradual development of mutual trust and cooperation*. It takes repeated experience of successful, varied, mutually beneficial cooperation to develop a solid basis for mutual trust between former enemies. In the early stages of reconciliation, when trust is required for cooperation, the former enemies may be willing to trust a third party (who agrees to serve as a monitor, inspector, or guarantor of any cooperative arrangement) but not yet willing

to trust one another if there is a risk of the other failing to reciprocate cooperation. Also in the early stages, it is especially important that cooperative endeavors be successful. This requires careful selection of the opportunities and tasks for cooperation so that they are clearly achievable as well as meaningful and significant.

How Applicable in Other Cultures Are the Theories Related to Conflict that Have Largely Been Developed in the United States and Western Europe?

I believe there is considerable confusion about this question. It would be presumptuous indeed to think that there exists, at this stage of the development of the field of conflict resolution, a theory which is universally valid across the various cultures, across historic time, and across different types of social actors (individuals, groups, organizations, and nations). There are some of us who hope such theory can ultimately be developed and some of us are even brash enough to think that some of the existing theoretical ideas (e.g. about cooperation–competition) may have considerable generality. However, even if we had a universally valid *theory* at the level of constructs, the operational definition of constructs (i.e. how they are defined empirically or in terms of phenomena) would inevitably differ in different cultures and even, within a given culture, from situation to situation. In Lewinian terminology, constructs are like *genotypes*, and the observational data are similar to *phenotypes*. A given genotype can be expressed in many different types of phenotypes (e.g. the color of two genotypically identical hydrangeas will differ as a function of the acidity of the soil in which they are planted). Similarly, a given construct, such as aggression, can be manifested in many ways depending on the culture and other characteristics of the specific situation in which the parties are involved.

Thus, whether or not we had a universally valid theory (which we don't),[4] we would still need to have detailed, specific knowledge of the culture in which we are employing whatever theoretical ideas or framework we use to orient ourselves to conflict and to cultural differences. A self-reflective practitioner will seek to be aware of his/her own framework and be open to its change in light of challenging, new experiences. S/he will also be sensitive to his/her own cultural assumptions about the power relations between him/herself and the people with whom s/he is working and their appropriateness in the culture within which s/he is working. In addition, s/he will be aware of his/her need to develop knowledge about the culture and background of the people with whom s/he is working by using existing knowledge, informants, coworkers from the culture, and by what Lederach (1995) has termed an "elicitive approach" as s/he works with people from a different culture. While the issue of "cultural" differences is obvious when comparing such differences across societies, it should be recognized that there are also "cultural" differences within societies—among the different socioeconomic classes, between the sexes, among occupations, etc. It is a common mistake to assume that cultures are homogeneous.

There are a number of excellent books which discuss specific differences among cultures as they deal with conflict and negotiation. They include Triandis (1972), Hofstede (1980),

[4] I believe that a number of psychological theories (e.g. equity theory) implicitly assume a culture that is individualistic and market-oriented. Sampson (1983) has an excellent critique of psychological theories from this perspective. In Deutsch and Coleman (2000, Chapter 1), I describe the values and social norms underlying our practice of conflict resolution.

Kimmel (1989), Hall and Hall (1990), Cohen (1991), Fisher (1998), Faure and Rubin (1993), Ross (1993), Rahim and Blum (1994), and Leung and Tjosvold (1998).

EVALUATION OF PROGRESS IN THE SOCIAL PSYCHOLOGICAL STUDY OF CONFLICT

I now turn to the important question: what progress, if any, has occurred during the past 70 years or so in the social psychological study of conflict? I am a biased observer, but, even taking my bias into account, I am strongly inclined to believe that significant scientific progress has been made and that important contributions to society are being derived from the scientific study of conflict. Let me briefly characterize the nature of the progress in the methodological, conceptual, empirical, and technological domains.

Methodological

There have been major methodological advances during the past 60 years in the study of cooperation–competition, conflict, bargaining, and negotiation. New and better techniques for studying these phenomena in the laboratory and also in the field have emerged.

Conceptual

In the course of this chapter, I have outlined some of the conceptual developments that have taken place in work on cooperation and competition; on understanding the nature and determinants of constructive and destructive processes of conflict resolution; and on understanding some of the determinants and consequences of different systems of distributive justice. We are beginning to have some understanding of the conditions and processes involved in intractable conflict. Some of the psychological issues involved in ethnic conflict have been highlighted by social identity theory. The functions of such third parties as mediators, the determinants of the effectiveness of mediation, and the nature of the processes involved in mediation are being clarified. This represents significant theoretical progress and a more systematic integration of our knowledge of the social psychological aspects of conflict and distributive justice.

Empirical

We know a great deal more, with considerably more certainty, about the empirical regularities associated with conflict. Thus, we know how such psychological processes as "autistic hostility," "self-fulfilling prophecies," "unwitting commitments," and "biased perceptions" operate to produce an escalation of conflict. We know the social psychological correlates of intensifying conflict and of de-escalating conflict. Thus, as conflict escalates there is an increased reliance upon a strategy of power and upon the tactics of threat, coercion, and deception. Also, there is increased pressure for uniformity of opinion and for leadership and control to be taken over by those elements organized for waging conflict. De-escalation of conflict is characterized by graduated reciprocation in tension reduction;

tactics of conciliation; accentuation of similarities; and enhancement of mutual understanding and goodwill. We are increasingly aware of the social psychological regularities associated with benign and malevolent conflict. We are reasonably sure of the typical effects of certain forms of bargaining strategies and tactics and can reliably conclude that many commonsense beliefs about bargaining are much too simple part-truths.

Technological

There have been many significant social consequences of the scientific study of conflict; not all of these can be attributed to the work of social psychologists. Social psychologists have been important contributors to some changes in thinking about conflict at the national level—as exemplified in Kennedy's American University speech and in the Kerner Commission reports. Also, in recent years, many of the ideas generated in the social psychological study of conflict have been employed in training administrators and negotiators, in schools, labor unions, industry, government, and community organizations, how to deal with conflict more effectively. "Conflict," "negotiation skills," and "mediation skills" workshops are now common features of training for work in organizations in the United States, Europe, and Japan. Osgood's (1962) strategy for de-escalating conflict—"graduated and reciprocated initiatives in tension reduction" (GRIT)—has received considerable experimental support, has been widely discussed in international and national meetings, and appears to have been the basis for the "Kennedy experiment" to end the Cold War. Key participants in the round-table negotiations in Poland between the Communist government and Solidarity have told me that our work on conflict resolution was consciously employed to facilitate successful negotiations. Problem-solving workshops, developed by such people as John Burton, Herbert Kelman, Leonard Doob, and Edward Azar, have been widely used in international and intercommunal conflict (Fisher, 1998).

Let me conclude by stating that although there has been significant progress in the study of conflict, the progress does not yet begin to match the social need for understanding conflict. We live in a period of history when the pervasiveness and intensity of competitive conflict over natural resources are likely to increase markedly. And currently ethnic and national conflicts pose a great danger to peace in many areas of the world. We also live in a period when hydrogen bombs and other weapons of mass destruction can destroy civilized life. The social need for better ways of managing conflict is urgent. In relation to this need, it is my view that too few of us are working on the scientific issues which are likely to provide the knowledge that will lead to more constructive conflict resolution of the many intensive conflicts which await us all.

REFERENCES

Adams, J. S. (1963). Toward an understanding of inequity. *Journal of Abnormal and Social Psychology, 67*, 422–436.

Adams, J. S. (1965). Inequity in social exchange. In L. Berkowitz (ed.), *Advances in Experimental Social Psychology* (Vol. 2). New York: Academic.

Adams, J. S. & Freedman, S. (1976). Equity theory revisited: comments and annotated bibliography. In L. Berkowitz & E. Walster (eds), *Advances in Experimental Social Psychology* (Vol. 9). New York: Academic.

Alinsky, S. D. (1971). *Rules for Radicals: A Practical Primer for Realistic Radicals.* New York: Random House.
Banton, M. (1967). *Race Relations*. New York: Basic Books.
Bartos, O. J. (1970). Determinants and consequences of toughness. In P. Swingle (ed.), *The Structure of Conflict*. New York: Academic.
Bazerman, M. H. & Neal, M. A. (1992). *Negotiating Rationally.* New York: Free Press.
Bodine, R. J. & Crawford, D. K. (1998). *The Handbook of Conflict Resolution Education.* San Francisco: Jossey-Bass.
Breslin, J. W. & Rubin, J. Z. (1991). *Negotiation Theory and Practice.* Cambridge, Mass.: Harvard Program in Negotiation.
Burton, J. W. (1969). *Conflict and Communication: The Use of Controlled Communication in International Relations.* London: Macmillan.
Burton, J. W. (1987). *Resolving Deep-rooted Conflict: A Handbook.* Lanham, Md: University Press of America.
Bush, R. A. B. & Folger, J. P. (1994). *The Promise of Mediation: Responding to Conflict through Empowerment and Recognition.* San Francisco: Jossey-Bass.
Cantril, H. (ed.) (1950). *Tensions that Cause Wars*. Urbana: University of Illinois Press.
Chamberlain, N. (1951). *Collective Bargaining*. New York: McGraw-Hill.
Christie, D. J., Wagner, R. V., & Winter, D. D. (eds) (2001). *Peace, Conflict, and Violence: Peace Psychology for the 21st Century.* Upper Saddle River, NJ: Prentice-Hall.
Cohen, R. (1991). *Negotiations across Cultures.* Washington, DC: United States Institute of Peace.
Coleman, P. T. (1997). Redefining ripeness: a social psychological perspective. *Peace and Conflict: Journal of Peace Psychology, 3*, 81–89.
Coleman, P. T. (2000). Intractable conflict. In M. Deutsch & P. T. Coleman (eds), *Handbook of Conflict Resolution: Theory and Practice*. San Francisco: Jossey-Bass.
Cummings, L. L. & Harnett, D. L. (1969). Bargaining behavior in a symmetric bargaining triad. *The Review of Economic Studies, 36*, 485–501.
Deutsch, M. (1949a). A theory of cooperation and competition. *Human Relations, 2*, 129–152.
Deutsch, M. (1949b). An experimental study of the effects of cooperation and competition upon group process. *Human Relations, 2*, 199–232.
Deutsch, M. (1973). *The Resolution of Conflict: Constructive and Destructive Processes*. New Haven: Yale University Press.
Deutsch, M. (1974). Awakening the sense of injustice. In M. Lerner & M. Ross (eds), *The Quest for Justice*. Toronto: Holt, Rinehart & Winston of Canada.
Deutsch, M. (1975). Equity, equality and need: what determines which value will be used as the basis of distributive justice? *The Journal of Social Issues, 31*, 137–150.
Deutsch, M. (1983). Preventing World War III: a psychological perspective. *Political Psychology, 3*(1), 3–31.
Deutsch, M. (1985). *Distributive Justice: A Social-psychological Perspective*. New Haven: Yale University Press.
Deutsch, M. (1988). On negotiating the non-negotiable. In B. Kellerman & J. Rubin (eds), *Leadership and Negotiation in the Middle East.* New York: Praeger.
Deutsch, M. & Coleman, P. T. (2000). *The Handbook of Conflict Resolution: Theory and Practice.* San Francisco: Jossey-Bass.
Deutsch, M. & Krauss, R. M. (1960). The effect of threat upon interpersonal bargaining. *Journal of Abnormal and Social Psychology, 61*, 181–189.
Diesing, P. (1962). *Reason in Society*. Urbana: University of Illinois Press.
Faure, G. I. & Rubin, J. Z. (1993). *Culture and Negotiation.* Newbury Park, Calif.: Sage.
Festinger, L. (1957). *A Theory of Cognitive Dissonance.* Evanston, Ill.: Row, Peterson.
Festinger, L. (1961). The psychological effect of insufficient reward. *American Psychologist, 16*, 1–11.
Fisher, G. (1988). *Mindsets.* Yarmouth, Me: Intercultural Press.
Fisher, R. J. (1997). *Interactive Conflict Resolution*. Syracuse, NY: Syracuse University Press.
Fisher, R. J. (1998). *Interactive Problem Solving*. Syracuse, NY: Syracuse University Press.
Fisher, R. J. (2000). Intergroup conflict. In M. Deutsch & P. T. Coleman (eds), *Handbook of Conflict Resolution: Theory and Practice.* San Francisco: Jossey-Bass.

Folger, J. B. & Bush, R. A. B. (1996). Transformative mediation and third-party intervention. Ten hallmarks of a transformative approach to practice. *Mediation Quarterly, 13*, 263–278.
Gurr, T. R. (1993). *Minorities at Risk: A Global View of Ethnopolitical Conflicts.* Washington, DC: US Institute of Peace Press.
Hall, E. T. & Hall, M. R. (1990). *Understanding Cultural Differences: Germans, French, and Americans.* Yarmouth, Me: Intercultural Press.
Hamner, W. C. & Baird, L. S. (1978). The effect of strategy, pressure to reach agreement and relative power on bargaining behavior. In H. Sauermann (ed.), *Contributions to Experimental Economics* (Vol. 7). Tübingen: Mohr.
Harnett, D. L. & Cummings, L. L. (1968). Bargaining behavior in an asymmetric triad: the role of information, communication, and risk-taking propensity. Mimeographed manuscript, University of Indiana.
Harnett, D. L., Cummings, L. L., & Hughes, C. D. (1968). The influence of risk-taking propensity on bargaining behavior. *Behavioral Science, 13*, 91–101.
Harnett, D. L. & Vincelette, J. P. (1978). Strategic influences on bargaining effectiveness. In H. Sauermann (ed.), *Contributions to Experimental Economics* (Vol. 7). Tübingen: Mohr.
Hofstede, G. (1980). *Culture's Consequences: International Differences in Work-related Value.* Thousand Oaks, Calif.: Sage.
Homans, G. C. (1961). *Social Behavior: Its Elementary Forms.* New York: Harcourt, Brace, Jovanovich.
Homans, G. C. (1974). *Social Behavior: Its Elementary Forms* (rev. edn). New York: Harcourt, Brace, Jovanovich.
Hull, C. L. (1938). The goal-gradient hypothesis applied to some "field-force" problems in the behavior of young children. *Psychological Review, 45*, 271–299.
Hyman, S. E. (1966). *The Tangled Bank.* New York: Grosset and Dunlap, University Library Edition.
Jervis, A. S. (1970). *The Logic of Images in International Relations.* Princeton: Princeton University Press.
Jervis, A. S. (1976). *Perception and Misperception in International Politics.* Princeton: Princeton University Press.
Johnson, D. W. & Johnson, R. T. (1989). *Cooperation and Competition: Theory and Research.* Edina, Minn.: Interaction.
Johnson, D. W. & Johnson, R. T. (2000). Teaching students to be peacemakers: results of twelve years of research. Unpublished paper, University of Minnesota.
Jones, T. S. & Kmitter, D. (eds) (2000). *Does it Work? The Case for Conflict Resolution Education in Our Nation's Schools.* Washington, DC: Conflict Resolution Education Network.
Kahn, N. (1965). *On Escalation: Metaphors and Scenarios.* New York: Praeger.
Kegan, R. (1994). *In over Our Heads: The Mental Demands of Modern Life.* Cambridge, Mass.: Harvard University Press.
Kelley, H. H. & Schenitzki, D. P. (1972). Bargaining. In C. G. McClintock (ed.), *Experimental Social Psychology.* New York: Holt, Rinehart & Winston.
Kelman, H. C. (1972). The problem-solving workshop in conflict resolution. In R. L. Merritt (ed.), *Communication in International Politics.* Urbana, Ill.: University of Illinois Press.
Kimmel, P. R. (1989). *International Negotiation and Intercultural Exploration: Toward Culture Understanding.* Washington, DC: US Institute of Peace Press.
Klineberg, O. (1964). *The Human Dimensions in International Relations.* New York: Holt, Rinehart & Winston.
Kressel, K. (2000). Mediation behavior. In M. Deutsch & P. T. Coleman (eds), *The Handbook of Conflict Resolution: Theory and Practice.* San Francisco: Jossey-Bass.
Kressel, K. & Pruitt, D. (1985). The mediation of social conflict. A special issue of the *Journal of Social Issues, 41*.
Kressel, K. & Pruitt, D. (1989). *Mediation Research.* San Francisco: Jossey-Bass.
Kritter, P. B. (1994). *Negotiating at an Uneven Table.* San Francisco: Jossey-Bass.
Lamm, H. & Kayser, E. (1978a). The allocation of monetary gain and loss following dyadic performance. *European Journal of Social Psychology, 8*, 275–278.
Lamm, H. & Kayser, E. (1978b). An analysis of negotiation concerning the allocation of jointly produced profit or loss. *International Journal of Group Tensions, 8*, 64–80.

Lederach, J. P. (1995). *Preparing for Peace: Conflict Transformation across Cultures.* Syracuse, NY: Syracuse University Press.

Lederach, J. P. (1997). *Building Peace: Sustainable Reconciliation in Divided Societies.* Washington, DC: US Institute of Peace Press.

Lerner, M. J. (1975). The Justice Motive in Social Behavior: Introduction. *Journal of Social Issues, 31*, 1–20.

LeVine, R. A. & Campbell, D. T. (1972). *Ethnocentricism: Theories of Conflict, Ethnic Attitudes, and Goup Behavior.* New York: Wiley.

Leung, H. & Tjosvold, D. (1998). *Conflict Management in the Asia Pacific.* New York: John Wiley & Sons.

Leventhal, G. S. (1976). *Fairness in Social Relationships.* Morristown, NJ: General Learning Press.

Lewicki, R. J. & Litterer, J. A. (1985a). *Negotiation: Readings, Exercises, and Cases.* Homewood, Ill.: Irwin.

Lewicki, R. J. & Litterer, J. A. (1985b). *Negotiation.* Homewood, Ill.: Irwin.

Lewicki, R. J., Saunders, D. M., & Minton, J. W. (1999). *Negotiation* (3rd edn). New York: McGraw-Hill.

Lewin, K. (1931). Environmental forces in child behavior and development. In C. Murchison (ed.), *A Handbook of Child Psychology.* Worcester, Mass.: Clark University Press.

Lewin, K. (1935). *A Dynamic Theory of Personality.* New York: McGraw-Hill.

Lewis, H. B. & Franklin, M. (1944). An experimental study of the role of the ego in work: II. The significance of task-orientation in work. *Journal of Experimental Psychology, 34*, 195–215.

Machiavelli, N. (1950). *The Prince and the Discourses.* New York: Modern Library.

Magenau, J. M. & Pruitt, D. G. (1978). The social psychology of bargaining: a theoretical synthesis. In G. M. Stephenson & C. J. Brotherton (eds), *Industrial Relations: A Social Psychological Approach.* London: Wiley.

Mahler, W. (1933). Ersatzhandlungen verschiedenen Realitätsgrades. *Psychologische Forschung, 18*, 27–89.

May, M. A. & Doob, L. W. (1937). *Competition and Cooperation.* Social Science Research Bulletin, No. 25. New York.

Mikula, G. & Schwinger, T. (1978). Intermember relations and reward allocation: theoretical considerations of affects. In H. Brandstatter, J. H. Davis, & H. Schuler (eds), *Dynamics of Group Decisions.* Beverly Hills: Sage Publications.

Miller, N. E. (1937). Analysis of the form of conflict reactions. *Psychological Bulletin, 34*, 720.

Miller, N. E. (1944). Experimental studies of conflict. In J. McV. Hunt (ed.), *Personality and the Behavior Disorders* (Vol. 1). New York: Ronald.

Minow, M. (1998). Between vengeance and forgiveness: South Africa's truth and reconciliation commission. *Negotiation Journal, 14*, 319–356.

Moore, C. W. (1996). *The Mediation Process: Practical Strategies for Resolving Conflict* (2nd edn). San Francisco: Jossey-Bass.

Murphy, G., Murphy, L. B., & Newcomb, T. M. (1937). *Experimental Social Psychology* (rev. edn). New York: Harper and Brothers.

Osgood, C. E. (1962). *An Alternative to War or Surrender.* Urbana, Ill.: University of Illinois Press.

Ovsiankina, M. (1928). Die Wiederaufnahme Unterbrochener Handlungen. *Psychologische Forschung, 11*, 302–379.

Potter, S. (1965). *The Theory and Practice of Gamesmanship.* New York: Bantam Books.

Pruitt, D. G. (1981). *Negotiation Behavior.* New York: Academic Press.

Pruitt, D. G. & Carnevale, P. J. (1993). *Negotiation in Social Conflict.* Pacific Grove, Calif.: Brooks/Col.

Pruitt, D. G. & Kimmel, M. J. (1977). Twenty years of experimental gaming: critique, synthesis, and suggestions for the future. *Annual Review of Psychology, 28*, 363–392.

Pruitt, D. G. & Olzack, P. V. (1995). Resolving seemingly intractable conflict. In B. B. Bunkey & J. Z. Rubin (eds), *Conflict, Cooperation, and Justice: Essays Inspired by the Work of Morton Deutsch*, pp. 39–58. San Francisco: Jossey-Bass.

Rahim, A. & Blum, A. A. (1994). *Global Perspectives on Organizational Conflict.* New York: Praeger.

Ross, M. H. (1993). *The Culture of Conflict.* New Haven: Yale University Press.

Ross, M. H. & Rothman, J. (1999). *Theory and Practice in Ethnic Conflict Management: Theorizing Success and Failure.* New York: St Martin's Press.

Rubin, J. Z. & Brown, B. R. (1975). *The Social Psychology of Bargaining and Negotiation*. New York: Academic.
Rubin, J. Z., Pruitt, D. G., & Kim, S. H. (1994). *Social Conflict: Escalation, Stalemate, and Settlement*. New York: McGraw-Hill.
Sampson, E. E. (1969). Studies of status congruence. In L. Berkowitz (ed.), *Advances in Experimental Social Psychology* (Vol. 4). New York: Academic.
Sampson, E. E. (1975). On justice as equality. *The Journal of Social Issues, 31*, 45–64.
Sampson, E. E. (1983). *Justice and the Critique of Peace Psychology*. New York: Plenum.
Schachtel, E. G. (1959). *Metamorphosis: On the Development of Affect, Perception, Attention, and Memory*. New York: Basic Books.
Schelling, T. C. (1960). *The Strategy of Conflict*. Cambridge: Harvard University Press.
Schelling, T. C. (1966). *Arms and Influence*. New Haven: Yale University Press.
Shriver, D. W., Jr (1995). *An Ethic for Enemies: Forgiveness in Politics*. New York: Oxford University Press.
Siegel, S. & Fouraker, L. E. (1960). *Bargaining and Group Decision Making: Experiments in Bilateral Monopoly*. New York: McGraw-Hill.
Snyder, G. H. & Diesing, P. (1977). *Conflict among Nations*. Princeton: Princeton University Press.
Staub, E. (1989). *The Roots of Evil: The Origins of Genocide and Other Group Violence*. New York: Cambridge University Press.
Stevens, C. M. (1963). *Strategy and Collective Bargaining Negotiation*. New York: McGraw-Hill.
Tajfel, H. (1978). *Differentiation between Social Groups: Studies in the Social Psychology of Intergroup Relations*. London: Academic Press.
Tajfel, H. (1981). *Human Groups and Social Categories: Studies in Social Psychology*. Cambridge: Cambridge University Press.
Tedeschi, J. T., Schlenker, B. R., & Bonoma, T. V. (1973). *Conflict Power and Games*. Chicago: Aldine.
Thompson, L. H. (1998). *The Mind and Heart of the Negotiation*. Upper Saddle River, NJ: Prentice-Hall.
Touval, S. & Zartman, I. W. (eds) (1985). *International Mediation in Theory and Practice*. Boulder, Colo.: Westview Press.
Triandis, H. (1972). *An Analysis of Subjective Culture*. New York: John Wiley & Sons.
Turner, J. C. (1987). *Rediscovering the Social Group: A Self-categorization Theory*. New York: Basil Blackwell.
Tyler, T. R., Boeckman, R. J., Smith, H. J., & Huo, Y. J. (1997). *Social Justice in a Diverse Society*. Boulder, Colo.: Westview Press.
Vinacke, W. E. & Arkoff, A. (1957). An experimental study of coalitions in the triad. *American Sociological Review, 22*, 406–414.
Von Neumann, J. & Morgenstern, O. (1944). *Theory of Games and Economic Behavior*. New York: Wiley.
Walster, E., Walster, G. W., & Berscheid, E. (1978). *Equity Theory and Research*. Boston: Allyn and Bacon.
Walton, R. E. & McKersie, R. B. (1965). *A Behavioral Theory of Labor Negotiations: An Analysis of a Social Interaction System*. New York: McGraw-Hill.
Wessels, M. & Monteiro, C. (2001). Psychosocial intervention and post-war reconstruction in Angola: interweaving traditional and Western approaches. In D. J. Christie, R. V. Wagner, & D. N. W. Winter (eds), *Peace, Conflict, and Violence: Peace Psychology for the 21st Century* (pp. 262–276). Upper Saddle River, NJ: Prentice-Hall.
Zartman, I. W. (1985). *Ripe for Resolution*. New York: Oxford University Press.
Zartman, I. W. (2000). Ripeness: the hurting stalemate and beyond. In *International Conflict Resolution after the Cold War*. Washington, DC: The National Academy of Science.
Zartman, I. W. & Berman, M. (1982). *The Practical Negotiator*. New Haven, Conn.: Yale University Press.
Zeigarnik, B. (1927). Uber das Behalten von erledigten und unerledigten Handlungen. *Psychologische Forschung, 9*, 1–85.

3

EVOLUTION OF COOPERATION

Martin Evans

COOPERATION

In this chapter I will explore a controversial topic in psychology: whether there might be evolutionary underpinnings to the cooperative activity that we see around us. In particular I will examine the evidence for a basic desideratum for cooperation to flourish: the ability to detect those who defect from the cooperative venture and pursue their own selfish ends to the detriment of those remaining in the cooperative activity. We will begin our search a long way from cooperation between individuals and groups in the modern organization: the environment in which our ancestors evolved as hunter gatherers during the Pleistocene. Our search will continue by drawing on evidence from the computer simulation of cooperative and uncooperative behaviors. We continue with an examination of scenario studies that look at puzzles designed to identify whether or not people can identify those who cheat them. We conclude our tour of the evidence by reviewing a number of behavioral studies which look at the cheater detection ability in real-time situations. The chapter concludes with a number of organizational implications.

CHARACTERISTICS OF COOPERATIVE ACTS

Cooperation occurs when one person or group helps another in carrying out a task whose outcome benefits both partners. Benefit in an evolutionary sense means that the life chances (and hence the probability of reproduction) are enhanced. In its simplest manifestation, a task may be too large or too complex to be carried out by a single individual, so the situation demands that each must work together if the task is to be completed. In this case, the interests of the two persons are directly and simultaneously aligned. Neither will receive positive outcomes unless they cooperate. In evolutionary terms, the survival fitness of both parties is enhanced if they work together.

This idea of task-induced cooperation is illustrated by Udy's (1959) study of present-day nonindustrial societies which are the nearest thing we have to the kinds of societies that existed in the Pleistocene. His aggregate data are presented in Table 3.1. These data are

International Handbook of Organizational Teamwork and Cooperative Working. Edited by M. A. West, D. Tjosvold, and K. G. Smith.

Table 3.1 Cooperation in nonindustrial societies

Activity	No. of instances	Task differentiation	Specialization of operations	Combined effort present or not
		Range: 1–5	*Range: 1–5*	*Range: 0–1*
Tillage	12	3.85	2.31	0.61
Hunting	20	1.04	2.10	0.85
Fishing	14	1.23	2.05	0.50
Collecting	9	1.22	1.55	0.11

Source: Udy, 1959.

based upon an examination of the organizational arrangements used by these societies to undertake the daily businesses of life: hunting, fishing, food collecting, crop cultivation.

Udy explores three indexes of complexity: task differentiation (the extent to which the activity comprised few or many different tasks: e.g. ground preparation, ploughing, sowing, watering, cultivation, harvesting, ground clearing), specialization of operations (the extent to which different persons performed these different tasks), and the presence or absence of combined effort (whether two or more actors performed the task simultaneously: e.g. one group of people drives game toward a second group who engage in the killing of the game). It is this last that we are interested in here: the presence or absence of combined and coordinated effort. We see that this is high in hunting, moderate in tillage and fishing, but virtually absent in collection (gathering). Furthermore, we see that at the aggregate level, task differentiation is positively associated with individual specialization ($r = 0.65$), the latter is positively associated with the presence of collaborative activity ($r = 0.72$); task differentiation and collaborative activity are not correlated. This suggests a model in which the need for collaboration and the presence of multiple tasks result in a high degree of specialization. This suggestion must be viewed with caution, as data were unavailable at the level of each nonindustrial organization (Udy, 2001, personal communication).

This, however, is not the only form of cooperation that we observe, and some of these other forms are more problematic for the evolutionary perspective to explain. We see parents making financial sacrifices in order to provide superior education for their children; we see unrelated persons sharing food; we even see unrelated vampire bats regurgitating blood to feed each other. In each of these cases where there is cooperation in sharing resources rather than generating them, the survival fitness of the giver is reduced. In evolutionary terms such people should be selected out and would have lower chances of reproducing. How, then, in evolutionary terms, did such forms of cooperation survive and prosper? Cooperation involving kinfolk (e.g. parents and children) is easy to explain; cooperation involving strangers in the absence of some outside authority forcing cooperation, more difficult.

Cooperation involving kinfolk: the selfish gene (Dawkins, 1976) does not care who carries it. It just wishes to be replicated. Replication through direct or collateral descent is just fine as far as the gene is concerned. This means that equal reproductive success is achieved, as far as the gene is concerned, by my survival, by the survival of two of my siblings (with whom I share 50 percent of genetic material), or two of my children (with whom I also share 50 percent of my genetic material), or even by the survival of eight of my first cousins (with whom I share 12.5 percent of my genetic material).

J. B. S. Haldane is known for having turned this idea into a joke. When asked, "Would you lay down your life for your brother?", Haldane replied, "No—but for two brothers, or

Table 3.2 Payoff matrix for the prisoners' dilemma

		Partner B		
		Cooperate—say nothing to the police	Defect—tell all to the police	R = Reward for mutual cooperation T = Temptation to defect S = Sucker's payoff P = Punishment for mutual defection Constraints: $T > R > P > S$; $R > (T + S)/2$
Partner A	Cooperate—say nothing to the police	A: $R = +3$ B: $R = +3$	A: $S = -2$ B: $T = +5$	
	Defect—tell all to the police	A: $T = +5$ B: $S = -2$	A: $P = 0$ A: $P = 0$	

eight cousins." In this way, the genetic material has the potential of continuing through to the next generation (Hamilton (1964a, b)). Note that in this case, the loss due to Haldane's death and the gain due to the survival of either siblings or cousins is equal. For Haldane's death to be beneficial to the survival of his genetic material he should be sacrificing himself for three siblings or nine cousins.

Cooperation involving nonkinfolk: here it is hard to understand why the selfish gene would surrender some of its life chances to help nonkinfolk. In such situations, the probability of the gene having its fitness enhanced is vanishingly small. Only if the individual carrying the gene can expect some reciprocity from the person being helped can there be any expectation of there being some improvement in the gene's own survival. This leads us to the solution of the problem of reciprocal altruism first laid out by Robert Trivers (1971). Trivers' insight was to frame the problem in the classical game-theoretic form of the "prisoners' dilemma" (see also Cosmides & Tooby (1992) on which this account is based). In the prisoners' dilemma the situation involves two partners in crime who are arrested and held in separate cells. The authorities offer each person a deal: squeal on your fellow prisoner and you will get set free. If neither squeal, the lack of evidence will enable both to get a relatively light sentence. If only one squeals, the squealer gets freedom, but the partner gets a heavy sentence. If they both defect, then both get a stiff sentence. This is set out in Table 3.2 showing the payoff matrix.

In this situation, if both cooperated with each other, they would be better off, yet individual rationality would lead to defection. Let us look at the situation from A's perspective. If A believes that B will cooperate, then if A chooses to defect A will get a higher payoff (T versus R). If A believes that B will defect, then A will also get a higher payoff if A defects (P versus S). Thus defection is the dominant strategy for A. The same is true for B. Thus in single plays of the prisoners' dilemma game the rational thing to do is defect. However, if we conceive of situations in which there are repeated plays of the game—an unlucky criminal partnership whose members are constantly being arrested—then when the players engage in the game for an unknown number of times,[1] alternatively cooperating and defecting will lead to a higher payoff $[(T + S)/2]$ and full cooperation will lead to the highest payoff of all (R).

This is exactly the structure of the situation facing our hunter/gathering ancestors when making a decision to share food. To share with kinfolk was noncontroversial, the chances of gene replication were increased. To share with strangers was more controversial. The argument is that in order to survive in an environment in which the availability of food and water was "lumpy" one needed to cooperate with strangers and that this cooperation entailed the sharing of food and water. Someone, or some clan, that was successful on one occasion would share with others; the others were expected to reciprocate when they got lucky. In the situation of reciprocal altruism, reproductive fitness would be enhanced for those members of the species who could detect (and punish) defection. In other words, if I did you a good turn, I needed to be aware if you failed to reciprocate. Those with this detection facility were less likely to die young and hence more likely to reproduce than those lacking the "cheater detector." More formally, Cosmides & Tooby (1992, p. 193) argue:

> The game theoretic models for the evolution of cooperation that could be reasonably applied... require the existence of some mechanism for detecting cheaters or otherwise excluding them from the benefits of cooperation. This is because the capacity to engage in social exchange could not have evolved in the first place unless the individuals involved could avoid being continually exploited by cheaters.

Thus four prerequisites are needed for the evolution of cooperation: continued interaction between partners (with no known end date); the ability to recognize partners; the ability to recognize whether or not one had been paid back within a reasonable time (what Cosmides and Tooby call the "cheater detection mechanism"); and the ability to assign value to the items exchanged for both self and other, that is we need to know whether or not the "terms of trade" are fair.

Implicit in the foregoing discussion is the fact that the cooperative events follow each other rather than occurring simultaneously. That is there is some time elapse between my giving help and the other party responding. It is this that makes things difficult. If I fail to reciprocate while you are providing help, it is easy to see that I have cheated; it is less easy if my helping response is not expected for some time. We shall see later that one of the most problematic situations of cooperation is intergenerational cooperation (Wade-Benzoni, 1999). A second issue is the target of reciprocity. Am I expected to repay my original benefactor, or can my repayment be made to a third party who in turn, either directly, or through a chain of others, repays my original benefactor?

In his seminal book, *The Evolution of Cooperation*, Axelrod (1984) demonstrated how a stable cooperative strategy could be stable in the most unpromising of conditions. He essentially ran the prisoners' dilemma game in a computer simulation that pitted a wide variety of strategies against each other. Despite altering various starting values such as the mix of actors using different strategies, the density of interaction, local versus widespread interaction, and the extent to which future interactions mattered, a relatively simple strategy dominated the simulation. This was a nice (it was never first to defect), forgiving (it never bore a grudge beyond one turn) strategy called "tit for tat" developed by Anatol Rapoport.

[1] It can be shown that there is no incentive to cooperate if we know how many times the game will be played. In the final game, the endgame strategy of defection is optimal; then the penultimate game is the last game for which the strategy of the other party is unknown, so defection is the optimal, and so on up to the first round of the game (Luce & Raiffa, 1957).

This began its interaction with another party by cooperating. It followed further cooperation with cooperation, and defection with defection. Once the other party cooperated again, it continued to cooperate. Thus with continued interaction with cooperators a culture of cooperation between partners would develop, so most actors would end up cooperating with each other. Only at extremely low levels of continued interaction did the superiority of the tit-for-tat strategy break down. Burt (1999) found that in this situation, actors that employed strategies involving an initial defection did better because they were unlikely to play additional rounds of the game with the same partner. This of course assumes that there was no other communication between actors, so that a "reputation" for defection did not get communicated around the set of actors. The common stereotype of the used-car market perhaps exemplifies this situation, with the purchaser being at the disadvantage.

REASONING-BASED STUDIES OF THE CHEATER DETECTION MECHANISM

What evidence is there that the cheater detection mechanism suggested by Cosmides and her coauthors (Cosmides, 1989; Cosmides & Tooby, 1992) evolved?[2] In a compelling series of studies, Cosmides has argued and claims to have demonstrated that such a mechanism does exist. She used as the vehicle of her demonstration Wason's reasoning task (Johnson-Laird & Wason, 1970). The Wason selection task was originally developed as a test of individual reasoning. It is based, like much of Wason's work, on the logic of scientific falsification developed by Popper (1959). The best description of the task is found in Kirby (1994, p. 2)—see Box 3.1.

Box 3.1 Wason selection task

In Wason's four-card selection task subjects are presented with four cards that are constrained to have instances from the sets P or not-P on one side and Q or not-Q on the other. A conditional statement describes an alleged relation between the fronts and the backs of the cards: if a P is on one side of the card, then a Q is on the other. Subjects' task is to select which of the cards should be turned over to determine whether the conditional relation holds.

Thus success on the task for a group of subjects, usually labeled the "hit rate," is provided by the proportion of the group that identifies both the P card *and* the not-Q card and no other card. The abstract form of this puzzle is stated in the following way:

- the subject is presented with four cards "A," "3," "D," and "7" and is told that there are numbers on one side of the card and letters on the other
- the announced rule is that "If there is an 'A' on one side of the card there must be a '3' on the other side"
- the subject is asked to point out the card or cards that has/have to be turned over to test whether or not the rule holds

[2] This section is based on Evans and Chang (1998).

When the task is represented simply in this form, few subjects (hit rate about 10 percent) solve the problem: the "A" must be turned over to ensure that there is a "3" on the other side and the "7" must be turned over to be sure that there is *not* an "A" on the other side. When the task is given the trappings of a familiar situation, hit rates go to about 15 percent. However this modest increase is often exceeded, and in some situations (e.g. Griggs & Cox's (1982) "bar scene"—see Box 3.2) the hit rate can be as high as 75 or 80 percent. Cosmides argues that the reason for this dramatic improvement is because we have a module of mind developed through evolutionary processes in the ancestral environment that is designed to detect cheats. That is, to return to our earlier discussion of how cooperation evolved, it did so through reciprocal altruism improving the chances for genetic replication (Trivers, 1971) and this could only take place when mechanisms to detect freeloaders evolved concurrently.

Box 3.2 Bar scene

In this scenario, the cards represent four persons who are described as sitting at a table in a bar. There is a law that states that a person has to be over 21 to drink alcohol. One of the persons at the table is known to be drinking beer, one is over 21, one under 20, one is drinking a soft drink. The subject is given the role of bouncer or bar tender and asked which person(s) need further investigation to make sure that the drinking age law is not being broken.

Although the hypothesis that there exists an evolved cheater detection mechanism is an attractive one, the supporting evidence based on the Wason task is both task specific and is subject to alternative explanations (see Box 3.3). So, if the results from the Wason task are ambiguous is there behavioral evidence for the existence of a cheater detection mechanism? We would argue that if cooperation evolved, and if its evolution was contingent on the presence of a "cheater detection" module, the module must have been operating in real time in face-to-face interactions with real people. Therefore, evidence from experimental studies using real people might be more informative than studies using "paper people." With the preponderance of studies involving the Wason task, there is a real danger that our investigation of this phenomenon has become "method bound" (Cook & Campbell, 1979).

Box 3.3 Alternative explanations for the effects of cheater detection in the Wason task

1. That the material being described in the stories (e.g. people in a bar) is very familiar to the respondents. This alternative has been convincingly refuted.
2. That people learn the rules of obligation and permission (deontic reasoning, e.g. if you mow the lawn, I will give you $5.00) during their childhood, so that Wason tasks framed in this way are easy to solve (Cheng & Holyoak, 1985, 1989). This position would suggest that (a) training in the reasoning task would *not* improve performance, and that (b) the logic of the reasoning task would apply equally well to identifying altruists as well as to cheats. Pure altruists (i.e. those not expecting reciprocation) would not be selected for—as Cosmides and Tooby (1992, p. 193) put it: "most models do not require the existence of a mechanism for detecting 'altruists,' individuals who follow the strategy of paying the required cost (thereby benefitting

the other party), but not accepting from the other party the benefit to which this act entitles them. Indeed because individuals who were consistently altruistic would incur costs but receive no compensating benefits, under most plausible scenarios they would be selected out." Unfortunately, neither of these explanations has been ruled out. Holyoak and his associates (Cheng et al., 1986) found that training did improve performance. Evans and Chang (1998) found that their subjects were equally effective in detecting cheaters and altruists.

3. That the stories prime the answer required. We ask them to detect cheats, so people are atuned to finding cheats. Again researchers have been unable to rule out this explanation (Politzer & Nguyen-Xuan, 1992; Schepmyer, 2001).

BEHAVIORAL STUDIES OF THE CHEATER DETECTION MECHANISM

There is some evidence from behavioral economics that people can identify potential defectors. Frank, Gilovich, and Regan (1993) had students mingle for half an hour before playing a single round of a prisoners' dilemma game. The students identified the persons with whom they would be willing to play a tit-for-tat strategy. Sure enough, a majority of those *not* chosen defected on the first round of the game! Evans et al. (2000) tried an alternative approach: whether people could identify defectors after each round of a step level public good game. In the game, individuals can make investments either in personal accounts or in a common pool. If the common pool reaches a certain minimum, then the sum is increased and, at the end of a round, the money in the common pool is shared equally among all players—whether they contributed or not. A selfish (defecting, cheating) strategy for a game player would be to contribute nothing, hope that others will contribute enough to meet the minimal requirements, and share in the division of the increased wealth. The expectation was that the players in the game would have a more accurate estimate of who had contributed what when another person had defected rather than cooperated. We found no evidence for this hypothesis.

It seems then that the existence of a specialized cheater detection mechanism is moot. We find it in many of the Wason task studies; we do not find it in others. We find it in one of the behavioral studies; we do not find it in the other. Further exploration is essential. I hope that this exploration will focus on behavior rather than the study of paper people. Some new ideas on trust (Lewicki, McAllister, & Bies, 1998) may also generate some testable implications of the cheater detection mechanism. They suggest two characteristics of trust: first, that it is multifaceted; second, that trust and mistrust are not opposite ends of the same continuum but that they are somewhat independent. Their view of the multifaceted nature of trust goes beyond the usual distinction between trust in the competence of the other and trust in the intention of the other (i.e. that the other person *can do* what he/she promises and that the other person *will do* what he/she promises). They also suggest that because individuals differ in their mix of skills, then if I am undertaking cooperative work with a colleague, I will trust my partner to perform some tasks while I will distrust him to perform others. They imply too (though do not give examples) that I will have differential trust about my partner's intention with respect to various tasks. My speculation would be that the underlying cheater detection mechanism would be fine-tuned to difference in the domain in which the failure to perform occurred, but that intention would be a more global undifferentiated (by domain) concept. This leads to the testable hypothesis that Lewicki, McAllister, and Bies (1998) are correct about multiplexity of trust vis-à-vis competence in different domains, but that (a) trust about intention will be highly correlated across domains, and (b) trust and distrust about intention will be at opposite ends of the same continuum.

IMPLICATIONS FOR ORGANIZATIONS

Most of organizational success depends upon cooperative work. The need for coordinated activity has been extensively documented by Lawrence and Lorsch (1964). The ways in which coordination can be achieved have been documented by these authors and more completely by Mintzberg (1979). He suggests several mechanisms each of which is appropriate depending on the nature of the organization's task environment: by face-to-face coordination, by supervisory authority, by plan, by outputs (budgets). Over the past 15 years, it has been recognized that many of these coordination activities (especially those occurring on a day-to-day basis) are not formally recognized in organizational job descriptions and reward systems. This has led to an increased focus on understanding the nature of organizational citizenship. This is defined as the extent to which people cooperate with and help their fellow employees, the extent to which individuals comply with organizational norms (e.g. exemplary attendance), the extent to which they disregard any minor inconveniences or impositions that may arise in daily work activities, the extent to which they are active in the polity of the organization (civic virtue), and the extent to which they are courteous to others; finally it includes the extent to which they take actions that are directed toward the prevention of problems encountered by work associates (Organ, 1988; Smith, Organ, & Near, 1983). If cheater detection mechanisms exist, it will be harder for us to identify good citizens (altruists) than it will be to recognize poor citizens.

A second example where the problem of cooperation seems less evident is in determining the content of decisions. By popular belief, we live in an age where managers are focused on the next quarter's bottom-line results. Taking such a short-time perspective may have long-term dysfunctions (consider the Enron implosion). Wade-Benzoni (1999) has argued that there are a number of barriers to bringing the future into the present for consideration of organizational decision makers. They are that the costs accrue to the present generation, the benefits accrue to later generations (often with a high degree of discounting); the costs are certain, the future benefits probabilistic, the decision maker incurs the costs, unspecified others reap the benefits (p. 7). She suggests that these can be overcome through two cognitive strategies. First, the decision maker should focus on the benefits that her/his generation has received from preceding generations (see Wade-Benzoni, 2000, for supporting evidence). This is expected to activate Gouldner's (1960) norm of reciprocity. Second, the decision maker should try to maximize the perceived affinity between her/himself and the beneficiaries.

Our third example comes from interorganizational relationships such as joint ventures. If the cheater detection mechanism does exist, and the altruistic detector mechanism is much weaker, there are some serious implications for managers. How can partners keep a joint venture alive and healthy, if the partner only sees my defaults, and I only see theirs, and neither of us can detect the times that we go out of our way to help each other beyond the terms of the contract? This then suggests that we can easily spot opportunism but not its reverse. The memory traces in managers' minds will be full of all those failures; this, as most members of Tolstoy's unhappy marriages will recognize, is no way to sustain a relationship.

A FINAL WORD

Nothing we have said in this section should be taken to suggest that our behavior and our actions are determined by our genes. Man is an infinitely malleable organism. We can develop techniques to enhance our cheater detection skills (e.g. auditors). We can do likewise to improve our skills for spotting cooperation (e.g. measures of organizational citizenship behavior).

REFERENCES

Axelrod, R. (1984). *The Evolution of Cooperation*. New York: Basic Books.

Burt, R. S. (1999). Private games are too dangerous. *Computational and Mathematical Organization Theory, 5*, 311–341.

Cheng, P. W. & Holyoak, K. J. (1985). Pragmatic reasoning schemas. *Cognitive Psychology, 17*, 391–416.

Cheng, P. W. & Holyoak, K. J. (1989). On the natural selection of reasoning theories. *Cognition, 33*, 285–313.

Cheng, P. W., Holyoak, K. J., Nisbett, R., & Oliver, L. (1986). Pragmatic versus syntactic approaches to training deductive reasoning. *Cognitive Psychology, 18*, 293–328.

Cook, T. D. & Campbell, D. T. (1979). *Quasi-Experimentation: Design and Analysis Issues for Field Settings*. Boston, Mass.: Houghton-Mifflin.

Cosmides, L. (1989). The logic of social exchange: has natural selection shaped how humans reason? Studies with the Wason selection task. *Cognition, 31*, 187–276.

Cosmides, L. & Tooby, J. (1992). Cognitive adaptations for social exchange. In J. H. Barkow, L. Cosmides, & J. Tooby (eds), *The Adapted Mind* (pp. 163–228). New York: Oxford University Press.

Dawkins, R. (1976). *The Selfish Gene*. Oxford, UK: Oxford University Press.

Evans, M. G. & Chang, Y. C. (1998). Cheater detection and altruistic behaviour: an experimental and methodological exploration. *Management and Decision Economics, 19*, 467–480.

Evans, M. G., Li, X., Cheung, Y.-T., & Sargent, L. (2000). Cheater detection *in vivo*. Working paper, Rotman School of Management, University of Toronto.

Frank, R. H., Gilovich, T., & Regan, D. T. (1993). Evolution of one shot cooperation. *Ethology and Sociobiology, 14*, 247–256.

Gouldner, A. W. (1960). The norm of reciprocity: a preliminary statement. *American Sociological Review, 25*, 161–179.

Griggs, R. A. & Cox, J. R. (1982). The elusive thematics material effect in Wason's selection task. *British Journal of Psychology, 73*, 407–420.

Hamilton, W. D. (1964a). The genetical evolution of social behaviour, Part I. *Journal of Theoretical Biology, 7*, 1–16.

Hamilton, W. D. (1964b). The genetical evolution of social behaviour, Part II. *Journal of Theoretical Biology, 7*, 17–32.

Johnson-Laird, P. N. & Wason, P. C. (1970). A theoretical analysis of insight into a reasoning task. *Cognitive Psychology, 1*, 134–148.

Kirby, K. N. (1994). Probabilities and utilities of fictional outcomes in Wason's four-card selection task. *Cognition, 51*, 1–28.

Lawrence, P. & Lorsch, J. (1964). *Managing Differentiation and Integration in Organizations*. Cambridge, Mass.: Division of Research, Harvard Business School.

Lewicki, R. J., McAllister, D. J., & Bies, R. J. (1998). Trust and distrust: new realities and relationships. *Academy of Management Review, 23*, 438–458.
Luce, R. D. & Raiffa, H. (1957). *Games and Decisions*. New York: Wiley.
Mintzberg, H. (1979). *The Structuring of Organizations*. Englewood Cliffs, NJ: Prentice-Hall.
Organ, D. W. (1988). *Organizational Citizenship Behavior: The Good Soldier Syndrome*. Lexington, Mass.: Lexington Books.
Politzer, G. & Nguyen-Xuan, A. (1992). Reasoning about conditional promises and warnings: Darwinian algorithms, mental models, relevance judgements, or pragmatic schemas. *Quarterly Journal of Experimental Psychology, 44*, 401–421.
Popper, K. R. (1959). *The Logic of Scientific Discovery*. New York: Basic Books.
Schepmyer, H. N. (2001). Priming perspective and the decision to look for cheaters: reassessing the determinants. Unpublished working paper, Rotman School of Management, University of Toronto.
Smith, C. A., Organ, D. W., & Near, J. P. (1983). Organizational citizenship behavior. *Journal of Applied Psychology, 68*, 653–663.
Trivers, R. L. (1971). The evolution of reciprocal altruism. *Quarterly Review of Biology, 46*, 35–57.
Udy, S. H. (1959). *Organization of Work: A Comparative Analysis of Production among Nonindustrial Peoples*. New Haven, Conn.: HRAF Press.
Wade-Benzoni, K. A. (1999). Thinking about the future: an intergenerational perspective on the conflict and compatibility between economic and environmental interests. *American Behavioral Scientist, 42*, 1393–1405.
Wade-Benzoni, K. A. (2000). A golden rule over time: reciprocity in intergenerational allocation decisions. Unpublished working paper, Stern School of Business, New York University.

ADDITIONAL READING

Pinker, S. (1997). *How the Mind Works*. New York: Norton.
Plomin, H. (1997). *Evolution in Mind*. Harmondsworth, UK: Penguin Books.
Wright, R. (1994). *The Moral Animal: Evolutionary Psychology and Everyday Life*. New York: Pantheon Books.

4

COOPERATION, TRUST, AND THE VALUES OF COMMUNITY

A POLITICAL AND INSTITUTIONAL PERSPECTIVE

Catherine Fieschi

The aim of politics is to allow human beings to live together as peacefully as possible; the practice of politics can be therefore thought of as the elaboration of plans to avoid or resolve conflict between individuals or groups of human beings. This statement contains two foundational factors: the first is that human beings live communally; the second, that communal living will lead to a measure of disagreement and conflict. The art of living together thus depends on elaborating a science of conflict avoidance, conflict diffusion, and conflict resolution. Thus the science of politics engages, on the one hand, in the prediction of cooperation breakdown and, on the other, in the elaboration of lasting structures (institutional and organizational) that will promote and maintain cooperation.

Two main questions arise. The first regards whether cooperation in the political realm comes naturally. Aristotle's individual as political animal (Aristotle, 1981) can easily be contrasted with Rousseau's reluctant social being, whose peaceful nature is perverted by greed through the emergence of community (and its handmaidens, work and property) (Rousseau, 1978), or with Hobbes's self-interested individual whose perpetual quest for what Hobbes terms "more intense delights" pushes him towards his famous "Warre of everyone against everyone" (Hobbes, 1968). These perspectives on human nature—and the politics that emanate from them—lead us to understand that, while living in communities may be natural, these communities may not necessarily bear the hallmark of voluntary or spontaneous cooperation. For Hobbes, cooperation must be engineered despite man's[1] deep-seated tendencies towards conflict; his conviction that there is "A general inclination of all mankind, a perpetual and restlesse desire of Power after power, that ceaseth only in death" (Hobbes, 1968, p. 161) drives him to attempt to specify a set of conditions under which self-interest may lead to something other than perpetual conflict. For Rousseau, co-operation brings the blissful state of nature to an end and is responsible for the evils that stem

[1] Where gender-specific language is used, it is adopted only insofar as the writings discussed are written in gender-specific mode.

International Handbook of Organizational Teamwork and Cooperative Working. Edited by M. A. West, D. Tjosvold, and K. G. Smith.

from organized communal life. Both of these understandings tell us that cooperating is not a natural thing to do; it must be engineered, contrived, achieved. It carries a price (loss of freedom and autonomy) and it may not bring peace or harmony to begin with. Aristotle's view of a fundamentally social being, whose existence is brought value and meaning by active participation in the community, is tempered along the way by these accounts that cast human communities into far less socially harmonious entities. This first question underscores the fact that cooperation is intrinsically linked to the different perceptions and depictions of communal life and, therefore, the value placed on community. Thus, the second question which arises concerns the aims of cooperation.

If community is an ideal state, if man truly is a political animal, then cooperation should be pursued as a means of maintaining a viable community, which is the only viable way of life for intrinsically social beings. Community, in this first scenario, is an end in itself. But if, on the other hand, the communal is perceived as a realm rife with conflict and war, a realm which must be tamed in order for men to cause the least possible damage to one another—as in the Hobbesian scenario—then cooperation, in this case, is a means to securing a context in which the individual might thrive unfettered by conflict. Finally, if the communal—as according to Rousseau—is a less than optimal natural development (a perversion even of the state of nature) that needs to be superseded and institutionally transcended in order to overcome the slavery which it naturally creates, then the end is an institutional context that builds on a transcendental vision of political and communal life in which both the individual (as a private subject and a public citizen) and the community become infinitely intertwined. In these latter two scenarios, cooperation is something that must be engineered only as a means to a series of ends.

While all of these scenarios address the value placed on the concept of community, they each also necessarily address a third and further question and that is, for whom is cooperation beneficial? The Aristotelian answer lies in a circular understanding of the benefits of community: while cooperation should be primarily pursued for the sake of the survival of the community, the survival of the community is necessary insofar as the latter is the only habitat for man. Here, the existence of the individual is so entwined with that of the community that pursuing cooperation for the sake of the community's equilibrium, survival, and development is the only way of addressing individual needs—but individual needs come second. For the other two scenarios, the community is not necessarily the object of protection. For Hobbes in particular, cooperation can be seen as pursued in order to create an order in which the individual is safe (from abuse by other individuals and from abuse by the monarch); he is in this respect laying the foundations for the development of what is often referred to as "protective democracy" (Held, 1987). For Rousseau, once the state of nature has been lost and the individual becomes—however reluctantly—a part of a community, that community must give itself laws and constitute a general will which will create a safe realm for the individual free from community interference, while at the same time creating a public, communal realm capable of evolving beyond the initial dependency–property–greed cycle created by communal life. In this last scenario, communal life is not the natural abode of individuals; on the contrary, it is something with which they have to make do, which they must, in a sense, "learn to choose" and organize so as to reclaim a measure of private autonomy while generating a publicly accepted concept of the common good. So, here, *both* the individual and the community are protected by the nature of the political cooperation envisaged.

We thus far have three main scenarios: one in which communal life has primacy and thus in which cooperation is an end in itself. One in which the individual and his interests hold pride of place and in which cooperation is pursued only in order to create enough order in the community to allow the individual to thrive; and finally, one in which cooperation serves the community and the individual in equal measure but in which individuality is intrinsically dependent on the protection and development of the community. These three scenarios find an articulation in the contemporary analyses of communal life and in political science understandings of cooperation. The authors cited should in no way be seen as the sole ancestors of the approaches (and their respective applications) delineated in the following sections, but rather, we should understand their questions as serving as the basis for the elaboration of the three main ways in which cooperation and the analyses of cooperation have been articulated in contemporary political theory and political science.

In this chapter the issue of cooperation in political science will thus be addressed in three parts. I will begin by giving an overview of rational choice approaches to cooperation as rooted in a Hobbesian liberal tradition and then move, in a second section, to communitarian explanations for cooperation which draw more specifically on an Aristotelian, classical conception of community. Finally, in the third section, I will draw parallels between Rousseau's view of institutions and recent developments in neo-institutionalist theory. These approaches should not be taken as superseding one another—while the three understandings of democracy and community delineated above can be taken as encapsulating a succession of developments over time (from classical, to protective, to developmental models of democracy), they inform contemporary political analyses and understandings equally. They have tended to develop in political science much as they have done in the other social sciences, but perhaps couched in slightly different terms. They have coexisted and continue to do so, though neo-institutionalist understandings have gained in importance and impact in the last 10–15 years, in part because of the latter's capacity to incorporate aspects of other approaches and explanatory tales.

I RATIONAL CHOICE APPROACHES TO COOPERATION

Rational choice approaches to cooperation should be understood as the descendants of the Hobbesian view of human nature and community. The basis for cooperation here is not the well-being of the community as a whole but, rather, the preservation of individual liberty, autonomy, and property within a community naturally defined by mistrust and conflict. The methodological individualism that characterizes rational choice approaches, therefore, is a reflection of the centrality of the individual and individual rationality in ultra-liberal political thought. Rational choice theory thus offers not an explanation for cooperation, but rather a set of partial (axiomatic) explanations for why it is rational for most human beings not to cooperate most of the time—although some rational choice theorists have engaged with the more optimistic pursuit of specifying the conditions under which a rational individual could be incentivized (to use the appropriate jargon) to cooperate. This being said, rational choice has, perhaps more than any other approach in politics, addressed the issue of cooperation relentlessly—in fact cooperation's elusive nature is central to the rational choice project.

Rational choice theory calls into question the assumptions of much pluralist and Marxist political analysis by starting from the premise that, even when there is a shared interest in the results of cooperation, this shared interest is not enough to prompt people to cooperate. Thus much of rational choice theory focuses on the question of how to make rational individuals cooperate when their self-interest dictates that they should let others shoulder the burden of participating and cooperating.

A Hobbes, Rationality and Political Cooperation: "The Warre of Everyone Against Everyone"

The combination of the core assumptions of rational choice theory (that individuals are self-interested, that all individuals have the capacity to make rational choices by ranking preferred outcomes, and that social science should build from the individual upward) has led to applications in a variety of areas. Most notably, rational choice theory has been applied to electoral behaviour (A. Downs' (1957) *An Economic Theory of Democracy* delivering the seminal framework which cast parties as products to be chosen by rational, economically aware political consumers rather than as representatives of an ideological stance) or international relations theory. As a discipline, international relations has been heavily influenced by rational choice approaches: realist approaches, cold-war theories of deterrence and mutually assured destruction (MAD) have, in particular, relied heavily both on the underlying assumption of the will to power and self-preservation that underpins Hobbes' natural law theory, and on the capacity to rationally order preferences and outcomes based on the gathering of information. Current research in international relations theory is no exception: the work of Albin, for instance (2001), entitled *Justice and Fairness in International Negotiation*, bears the mark of rational choice theory. Works such as these take the approach that international cooperation is the sought-after public good, but cooperation here does not refer so much to the end-result or "equilibrium" achieved, so much as the willingness to participate in a rational game of negotiation over time. The challenge for these writers is in the overcoming of country behaviour which is seen as a hindrance to this game.

Rational choice approaches to cooperation have, however, been even more prevalent in the study of mobilization and collective action. For understandings of collective action, rational choice theory has served as a prism through which to interpret the motivations behind political participation, and more pointedly, political non-participation. Mancur Olson's *The Logic of Collective Action* (1965) is an archetype of rational choice interpretations of collective mobilization. Noting that rational individuals will always choose to "free-ride" (that is, not to participate or contribute to the securing of a collectively available public good), Olson attempted to specify the circumstances under which rational individuals will perceive cooperation as being in their interest. For this, Olson argues, incentives—over and above the sought-after public good—must be provided that are only available to those who participate or "cooperate" in securing the good. For example, to recruit individuals in a movement whose aims are cleaner air, one must make available, to the participants in the movement, privileges, gains, prizes that will—unlike the resulting clean air—not be available to those whose cooperation was not secured. Olson's logic of collective action and its attendant "free-rider" problem have given rise to a vast literature attempting to explain all sorts of forms of non-cooperation from draft-dodging (Levi, 1998) to difficulties faced by nationalist movements (Meadwell, 1993; Pinard & Hamilton, 1984).

Rational choice approaches to cooperation have contributed significantly to our understanding of political cooperation—they have done so in part by addressing the issue of non-cooperation, or non-participation. In their focus on individual motivations they have forced political science to address, much more directly than was previously the case, the role and status of individuals in the collective projects of politics. The use of the prisoners' dilemma to represent how people choose when their choices are interdependent (Tsebelis, 1990), or the application of game-theoretic models over time to explain the failure of processes such as wage bargaining (Lange & Garrett, 1985), have placed at the heart of political science as a discipline a much more powerful, discerning, and somewhat fickle individual—this has contributed to a better understanding of political motivation, participation, and cooperation in (or between) mass democracies. Yet, precisely because of this focus, it is difficult not to come to the conclusion that rational choice theory takes the politics out of politics, namely by reducing the collective or communal to, at best, aggregation.

B Hobbes, Rationality and Organizational Dynamics: A Dog-Eat-Dog World

However misguided the reasoning, many of the work organizations who espouse Hobbesian/rational choice management practices do so in part because of the outlook they cast outward rather than inward; those organizations apply to their internal workings a reasoning based on the business equivalent of Hobbes' "homo homini lupus" (man to man is a wolf)—in other words, "it's a dog-eat-dog world". An open, competitive market economy is cut-throat (though most analysts would tell you—Greenspan included—that markets are not jungles; that there are rules and that breaking these rules endangers the workings of the market and potential gains for everyone), and a manager engaged in a particularly competitive sector can only be forgiven for perceiving and acting upon what is the reality of the context: unpredictable, ruthless, threatening. But for our purposes here, it is interesting to note that turning such reasoning inward and thereby assuming that the threats on the outside will be replicated on the inside presents a series of paradoxes and serious problems for organizations.

It is perhaps by starting from the notion of community as an aggregation of individuals that the attraction and shortcomings of rational choice approaches as applied to work organizations are best illustrated. The premises of the Hobbesian model—and much of rational choice—entail work organizations that are loosely knit, created out of necessity rather than choice (recognizing the necessity of, and advantages to, a loose association is testimony to the rationality of those involved and to the rationality of their choice), defined by threat rather than trust, individualized tasks and rewards rather than teamworking and collectively embraced goals and rewards (as one employee put it, "Teamwork stops feeling so amicable when you are competing with your teammates for your livelihood", Putnam, 2000, p. 90). Cooperation here is, much as in Hobbes' mind, the product of a decision designed to allow each person in the organization as much freedom and autonomy as possible, and the leeway necessary to complete their tasks or apply their expertise unhindered by the needs of others. The organization is presented as deriving benefits as a result of the benefits derived by individuals. The organization, therefore, is a world of autonomous beings whose association with one another does not define them but simply allows them to accomplish tasks and reap individual rewards. There are attractions to this model—an organization along these lines allows one to dream of unprecedented individual success (financial and other), autonomy, power, and flexibility. The figure of the "self-made", maverick entrepreneur, was for a long time associated with a sort of environment that offered nothing but opportunities for an individual able to fend for themselves. Further, for unskilled or only partially skilled workers, this image of success was adapted and downgraded rather perversely through the Fordist model of production: a simple individualized task, reduced to its most basic elements, repeated ad infinitum rewarded by the prospect of buying . . . a Ford. It is arguable that Fordism can be held accountable for the manufacturing sector's lingering infatuation with certain management practices.

But for work organizations, the problematic aspects of such a model can make themselves felt through a paradox. Hobbes recognized the need for a measure of cooperation—however, this cooperation exists in a context where everyone assumes the worst of everyone. Employees assume the worst of each other and of their employer, and vice versa. In other words, the context is one of very low, if not altogether absent trust. The basic, necessary level of cooperation is created by a contract, a set of minimum, basic rules. The problem with this scenario is that in the absence of trust, one needs more rules: over time this sort of organization tends to generate a spiralling amount of control mechanisms, monitoring tactics, enforcement procedures, and perhaps even reprisals (which will further contribute to a reduction of trust). Yamagishi and Yamagishi (1994) make this same point by highlighting the distinction between trust (that does not necessarily require explicit agreements) and assurance (based on agreements and explicit incentive structure). Molm, Takahashi, and Peterson (2000) find that organizations based on reciprocal exchanges (i.e. those organizations where there are many unregulated exchanges between individuals) are characterized by trust, whereas organizations based on rules are characterized by assurances. For our purposes here, it is the opposite which interests us: that organizations characterized by assurances, agreements, explicit contracts, etc., contain a plethora of rules and rule-bound behaviour. Precisely the opposite of what our ultra-liberal model sets out to accomplish.

In practical terms, the Hobbesian organization may become both cumbersome and expensive, but more importantly it never fails to stamp out the individuality it initially sets out to preserve. Forced bureaucratization (and associated costs) may cut into the organization's innovative capacity, gnaw away at budgets, and reduce its adaptability. Staff turnover—and training costs—are typically high and the atmosphere of autonomous innovation and creativity is transformed into one characterized by a degree of threat incompatible, for most individuals, with the risks associated with creativity and innovation.

The Nordstrom chain of American department stores and the management practices associated with the "Nordstrom way" are a good illustration of the benefits and costs associated with this type of organization. More interestingly, the Nordstrom case illustrates almost flawlessly the enormous paradoxes created by such management practices: the autonomy of the individual is almost entirely sacrificed to the myriad scripted and unscripted rules of behaviour, while the loosely knit association of autonomous players is based, in practice, on an extremely powerful—though often hidden or unacknowledged—set of beliefs about the organization. This paradox mirrors the political argument often made by detractors of liberalism about its professed "neutrality"—that, in practice, liberalism works not as a set of neutral, minimum rules but as a powerful ideology.

Nordstrom's management practices look like a type of Hobbesian organizational blueprint: the company offers little or no formal training, everyone starts on the "floor" and works their way up, impeccable service to the customer is—apparently—the only guideline for conduct, each employee works entirely autonomously to fulfil his or her sale quota (which is measured, monitored, and controlled at all times and can be accessed by any other employee), rewards are commensurate with performance and distributed on a strictly individual basis. There is no real teamworking (only pseudo-teams), only an intricate and very clearly spelled out hierarchy capable of whipping sets of individuals into a performance frenzy through a system of rewards and threats (Buller & Schuler, 2000). What is striking in the case of Nordstrom is, firstly, the gap between the rhetoric of—almost—savage individualism and practices which are clearly designed to reduce individual autonomy to very little. Nordstrom employees are happy to confirm that the only two pieces of advice they were given upon being hired was "use your best judgement" and "do whatever it takes to make the customer happy" (Buller & Schuler, 2000, p. 260), but the same case study also gives detailed accounts of the countless, compulsory early morning management meetings that are "off the clock", i.e. on unpaid time, the obligation to send thank you notes to customers and log these in a "manager's book", smile contests, the daily recital of "affirmations", motivational skits, and, perhaps most significantly for our purposes here, the intricate systems of goal setting and management, performance charts, and commission control and calculations (Buller & Schuler, 2000, pp. 253–598). Two points are of relevance here; the first is the amount of control exercised by this so-called "hands off" approach. Quite clearly, performance is not only encouraged, it is ceaselessly monitored by both managers as well as employees. This fits well within the model of cooperation outlined earlier in which a desire for a minimum set of rules in a context of lack of trust creates the need for further rules and controls. It also echoes the findings of Molm, Takahashi, and Peterson (2000), for here is an organization in which rules and assurances, as well as explicitly monitored expectations, stand in for trust.

What is of even greater interest is the company's (and its employees') refusal to acknowledge the organization's true nature, i.e. their persistence in the belief that the organization is low on rules and regulations as well as low on control mechanisms. To some extent, the controls and monitoring systems in place are effective: aside from a few hundred dissatisfied employees, Nordstrom is extremely successful and enough "Nordies" are satisfied on the inside for the company to think that it is doing something right. And if employees want more autonomy they are free to leave—Nordstrom, with its very high rate of turnover, has a seemingly endless supply of willing employees and enormous profit margins. The fact that most of us would find working for Nordstrom unbearable, that such an employer also clearly benefits from cultural and political factors absent in most of Europe for example, that most Nordstrom employees, despite the lip-service paid to initiative, do not seem to benefit from the leeway necessary for any meaningful sort of initiative, and that, finally, high costs are associated with such levels of control, all of this is not as interesting as the fact that Nordstrom is a success story whose success is partially premised on not telling the real story (of control and regulations) that lurks behind the liberal rhetoric.

Nordstrom has done no more than recognize that for employees to give their all they must be financially rewarded, but that for them to "outperform" each other, they must, much as Olson suggested, be "incentivized". Even more crucially, Nordstrom long ago acknowledged, however quietly, that employees must comport themselves as if they buy wholeheartedly and enthusiastically (whether they do or not) into the organization's internal norms. In other words, Nordstrom has become more and more of an institution. Far from the loosely knit, autonomy-based management it claims to endorse, Nordstrom has implemented the opposite of this. It replaced its 20-page rule book with a single sheet of advice (Buller & Schuler, 2000, p. 253), but it has also done something more effective:

strengthened a set of rules with a system of beliefs, with rituals and ceremonies. Worryingly, however, Nordstrom has endorsed the practices of a non-democratic, perhaps even a coercive, institution. Beliefs and rituals though they are (and they are distinctly recognizable to the outsider since outsiders are familiar with the "Nordie way"), the mechanisms whereby this institutionalization is achieved are not acknowledged, are not publicly arrived at, and not explicitly endorsed by the management or employees. Nordstrom seems to have taken on all of the negative, coercive elements of institutionalization (controls, rules, punishment, monitoring) without any of the positive practices that ensure that the institutionalization is democratic. The result is that the Nordie employee—the rational, free individual—tells a story that is disconnected from the practices that regulate his or her work life and displays ignorance regarding the company's aims. This sheds light on the nature of such a model: this model of a minimum cooperation for the individual's sake and for the maintenance of his/her autonomy not only fails to deliver meaningful autonomy but creates a situation whereby the success of the organization is linked (a) to the creation of a set of beliefs and the hyperinstitutionalization of practices into rituals and (b) to a set of beliefs that are implicitly designed to make the individual dependent on the collective (or anti-collective) without his or her being aware of this. Ultimately this amounts to a degree of manipulation rather than management, and the creation, not of an institutionalized inclusive culture but, rather, of an institution without community.

The next two sets of approaches to the study of cooperation reject much of rational choice theory's basic assumptions; by taking the pursuit of cooperation as the core of politics rather than as a counterfactual, they lose the parsimony inherent to rational choice theory yet gain in their capacity to observe and analyse complex collective phenomena.

II COMMUNITARIAN APPROACHES TO COOPERATION

The aim here is not to analyse the strands of communitarianism; I use the term "communitarian" because under this heading we can group together effectively theories of politics which place community and cooperation at the heart of the political project and at the centre of political and social analysis. As outlined at the start of this chapter, the roots of such analysis lie in a classical Aristotelian understanding of politics. From this perspective, the springs, or motivation, for cooperation are seen to be human nature's intrinsically social fabric and an individual's fundamental need for a societal or communal context. Such theories are based on an understanding of human beings as inseparable from their social, or even communal, surroundings: cooperation is not only desirable, it is necessary for its own sake as well as the basis upon which to secure the community's existence—the community being that without which an individual cannot exist. Cooperation is the basis of the virtuous circle of politics—because without it there is no possibility of community, which is the condition for the flourishing of human potential.

In contemporary terms, the communitarian position informs understandings of cooperation which serve as the basis for a series of normative analyses. The first point to make is that, remaining true to their founding moment, communitarian political analyses often use cooperation as a synonym for active membership or participation in the community or the wider society. Joining into the rituals, events (formal and informal) that make up the life of the polis *is* cooperating with the spoken and unspoken, formal and informal rules of the community. But, while cooperation is pivotal to the life of the community—indeed it defines it—it is also, to a large extent, the "dark matter" of communitarian theory: it is everywhere but difficult to locate—replaced by near-equivalents such as collaborative behaviour, participation, engagement (I use the term as Putnam and others do)—and often simply assumed to be in a parasitic, and therefore largely subservient, relationship to the concept of community.

This basic assumption about the tight relationship between cooperation and participation (and, more broadly, political engagement) provides the impetus for a number of important interpretations of political behaviour, political action, and the value of each of these. Communitarian understandings of cooperation have made very distinct contributions to political science and political theory. Starting with the basic assumptions outlined above, they have contributed to the analysis of participation at various levels. Research on new social movements (feminist, green, peace movements and groups), for example, has often stressed the groups' reliance on a rhetoric or discourse of community however defined; further, participation in these movements was often understood as stemming from a desire to participate in the building of a new form—or alternative—of community or to inject new types of values into older and already defined communities (Inglehart, 1990). Until the behavioural revolution, political science was dominated by these understandings of mobilization that were strictly based on a collective unit of analysis (the group, the community, the nation, etc.), and the success of rational choice applications to the study of collective action can be explained in great part by the hitherto unquestioned dominance of the more community-based approaches to the study of mobilization.

A Social Capital Theory: The Rescuing of the Modern Community

Perhaps the most influential manner in which communitarian theories have pervaded political analysis in recent years is through the elaboration, articulation, and application of social capital theory. Robert Putnam's *Making Democracy Work: Civic Traditions in Modern Italy* (1993) and its companion or sequel—and more widely known—tome *Bowling Alone* (2000) have contributed to, and served as the hallmark of, political science's renewed interest in the value of community.

Social capital theory fits under the communitarian heading because the community is the starting point as well as the end of the analysis which, to summarize it in a nutshell, hails and extols the benefits of "civic vitality" (Putnam, 2000, p. 18). Putnam's is a comparative analysis of communal life in the United States as it was in the 1950s and 1960s, with what is taken to be its slow decline over the three decades following—three decades over which the United States went from being a nation in which, just as Putnam's title indicates, people bowled in leagues to one in which people bowl alone. The basis of Putnam's argument is that a sharp decline in communal life is responsible for a sharp decline in standards of living. Social networks have value, writes the author: "Just as a screwdriver (physical capital) or college education (human capital) can increase productivity (both individual and collective), so too can social contacts affect the productivity of individuals and groups" (Putnam, 2000, p. 19).

Social capital thus refers to the connections among individuals "and the norms of reciprocity and trustworthiness that arise from them" (Putnam, 2000, p. 19). According to Putnam's study, high social capital makes for a more efficient society (lower transaction costs associated with smoother and more straightforward negotiations, the capacity to identify problems and areas of conflict before they become unresolvable, the potential for increased circulation of information and thus a growth in shared values and understanding. Finally, and resulting from all of these, the decline of social conflict). Putnam's diagnosis therefore pins the increase in social conflict and the declining efficiency of American society as a whole on the decline in social capital. Conversely—and this was the basis for Putnam's earlier analysis of Italy—higher societal efficiency and standards of living exist where organized communal life is highly developed, where individuals belong to dense social networks—in other words where social capital is high.

Social capital theory's argument is not new. Putnam himself acknowledges his debt to previous iterations of social capital theory (Putnam, 2000, pp. 19–20) and the first section of this chapter allows one to trace social capital's heritage back to early theories regarding the centrality of community life and the benefits inherent to one's commitment to it. Further, it could be argued that Putnam is the latest in a long line of admirers of a quintessentially American conception of civic engagement and political participation. While Putnam's argument revolves around a broad range of types of engagement—and not political engagement *sensu stricto*—he is, nevertheless, not far removed from the marvelling Tocqueville when the latter found himself confronted with the American communities of the East Coast and their thriving local groups and organizations (Tocqueville, 1969).

Putnam's analysis is valuable in two original and particular ways: the first is the variety and amount of data on which he draws in order to make his argument. The second is the boldness with which the argument is made given American society's—and, correspondingly, American social science's—veneration of the pursuit of individual goals and individual happiness. In such a context—in which the pursuit of individual happiness is constitutionally enshrined—arguments about the value of community and participation need to be made along particular lines. These lines are those traced by a political and economic tradition (precisely the one of which Tocqueville was in awe) which, as much as it reveres and protects the rights of the individual, is nevertheless a version of the classical republican tradition in which society or community as a whole is greater than the sum of its parts (along the lines stipulated by Aristotle).

How is social capital theory, however, connected to cooperation? For our purposes here, we can argue that social capital theory is a version—a thick version—of cooperation. As alluded to previously, communitarian theories make too little of the concept of cooperation upon which they are nevertheless premised. Social capital theory is no exception: while the whole aim of social capital is to increase cooperation among individuals through dense social networks, the term "cooperation" is only intermittently used, yet the dense social networks of social capital theory enhance both the ability and the opportunities of individuals to work together—to cooperate. That which these networks are based upon, and the concept upon which their capacity to affect cooperation is pinned, is a (thin) version of the concept of "trust" or what Putnam refers to as "norms of reciprocity" (Putnam, 2000, p. 134). These norms of reciprocity are a combination, Putnam writes, of "short term altruism and long term self-interest" (Putnam, 2000, p. 134). Tellingly, Putnam quotes Tocqueville here and defines generalized reciprocity as "self-interest rightly understood" (Putnam, 2000, p. 135). The norms of reciprocity and the generalized reciprocity (virtuously) resulting from high social capital have thus become the focus of analysis for theories of social capital and their application. It is clear that social capital theory is the late twentieth century's most articulate development of an argument that links the success and efficiency of a community to its members' capacity to transcend their narrow individual self-interests in favour of cooperative modes of behaviour that reinforce rather than deplete the realm of the communal, and more broadly of the societal.

There is, however, a lingering doubt about social capital theory—a sense in which the theory, while cloaked in the language of community, is nevertheless simply a more long-term, more patient—perhaps more caring—view of the pursuit of individual well-being. The suspicion is that, beyond collective values, beyond the protection of the community, it is the wealth and the autonomy of individual citizens that is being pursued—that, in a word, this is simply an instrumentalization of community, trust, and cooperation. Perhaps, even, a version of rational choice theory in thick sheep's clothing. The answer to this objection, without making too much of it, is that it is both valid and invalid. It is invalid because the evaluation of social capital's value is based first and foremost on an assessment of its contribution to communal and societal efficiency. A good illustration of this is Putnam's generic tale of Bob and Rosemary Smith whose concern for their child's education pushes them to take part in a range of activities which increase their own and their community's social capital (Putnam, 2000, pp. 289–290). While the concern is initially expressed for an individual child, it is immediately articulated and assuaged at the collective level. The unit of analysis in social capital theory is collective; the benefits of increased social capital are collective—they only become individualized as a result of a trickle-down effect, and not the other way around.

The objection referred to above, however, cannot be entirely dismissed: yes, social capital theory also delineates the individual gains to be made from increased social capital. But this should not lead one to conclude that pre-eminence is given to those gains—social capital theory is firmly within the realm of approaches to cooperation which stipulate that the needs of the community determine those of the individual—or rather that individual needs are such that the nature of the community is primordial in being able to satisfy them. However, social capital theory acknowledges the existence of such a thing as an individual; it recognizes also the individual's need for autonomy, privacy, self-esteem, and independence of thought and preferences. In other words, in contrast to the early Aristotelian theories, social capital theory capitalizes on the gains of modernity, on the values of the Enlightenment, on the development of the liberal view of the individual—it is a *modern* theory which grants the individual duties *and* rights within the community or society in which he or she evolves. It should be argued, however, that this does not detract from its aims, it simply places it firmly alongside those social science theories able to recognize that contemporary politics are structured, in part, by the tension between the inescapable Aristotelian fact and the modern state's duty to foster individual autonomy and protect individual rights. Social capital theory attempts a synthesis which nevertheless gives pre-eminence to cooperative behaviour as an end in itself.

B Social Capital and Work Organizations: The Organization as Community

Putnam explicitly addresses the relationship between social capital and work organizations in his volume. Given his focus, the relationship is addressed from the point of view of society's (or the wider community's) gain in social capital through work organizations. The argument is, therefore, relatively predictable: America's social capital has declined in part because work organizations have become loosely knit and no longer represent the social "hub" they once represented in people's lives. Disregarding momentarily the fact that Putnam's data are at their thinnest on this matter, let us assume that he is not guilty of oversimplification when he writes:

> I know of no evidence whatever that socialising in the workplace, however common, has actually increased over the last several decades. . . . Social connectedness in the workplace might be described as a glass half-empty, not merely as a glass half-full. Most studies of personal networks find that co-workers account for less than 10 percent of our friends. Workplace ties tend to be casual and enjoyable, but not intimate or supportive (Putnam, 2000, p. 87).

For Putnam this is the direct result of the management practices of the 1980s and 1990s and, while he lists a number of problems related to "downsizing", "rightsizing", "re-engineering", and "restructuring" (such as, for example, increased employee anxiety), what he focuses on more explicitly is the retreat of most employees into a narrower and narrower social circle as a result of the onslaught. The loss of confidence set in train by the breaking of the old, tacit employment contract is held up as the major explanatory variable behind the decline of "long term individual investments such as home ownership and college education for children, community ties and the stability they bring" (Putnam, 2000, p. 89); in other words, the decline of the traditional workplace is seen as heralding a decline in American social capital. So, in Putnam's argument, the workplace as community is valuable because it is just one more area in which we forge the social links that create the networks that spill over onto the rest of society, thus increasing its overall social capital.

But what of the role of social capital from the point of view of the work organization itself? Adopting some of the basic tenets of social capital theory leads an organization to explicitly recognize its importance not only to the wider community but *as* a community. Typically, the networks that are intrinsic to social capital yield three reinforcing results: teamworking, better communication, and trust. Aside from creating a workplace that fulfils some basic social needs, a social capital-based organization can also expect a decline in employee anxiety, thus creating a workplace in which employees may feel more able to take risks associated with creative behaviour. This in turn will allow them to build a network of people with whom they share information and whom they trust. Further, the sharing of information is a crucial variable in enabling problem solving before the problem becomes unmanageable and/or turns into a crisis. In a 2002 *New Yorker* article entitled "The Talent Myth", Malcolm Gladwell recounts the story of the battle of eastern Pearl Harbor. This Second World War story draws on Admiral Ernest Jones King's leadership: brilliant, arrogant, and based on what Gladwell refers to as the "McKinsey talent mindset". King's motto was to never tell "subordinates 'how' as well as 'what to do'", to give subordinates minimum information regarding a mission, and, rather peculiarly for a Navy man, to encourage individual initiative. However, his legend draws mostly on his spectacular failure to counter German U-boat attacks on American warships in 1942. Only when, against his advice, the American Navy set up a centralized unit to coordinate submarine warfare, only when it agreed to take operational lessons from the British, only when American–British teams were set up to detect the U-boats—in other words, only when a network of anti-submarine warfare was set up—did the American Navy learn to know where the German U-boats were and begin to defeat them. Here Gladwell concludes, "The talent myth assumes that people make organizations smart. More often than not, it's the other way around" (Gladwell, 2002, p. 32).

Applied to work organizations, social capital theory points to a version of this premise: that collective working, teamworking, make organizations smart by allowing individuals to be far more effective. Returning momentarily to the case of Nordstrom, the contrast is striking: at Nordstrom the individual is encouraged to perform individually and for him/herself. The people are taken to make the organization successful but this is held up, somewhat misleadingly, as a by-product of individual success. Where the principles of social capital theory might be applied, the organization works for the community—and individual happiness (for example living in a post-1945 democracy) is a by-product of collective success.

The two sets of theories we have examined so far are, respectively, descendants of the early liberal and classical theories of community: the first is a liberal paradigm stressing reason, freedom, the priority of individual nature over the communal, and competition (not only, in fact, a liberal paradigm but a paradigm for a market society). The second is a classical, more conservative paradigm reaching back to notions of community, tradition, cooperation, but also, often, hierarchy and authority. Social capital theory, as one of the last in a long series of modern communitarian theories, struggles more consciously to find a resolution to the tension between these two paradigms but ultimately fails to do so, hence the haziness and somewhat tautological nature of the theory. Both of these approaches contain valuable elements: the first allows for an unprecedented degree of autonomy within an organization. However limited that autonomy might be and whatever its toll, management practices such as those associated with Nordstrom are at the root of spectacular success stories for individuals, and perhaps in particular for individuals who might have previously been hindered by their backgrounds (social or educational), their race, or their gender. Such organizations have broken not only with some commendable traditions but also with a series of lamentable—bureaucratic, nepotistic, paternalistic, sexist, racist—ones. As for social capital theory, despite its shortcomings, its understanding of human beings as social beings leads to the acknowledgement that work organizations—where individuals spend at least one-quarter of their lives—should be treated as possible versions of community. This realization can contribute to making the workplace somewhere where employees might be more tempted to bring a variety of talents, thus benefiting the organization.

There are significant limits to social capital theory's contribution to our understanding of communities and work communities in particular; these stem from its significant underspecification and undertheorization of the role of institutions. Despite the *implicit* recognition of the centrality of institutions in building social capital, social capital theory does not grant institutions proper analytical attention. Yet, paying more attention to institutions would allow analyses rooted in social capital theory to clarify propositions that claim, for example, that dilemmas of collective action are best solved "by an institutional mechanism with the power to ensure compliance with the collectively desirable behaviour" (Putnam, 2000, p. 288). This, in turn, would lead to a far more effective exploration of how institutions—and the manner in which they are studied—are attempts to foster cooperation and to transcend the tension between the individual and the collective in political practice. Neo-institutionalist theories appear to be able to transcend the perennial tension between communal aims and individual needs by shedding a new light on the nature and the role of institutions. In this respect, neo-institutionalist approaches might help in elaborating a model for work organizations that enables organizations to become smarter by treating people as smart.

III NEO-INSTITUTIONALIST APPROACHES TO COOPERATION

The tensions between the classical and the liberal views of community and cooperation place us in a difficult analytical situation. In many ways, we are unable to think of ourselves outside the modern liberal paradigm. We may hark back to classical antiquity and its "community for community's sake" but we are also conditioned to be competitive, to assert our autonomy, our independence as individuals. Yet, as we try to suppress the communal/societal side of our existence, we never succeed in making it disappear, but we have great difficulty conceiving of it within the limits of our modern selves. Rousseau's writings can be understood as the first attempt to theorize and overcome this difficulty, to provide us with a higher form of social individuality.

Having identified what he referred to as Hobbes' mistake (namely the misrepresentation of the state of nature), what Rousseau discovers is that when one breaks society down into parts what one finds is neither an idiot (in the Greek sense of "he who keeps to himself"), nor an individual motivated by Hobbes' "ceaseleth desire for power". Rather what we find is, first, a proto-human and then, over time and transformation, an irretrievably social human who is capable of looking into himself and asking "what, as a rule, would be best for me as a member of this society—for that is what I am". As such, Rousseau moves early on beyond the Enlightenment's liberal premises to recognize that law and society shape the very desires of the "autonomous" individuals, but that their knowledge of themselves is the most unfailing instrument in the search for a just society—only when these two propositions are brought together can the oppressive nature of both the classical and liberal communities be transcended.

For Rousseau, as referred to earlier in this chapter, neither community nor cooperation are straightforwardly positive concepts. In fact, both are associated with a loss of innocence. They become rehabilitated by his realization that to move beyond the conundrum (and chaos) created by the tension between individual freedom on the one hand, and the social bond on the other, cooperation must be obtained not by communal pressure, not by moral obligation, not by appealing to self-interest alone, but by effecting cooperation through a commonly agreed set of institutions which both guarantee individual freedom and transcend it. The social contract according to Rousseau would

> allow men to find a form of association which will defend and protect with the whole common force the person and goods of each associate, and in which each, while uniting himself with all, may still obey himself alone, and remain as free as before (Rousseau, 1993, p. 191).

What is key in Rousseau's approach is that the manner in which political processes are organized has a determining impact on the nature, quality, and justice of political decisions. As such it is not preferences that are the decisive factor here, but rather the political processes by which these preferences are inevitably shaped. Institutions become the sphere in which the individual/social opposition is transcended because they are the result of a publicly agreed upon conception of the common good, itself based on the knowledge of one's self as part of a community.

For political analysts, by spelling out the rules of the political game—whatever these rules might be—institutions set out the desirable aims of politics and enshrine the collective goals of a given community. In this sense, institutions are designed primarily to set out the rules, thus allowing for a collectively perceived and publicly sanctioned routinization of political practice. Institutions are thus both the result of cooperation (the rules being agreed upon) and the guarantee that cooperation can be and will be made easier by reducing the possibility of costly political and/or economic conflict arising by shaping political preferences and behaviour.

Recent institutional analyses, however, place greater emphasis on the role of institutions in affecting and increasing cooperative behaviour, rather than simply on routinization and the corresponding decrease of the possibility of conflict. In this respect these recent analyses are the heirs to Rousseau's argument that institutions are malleable, transformable, that the procedures are amendable and can be made to reflect changing aims and objectives, new difficulties, and that they shape both behaviour and preferences.

A The Claims of the New Institutionalism

This neo-institutionalist literature is concerned with the manner in which institutions are conceived in their relationship to society and to a variety of actors, and March and Olsen's (1984) now classical statement of the aims of the new institutionalism is testimony to this:

> The ideas de-emphasize the dependence of the polity on society in favour of an interdependence of relatively autonomous social and political institutions; they de-emphasize the simple primacy of micro-processes and efficient histories in favour of relatively complex processes and historical inefficiency; they de-emphasize metaphors of choice and allocative outcomes in favour of other logics of action and the centrality of meaning and symbolic action (March & Olsen, 1984, p. 738).

The shift away from the traditional, rule-bound approach to institutions (static, rigid, and immobile) to a more fluid, and more complex, conception of institutions is obvious; as classical institutionalists held, institutions *do* structure political relations among various actors in the political and social and economic spheres, but—and this is one of the main contributions of neo-institutionalist approaches—they do so partly through the relationships they have with one another—from institution to institution, through the relationships (practical and symbolic) they construct between political actors (which are or are not yet fully institutionalized), and through the manner in which all of these processes are perceived by the public.

The emphasis on the links between institutions as one of the constitutive features of institutionalization contributes to a conception of institutions as three-dimensional: they are at once a framework of rules, the relationships enacted within this framework, and the pattern of these relationships over time (March & Olsen, 1984). Because they structure the relationship between politics and individuals their role in building trust and enhancing cooperative behaviour in communities is crucial. Thus, neo-institutionalist theories (drawing on Rousseau's conception of political processes and institutions) have drawn attention to the fact that institutions are a key variable in the building and maintenance of trust and cooperation.

B Institutions as Builders of Trust and Cooperation

It can be argued that social capital theory's weakness is its undertheorization of trust which results in an undertheorization—or at least underspecification—of the role of institutions in building social capital. Yet, trust and institutions are central to contemporary political understandings of cooperation and the cooperative behaviour upon which social capital theory is premised. Neo-institutionalist theory makes a significant contribution to our understanding of the mechanisms that help to foster trust, and thus cooperation, by specifying *how* democratic institutions suitably structured can generate trust and engender cooperation.

Part of Rousseau's dilemma concerning the role of institutions, and more broadly the place of the individual in modern communities, was that the emphasis on individual freedoms and autonomy combined with the size of the communities in question made the emergence of trust seem even more unlikely. Yet we remain convinced that one of the fundamental requirements of democratic politics is the ability to associate, thereby making cooperation the lifeblood of society. Rousseau's social contract experimented with whether forms of cooperation might be induced by political and institutional design; neo-institutional theory has furthered this project by expanding on the relationship between trust and cooperation on the one hand as well as trust and government on the other, in increasingly complex and heterogeneous societies. As Warren notes, generating trust is "one means of engaging in extensive social cooperation that does not generate the experience that in working with others, one is compromising one's freedom" (Warren, 1999, p. 346).

Yet to relate trust to institutions is problematic—and Rousseau was well aware of this—because trust is something that we experience primarily on an interpersonal level. Authors such as Hardin, for example, go as far as to argue that it makes no sense to trust a specific institution or set of institutions because we do not have sufficient knowledge of them to base our trust on anything significant (Hardin, 1991, 1996). Similarly, Putnam's conception of trust fudges the issue as to how one moves from particularized (interpersonal) trust to generalized trust (trust in strangers). It is quite clear that we have at least two different types of trust at play here: one type is rooted in Hardin's notion that we can only trust someone if we have reason to think that they will act in our interest or "as our agent", as Hardin puts it, on a specific matter. This is the case of particularized trust. The other type of trust, however, which affects cooperative behaviour in the larger society, is in fact based on the very opposite of Hardin's premise, namely on the assumption that an institution will be no one's agent and will not act on behalf of particular interests (Rothstein, 2000). We place our trust in institutions precisely because we "trust" that they will act impartially. And this trust stems from the fact that, while the outcome of an institutional process may not be "in our favour", the process itself was impartial. The nature of the *process*, therefore, is what in great part legitimates trust in an institution. For this trust in the process to exist that process must be publicly debated, agreed upon, and transparent throughout. Reconnecting with Rousseau's vision, neo-institutionalism underscores the fact that the process by which the rules are agreed upon and the transparency of that process form the basis of the institution itself. Part of the trust stems from our having been (however remotely) engaged in the process of deciding upon the nature of the legitimate process to be adopted from now on. We cooperate in creating the venues for cooperative behaviour.

What this also points to, however, is yet another underspecified area of social capital theory, and that is the mechanism by which—if any—one moves from one type of trust to the other. Putnam assumes that they are related. Neo-institutionalists have shown *how* this is so by opening up the contents of the institutional black box to reveal the role of individuals within them and by highlighting the nature of the links between civil society and institutions.

Fukuyama (1995), for example, argued that democratic societies draw on stored social capital. He roots social capital in what he calls "pre-modern cultural habits" which are based on the face-to-face relations of small communities. The growth of communities and the development of a "rights" culture are, according to him, what accounts for the erosion of social capital, the decline of cooperative behaviour, and, as a result, the decline of both American capitalism and American democracy. Yet authors such as Zucker (1986) have argued convincingly that the US economy began to grow at its most rapid when it was able to separate trust from the characteristics that Fukuyama attaches to small communities. According to Zucker, the US economy began to develop institutional means of producing trust in the second half of the nineteenth century, a period corresponding to the emergence of the United States as a superpower.

In other words, once the community had given itself the means to transcend the limits of interpersonal trust, it was able to generate the forms of cooperation necessary for its expansion and thriving. Luhmann (1979, 1988) also notes that social systems will be able to gain from complexity when exchanges can also occur autonomously from face-to-face relationships. These arguments confirm that there are two types of trust operating in large-scale and complex societies, and that institutions are instrumental in generating the type of trust needed for high and complex levels of cooperation.

Institutions are key in creating generalized trust and cooperation because inherent to an institution is what Offe refers to as their "triadic" nature. He clarifies the point by citing Ostrom:

> Working rules must be common knowledge and must be monitored and enforced. Common knowledge implies that every participant knows the rules, knows that others know the rules, and knows that others also know that the participants know the rules (Ostrom, in Offe, 1996, p. 204).

We have shared knowledge of institutional rules: not only are we able to sanction, in some measure, institutional design, but one of the primary functions of institutions is to publicize their own procedural legitimacy.[2]

Offe adds to this argument by pointing out that we can extend trust to institutions without even relying on dense social networks (though dense networks rely on trust) because

> Institutions provide normative reference points and values that can be relied upon to make sense of [their] rules.... [I]t is this implied normative meaning of institutions and this moral plausibility I assume it will have for others which allows me to trust those that are involved in the same institution. Although they are strangers and not personally known to me (Offe, 1999, p. 70).

The answer to why we should trust institutions whereas we do not personally "know" them, is that we should trust institutions because they allow us to know strangers more than we would otherwise. This is a more encouraging and more feasible strategy than Putnam's. According to social capital theory we should strive to know as many people as we can in order to minimize our perception of being surrounded by strangers whom we cannot trust—the process of generalization of trust stems from a sociological ripple effect from the individual

[2] This is how one can understand Rawls' statement that a "just system must generate its own support". The design of government institutions is crucial for their popular support which implies that they should be designed to increase support (Rawls, 1971, p. 271).

outward. But it is a ripple effect that makes individuals dependent on intensely cultivated, relentlessly pursued social networks. The neo-institutionalist view is infinitely more suited to a society, or set of communities in which (a) contact of the sort that Putnam bemoans is necessarily increasingly restricted and (b) where democratic freedom also entails the possibility of "opting out". Not of everything, but of some things—I may, for instance, feel that there is nothing wrong with the local PTA, but I may choose not to attend the meetings. Or, in fact, I may feel that there is something wrong with the local PTA and therefore choose not to attend the meetings. It may be that I really am not keen on giving up my evenings for whatever group because I want to spend time on my own meditating. The difference between us and the Greek polis is that it is entirely acceptable that I should do so and, while my social standing in the community may not get my lawn mowed for free by the neighbourhood kids, it will not affect my political rights or those of my community as a whole. Institutions cater for the possibility of cooperation at a political level, ensuring that we need no longer be entirely dependent on social cooperation for the development of trust and the thriving of democracy. There is an element of social control inherent to Putnam's argument which has put up the hackles of those who have not shed tears over the demise of the Tupperware party or the declining ubiquity of the bowling league. These are, after all, the same "dense networks" that lead to the manicured lawns of the Boston suburbs—pretty, but what if you like jungles?

This is not to say that social capital theory and its valorization of social networks and cooperative behaviour are to be discarded. Much of what Putnam and others put forth is a valuable reminder of the need to tend to the social fabric of our communities. However, it seems that one of the great advantages of democratic institutions is that they allow the ripple effect to be somewhat reversed—in other words they allow us to trust others because we trust in institutions, the norms they represent, and the institutional processes by which they are maintained and amended, and that we know that others also identify with them and trust them. Social cooperation is secured because political cooperation is enshrined in the institutional norms of a society. The two spheres are mutually dependent, intrinsically linked—but they are not synonymous. And the sequence of the relationship between the two in a post-modern, mass democracy is reversed: it is the political institutions to which we need to pay attention first in order to secure the continued existence of social and work organizations and networks.

C Cooperation in Work Organizations: The Institutionalization of Trust

There are two ways in which a neo-institutional analysis is applicable to work organizations. Earlier on in this section we alluded to the notion that there are at least two types of trust. Social capital-based models help elaborate the first type of trust—an interpersonal trust—that is reliant on face-to-face exchanges and contact over time. This trust is created and enhanced by teamworking, communication, and the networks resulting from both of these. Our argument here, however, is that organizations also need another type of trust that caters to the needs of large and complex communities and relieves individuals of the burden that might come from relentless networking or from the potentially oppressive nature of tightly knit communities. This is the type of institutional trust created by shared norms and collectively elaborated rules and can be understood to flow from the top down, from the edges inward rather than, as implicitly held by Putnam, from the ground up and from the network out. Employee involvement initiatives are a good illustration of the type of institutional trust that might be generated and how it might benefit an organization.

While employee involvement may be defined in a number of ways, we take it to refer to practices that seek to involve employees in meaningful ways in the elaboration and implementation of the norms and practices that define their place of work. Such initiatives will have foreseen and unforeseen consequences, but two are particularly relevant for our purposes. The first expectation is that such initiatives will reinforce communication and knowledge of the organization, and this in two ways: by helping employees to know more about the overall aims and goals of the organization and, depending on the specific nature of the initiatives involved, by allowing them to contribute to setting these goals. The second expectation is that, much as specified earlier, such initiatives create a climate in which—in particular in the case of a very large organization—employees, at whatever level, who do not know each other can nevertheless assume that they share a number of goals and that, having been consulted about and involved in the elaboration of some of the organization's structures, they can make judgements about each other's preferences and values. In short, they come to know and trust each other because they can make these assumptions. Much like we can infer a number of things about our fellow citizens because we share in the norms and procedure of institutional elaboration, so can fellow workers make a number of assumptions about each other because they share not only in the results of the organization's work but also in determining what that work will be. In work organizations such as hospitals, for instance, in which employees have little contact beyond their department and, sometimes, their ward, the ability to trust other employees can create significant opportunities for information and best-practice sharing beyond the department or ward. Unlike the Nordstrom employees or Admiral King's hapless subordinates they are, at least in part, involved in the "big picture" which—provided the training is commensurate with the responsibilities—will allow them to work smarter in a smart organization. More importantly for the creation of institutional trust, it is obvious that initiatives such as employee involvement send out a message regarding the management's perception of what individuals and groups of individuals have to bring to the organization; it also sends out a message about the values and norms held by the management as a group, and thus a possibility for employees to make inferences about those who are closest to the organization's driving structures.

This leads us to a final point: employee involvement initiatives can also contribute to increasing the organization's institutional component by publicizing, as Offe puts it, "its own legitimacy". Institutionalization—through whatever means—can provide the organization with a measure of legitimacy which can, aside from approval from customers and clients, reinforce employee trust in the organization based on the fact that their workplace abides by and promotes rules and norms that are commensurate with those they find operating in the other communities of which they are a part or in which they choose to participate. The perception that a place of work—an organization in which we spend so much of our lives—is prepared to reflect some of the expectations we hold about other communities, circles, and organizations to which we belong integrates some of our publicly and personally held goals into our work lives—much like institutions integrate personally held values into the public sphere—thus creating a situation from which both the individual and the organization stand to gain.

Institutionalization is, in many ways, inescapable, both in terms of routinization as well as in terms of the creation (purposely or not) of rituals and ritualized behaviour. Employee involvement initiatives are a way in which an organization can use institutional processes to its advantage as well as to the advantage of its employees. Unlike the institutionalized behaviour inside Nordstrom, this institutionalization is publicly endorsed as one of the organization's goals, not a by-product of manipulative practices.

CONCLUSION

Rousseau was acutely aware of the need to supplement communities—especially organized communities—with institutional norms lest they become oppressive, and then, anarchic. Yet for organizational theorists, institutionalization is often associated with the less dynamic aspects of a community: routinization, staleness—in a word, the non-creative. The challenge for many contemporary organizations, and particularly work organizations, is to be able to develop a measure of institutionalization so as to guarantee their continued functioning over time and the creation of a stable community—conducive to both individual well-being and organizational effectiveness and innovation.

While institutions and organizations are distinct, for some—and for economists in particular—the distinction is drawn in stark and unproductive terms: Khalil, for example, states that where an organization denotes the agent pursuing ends, the institutions are about the means to pursue the ends (Khalil, 1995, p. 447). North addresses the distinction by stating that

> Conceptually, what must be clearly differentiated are the rules from the players. The purpose of the rules is to define the way the game is played. But the objective of the team within that set of rules is to win the game (North, 1990, fn. 4).

The starkness of the contrast here is illustrative of the preoccupations of economic theories which are concerned with the systems that regulate economic exchanges. The analytical question is the efficacy of different systems of governance on transaction costs rather than concern for "the institutional rules of the game: customs, laws, politics" (Williamson, 1991, p. 26).

Neo-institutionalist analysis posits a deep connection between rules and players, institutions and organizations. They remind us that the process of elaborating the rules conditions the players, and thus dictates how they will play to win the game (if there is the appearance of few rules, the players may feel justified in assuming that this is an ultra-competitive game in which—almost—anything goes), in fact, which game they might choose to play to win (if employees are not consulted or involved in elaborating the rules of a game, they may choose to go work elsewhere where gains are higher; or where they are involved). Further, that the process of elaborating the rules might lead to a very different picture of the game itself, and thus of the meaning of victory or defeat (financial gain vs employment security). Finally, they remind us that individuals are involved in playing in many games at once and thus come into contact with different players. For the players to continue to be efficient in any one game the rules by which they play must span a number of games. The work that has been done on trust in organizations (Sachs, 1994; Kramer, 1999; Nyhan, 2000) demonstrates that cooperation is increased in organizations with high levels of trust; when cooperation is increased so are the levels of innovation. In other words, a secure trusting environment is also one in which individuals and teams feel that they can take the risks necessary to innovate. What neo-institutionalists tell us is that trust may stem firstly from trust in those components of the organization which are explicitly tied into the broader institutional framework and are seen to uphold the norms of the society of which the organization is a part. Rather than posit a one-way building of trust (and cooperation) from individuals, to teams, to networks of teams upward (an organizational capital), it may prove useful to look to the manner in which the trust cascades down from institutions, to organizations, to networks through to teams and individuals.[3] In this respect the organization can be said to become, truly, a citizen.

REFERENCES

Albin, C. (2001). *Justice and Fairness in International Negotiation.* Cambridge: Cambridge University Press.

Aristotle (1981). *The Politics.* Harmondsworth: Penguin.

Berger, P. & Luckmann, T. (1967). *The Social Construction of Reality.* New York: Doubleday Anchor.

Buller, P. F. & Schuler, R. (2000). *Managing Organizations and People: Cases in Management, Organizational Behaviour and Human Resource Management* (6th edn). Cincinnati, Ohio: South Western College Publishing/Thomson Learning.

Downs, A. (1957). *An Economic Theory of Democracy.* New York: Harper and Row.

Fukuyama, F. (1995). *Trust. The Social Virtues and the Creation of Prosperity*, New York: Free Press.

Gergen, K. J. & Davis, K. E. (1985). *The Social Construction of the Person.* New York: Springer-Verlag.

Gladwell, M. (2002). The talent myth. *The New Yorker*, 22 July, pp. 28–33.

Hardin, R. (1991). Trusting persons, trusting institutions. In R. J. Zeckhauser (ed.), *Strategy and Choice* (pp. 185–209). Cambridge: MIT Press.

Hardin, R. (1996). Trustworthiness. *Ethics, 107*, 26–42.

Held, D. (1987). *Models of Democracy.* Stanford, Calif.: Stanford University Press.

Hobbes, T. (1968) [1651]. *Leviathan*, C. B. Macpherson (ed.). Harmondsworth: Penguin.

Inglehart, R. (1990). *Culture Shift in Advanced Industrial Society.* Princeton, NJ: Princeton University Press.

Khalil, E. (1995). Organizations versus Institutions. *Journal of Institutional and Theoretical Economics, 151*(3), 445–466.

Kramer, R. M. (1999). Trust and distrust in organizations: emerging perspectives, enduring questions. *Annual Review of Psychology, 50*, 569–598.

Krasner, S. (1988). Sovereignty: an institutional perspective. *Comparative Political Studies, 21*(1), 66–94.

Lange, P. & Garrett, M. (1985). The politics of growth: strategic interaction and economic performance in the advanced industrial democracies 1974–1980. *Journal of Politics, 47*(3), 792–827.

Levi, M. (1998). *Consent, Dissent and Patriotism.* New York: Cambridge University Press.

Luhmann, N. (1979). Trust: a mechanism for the reduction of social complexity. In *Trust and Power: Two Works by Nikeas Luhmann.* Chichester: John Wiley & Sons.

Luhmann, N. (1988). Familiarity, confidence, trust. Problems and alternatives. In D. Gambetta (ed.), *Trust. Making and Breaking Cooperative Relations.* Oxford: Blackwell.

March, James G. & Olsen, J. P. (1984). The new institutionalism: organizational factors in political life. *American Political Science Review, 78*, 734–749.

Meadwell, H. (1993). The politics of nationalism in Quebec. *World Politics, 45*(2), 203–241.

Meyer, J. W. & Rowan, B. (1991). Institutionalized organizations: formal structure as myth and ceremony. In W. W. Powell & P. J. DiMaggio (eds), *The New Institutionalism in Organizational Analysis* (pp. 41–62). Chicago: The University of Chicago Press.

[3] While some work has been done on this (Meyer & Rowan, 1991; Powell & DiMaggio, 1991), it has been done mainly by sociological institutionalists who have posited an abolition of the distinction between institutions and organizations through a process of isomorphism. What I suggest here hinges on the distinction being maintained but recast.

Molm, L., Takahashi, N., & Peterson, G. (2000). Risk and trust in social exchanges: an experimental test of a classical proposition. *American Journal of Sociology, 105*(5), 1396–1427.
North, D. (1990). *Institutions, Institutional Change and Economic Performance*. Cambridge: Cambridge University Press.
Nyhan, R. C. (2000). Trust and its role in public sector organizations. *American Review of Public Administration, 30*(1), 87–109.
Offe, C. (1996). Institutions in East European transitions. In R. E. Goodin (ed.), *The Theory of Institutional Design* (pp. 199–226). Cambridge: Cambridge University Press.
Offe, C. (1999). How can we trust our fellow citizens? In M. E. Warren (ed.), *Democracy and Trust* (pp. 42–87). Cambridge: Cambridge University Press.
Olson, M. (1965). *The Logic of Collective Action: Public Goods and the Theory of Groups*. Cambridge: Harvard University Press.
Ostrom, E. (1992). *Crafting Institutions for Self-governing Irrigation Systems*. San Francisco, Calif.: CS Press.
Pinard, M. & Hamilton, R. (1984). The class bases of the Quebec independence movement: conjectures and evidence. *Ethnic and Racial Studies, 7*, 11–54.
Powell, W. W. & DiMaggio, P. J. (eds) (1991). *The New Institutionalism in Organizational Analysis*. Chicago: The University of Chicago Press.
Putnam, R. (1993). *Making Democracy Work: Civic Traditions in Modern Italy*. Princeton: Princeton University Press.
Putnam, R. (2000). *Bowling Alone: The Collapse and Revival of American Community*. New York, London: Simon and Schuster.
Rawls, J. (1971). *A Theory of Justice*. Cambridge, Mass.: Belknap Press of Harvard University.
Rothstein, Bo (2000). Social capital and institutional legitimacy. Paper prepared for delivery at the Annual Meeting of the American Political Science Association. Washington, DC: August 31–September 3.
Rousseau, J.-J. (1978). Discourse on the origins of inequality. In R. D. Masters (ed.), *On the Social Contract*. New York: St Martin's Press.
Rousseau, J.-J. (1993) [1762]. The social contract. In *The Social Contract and Discourses*. London: Everyman.
Sachs, S. M. (1994). Building trust in democratic organizations. *Psychology, 31*(2), 35–44.
Tocqueville, A. de (1969). *Democracy in America*, G. Lawrence translation, G. P. Mayer (ed.). Garden City, NY: Doubleday.
Tsebelis, G. (1990). *Nested Games*. Berkeley, LA, and Oxford: University of California Press.
Warren, M. E. (1999). Democratic theory and trust. In M. E. Warren (ed.), *Democracy and Trust* (pp. 310–345 and 346–360). Cambridge: Cambridge University Press.
Williamson, O. E. (1991). Comparative economic organizations: the analysis of discreet structural alternatives. *Administrative Science Quarterly, 36*, 269–296.
Yamagishi, T. & Yamagishi, M. (1994). Trust and commitment in the United States and Japan. *Motivation and Emotion, 18*, 129–166.
Zucker, L. (1986). Production of trust: institutional sources of economic structures, 1840–1920. *Research in Organizational Behaviour, 8*, 53–111.

5

CONTEXTUALIZING COOPERATION

Greg Young

No man can be acquainted with all of psychology today.

(L. J. Cronbach, 1957)

INTRODUCTION

This chapter uses theory and empirical studies to provide a contextually based analysis of the dimensions of human social relationships, with a specific focus on the concepts of cooperation and competition. It emphasizes the value of a psychological orientation to understand the dynamics of cooperation in all its complex forms, and the cognitive orientations that may be associated with them.

As the Cronbach quote above suggests, a psychological orientation to understand the context of cooperative and competitive conduct lends itself to multidimensional, multi-process, and multidirectional models that are difficult, if not impossible, to approach comprehensively. Accordingly, this chapter draws on established literature from multiple theoretical domains to examine these contextual factors individually, and we do not attempt to offer a unifying theory. The chapter, however, links these multiple perspectives around a single core theme: an individual's psychological processes are purposeful mechanisms that recognize, interpret, and interact with physical phenomena and social relationships to rationally guide behavior. In this thematic view, cognition of goal interdependence influences an individual's conduct in social relationships, and this influence is moderated by multiple contextual factors.

In this chapter, we define an individual actor's social conduct in terms of his/her pattern of action relative to interdependent others. We apply a goal-based theory of behavior (Locke & Latham, 1990; Pervin, 1989), well-received game-theoretic models (Bonacich, 1995; McMillan, 1992), and social cognition theory (Bandura, 1986; Wood & Bandura, 1989) to examine the context of cooperative and competitive patterns of action. The chapter argues first that an individual's social conduct is directly influenced by his/her perception of the association between his/her own goals and the goals aspired to by others. Second,

International Handbook of Organizational Teamwork and Cooperative Working. Edited by M. A. West, D. Tjosvold, and K. G. Smith.

we frame social conduct as a multidirectional function of the individual actor's internal (*psychological*) and external (*material, action, and social*) situational context.

The direct theoretical relationship between perceived goal association and an individual's social conduct is not the focus of this chapter. This chapter addresses the context in which this direct influence operates: the individual's identity in psychological, action, and social domains operating in, influencing, and being influenced by a material environment. This context includes all those internal and external factors that moderate the direct influence on conduct from an individual's perception of goals and interdependencies in social relationships. The focus of this chapter, then, is an individual level of analysis of the moderating factors from the internal and external context of cooperative and competitive conduct in human social relationships.

The next section of this chapter discusses interdependence in social relationships, and frames interdependence as an individual's perception that there is an association between his/her own goals and those aspired to by others. This section defines cooperative, competitive, and other forms of social conduct as an individual's pattern of action that is likely to arise from the direction and significance of this perceived association between the goals of self and the goals of others. The discussion here considers the influence of goal difficulty and network structures composed of distal social relationships connected to a proximal interdependent relationship of interest.

The chapter then discusses prior literature concerning the appraisals that individuals apply to social relationships. These appraisal criteria include trustworthiness, vengefulness, and skillfulness. This section of the chapter argues that, *ceteris paribus*, the direct relationship between goal association and social conduct is moderated by a positive or negative appraisal on these criteria. For example, an individual who perceives a positive goal association with another party, such as in a "win–win" situation of mutually compatible goals, is expected to prefer cooperative behavior. The magnitude of this preference, however, is likely to be moderated by the focal individual's appraisals of the interdependent other. On a criterion of *trustworthiness*, for example, a negative appraisal (untrustworthy other) is expected to reduce the focal individual's tendency to behave cooperatively in an otherwise "win–win" situation, but a positive appraisal (trustworthy other) should increase such behavior.

Next, the chapter presents a decision-making perspective of social conduct. This section focuses on game theory, with particular attention to the well-received prisoners' dilemma. Game theory is a useful framework to illustrate the information and incentive structures embedded in the dynamics of cooperative and competitive conduct in social relationships.

The chapter then proceeds to examine the external context of cooperative and competitive conduct. Here we consider networks of social relationships, task structures, and resources.

Finally, the chapter discusses research implications derived from a cognitive and psychological orientation to the context of social conduct.

A COGNITIVE PERSPECTIVE OF CONTEXT

In general theories of behavior (e.g. Spencer, 1897, p. 39; Tschacher & Dauwalder, 1999, p. 83) and cognitive science there is a well-established focus on purposeful goal-oriented actions. In normal human functioning, psychological processes are goal directed (Wood &

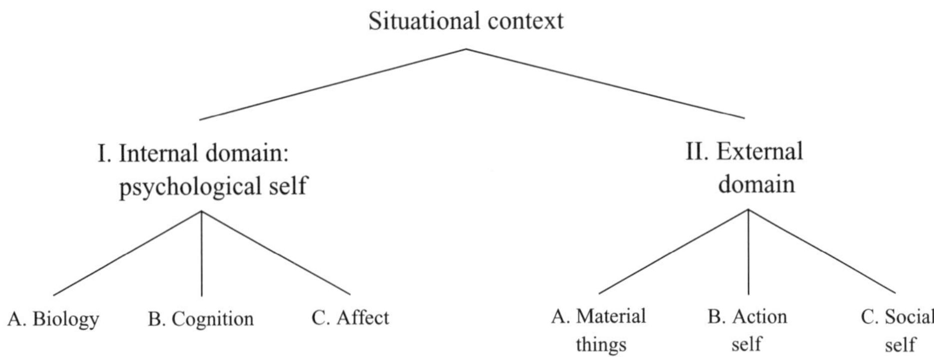

Figure 5.1 Top-level decomposition of the situational context for one individual

Bandura, 1989, p. 362), goal-oriented behavior operates in action and social domains, and each individual interacts with an environment of material things and other people. As Richardson (1997, p. 10) writes:

> ...the contents and the strategies of human cognition are acquired through experience with the social and physical world, and they are organized by means of a rich network of generic knowledge structures that are constituted and transmitted by means of sociocultural practices. In principle, then, individual differences in human cognitive functioning could originate in either biological or sociocultural processes.

Our actions have purposes and consequences in a personal world of social cognition (Bandura, 1986; Wood & Bandura, 1989) that is composed of multidirectional, reciprocating interactions among our inner psychological domain, our behavioral presence, our social dimension, and the material things in our environment. Figure 5.1 graphically displays the integration of these multiple domains into one individual's situational context.

For each of us, our biological sense organs take sensory information from the external domains outside of our mind, and our psycho-physiological processes transduce this sensory information to inform, and to be informed by, our cognitive processes and emotions (Gleitman, 1995). How we conduct ourselves in our behavior is viewed here as an outcome of a reciprocating system in which this psycho-biological process is influenced by, and influences, its environment (Bandura, 1986; Wood & Bandura, 1989). In this view, cognition is an internal psycho-biological mechanism focused on goal achievement in a specific situational context. This cognitive perspective addresses, in part, how personal perceptions, memories, thoughts, motivations, language, and knowledge about the self and the environment are organized, combined, or integrated into behavior (Green, 1996; Martin & Clark, 1990, p. 266). Figure 5.2 decomposes the psychological domain of the situational context to a more granular level of detail. Figure 5.3 shows in more detail the external domain of the situational context.

As Figures 5.1–5.3 show, an individual's conduct in social relationships is a function of all his/her psychological processes working together and interacting with all the components in his/her external domain. That is, an individual's internal psychological domain recognizes social interdependence with others, and the individual's conduct is guided by the interaction of this perception with the external situational context and with his/her internal processes

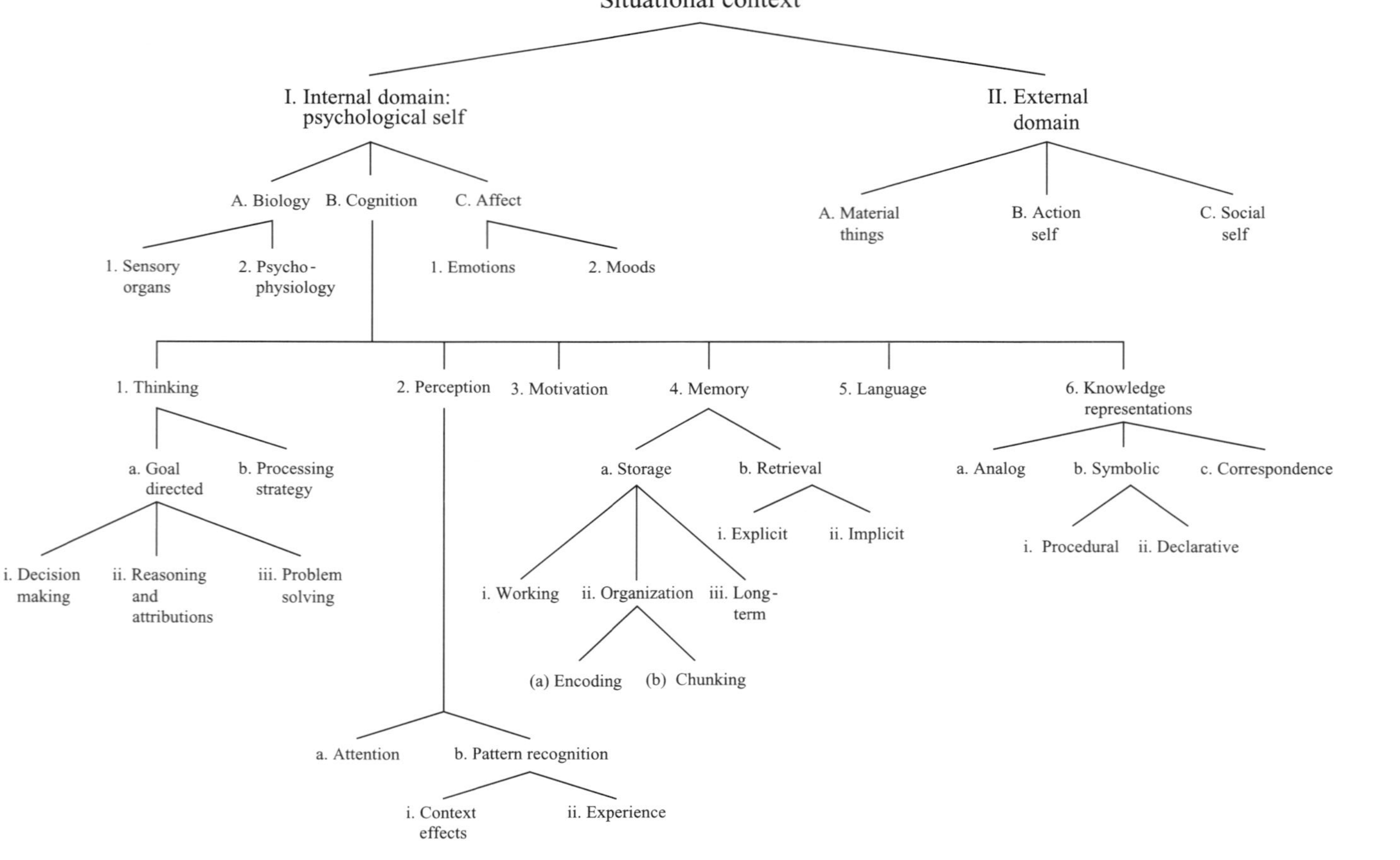

Figure 5.2 Situational context of a focal individual: decomposition of the internal psychological self

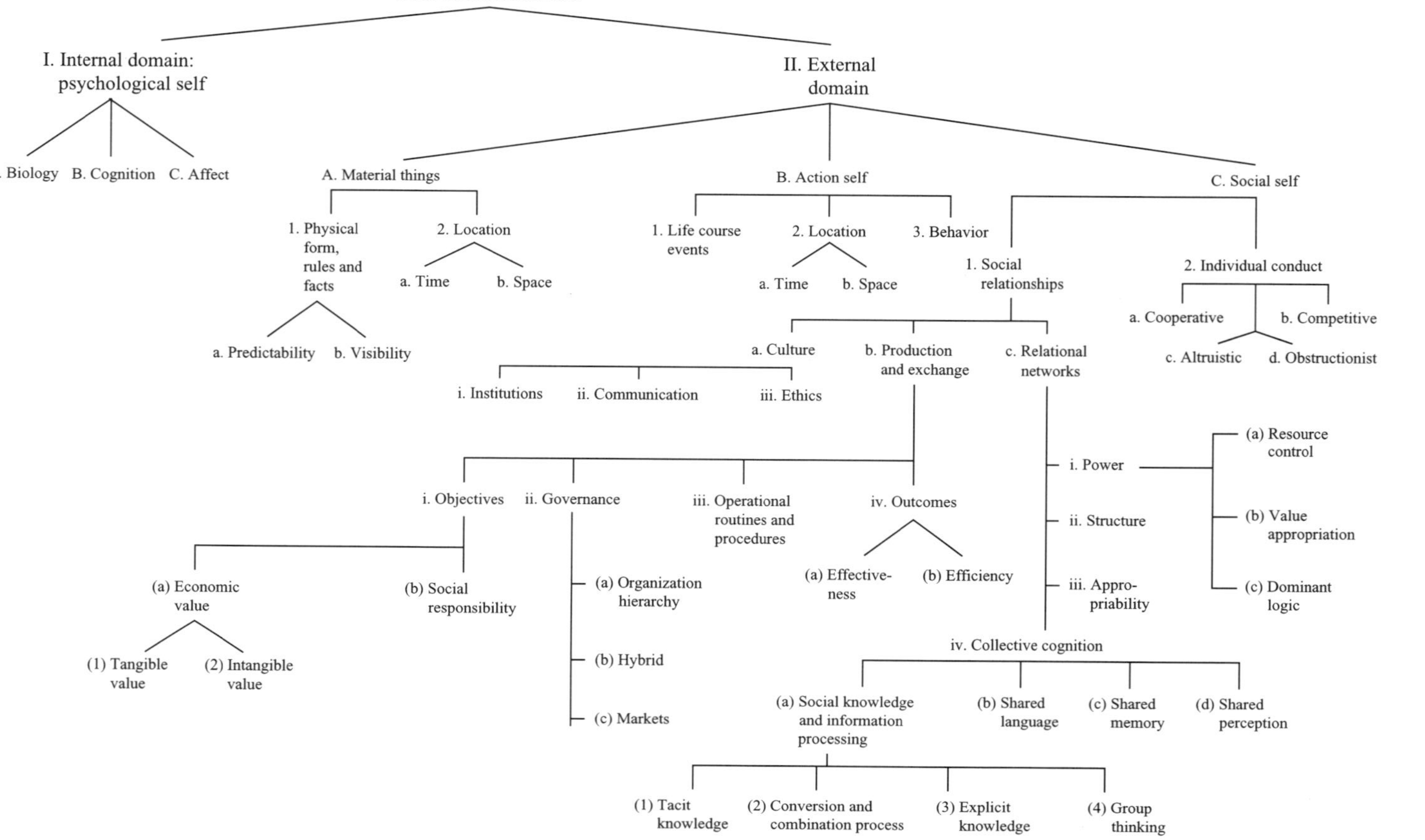

Figure 5.3 Situational context of a focal individual: decomposition of the external domain

of cognition (including goal-directed thinking, perception, motivation, memory, language, knowledge), biology, and affect.

This chapter applies a cognitive perspective to examine the context of cooperative and competitive social conduct. As presented in Figures 5.1–5.3, this context is composed of psychological, material, action, and social dimensions that are perceived by a focal goal-oriented individual. In this context, the individual takes actions that are instrumental to make progress toward his/her own goals, and these actions and goals may be associated with other individuals in the social context.

The next section discusses an individual's perception of interdependence with others. It examines the characteristics of this interdependence that may influence that individual to behave cooperatively or competitively in his/her social relationships.

INTERNAL PSYCHOLOGICAL DOMAIN: INTERDEPENDENCE AS A FUNCTION OF PERCEPTION AND GOALS

This chapter defines social conduct (e.g. cooperation and competition) as a pattern of action that an individual actor executes within social relationships to accomplish goals. We follow goal-setting theory to define goals as "an action's object or aim composed of a specific standard of proficiency to be attained on a given task, usually within a given time" (Locke & Latham, 1990, pp. 25–26).

In social relationships, an individual may be cognizant of an association between his/her own goal accomplishment and the accomplishment of goals held by others. Put another way, goal association is a cognitive description of a situation as it is perceived by one person (*call them* $PERSON_A$). In this situation, $PERSON_A$ desires to accomplish a goal or set of goals (*call it* $GOALS_A$), progresses toward $GOALS_A$ with instrumental actions ($ACTIONS_A$), and knows that $PERSON_B$ desires $GOALS_B$ and progresses with $ACTIONS_B$. In this situation, goal association is the perception held by $PERSON_A$ that there is a (positive or negative) relationship, or association, between $GOALS_A$ and $GOALS_B$. This chapter frames this association as an individual's subjective thinking, perceptions, motivation, memory, language, and knowledge about the instrumentality for self-goals that is embedded in the goals of others.

We define interdependency as a nonzero association between the goals held by a focal actor and the goals of others. There are multiple forms of interdependency (*action-based, structural, and outcome-based*) in which a focal actor may perceive goal association. The logic of goal association may alert the focal individual to the presence of an action-based interdependency with the other person(s) in the relationship. That is, if $PERSON_A$ recognizes that $GOALS_A$ are associated with $GOALS_B$, and $ACTIONS_B$ are instrumental for $GOALS_B$, then $PERSON_A$ may recognize that both s/he and $PERSON_B$ are mutually dependent on $ACTIONS_B$. Figure 5.4 extends this logic to show that not only actions but also temporal–spatial structures and outcomes are paths through which an individual may recognize interdependencies that arise from goal association with another.

For a goal-oriented individual in a social environment, his/her cognition of goal association is informed by the historical, contemporaneous, and anticipated patterns of structure, actions, and outcomes embedded in the external situational context. For example, the temporal–spatial structure of an external situation may locate the individual remotely from

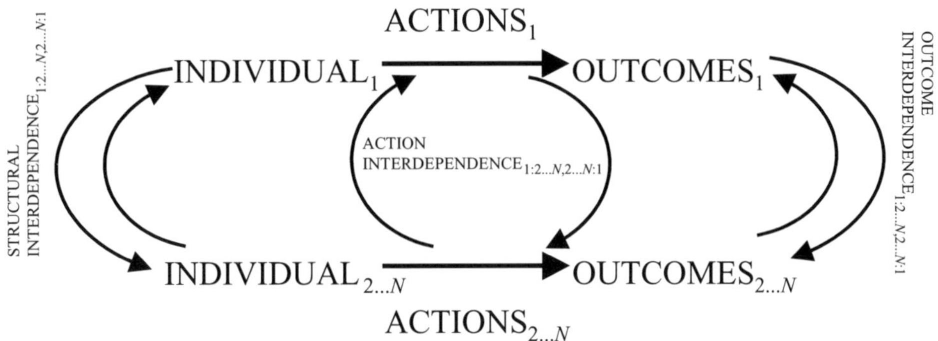

Figure 5.4 Social relationship within the situational context of INDIVIDUAL_X

others or with other(s) in proximity of space and time, concentrate material resources into a small space and time or disperse them widely, persist over a long period of time or be short-lived. The individual's actions may be contemporaneous with others on one activity, or his/her actions may be part of a system of activities so that the outcome of one affects the situation of others.

In Figure 5.4, the focal individual (Individual_1) may have some combination of structural, action-based, or outcome interdependencies with one (Individual_2) or with many other people (Individual_2 through Individual_N). For example, the notation ACTION $\text{INTERDEPENDENCE}_{1:2\ldots N,2\ldots N:1}$in Figure 5.4 indicates that the GOALS of Individual_1 depend on the ACTIONS of $\text{Individuals}_{2\ldots N}$ (ACTION $\text{INTERDEPENDENCE}_{1:2\ldots N}$) and the GOALS of $\text{Individuals}_{2\ldots N}$ depend on the ACTIONS of Individual_1 (ACTION $\text{INTERDEPENDENCE}_{2\ldots N:1}$).

That these paths may exist is not to say anything about how they come about. Linkages of interdependence based on structure, actions, and/or outcomes may be due to explicit, intended design, or emerge from unintended consequences of history, or come from tacit understanding. No matter their origin, interdependence is an individual's perception of his/her relationship with another. This perception is grounded in the individual's psychological connection to his/her external environment in which s/he is an action agent to accomplish self-goals. The subjectivity of individual psychological processes suggests that each party in a given social environment can asymmetrically recognize the interdependence of his/her own goals relative to those held by the other.

When an individual believes that his/her goals are *interdependent* with others, s/he perceives a positive or negative association with the goals held by others. The perception of significant nonzero goal association with interdependent others makes salient the role of the individual in social relationships, and guides his/her psychological processing and conduct in social interactions (Deutsch, 1949; Alper, Tjosvold, & Law, 1998). A contingency perspective on conduct, for example, suggests that people may interpret the context of their interdependencies in social relationships so that they behave in a manner that fits the situation, and the behavior is likely to be sustained for the duration of the contextual configuration. In this way, interdependencies may develop over time into patterns of behavior. Prior literature has described the available patterns of social conduct (*individual behavior that persists over time in social relationships*) as cooperative, competitive, altruistic, and obstructionist (Alper, Tjosvold, & Law, 1998; Williams, 2001).

The next section discusses these patterns of behavior in terms of an individual's perception of an association between his/her own and others' goal achievement. Importantly, this discussion frames interdependence as an asymmetric description of a focal individual's psychological connection to a social relationship, and not as a description of the relationship itself.

Cooperative Interdependence

In interdependence, a positive goal association means that an individual recognizes that as others successfully move toward their goal attainment, s/he moves toward reaching his/her own goals as well. Interestingly, positive goal association may be asynchronous ("they are helpful to me"), or bisynchronous ("We are mutually helpful to each other").

Asynchronous positive goal association is the perception held by PERSON_{A} that s/he moves closer to his/her GOAL_{A} as PERSON_{B} takes $\text{ACTIONS}_{\text{B}}$ to achieve GOAL_{B}, but progress toward GOAL_{A} is not instrumental for progress toward ACTION_{B} or GOAL_{B}. In other words, in asynchronous positive goal association PERSON_{A} believes PERSON_{B} is instrumental but does not think him/herself instrumental for PERSON_{B}. For example, imagine a task to schedule time on scarce equipment for which all parties have commonly held goals of resource accessibility and efficiency. Assume PERSON_{A} requires equipment time to accomplish GOAL_{A} but s/he cannot start until PERSON_{B}, ahead in the queue, finishes with the equipment. In this case, PERSON_{A} may request that PERSON_{B} cooperate by hurrying it along.

Bisynchronous positive goal association modifies the asynchronous form so PERSON_{A} believes his/her own goals and those of PERSON_{B} are mutually compatible and both parties are instrumental for each other. That is, PERSON_{A} perceives that as PERSON_{B} takes $\text{ACTIONS}_{\text{B}}$ to achieve GOAL_{B}, there is progress toward GOAL_{A}, and as s/he moves closer to GOAL_{A}, PERSON_{B} progresses toward GOAL_{B}. In the scheduling example, PERSON_{A} may now actively support PERSON_{B}'s productivity and efficiency so that the *total time on equipment* of A and B together is less.

The scheduling example places $\text{PERSONS}_{\text{A and B}}$ in a context of scarce resources, but variation in expected conduct arises from differences in perceived synchronicity, or instrumentality, in the goal association. Asynchronous positive goal association leads to a preference for others to cooperate with the self, bisynchronous positive goal association leads to a preference for the self to act cooperatively as well.

Figure 5.5 shows that we expect to observe cooperative conduct from an individual who highly values both the accomplishment of his/her own goals as well as those held by interdependent others (the upper left quadrant of the figure). This cell may describe the instrumentality of either an asynchronous or a bisynchronous positive goal association, although we expect that only the mutually compatible cooperative conduct of the latter type will persist over time. This expectation is grounded in assumptions including goal-directed intentionalism of psychology from general theories of behavior (e.g. Spencer, 1897, p. 39; Tschacher & Dauwalder, 1999, p. 83), cultural norms of reciprocity (Ariño, 1997), economic rationality, and learning over time in a subjective process of symbolic interaction (Jones & George, 1998).

Goal-directed intentionalism suggests a preference for actions and other people who are instrumental for the attainment of goals. Put another way, if PERSON_{A} is motivated to

Valence to focal actor from interdependent others' goal accomplishment

Valence to focal actor from self-accomplishment of goals	High	Low
High	Cooperative conduct	Competitive conduct
Low	Altruistic conduct	Obstructionist conduct

Figure 5.5 Valence-based typology of social conduct from the perspective of a focal actor

achieve his/her own goals, and if s/he believes that PERSON_B is instrumental toward this end, then PERSON_A is likely to prefer that PERSON_B accomplish his/her GOALS_B, and PERSON_A is likely to be motivated by this preference to take action helpful to PERSON_B. Second, the norm of reciprocity, present in all cultures (Ariño, 1997), frames cooperative action offered by another, such as may be prompted by a focal individual's cognition of asynchronous positive goal association, as a social debt that must be repaid in kind. The absence of such repayment visibly violates an omnipresent cultural value so that additional cooperation in that social relationship is likely not to be forthcoming. Third, a rational process of symbolic interaction suggests that a thinking individual, learning about his/her social situation and the other's needs and goals (Jones & George, 1998), is likely to discover available actions for mutual gain for which the fair share of the total expected benefits exceeds the expected costs. We label such actions cooperative, and we assume, all else equal, that as long as PERSON_A has not satisfied his/her motivation, s/he will take all such actions whose expected benefits exceed expected costs. Accordingly, we suggest that unreciprocated cooperative conduct is not sustainable, and over time asynchronous positive goal association is likely either to die out or to evolve into the bisynchronous form of mutual instrumentality. Cooperation that persists likely is an individual's conduct that helps others, and such cooperation arises from the focal actor's cognition of bisynchronous positive goal association.

Examples of Cooperative Conduct

Cooperation may be direct between participants co-located in time on one activity, or it may be an indirect behavior in which the participants are separated either by time or by an intermediary relationship. For example, cooperative action may be undertaken as a consequence of prior conduct or in the expectation of a future reciprocal action from another party. PERSON_A also may cooperate with PERSON_B indirectly by helping parties from PERSON_B's other relationships.

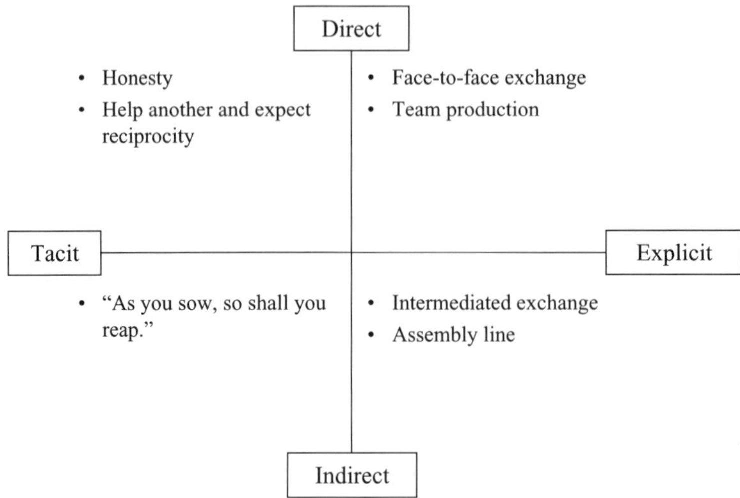

Figure 5.6 Examples of cooperative conduct

In addition to its direct or indirect characteristic, cooperation may be explicit conduct with clear intention communicated by the actor to the beneficiary, or tacit conduct in which there is no communication of intention to the interdependent beneficiary. Figure 5.6 lists some examples of direct–indirect, and explicit–tacit cooperative conduct.

Attributes of cooperative conduct include truthfulness, honest dealing, commitment, fair play, and complying with agreements (Das & Teng, 1998). Alper, Tjosvold, & Law (1998) discuss prior studies of cooperative conduct that show people "share information, acknowledge each other's perspective, communicate and influence effectively, exchange resources, assist and support each other, discuss opposing ideas openly, and use higher-quality reasoning . . . fostering attraction, and strengthening work relationships and confidence in future collaboration."

It is useful to note here that cooperative conduct is not constrained to the absence of conflict or controversy. For example, prior research has documented that controversy is useful for solving problems when conducted within a cooperative context. Cooperative people who disagree with one another will communicate and clarify more, create more alternatives, and be more likely to reach an agreement that is mutually beneficial (Alper, Tjosvold, & Law, 1998).

In sum, this chapter frames cooperation in terms of an individual's conduct in social relationships. It defines cooperation to be either (a) the pattern of action a focal individual prefers from instrumental others, or (b) the pattern of action undertaken by a focal individual to benefit goals held by the actor and instrumental others; but the chapter suggests the asynchronous form likely leads to the bisynchronous. Accordingly, the chapter focuses on the focal individual as cognizant actor, and argues that cooperative conduct comes about when s/he is aware of a positive association between self-goals and those held by others. The direct theoretical relationship is between the individual's perception of a "win–win" association and the cooperative conduct that arises from this perception. The situational context, then, consists of all those internal and external factors that moderate this direct influence.

Competitive Interdependence

In interdependence, a negative goal association means that a focal individual believes that his/her own goal attainment is incompatible with the goal attainment of the interdependent others. Reasoning from this perception, s/he is better off when interdependent others act ineffectively and, therefore, self-interest motivates a preference that others should not accomplish their goals. This is the situation, described in the upper right quadrant of Figure 5.5, in which we expect to observe competitive conduct.

In negative goal association, another's win is a loss for self and valued outcomes are contested. The direct theoretical relationship of interest is between the individual's perception of a "win–lose" relationship and the competitive conduct that arises from this perception. All internal and external factors that moderate this direct relationship compose the situational context that is the subject of this chapter.

We expect that in the absence of an overriding cooperation on group ethics, attributes of competitive conduct might include dishonest dealing and failure to comply with agreements. Ethical competitive conduct might include withholding information, resources, and support as well as striving for positions of advantage that are incompatible with others.

Other Forms of Social Conduct

Figure 5.5 shows that altruism and obstructionism are other types of social conduct that can arise from an individual's perception of goal association between self and interdependent others. Both altruism and obstructionism hinder the achievement of self-goals.

Altruistic conduct advances the interests of others at the expense of self. It is a form of "I am helpful to them" in which PERSON_A perceives that as s/he takes ACTIONS_A s/he is instrumental in PERSON_B's progress toward GOALS_B, but ACTIONS_A are not instrumental for progress toward any GOAL_A. For PERSON_A, the time, effort, and expense are opportunity costs that, perhaps, could have been allocated elsewhere for some GOAL_A. Altruistic behavior does not require that PERSON_A perceive opportunity costs, but it may require that the focal actor not have a goal to be an altruist. An attribution of altruism may lead to trust (Doney, Cannon, & Mullen, 1998), and, with a norm of reciprocity, over time altruism may lead to cooperation.

Obstructionism has been described in terms of negative exchange relations and behaviors such as interference, threats, sabotage, and rejection, as well as imitative responses to such behaviors (Sparrowe et al., 2001, p. 318). More precisely, obstructionism is social conduct in which PERSON_A perceives that as s/he takes ACTION_A s/he is instrumental in PERSON_B's loss of progress relative to GOAL_B, and ACTION_A also loses progress for GOALS_A as well. For example, individuals who were identified by coworkers as hindering the work of others were rated by managers as relatively lower on performance (Sparrowe et al., 2001).

Altruism and obstructionism are interesting and important types of social conduct that to our knowledge have not been extensively studied. This chapter, however, focuses on cooperative and competitive social conduct in interdependent relationships.

Discussion of Situational Context and Social Conduct

This chapter defines social conduct in terms of the pattern of an individual's actions in social relationships, and argues that this pattern (1) is directly influenced by the perceived association between the attainment of self-goals and the goals of others; and (2) is contingent on the internal and external situational context. The focus of this chapter is the latter—an individual level of analysis of the internal and external factors that moderate the direct influence of perceived goal association on conduct in social relationships.

A psychological perspective suggests that an individual's cognition of goal association is informed by patterns of structure, actions, and outcomes embedded in interdependent relationships grounded in the internal and external situational context. In this context, the individual's behavior is guided by a multidirectional, multi-process consideration of the instrumentality of others for the accomplishment of self-goals and the valence to the focal individual of these self-goals and those held by others.

The discussion of cooperation and competition accommodates the possibility that both types of conduct might be observed from the same individuals in a social dyad. This is a common situation in business, for example, when two people employed by the same firm cooperate on projects while competing for the same job promotion. In this example, we note that the context changes (from a team structure to a pyramid-like hierarchical careerist power structure). It is the richness of context that is the subject of this chapter.

Building on this chapter's focus on an individual's subjective calculus in a process of symbolic interaction, we argue that valuable insight into social conduct (*whether a cooperative, competitive, altruistic, or obstructionist pattern of action*) will incorporate a cognitive perspective into theory-building. Accordingly, this chapter frames its contextual analysis at the individual level of the actor, and integrates the internal representations and external environment in a multidirectional model of social cognition (e.g. Bandura, 1986; Wood & Bandura, 1989).

The next section of this chapter discusses the attributions, appraisals, flexibility, and decision-making processes that individuals apply to social relationships.

INTERNAL PSYCHOLOGICAL DOMAIN: INDIVIDUAL ATTRIBUTIONS AND APPRAISALS IN SOCIAL RELATIONSHIPS

This section of the chapter argues that the direct relationship between perceived goal association and social conduct is positively or negatively moderated by appraisal of the interdependent party's attributes. The discussion here focuses on the role of trustworthiness, vengefulness, and skillfulness as specific appraisal criteria. For example, an individual who perceives a positive association of goals with another person is expected to behave cooperatively (the upper left quadrant of Figure 5.5). The cooperative conduct that is expected in a "win–win" situation, however, may be mitigated if the actor perceives an "untrustworthy" attribute in the interdependent party. Following classic appraisal theory (Scherer, 1999, p. 638), the magnitude of mitigation in this example is a function of the importance the actor places on trustworthiness and his/her ability to influence or cope with the consequences of an "untrustworthy" partner.

Trustworthiness

Prior literature has identified trust as a valuable enabler of cooperative conduct (Williams, 2001). Practicing managers, for example, consistently say that trust is indispensable to the success of alliances (Badaracco, 1991, p. 142). Individuals are more inclined to engage in cooperation with partners who have demonstrated their trustworthiness directly in proximal relationships or by reputation in distal relationships (Blankenburg, Eriksson, & Johanson, 1997).

We define trust as an individual's belief and expectation that his/her assets at risk are reliably safe in the presence of another party—"by definition, trust is the degree to which the trustor holds a positive attitude toward the trustee's goodwill and reliability in a risky exchange situation" (Das & Teng, 1998). Trust is one important relational dimension that influences interpersonal proximity, value incentives, and the motivation to cooperate (Nahapiet & Ghoshal, 1998; Tsai & Ghoshal, 1998). The perception of a trustworthy attribute in another brings with it the expectation of reciprocity, and the other person may return the positive psychological orientation. The positive attribution motivates the individual more often to be physically available to the other and to anticipate a higher reward because vulnerabilities will not be exploited.

Dyer & Singh (1998) note that trust based on the credible goodwill of another offers performance advantages over other forms of safeguards. For example, carefully specified legal contracts that anticipate all future situations are costly to write, monitor, and enforce. In comparison with third-party enforcement of such contracts, safeguards based on trust from goodwill offer lower transaction costs related to bargaining and monitoring and therefore enhance performance (Dyer & Singh, 1998, p. 669).

Even with perceived positive goal association among interdependent parties, it is difficult (if not impossible) to explicitly contract in advance for value-creation activities such as sharing fine-grained tacit knowledge, exchanging resources that are difficult to price, or commercializing innovations with untested market value (Ring & Van de Ven, 1994). With safeguards based on trust, however, an individual is more likely to cooperate in these activities because they believe they have credible assurances that they will be rewarded.

In short, and not surprisingly, an individual should have more confidence in a beneficial outcome from cooperative combination and exchange of resources with trusted rather than distrusted others (Das & Teng, 1998). Accordingly, the influence of a positive goal association on cooperative conduct likely is stronger for an individual who appraises the interdependent party to be trustworthy, weaker for an individual who appraises the interdependent party to be untrustworthy. We expect, however, that the moderating influence of trust on cooperation is itself moderated by the goal-related salience of trust for the focal individual.

Further, the competitive conduct outcome expected in negative goal association is weaker when the focal individual appraises the other party to be trustworthy. Trustworthy rivals offer credible commitments to forbear from behavior that could destroy value available for distribution. As Axelrod (1984) found, trustworthy commitments to forbear preserve value and encourage reciprocity. Conversely, competitive conduct should be stronger from an individual who appraises the interdependent party to be untrustworthy. In this case, aggressive competitive actions may be costly but still necessary to seize value before it is irretrievably lost.

Substitutes for Trust

The basis for credible trust does not need to rest solely on an assumption of goodwill. Das and Teng (1998) note that control mechanisms designed to monitor and regulate the interaction between the parties can make cooperative behavior more likely even when trust based on goodwill is lacking.

There is much support for control mechanisms as substitutes for trust in interdependent relationships, though there is controversy about whether the use of control mechanisms damages trust within the relationship. Das & Teng (1998) argue against substitutability because "a firm is free to build more trust without being required to reduce controls . . . and it may pursue changing both trust and control simultaneously and in a parallel fashion, without any zero-sum complementarity constraints linking trust and control." Rather than substitution between trust and control, they call for a contingency perspective that fits task characteristics with the control mechanisms employed.

Their contingency argument differs from the one put forward here in their omission of a well-articulated appraisal process as a dimension of fit. This chapter argues that the debate concerning a complementary or substitution relationship between trust and control, and whether control damages trust, is likely to be resolved by formally considering the psychological appraisal process of the decision maker who selects the control mechanisms for the relationship. This approach calls attention to the salience of an attribute for an individual, and to the coping mechanisms with which an individual can deal with the consequences of an attribute. From the psychological perspective, substitutability and complementarity are not objective descriptions of the trust or control constructs but are better understood as outcomes of a subjective cognitive calculus embedded in an individual's appraisal processes. This subjective calculus means that for given mechanisms of trust and control, substitutability and complementarity are asymmetric across individuals.

Vengefulness and Learning to Trust over Time

The development of cooperation within exchange relationships is a process that evolves over time. Whitener et al. (1998) suggest that trust-building is a mechanism of social exchange over time that reduces the threat of competitive behavior. Trust-building is a social–psychological process of learning, recognition of patterns of behavior and contextual configurations, and reasoning from attributions. In this process, patterns of action in a social relationship lead to a perception of trustworthiness as an attribute of the interdependent counterpart. The components of this process include two or more interdependent parties characterized by some magnitude of fairness and equity, communication, and flexibility among themselves, with resources at risk in the relationship (Das & Teng, 1998).

Somewhat surprisingly, these desirable characteristics are likely to be associated with a party whose reputation is for retaliation against anyone who defects from such behaviors. Well-received prior literature recognizes that trust and long-term cooperative behavior are supported by "tit-for-tat" retaliation that punishes and deters defections (Axelrod, 1984; Doney, Cannon, & Mullen, 1998; Heide & Miner, 1992).

Early in the trust-building process, small transactions with little risk require relatively low levels of trust (Knez & Camerer, 2000). These small exchanges are useful experiences, however, during which each party stores cognitions that support an appraisal regarding the other's trustworthiness. For example, an individual might be more likely to trust another party who demonstrated internal locus of control or goal commitment in an earlier interaction (Lepine & van Dyne, 2001). One mechanism to demonstrate such commitment is to retaliate against anyone whose behavior undermines the mutual accomplishment of goals.

In a cognitive trust-building process, the individual first senses the experience, recognizes the pattern, then makes the attribution. The attribution informs a reasoning process that, first, the partner will sustain in a riskier situation the desirable attribute experienced in an earlier less risky situation, and second that the interdependent parties can appropriate (or "reuse") their relationship from a less risky situation for a subsequent riskier situation. While this process appears sequential, it might emerge in fits and starts, with loop-backs and interruptions.

A trust-building process is grounded, in part, on the actor's anticipation that the other party will sustain their trustworthy attribute into the future. The reasonableness of this assumption, and the feasibility of a well-intentioned other party to actually sustain the desirable attribute over time, are supported by Axelrod's (1984) well-known "tit-for-tat" strategy in a game-theoretic computer simulation. We discuss game theory in some detail later in this chapter. For now, we only wish to point out that Axelrod's (1984) simulation demonstrated that trustworthy behavior is sustained over time once the parties learn that defection from cooperation is immediately punished. Accordingly, we expect that the influence of a positive goal association on cooperative conduct is stronger as the focal actor increasingly attributes the interdependent party with vengefulness against defections from cooperation.

Skillfulness

An individual with cognitive understanding of trust-building as a process (evident, for example, in his/her thinking, memory, language, and knowledge representations) has the mental foundation to be skillful at cooperative behavior. Cooperative conduct is, in part, a learned behavior, and those who learn it in one relationship may be able to transfer that learning to other relationships as well (Blankenburg, Eriksson, & Johanson, 1997). In this way, the tendency of an individual to behave cooperatively is moderated by his/her prior experience at trust-building, the cognitive consequences of this experience, and the retrieval of those cognitions in the new relationships. Prior experience at cooperative conduct offers potential time compression economies for cooperative conduct, so that an individual may be faster to cooperate in subsequent interdependent relationships. Accordingly, here we propose that the cooperative conduct outcome expected in positive goal association is stronger when the focal actor increasingly attributes the interdependent party to be endowed with learned trust-building and cooperative skills. For example, an individual who has the experience of good group communication and effort is likely to have the confidence that the group can cooperate successfully. Conversely, without this experience, the individual team member is likely to be skeptical that the group has the wherewithal to cooperatively accomplish goals (Alper, Tjosvold, & Law, 1998).

In addition to skills in the dynamics of cooperation, complementary goal-specific skills are important as well. These skills are discussed in more detail in a later section on task structure and social networks. Here we point out that appraisal of the interdependent party's attributes of task skillfulness should influence the focal actor's assessment of the group efficacy. Efficacy research suggests that an individual who perceives his/her group to be highly efficacious is more likely to be willing to behave cooperatively. The assumption, then, is that an individual's confidence or skepticism concerning relational efficacy moderates the influence of goal association and cooperative conduct. Specifically, the cooperative conduct outcome expected in positive goal association is stronger when the individual perceives high relational efficacy, weaker when the individual perceives low relational efficacy. The focal actor is likely to perceive relational efficacy is higher when partners are attributed to be increasingly skillful.

It is interesting to consider the role of relational efficacy in a competitive situation characterized by the individual's perception that self-goals are negatively associated with others. Porter (1985, pp. 201–228) discusses the importance of selecting a good competitor whose conduct will not be so aggressive that they destroy the potential value available to be captured in the external environment. We expect, then, that the individual's confidence or skepticism concerning relational efficacy moderates the influence of negative goal association and competitive conduct. Specifically, the competitive conduct outcome expected in negative goal association is weaker when the individual perceives the interdependent party to have little skill at the competitive process and potentially destructive of the total value to be distributed.

Flexibility

We define *flexibility* as the willingness of an individual to adapt, change, or adjust to new knowledge, processes, or new resource configurations without resorting to a series of new contracts or renegotiations with interdependent others (Volberda, 1996). This definition of flexibility focuses on the cognitive attitudes and behaviors with which an individual governs his/her response to change.

Flexibility has been proposed to be an important influence on the accomplishment of goals. Processes to exchange resources and substitute more valuable for less valuable resources are subject to transfer barriers. In the presence of such barriers, however, an individual's flexibility influences the speed, ease, and cost of responding to innovation, new knowledge, new technologies, or other developments that arise during the course of work (Conner & Prahalad, 1996; Sanchez & Mahoney, 1996, p. 66). Indeed, the flexibility with which partner relationships are governed may have more to do with successful performance outcomes than does an initial formal agreement (Doz & Hamel, 1998, p. xv). For example, *ex ante* differences and knowledge asymmetries between trading partners can lead to divergent judgements and expectations (Conner & Prahalad, 1996), reduce each party's willingness to accept at face value the statements of the other, and add time and cost to resource sharing and exchange. Flexibility, however, is a coping mechanism to adapt efficiently and quickly and to mitigate the influence of such divergence. In short, flexibility reduces barriers to change.

We propose here that the influence on social conduct from a perceived goal association between individuals is moderated by the flexibility of the relational context. Specifically, the expected relationship between cooperative conduct and perceived positive goal association between individuals is likely to be stronger as the level of flexibility with trading partners increases. That is, more cooperative conduct is enabled as the dynamics of the relationship are handled with more flexibility.

The moderating influence of flexibility on the relationship between an individual's perceived negative goal association with others and competitive conduct is more complex. We expect that an individual who is more flexible can take more competitive actions in a given period of time than a less flexible individual. In this way, flexibility strengthens the relationship between incompatible goals and competitive conduct. Implicit in this simple proposition, however, is the assumption that flexibility is constrained so that it does not include the capacity to change goals or position to convert the goal association from negative to positive.

This constrained definition of flexibility may not describe all situations. In a less constrained definition, we expect an individual is less likely to strive for goals that are incompatible with those held by a stronger rival if the weaker has the flexibility to retreat from the struggle. Stronger rivals, on the other hand, have no rational incentive to retreat even if flexibility gives them the capability.

Discussion of the Role of Flexibility and Appraisal in the Psychological Self

Models that incorporate appraisal are likely to be multi-process and multi-criteria (Scherer, 1999), and this richness should add value compared to simpler models that might be based on a single contingency mechanism. In this regard, we suggest that additional research is required to understand the influence of flexibility and appraisal on social conduct. For example, we do not know if a moderating or mediating combinatory model is more appropriate. In the former, the role of flexibility to enable cooperative conduct likely is stronger as appraisals of interdependent parties are more positive. In the latter, the influence of flexibility is indeterminate in the absence of appraisal, or flexibility is a reciprocating behavior generated by an appraisal of a flexible interdependent party.

In the next section, the chapter presents a decision-making perspective of social conduct. Here we address the information and incentive structures embedded in the dynamics of social relationships.

Decision-making Perspective of Social Conduct

This section applies game theory, with particular attention to the prisoners' dilemma, as a framework to understand the information and incentive structures that influence an actor's choice to be cooperative or competitive. As Pinker (1997, p. 38) suggested, "To understand cooperation and conflict, we have to look to the mathematics of games and to economic modeling." Here we focus on a focal actor's conjectural, or a priori, assessment of information about rewards that are contingent on his/her own behavior in a situational context defined by an interdependent party's behavior.

Game Theory

Game theory, contrary to its name, is less a theory and more a tool that imposes logical structure to a decision-making problem (Postrel, 1991). In this structure, one must anticipate what others will choose to do in order to select the best action for oneself (McMillan, 1992, p. 19). We present a game-theoretic framework to illustrate the structure of interdependencies and stimulate some testable implications for the context of cooperation.

Game theory typically presents choice problems as decision tables that arrange alternative acts in rows, a column for each alternative situational state, and an entry in each

Other's choices

Choices for self	Confess	Do not confess
Do not confess	(15, 1)	(4, 4)
Confess	(10, 10)	(1, 15)

Note that a smaller number is preferred—it is a lighter punishment.

Figure 5.7 Net outcomes from decisions in a prisoners' dilemma decision structure

cell corresponding to the outcome for that act and state (Resnik, 1987, p. 7). Figure 5.7 presents the prisoners' dilemma game (PDG), an example of a well-known game-theoretic decision problem (Bonacich, 1995; Lodewijkx, 2001; McMillan, 1992). In this problem, two interdependent players must decide whether to cooperate or compete with one another, and the net benefit of each possible choice combination is shown in the coordinate information listed in the cells of the figure (with the net benefit for a focal player listed first).

According to the story of the game, the prisoners know the sentences to be handed down for each combination of choices (listed in Figure 5.7). Each sees that no matter what they choose to do, the other is better off to confess (*the lighter sentence preferred by the other prisoner is the smaller second number in each row*). Accordingly, each looks up their own sentence for the situation (*column*) in which the other confesses, and sees they are better off confessing as well (*the smaller first number in the Other Confesses column*). Here is the dilemma: the prisoners make a rational choice to confess and compete with one another for the lighter sentence, even though the known outcomes clearly inform them that each would have a lighter sentence by cooperating with one another by not confessing.

To understand the dynamics of such conduct, we assume that each is rationally motivated and prefers the highest possible benefit (in this case, the lowest sentence). In the incentive structure of the prisoners' dilemma, a person achieves the highest performance if s/he undertakes a competitive action for unilateral advantage (*compete for the lighter sentence by confessing*) while their rival forbears from such competitive conduct. A move for unilateral gain, however, risks competitive retaliation and erosion of performance below the mutual forbearance level. The game pays the highest aggregate rewards when the prisoners cooperate with each other and forbear from choosing to confess. The dilemma for each is that, should s/he forbear in anticipation of mutual benefit, their own performance will be lowest if the other defects from forbearance by confessing. Thus, mutual forbearance is more profitable when the outcomes for both are considered in the aggregate, but it is unattainable or unstable because either individual could improve their performance by moving unilaterally to a more rivalrous position.

To resolve the prisoners' dilemma, additional mechanisms are required to secure mutual forbearance behavior between rivals (Bonacich, 1995). Mechanisms useful for this purpose are those that signal trustworthiness, deter rivalrous behavior, and/or enforce rules of forbearance against defectors (Axelrod, 1984; Caves & Porter, 1977, p. 249; Porter, 1980, p. 105). For example, a reputation for credible retaliation, or vengefulness, may motivate rivals to refrain from competitive action they may contemplate. Other useful mechanisms come from social categorization processes that shift individual identity to group identity (De Cremer & van Vugt, 1998; Hogg & Terry, 2000).

We recognize that many choices come from bounded rationality and psychological preferences rather than the outcome of rational analysis and full consideration of the likely choices of interdependent others in a game-theoretic framework (Zajac & Bazerman, 1991). Still, the structure of the prisoners' dilemma is useful to focus attention on the contextual features that might make cooperative conduct more likely. Four of these contextual dimensions include the visibility of the behavior, the costs of not cooperating, the cognitive skills of the interdependent party, and the frequency of the actors' interaction.

The logic of the prisoners' dilemma seems to depend on the lack of a communication channel on which the players can signal to one another their intent to cooperate (Bonacich, 1995). If such a channel is made available and used, then the players can arrange their cooperation. But is such an arrangement credible? Should one prisoner communicate their intent to cooperate, the logic of the game offers a powerful incentive for the other prisoner to defect from the cooperative arrangement rather than abide by it (for the defector, this situation is the lightest sentence of all shown in Figure 5.7).

Accordingly, it is not the lack of a communication channel alone that hinders cooperation. Rather, a prisoner must use such a channel to carry a message that actions are monitored and a credible threat of retaliation raises the costs of competitive conduct to exceed the benefits. Cooperation is more likely to be chosen if the threat of retaliation changes the payoff structure of the outcomes so that the net utility from cooperating is higher than the net utility of not (Ariño, 1997). As Pinker (1997, pp. 503–504) noted:

> The problem with delayed exchanges, or reciprocation, is that it's possible to cheat . . . to accept a favor now and not return it. . . . The emotions making up the moral sense could evolve when parties interacted repeatedly and could reward cooperation now with cooperation later and punish defection now with defection later. Cooperativeness can evolve when the parties interact repeatedly, remember each other's behavior, and reciprocate it.

What is required for a threat of retaliation to be credible? First, the offending competitive act and outcome must be observable. If the probability of any particular outcome from one or more of the acts is unknown, the would-be enforcer may consider it too risky to select a retaliatory "decision under ignorance or uncertainty" (Heide & Miner, 1992; Resnik, 1987, p. 14). Second, the enforcing actor must be capable of executing a retaliatory threat (Doney, Cannon, & Mullen, 1998; Mayer, Davis, & Schoorman, 1995). This capability calls for the enforcer to be cognizant of the other's behavior, and also to have sufficient retaliatory power to raise the offending actor's costs to exceed the benefits from a competitive act. Third, the potential offender must understand that the enforcing actor's sensory apparatus is alert and the enforcer's retaliatory capability is in the feasible set of actions. Finally, the interaction of the parties must be more frequent than a one-time competitive act so there is an opportunity to punish the offending behavior (Lodewijkx, 2001; McMillan, 1992, p. 28).

The communication channel is a mechanism that may increase cooperation. For this to happen, however, the parties must use it to convey information about intentions, plans, and the credibility of retaliatory threats. As (Lodewijkx, 2001, p. 169) noted:

> Communication will increase mutual cooperation in iterated interactions because it permits parties (1) to share and develop insights about the interdependence structure of the PDG; (2) to communicate cooperative intentions; and (3) to warn each other that noncooperation will be reciprocated. Opportunities to communicate further enable parties (4) to coordinate their choices and (5) effectively reduce the confusion that is inherent to the process of sorting out which part of the opponent's behavior reflects his strategy, and which part reflects the opponent's reactions to one's own actions. All these factors will promote both the long-term goal of mutual cooperation and the expectation that the opponent will strive for this goal, and they will do so to an equal extent for individuals and groups.

This discussion has suggested that important dimensions of context include (a) the availability of communication channels; (b) the effectiveness of communication skills; (c) the transferability of information about interdependence, intentions, acts, and outcomes; (d) the credibility, feasibility, and effectiveness of retaliatory capability; (e) the skillfulness of interdependent parties to cognitively apply the communicated information; and (f) the repetitiveness of interaction. We suggest that over time the multiple processes of these six contextual dimensions reciprocally interact with each other and with associated attributes of the interdependent parties' power, resources, and predictability to build trust and enable cooperative conduct.

Game theory is often criticized as an overly rational approach to explain actors who often are not rational (Camerer, 1991; Zajac & Bazerman, 1991). Further, game theory can be mathematically complex, used to explain anything, and lends itself to be so customized for specific circumstances that it loses generalizability (Camerer, 1991). In addition, the payoff structure of the game needs to consider that the incentive power of payoffs is a function of the player's utility preferences for that payoff. In other words, a prison sentence of 10 years may be a powerful incentive for a free person, but much less powerful for someone already doing a life term. Experimental research on social conduct needs to consider the role of incentives to induce behavior and the subjective utility valence structure associated with these incentives as well. Bonacich (1995) discusses several different forms of payoff structures that could generate different decision choices.

We are sensitive to these concerns and address them by limiting our use of a game-theoretic framework to help illustrate the structure of interdependence and stimulate some testable implications. Specifically, we draw on prior literature (e.g. Doney, Cannon, & Mullen, 1998; Heide & Miner, 1992; Lodewijkx, 2001; Mayer, Davis, & Schoorman, 1995) to suggest that the relationship of a perceived positive goal association on cooperative conduct is stronger in the presence of available communication channels, effective communication skills, transferable information, credible retaliatory threats, repeated interaction, valued payoffs, and cognizant interdependent parties.

These contextual factors assume, in part, rational reasoning grounded in the exchange of known values and costs. Not all interdependencies can be so described. Interdependencies based not on economic exchange but on shared cultural norms or relational networks such as clan (Ouchi, 1980) or family or other social affiliation are more likely to have tacit values and affect-based motivations that do not lend themselves to calculation. For example, the

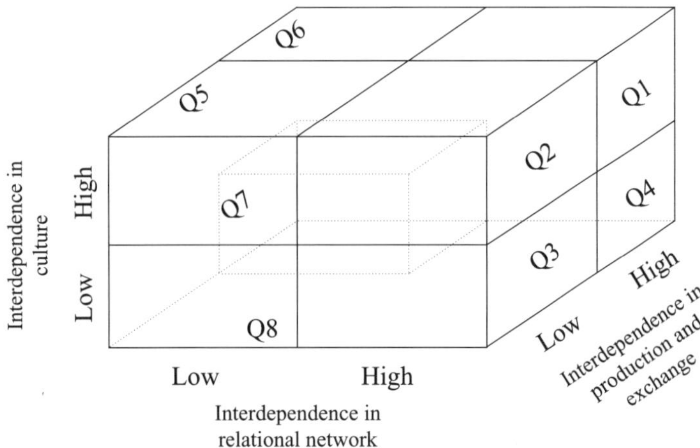

Figure 5.8 Typology of interdependence between an individual and his/her social relationships

costs and benefits of social capital cannot be measured in other than a metaphorical sense (Adler & Kwon, 2002, p. 22). Jones and George (1998) suggest that unconditional trust is critical for cooperation that involves tacit knowledge.

Compounding this calculation difficulty is that the contextual components of cooperative and competitive social conduct may not always be easily distinguished as either economic or cultural or a social relationship such as family. For example, do I work as an employee of a specific employer because of my calculation of the net value of exchanging my labor for pay and benefits, or because I want to support the family that I love, or because in my culture self-worth and identity are derived, in part, from employment? The answer is probably some combination from these economic, cultural, and relational types of interdependencies. Figure 5.8 combines these three types to suggest eight profiles that vary according to the magnitude of each interdependency type. Descriptions of social relationships and the subjective utility derived from them may be a combinatory function of these three dimensions that is difficult to disaggregate.

While future research needs to be parsimonious, nevertheless the inner psychological domain is confronted with a multidimensional external context. Future research models should explicitly recognize their conceptual boundaries and be sensitive to the limits of accuracy and generalizability that arise from these boundaries. For example, Pillutla and Chen (1999) found that the dynamics of cooperation changes within the same group as the context shifts from social to economic interdependence.

The next section examines the external context of cooperative and competitive conduct. Here we consider networks of social relationships, task structures, and resources.

EXTERNAL DOMAINS OF SELF, RELATIONSHIPS, MATERIAL THINGS, AND SOCIAL CONDUCT

This section discusses the external domain of the self as a physical actor exhibiting social conduct in interdependent relationships. Here we pay particular attention to the role of proximal and distal social relationships as important components of context. These relationships provide tangible and intangible resources to the goal-directed actor.

Networks of Social Relationships

A direct, or proximal, dyadic relationship, as shown in Figure 5.4, links a focal individual to another person through interdependencies of structure, action, or outcomes. The focus on dyadic relationships in this chapter has been only a device to simplify explanation. Social network analysis (e.g. Granovetter, 1985; Rowley, 1997), however, broadens perspective beyond the dyadic to better understand the impact of social structure and social relations on human action. As Rowley (1997, p. 894) notes, "The primary focus of social network analysis is the interdependence of actors and how their positions in networks influence their opportunities, constraints, and behaviors."

An analysis of the position of an individual in a social network provides information about his/her effectiveness as a communicator, relative power for the enforcement of behavior norms, and access to resources. For example, as the individual's position is increasingly central in the network, his/her effectiveness in these areas increases (Rowley, 1997, pp. 898–899). As discussed earlier, communication effectiveness, credible enforcement of behavior, and resource availability are key contextual dimensions of cooperative conduct. To understand the influence of network relationships, however, analysts should first classify the power of the focal actor (Lovaglia et al., 1995; Markovsky et al., 1993).

A network analysis of the relationships of others linked to the focal actor also provides important contextual information. The interdependent person, in addition to his/her role in the proximal social relationship, may have relationships that are not directly linked to the focal individual. That is, the proximal interdependent party is the nexus between the focal individual in the proximal relationship and a distal social network. Figure 5.9 extends the proximal social relationship to a relational network that includes a distal social relationship composed of the interdependent other party from the proximal relationship and another individual.

Though a social relationship may be distal, it still may inform and influence the situational cognition, affect, and behavior of the focal individual within a proximal social relationship (Williams, 2001). For example, the focal individual may use information from the distal relationships to make judgements and evaluations about the interdependent party's reputation for cooperative behavior and trustworthiness (Blankenburg, Eriksson, & Johanson, 1997; Williams, 2001).

The discussion here assumes a focal actor is somehow assigned to proximal and distal relationships. Of course, this is not a necessary condition. As Whitmeyer (1997) points out, actors may have a choice of networks, and they may have a set of feasible behaviors from which to choose. This suggests that the availability of network structures is an important dimension of context.

Access to Material Things through Networks of Social Relationships

Social resource theory (Lin, Einsel, & Vaughn, 1981) describes how the distal network not only informs the proximal one, but also may create resource-based incentives for

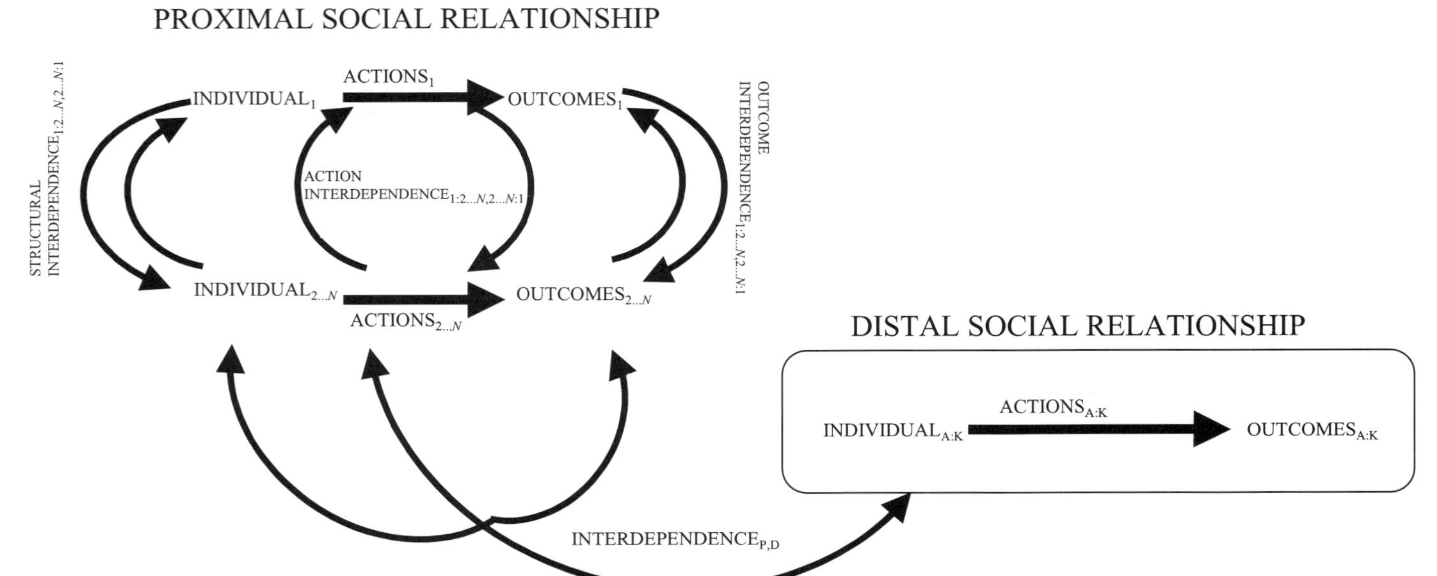

Figure 5.9 Relational networks within the situational context of INDIVIDUAL$_X$

cooperation in the proximal relationship (Blankenburg, Eriksson, & Johanson, 1997, p. 246). Social resource theory argues that the proximal interdependent party has access to the tangible and intangible resources of the distal network and may be able to convert, adapt, or transfer them for value creation in the proximal relationship. For example, an interdependent party with good relationships with the financial community might cosign loans to transfer financial resources to the focal actor in the proximal relationship, or make introductions to the gatekeepers of capital. In short, the appropriability of value from the distal social network to the proximal one is an incentive for the focal individual to support the proximal interdependent party's value-creating goals in the distal relationship. An analogous argument from organization theory is that cooperation in a dyadic relation should be analyzed within the context of the exchange network surrounding the dyad (Blankenburg, Eriksson, & Johanson, 1997). Here we propose that the influence of a perceived positive goal association on cooperative conduct is stronger for an individual as their cognizance of appropriable value in the aggregated proximal and distal social network increases.

Conversely, in a competitive situation we expect that an actor's goals are more difficult to achieve as the resources of a proximal rival increase. This difficulty represents (1) the increasing cost of action and responses that might displace an endowed rival from progress toward his/her goals, and (2) the increasing effectiveness of the actions undertaken by an endowed rival. One source of the proximal rival's endowment is his/her access to the tangible and intangible resources in his/her distal network. In sum, we suspect that a focal individual is increasingly deterred from competition as the costliness of action increases and as rivals grow increasingly effective. Accordingly, we propose that the influence of a perceived negative goal association on competitive conduct is weaker for an individual as his/her rival's capability to appropriate value, and the absolute value of the appropriated value, from the aggregate of proximal and distal social networks increases.

Task Structure

The attributes of the task may influence the cooperative approach (Milgrom & Roberts, 1992, p. 90). For example, Williams (2001) reported that people from dissimilar professional backgrounds working together on complex tasks developed trust quickly because they believed that everyone on the task held shared goals and that everyone would personally benefit from the project's success. Earlier we specified that the influence on cooperative conduct that comes from shared goals in positive association is the direct theoretical relationship of interest, though outside the scope of this chapter. Here we focus instead on the activity-related mechanisms in task design, such as participant proximity and task complexity, that may moderate this direct relationship.

An individual may undertake simple tasks alone, but prefer to cooperate on complex tasks with others whose goals converge on that task (Locke & Latham, 1990, p. 97). One approach for an individual to increase the number of different goals s/he can handle is to cooperate with others to whom tasks can be delegated (Locke & Latham, 1990, p. 54). More difficult goals may be attainable if the task design permits delegation and complementary effort. In sum, the cooperative conduct outcome expected in positive goal association is stronger as the individual perceives task design (1) to increase in complexity, (2) to have more decomposable parts, and (3) to require complementary skills that match with those possessed by interdependent others.

Task design structures may vary in their coordination and communication requirements. Two examples of these different requirements are synchronization tasks and assignment tasks. In synchronization tasks, all participants must take the same action on the same task at the same time (e.g. a tug-of-war in which all must pull on the rope simultaneously). In this type of task, coordination requires centralized decision making, so responsiveness to the local needs of each participant suffers. Communication tends to be unidirectional—from a synchronizer to the participants. Assignment tasks, on the other hand, are those in which a task has component subtasks, and participants must be assigned individually to unique subtasks so that the entire task is efficiently accomplished. A business with employees to be assigned to multiple functional activities is a typical example. Communication is multidirectional—from the manager of the overall task, across the subtasks, and from the subtasks upward to the overall manager.

Some task designs arrange work to flow in an assembly line fashion. In this operational arrangement, there may be little opportunity for line workers to communicate with one another. In a cellular work group layout, however, workers are arranged in teams whose members communicate rich work-related information within their group and also negotiate the work flow and requirements with adjacent teams. While workers in both assembly and cellular layout arrangements may have common goals related to standards of productivity and quality, the cellular work group structurally co-locates cross-functionally skilled individuals and applies them to common tasks.

Synchronization and assignment tasks, and assembly and cellular layout operations, are all cooperative forms of arranging work harmoniously among multiple participants. These examples highlight the role of complementary skills and the nature of communication and work flows. We propose here that an observer will find the relationship between positive goal association and cooperative conduct is stronger (1) as the interdependent parties' skills in proximity are increasingly complementary, and (2) as communication flow among the interdependent parties becomes more multidirectional and rich.

This section has examined three dimensions of task structure that moderate the relationship between goals and cooperative conduct: task complexity, the proximity of complementary skills, and the characteristics of communication flow. We do not know, however, if these three task-related dimensions moderate cooperative conduct directly or instead might be mediated by appraisal criteria including trust, skill, vengefulness, and flexibility.

Resources as Context of Cooperation

When valuable resources are asymmetrically distributed in the external environment, the stock of resources accessible to an individual may not be sufficient to satisfy his/her goals, and the best resources may be held by another. Here we draw on resource-based theories to discuss constructs that recently have been developed at the level of the organization or collective. As Locke (1999) noted, however, "A collective is not an entity but a group of individuals." Moreover, the resource-based theories themselves have their conceptual roots in the biological survival mechanisms observed in all individuals.

In a condition of resource scarcity and positive goal association with others, accomplishment of self-goals may depend on the integration of critical resources from multiple contributors and the integration of the individual's knowledge and resources with that held by others (Grant, 1996, p. 383; Nordberg, Campbell, & Verdeke, 1996, pp. 966–967). In this way, the focal individual applies a more complete resource set to the task, and shares the cost of these resources with many people rather than bearing it alone in its entirety (Kessler & Chakrabarti, 1996; Mowery, Oxley, & Silverman, 1996, p. 79). Thus, we expect that the direct influence between positive goal association with others and cooperative conduct is stronger in the presence of resource scarcity. Conversely, when valuable resources are abundantly available, we expect that an individual can independently and cost-effectively acquire all required resources. In this case, the relationship between positive goal association and cooperative conduct should be weaker.

Scarcity of valuable resources may seem to define competition and a negative goal association between interdependent parties, but such a linkage fails to consider the subjective utility derived from the resources. A simple thought experiment to introduce utility demonstrates that resource scarcity and negative goal association are independent constructs. In this experiment, we define employment and wealth as valuable resources for survival, and let two people compete for the same higher-paying job promotion so that if one gets it the other does not. This negative goal association leads to competitive conduct for the job, but what will be the intensity of the competition? If one of the individuals is very wealthy, or perceives other high-paying employment opportunities to be abundant, then they are likely to be a less aggressive competitor for the job promotion in question. Conversely, if other employment opportunities are scarce, or one of the rivals is poverty-stricken, then the competitive conduct should be very intense for this one available promotion. We generalize from this thought experiment to propose that the direct influence between negative goal association with others and competitive conduct is stronger when valuable resources are scarce, and weaker when valuable resources are abundant.

Resource Hostages

Some individuals may meet each other in multiple relational structures each with different goals and resources. For example, the same people may meet at work as colleagues, meet also in community sports leagues, and meet again as members in the same organized religious activities. For interdependent individuals who meet each other in multiple relational structures, actions in one relationship may bring about a response in another relationship where they meet. Earlier in this chapter we discussed retaliation to deter defections from cooperative behavior. Here we apply mutual forbearance theory (Edwards, 1955) to note that, for parties who meet in more than one relationship, an actor's resources in a nonfocal relationship can be "hostages" to enforce cooperative behavior in the proximal relationship in which the parties meet (Barnett, 1993). Similar to the logic in the earlier discussion of retaliation to deter competitive behavior, we suggest that the relationship of a positive goal association between interdependent actors on cooperative conduct is stronger in the presence of credible retaliatory threats in other relationships where the parties meet. Further, we expect that the relationship of a negative goal association between interdependent actors on competitive conduct is weaker in the presence of credible retaliatory threats in other relationships where the parties meet.

THE PSYCHOLOGICAL ORIENTATION APPLIED TO THE CONTEXT OF SOCIAL CONDUCT

The focus of this chapter is an individual level of analysis of the moderating factors from the internal and external context of cooperative and competitive social conduct. Psychologists have been aware of the importance of context for quite some time (Allport, 1940). According to Mohrman, Gibson, and Mohrman (2001, p. 359), "... human behavior and understanding are contextual, guided by contextually determined interpretive schemes, norms, and power relationships that shape 'sense making.'" Schoorman, Mayer, and Davis (1996) call for additional research into the moderating influence of social context in order to fully understand the development of trust in relationships. As these authors note, however, it is overly complex and often infeasible to account for all contextual variables.

The subjectivity of context compounds the difficulty that arises from its complexity. Behavior in social situations is grounded in meanings learned through interactions with other people over time. In this way, the dynamics of the group are uniquely created and defined, and the researcher must find theory to explain individual perception of a socially defined experience. For example, Jones and George (1998) note that there are multiple categories of trust, and "it is necessary to understand how trust in others is experienced psychologically before its impact on behavioral expectations and outcomes, such as the level of cooperation between people in an organization, can be adequately analyzed."

Despite this complexity and subjectivity, or because of it, a theoretical grounding in individual cognition is important to account for variation across individuals within a given situational context and social relationship, as well as to account for the variability in one focal actor across types of interdependencies or situational contexts. This chapter has identified dimensions of merit in the situational context, summarized in Figure 5.10, that are likely to moderate social conduct. Future research that recognizes a reciprocating relationship between these internal and external domains of context is more likely to add to our understanding of social conduct than is feasible from more narrowly articulated theoretical models. In addition, we suggest that future research considers the dimensions of the situational context listed in Figures 5.2 and 5.3 but not found in the literature summarized in Figure 5.10.

Figure 5.11 draws on the focal actor's individual domains of self presented earlier in Figures 5.1–5.3. Here we suggest that the five psychological perspectives *(personal identity, social identity, social-psychology, social impact, and physiological psychology*) that describe the interaction between these domains are particularly appropriate to study the situational context of social conduct described in this chapter. Researchers in these root disciplines, however, need to carefully consider the methods, level of analysis, and theoretical integration with which they study the cognitive orientation of social conduct. This chapter discusses these issues below.

Methods

This chapter has suggested that the structure of social relationships over time is a critical dimension of the context of social conduct. Analysis of short-term phenomena, common in research conducted in laboratory experiments, may not be generalizable to social conduct outside the laboratory (Schoorman, Mayer, & Davis, 1996). Perhaps the field methods used

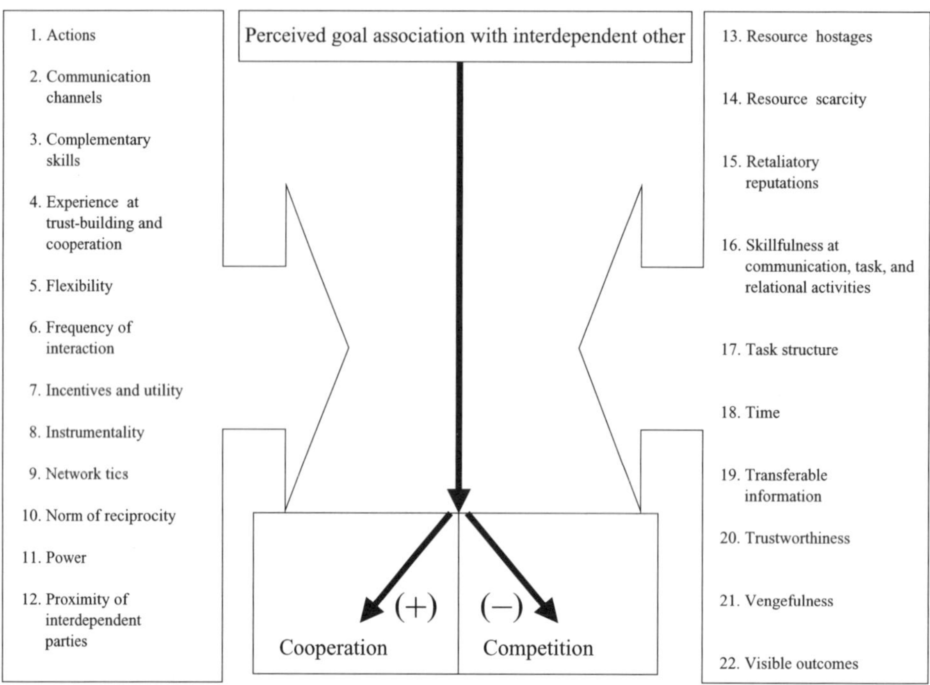

Figure 5.10 The context of social conduct

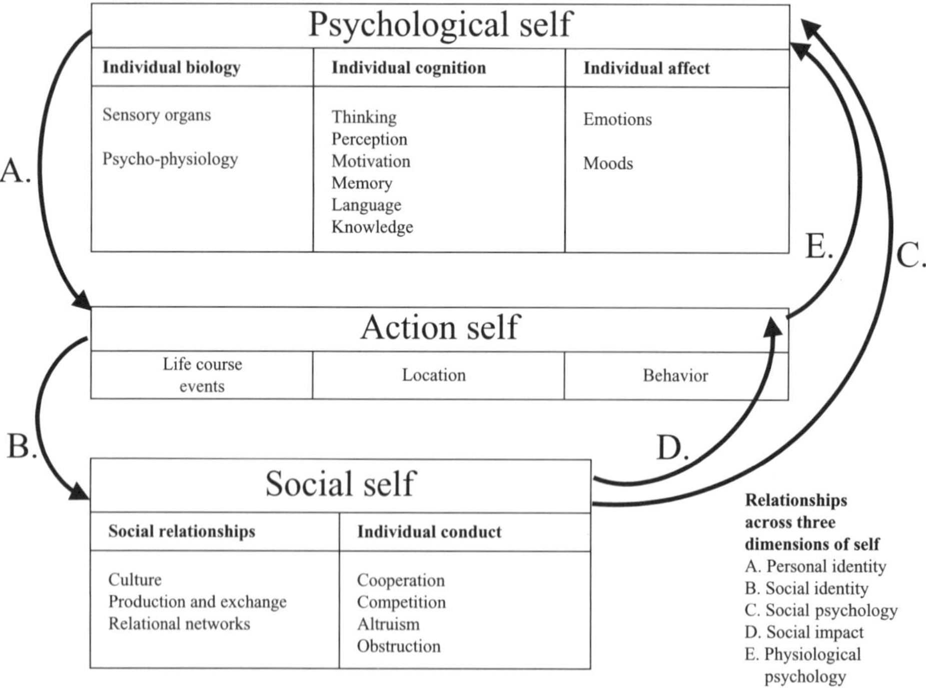

Figure 5.11 Psychological, action, social context of individual conduct

to map cognitive schemas of managers (Huff, 1990) can be usefully applied for insight into the psychological orientation associated with social conduct.

Watters, Ball, and Carr (1996) have suggested that nonlinear dynamical systems theory, such as "chaos" theory, catastrophe models, and self-organizing networks research methodology are particularly appropriate to study social phenomena such as cooperation and competition. These perspectives explicitly consider the role of time, an important contextual dimension that captures the dynamic nature of social processes.

Levels of Analysis

This chapter has applied a psychological and cognitive orientation to describe social conduct at the level of the individual actor. We recognize, however, that cognitive science today is progressing at levels of detail down to the neuron and lower. Nevertheless, there appears to be some disjointedness, if not controversy, concerning the appropriate level at which consciousness can be understood (Salo, 1996). This chapter suggests a convergence of multiple theoretical and analytical perspectives is appropriate in order to recognize that social behavior arises from a convergence of multiple processes. As Grimshaw and Berenbaum (2000) propose, this pan-theoretic approach holds much excitement for a new millennium of research in cognition and the social sciences:

> Our hope for behavioral neuroscience in the first century of the present millennium is for a broad conceptualization of cognition that builds upon the foundations of our field. We see the future in work that recognizes the reciprocal interplay of cognition with affect, personality, and social reasoning, and that honors a multitude of methodological approaches, maintaining the best traditions of behavioral neuroscience while taking advantage of new technologies as appropriate. Cognitive neuroscientists have traditionally worked within the limited domain of intellectual abilities, but this provides an incomplete answer to our fundamental question: "What are people actually doing and how are they doing it?" The answer to this question requires good behavioral observation with strong methodological control.... [S]ocial and affective processes are part of a full understanding of the relations between brain and behavior, and they suggest that consideration of these processes will provide a rich and coherent picture of the neural substrates of both normative behavior and its variations.... [T]his expanded view of cognition is best served by maintaining divergent methodologies that permit analysis of behavioral *processes* as well as products.... [A]n appreciation of related disciplines... will enable investigators to work independently on discipline-specific problems and in collaboration with those in other disciplines on broader questions, with shifting collaborations depending on the nature of the questions.... Nevertheless, progress depends not on giant conceptual or technological leaps, but rather on incremental steps that emphasize behavioral analysis. Our strength is in our sensitivity to the nuances of behavior, not in our technological prowess.[1]

While neuroscience brings understanding of the cognition of behavior to the most granular level possible, fuller insight requires consideration of the dynamics of the group relationship as a particularly important component of social conduct. The group as the unit of analysis is important because social conduct, as defined in this chapter, is the behavior of an individual in a group. For example, the literature on social identity suggests that positive beliefs about in-group members influence trust, cooperation, and efficacy (De Cremer & van Vugt, 1998; Williams, 2001). In addition, the role of trust and efficacy as moderators of cooperative

[1] This extract is reprinted from Grimshaw and Berenbaum (2000) with permission from Elsevier Science.

conduct may vary as an individual's self-categorization switches from the self to the group (De Cremer & van Vugt, 1998). As Hogg and Terry (2000) note, a social categorization process produces collective behavior that may include cooperation but "cognitively assimilates self to the in-group prototype and, thus, depersonalizes self-conception."

What happens as an individual's self-categorization switches from the self to the group? Importantly, the processes of group behavior cannot be assumed to be identical to those that explain the behavior of individuals (Lodewijkx, 2001). Research needs to clearly articulate aggregation mechanisms for cross-level process models that account for development over time from individual self-categorization to group social categorization. Such research is likely to benefit from new methods and perspectives.

Catastrophe models grounded in nonlinear dynamical systems theory may be one useful approach to simulate such process models. Moreover, this approach introduces the dimension of time into social identity models, an important dimension of context discussed in this chapter, but which Hogg and Terry (2000) find has been absent in prior research.

CONCLUSION

This chapter has offered a psychological orientation to understand the context of cooperative and competitive conduct. In this review, we have defined cooperative, competitive, and other forms of social conduct as an individual's pattern of action that is likely to arise from the direction and significance of the perceived association between the goals of self and the goals of others. The chapter presented social conduct as a multidirectional function of the individual actor's internal (*psychological*) and external (*material, action, and social*) situational context and addressed the context in which the influence of goal association with others operates. This context includes all those internal and external factors that moderate the direct influence on conduct from an individual's perception of goals and interdependencies in social relationships.

We applied goal-based theory of behavior, well-received game-theoretic models, and social cognition theory to examine the context of cooperative and competitive patterns of action. The chapter considered the influence of goal difficulty and network structures composed of distal social relationships connected to a proximal interdependent relationship of interest, and discussed prior literature concerning the appraisals that individuals apply to social relationships.

The chapter argued that, *ceteris paribus*, the direct relationship between goal association and social conduct is moderated by a positive or negative appraisal on criteria of trustworthiness, vengefulness, flexibility, and skillfulness. We also presented a decision-making perspective of social conduct that focused on game theory, with particular attention to the well-received prisoners' dilemma. This section highlighted the role of communication, retaliation, skills, transferable information, and cognition. The chapter then examined the external context of cooperative and competitive conduct with particular attention to networks of social relationships, task structures, and resources.

The multidimensional, multi-process, and multidirectional models suggested by prior literature are difficult, if not impossible, to approach comprehensively. Nevertheless, we suggest that exciting future research will apply cross-disciplinary perspectives of cognition and social conduct to integrate multiple levels of analysis with clearly articulated processes of integration and development over time. This chapter has drawn on multiple theoretical fields to examine 22 contextual factors individually (listed in Figure 5.10), and we attempted to link these multiple factors around a single core theme. In this thematic view, an individual's psychological processes are purposeful mechanisms that recognize, interpret, and interact with physical phenomena and social relationships to rationally guide behavior; cognition of goal interdependence influences an individual's conduct in social relationships, and this influence is moderated by the subjective perception of the situational context that arises from the interaction among that individual's psychological, material, action, and social domains.

REFERENCES

Adler, P. S. & Kwon, S.-W. (2002). Social capital: prospects for a new concept. *Academy of Management Review, 27*(1), 17–40.

Allport, G. W. (1940). The psychologist's frame of reference. *Psychological Bulletin, 37*, 1–28. [Allport's APA Presidential Address.]

Alper, S., Tjosvold, D., & Law, K. (1998). Interdependence and controversy in group decision making: antecedents to effective self-managing teams. *Organizational Behavior and Human Decision Processes, 74*(1), 33–52.

Ariño, A. (1997). Veracity and commitment: cooperative behavior in first-time collaborative ventures. In Paul W. Beamish & J. Peter Killing (eds), *Cooperative Strategies: European Perspectives* (pp. 215–241). San Francisco: The New Lexington Press.

Axelrod, R. (1984). *The Evolution of Cooperation*. New York: Basic Books.

Badaracco, J. L. (1991). *The Knowledge Link: How Firms Compete through Strategic Alliances*. Boston, Mass.: Harvard Business School Press.

Bandura, A. (1986). *Social Foundations of Thought and Action: A Social Cognitive Theory*. Englewood Cliffs, NJ: Prentice-Hall.

Barnett, W. P. (1993). Strategic deterrence among multipoint competitors. *Industrial and Corporate Change, 2*, 249–278.

Blankenburg, D., Eriksson, K., & Johanson, J. (1997). Business networks and cooperation in international business relationships. In Paul W. Beamish & J. Peter Killing (eds), *Cooperative Strategies: European Perspectives* (pp. 242–266). San Francisco: The New Lexington Press.

Bonacich, P. (1995). Four kinds of social dilemmas within exchange networks. *Current Research In Social Psychology, 1*(1), 1–7.

Camerer, C. F. (1991). Does strategy research need game theory? *Strategic Management Journal, 12*, 137–152.

Caves, R. E. & Porter, M. (1977). From entry barriers to mobility barriers: conjectural decisions and contrived deterrence to new competition. *Quarterly Journal of Economics, 91*, 241–262.

Conner, K. R. & Prahalad, C. K. (1996). A resource-based theory of the firm: knowledge versus opportunism. *Organization Science, 7*(5), 477–501.

Cronbach, L. J. (1957). The two disciplines of scientific psychology. *American Psychologist, 12*, 671–684. [online] http:psychclassics.yorku.ca/Cronbach/Disciplines

Das, T. & Teng, B. (1998). Between trust and control: developing confidence in partner cooperation in alliances. *Academy of Management Review, 23*, 491–512.

De Cremer, D. & van Vugt, M. (1998). Collective identity and cooperation in a public goods dilemma: a matter of trust or self-efficacy? *Current Research In Social Psychology, 3*(1), 1–11.

Deutsch, M. (1949). A theory of cooperation and competition. *Human Relations, 2*, 129–152.

Doney, P. M., Cannon, J. P., & Mullen, M. R. (1998). Understanding the influence of national culture on the development of trust. *Academy of Management Review, 23*(3), 601–620.

Doz, Y. L. & Hamel, G. (1998). *Alliance Advantage*. Boston: Harvard Business School Press.

Dyer, J. H. & Singh, H. (1998). The relational view: cooperative strategy and sources of interorganizational competitive advantage. *Academy of Management Review, 23*(4), 660–679.

Edwards, C. D. (1955). Conglomerate bigness as a source of power. In *Business Concentration and Price Policy*, NBER Conference Report.

Gleitman, H. (1995). *Psychology* (4th edn). New York: W. W. Norton & Company.

Granovetter, M. (1985). Economic action and social structure: the problem of embeddedness. *American Journal of Sociology, 91*(3), 481–510.

Grant, R. M. (1996). Prospering in dynamically-competitive environments: organizational capability as knowledge integration. *Organization Science, 74*, 375–387.

Green, C. (1996). Where did the word "cognitive" come from anyway? *Canadian Psychology, 37*, 31–39.

Grimshaw, G. M. & Berenbaum, S. A. (2000). Achieving convergent evidence through divergent approaches. *Brain and Cognition, 42*, 85–88.

Heide, J. B. & Miner, A. S. (1992). The shadow of the future: effects of anticipated interaction and frequency of contact on buyer–seller cooperation. *Academy of Management Journal, 35*(2), 265–291.

Hogg, M. A. & Terry, D. J. (2000). Social identity and self-categorization processes in organizational contexts. *Academy of Management Journal, 25*(1), 121–140.

Huff, A. S. (1990). *Mapping Strategic Thought*. New York: Wiley.

Jones, G. & George, J. M. (1998). The experience and evolution of trust: implications for cooperation and teamwork. *Academy of Management Review, 23*(3), 531–546.

Kessler, E. H. & Chakrabarti, A. K. (1996). Innovation speed: a conceptual model of context, antecedents, and outcomes. *Academy of Management Review, 21*(4), 1143–1191.

Knez, M. & Camerer, C. (2000). Increasing cooperation in prisoners' dilemmas by establishing a precedent of efficiency in coordination games. *Organizational Behavior and Human Decision Processes, 82*(2), 194–216.

Lepine, J. A. & van Dyne, L. (2001). Peer responses to low performers: an attributional model of helping in the context of groups. *Academy of Management Review, 26*(1), 67–84.

Lin, N., Einsel, W. M., & Vaughn, J. C. (1981). Social resources and strength of ties. *American Sociological Review, 46*, 393–405.

Locke, E. A. (1999). Some reservations about social capital. *Academy of Management Review, 24*(1), 8–9.

Locke, E. A. & Latham, G. P. (1990). *A Theory of Goal Setting and Task Performance*. Englewood Cliffs, NJ: Prentice-Hall.

Lodewijkx, H. F. M. (2001). Individual–group continuity in cooperation and competition under varying communication conditions. *Current Research in Social Psychology, 6*(12), 166–182.

Lovaglia, M. J., Skvoretz, J., Markovsky, B., & Willer, D. (1995). Assessing fundamental power differences in exchange networks: iterative GPI. *Current Research in Social Psychology, 1*(2), 8–15.

McMillan, J. (1992). *Games, Strategies, and Managers*. New York: Oxford University Press.

Markovsky, B., Skvoretz, J., Willer, D., Lovaglia, M. J., & Erger, J. (1993). The seeds of weak power: an extension of network exchange theory. *American Sociological Review, 58*, 197–209.

Martin, L. L. & Clark, L. F. (1990). Social cognition: exploring the mental processes involved in human social interaction. In M. W. Eysenck (ed.), *Cognitive Psychology: An International Review* (pp. 265–310). New York: John Wiley & Sons.

Mayer, R. C., Davis, J. H., & Schoorman, F. D. (1995). An integrative model of organizational trust. *Academy of Management Review, 20*(3), 709–734.

Milgrom, P. & Roberts, J. (1992). *Economics, Organization and Management*. Upper Saddle River, NJ: Prentice-Hall.

Mohrman, S. A., Gibson, C. B., & Mohrman, A. M. (2001). Doing research that is useful to practice: a model and empirical exploration. *Academy of Management Journal, 44*(2), 357–375.

Mowery, D. C., Oxley, J. E., & Silverman, B. S. (1996). Strategic alliances and interfirm knowledge transfer. *Strategic Management Journal, 17*(Special issue: Winter), 77–91.

Nahapiet, J. & Ghoshal, S. (1998). Social capital, intellectual capital and the organizational advantage. *Academy of Management Review, 23*(2), 242–266.

Nordberg, M., Campbell, A., & Verbeke, A. (1996). Can market-based contracts substitute for alliances in high technology markets? *Journal of International Business Studies, 27*(5), 963–980.

Ouchi, W. (1980). Markets, bureaucracies, and clans. *Administrative Science Quarterly, 25*, 129–141.

Pervin, L. A. (1989). Persons, situations, interactions: the history of a controversy and a discussion of theoretical models. *Academy of Management Review, 14*(3), 350–360.

Pillutla, M. M. & Chen, X.-P. (1999). Social norms and cooperation in social dilemmas: the effects of context and feedback. *Organizational Behavior and Human Decision Processes, 78*(2), 81–103.
Pinker, S. (1997). *How the Mind Works*. New York: W. W. Norton & Co.
Porter, M. E. (1980). *Competitive Strategy: Techniques for Analyzing Industries and Competitors*. New York: Free Press.
Porter, M. E. (1985). *Competitive Advantage: Creating and Sustaining Superior Performance*. New York: Free Press.
Postrel, S. (1991). Burning your britches behind you: can policy scholars bank on game theory? *Strategic Management Journal, 12*, 153–155.
Resnik, M. D. (1987). *Choices: An Introduction to Decision Theory*. Minneapolis: University of Minnesota Press.
Richardson, J. T. E. (1997). Introduction to the study of gender differences in cognition. In P. J. Caplan, M. Crawford, J. S. Hyde, & J. T. E. Richardson (eds), *Gender Differences in Human Cognition* (pp. 3–29). New York: Oxford University Press.
Ring, P. S. & Van de Ven, A. H. (1994). Developmental processes of cooperative interorganizational relationships. *Academy of Management Review, 19*(1), 90–118.
Rowley, T. (1997). Moving beyond dyadic ties: a network theory of stakeholder influences. *Academy of Management Review, 22*(4), 887–910.
Salo, P. (1996). *Methodological Issues in Cognitive Science*. http://www.helsinki.fi/hum/kognitiotiede/methodology.html
Sanchez, R. & Mahoney, J. T. (1996). Modularity, flexibility, and knowledge management in product and organization design. *Strategic Management Journal, 17*(Special issue: Winter), 63–76.
Scherer, K. R. (1999). Appraisal theory. In T. Dalgleish & M. J. Power (eds), *Handbook of Cognition and Emotion* (pp. 637–663). New York: Wiley.
Schoorman, F. D., Mayer, R. C., & Davis, J. H. (1996). Social influence, social interaction, and social psychology in the study of trust. *Academy of Management Review, 21*(2), 337–339.
Sparrowe, R. T., Liden, R. C., Wayne, S. J., & Kraimer, M. L. (2001). Social networks and the performancec of individuals and groups. *Academy of Management Journal, 44*(2), 316–325.
Spencer, H. (1897). *The Principles of Ethics* [1978, Liberty Fund, Inc. edn] (Vol. I). New York: D. Appleton and Co.
Tschacher, W. & Dauwalder, J.-P. (1999). Situated cognition, ecological perception, and synergetics: a novel perspective for cognitive psychology. In W. Tschacher & J.-P. Dauwalder (eds), *Dynamics, Synergetics, Autonomous Agents: Nonlinear Systems Approaches to Cognitive Psychology and Cognitive Science* (Vol. 8). Studies of Nonlinear Phenomena in Life Science. Singapore: World Scientific Publishing Co. Pte. Ltd.
Tsai, W. & Ghoshal, S. (1998). Social capital and value creation: the role of intrafirm networks. *Academy of Management Journal, 41*(4), 464–476.
Volberda, H. W. (1996). Toward the flexible form: how to remain vital in hypercompetitive environments. *Organization Science, 7*(4), 359–374.
Watters, P. A., Ball, P. J., & Carr, S. C. (1996). Social processes as dynamical processes: qualitative dynamical systems theory in social psychology. *Current Research in Social Psychology, 1*(7), 60–68.
Whitener, E. M., Brodt, S. E., Korsgaard, M. A., & Werner, J. M. (1998). Managers as initiators of trust: an exchange relationship framework for understanding managerial trustworthy behavior. *Academy of Management Review, 23*(3), 513–530.
Whitmeyer, J. (1997). Applying general equilibrium analysis and game theory to exchange networks. *Current Research in Social Psychology, 2*(2), 13–23.
Williams, M. (2001). In whom we trust: group membership as an effective context for trust development. *Academy of Management Review, 26*(3), 377–396.
Wood, R. & Bandura, A. (1989). Social cognitive theory of organizational management. *Academy of Management Review, 14*(3), 361–384.
Zajac, E. J. & Bazerman, M. H. (1991). Blind spots in industry and competitor analysis. *Academy of Management Review, 16*(1), 37–56.

Section II

THE PSYCHOLOGY OF INDIVIDUALS IN GROUPS

6

TRUST, IDENTITY, AND ATTACHMENT

PROMOTING INDIVIDUALS' COOPERATION IN GROUPS

M. Audrey Korsgaard, Susan E. Brodt, and Harry J. Sapienza

This chapter sets out to take a new look at trust and cooperation in work groups by focusing on individuals' attitudes toward the group as a whole, rather than simply assuming that interpersonal relationships within the group "add up" to trust (or distrust) and cooperativeness (or uncooperativeness). We approach the issue of trust in groups with the assumption that an individual's trust in the group is an attitude that is quite distinct from interpersonal trust. Trust in the group is not simply the aggregate or average of a member's interpersonal relationships with other group members. Instead, it is an attitude the individual holds toward the group as a collective. Furthermore, we reinvigorate the discussion by looking beyond presumptive and structural factors to the group processes and individual differences that shape trust and cooperation over the long term.

We believe that the dynamics within the group are important determinants of an individual's trust in the group as a whole. We identify two critical conditions that are necessary for trust in and sustained cooperation with the group: group identity and psychological attachment to the group. Identification, which refers to the extent to which individuals define themselves in terms of their membership in a particular group, is influenced by a wide array of contextual and process factors. We focus on intragroup processes that affect identification, using the lens of procedural justice to identify key processes and behaviors within the group that determine the degree to which individuals identify with the group. Second, drawing on the literature on attachment styles, we introduce the concept of group attachment style, an attribute that reflects a person's propensity to seek and feel secure in group situations. We argue that group attachment styles influence both the propensity to become identified with a group and the relationship between group identification and the individual's trust in the group.

This chapter is laid out as follows. First, we briefly examine the meaning, importance, and challenge of strong forms of cooperation in work groups. Next, we review research on the nature and consequences of trust to argue that trust in the group is a critical and immediate determinant of cooperation in groups. We then review the social identity literature and argue that the extent to which individuals define themselves in terms of group identities promotes

International Handbook of Organizational Teamwork and Cooperative Working. Edited by M. A. West, D. Tjosvold, and K. G. Smith.

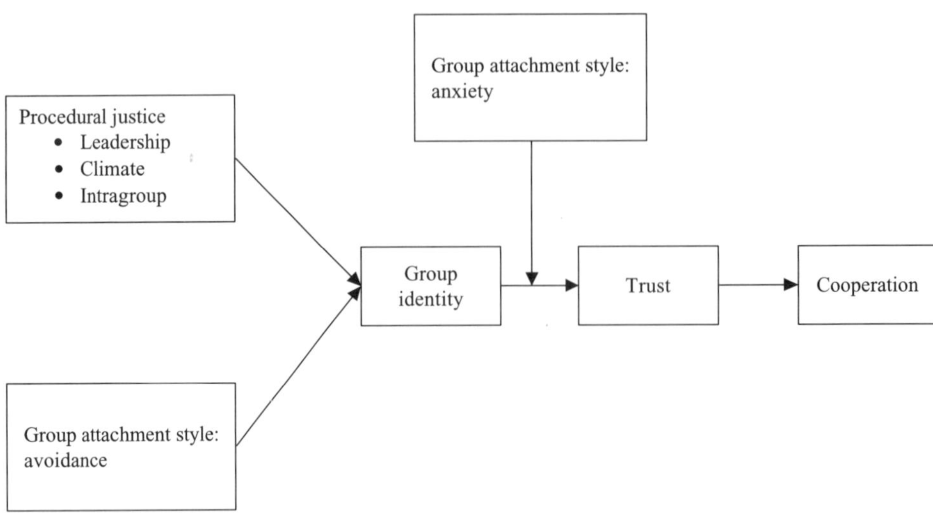

Figure 6.1 A model of the relationships between identity, attachment, trust, and cooperation in groups

trust and cooperation. In establishing the link between identity and trust, we rely on the procedural justice literature to identify antecedents of identification and trust. Drawing on emerging theory and research on group attachment styles, we then illustrate how the nature of attachment in previous group relationships and the formation of interpersonal relationships within the group influence identity and trust in the group. We conclude with a discussion of implications and directions for future research.

The analysis presented in this chapter explicates our model of individuals' trust in and cooperation with groups (see Figure 6.1). Briefly, at the center of this model is group identity, which we view as critical to fostering individuals' trust in and cooperation with their work groups. In essence, individuals form part of their self-concept based on membership in groups, and this identification with the group promotes cooperation. The mechanism by which such cooperation occurs is trust, i.e. identity engenders trust, and trust promotes cooperation. The model identifies two important factors in the development of group identity, namely procedural justice and individual differences in group attachment styles. We argue that fair treatment within the group and individual differences in group attachment styles have a direct effect on group identification. Further, the model suggests that group attachment styles moderate the effect of identification on trust. A particular innovation in our model is our emphasis on a new construct, psychological attachment to the group.

THE CHALLENGE OF COOPERATION IN WORK GROUPS

We define an individual's cooperation with the group as the active and persistent pursuit of the goals of the work group, regardless of personal or interpersonal interests. In its purest form, this definition of cooperation implies an intuitive and/or conscious awareness of what the group wants and a willingness to make one's own interests secondary to those of the group. The type of cooperation we intend implies much more than mere compliance or conformity. Compliance and conformity may be passive and may even thwart group goals when initiative is required. The active component we stress here is analogous to the dichotomy identified by Tyler and Blader (2000, 2001) who distinguish cooperation based on mandatory behavior (i.e. behaviors specifically required by the organization) versus discretionary behavior (i.e. behavior that is voluntary and outside organizational guidelines). Tyler and Blader (2000, 2001) argue that the latter type of cooperation, i.e. that based on discretionary behaviors, is key to the success of groups because groups cannot specify in advance what its members should do in all circumstances.

Besides proactivity, the other key dimension of our definition is the emphasis on proactivity on behalf of the group rather than oneself or favored individuals within the group. Thus, for the purposes of our theorizing we further qualify Tyler and Blader's (2000, 2001) concept of voluntary cooperative behavior to be that which is in reference to the group as a whole. Full cooperation requires a vigilance in raising issues that move the group toward shared goals, not just those of a subset or "lead" set of individuals; it means that self- or friendship interests must sometimes be willingly suppressed. Cooperation may result in challenging others in order to ensure that the group remains on track.

Importance of Cooperation for Work Group Effectiveness

There are numerous reasons why cooperation is essential to long-term group effectiveness. First, cooperation among group members ensures that group efforts will be coordinated toward a common goal, thus enabling the group to perform more effectively (Gladstein, 1984). Moreover, Podsakoff, Ahearn, and MacKenzie (1997) argue that cooperative behavior such as organizational citizenship behavior can directly enhance the productivity of group members. Further, cooperation may promote the efficient use of group resources. Pursuit of individual or subgroup goals can undermine group success either directly by diverting resources or indirectly by weakening the resolve of other group members to continue voluntarily to provide effort on behalf of the group (Korsgaard, Sapienza, & Schweiger, 2001). Cooperation reduces the need to devote the group's resources to group maintenance functions, thereby freeing up resources for more productive purposes (Podsakoff, Ahearn, & MacKenzie, 1997; Podsakoff et al., 2000).

Research on groups and teams in organizations supports a direct relationship between cooperation among group members and group effectiveness. For example, organizational citizenship behavior directed at group members has a positive effect on both the quality and the quantity of performance, as well as customer service (Podsakoff, Ahearn, & MacKenzie, 1997; Podsakoff et al., 2000). The level of cooperation in teams is also positively related to group member satisfaction, effort, and performance evaluations (Campion, Medsker, & Higgs, 1993; Campion, Papper, & Medsker, 1996; Lester, Meglino, & Korsgaard, 2002). Moreover, cooperation in groups indirectly affects performance by enhancing the group's sense of efficacy in its ability to resolve conflicts and perform effectively (Alper, Tjosvold, & Law, 2000; Lester, Meglino, & Korsgaard, 2002).

Despite the positive effect of cooperation on group member attitudes, cooperation in groups need not imply an absence of conflict. Conflict is an inevitable and often desirable fact of work group life (Alper, Tjosvold, & Law, 2000). Indeed, open and productive confrontation of task-based conflict is likely to enhance decision making (Johnson, Johnson, & Tjosvold, 2000), but the process of resolving conflicts has the potential to undermine the group itself (Amason & Sapienza, 1997; Korsgaard, Sapienza, & Schweiger, 2001; Korsgaard, Schweiger, & Sapienza, 1995; Simons & Peterson, 2000). Effective group functioning depends on high-quality decisions, commitment to and understanding of the decisions reached, and group continuity (Korsgaard, Sapienza, & Schweiger, 2001). Research suggests that a cooperative orientation to confronting and resolving conflicts with the group can both enhance the quality of decision making and group members' attitudes and motivation as well (Alper, Tjosvold, & Law, 1998, 2000; Korsgaard, Sapienza, & Schweiger, 2001). For example, Amason and Sapienza (1997) showed that norms of mutuality within top management groups encouraged team continuity without limiting the cognitive or task conflict necessary for reaching effective group decisions.

We have argued that if a work group is to be effective over time, its members must fully cooperate. Mere compliance or conformity is inadequate to meet changing requirements. Further, we have argued that the effectiveness of the group will depend to some extent on the willingness of individuals to take actions that preserve the integrity of the group, regardless of their own interests. Consider, as an example, faculty within a department of a university. These groups face a myriad of tasks such as selecting doctoral candidates for admission, screening job candidates, determining course and class scheduling, and allocating merit raises. Time demands preclude the full involvement of everyone in every task, even if such involvement were desirable. Our foregoing discussion suggests that for the good of the department as a whole, individual faculty must cooperate by supplying adequate effort, sharing information freely and honestly, and suppressing the pursuit of personal or subgroup outcomes. We describe in the next section why we consider trust in the group the essential attitude that enables such strong cooperation to exist in work groups.

The Nature of Trust and its Importance to Work Group Cooperation

Although many different attitudes may be associated with cooperation, trust has emerged as the attitude most critical to the formation of cooperation within groups and organizations (Smith, Carroll, & Ashford, 1995). In a special issue of the *Academy of Management Journal* on cooperation in organizations, Smith, Carroll, and Ashford (1995, p. 10) argued that a difficulty in making sense of organizational research on cooperation is attributable in part to the diversity of definitions of the cooperation construct. Nonetheless, they concluded (pp. 10–11) that "virtually all scholars have agreed that one especially immediate antecedent [of cooperation] is trust." Consistent with definitions of interpersonal trust (e.g. Rousseau et al., 1998; Whitener et al., 1998; Williams, 2001), we define trust in the work group as an individual's intention to accept vulnerability to the group based on the expectation but not the guarantee that the group will act in a considerate and benevolent manner toward the individual. We will argue that this *attitude* is based in large part on the individual's identification with and attachment to the group and on the quality of group processes.

Empirical research supports a relationship between interpersonal trust and cooperation in the workplace. In a meta-analysis of research on interpersonal trust in work organizations, Dirks and Ferrin (2002) found that trust was positively related to organizational citizenship behavior. This relationship holds for both trust in peers (McAllister, 1995) and trust in managers (Korsgaard, Brodt, and Whitener, 2002). Research on procedural justice and contract violations also indicates that trust is an immediate determinant of cooperative behavior (Konovsky & Pugh, 1994; Robinson & Morrison, 1995). Indirect evidence of this relationship is also seen in studies demonstrating a positive relationship between managers' trust-building behavior and employee cooperative behavior (Deluga, 1994; Korsgaard, Brodt, & Whitener, 2002). Although much of the empirical and theoretical work in this area has concerned interpersonal trust, there are reasons to expect a similar relationship between trust in the work group and cooperation.

A consideration of our definition of cooperation and its challenges provides insight into why trust in the group is essential to cooperation. First, individuals who do not believe in the benevolence of the group and who are not willing to be vulnerable to the group are very unlikely to engage in proactive, voluntary behavior because such behavior requires, at minimum, exposure to the threat of censure. Further, cooperation often exposes one to uncertain payoff, lack of reciprocation, and distributive inequity. In short, trust is important because as Kramer, Brewer, and Hanna frame it (1996, p. 358), "In the absence of some basis for thinking that others will reciprocate, therefore, individuals may find it hard to justify the decision to cooperate themselves."

Trust in the work group is especially important because it also enables cooperative behavior that nonetheless challenges the group or individuals in it. Trust in the group frees individuals to respond rapidly to emerging circumstances without waiting for signals of approval (Lind, 2001) and to interpret ambiguous group actions as benign and to respond in kind (Amason & Sapienza, 1997). Simons and Peterson (2000) provided empirical support for the potential beneficial effects of trust in the work group on cooperation by showing that trust in the group attenuates the tendency of individuals to interpret task conflict as relationship conflict. This finding is significant in relation to our definition of cooperation because task conflict involves challenging the group to reach optimal performance, but relationship conflict tends to lead to uncooperativeness and group dissolution (Amason & Sapienza, 1997; Korsgaard, Sapienza, & Schweiger, 2001; Simons & Peterson, 2000).

Although the arguments regarding the effects of cooperation on trust in the work group are intuitively appealing, direct theoretical argumentation and empirical evidence are somewhat scant. Moreover, the antecedents of trust in the work group have rarely been examined explicitly in the literature. Insight into the causes and consequences of trust in the work group can be gleaned from recent theoretical work on the formation of trust and trust in social dilemmas. Theory and research on swift trust highlight the role of group identity in facilitating the formation of trust (McKnight, Cummings, & Chervany, 1998; Meyerson, Weick, & Kramer, 1996). This perspective suggests that group membership confers trust in the collective, for the group is a type or symbol of the individual him/herself. That is, groups formed to complete some special task may engage in a categorization process whereby they see the group as being select or special and therefore will adopt positive expectations of the group.

The limited empirical research on trust in groups or collectives also provides strong arguments for the validity of viewing trust in the collective as a legitimate and important construct. For example, Dirks (1999) examined the effect of trust on group process, although he examined the aggregate of interpersonal trust rather than trust in the group. Simons and Peterson (2000) demonstrated the impact of trust in the group on limiting counterproductive group conflict. Similarly, research on the role of trust in social dilemmas (Kramer, Brewer, & Hanna, 1996) not only provides support for the positive effects of collective trust on cooperation (Kramer, 1999), it also suggests that identification with the group is an important determinant of trust in the collective (Kramer, Brewer, & Hanna, 1996). Given the importance of identity to trust, we next examine the concept of social identity and the intragroup processes related to identification.

SOCIAL IDENTITY

Psychologists have long acknowledged the notion of the self or self-concept and its role in regulating thought and action (e.g. James, 1948). An individual's self-concept contains many facets or aspects that serve to define the self. Social identity is that aspect of a person's self-concept that is determined by her/his membership in a particular group. That is, individuals to a greater or lesser extent define themselves in terms of their membership in various groups. These groups may include demographic, political, religious, social, and work groups. This aspect of the self is at the center of theoretical perspectives on group identity such as social identity theory (Tajfel & Turner, 1979; Brown, 2000), self-categorization theory (Hogg, 2001; Turner et al., 1987), and organizational identity (Ashforth & Mael, 1989; Dutton, Dukerich, & Harquail, 1994). These theories concern the processes by which individuals form identities with groups and the effects such identities have on judgment and action.

The impetus for early work on social identity was to understand intergroup relations, and, today, the emphasis on intergroup issues remains in much of the theory and research on identity. The main thrust of this research is the impact of group identity on ingroup bias. Generally, this literature shows that social identity leads to more favorable evaluations and treatment of ingroup members (i.e. the set of people in the focal individual's group) compared to the evaluation and treatment of outgroup members (i.e. those in groups other than the focal individual's group) (Brown, 2000).

Despite the prevailing interest in intergroup relations, social identity has strong implications for intragroup relations as well. In fact, organizational identity, a particular form of identity associated with a work organization (Ashforth & Mael, 1989), specifically focuses on how identity influences the dynamics within the organization. Consistent with this view, we examine the impact of social identity on relations within the group. Unique to our analysis, however, is a focus on the work group rather than the organization as a whole and especially on the impact of intragroup processes on work group identity.

Importance of Social Identity to Intragroup Cooperation and Trust

Research suggests that identity generally fosters prosocial or cooperative relations within the group. Social dilemma studies have demonstrated the impact of group identity on prosocial or altruistic behavior toward the group (Dawes, van de Kragt, & Orbell 1988; De Cremer & van Vugt, 1999; Kramer, 1993). These studies involved social dilemma-type tasks in which participants decide how to allocate resources within the group. Results consistently showed that participants were more self-sacrificing and cooperative in their allocations when they had formed even a minimal group identity. Similarly, in their study of alumni's identification with their alma mater, Mael and Ashforth (1992) found that identification was related to the altruistic behavior of donating to the organization. A similar relationship between identity and prosocial behavior in the form of organizational citizenship behavior has been observed in work organizations (Bergami & Bagozzi, 2000; O'Reilly & Chatman, 1986).

Some scholars have argued that the effect of social identity on cooperation is largely due to the effect of identity on trust (Kramer, 1993; Kramer, Brewer, & Hanna, 1996; Meyerson, Weick, & Kramer, 1996; Williams, 2001). This interpretation is consistent with research on the ingroup bias effects of social identification (Brewer, 1979) wherein group members tend to ascribe positive attributes such as trustworthiness and cooperativeness to other ingroup members. These inferences are thought to result from the effect identification has on categorization processes (Kramer, Brewer, & Hanna, 1996). Specifically, inferences regarding group members are based on beliefs regarding the group or category rather than on current specific information about the members (Brodt & Ross, 1998; Williams, 2001). It is noteworthy that this form of trust does not require any direct experience with particular individuals within the group and is, in effect, "presumptive" (Kramer, 1993, p. 252).

There is little direct empirical evidence of the effect of identity on trust, and the findings are not fully consistent with theory. For example, a recent study examined the effect of school affiliation (used as a proxy for social identity) on negotiations and found that dyads who shared an affiliation were significantly more cooperative and outperformed mixed dyads but were no higher on trust (Moore et al., 1999). However, another study, one involving permanent versus temporary employees, provided limited support for the relationship between identity and trust (Chattopadhyay & George, 2001). In this study, identity was operationalized in terms of the diversity of permanent versus temporary employees in a work group. The findings indicated a significant relationship between shared identity and trust, but only in groups that were composed predominantly of temporary employees.

In summary, research indicates that group identification has a positive impact on intragroup cooperation. Theory also suggests that this relationship is explained, at least in part, by the impact of group identification on trust in the group. Thus, an exploration of group processes leading to group identification should provide understanding of how to foster trust in group and intragroup cooperation.

Most of the antecedents examined in theories of social identity do not involve intragroup processes. Rather, because of the emphasis on intergroup relations, the social identity literature has focused on the impact of the group's broader social and task environment on identity. For example, attractiveness and distinctiveness are thought to increase identity because they enhance the collective esteem of the group relative to other groups in the social environment. That is, individuals are apt to identify more strongly with groups that possess some relatively attractive or unique attribute (Ashforth & Mael, 1989; Mael & Ashforth, 1992). Another antecedent that is related to the social context of the group is salience, which heightens awareness of the ingroup and outgroups and leads individuals to identify more strongly with the group (Ashforth & Mael, 1989; Haslam et al., 1999). Other antecedents are associated with the uncertainty in the social or task environment. For example, factors such as the lack of clear feedback and task ambiguity (Grieve & Hogg, 1999; Mullin & Hogg, 1998, 1999) have a positive impact on group identity.

The emphasis on the broader social or task environment among these antecedents is consistent with the emphasis on intergroup relations that predominates theories of social identity. However, these antecedents provide limited insight into how dynamics *within* the group influence identity. In consequence, our interest in the internal workings of the group points us in the direction of antecedents suggested by related theory and research on procedural justice.

Social Identity and Procedural Justice

Procedural justice provides a useful framework for examining how group process influences identity. This perspective suggests a distinct motivational function of group identity, namely enhancing or maintaining the individual self-esteem of group members. In contrast to collective esteem enhancement, which involves the group's standing relative to other groups in the social context, individual self-esteem concerns members' status within the group and how it is affected by members' treatment within the group. That is, procedural justice theory suggests that an individual will identify more strongly with a group in which his/her individual worth and status as a member are validated by fair treatment. Theories of procedural justice, in particular the relational model (Tyler & Blader, 2000) and fairness heuristic theory (Lind, 2001), suggest that group members have two main concerns in their social exchanges within the group or organization. First, they are concerned with the prospect that their contributions to the group will not be reciprocated (i.e. they will not be fairly compensated for their efforts). Second, individuals are concerned that, if they link their identity to the group, they are in danger of rejection by the group. This latter concern is thought to be the more powerful motive (Lind, 2001) and to lead to individuals being sensitive to cues regarding their status and value to the group. In consequence, this theory suggests that group identity is central to fostering cooperation (Tyler & Blader, 2001).

Intragroup interactions, viewed through the lens of procedural justice, provide important information to the individual regarding his or her status within the group. That is, being treated in a procedurally just fashion signifies that the individual is a member in good standing within the group or organization. The self-esteem enhancing effect of having their status in the group affirmed leads members to identify strongly with the group. Consequently, procedurally fair treatment is positively associated with favorable attitudes toward the group (Korsgaard, Schweiger, & Sapienza, 1995; Phillips, Douthitt, & Hyland, 2001). In contrast, when an individual's standing in the group is threatened, as is the case when the individual is treated unfairly, and he/she is less likely to use the group as a basis for identity (Mussweiler, Gabriel, & Bodenhausen, 2000).

Procedural justice concerns the fairness of procedures used to make decisions and the fairness of the treatment of individuals when enacting those procedures. Numerous aspects of procedures and treatment result in the perception of procedural justice. The most extensively documented factor is the opportunity for input or voice in the process of making the decision (Lind & Tyler, 1988). Based on the work of Leventhal (1980), several additional procedural criteria have been investigated, including judgment based on evidence, correctability or refutability of the decision, and consistent application of procedures (Folger, Konovsky, & Cropanzano, 1992; Kim & Mauborgne, 1993). Researchers have drawn the distinction between determinants of procedural justice that pertain to formal procedures and those that pertain to the decision maker's conduct, the latter being referred to as interactional justice (Tyler & Bies, 1990). Interactional justice is determined by two sets of factors, interpersonal sensitivity factors—the extent to which individuals are treated with respect and dignity—and informational factors—the extent to which individuals are given adequate and timely information regarding the decision procedure and outcome. Both procedural and interactional factors give rise to judgments of procedural justice, although the relevance or importance of particular factors may vary somewhat depending on the decision context (Greenberg, 1993). Generally, however, to the extent that decisions are made in a fair manner, individuals are likely to be more trusting and behave more cooperatively within the group (Colquitt et al., 2001; Korsgaard, Schweiger, & Sapienza, 1995; Korsgaard & Roberson, 1995; Sapienza & Korsgaard, 1996).

Theory and research on procedural justice have focused primarily on the impact of a group leader or decision-making authority's (e.g. manager's) treatment of individuals. However, there is increasing evidence that procedural justice may also be a collective phenomenon. Recent research has demonstrated the existence of a procedural justice climate or context, a shared perception of procedural justice in work groups (Colquitt, Noe, & Jackson, 2002; Mossholder, Bennett, & Martin, 1998; Naumann & Bennett, 2000). The data suggest that a justice climate has a positive impact on organizational commitment (Johnson, Korsgaard, & Sapienza, 2002), a concept closely related to organizational identification, as well as cooperative behavior (Naumann & Bennett, 2000), performance (Colquitt, Noe, & Jackson, 2002), and satisfaction (Mossholder, Bennett, & Martin, 1998).

To summarize, theory and research in social identity suggest that group identity is important to fostering cooperation within the group. Theory would also suggest that identity directly influences trust, which functions as a mediator of the identity–cooperation relationship. These relationships underscore the importance of identity to fostering cooperative relationships within a group. The centrality of group identity leads us to an examination of the causes and mechanisms underlying group identification. Many of these antecedents involve the broader social context and therefore are beyond the scope of our examination of intragroup processes. However, procedural justice theory provides a useful framework for understanding the effect of group process on group identification. Specifically, it suggests that the degree of fairness of decision-making procedures employed by the group or the group leader influences group members' perceptions of their status and worth to the group and, hence, identification with the group. These relationships are summarized in Figure 6.1.

Two important questions regarding the formation and impact of group identity on trust and cooperation in the group remain unanswered: why have the empirical results regarding the relationship between group identification and trust been inconsistent? And, what role might individual differences play in the formation and effects of group identification? First, although theory suggests that trust mediates the impact of identity on cooperation, evidence of the effect of group identification on trust in the group is mixed. Such inconsistency in findings may result from unidentified moderators in the relationship between identity and trust. Second, evidence suggests that individual differences in propensity to form attachments may play a role in identification and its consequences. For example, Mael and Ashforth (1995) demonstrated that one dimension of past experience (i.e. biodata) influenced individuals' propensity to become identified with a given organization. The authors speculated that this dimension, which they identified as "group orientation," may reflect a generalized tendency toward organizational identification. This view is consistent with research by Smith and colleagues (Smith, Coats, & Murphy, 2001; Smith, Murphy, & Coats, 1999) indicating that individual differences in attachment styles influence group identification. To date, however, the role of individual differences in shaping social identity and in influencing the impact of identity on trust and cooperation in groups is unclear.

We posit that insight into the answers to these questions lies in research and theory on psychological attachment to the group. In the next section, we review this perspective, discuss its implications for trust and cooperation, and integrate it into our model.

PSYCHOLOGICAL ATTACHMENT TO THE GROUP

Psychological attachment to the group, in addition to identification, is necessary for trust and sustained cooperation. Attachment style, with its roots in research on psychological attachment, was a concept initially used in child development (Bowlby, 1982) to describe the affective bonds between a child and caregiver. Psychological attachment styles are presumed to organize the development of personality and guide social behavior not only in infancy but also throughout adult life (Hazan & Shaver, 1987; Main, Kaplan, & Cassidy, 1985). Researchers subsequently applied this concept to adult relationships and found adult attachment styles related to such topics as fear of personal death (i.e. the ultimate separation; Mikulincer, Florian, & Tolmacz, 1990), support seeking and caregiving in romantic relationships (Feeney & Collins, 2001), the suppression of unwanted thoughts (Fraley & Shaver, 1997), affect regulation (Mikulincer, Orbach, & Iavnieli, 1998), intergroup bias (Mikulincer & Shaver, 2001), and even the issues of love and work and the balance of work and family (Hazan & Shaver, 1990).

Extending this work, researchers have recently developed the concept of group attachment style, which describes a group member's propensity to seek and feel secure in group situations (Brodt, forthcoming; Brodt & Korsgaard, 2002; Smith, Coats, & Murphy, 2001; Smith, Murphy, & Coats, 1999). For anyone who has managed work groups or project teams, the concept has intuitive appeal. When a project deadline approaches, the range of reactions can be dramatic: some individuals turn quickly to their groups bringing everyone together whereas others hole up alone and work to complete the task themselves. Yet others, those who work exclusively within their groups, pull even closer together to their "secure base" (Brodt, forthcoming) to get the job done. These behavioral differences are believed to reflect different mental representations or "working models" of the self-as-group-member that develop from the group's availability and responsiveness to the individual. The securely attached group member feels safe and comfortable in his/her organizational environment and knows that his/her group will be available and respond to his/her needs (Brodt, forthcoming). As a consequence, s/he will work independently and freely share information among group members, but also keep in touch with his/her group as deadlines and other urgent group needs arise (Brodt, forthcoming; Brodt & Korsgaard, 2002). As this description suggests, the concept underscores the adaptive significance of group attachment and individuals' strong bonds to a group; it is based on the premise that group attachment styles (including closeness and security) both affect group identification and alter the impact of that identification on intragroup cooperation and performance.

Research on group attachment is in its infancy. However, recent work shows promise on both conceptual and empirical fronts. Smith and colleagues (Smith, Coats, & Murphy, 2001; Smith, Murphy, & Coats, 1999) paved the way for researchers by defining the concept and developing a measure of group attachment. On the conceptual front, they analyzed the relationship between group attachment and identification, proposing that these two psychological processes are complementary. Specifically, they pointed out that social identity theory and research typically focus on identification with the group as an entity and on a single dimension, namely an individual's evaluation of the group (i.e. favorable, unfavorable). Attachment theory underscores individual variation in the type of relationships individuals have to a group and its members. That is, among group members, there are multiple mental models of the self as group member corresponding to differences in attachment styles. Brodt (forthcoming) further developed the concept, emphasizing the role of the group as a secure base from which group members may venture, take risks, and work independently but on behalf of the group. Her analysis includes both group attachment and interpersonal attachment (e.g. attachment to a boss or superior).

On the empirical front, Smith and colleagues developed a measure of group attachment (Smith, Murphy, & Coats, 1999). Borrowing from research on adult attachment (Bartholomew & Horowitz, 1991; Brennan & Shaver, 1995; Fraley & Waller, 1998), they proposed two dimensions—avoidance and anxiety—and developed a scale to measure the attitudes, feelings, and behaviors of individuals. The two dimensions are nearly orthogonal so that individuals can be high on both or low on both as well as high on one or the other. Other researchers have used their attachment measure (Brodt, forthcoming; Brodt & Korsgaard, 2002), creating an emerging literature on group attachment styles.

In the next section, we describe these two components or dimensions of the attachment relationship, and we describe how group attachment styles influence facets of cooperation. We conclude with a discussion of the relationship between group attachment styles and our model.

Group Attachment Avoidance

One aspect of an individual's relationship to a group is typically defined in terms of the extent to which the individual desires to be distant from or independent of the group. This dimension of group attachment is called avoidance and is measured by items such as "I prefer not to depend on my group or to have my group depend on me" and "I want to feel completely at one with my group" (reverse coded) (Smith, Murphy, & Coats, 1999, p. 110). Individuals who report low attachment avoidance accept and value closeness or dependence on groups and attempt to maintain that type of relationship. Part of a secure group attachment style is scoring *low* on this avoidance dimension, implying a desire to be part of a group and an expectation that groups are valuable (Smith, Murphy, & Coats, 1999). In their research, Smith, Murphy, and Coats (1999) found that avoidance was strongly negatively related to group identification and commitment, and positively related to plans to leave the group. Furthermore, Brodt (forthcoming) found that avoidance was strongly positively correlated with behavior aimed at fulfilling self-interest rather than group or organization interest.

Group Attachment Anxiety

The other aspect of group attachment reflects a worry or anxiety about being accepted by one's group. This dimension is measured by items such as "I often worry my group will not always want me as a member," and "I sometimes worry that my group doesn't value me as much as I value my group" (Smith, Murphy, & Coats, 1999, p. 110). Individuals with high group attachment anxiety report a sense of being "unworthy as a group member and feelings of worry and concern regarding acceptance by valued groups" (Smith, Murphy, & Coats, 1999, p. 96). Behaviorally, these individuals are believed to seek to conform in order to "fit in" and be accepted by their groups. Hence, individuals high in group attachment anxiety are unlikely to question the group or to engage in positive group conflict to ensure that the group remains on track. In contrast, individuals who report low attachment anxiety expect to be accepted by the group and are less concerned about group approval. Smith, Murphy, and Coats (1999) found that individuals higher in attachment anxiety perceived fewer and less satisfying social supports within the group and exhibited greater negative affect.

Group Attachment Styles and Cooperation in Groups

Our discussion about psychological attachment and its implications for our analysis of identification, trust, and cooperation within groups are reflected in our model shown in

Figure 6.1. In general, the attachment research has implications for both the development of group identity and for the link between identity and trust in groups. Specifically, the reliable individual differences in group attachment avoidance regarding preference for working alone or with others suggest a direct effect of attachment avoidance on group identification. Persons high in group attachment avoidance will be less likely to identify with a group because they see the self as autonomous and place a low value on closeness. These individuals have a lower need for group identity.

Group attachment anxiety, however, should moderate the relationship between identity and trust. Persons who are high in group attachment anxiety will develop less trust even if they strongly identify with a group because they tend to view others as inconsistent and untrustworthy. That is, even though these individuals may show strong identification with a group, they will not show the expected positive relationship between identification and trust. For these individuals, group identification and attachment stem from a desire for closeness but are tempered by a fear of rejection. By including attachment style as an individual difference in our model, we should increase its predictive power in these specific ways.

CONCLUSIONS

We set out in this chapter to develop an understanding of the factors contributing to trust and cooperation in work groups. The cooperation of individual group members is essential to the collective performance of the group, and trust is a powerful motivator of cooperation. In contrast to interpersonal trust, we focused on individuals' trust in the group. Viewing trust in the group in this way, we sought to explore the role of the intragroup context and of the group's broader social context in this unique form of trust. The preceding review and synthesis of a variety of literatures, principally trust and cooperation, social identity, procedural justice, and psychological attachment, point to three key factors in building individuals' trust in the group, and hence, cooperation: fair treatment in the group, identification with the group, and group attachment styles. We hope that this focus will stimulate research that takes a new approach to intragroup cooperation and effective group processes. To that end we highlight some implications and potentially rewarding avenues for further research.

One important implication of our model is the extension of procedural justice effects to trust in the group. Although the impact of procedural justice on identity and trust is well documented, such research has mainly focused on the dyadic relationship between the decision-making authority (i.e. the manager) and the person affected by the decision. Although researchers have recently begun to investigate the collective experiences and perceptions of groups (Colquitt et al., 2001; Johnson, Korsgaard, & Sapienza, 2002; Mossholder, Bennett, & Martin, 1998; Naumann & Bennett, 2000), these approaches still focus on the impact of a decision-making authority or manager on the groups' perceptions. What has not been examined is the team itself as a decision-making body. That is, little is known about the dynamics of fairness in the exchanges among peers. Given the prevalence of self-managed teams, group members' perceptions of fair treatment in dealings with the group and its members—rather than the supervisor's fairness—may be a more critical determinant of group identity.

Another implication of our model is the specification of the role of individual differences in group attachment styles in the development and effects of identity on trust and cooperation. To date, most of the research on identity, cooperation, and trust has ignored or minimized the role of individual differences. Preliminary research suggests, however, that there is substantial individual variation in the propensity to form attachments to groups (i.e. group attachment avoidance), which may also influence the propensity to identify with a group and, consequently, to trust the group and be truly cooperative. Our model also proposes a moderating effect of the other main dimension of group attachment styles, anxiety. Specifically, research suggests that group attachment anxiety may exert an independent influence on trust in the group. We therefore propose that this dimension of group attachment may work against the positive effects of identity on trust and, hence, cooperation.

The proposed interaction of identity and group attachment has implications for clarifying the centrality of trust to cooperation. As noted earlier, direct empirical evidence of the impact of identity on trust is weak and limited, whereas the documented impact of identity on cooperation is substantial. This inconsistency suggests that perhaps trust is not essential to fostering cooperation and that identity has a direct impact on cooperation or an indirect one through some other mechanisms. Indeed, some researchers using the social dilemma paradigm have suggested that identity effects on cooperation do not require any positive expectations of reciprocation or cooperation on the part of other group members (Dawes, van de Kragt, & Orbell, 1988). Further, some studies have failed to demonstrate a direct impact of trust on cooperation, finding rather that trust interacts with other variables to influence group process and outcomes (Dirks, 1999; Dirks & Ferrin, 2001). We, on the other hand, assert that trust is indeed essential to cooperation, as is evidenced by the strong link between trust and cooperation, and we assert that trust is central to the effect of identity. However, our model suggests that the lack of empirical evidence for the effect of identity on trust may be attributable to past researchers overlooking the moderating role of group attachment anxiety. This implication awaits empirical validation.

Although group attachment styles are considered an individual difference, it is worth noting that it is not necessarily a stable trait (Smith, Murphy, & Coats, 1999). Thus, it is possible that, over time, an individual's experience with various work groups over his or her career may shape that person's attachment style in groups. For example, individuals who have several successful experiences with temporary work teams early in their career may develop a secure attachment style toward teams and quickly identify and cooperate with newly formed teams in the future. Indeed group attachment style may be a latent factor—what managers commonly refer to as "being a good team player." Furthermore, a relationship unexplored in our model, but not inconsistent with thinking in procedural justice, is the possibility that the procedural justice in groups may have some impact on group attachment styles. For example, given that group attachment styles are posited to be affected by group experience, it is possible that over time, an individual's level of group attachment anxiety may change as a result of consistently fair or unfair treatment in a group.

Our model does not define an exhaustive set of the causes and consequences of trust; rather, it explores the role of group and interpersonal factors in engendering trust in the group. Although not specified in our model, it is equally possible that variations in avoidant group attachment style may moderate the antecedents of identity as well. For example, group attachment avoidance may influence reactions to procedural justice within the group. Recall that the procedural justice perspective suggests that procedurally fair treatment provides information about an individual's standing in the group and should therefore reinforce their identification with the group. Persons who are prone to identify with a group (i.e. low in avoidance) may be particularly sensitive to justice cues about their standing, whereas avoidant persons may be relatively indifferent to such cues.

Another possible extension of the model concerns the potential direct effect of procedural justice on trust and cooperation. Identity is only one of several mechanisms underlying the effects of procedural justice. For example, the fairness heuristic theory (Lind, 2001) suggests that individuals respond favorably to fair procedures because they provide diagnostic information about the trustworthiness of authorities and future outcomes in the exchange relationship. Similarly, the self-interest model of procedural justice (Lind & Tyler, 1988) indicates that individuals care about fair procedures because they help assure that over time, their self-interests will be protected. Fairness accountability theory (Folger & Cropanzano, 2001) suggests that fair procedures provide information about the accountability and intent of decision makers. These alternative models, which share a common emphasis on protection of self-interests, suggest that procedural justice may directly contribute to trust in the group as well as indirectly through building identity. However, it is not yet clear whether satisfaction of self-interest concerns described in these models of justice will motivate the level of cooperation that is emphasized in our model.

Another issue worthy of further investigation is the possibility of reciprocal causality or feedback loops. Specifically, research suggests that, in addition to the effect of trust on cooperation, cooperation has a causal impact on trust in the other party (Ferrin, Bligh, & Kohles, 2002). Further, trust in the group may have important consequences for group processes and outcomes beyond those specified by our model. For example, trusting one's manager or co-worker and being trusted by co-workers has a positive impact on in-role performance (Dirks & Ferrin, 2002; Dirks & Skarlicki, 2002). Research also suggests that trust has a negative impact on monitoring (Ferrin, Bligh, & Kohles, 2002). These consequences of interpersonal trust may well extend to the group's overall functioning.

Our purpose in this chapter was to bring recognition to the issues of the causes of an individual's trust and cooperation in work groups. As prior work had largely focused on the development of interpersonal trust, one of our objectives was to clarify how and why formation of trust in the group differs from interpersonal trust. We posited group identity as the immediate determinant of trust and considered two basic antecedents to group identity, including the procedural justice of group processes and individual differences in the avoidance dimension of group attachment style. Finally, we posited a moderating role for the anxiety dimension of group attachment style on the relationship between group identity and trust in the group. We believe that these ideas help to clarify a previously under-recognized distinction between interpersonal trust and trust in groups.

REFERENCES

Alper, S., Tjosvold, D., & Law, K. S. (1998). Interdependence and controversy in group decision making: antecedents to effective self-managing teams. *Organizational Behavior and Human Decision Processes, 74*, 33–52.

Alper, S., Tjosvold, D., & Law, K. S. (2000). Conflict management, efficacy, and performance in organizational teams. *Personnel Psychology, 53*, 625–642.

Amason, A. C. & Sapienza, H. J. (1997). Effects of top management team size and interaction norms on cognitive and affective conflict. *Journal of Management, 23*, 495–516.

Ashforth, B. E. & Mael, F. (1989). Social identity theory and the organization. *Academy of Management Review, 14*, 20–39.

Bartholomew, K. & Horowitz, L. (1991). Attachment styles among young adults: a test of a four-category model. *Journal of Personality and Social Psychology, 61*, 226–244.

Bergami, M. & Bagozzi, R. P. (2000). Self-categorization, affective commitment and group self-esteem as distinct aspects of social identity in the organization. *British Journal of Social Psychology, 39*, 555–577.

Bowlby, J. (1982). *Attachment and Loss*: Vol 1. *Attachment* (2nd edn). New York: Basic Books.

Brennan, K. & Shaver, P. (1995). Dimensions of adult attachment, affect regulation, and romantic relationship functioning. *Personality and Social Psychology Bulletin, 21*, 267–283.

Brewer, M. B. (1979). Ingroup bias in the minimal intergroup situation: a cognitive–motivational analysis. *Psychological Bulletin, 86*, 307–324.

Brodt, S. (forthcoming). Trust is at the heart of negotiating. In R. Kramer & K. Cook (eds), *Trust and Distrust in Organizational Contexts: Enduring Questions, Emerging Perspectives*. Sage.

Brodt, S. & Korsgaard, M. A. (2002). The role of group attachment and trust in group problem solving by newly formed and existing groups. Manuscript in preparation.

Brodt, S. & Ross, L. (1998). The role of stereotypes in overconfident social prediction. *Social Cognition, 16*, 225–252.

Brown, R. (2000). Social identity theory: past achievements, current problems and future challenges. *European Journal of Social Psychology, 30*, 745–778.

Campion, M. A., Medsker, G. J., & Higgs, A. C. (1993). Relations between work group characteristics and effectiveness: implications for designing effective work groups. *Personnel Psychology, 46*, 823–850.

Campion, M. A., Papper, E. M., & Medsker, G. J. (1996). Relations between work team characteristics and effectiveness: a replication and extension. *Personnel Psychology, 49*, 429–452.

Chattopadhyay, P. & George, E. (2001). Examining the effects of work externalization through the lens of social identity theory. *Journal of Applied Psychology, 86*, 781–788.

Colquitt, J. A., Conlon, D. E., Wesson, M. J., Porter, C. O. L. H., & Ng, K. Y. (2001). Justice at the millennium: a meta-analytic review of 25 years of organizational justice research. *Journal of Applied Psychology, 86*, 425–445.

Colquitt, J. A., Noe, R. A., & Jackson, C. L. (2002). Justice in teams: antecedents and consequences of procedural justice climate. *Personnel Psychology*. *55*, 83–109.

Dawes, van de Kragt, A. J. C., & Orbell, J. M. (1988). Not me or thee but we: the importance of group identity in eliciting cooperation in dilemma situations: experimental manipulations. *Acta Psychologica, 68*, 83–97.

De Cremer, D. & van Vugt, M. (1999). Social identification effects in social dilemmas: a transformation of motives. *European Journal of Social Psychology, 29*, 871–893.

Deluga, R. J. (1994). Supervisor trust building, leader–member exchange and organizational citizenship behaviour. *Journal of Occupational and Organizational Psychology, 67*, 315–326.

Dirks, K. T. (1999). The effects of interpersonal trust on work group performance. *Journal of Applied Psychology, 84*, 445–455.

Dirks, K. T. & Ferrin, D. L. (2001). The role of trust in organizational settings. *Organization Science, 12*, 450–467.

Dirks, K. T. & Ferrin, D. L. (2002). Trust in leadership: meta-analytic findings and implications for research and practice. *Journal of Applied Psychology, 87*, 611–628.

Dirks, K. T. & Skarlicki, D. P. (April, 2002). *The relationship between coworker trust and performance*. Paper presented at the annual meeting of the Society for Industrial and Organizational Psychology, Toronto, Ontario, Canada.

Dutton, J. E., Dukerich, J. M., & Harquail, C. V. (1994). Organizational images and member identification. *Administrative Science Quarterly, 39*, 239–263.

Feeney, B. & Collins, N. (2001). Predictors of caregiving in adult intimate relationships: an attachment theoretical perspective. *Journal of Personality and Social Psychology, 80*, 972–994.

Ferrin, D. L., Bligh, M. C., & Kohles, J. C. (April, 2002). *Trust, monitoring and cooperation in mixed-motive negotiations: a causal examination of competing theories and a comparison across levels*. Paper presented at the annual meeting of the Society for Industrial and Organizational Psychology, Toronto, Ontario, Canada.

Folger, R. & Cropanzano, R. (2001). Fairness theory: justice as accountability. In J. Greenberg & R. Cropanzano (eds), *Advances in Organizational Justice* (pp. 1–55). Stanford, Calif.: Stanford University Press.

Folger, R., Konovsky, M. A., & Cropanzano, R. (1992). A due process metaphor for performance appraisal. In B. M. Staw & L. L. Cummings (eds), *Research in Organizational Behavior* (Vol. 14, pp. 129–177). Greenwich, Conn.: JAI Press.

Fraley, R. & Shaver, P. (1997). Adult attachment and the suppression of unwanted thoughts. *Journal of Personality and Social Psychology, 73*, 1080–1091.

Fraley, R. C. & Waller, N. G. (1998). Adult attachment patterns: a test of the typological model. In J. Simpson & W. Rholes (eds), *Attachment Theory and Close Relationships* (pp. 78–114). New York: Guilford Press.

Gladstein, D. (1984). A model of task group effectiveness. *Administrative Science Quarterly, 29*, 499–517.

Greenberg, J. (1993). The social side of fairness: interpersonal and informational classes of organizational justice. In R. Cropanzano (ed.), *Justice in the Workplace: Approaching Justice in Human Resource Management* (pp. 79–103). Hillsdale, NJ: Lawrence Erlbaum Associates.

Grieve, P. G. & Hogg, M. A. (1999). Subjective uncertainty and intergroup discrimination in the minimal group situation. *Personality and Social Psychology Bulletin, 25*, 926–940.

Haslam, S. A., Oakes, P. J., Reynolds, K. J., & Turner, J. C. (1999). Social identity salience and the emergence of stereotype consensus. *Personality and Social Psychology Bulletin, 25*, 809–818.

Hazan, C. & Shaver, P. (1987). Romantic love conceptualized as an attachment process. *Journal of Personality and Social Psychology, 52*, 511–524.

Hazan, C. & Shaver, P. (1990). Love and work: an attachment–theoretical perspective. *Journal of Personality and Social Psychology, 59*, 270–280.

Hogg, M. A. (2001). Social identity and the sovereignty of the group: a psychology of belonging. In C. Sedikides & M. B. Brewer (eds), *Individual Self, Relational Self, Collective Self* (pp. 125–142). Philadelphia, Pa: Psychology Press.

James, W. (1948). *Psychology*. New York: World Publishing Company.

Johnson, D. W., Johnson, R. T., & Tjosvold, D. (2000). Constructive controversy: the value of intellectual opposition. In M. Deutsch & P. T. Coleman (eds), *The Handbook of Conflict Resolution: Theory and Practice* (pp. 65–85). San Francisco, Calif.: Jossey-Bass, Inc.

Johnson, J. P., Korsgaard, M. A., & Sapienza, H. J. (2002). Perceived fairness, decision control, and commitment in international joint venture management teams. *Strategic Management Journal, 23*, 1141–1160.

Kim, W. C. & Mauborgne, R. A. (1993). Procedural justice, attitudes, and subsidiary top management compliance with multinationals' corporate strategic decisions. *Academy of Management Journal, 26*, 502–506.

Konovsky, M. A. & Pugh, S. D. (1994). Citizenship behavior and social exchange. *Academy of Management Journal, 37*, 656–669.

Korsgaard, M. A., Brodt, S. E., & Whitener, E. M. (2002). Trust in the face of conflict: the role of managerial trustworthy behavior and organizational context. *Journal of Applied Psychology, 87*, 312–319.

Korsgaard, M. A. & Roberson, L. (1995). Procedural justice in performance evaluation. *Journal of Management, 21*, 657–699.

Korsgaard, M. A., Sapienza, H. J., & Schweiger, D. M. (2001). Organizational justice in strategic decision making. In R. Cropanzano (ed.), *Justice in the Workplace* (Vol. 2, pp. 209–226). Hillsdale, NJ: Lawrence Erlbaum Associates.

Korsgaard, M. A., Schweiger, D. M., & Sapienza, H. J. (1995). The role of procedural justice in building commitment, attachment, and trust in strategic decision-making teams. *Academy of Management Journal, 38*, 60–84.

Kramer, K. M. (1999). Trust and distrust in organizations: emerging perspectives, enduring questions. *Annual Review of Psychology, 50*, 569–598.

Kramer, R. M. (1993). Cooperation and organizational identification. In J. K. Murninghan (ed.), *Social Psychology in Organizations* (pp. 244–267). Englewood Cliffs, NJ: Prentice-Hall.

Kramer, R. M., Brewer, H. B., & Hanna, B. A. (1996). Collective trust and collective action: the decision to trust as a social dilemma. In R. M. Kramer & T. R. Tyler (eds), *Trust in Organizations* (pp. 357–389). Thousand Oaks, Calif.: Sage.

Lester, S., Meglino, B. M., & Korsgaard, M. A. (2002). The antecedents and consequences of group potency: a longitudinal investigation of newly formed groups. *Academy of Management Journal, 45*, 352–369.

Leventhal, G. S. (1980). What should be done with equity theory? In K. J. Gergen, M. S. Greenberg, & H. R. Willis (eds), *Social Exchange: Advances in Theory and Research* (pp. 27–55). New York: Plenum Press.

Lind, E. A. (2001). Fairness heuristic theory: justice judgments as pivotal cognitions in organizational relations. In J. Greenberg & R. Cropanzano (eds), *Advances in Organizational Justice* (pp. 56–88). Stanford, Calif.: Stanford University Press.

Lind, E. A. & Tyler, T. R. (1988). *The Social Psychology of Procedural Justice*. New York: Plenum.

McAllister, D. J. (1995). Affect- and cognition-based trust as foundations for interpersonal cooperation in organizations. *Academy of Management Journal, 38*, 24–59.

McKnight, D. H., Cummings, L. L., & Chervany, N. L. (1998). Initial trust formation in new organizational relationships. *Academy of Management Review, 23*, 473–490.

Mael, F. & Ashforth, B. E. (1992). Alumni and their alma mater: a partial test of the reformulated model of organizational identification. *Journal of Organizational Behavior, 13*, 103–123.

Mael, F. A. & Ashforth, B. E. (1995). Loyal from day one: biodata, organizational identification, and turnover among newcomers. *Personnel Psychology, 48*, 309–333.

Main, M., Kaplan, N., & Cassidy, J. (1985). Security in infancy, childhood, and adulthood: a move to the level of representation. In I. Bretherton & E. Waters (eds), *Growing Points of Attachment Theory and Research. Monographs of the Society for Research in Child Development, 50*(1–2, Serial No. 209), 66–104.

Meyerson, D., Weick, K. E., & Kramer, R. M. (1996). Swift trust and temporary groups. In R. M. Kramer & T. R. Tyler (eds), *Trust in Organizations* (pp. 166–195). Thousand Oaks, Calif.: Sage.

Mikulincer, M., Florian, V., & Tolmacz, R. (1990). Attachment styles and fear of personal death: a case study of affect regulation. *Journal of Personality and Social Psychology, 58*, 273–280.

Mikulincer, M., Orbach, I., & Iavnieli, D. (1998). Adult attachment style and affect regulation: strategic variations in subjective self–other similarity. *Journal of Personality and Social Psychology, 75*, 436–448.

Mikulincer, M. & Shaver, P. (2001). Attachment theory and intergroup bias: evidence that priming the secure base schema attenuates negative reactions to out-groups. *Journal of Personality and Social Psychology, 81*, 97–115.

Moore, D. A., Kurtzberg, T. R., Thompson, L. L., & Morris, M. W. (1999). Long and short routes to electronically mediated negotiations: group affiliations and good vibrations. *Organizational Behavior and Human Decision Processes, 77*, 22–43.

Mossholder, K. W., Bennett, N., & Martin, C. L. (1998). A multilevel analysis of procedural justice context. *Journal of Organizational Behavior, 19*, 131–141.

Mullin, B. A. & Hogg, M. A. (1998). Dimensions of subjective uncertainty in social identification and minimal intergroup discrimination. *British Journal of Social Psychology, 37*, 345–365.

Mullin, B. A. & Hogg, M. A. (1999). Motivations for group membership: the role of subjective important and uncertainty reduction. *Basic and Applied Social Psychology, 21*, 91–102.

Mussweiler, T., Gabriel, S., & Bodenhausen, G. V. (2000). Shifting social identities as a strategy for deflecting threatening social comparisons. *Journal of Personality and Social Psychology, 79*, 398–409.

Naumann, S. E. & Bennett, N. (2000). A case for procedural justice climate: development and test of a multilevel model. *Academy of Management Journal, 43*, 881–889.

O'Reilly, C., III & Chatman, J. (1986). Organizational commitment and psychological attachment: the effects of compliance, identification, and internalization on prosocial behavior. *Journal of Applied Psychology, 71*, 492–499.

Phillips, J. M., Douthitt, E. A., & Hyland, M. M. (2001). The role of justice in team member satisfaction with the leader and attachment to the team. *Journal of Applied Psychology, 86*, 316–325.

Podsakoff, P. M., Aherne, M., & MacKenzie, S. B. (1997). Organizational citizenship behavior and the quantity and quality of work group performance. *Journal of Applied Psychology, 82*, 262–270.

Podsakoff, P. M., MacKenzie, S. B., Paine, J. B., & Bachrach, D. G. (2000). Organizational citizenship behaviors: a critical review of the theoretical and empirical literature and suggestions for future research. *Journal of Management, 26*, 513–563.

Robinson, S. L. & Morrison, E. W. (1995). Psychological contracts and OCB: the effect of unfulfilled obligations on civic virtue behavior. *Journal of Organizational Behavior, 16*, 289–298.

Rousseau, D. M., Sitkin, S. B., Burt, R. S., & Camerer, C. (1998). Not so different after all: a cross-discipline view of trust. *Academy of Management Review, 23*, 405–421.
Sapienza, H. J. & Korsgaard, M. A. (1996). The role of procedural justice in entrepreneur–investor relations. *Academy of Management Journal, 39*, 544–574.
Simons, T. L. & Peterson, R. S. (2000). Task conflict and relationship conflict in top management teams: the pivotal role of intragroup trust. *Journal of Applied Psychology, 85*, 102–112.
Smith, E. R., Coats, S., & Murphy, J. (2001). The self and attachment to relationship partners and groups: theoretical parallels and new insights. In C. Sedikides & M. B. Brewer (eds), *Individual Self, Relational Self, Collective Self* (pp. 109–124). Philadelphia, Pa: Psychology Press.
Smith, E. R., Murphy, J., & Coats, S. (1999). Attachment to groups: theory and measurement. *Journal of Personality and Social Psychology, 77*, 94–110.
Smith, K. G., Carroll, S. J., & Ashford, S. J. (1995). Intra- and interorganizational cooperation: toward a research agenda. *Academy of Management Journal, 38*, 7–23.
Tajfel, H. & Turner, J. C. (1979). An integrative theory of intergroup conflict. In W. G. Austin & S. Worchell (eds), *The Social Psychology of Intergroup Relations* (pp. 33–47). Monterey, Calif.: Brooks/Cole.
Turner, J. C., Hogg, M. A., Oakes, P. J., Reicher, S. D., & Wetherell, M. S. (1987). *Rediscovering the Social Group: A Self-categorization Theory*. Oxford, UK: Blackwell.
Tyler, T. R. & Bies, R. J. (1990). Beyond formal procedures: the interpersonal context of procedural justice. In J. Carroll (ed.), *Applied Social Psychology and Organizational Settings* (pp. 77–98). Hillsdale, NJ: Lawrence Erlbaum Associates.
Tyler, T. R. & Blader, S. L. (2000). *Cooperation in Groups*. Philadelphia, Pa: Taylor & Francis.
Tyler, T. R. & Blader, S. L. (2001). Innovations in organizational justice. Paper presented at the International Round Table on Innovations in Organizational Justice. Vancouver.
Whitener, E., Brodt, S., Korsgaard, M. A., & Werner, J. (1998). Managers as initiators of trust: an exchange relationship framework for understanding managerial trustworthy behavior. *Academy of Management Review, 23*, 513–530.
Williams, M. (2001). In whom we trust: group membership as an effective context for trust development. *Academy of Management Review, 26*, 377–396.

7

THE ROLE OF COGNITION IN MANAGING CONFLICT TO MAXIMIZE TEAM EFFECTIVENESS

A TEAM MEMBER SCHEMA SIMILARITY APPROACH*

Joan R. Rentsch and Jacqueline A. Zelno

Researchers in organizational behavior, industrial/organizational psychology, social psychology, sociology, political science, and strategic management have long had an interest in intrateam conflict. Early conflict researchers' ideas that conflict is inevitable and that it can be productive remain highly influential today (e.g. Bales, 1955; Boulding, 1962; Coser, 1956; Deutsch, 1969; Mack & Snyder, 1957). Productive conflict, in particular, remains a focus of many contemporary team conflict researchers (e.g. De Dreu & van de Vliert, 1997; Tjosvold, 1991). The purpose of this chapter is to continue to explore productive conflict within teams and to suggest that a cognitive perspective may provide another vantage point from which to approach this area of research. We examine the role of cognition among team members, specifically the role of team member schema similarity, in the development of productive conflict and high team effectiveness.

We placed several boundaries on our presentation. First, we focused our research on work teams. We defined a work team as: two or more individuals interacting interdependently and cooperatively to achieve a common objective (Cannon-Bowers, Salas, & Converse, 1993; Ilgen, 1999). Second, we concentrated exclusively on the dynamics existing within a team and among team members rather than on relationships between teams and external entities. Third, we centered our work on research, conducted in the field and in the laboratory, involving work teams that engage in complex ill-defined tasks such as strategic decision making (e.g. Amason, 1996; Tjosvold, 1991), case resolution (e.g. Sessa, 1996), and problem solving (e.g. Rentsch et al., 1999). Furthermore, we did not include the extensive research literatures on negotiation, sports teams, and team/group competition.

* The authors wish to thank Michael A. West and Scott Hutchison for their comments on an earlier version of the chapter.

International Handbook of Organizational Teamwork and Cooperative Working. Edited by M. A. West, D. Tjosvold, and K. G. Smith.

We begin by presenting a focused overview of conceptualizations of conflict and the research that is relevant to productive conflict in teams. Then, we describe team member schema similarity as an approach to the study of cognition in teams, and we integrate this approach with conflict research in an effort to enrich both literatures. Finally, we discuss several mechanisms that promote team member schema similarity.

PRODUCTIVE CONFLICT IN TEAMS

Competition, or a win–lose mentality, typically evidenced by goal incompatibility, is the core of many concepts of conflict (e.g. Baron, 1997; Mack & Snyder, 1957). Conflict has been generally defined as occurring when individuals perceive incompatibilities in interests, goals, or behaviors (Deutsch, 1973; Rubin, Pruitt, & Kim, 1994; Tjosvold, 1997). Perceived incompatibilities may have many sources including power differentials, competition over resources, tendencies to differentiate rather than to converge in decision making, ambiguities, denial of self-concepts or values, and anything else perceived to be annoying (De Dreu & van de Vliert, 1997).

Conflict within teams appears to have a complex relationship with team effectiveness. Research has produced evidence that conflict is negatively associated with such indicators of team effectiveness as productivity, satisfaction, and decision-making quality (e.g. Gladstein, 1984; Guetzkow & Gyr, 1954; Schwenk & Cosier, 1993). In contrast, evidence exists showing conflict to be positively associated with such team effectiveness indicators as flexibility, adaptability, growth, stability (Putnam, 1997), decision quality, performance (e.g. Amason, 1996; Jehn, 1994, 1995), mutual understanding, creativity, integration of diverse ideas (De Dreu, 1997; Tjosvold, 1991), establishment of boundaries, cohesion, establishment of group norms, clarification of goals, and the exploration of common aims (Mack & Snyder, 1957). These latter findings support the long-held view that conflict is potentially productive and even essential for effective team performance (e.g. Coser, 1956; Deutsch, 1969).

Early researchers' distinction between different types of conflict (Mack & Snyder, 1957) offers an explanation for the conflicting research results and serves as a basis of current conceptualizations of conflict. One such distinction was between realistic and nonrealistic conflict (e.g. Coser, 1956; Mack & Snyder, 1957). Realistic conflict referred to interactionally based conflict stemming from incompatibility of means, ends, values, or interests typically exacerbated by resource scarcity. Nonrealistic conflict referred to interpersonally based conflict that occurred between individuals and tended to be related to the need for tension release (Mack & Snyder, 1957).

More recently, researchers attempting to exploit the advantages of conflict have yielded a similar two-dimensional model. This model has its roots in the works of such scholars as Bales (1955), Guetzkow and Gyr (1954), Torrance (1957), and others (Mack & Snyder, 1957), who observed that conflict could be categorized as centering on either task or socio-emotional issues. Task conflict (sometimes referred to as cognitive conflict) is similar to realistic conflict and involves disagreements among team members about task issues (e.g. allocation of resources, policies, procedures, roles). Task conflict tends to be associated with constructive conflict management strategies and with positive team outcomes (Tjosvold, 1997). It is through task conflict that team members are thought to identify, extract, and combine their diverse perspectives to maximize performance (Amason & Schweiger, 1994). Task conflict is expected to increase team members' commitment to the team and to its decisions by providing them with an elaborated and common understanding of the rationale underlying the team's decisions and behaviors. In addition, by engaging in task-related debate and thereby gaining a common understanding of decisions, team members are likely to perceive a just process in which members experience a sense of voice and believe that teammates are considering their opinions (Tjosvold, 1991).

Socio-emotional conflict (sometimes referred to as affective conflict) is similar to non-realistic conflict and involves interpersonal incompatibilities among team members (e.g. issues related to norms, values, identity; Amason & Sapienza, 1997; De Dreu, 1997). Socio-emotional conflict usually yields nonproductive conflict management strategies (De Dreu, 1997) and is associated negatively with team effectiveness variables. Socio-emotional conflict tends to be more threatening to individuals than task conflict because it involves negative emotions and may implicate deep psychological factors such as one's identity (De Dreu, 1997). It is personalized and individually oriented disagreements that are characterized by friction, frustration, and personality clashes. Socio-emotional conflict can obstruct the exchange of information between team members and erode their commitment to the team and to its decisions (Amason & Sapienza, 1997). It detracts from performance because it causes team members to focus on reducing threats, increasing power, and attempting to build cohesion rather than on completing the team's task (Evan, 1965; Jehn, 1997). Furthermore, research results indicate that socio-emotional conflict tends to hinder individuals' processing of complex information, thus further inhibiting task performance (Baron, 1997).

The two-dimensional approach to the study of conflict seems to simplify a complex conflict–team effectiveness relationship. However, this approach has its own complexity. Although there are clear theoretical and empirical distinctions between task and socio-emotional conflict, they are frequently found to co-vary positively (Amason & Sapienza, 1997; Jehn, 1994; Pelled, Eisenhardt, & Xin, 1999).

Several explanations for this covariance exist. The most probable explanation is that team members may take task-related conflicts personally thereby generating socio-emotional conflict. Task conflict involves such behaviors as scrutinizing and challenging others' ideas and opinions that can easily be misinterpreted as personal criticism. For example, Bales (1955) observed that giving suggestions, which is a required process for problem solving, usually elicits more negative reactions than giving information or opinions. Furthermore, people tend to view disagreements or criticisms of their ideas as personal rejection (Torrance, 1957).

A key to achieving productive conflict seems to be to minimize socio-emotional conflict while concurrently increasing task conflict. As Torrance (1957) wrote, "...what we are looking for is a group which can tolerate disagreements without becoming emotionally involved" (p. 318). This is likely to be accomplished when team members perceive their teammates' behaviors as well-intended (i.e. task-oriented and constructive) rather than as personal attacks. In other words, the perception of conflict in a team is based on team members' interpretations of the intentions underlying their teammates' actions.

The recent research on cognition in teams offers a perspective from which to examine how interpretations of team members' behaviors may be associated with intrateam conflict. A cognition in teams perspective also offers mechanisms that influence team members' cognitions through which intrateam conflict can be managed.

A COGNITION IN TEAMS PERSPECTIVE ON PRODUCTIVE INTRATEAM CONFLICT

Cognition in teams has been shown to be related to team processes. However, the major variables, team cognition and team processes, have been conceptualized and operationalized at rather general levels (e.g. Mathieu et al., 2000). The application of a cognitive approach to the study of intrateam conflict will likely be most effective when these variables are conceptualized and operationalized with specificity. Therefore, we propose specific forms and contents of team member cognitions that may be related to intrateam conflict. We propose that members who understand functional teamwork behaviors similarly will not perceive intrateam conflict, but instead they will perceive a productive teamwork process.

Teamwork is a process aimed at facilitating team member interactions through effective communication, coordination, and cooperation in an effort to promote successful task completion and to develop high-quality relationships among team members (Cannon-Bowers, Salas, & Converse, 1993; Salas et al., 1988). The research on team cognition has focused primarily on congruence among team members' cognitions (e.g. Cannon-Bowers, Salas, & Converse, 1993; Rentsch & Hall, 1994). According to most models of team cognition, team members possessing high cognitive congruence will experience efficient and effective interactions, because they will be able to compensate for, anticipate, facilitate, and understand one another's actions (e.g. Nieva, Fleishman, & Reick, 1985); to communicate effectively (Dyer, 1984); to coordinate their behaviors (Klimoski & Mohammed, 1994); and to minimize process losses (Steiner, 1972).

Forms of Team Member Cognition

Schemas regarding teamwork and other team-relevant information are the mechanisms by which team members interpret each other's behavior. Schemas serve to organize knowledge and thereby represent ways of thinking about, interpreting, predicting, and remembering events (Lord & Maher, 1991). Any team-relevant domain may constitute the content of team members' schemas (Cannon-Bowers, Salas, & Converse, 1993). Team members possess similar teamwork schemas when their schemas contain compatible knowledge structures for organizing and understanding teamwork-related phenomena (Rentsch & Hall, 1994). Team member schema similarity (TMSS) may take the form of *schema congruence*,[1] which exists when team members' schemas are comparable in content and/or structure. In Figure 7.1, team member schema congruence is represented by the overlap of Donna's and Mitch's schemas of teamwork (i.e. both schemas contain "trust" and "supporting others").

TMSS may also take the form of *schema accuracy*. A team member's schema is accurate if it is similar to a "true score" or to a target. For example, training effectiveness can be evaluated by examining the degree to which trainees' schemas match the instructor's schema at the conclusion of training (Smith-Jentsch et al., 2001). Schema accuracy also exists to the degree that a team member's schema of a target matches the target's schema. Of primary interest here is the degree to which team members form accurate schemas of their teammates' schemas of teamwork. As illustrated in Figure 7.1, Donna's schema of Mitch's teamwork schema is accurate to the extent that she thinks that for Mitch "getting along"

[1] We use the term "schema congruence" to refer to what Rentsch and Hall (1994) referred to as schema agreement.

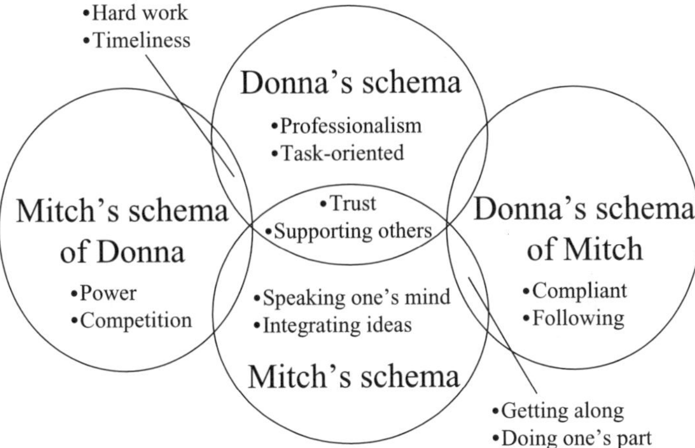

Figure 7.1 Illustration of schema congruence and schema accuracy

and "doing one's part" are important components of teamwork, and Mitch actually believes that "getting along" and "doing one's part" are important parts of teamwork. However, as shown in Figure 7.1, Donna's schema of Mitch is deficient because she does not realize that "speaking one's mind" and "integrating ideas" are parts of Mitch's schema. In addition, her schema of Mitch's schema is contaminated because she thinks that for Mitch "being compliant" and "following" are components of teamwork, but these components are not parts of Mitch's teamwork schema. Because Donna's schema of Mitch is inaccurate, when she observes Mitch adapting his ideas to accommodate other teammates' ideas, she interprets this behavior as compliant and believes that Mitch is a follower. Mitch, on the other hand, believes that he is speaking his mind in an effort to integrate his ideas with his teammates' ideas. Thus, schema accuracy can play a role in team members' interpretations of one another's behaviors.

Accumulating empirical research evidence supports team member schema congruence and team member schema accuracy as correlates of team effectiveness (e.g. Mathieu et al., 2000; Rentsch et al., 1999; Rentsch & Klimoski, 2001). With regard to conflict in teams, teams in which members interpret teammates' behaviors differently or inaccurately will likely experience nonproductive conflict (cf. Baron, 1997; Ensley & Pearce, 2001; Pinkley & Northcraft, 1994). For example, team members may interpret the behaviors of pointing out the weaknesses of arguments (Tjosvold, 1991) and offering dissenting opinions (Amason & Sapienza, 1997) quite differently. Some members may interpret these behaviors, intended as efforts to collaborate, as personal attacks. Team members who interpret their teammates' behavior as personal attacks may begin to believe that their goals and those of their teammates are incompatible. Misinterpretation of behaviors intended to support task conflict as threats or as indicators of goal incompatibility is a potential source of emotional responses that may promote nonproductive conflict (Baron, 1988; Ensley & Pearce, 2001).

Torrance (1957) provides an excellent example of how misinterpretations can result in ineffective team performance, due to nonproductive conflict. He reported an incident in which, following a blizzard, trainees and their instructors crossed an unfrozen creek and continued onward for several hours before pitching camp and drying out. The delay in drying out resulted in a number of the men experiencing severe frostbite. In post-training interviews, trainees and instructors reported that they believed the group should have stopped to dry out earlier than it did. The trainees also reported that they did not express their desire to stop because they believed the instructors to be "unusually intolerant of expressions of disagreement" (p. 315; particularly with regard to a trainee who was perceived to be the trainees' natural leader). The instructors stated that they did not stop the group because they believed the trainees to be apathetic due to the trainees' silence. Misinterpretations, due to low schema congruence and schema accuracy, led to ineffective team performance. Most likely instructors had misinterpreted earlier disagreements with trainees (particularly disagreements with powerful trainees) as threats (i.e. socio-emotional conflict evolved within the group). Therefore, they expressed intolerance for disagreements, which caused trainees to be unwilling to express their desires following the blizzard (i.e. task conflict was squelched within the group).

Influences of Schema Congruence and Schema Accuracy on Productive Conflict

Team member schema congruence and schema accuracy may be related differentially to elements of productive conflict. When teamwork schema congruence is low among team members, then the team members are not thinking similarly with respect to the process of teamwork, and this may produce differential interpretations of teammates' behaviors. For example, some team members may think that effective teamwork involves heated debates in which each team member fights for his or her viewpoint. Other team members may believe that considering the strengths and weaknesses of all perspectives in turn is essential for effective teamwork. In such a situation of low congruence, team members may quickly withdraw from task conflict either by fighting opposing perspectives or by withholding opinions and analyses. Conversely, if team members possess functional and highly congruent schemas regarding the process of teamwork, then they will be likely to interpret behaviors intended to be collaborative as such. This common interpretation will result in members actively engaging in appropriate teamwork behaviors that stimulate and support task conflict. See Figure 7.2.

Low team member schema accuracy is expected to be related to high socio-emotional conflict, because low schema accuracy is likely to produce misattributions (Baron, 1997). As illustrated in Figure 7.1, if Mitch thinks that for Donna "hard work" and "timeliness" are important components of teamwork, and Donna actually believes that "hard work" and "timeliness" are important parts of teamwork, then Mitch's schema of Donna's teamwork schema is accurate. However, as shown in Figure 7.1, Mitch's schema of Donna is deficient because he does not realize that "professionalism" and "being task-oriented" are parts of Donna's schema. Mitch's schema of Donna's schema is also contaminated, because he believes that she thinks "power" and "competition" are components of teamwork, but these components are not in her schema of teamwork. Because Mitch's schema of Donna is inaccurate, when he observes Donna cut off teammates' tangential conversations, he interprets this behavior as power hungry and competitive. Mitch then feels threatened and begins to subtly undercut Donna's suggestions. Donna, on the other hand, believes that she is simply being task-oriented and professional. Therefore, she perceives Mitch's reaction

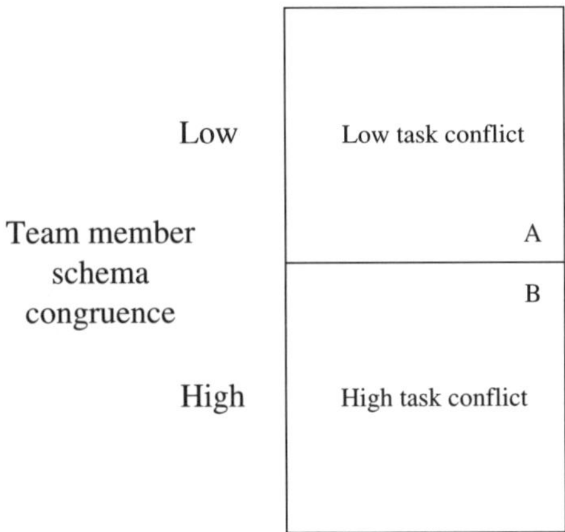

Figure 7.2 Proposed effects of team member schema congruence on task conflict

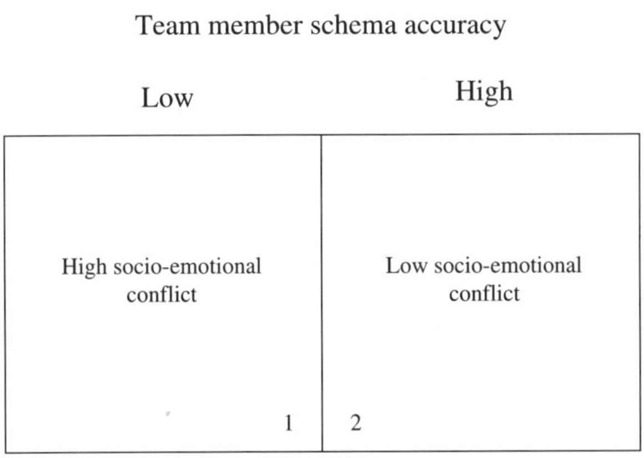

Team member schema accuracy

Low	High
High socio-emotional conflict 1	Low socio-emotional conflict 2

Figure 7.3 Proposed effects of team member schema accuracy on socio-emotional conflict

as irritating and distracting, so she begins to disregard his comments. Mitch may react with additional negative emotions and the socio-emotional conflict between Donna and Mitch continues to escalate.

When schema accuracy is high, then team members understand how their teammates think about teamwork and therefore are less likely to interpret potentially offensive behavior (e.g. critiquing an idea) as a personal attack. They will have accurate explanations for their teammates' behavior and will be able to understand and predict their teammates' reactions. They will be able to modulate their own emotional responses to their teammate's behavior. See Figure 7.3.

Schema congruence and schema accuracy may offer an explanation for the positive and significant correlations between task conflict and socio-emotional conflict obtained in the empirical research (e.g. Ensley & Pearce, 2001; Pelled, Eisenhardt, & Xin, 1999; Simons & Peterson, 2000). A positive relationship between the two types of conflict may occur

		Team member schema accuracy	
		Low	High
Team member schema congruence	Low	Low task conflict High socio-emotional conflict *Noxious nonproductive conflict* A1	Low task conflict Low socio-emotional conflict *Innocuous nonproductive conflict* A2
	High	B1 High task conflict High socio-emotional conflict *Costly productive conflict*	B2 High task conflict Low socio-emotional conflict *Optimal productive conflict*

Figure 7.4 Proposed effects of team member schema accuracy and team member schema congruence on task and socio-emotional conflict

when team members have either low schema congruence and high schema accuracy or high schema congruence and low schema accuracy. These cases are represented in Cells A2 and B1 of Figure 7.4. Cell A2 represents innocuous nonproductive conflict in which the team experiences little task conflict (therefore little task-related activity), but team members are not experiencing negative emotional reactions to the team. Cell B1 represents a costly productive conflict in which the team engages in task conflict (and therefore is actively working on its task), but there is an associated emotional cost. For example, techniques designed to promote critical evaluation of alternatives (i.e. increase task conflict), such as dialectical inquiry and devil's advocacy, can also produce bitterness and lingering resentment (Amason & Sapienza, 1997; Schweiger, Sandberg, & Rechner, 1989).

The cases shown in Cells A1 and B2, representing a negative relationship between the two types of conflict, appear to be rare. Cell A1 represents perhaps the most undesirable case, noxious nonproductive conflict, in which task conflict is low and socio-emotional conflict is high. The team is not engaging in task conflict (or in task-related behaviors) and the team members are feeling negatively about each other and/or the team's processes.

The case that represents optimal productive conflict is Cell B2. High congruence and high accuracy represent a state of consensus (Poole & McPhee, 1983) and is a form of schema similarity that is likely to be related to high levels of team effectiveness (Rentsch & Hall, 1994). In this case, task conflict is high and socio-emotional conflict is low, because team members will have congruent conceptualizations about teamwork and will accurately interpret teammates' team-related behaviors.

We have assumed in the cases of high schema congruence and high schema accuracy that the content of the schema is functional. Although research evidence indicates that high TMSS is related to team effectiveness, it is similarity of functional schemas that is likely to be most strongly related to team effectiveness (Rentsch & Hall, 1994). Achieving productive conflict through TMSS requires addressing the specific content of teamwork schemas. Below, we describe elements of functional schemas that are likely to be related to productive conflict.

Content of Team Member Schemas: Schema Congruence and Task Conflict

Team member schema congruence is expected to be related positively and strongly to task conflict when the schema content is functional. Teamwork schemas conducive to productive conflict include organized knowledge regarding many functional aspects of teamwork. Two examples are those related to supporting cooperative goal interdependence and to encouraging constructive normative behavior.

Cooperative goal interdependence exists when team members believe there is a positive relationship between the attainment of their own goals and the attainment of their teammates' goals. With such beliefs, they are likely to engage in behaviors related to task conflict. These behaviors include actively participating in discussions, attending to others, being influenced by teammates, encouraging and assisting teammates, correcting errors, pooling information, and integrating perspectives (cf. Deutsch, 1949; Tjosvold, 1984).

Team members' perceptions of the degree and type of goal interdependence existing within the team are based, in part, on their interpretations of behaviors occurring within the team (Tjosvold, 1984, 1997). These interpretations are driven by their teamwork schemas. Team members whose teamwork schemas enable them to interpret their teammates' potentially personally offensive behaviors (e.g. correcting errors) as consistent with cooperative goal interdependence are likely to engage in behaviors supportive of task conflict (Alper, Tjosvold, & Law, 1998; Deutsch, 1949). However, if team members misinterpret such behaviors they may avoid these types of behaviors, which would result in minimal task conflict.

When team members possess congruent schemas regarding cooperative goal interdependence, they will develop a high performance spiral. For example, if Mitch and Donna have congruent schemas regarding cooperative goal interdependence, then Mitch will interpret Donna's critique of his ideas as consistent with cooperative goal interdependence. Therefore, he will feel free to respond by disagreeing with her critique. Donna would understand that he intended his response to support cooperative goal interdependence and would listen carefully to his remarks. This cycle of behavior and interpretation would strengthen their congruent schemas of cooperative goal interdependence.

This example illustrates how team members possessing functional and congruent teamwork schemas that enable them to interpret behaviors, such as discussing dissenting views, as indicative of cooperative goal interdependence will be likely to engage in task conflict (Alper, Tjosvold, & Law, 1998; Tjosvold, 1991). They will be prone to believe that they can promote their own welfare by promoting the interests of their teammates (Tjosvold, 1991; Tjosvold & Tjosvold, 1995). They will also expect their teammates to want them to be effective and that their teammates will reciprocate effort and risk-taking (Tjosvold & Tjosvold, 1995).

Congruent teamwork schemas should also include an understanding of constructive normative behaviors. Although many constructive normative behaviors may contribute to task conflict, openness behaviors, such as sharing information, expressing opinions, raising doubts, airing objections, challenging ideas, and evaluating ideas of others, have been shown to be of particular significance (Amason & Sapienza, 1997; Janis, 1982). Many openness behaviors, although conducive to task conflict, may cause team members discomfort if they do not interpret them as well-intended. In order to avoid or minimize uncomfortable or anxiety-arousing situations within the team, members of newly formed teams are not likely to develop behavioral patterns that support task conflict (Cosier & Schwenk, 1990; Hackman & Morris, 1975; Mitchell & Mitchell, 1984). However, behavioral patterns that support openness result in high-quality, innovative solutions, and consensual agreements (Tjosvold, 1991), and are positively related to reported levels of task conflict (Amason & Sapienza, 1997).

Thus, team members who have congruent schemas regarding openness behaviors are likely to engage in task conflict. For example, if team members' teamwork schemas include openness behaviors, then when one team member presents a suggestion for approaching the team's task, another member may immediately begin to articulate the weaknesses of the idea. The first team member will understand that this behavior is an attempt to evaluate the quality of the suggested idea. Schema congruence will enable team members to engage in openness behaviors that their teammates will interpret as supportive of task conflict.

Content of Team Member Schemas: Schema Accuracy and Socio-emotional Conflict

As shown in Figure 7.3, team member schema accuracy is hypothesized to be negatively related to socio-emotional conflict. Although this is likely to be true for teamwork schemas containing cooperative goal interdependence and openness, a stronger relationship may exist for schemas containing accurate information about other team members. Specifically, socio-emotional conflict may be negatively associated with the degree to which team members possess schema accuracy with respect to the other team members' characteristics. Three team member characteristics that may be highly relevant are expertise, internal frames of reference, and task-related constraints.

Team members who have accurate schemas of each other will be able to interpret each other's behaviors nonemotionally. Accurate schemas about teammates are likely to reduce cognitive biases, such as stereotyping and attribution biases, typically used to understand others' behavior. Stereotypes are schemas about specific social groups that influence information processing, and upon activation, may not only affect cognition, but may also elicit strong emotional reactions (Baron, 1997). Therefore, rather than activating stereotypic schemas to interpret teammates' behavior, teams are likely to be more effective, and minimize emotional reactions, if members invoke schemas containing information unique to each teammate (cf. Baron, 1997). If team members have accurate schemas about individual team members then stereotyping and its associated problems may be diminished.

With respect to attributions, if team members perceive the behavior exhibited by another member as undesirable and they have accurate schemas of the "offending" person, then they may be able to correctly attribute the behavior to external forces, such as the individual's personal constraints, rather than to internal forces. If team members do not have accurate schemas of team members' characteristics, then they may find it difficult to interpret evocative behaviors exhibited by teammates. In particular, the hostile attribution bias, associated with aggressive behavior, is likely to be triggered in ambiguous situations. An accurate schema may enable team members to avoid the hostile attribution bias and, thus, enable them to attribute any potentially confrontational action to unintentional causes (Zillmann, 1993). Moreover, making an appropriate external attribution will minimize negative emotional reactions.

In our example above, Donna and Mitch are members of a construction team. Donna is very knowledgeable about the client's financial resources, and Mitch is very knowledgeable about the engineering aspects of construction. If Donna's schema of Mitch contains information that he is an engineering expert, then her schema of Mitch is accurate with respect to his expertise. Mitch's frame of reference as an engineer leads him to suggest the use of high-quality materials without regard for their associated cost. In this case, if Donna has an accurate schema regarding Mitch's frame of reference, she will be able to understand why he focuses on quality materials and tends to disregard cost. Having the knowledge to make an external attribution will assuage the possibility of creating emotional conflict (Baron, 1997).

In addition, members in teams characterized by highly accurate schemas for team members' characteristics will likely justify their own perspectives to their teammates. To continue with our example, Donna responds to Mitch's suggestion by arguing strongly for adhering to a tight budget. Because she has an accurate schema of Mitch's perspective as an engineer, in making her argument she also reveals that she has a task-related constraint due to pressure from the client to work within a budget. As Mitch's schema of Donna becomes increasingly accurate regarding her task-related constraint, he will be able to understand that she has no choice in making her argument. He is therefore likely to accept these justifications rather than misattributing them and exacerbating socio-emotional conflict.

Summary Model of Team Member Schema Similarity and Productive Conflict

Teams with members who have highly accurate schemas and highly congruent schemas are proposed to experience optimal productive conflict (Cell B2 in Figure 7.4). Specifically, congruent schemas regarding functional teamwork processes (e.g. cooperative goal interdependence and openness) are proposed to be related positively to task conflict, and accurate schemas regarding team members' characteristics (e.g. expertise, task-related constraints, internal frames of reference) are proposed to be negatively related to socio-emotional conflict.

Figure 7.4 illustrates the integration of the effects of schema congruence and schema accuracy on intrateam conflict that are shown in Figures 7.2 and 7.3. The specific relationships depicted in Figures 7.2–7.4 are likely to be less distinct than presented. We propose that high schema congruence will be strongly associated with high task conflict, but it may also have a weaker relationship with socio-emotional conflict. For example, if team members achieve the high performance spiral of behavior and interpretations of behavior that support cooperative goal interdependence, then their experience of socio-emotional conflict may be minimized. The same may be true for accurate schemas. We suggest that increased schema accuracy will be strongly associated with decreased socio-emotional conflict, but it may also have some, albeit weaker, relationship with task conflict. For example, if team members understand a teammate's areas of expertise, they may be open to or even probe for that teammate's expert opinions, which will contribute to increased task conflict.

The benefit of this model is that it offers an approach for eliminating, reducing, or reversing the positive correlation typically found between task conflict and socio-emotional conflict, because forces are exerting differential pressure on each type of conflict. Consistent with previous research findings, the resulting productive conflict is expected to be related to team effectiveness variables such as team viability, member growth, client satisfaction, creativity/innovation, and commitment to the teams' decision or product. Members of teams experiencing productive conflict are less likely to be distracted by concerns about each other's underlying assumptions and goals, and they are less likely to undermine task conflict by engaging in opportunistic and self-serving behaviors (Ensley & Pearce, 2001). Essentially, they will be able to focus on task work and to engage in it without undue negative emotional reactions.

DEVELOPMENT OF APPROPRIATE SCHEMA FORMS AND CONTENTS

Several mechanisms may facilitate the development of these specific forms (i.e. schema congruence and schema accuracy) and contents (e.g. goal interdependence, openness, team member expertise, constraints, and frames of reference) of team members' cognitions. Three such mechanisms are team member characteristics, training, and technology.

Team Member Characteristics

Many team member characteristics may play a role in the development of schema congruence and schema accuracy. We will focus on experience as a major determinant of schema congruence and on individual differences (i.e. trust, perspective taking, and social anxiety) as influencing schema accuracy.

Similar experiences among team members are expected to increase their *schema congruence* (Rentsch & Hall, 1994). Experience takes many forms, including team, functional, organizational, and industry experience, and experiences related to the team's task. Team members' team experience, which refers to the extent of their experience working in teams (this may include experience working with any particular team), has been shown to be related to schema congruence among team members (e.g. Rentsch & Klimoski, 2001). With respect to functional background (e.g. marketing or production), team members from the same functional background were found to attend to information that relates to the goals of their functional area (Dearborn & Simon, 1958). This tendency indicates that members with similar experience related to function may have congruent schemas. Evidence also indicates that team members who have similar organizational and industry experience may possess schema congruence (Smith et al., 1994). Heterogeneity of team members' organizational and industry experience was found to be negatively related to informal communication (Smith et al., 1994). A lack of schema congruence may be what causes the team members to resort to formal channels of communication.

The development of *schema accuracy* among team members will involve person perception processes. Person perception depends extensively on the perceiver observing and processing information and on the target disclosing information and behaving consistently (London, 1995; Mischel, 1983). Several individual difference variables, including trust, perspective taking, and social anxiety, may be related to these tendencies. High levels of trust among team members will increase their willingness to disclose teamwork-related information (e.g. expertise, task constraints, and frames of reference; Morgan & Hunt, 1994; Pistole, 1993). They may also be willing to accept teammates' disclosures (Alper, Tjosvold, & Law, 1998). This free exchange of information may enable them to develop high team member schema accuracy. Perspective taking is also likely to be related to team member schema accuracy, because high perspective-taking targets tend to communicate so that others may understand them easily (i.e. tend to self-disclose; Feffer & Suchotliff, 1966). In addition, high perspective-taking perceivers tend to understand others' messages and perspectives accurately (Johnson, 1971). Burnett, Rentsch, and Zelno (2002) reported evidence supporting the relationship between team members' levels of trust and perspective taking and their ability to accurately report their teammates' schema of teamwork.

Social anxiety is also expected to be related to schema accuracy. Highly anxious individuals tend to be more self-focused than less anxious individuals, and when people are overly self-focused (e.g. concerned about how others will view them) they exert most of their cognitive efforts on behavior management at the expense of person perception (Patterson, 1996). Not only are low anxiety team members likely to have the cognitive resources to devote to developing schema accuracy, but they will also be likely to gaze at teammates, to engage in nonverbal interactions, and to rely minimally on stereotyping and attribution biases (Patterson, 1996). All of these tendencies are likely to increase their ability to form accurate schemas about their teammates.

Team member characteristics are expected to influence the development of schema congruence and schema accuracy. However, they are expected to contribute less to the development of specific schema content than will training and technology.

Training

One purpose of training is to alter cognitive structures. Training focused on specific schema content should result in team members developing congruent schemas that promote productive conflict. Training related to teammates' perspectives and roles (e.g. cross-training) should enhance team member schema accuracy regarding teammates. Another purpose of training is to broaden and deepen behavioral repertoires through skill development. In order for schema congruence and schema accuracy to manifest productive conflict, team members must possess the skills to execute the schema consistent behaviors.

Training designed to increase team member *schema congruence* should include a knowledge component that focuses on the development of declarative knowledge aimed at defining cooperative goal interdependence and openness, and on recognizing behaviors that support these notions. Because knowledge development does not ensure skill development (Smith-Jentsch, Salas, & Baker, 1996; Tjosvold & Tjosvold, 1995), training should also include a practice-based component that complements the knowledge-based component. For example, with respect to openness, trainees could be instructed on giving and receiving communicative signals that are reliable and straightforward and that help to ensure that each party understands the other (Mitchell & Mitchell, 1984). This would include summarizing, clarifying, asking focused questions, and cueing active listening (Tjosvold, 1991). Skill development is important to the application of schema-based knowledge, but the combination of well-developed skills and well-developed teamwork knowledge is essential for perpetuating schema congruence among team members. Training should also include a feedback component by which team members learn to support and teach each other about cooperative goal interdependence and openness as the team engages in its task. These three training components should produce teams capable of functioning as high performance systems that will continually strengthen functional teamwork schema congruence (and, therefore, task conflict).

Training designed to increase *schema accuracy* regarding teammates should include cross-training and opportunities for team members to share frames of reference (Mitchell, 1986). Cross-training, which requires team members to be trained on their teammates' tasks and responsibilities, enables team members to understand their teammates' task constraints and expertise (Volpe et al., 1996). Verbal training and position rotation are two effective methods for cross-training team members with respect to task functions that provide them with their teammates' perspective (Cannon-Bowers et al., 1998; Volpe et al., 1996).

Sharing frames of reference, which typically highlights personal and interpersonal issues, complements the task focus associated with cross-training. Team members will possess an internal frame of reference for aligning their self-interests with their job demands (Mitchell, 1986). When team members share their internal frames of reference they increase their understanding of one another's alignments and increase their schema accuracy.

Technology

Technology designed to facilitate schema-related communications should increase schema congruence and schema accuracy. The use of innovative technologies applies to many types of teams, but it has perhaps the most relevance to virtual teams (i.e. teams in which members are distributed) and to teams working in virtual environments. These types of teams are unable to engage in information-rich face-to-face interactions that can accelerate, strengthen, and enhance the development of schema congruence and accuracy. For example, geographically distributed team members must interact using communications technologies (sometimes equipped with special programs designed to support group processes; Andriessen & van der Velden, 1995). Technologies that promote communications among team members that support a common understanding of teamwork will aid in the development of schema congruence. Technologies designed to provide information about teammates will promote the development of schema accuracy.

Technologies designed to ease frequent and explicit communications among team members promote the development of *schema congruence*. Distributed team members rely on technology to cultivate friendships and working alliances with their teammates. Therefore, the technology should be designed to enable them to engage in many of the social "niceties" that are frequently absent in a virtual world (e.g. a "virtual handshake"; cf. Nunamaker, 1997), as well as to engage in task-related activities.

One challenge is to design technology that supports the development of specific schema content related to productive conflict (e.g. goal interdependence and openness). This challenge may be met by designing technologies using the advanced cognitive engineered intervention technologies approach (ACE-IT; Rentsch & Hutchison, 1999a). The ACE-IT approach involves conducting a collaborative task analysis, which is an analysis of the social and cognitive requirements associated with the team's work (McNeese & Rentsch, 2001). One result of the analysis is the identification of the ideal content for the given team members' schemas with respect to that team's particular task. The ideal content is integrated with the team members' existing schemas to develop functional schema content using team enhanced action mediators (TEAMs; Rentsch & Hutchison, 1999a). TEAMs may consist of combinations of software mediators, intelligent agents, and technological interventions with the purpose of enhancing team member schema congruence. For example, embedded software prompts, designed to encourage openness behaviors and positive interpretations of these behaviors, presented to team members at regular intervals as they work on the team task, will enhance team members' communication of schema-relevant information. Prompts as simple as: "Ask your teammates to point out the strengths and weaknesses of your suggestion" and "Provide assistance to your teammates so the team can meet its goal" are likely to enhance team performance and may increase schema congruence (Rentsch & Hutchison, 1999b).

The ACE-IT approach to the technology design may also increase team member *schema accuracy* about team members. In general, virtual reality technology presents a multitude of opportunities to increase schema accuracy. Three examples are intelligent agents, avatars, and replaying virtual reality experiences.

Intelligent agents that remind team members about each other's constraints can increase schema accuracy regarding team members. To return to our example, Donna and Mitch are now members of a virtual team using a technologically enhanced communication system. As they plan the construction project, Donna mentions that she is constrained by the client's budget. An intelligent agent, which is part of the communication technology, recognizes this type of task constraint information and stores it in memory. In a later meeting, Donna and Mitch are discussing building materials. Mitch is about to suggest using a high-quality but expensive material when the intelligent agent reminds him of Donna's task constraint regarding budget. In response to this reminder, Mitch suggests a material that he believes will provide acceptable quality and will be in line with the client's budget.

Technology can also increase schema accuracy through the careful design of avatars, the multidimensional images that represent team members in a computerized virtual environment. Avatars can affect interactions, because they tend to become associated with the personalities and behaviors of the individuals they represent (Nunamaker, 1997). They can also convey information about expertise. The technology that Donna and Mitch are using could contain avatars representing each of them. Mitch's avatar could be a headshot of him wearing a tie with equations and buildings on it to remind his teammates of his engineering expertise.

Virtual reality technology also provides the opportunity for team members to experience their teammates' frames of reference. For example, while the team completes a task, each team members' sensory experience and behaviors could be recorded. The recordings could be replayed so each team member could experience the activity from their teammates' perspectives.

SUMMARY AND CONCLUSION

In summary, we have explored a possible role of cognition among team members in the development of productive conflict and high team effectiveness. The proposed relationships

Mechanism	Team Member Schema	Conflict	Team Effectiveness
Member characteristics related to similar experiences			Commitment Team viability Member growth Client satisfaction Creativity/innovation
Training focused on functional teamwork knowledge and skills	Congruent schemas of functional teamwork	Increased task conflict	
Technology designed to cultivate friendships and working alliances			
Member characteristics related to person perception			
Training focused on teammates' roles and perspectives	Accurate schemas of team members	Decreased socio-emotional conflict	
Technology designed to provide information about teammates			

Figure 7.5 Proposed model of team member schemas and productive team conflict

are summarized in Figure 7.5. The core relationship is the effect of TMSS on intrateam conflict. A primary contribution of this paper is the identification of specific forms and contents of team members' schemas that we expect to be related to specific types of intrateam conflict. We propose that congruent schemas containing functional teamwork knowledge (e.g. cooperative goal interdependence and openness) will be associated with increased task conflict. We expect that accurate schemas regarding team members (e.g. expertise, task-related constraints, and frames of reference) will be related to decreased socio-emotional conflict. The resulting high task conflict and low socio-emotional conflict define optimal productive conflict, which is expected to be positively related to team effectiveness variables. A second contribution of the chapter is the identification of forces that exert differential pressure on each type of conflict. Management of these forces offers a potential means for eliminating, reducing, or reversing the positive correlation typically found between task and socio-emotional conflict. Another contribution is the specification of the mechanisms by which schema congruence and accuracy may be developed and managed. Schema congruence and accuracy are expected to be affected by different forms of these mechanisms (i.e. training, technology, team member characteristics).

In conclusion, several issues require brief clarification. First, the schema and conflict variables are presented in Figures 7.2–7.4 as dichotomous. This was done to simplify the discussion of the fundamental concepts and their relationships. However, it should be noted that we believe these variables to be continuous. In addition, the two-dimensional model of conflict may be oversimplifying a complex phenomenon. We suggest that researchers might alternate their attention between the two-dimensional model and a more holistic perspective such as that represented by Tjosvold's (1984) long-standing notion of constructive controversy. This type of "figure-ground" approach might yield a richer understanding of the conflict process. Second, we focused on schema congruence and accuracy, but other forms of TMSS may exist. In addition, we identified specific schema contents, but other schema contents relevant to intrateam conflict no doubt exist. In this chapter, we chose to detail schema forms and contents that are most likely to be highly related to conflict. Third, we discussed each mechanism for creating schemas in isolation, but we expect that they may operate most effectively in combination. For example, technology designed to increase schema congruence and accuracy can be used to train teams whose members have been selected based on their characteristics (e.g. experience). Fourth, the conflict process is complex and we presented a simplified account of the relationships between the types of conflict and team outcomes to illustrate the potential role of team member schemas. However, in order to isolate the effects of each type of conflict on team outcomes, it is necessary to account for other influential variables such as team type and task complexity (De Dreu & Weingart, Chapter 8 this volume). Although the model we presented is intended to be applicable to many types of teams, we expect that it will be most applicable to teams performing complex, ill-defined tasks such as problem solving and strategic decision making. Fifth, given that we expect our model to be most applicable to these types of teams, we focused on a specific set of team effectiveness variables that included attitudinal reactions to the team's process and outputs. However, we recognize that many forms of team outcomes (e.g. satisfaction, individual well-being, objective performance; De Dreu & Weingart, Chapter 8 this volume) are appropriate for understanding the effects of conflict on teams.

REFERENCES

Alper, S., Tjosvold, D., & Law, K. S. (1998). Interdependence and controversy in group decision making: antecedents to effective self-managing teams. *Organizational Behavior and Human Decision Processes, 74*(1), 33–52.

Amason, A. C. (1996). Distinguishing the effects of functional and dysfunctional conflict on strategic decision making: resolving a paradox for top management teams. *Academy of Management Journal, 39*, 123–148.

Amason, A. C. & Sapienza, H. J. (1997). The effects of top management team size and interaction norms on cognitive and affective conflict. *Journal of Management, 23*(4), 495–516.

Amason, A. C. & Schweiger, D. M. (1994). Resolving the paradox of conflict, strategic decision making, and organizational performance. *The International Journal of Conflict Management, 5*(3), 239–253.

Andriessen, J. H. E. & van der Velden, J. M. (1995). Teamwork supported by interaction technology: the beginning of an integrated theory. In J. M. Peiro, F. Prieto, J. L. Melia, & O. Luque (eds), *Work and Organizational Psychology: European Contributions of the Nineties* (pp. 155–169). Oxford: Erlbaum (UK) Taylor & Francis.

Bales, R. F. (1955). How people interact in conferences. *Scientific American, 192*(3), 31–35.

Baron, R. A. (1988). Attributions and organizational conflict: the mediating role of apparent sincerity. *Organizational Behavior and Human Decision Processes, 41*, 111–127.

Baron, R. A. (1997). Positive effects of conflict: insights from social cognition. In C. K. W. De Dreu & E. van de Vliert (eds), *Using Conflict in Organizations* (pp. 177–191). London: Sage Publications.

Boulding, K. (1962). *Conflict and Defense*. New York: Harper and Row.

Burnett, D. D., Rentsch, J. R., & Zelno, J. A. (2002). Composing great teams: the role of person perception in building team member schema similarity. In T. Halfhill (Chair), *Work Group Composition and Effectiveness: Personality, Diversity, and Citizenship*. Symposium presented to the 17th Annual Conference of the Society for Industrial and Organizational Psychology, Toronto, Ontario, Canada, April 12–14, 2002.

Cannon-Bowers, J. A., Salas, E., Blickensderfer, E., & Bowers, C. A. (1998). The impact of cross-training and workload on team functioning: a replication and extension of initial findings. *Human Factors, 40*, 92–101.

Cannon-Bowers, J. A., Salas, E., & Converse, S. (1993). Shared mental models in expert team decision making. In N. J. Castellan (ed.), *Individual and Group Decision Making* (pp. 221–246). Hillsdale, NJ: Lawrence Erlbaum Associates.

Coser, L. A. (1956). *The Functions of Social Conflict*. New York: Free Press.

Cosier, R. A. & Schwenk, C. R. (1990). Agreement and thinking alike: ingredients for poor decisions. *Academy of Management Executive, 4*(1), 69–74.

Dearborn, D. C. & Simon, H. A. (1958). Selective perception: a note on the departmental identifications of executives. *Sociometry, 21*, 140–144.

De Dreu, C. K. W. (1997). Productive conflict: the importance of conflict management and conflict issue. In C. K. W. De Dreu & E. van de Vliert (eds), *Using Conflict in Organizations* (pp. 9–22). London: Sage Publications.

De Dreu, C. K. W. & van de Vliert, E. (1997). *Using Conflict in Organizations*. London: Sage Publications.

Deutsch, M. (1949). A theory of co-operation and competition. *Human Relations, 2*(2), 129–152.

Deutsch, M. (1969). Conflicts: productive and destructive. *Journal of Social Issues, 25*(1), 7–41.

Deutsch, M. (1973). *The Resolution of Conflict: Constructive and Destructive Processes*. New Haven, Conn.: Yale University Press.

Dyer, J. L. (1984). Team research and team training: a state-of-the-art review. In F. A. Muckler (ed.), *Human Factors Review: 1984* (pp. 285–323). Santa Monica, Calif.: The Human Factors Society, Inc.

Ensley, M. D. & Pearce, C. L. (2001). Shared cognition in top management teams: implications for new venture performance. *Journal of Organizational Behavior, 22*, 145–160.

Evan, W. M. (1965). Conflict and performance in R&D organizations. *Industrial Management Review, 7*, 37–46.

Feffer, M. & Suchotliff, L. (1966). Decentering implications for social interaction. *Journal of Personality and Social Psychology, 4*, 415–422.

Gladstein, D. L. (1984). Groups in context: a model of task group effectiveness. *Administrative Science Quarterly, 29*, 499–517.

Guetzkow, H. & Gyr, J. (1954). An analysis of conflict in decision making groups. *Human Relations, 7*, 367–381.

Hackman, J. R. & Morris, C. G. (1975). Group tasks, group interaction process, and group performance effectiveness: a review and proposed integration. In L. Berkowitz (ed.), *Advances in Experimental Social Psychology* (pp. 45–99). New York: Academic Press.

Ilgen, D. (1999). Teams embedded in organizations: some implications. *American Psychologist, 54*, 129–139.

Janis, I. L. (1982). *Groupthink: Psychological Studies of Foreign Policy Decisions and Fiascoes* (2nd edn). Boston, Mass.: Houghton-Mifflin.

Jehn, K. A. (1994). Enhancing effectiveness: an investigation of advantages and disadvantages of value-based intragroup conflict. *The International Journal of Conflict Management, 5*(3), 223–238.

Jehn, K. A. (1995). A multimethod examination of the benefits and detriments of intragroup conflict. *Administrative Science Quarterly, 40*, 256–282.

Jehn, K. A. (1997). A qualitative analysis of conflict types and dimensions in organizational groups. *Administrative Science Quarterly, 42*, 530–557.

Johnson, D. W. (1971). Role reversal: a summary and review of the research. *International Journal of Group Tensions, 7*, 318–334.

Klimoski, R. & Mohammed, S. (1994). Team mental model: construct or metaphor? *Journal of Management, 20*(2), 403–437.

London, M. (1995). *Self and Interpersonal Insight*. New York: Oxford University Press.

Lord, R. G. & Maher, K. J. (1991). Cognitive theory in industrial and organizational psychology. In M. D. Dunnette & L. M. Hough (eds), *Handbook of Industrial and Organizational Psychology* (Vol. 2, pp. 1–62). Palo Alto, Calif.: Consulting Psychologists Press.

Mack, R. W. & Snyder, R. C. (1957). The analysis of social conflict: toward an overview and synthesis. *Journal of Conflict Resolution, 1*(2), 212–248.

McNeese, M. D. & Rentsch, J. R. (2001). Social and cognitive considerations of teamwork. In M. D. McNeese, E. Salas, & M. Endsley (eds), *New Trends in Cooperative Activities: Understanding System Dynamics in Complex Environments* (pp. 96–113). Santa Monica, Calif.: Human Factors and Ergonomics Society Press.

Mathieu, J. E., Heffner, T. S., Goodwin, G. F., Salas, E., & Cannon-Bowers, J. A. (2000). The influence of shared mental models on team process and performance. *Journal of Applied Psychology, 85*, 273–282.

Mischel, W. (1983). Alternatives in the pursuit of the predictability and consistency of persons: stable data yield stable interpretations. *Journal of Personality, 51*, 578–604.

Mitchell, R. (1986). Team building by disclosure of internal frames of reference. *The Journal of Applied Behavioral Science, 22*(1), 15–28.

Mitchell, R. C. & Mitchell, R. R. (1984). Constructive management of conflict in groups. *Journal for Specialists in Group Work, 9*(3), 137–144.

Morgan, R. M. & Hunt, S. D. (1994). The commitment–trust theory of relationship marketing. *Journal of Marketing, 58*, 20–38.

Nieva, V. F., Fleishman, E. A., & Reick, A. (1985). *Team Dimensions: Their Identity, Their Measurement, and Their Relationships*. Washington, DC: Advanced Research Resources Organization.

Nunamaker, J. F., Jr (1997). Future research in group support systems: needs, some questions and possible directions. *International Journal of Human–Computer Studies, 47*(3), 357–385.

Patterson, M. L. (1996). Social behavior and social cognition. In J. L. Nye & A. M. Brower (eds), *What's Social about Social Cognition?: Social Cognition Research in Small Groups* (pp. 87–105). London: Sage Publications.

Pelled, L. H., Eisenhardt, K. M., & Xin, K. R. (1999). Exploring the black box: an analysis of work group diversity, conflict, and performance. *Administrative Science Quarterly, 44*, 1–28.

Pinkley, R. L. & Northcraft, G. B. (1994). Conflict frames of reference: implications for dispute processes and outcomes. *Academy of Management Journal, 37*(1), 193–205.

Pistole, M. C. (1993). Attachment relationships: self-disclosure and trust. *Journal of Mental Health Counseling, 15*, 94–106.

Poole, M. S. & McPhee, R. D. (1983). A structurational analysis of organizational climate. In L. L. Putnam & M. E. Pacanowsky (eds), *Communication and Organizations: An Integrative Approach* (pp. 195–219). Beverly Hills, Calif.: Sage Publications.

Putnam, L. L. (1997). Productive conflict: negotiation as implicit coordination. In C. K. W. De Dreu & E. van de Vliert (eds), *Using Conflict in Organizations* (pp. 147–160). London: Sage Publications.

Rentsch, J. R., Burnett, D. D., McNeese, M. D., & Pape, L. J. (1999). Team member interactions, personalities, schemas, and team performance: Where's the connection? Paper presented to the Fourteenth Annual Conference of the Society of Industrial and Organizational Psychology, Atlanta, Georgia, April 30–May 2.

Rentsch, J. R. & Hall, R. J. (1994). Members of great teams think alike: a model of team effectiveness and schema similarity among team members. In M. M. Beyerlein, D. A. Johnson, & S. T. Beyerlein (eds), *Advances in Interdisciplinary Studies of Work Teams: Theories of Self-managing Work Teams* (Vol. 1, pp. 223–261). Greenwich, Conn.: JAI Press, Inc.

Rentsch, J. R. & Hutchison, A. S. (1999a). *Advanced Cognitive Engineered Intervention Technologies (ACE-IT)*. Knoxville, Tenn.: Organizational Research Group.

Rentsch, J. R. & Hutchison, A. S. (1999b). *Assessment and Measurement of Team Member Schema Similarity in BMC3I demonstrations*. Knoxville, Tenn.: Organizational Research Group.

Rentsch, J. R. & Klimoski, R. J. (2001). Why do "great minds" think alike?: antecedents of team member schema agreement. *Journal of Organizational Behavior, 22*, 107–120.

Rubin, J. Z., Pruitt, D. G., & Kim, T. (1994). *Social Conflict: Escalation, Stalemate and Settlement*. New York: McGraw-Hill.

Salas, E., Montero, R. C., Glickman, A. S., & Morgan, B. B. (1988). Group development, teamwork skills, and training. Paper presented at the American Psychological Association Meetings, Atlanta, Georgia, August.

Schweiger, D. M., Sandberg, W. R., & Rechner, P. L. (1989). Experiential effects of dialectical inquiry, devil's advocacy, and consensus approaches to strategic decision making. *Academy of Management Journal, 32*(4), 745–772.

Schwenk, C. & Cosier, R. (1993). Effects of consensus and devil's advocacy on strategic decision making. *Journal of Applied Social Psychology, 23*, 126–139.

Sessa, V. I. (1996). Using perspective taking to manage conflict and affect in teams. *Journal of Applied Behavioral Science, 32*(1), 101–115.

Simons, T. L. & Peterson, R. S. (2000). Task conflict and relationship conflict in top management teams: the pivotal role of intragroup trust. *Journal of Applied Psychology, 85*(1), 102–111.

Smith, K. G., Smith, K. A., Olian, J. D., Sims, H. P., Jr, O'Bannon, D. P., & Scully, J. A. (1994). Top management team demography and process: the role of social integration and communication. *Administrative Science Quarterly, 39*, 412–438.

Smith-Jentsch, K. A., Campbell, G. E., Milanovich, D. M., & Reynolds, A. M. (2001). Measuring teamwork mental models to support training needs assessment, development, and evaluation: two empirical studies. *Journal of Organizational Behavior, 22*, 179–194.

Smith-Jentsch, K. A., Salas, E., & Baker, D. P. (1996). Training team performance-related assertiveness. *Personnel Psychology, 49*, 909–936.

Steiner, I. D. (1972). *Group Process and Productivity*. New York: Academic Press.

Tjosvold, D. (1984). Cooperation theory and organizations. *Human Relations, 37*(9), 743–767.

Tjosvold, D. (1991). Rights and responsibilities of dissent: cooperative conflict. *Employee Responsibilities and Rights Journal, 4*(1), 13–23.

Tjosvold, D. (1997). Conflict within interdependence: its value for productivity and individuality. In C. K. W. De Dreu & E. van de Vliert (eds), *Using Conflict in Organizations* (pp. 23–37). London: Sage Publications.

Tjosvold, D. & Tjosvold, M. M. (1995). Cross-functional teamwork: the challenge of involving professionals. *Advances in Interdisciplinary Studies of Work Teams, 2*, 1–34.

Torrance, E. P. (1957). Group decision-making and disagreement. *Social Forces, 35*, 314–318.

Volpe, C. E., Cannon-Bowers, J. A., Salas, E., & Spector, P. E. (1996). The impact of cross-training on team functioning: an empirical investigation. *Human Factors, 38*, 87–100.

Zillmann, D. (1993). Mental control of angry aggression. In D. M. Wegner & J. W. Pennebaker (eds), *Handbook of Mental Control* (pp. 370–392). Upper Saddle River, NJ: Prentice-Hall.

8

A CONTINGENCY THEORY OF TASK CONFLICT AND PERFORMANCE IN GROUPS AND ORGANIZATIONAL TEAMS

Carsten K. W. De Dreu and Laurie R. Weingart

INTRODUCTION

Where people come together to work, there is a need to coordinate their knowledge, skills, abilities, and activities. Coordination is critical to organizations and the quest for optimal coordination is perhaps the oldest and most enduring problem organizational leaders and management scientists face (Jaffee, 2000). For instance, in their classical work on the social psychology of organizations, Katz and Kahn (1978) observe that "...every aspect of organizational life that creates order and coordination of effort must overcome tendencies to action, and in that fact lies the potentiality for conflict" (p. 617).

To many organizational leaders and managers, conflict is a threat to coordination and effective functioning and thus should be avoided and prevented. This traditional view is reflected in the large number of academic and practitioner-oriented writings that have appeared in recent years, bearing such titles as "barriers to dispute resolution" (Arrow et al., 1995), "controlling the cost of conflict" (Slaikeu & Hasson, 1998), and "difficult conversations" (Stone, Patton, & Heen, 1999). Furthermore, there is a tendency in both the academic and the practitioner-oriented literature to denote collaboration and problem solving as the single best solution to emerging conflict in groups (for discussions, see Blake & Mouton, 1964; Pruitt & Rubin, 1986; van de Vliert, 1997; Weingart & Jehn, 2000). In this chapter, we will argue that the traditional view that task conflict is bad is one-sided, and that the suggestion that problem solving is the one-best-way approach to solving task conflict is erroneous. We review research that suggests that conflict can be functional to teamwork at times and detrimental at others. We develop a contingency perspective that views group performance as a function of the interaction between type of task conflict, conflict management strategy, and group tasks.

International Handbook of Organizational Teamwork and Cooperative Working. Edited by M. A. West, D. Tjosvold, and K. G. Smith.

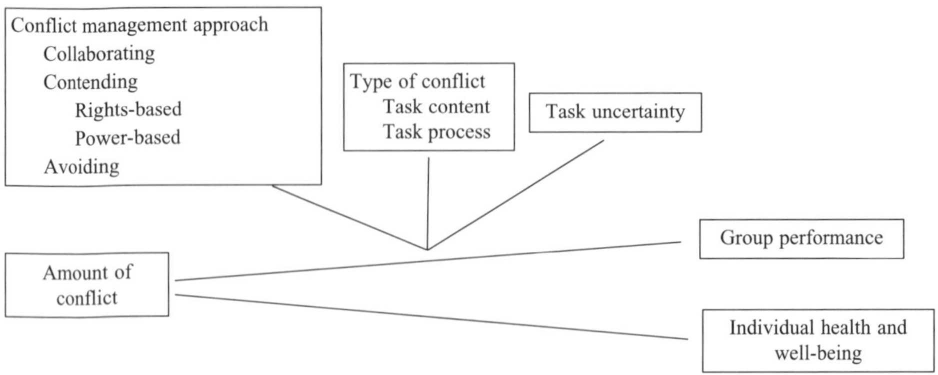

Figure 8.1

Overview of the Contingency Perspective

Figure 8.1 gives an overview of the contingency perspective we will develop in this chapter. A fundamental assumption underlying the model is that conflict affects individuals and the social system in which they function in different ways. Accordingly, we cannot focus exclusively on one outcome variable, such as group performance, and expect to obtain a thorough understanding of conflict at work. Instead, a multifaceted approach that includes multiple outcome variables is necessary. In this chapter, we consider both group performance and individual health and well-being as key outcome variables. We choose these two outcome variables because they represent two levels of aggregation (individual and group) that are the most proximal to many conflict episodes. The impact of task conflict on group performance and individual well-being is considered to depend on (a) the type of conflict (task content or task process); (b) the level of task uncertainty (the extent to which the group tasks are routine versus complex and ill-defined); and (c) whether the group approaches the conflict through collaborating, contending, or avoiding.

In the remainder of this first section we introduce the building blocks of our contingency model. Consecutively, we discuss group performance and individual well-being, the role of task uncertainty, the differences between task-content and task-process conflicts, and conflict management strategies groups may use. In the second section, we review evi dence pointing toward the efficacy of a contingency perspective and we develop a set of propositions pertaining to the more novel aspects of the model. We conclude this chapter with some general conclusions and we highlight several fundamental questions awaiting research.

Group Performance and Individual Well-being

In this chapter the terms "group" and "team" are used interchangeably and refer to ongoing (semi)-autonomous sets of interdependent individuals who have a joint responsibility for accomplishing a set of tasks (West, Borrill, & Unsworth, 1998). While the tasks groups perform may vary widely (for discussions and taxonomies, see McGrath, 1984, and Steiner, 1972), a particularly useful distinction when it comes to understanding the effects of conflict relates to the level of task uncertainty (van de Ven, Delbecq, & Koenig, 1976). Task uncertainty refers to the variability (i.e. routineness) and difficulty (i.e. complexity) experienced when performing the task. Variability has been operationalized as the number of work exceptions encountered by a work unit (Perrow, 1967) and the variety of methods used in task processes (Hall, 1972). Difficulty relates to predictability of work methods. Thus the task uncertainty distinction is largely between simple, routine tasks on the one hand, and complex, ill-defined tasks on the other. Examples of more certain (i.e. simple, routine) tasks include signal detection tasks, routine planning and design in logistics, and routine execution tasks in production and manufacturing. Examples of more uncertain tasks include group decision making, creative tasks, or nonroutine production tasks. The task uncertainty dimension is one of three factors important to group performance in our contingency model of conflict (see Figure 8.1).

Researchers have used a variety of indicators of group performance, including productivity, innovativeness, and adherence to constraints. Examples include the team's average productivity (Jehn, 1995), self-assessments of the quality of group decisions (Amason, 1996), the number of innovations (De Dreu & West, 2001), or adherence to time and budget constraints (Lovelace, Shapiro, & Weingart, 2001). To some extent, however, these different indicators all tap into the general construct of *group effectiveness*—the extent to which a group reaches its goals (Hackman, 1983). As we will see below, many studies on conflict and group performance indeed used a global measure of team effectiveness.

The use of a wide range of group performance measures is due to at least two factors. First, relevant indices of group performance can only be identified based on an understanding of the specific group task (Steiner, 1972), thus different group tasks necessitate different performance measures. For example, innovation is a more relevant performance indicator to new product development teams than to production teams. As a result, multiple measures of group performance are necessary to compare conflict effects across multiple studies. Second, in field research one often has to settle for those indicators that are or can be made available.

Individual well-being reflects an individual's evaluation of his/her work environment. The experiences at work may affect an individual in several ways, ranging from depression and despair to elation and work satisfaction. Although frameworks and definitions of well-being exist (e.g. Warr, 1987), a generally accepted conceptualization of well-being is lacking. In studies that explore the impact of conflicts on individual well-being, the emphasis lies on stress and burnout. *Stress* is an ambiguous word that is used as an overarching rubric encompassing, among other things, the (failing) adaptation of individuals to their environment, and feelings of distress resulting in various physiological, behavioral, and psychological consequences (Quick et al., 1997). In the stress literature one may differentiate between the stressor, the stress response, and distress. Within organizations, an example of stressors are the demands in the workplace. These demands bring about the stress response: a generalized, patterned unconscious mobilization of the body's natural energy. We may feel an elevated heart rate, increased respiration, a dry mouth, and an increased alertness. This mobilization becomes detrimental for an individual's well-being if the demands tax or exceed his or her adaptive resources over longer periods of time. Such distress can manifest itself in various ways, including behavioral consequences (e.g. absenteeism, accident proneness, drug abuse), psychological consequences (e.g. depression, psychosomatic complaints, burnout), and medical consequences (e.g. heart disease) (Quick et al., 1997).

Burnout can be considered as a long-term stress reaction that is caused by the prolonged exposure to job stress. The term "burnout" is a metaphor that refers to the draining of energy, that is more energy is lost than replenished, comparable to a car battery which will run empty if not enough energy is generated from the dynamo (Schaufeli & Enzmann, 1998). Burnout is nowadays defined as a syndrome consisting of three dimensions: exhaustion, cynicism, and ineffectiveness (or reduced personal accomplishment) (Maslach & Leiter, 1997).

Conflict in Groups

In everyday speech, conflict is seen as a fight, a struggle, or the clashing of opposed principles (e.g. *Concise Oxford Dictionary*, 1983). As a result, conflict is often avoided, and when confronted, is difficult to reconcile given this negative and active view of conflict (Kolb & Bartunek, 1992; O'Connor, Gruenfeld & McGrath, 1993). Students of conflict, however, have noted that such a definition is problematic because it confounds what the conflict is about, how the conflict is experienced, and how the conflict is managed (Deutsch, 1973; Pondy, 1967). An alternative is to define conflict as a process that begins when one individual or group perceives differences between oneself and another individual or group over something that is important (Thomas, 1992). Perceived differences about issues that matter produce psychological states, including feelings and motivational goals, that in turn drive behaviors intended to intensify, reduce, or solve the tension (De Dreu, Harinck, & van Vianen, 1999; Pruitt, 1998; Thomas, 1992; Wall & Callister, 1995).

CONFLICT TYPE

Critical in the contingency model we outlined in Figure 8.1 is the content of the problem producing the tension. Given that task performance-related activities include those that have to do with the actual task and others that have to do with the process of performing the task or delegating resources and duties, conflicts in work teams can be differentiated into task-content and task-process conflict.[1] *Task-content conflicts* are disagreements among group members' ideas and opinions about the task being performed, such as disagreement regarding an organization's current hiring strategies or determining the information to include in an annual report. Task-content conflicts include debates over facts (driven by data, evidence) or opinions (De Dreu, Harinck, & van Vianen, 1999) and are sometimes referred to as information conflicts (Levine & Thompson, 1996), or cognitive conflicts (Brehmer, 1976; Jehn, 1997). *Task-process conflicts* are about logistical and delegation issues such as how task accomplishment should proceed in the work unit, who is responsible for what, and how things should be delegated (Jehn, 1997). Since task-process conflicts often involve the distribution of scarce resources, whether tangible or intangible, task-process conflict is sometimes equated with resource conflict, a conflict of interest (e.g. De Dreu, Harinck, & van Vianen, 1999; Harinck, De Dreu, & van Vianen, 2000). For example, a cross-functional

[1] In some studies, task-content and task-process conflicts have been differentiated from relationship conflicts. Relationship conflicts are personal in nature, including interpersonal conflicts, personality clashes, and disagreements about extracurricular issues. Relationship conflict is generally dysfunctional to team performance. Research suggests that effective teams manage relationship conflicts through avoiding and ignoring the issues, whereas ineffective teams with relationship conflict manage these conflicts in a more active way, through forcing or problem solving (De Dreu & van Vianen, 2001; Jehn, 1997; Murnighan & Conlon, 1991). Avoiding and ignoring personality differences and relationship conflict may prevent the conflict intensifying and translating into nonproductive task conflict.

product development team might disagree about the optimal design for a new product—a task-content conflict. Or they might have a conflict over the timing of completion of an aspect of the aesthetic design—a task-process conflict.

CONFLICT MANAGEMENT

Conflict management refers to the behavior oriented toward the intensification, reduction, and resolution of the conflict. Although an infinite number of conflict management strategies may be conceived of, conflict research and theory tend to converge on a four-way typology distinguishing between (a) collaborating, (b) contending, (c) conceding, and (d) avoiding (Blake & Mouton, 1964; De Dreu et al., 2001; Pruitt & Rubin, 1986; Thomas, 1992). *Collaborating* is oriented toward an agreement that satisfies both own and other's aspirations as much as possible. It involves an exchange of information about priorities and preferences, showing insights, and making trade-offs between important and unimportant issues. Collaboration is related to "constructive controversy" (Tjosvold, 1998), which is defined as the open-minded discussion between parties with opposing points of view but compatible goals. *Avoiding* involves reducing the importance of the issues, and attempts to suppress thinking about the issues. *Contending* involves threats and bluffs, persuasive arguments, and positional commitments. *Conceding*, which can be seen as the flip side of contending, is oriented toward accepting and incorporating the other's will. It involves unilateral concessions, unconditional promises, and offering help. When both parties use a contending strategy, the conflict tends to escalate. Alternatively, a party can concede in response to contention from the other party, resulting in progress toward potential resolution of the conflict.

Ury, Brett, and Goldberg (1993) further differentiated contending strategies into two subcategories, rights and power, in their taxonomy of approaches to dispute resolution. We adopt this distinction because while rights and power are both contending strategies, they are differentially effective. When using a rights-based approach, the parties attempt to resolve the dispute by applying some standard of fairness, precedent, contract, or law. A focus on rights is likely to lead to a distributive agreement in which each party has to give something up to reach an agreement, with the possibility of one party giving much more than receiving. A power-based approach results in the dispute being resolved by determining who is able to force their desired outcome—who is stronger, has higher status, is able to coerce the other, or can force a concession from the other party. A power-based approach usually leads to distributive agreements that have the potential to escalate due to feelings of resentment and a desire for revenge (Brett, Shapiro, & Lytle, 1998; Lytle, Brett, & Shapiro, 1999; Tinsley, 1998, 2001). While either a rights-based or power-based approach can lead to concessions from the other party, rights-based concessions are usually evidenced when there is agreement about a standard, whereas power-based concessions reflect submission to a greater force.

In this model we use four categories of conflict management strategies: collaborating, avoiding, contending rights, and contending power. We do not consider conceding as a separate category because it is a reactive rather than proactive strategy that is often paired with contending. In the next section we explore the role that these conflict management strategies play, along with type of conflict and task uncertainty in our contingency model of conflict on group performance.

A CONTINGENCY PERSPECTIVE OF GROUP CONFLICT

This section develops the contingency model further. We begin by discussing the relationship between conflict at work and individual health and well-being because this relationship is the most straightforward within our model (cf. Figure 8.1). Subsequently, we discuss the relationship between task-related conflict and group effectiveness. We review research and summarize results using meta-analytic techniques. This review provides the input for the third and final part of this section, in which we advance hypotheses about the moderating role of conflict management strategies in high and in low complexity group tasks.

Conflict and Individual Well-being

Conflict is an emotional situation and elicits anger, disgust, and fear. Being in conflict threatens one's self-esteem and requires cognitive resources to cope with the situation. Negative emotions, threatened self-esteem, and heightened cognitive effort impact the physiological system in a multitude of ways: adrenaline levels go up, heartbeat accelerates, and muscle tension increases (Quick et al., 1997). Quite obviously, in the short run conflict and conflict interaction have rather negative consequences for individual health and well-being. When conflict is not resolved but persists over longer periods of time, serious health threats may result. Research suggests that enduring high levels of stress hormones deplete the physiological system and result in psychosomatic complaints including enduring headaches, upset stomach, and the like (Pennebaker, 1982). In addition, enduring conflict at work may increase alcohol intake, and trouble sleeping, which in turn affects the physical and psychic well-being of the individuals involved (Dana & Griffin, 1999).

The notion that enduring conflict at work may have serious consequences for individual health and well-being is supported by various studies. Spector and Jex (1998) summarize the findings of 13 samples involving over 3000 employees and find a positive and significant correlation between conflict at work and physical health complaints. A similar finding was reported in a more recent study by Spector, Chen, and O'Connell (2000). These authors measured conflict at work, anxiety, frustration, and physical complaints. Analyses revealed positive and moderate correlations between conflict at work and anxiety and frustration, and a small but significant correlation between conflict at work and physical complaints. This general pattern is substantiated in various other studies. For instance, Shirom and Mayer (1993) found a small but significant correlation between conflict and burnout among Israeli high-school teachers. Several other studies reported moderately positive correlations between conflict at work and the exhaustion dimension of burnout (e.g. Taylor et al., 1990; van Dierendonck, Schaufeli, & Buunk, 2001; van Dierendonck, Schaufeli, & Sixma, 1994).

Conflict at work not only affects overall stress levels, but translates into psychosomatic complaints. For instance, research has established positive relationships between conflict and psychosomatic complaints, including gastrointestinal symptoms (e.g. nausea, stomach cramps), respiratory symptoms (e.g. pressure on chest, hyperventilation), cardiac symptoms (e.g. rapid heart rate, pounding of heart), dizziness and fainting, headaches, and tingling sensations in the limbs (for reviews, see De Dreu, van Dierendonck, & De Best Waldhober, 2002; Spector & Jex, 1998). Finally, the relationship between conflict at work and stress appears to hold up also when task-related conflict is considered. In a study of 82 hospital staff members, Friedman et al. (2000) found that stress was positively related to task-related conflict. De Dreu, van Dierendonck, and De Best Waldhober (2002) reviewed some of their own (unpublished) research findings showing them to be consistent with Friedman et al., indicating the negative relationship between task-related conflict and stress is robust and generalizes to other organizations, including manufacturing organizations.

The work on conflict and individual health and well-being did not consider the distinction between task-content and task-process conflicts and this is an important area for future research. Task-process conflicts are associated with distribution and fairness to a greater extent than task-content conflicts (Harinck, De Dreu, & van Vianen, 2000), and injustice and violations of basic principles of fairness constitute major threats to individual health and well-being (van Dierendonck, Schaufeli, & Buunk, 1998). In other words, future research could test the hypothesis that task-process conflicts impact individual health and well-being more than task-content conflicts.

While the relationship between individual well-being and conflict management strategies has not been the focus of systematic research, several empirical studies exist. De Dreu, van Dierendonck, and De Best-Waldhober (2002) reviewed these studies, and concluded that a passive and obliging way of dealing with conflict has more negative consequences for health and individual well-being than a more proactive and collaborating approach to conflict. This conclusion is consistent with the idea that collaborating in conflict strengthens interpersonal relationships, and increases self-esteem, feelings of self-efficacy, and satisfaction (De Dreu, Weingart, & Kwon, 2000; Rubin, Pruitt, & Kim, 1994).

Before moving to a discussion about the relationships between conflict and group effectiveness, a word of caution is needed. Without exception, the work on conflict and individual health and well-being is cross-sectional and based on self-report. Although valid scales were used and results were consistent across studies, it cannot be excluded that reduced well-being produces conflict rather than the reverse. We need research using experimental or longitudinal designs to increase our confidence in these results. Also, we would benefit from going beyond self-reports as sole indicators of (deteriorated) health and well-being, and instead incorporate in future studies more objective measures of stress (e.g. hormone levels) and psychosomatic complaints (e.g. number of doctor visits and number of sick days). Finally, future research should focus on teasing apart task-content from task-process conflict.

Conflict and Group Effectiveness

As mentioned at the outset, conflict is inherent to groups and organizations and many see it as inherently bad. It has been argued, however, that there exists a curvilinear relationship between individual and group effectiveness and the level of conflict between individuals or within that group (Robbins, 1974; Walton, 1969). That is, it has been argued that some conflict is better than no conflict at all, and that some conflict is better than intense conflict. Consistent with this, research has shown that when conflict escalates and becomes very intense the social system shuts down and performance suffers badly (Jehn, 1995; Walton, 1969). On the other hand, research on groupthink (Janis, 1972) as well as studies on the role of devil's advocacy in group decision making (Schwenk, 1990) have shown that extreme concurrence seeking in groups (i.e. the avoidance of conflict) may lead to ineffective decision making with sometimes disastrous consequences. Defective decision making is, however, reduced when conflict is stimulated rather than suppressed (Nemeth, 1986; Turner & Pratkanis, 1997).

Table 8.1 Average correlations between task conflict and group performance

Amason & Mooney (2000)	−0.25
De Dreu & West (2001)	−0.21
Janssen, van de Vliert, & Veenstra (2000)	−0.27
Jehn (1994)	+0.38
Jehn & Mannix (2001)	−0.16
Friedman et al. (2000)	−0.39
Amason (1996)	−0.09
Jehn (1995)	−0.29
Jehn et al. (1999)	−0.11
Pelled, Eisenhardt, & Xin (1999)	+0.05
Porter & Lilly (1996)	−0.35
Effect size (Cohen's *d*)	−0.43
95% Confidence interval	−0.51/−0.35
Average *r*	−0.21***
Homogeneity Q_w	92.04***

Note: ***$p < 0.001$.

Table 8.1 uses meta-analytic techniques (Johnson, 1989) to summarize the findings from research published between 1994 and 2000 that considered task conflict as the independent variable and group effectiveness as the dependent variable. Most studies measured task conflict with a scale developed by Jehn (1995), but studies varied considerably in how group performance was assessed. Some studies used supervisor ratings of team effectiveness (e.g. Amason, 1996; Jehn, 1994), while others included objective performance measures such as average production per day (e.g. Jehn, 1995). Some studies reported multiple measures of group performance, in which case we took the correlation with the least objectionable performance measure (e.g. we preferred external source data to self-reports, and objective data to subjective assessments of performance).

As can be seen in Table 8.1, there is little evidence for the idea that task conflict has positive consequences for group performance. In fact, the average effect size (i.e. the average correlation, allowing for different sample sizes across the studies) between task conflict and group performance across all studies is negative, significantly different from zero, and moderate in size. Thus, when looking at the average effect sizes across published studies, we have to conclude that task conflict is detrimental to group performance. Interestingly, the variance in correlations between task conflict and group performance is large and significant (as indicated by the homogeneity measure, Q_w).

The large variation in effect size noted in Table 8.1 indicates that moderators of the relationship between task-related conflict and group effectiveness exist. One important moderator may be the way in which task conflict is managed. Weingart and Jehn (2000) have argued that the key to team effectiveness is collaboration. Open-minded debates may be particularly useful in task-content conflict where creativity and novel solutions are key to resolving a dispute. Collaboration is also related to integrative negotiation (Pruitt, 1998), which involves a problem-solving approach to settle divergent interests through substantial information exchange and logrolling (trading unimportant issues for important ones). Integrative negotiation may be particularly useful in task-process conflict where group members have opposing interests.

Some first evidence for the idea that collaboration is a prerequisite for task-related conflict to become productive (or at least not unproductive) comes from a study by Lovelace, Shapiro, and Weingart (2001). In a study of cross-functional new product development teams, they examined the effects of both collaborative (i.e. more objective and problem-focused) and contentious (i.e. emotional and personal) conflict communication on team performance. In general, task conflict was negatively related to team performance in terms of product innovation as well as budget and time constraint adherence. Results showed that teams that used collaborative communication did not suffer from the deleterious effect of conflict on innovation and constraint adherence. However, these collaborative teams did not enjoy any positive effects of conflict. They merely avoided the potential negative effects. Interestingly, contentious communication played a pivotal role in determining constraint adherence. Contentious communication greatly exacerbated the negative effect of task conflict on constraint adherence, to an even greater degree than collaborative communication eliminated the effect.

Additional evidence for the importance of collaboration in task-content conflict comes from a study by De Dreu and West (2001) on innovation in self-managed teams. They assessed, through questionnaires, the extent to which self-managed teams were characterized by task-content conflict (operationalized as minority dissent), as well as the extent to which the team members participated in the decision-making process—a proxy to collaboration. Results showed more innovations when minority dissent was high *and* teams had high levels of participation in decision making. This suggests, indeed, that task-content conflict may be beneficial provided that group members collaborate and participate in the decision-making process.

The results of these two studies are consistent with the results from an extensive program of research by Tjosvold and colleagues on constructive controversy (e.g. Tjosvold, 1991, 1997, 1998). This work reveals that when individuals with task conflict perceive their own and their conflict opponent's goals as cooperative and compatible, they are more likely to engage in "constructive controversy" and debate in an open-minded way about their opposing views, beliefs, and opinions. When, in contrast, they perceive their own and their opponent's goals as competitive and incompatible, they are unlikely to engage in constructive controversy and instead work hard to win from the other. Constructive controversy has been shown to result in stronger interpersonal relations, better and richer understanding of the issues under debate, and more effective employees and work teams.

Conflict Type and Task Uncertainty

Our review so far suggests that task-related conflict appears to require mutual problem solving and collaborating for groups to become effective. While incorporating conflict management strategies into the analysis may account for some of the variation in the relationship between conflict and group performance, additional moderators may exist. We suggest that in addition to conflict management strategies, task uncertainty and conflict type determine the effect of conflict on group performance.

The nature of the task at hand will partly determine whether conflict will be productive rather than dysfunctional. Research suggests that task uncertainty may play an important role. Provided that the group performs uncertain tasks in which standard solutions do not suffice, task conflict may be beneficial (Amason, 1996; De Dreu, 1997; Jehn, 1994,

1995, 1997; Turner & Pratkanis, 1997). The basic premise is that task conflict increases group members' tendency to scrutinize task issues and to engage in deep and deliberate processing of task-relevant information. This fosters learning and the development of new and sometimes highly creative insights, leading the group to become more effective and innovative (De Dreu & West, 2001).

Evidence of the moderating role of task uncertainty comes from a study of intensive care units, which suggests that diagnostic diversity (the array of medical and surgical cases admitted to the same ICU) moderates the effect of conflict management approach (conflict avoidance vs problem solving) on unit performance (Pearce et al., 2001). Pearce et al. (2001) found that in units facing lower diagnostic diversity, more conflict avoidance was associated with better performance (i.e. lower mortality rates, controlling for expected mortality rates), while more active problem solving was associated with worse performance. The performance of the units with high diagnostic diversity was not affected by the conflict management approach taken. It appears that conflict avoidance in units facing more homogeneous, but still complex, tasks may allow team members to focus on standard operating procedures (e.g. use of patient care protocols), thereby improving team performance (i.e. decreasing mortality rates).

It thus appears that task uncertainty matters in determining the effects of conflict management approaches on different types of conflict. High uncertainty tasks require the integration of large amounts of information, multiple perspectives, and many potential actions. These tasks require an active approach to both task-content and task-process conflict as a way to manage potentially contradictory desires and information, and therefore this conflict should not be avoided. Collaboration can be an ideal approach for resolving conflicts that occur when working on uncertain tasks.

In contrast, low uncertainty tasks involve more routine behavior and allow reliance on a set of well-learned, a priori established principles and working assumptions. Collaborating to resolve conflict on low uncertainty, clearly defined tasks only seems appropriate when the group has relied on erroneous assumptions and used the wrong heuristics in making judgements and decisions. Otherwise, intensive collaboration may lead the group to rediscover that their original assumptions and heuristics worked best. Indeed, research on the added value to group decision making of a devil's advocate has shown that task conflict induced by a devil's advocate is counterproductive when the group performs a routine task *and* proceeded on the basis of correct assumptions (Schwenk, 1990). In other words, approaching task-content conflicts with collaborating and creative problem solving is expected to be variable in its consequences for group effectiveness because it risks solving the wrong problem based on incorrect assumptions. Often, dealing with conflict about clearly defined tasks may be best settled through rights-based forms of contending. A rights-based approach shifts the focus to determining the appropriate standard, assumptions, or approach to the problem.

The efficacy of the different conflict management approaches also depends on whether the conflict is driven by scarce resources (a conflict of interest) or by differing opinions about optimal solutions with adequate resources available (a conflict of understanding). Task-process conflict often involves the allocation and distribution of scarce resources like time, money, or people. In this context, rights-based forms of contending may help the group deal with opposing interests regarding allocation in a fair and efficient way. In contrast, task-content conflict is often about verifiable issues, about a matter of taste, or about sacred values, and in such conflicts normative standards cannot be used and fairness principles do not apply (Druckman, 1994; Harinck, De Dreu, & van Vianen, 2000). Instead, parties need either a creative solution that bridges both sides, or one party needs to be truly and profoundly convinced of the superiority of the other party's position. In these task-content conflicts collaborating and creative problem solving may be key, and rights-based (or power-based) forms of contending are considered less optimal.

So far we have proposed independent effects of conflict type, conflict management approach, and task complexity on group performance. But some interesting joint effects occur when the moderators are considered simultaneously. For example, a collaborative approach, while ideal for *task*-content conflicts that are *complex*, might be less so when the conflict is about the *process* or the task is *simple* (where rights-based contention might be more appropriate). In contrast, the use of power, at one extreme, or avoidance, at the other, would be dysfunctional for any high complexity task (task or process conflict) and potentially of mixed effectiveness for low complexity tasks. Table 8.2 provides a look at the possible predictions that could be made when task uncertainty, task conflict type, and conflict management approach are considered together.

CONCLUSIONS AND AVENUES FOR FUTURE RESEARCH

The contingency perspective proposed in this chapter and summarized in Figure 8.1 is consistent with past research on conflict and group performance, yet also contains new elements and predictions that require empirical testing. In this section we summarize the main conclusions that derive from our review and theorizing, and we highlight some important areas for further research.

One first area for future work is to study the interactions between conflict type, conflict management, and individual health and well-being. While an increasing number of studies attests to the negative relationship between conflict at work and health parameters such as stress, psychosomatic complaints, and burnout, research is needed to examine the moderating role of conflict management and conflict type. Some initial evidence suggests that an active approach to conflict, including collaborating and contending, is more positive (or less negative) than a more passive strategy that involves conceding and avoiding. However, the cause–effect sequences need examination, and we need to know whether it matters whether the conflict is about content or process issues.

A second area for future research is to examine the moderating role of conflict management in task-content and task-process conflicts. We have argued that in highly complex tasks, collaborating and creative problem solving are highly effective in task-content conflicts, but that in task-process conflicts a rights-based form of contending may often settle the issue in an effective *and* efficient way. We based this speculation on indirect evidence, and research testing these hypotheses is needed.

At least in some instances, a focus on health rather than group performance leads to rather different prescriptions. For example, with regard to health it appears that collaborating is to be preferred regardless of the type of conflict, while with regard to group effectiveness rights-based forms of contending may be more effective than collaborating and creative problem solving, especially in task-process conflicts. This points to a potentially paradoxical situation group managers and team leaders may find themselves in—the need to stimulate group effectiveness requires a different approach to conflict than the need to safeguard individual health and well-being.

Table 8.2 Joint influence of type of conflict and conflict management approach on group performance when group tasks have high or low levels of uncertainty

		Collaborating	Contending		Avoiding
			Rights	Power	
Examples		Interests-based, problem solving, logrolling, informational influence	Rules, precedent, normative standards	Formal authority, status, coercion	
Task uncertainty	Conflict type				
High uncertainty	Task content	Ideal	Variable	Dysfunctional	Dysfunctional
	Task process	Variable	Ideal	Dysfunctional	Dysfunctional
Low uncertainty	Task content	Variable	Ideal	Variable	Variable
	Task process	Variable	Ideal	Variable	Variable

Despite the limitations noted, we believe the contingency approach provides a fruitful avenue for future research. We need to test the basic propositions that task type, type of conflict, and bases for dispute resolution interact to predict group performance. Such tests can be conducted in the laboratory as well as in the field with ongoing work teams. For instance, in the laboratory one can manipulate task type and prime different ways of dispute resolution. In ongoing work teams, long-term effects can be studied and nontask conflicts are more likely to emerge. In addition to testing the core relationships predicted by the contingency theory, research is needed to examine whether the type of group matters. That is, the question is whether the contingency perspective is equally valid in ongoing teams as in temporary, ad hoc teams that exist only to perform one specific task once.

The contingency perspective is in its infancy. However, it connects better with the general notion in the social sciences that human behavior is a function of the interaction between several key variables than the one-best-way approach to conflict and conflict management we often encounter in organizations, and sometimes in the academic literature. While much more research is needed, we can confidently reject the idea that collaborating is always good, and that conflict in work teams is always bad. The contingency perspective advanced here reveals that group conflict is a multifaceted phenomenon that requires tailor-made interventions that recognize that different types of conflict require different modes of dispute resolution.

ACKNOWLEDGEMENTS

This work was facilitated by a grant from the Carnegie Bosch Institute awarded to Laurie R. Weingart and Carsten K. W. De Dreu, and grant 490-22-173 of the Netherlands Foundation for Scientific Research awarded to Carsten K. W. De Dreu. We thank Dean Tjosvold and Michael A. West for providing us with comments on an earlier version of this chapter.

REFERENCES

Amason, A. C. (1996). Distinguishing the effects of functional and dysfunctional conflict on strategic decision making: resolving a paradox for top management groups. *Academy of Management Journal, 39*, 123–148.

Amason, A. C. & Mooney, A. C. (2000). Past performance as an antecedent of top management team conflict: the effects of financial condition on strategic decision making. *International Journal of Conflict Management, 10*, 340–359.

Arrow, K., Mnookin, R. H., Ross, L., Tversky, A., & Wilson, R. (1995). *Barriers to Dispute Resolution*. New York: Norton.

Blake, R. & Mouton, J. S. (1964). *The Managerial Grid*. Houston, Tex.: Gulf.

Brehmer, B. (1976). Social judgement theory and the analysis of interpersonal conflict. *Psychological Bulletin, 83*, 985–1003.

Brett, J. M., Shapiro, D. L., & Lytle, A. L. (1998). Breaking the bonds of reciprocity in negotiations. *Academy of Management Journal, 41*(4), 410–424.

Concise Oxford Dictionary (1983). Oxford, UK: Oxford University Press.

Dana, K. & Griffin, R. W. (1999). Health and well-being in the workplace: a review and synthesis of the literature. *Journal of Management, 25*, 357–384.

De Dreu, C. K. W. (1997). Productive conflict: the importance of conflict issue and conflict management. In C. K. W. De Dreu & E. van de Vliert (eds), *Using Conflict in Organizations* (pp. 9–22). London: Sage.

De Dreu, C. K. W., Evers, A., Beersma, B., Kluwer, E. S., & Nauta, A. (2001). Toward a theory-based measure of conflict behavior in the work place. *Journal of Organizational Behavior, 22*, 645–668.
De Dreu, C. K. W., Harinck, F., & van Vianen, A. E. M. (1999). Conflict and performance in groups and organizations. In C. L. Cooper & I. T. Robertson (eds), *International Review of Industrial and Organizational Psychology* (Vol. 14, pp. 376–405). Chichester: Wiley.
De Dreu, C. K. W., van Dierendonck, D., & De Best-Waldhober, M. (2002). Conflict at work and individual well-being. In M. J. Schabracq, Jac. Winnubst, & C. L. Cooper (eds), *International Handbook of Occupational and Health Psychology* (2nd edn). Chichester, UK: Wiley.
De Dreu, C. K. W. & van Vianen, A. E. M. (2001). Responses to relationship conflict and team effectiveness. *Journal of Organizational Behavior, 22*, 309–328.
De Dreu, C. K. W., Weingart, L. R., & Kwon, S. (2000). Influence of social motives in integrative negotiation: a meta-analytic review and test of two theories. *Journal of Personality and Social Psychology, 78*, 889–905.
De Dreu, C. K. W. & West, M. A. (2001). Minority dissent and team innovation: the importance of participation in decision making. *Journal of Applied Psychology, 86*, 1191–1201.
Deutsch, M. (1973). *The Resolution of Conflict: Constructive and Destructive Processes*. New Haven, Conn.: Yale University Press.
Druckman, D. (1994). Determinants of compromising behavior in negotiation. *Journal of Conflict Resolution, 38*, 507–556.
Friedman, R. A., Tidd, S. T., Currall, S. C., & Tsai, J. C. (2000). What goes around comes around: the impact of personal conflict style on work group conflict and stress. *International Journal of Conflict Management, 10*, 577–589.
Hackman, R. (1983). The design of effective work groups. In J. W. Lorsch (ed.), *Handbook of Organizational Behavior* (pp. 315–342). Englewood Cliffs, NJ: Prentice-Hall.
Hall, R. (1972). *Organizations, Structures, Processes, and Outcomes*. Englewood Cliffs, NJ: Prentice-Hall.
Harinck, F., De Dreu, C. K. W., & van Vianen, A. E. M. (2000). The impact of conflict issue on fixed-pie perceptions, problem solving, and integrative outcomes in negotiation. *Organizational Behavior and Human Decision Processes, 81*, 329–358.
Jaffee, D. (2000). *Organization Theory: Tension and Change*. New York: McGraw-Hill.
Janis, I. L. (1972). *Victims of Groupthink: A Psychological Study of Foreign-policy Decisions and Fiascos*. Boston: Houghton-Mifflin.
Janssen, O., van de Vliert, E., & Veenstra, C. (2000). How task and person conflict shape the role of positive interdependence in management groups. *Journal of Management, 25*, 117–141.
Jehn, K. (1994). Enhancing effectiveness: an investigation of advantages and disadvantages of value-based intragroup conflict. *International Journal of Conflict Management, 5*, 223–238.
Jehn, K. (1995). A multimethod examination of the benefits and detriments of intragroup conflict. *Administrative Science Quarterly, 40*, 256–282.
Jehn, K. (1997). A qualitative analysis of conflict types and dimensions in organizational groups. *Administrative Science Quarterly, 42*, 530–557.
Jehn, K. & Mannix, E. (2001). The dynamic nature of conflict: a longitudinal study of intragroup conflict and group performance. *Academy of Management Journal, 44*, 238–251.
Jehn, K., Chadwick, C., & Thatcher, S. M. B. (1997). To agree or not to agree: the effects of value congruence, individual demographic dissimilarity, and conflict on work group outcomes. *International Journal of Conflict Management, 8*, 287–305.
Johnson, B. T. (1989). *DSTAT: Software for the Meta-analytic Review of Research Literatures*. Hillsdale, NJ: Lawrence Erlbaum.
Katz, D. & Kahn, D. (1978). *The Social Psychology of Organizing*. New York: McGraw-Hill.
Kolb, D.M. & Bartunek, J. M. (eds) (1992). *Hidden Conflict in Organizations: Uncovering Behind-the-scenes Disputes*. London: Sage.
Levine, J. M. & Thompson, L. L. (1996). Conflict in groups. In E. T. Higgins & A. W. Kruglanski (eds), *Social Psychology: Handbook of Basic Principles* (pp. 745–776). New York: Guilford.
Lovelace, K., Shapiro, D. L., & Weingart, L. R. (2001). Maximizing cross-functional new product teams' innovativeness and constraint adherence: a conflict communications perspective. *Academy of Management Journal, 44*, 779–783.

Lytle, A. L., Brett, J. M., & Shapiro, D. L. (1999). The strategic use of interests, rights, and power to resolve disputes. *Negotiation Journal, 15*(1), 31–49.

McGrath, J. E. (1984). *Groups, Interaction and Performance*. Englewood Cliffs, NJ: Prentice-Hall.

Maslach, C. & Leiter, M. P. (1997). *The Truth about Burnout. How Organizations Cause Personal Stress and What to Do about it*. San Francisco: Jossey-Bass.

Murnighan, J. K. & Conlon, D. E. (1991). The dynamics of intense work groups: a study of British string quartets. *Administrative Science Quarterly, 36*, 165–186.

Nemeth, C. (1986). Differential contributions of majority and minority influence processes. *Psychological Review, 93*, 10–20.

O'Connor, K. M., Gruenfeld, D. H., & McGrath, J. E. (1993). The experience and effects of conflict in continuing work groups. *Small Group Research, 24*, 362–382.

Pearce, B. M., Rousseau, D. M., Shortell, S. M., & Gillies, R. R. (2001). Conflict management and group performance: how context alters the effects of problem solving and avoidance. Working paper, Heinz School of Public Policy and Management, Carnegie Mellon University.

Pelled, L. H., Eisenhardt, K. M., & Xin, K. R. (1999). Exploring the black box: an analysis of work group diversity, conflict, and performance. *Administrative Science Quarterly, 44*, 1–28.

Pennebaker, J. W. (1982). *The Psychology of Physical Symptoms*. New York: Springer-Verlag.

Perrow, C. (1967). A framework for the comparative analysis of organizations. *American Sociological Review, 32*, 194–208.

Pondy, L. (1967). Organizational conflict: concepts and models. *Administrative Science Quarterly, 17*, 296–320.

Porter, T. & Lilly, B. (1996). The effects of conflict, trust, and task commitment on project team performance. *International Journal of Conflict Management, 1*(4), 361–376.

Pruitt, D. G. (1998). Social conflict. In D. Gilbert, S. T. Fiske, & G. Lindzey (eds), *Handbook of Social Psychology* (4th edn, Vol. 2, pp. 89–150). New York: McGraw-Hill.

Pruitt, D. G. & Rubin, J. Z. (1986). *Social Conflict: Escalation, Stalemate, and Settlement*. New York: Random House.

Quick, J. C., Quick, J. D., Nelson, D. L., & Hurrel, J. J. (1997). *Preventive Stress Management in Organizations*. Washington, DC: American Psychological Association.

Robbins, S. P. (1974). *Managing Organizational Conflict: A Nontraditional Approach*. Englewood Cliffs, NJ: Prentice-Hall.

Rubin, J., Pruitt, D. G., & Kim, S. (1994). *Social Conflict: Escalation: Stalemate and Settlement*. New York: McGraw-Hill.

Schwenk, C. R. (1990). Effects of devil's advocacy and dialectical inquiry on decision making: a meta-analysis. *Organizational Behavior and Human Decision Processes, 47*, 161–176.

Shirom, A. & Mayer, A. (1993). Stress and strain among union lay officials and rank-and-file members. *Journal of Organizational Behavior, 14*, 401–413.

Slaikeu, K. A. & Hasson, R. H. (1998). *Controlling the Cost of Conflict*. San Francisco: Jossey-Bass.

Spector, P. E., Chen, P. Y., & O'Connell, B. J. (2000). A longitudinal study of relations between job stressors and job strains while controlling for prior negative affectivity and strains. *Journal of Applied Psychology, 85*, 211–218.

Spector, P. E. & Jex, S. M. (1998). Development of four self-report measures of job stressors and strain: Interpersonal Conflict at Work Scale, Organizational Constraints Scale, Quantitative Workload Inventory, and Physical Symptoms Inventory. *Journal of Occupational Health Psychology, 3*, 356–367.

Steiner, I. D. (1972). *Group Processes and Productivity*. New York: Academic Press.

Stone, D., Patton, B., & Heen, S. (1999). *Difficult Conversations*. New York: Viking.

Taylor, A., Daniel, J. V., Leith, L., & Burke, R. J. (1990). Perceived stress, psychological burnout and paths to turnover intentions among sport officials. *Applied Sport Psychology, 2*, 84–97.

Thomas, K. W. (1992). Conflict and negotiation processes in organizations. In M. D. Dunnette & L. M. Hough (eds), *Handbook of Industrial and Organizational Psychology* (2nd edn, pp. 651–717). Palo Alto, Calif.: Consulting Psychologists Press.

Tinsley, C. H. (1998). Models of conflict resolution in Japanese, German, and American cultures. *Journal of Applied Psychology, 83*, 316–323.

Tinsley, C. H. (2001). How negotiators get to yes: predicting the constellation of strategies used across cultures to negotiate conflict. *Journal of Applied Psychology, 86*, 583–593.

Tjosvold, D. (1991). *The Conflict-positive Organization*. Reading, Mass.: Addison-Wesley.
Tjosvold, D. (1997). Conflict within interdependence: its value for productivity and individuality. In C. K. W. De Dreu and E. van de Vliert (eds), *Using Conflict in Organisations* (pp. 23–37). London: Sage.
Tjosvold, D. (1998). Cooperative and competitive goal approaches to conflict: accomplishments and challenges. *Applied Psychology: An International Review, 47*, 285–342.
Turner, M. E. & Pratkanis, A. (1997). Mitigating groupthink by stimulating constructive conflict. In C. K. W. De Dreu and E. van de Vliert (eds), *Using Conflict in Organizations* (pp. 53–71). London: Sage.
Ury, W. L., Brett, J. M., & Goldberg, S. B. (1993). *Getting Disputes Resolved: Designing Systems to Cut the Costs of Conflict*. Cambridge, Mass.: PON.
Van de Ven, A. H., Delbecq, A. L., & Koenig, R. (1976). Determinants of coordination modes within organizations. *American Sociological Review, 41*(2), 322–338.
Van de Vliert, E. (1997). *Complex Interpersonal Conflict Behaviour*. Hove, UK: Psychology Press.
Van Dierendonck, D., Schaufeli, W., & Buunk, B. (1998). The evaluation of an individual burnout intervention program: the role of inequity and social support. *Journal of Applied Psychology, 83*, 392–407.
Van Dierendonck, D., Schaufeli, W. B., & Buunk, B. P. (2001). Toward a process model of burnout. Results from a secondary analysis. *European Journal of Work and Organizational Psychology, 10*, 41–52.
Van Dierendonck, D., Schaufeli, W. B., & Sixma, H. (1994). Burnout among general practitioners: a perspective from equity theory. *Journal of Social and Clinical Psychology, 13*, 86–100.
Wall, J. & Callister, R. (1995). Conflict and its management. *Journal of Management, 21*, 515–558.
Walton, R. E. (1969). *Interpersonal Peacemaking: Confrontations and Third Party Consultation*. Reading, Mass.: Addison-Wesley.
Warr, P. (1987). *Work, Unemployment and Mental Health*. Oxford, UK: Clarendon.
Weingart, L. R. & Jehn, K. A. (2000). Manage intra-team conflict through collaboration. In E. A. Locke (ed.), *The Blackwell Handbook of Principles of Organizational Behavior* (pp. 226–238). Oxford, UK: Blackwell Publishers.
West, M. A., Borrill, C. S., & Unsworth, K. (1998). Team effectiveness in organizations. In C. L. Cooper & I. T. Robertson (eds), *International Review of Industrial and Organizational Psychology* (Vol. 13, pp. 1–48). Chichester: Wiley.

9

TRAINING FOR COOPERATIVE GROUP WORK

David W. Johnson and Roger T. Johnson

INTRODUCTION

There are few skills more essential for the modern organization than the ability to work effectively in groups. The practical aspects of group work are directly based on both theory and research. In this chapter the nature of social interdependence theory and cooperative group work are defined, a meta-analysis of the research on cooperation among adults is presented, the essential elements of cooperation are discussed, and the factors that enhance the effectiveness of cooperation are presented. Group members must be quite skilled in creating and maintaining cooperation if they are to realize the advantages of collaborative efforts.

COOPERATIVE GROUP WORK

In order to discuss the need to train individuals to work effectively in cooperative groups, it is first necessary to define cooperation. By far the most important theory dealing with co-operation is social interdependence theory. *Social interdependence* exists when individuals share common goals and each individual's outcomes are affected by the actions of the others (Deutsch, 1949, 1962; Johnson & Johnson, 1989; Tjosvold, 1986). It may be differentiated from *social dependence* (i.e. the outcomes of one person are affected by the actions of a second person but not vice versa) and *social independence* (i.e. individuals' outcomes are unaffected by each other's actions). There are two types of social interdependence: cooperative and competitive. The absence of social interdependence and dependence results in individualistic efforts.

Cooperation exists when individuals work together to accomplish shared goals (Deutsch, 1949, 1962; Johnson & Johnson, 1989). When a situation is structured cooperatively, individuals' goal achievements are positively correlated; individuals perceive that they can reach

International Handbook of Organizational Teamwork and Cooperative Working. Edited by M. A. West, D. Tjosvold, and K. G. Smith.

their goals if and only if the others in the group also reach their goals. Thus, individuals seek outcomes that are beneficial to all those with whom they are cooperatively linked. *Competition* exists when individuals work against each other to achieve a goal that only one or a few can attain (Deutsch, 1949, 1962; Johnson & Johnson, 1989). When a situation is structured competitively, individuals' goal achievements are negatively correlated; each individual perceives that when one person achieves his or her goal, all others with whom he or she is competitively linked fail to achieve their goals. Thus, individuals seek an outcome that is personally beneficial but detrimental to all others in the situation. Finally, *individualistic efforts* exist when each individual works by him- or herself to accomplish goals unrelated to the goals of others (Deutsch, 1962; Johnson & Johnson, 1989). When a situation is structured individualistically, there is no correlation among participants' goal attainments. Each individual perceives that he or she can reach his or her goal regardless of whether other individuals attain or do not attain their goals. Thus, individuals seek an outcome that is personally beneficial without concern for the outcomes of others.

The *basic premise* of social interdependence theory is that the type of interdependence structured in a situation determines how individuals interact with each other which, in turn, determines outcomes (Deutsch, 1949, 1962; Johnson & Johnson, 1989). Positive interdependence tends to result in promotive interaction, negative interdependence tends to result in oppositional or contrient interaction, and no interdependence results in an absence of interaction. Depending on whether individuals promote or obstruct each other's goal accomplishments, there is *substitutability* (i.e. the actions of one person substitute for the actions of another), *cathexis* (i.e. the investment of psychological energy in objects and events outside of oneself), and *inducibility* (i.e openness to influence) (Deutsch, 1949). In cooperative situations, the actions of participants substitute for each other, participants positively cathect to each other's effective actions, and there is high inducibility among participants. In competitive situations, the actions of participants do not substitute for each other, participants negatively cathect to each other's effective actions, and inducibility is low. When there is no interaction, there is no substitutability, cathexis, or inducibility. The relationship between the type of social interdependence and the interaction pattern it elicits is bidirectional. Each may cause the other.

OUTCOMES OF COOPERATIVE GROUP WORK

There are hundreds of studies conducted during the last 100 years on the effectiveness of cooperative group work compared with competitive and individualistic efforts (Johnson & Johnson, 1989). The numerous dependent variables studied may be subsumed in three broad and interrelated outcomes (Johnson & Johnson, 1989): effort to achieve, quality of relationships, and psychological health.

Effort to Achieve

Over the past 100 years over 375 studies have been conducted on the relative impact of cooperative, competitive, and individualistic efforts on productivity and achievement (Johnson & Johnson, 1989). Of those studies, 165 measured performance of adults (individuals 18 years and older). The studies on adults focused on two questions:

1. Do groups outperform individuals? In these studies, group performance was compared with the performance of individuals working alone competitively or individualistically (group performance was the dependent measure).
2. Do individuals working in groups outperform individuals working alone? In these studies, the performance of individual group members was compared with the performance of individuals working alone competitively or individualistically (individual performance was the dependent measure).

GROUPS VS INDIVIDUALS

Since 1928 over 57 studies have compared the relative effectiveness of groups and individual efforts (see Table 9.1). The majority of these studies were conducted before 1970. Group efforts resulted in higher group productivity than did individual efforts structured either competitively or individualistically (effect sizes of 0.63 and 0.94 respectively). When only the methodologically high-quality studies were included in the analysis, group efforts were still more effective than competitive or individualistic efforts (effect sizes of 0.96 and 0.66 respectively). Groups tend to perform higher, make better decisions, and solve problems better than do individuals.

The studies used a wide variety of tasks (see Table 9.2). The tasks were classified into those that required verbal skills to complete (such as reading, writing, and orally presenting), mathematical skills to complete, or procedural skills to present (such as sports like swimming, golf, and tennis). When the results were analyzed for type of task, groups outperformed individual efforts structured competitively and individualistically on verbal tasks (effect sizes = 0.73 and 1.47 respectively), on mathematical tasks (effect sizes = 0.26 and 0.86 respectively), and on procedural tasks (effect sizes = 1.37 and 0.95 respectively). From these results it may be concluded that group efforts promoted higher group performance than did individual efforts on all three types of tasks. There is reason to believe, however,

Table 9.1 Achievement

Conditions	Effect size	Standard deviation	Cases
Group performance			
Cooperation vs competition	0.63	0.98	16
Cooperation vs individualistic	0.94	1.34	34
Competitive vs individualistic	−0.66	0.00	1
High-quality studies			
Cooperation vs competition	0.96	0.88	10
Cooperation vs individualistic	0.66	0.68	19
Competitive vs individualistic	−0.66	0.00	1
Individual performance			
Cooperation vs competition	0.54	0.86	29
Cooperation vs individualistic	0.41	0.43	52
Competitive vs individualistic	0.63	0.77	13
High-quality studies			
Cooperation vs competition	0.61	0.99	9
Cooperation vs individualistic	0.35	0.35	31
Competitive vs individualistic	0.34	0.80	7

Table 9.2 Type of task

Conditions	Effect size	Standard deviation	Cases
Group performance			
Cooperative vs competitive			
Verbal	0.73	0.22	3
Math	0.26	0.86	9
Procedural	1.37	1.29	4
Rote/decoding	0.00	0.00	0
Cooperative vs individualistic			
Verbal	1.47	1.37	8
Math	0.86	1.41	21
Procedural	0.95	0.29	2
Rote/decoding	0.00	0.00	0
Individual performance			
Cooperative vs competitive			
Verbal	0.36	0.35	29
Math	0.45	0.52	17
Procedural	0.95	0.29	2
Rote/decoding	0.00	0.00	0
Cooperative vs individualistic			
Verbal	0.66	0.68	19
Math	1.32	1.90	14
Procedural	1.06	0.00	1
Rote/decoding	0.00	0.00	0

that on brainstorming tasks individuals may do just as well as groups (Johnson & Johnson, 2000a).

GROUP MEMBERS VS INDIVIDUALS

Over 120 studies have compared the relative efficacy of group and individual efforts on individual performance. While the first study was conducted in 1924, 70 percent of the studies have been conducted since 1970. In these studies, working in a group resulted in higher individual performance than did working alone competitively or individualistically (effect sizes of 0.54 and 0.51 respectively). When only the methodologically high-quality studies were included, working in a group still promoted greater individual productivity than did competitive or individualistic efforts (effect sizes of 0.61 and 0.35 respectively). These results indicated that there was greater group-to-individual transfer than there was individual-to-individual transfer. Hagman and Hayes (1986) conducted two studies in which they demonstrated that the superiority of group-to-individual transfer over individual-to-individual transfer increased as participants worked toward a group (as opposed to an individual) reward and as the size of the group got smaller. Groups in which members (a) interacted with each other and discussed the material being learned and (b) received a group reward, had the greatest amount of group-to-individual transfer. In a study involving children as participants, learning in a group resulted in greater individual transfer than did learning as an individual for complex higher-level tasks, but not for simple lower-level tasks (Gabbert, Johnson, & Johnson, 1986). In a recent study, Jensen, Johnson, and Johnson (in press) had college students take a series of quizzes and biweekly examinations. Students were randomly assigned to conditions. Students who took the quizzes in small groups achieved higher on the subsequent biweekly examinations taken individually than did students who took the quizzes alone.

When the results were analyzed for type of task, individuals working in groups outperformed individuals working alone competitively or individualistically on verbal tasks (effect sizes = 0.36 and 0.66 respectively), on mathematical tasks (effect sizes = 0.45 and 1.32 respectively), and on procedural tasks (effect sizes = 0.95 and 1.06 respectively). From these results it may be concluded that working in a group promoted higher individual proficiency and knowledge than did working alone competitively or individualistically on all three types of tasks.

Positive Relationships and Social Support

GROUPS VS INDIVIDUALS

Since the 1940s there have been over 22 studies on group performance in which the quality of relationships among individuals was examined. Within groups, there tends to be greater

Table 9.3 Results for interpersonal attraction, social support, and self-esteem

Conditions	Mean	Standard deviation	Cases
Group performance			
Interpersonal attraction			
Cooperation vs competition	0.64	0.51	14
Cooperation vs individualistic	0.39	0.97	7
Competitive vs individualistic	0.70	0.00	1
Social support			
Cooperation vs competition	0.13	0.59	10
Cooperation vs individualistic	0.38	0.37	5
Competitive vs individualistic	−0.30	0.00	1
Self-esteem			
Cooperation vs competition	0.86	1.70	6
Cooperation vs individualistic	0.68	0.00	1
Competitive vs individualistic	0.21	0.00	1
Individual performance			
Interpersonal attraction			
Cooperation vs competition	0.68	0.54	57
Cooperation vs individualistic	0.55	0.62	31
Competitive vs individualistic	−0.04	0.96	7
Social support			
Cooperation vs competition	0.60	0.43	54
Cooperation vs individualistic	0.51	0.39	35
Competitive vs individualistic	−0.29	0.32	11
Self-esteem			
Cooperation vs competition	0.47	0.40	39
Cooperation vs individualistic	0.29	0.41	24
Competitive vs individualistic	−0.35	0.37	14

interpersonal attraction than among individuals working competitively (effect size = 0.64) or individualistically (effect size = 0.39).

In addition to liking, relationships among individuals may be characterized by social support. *Social support* involves the exchange of resources intended to enhance mutual well-being and the existence and availability of people on whom one can rely for emotional, instrumental, informational, and appraisal aid. The studies focusing on group performance found that cooperation promoted greater social support than did individualistic (effect size = 0.38) efforts, but surprisingly, the difference between cooperative and competitive efforts (effect size = 0.13) was lower than one would expect.

GROUP MEMBERS VS INDIVIDUALS

Since the 1940s, there have been 95 studies on the performance of individual group members in which the quality of relationships among individuals was examined. Individual group members liked each other better than did individuals working alone competitively (effect size = 0.68) or individualistically (effect size = 0.55).

In the studies focusing on individual performance of individuals, group efforts promoted greater social support than did individual efforts structured competitively (effect size = 0.60) or individualistically (effect size = 0.51).

Psychological Health and Self-esteem

PSYCHOLOGICAL HEALTH

Several studies have directly measured the relationship between social interdependence and psychological health (Crandall, 1982; Hayes, 1976; James & Johnson, 1983; James & Johnson, 1988; Johnson, Johnson, & Krotee, 1986; Johnson & Norem-Hebeisen, 1977; Norem-Hebeisen et al., 1984). The samples studied included university individuals, older adults, suburban high-school seniors, juvenile and adult prisoners, step-couples, and Olympic hockey players. The results indicate that cooperative attitudes are highly correlated with a wide variety of indices of psychological health, competitiveness was in some cases positively and in some cases negatively related to psychological health, and individualistic attitudes were negatively related to a wide variety of indices of psychological health.

SELF-ESTEEM

In regard to self-esteem, the studies focusing on group productivity found that group efforts promoted higher self-esteem than did competitive (effect size = 0.86) or individualistic (effect size = 0.68) efforts. The studies focusing on individual proficiency found that individuals working in groups had higher self-esteem than did individuals working alone competitively (effect size = 0.47) or individualistically (effect size = 0.29). Not only is the level of self-esteem affected by being part of a group effort, but the process by which individuals make judgments about their self-worth is also. Norem-Hebeisen and Johnson (1981) conducted four studies involving 821 white, middle-class, high-school seniors in a midwestern suburban community. They found that cooperative experiences promoted basic self-acceptance, freedom from conditional acceptance, and seeing oneself positively compared to peers. Competitive experiences were related to conditional self-acceptance and individualistic attitudes were related to basic self-rejection, including anxiety about relating to other people. Cooperative, group-based experiences seem to result in (a) the internalizing perceptions that one is known, accepted, and liked as one is, (b) internalizing mutual success, and (c) developing multidimensional views of self and others that allow for positive self-perceptions (Johnson & Johnson, 1989).

ENSURING GROUP WORK IS COOPERATIVE: THE BASIC ELEMENTS OF COOPERATION

Potential Group Performance

Not all groups are effective (Johnson & Johnson, 2000a). Placing people in the same room, seating them together, telling them they are a group, and advising them to "work together," does not mean they will work together effectively. Project groups, lab groups, committees, task forces, departments, and councils are groups, but they are not necessarily effective. Many groups are ineffective and some are even destructive. Almost everyone has been part of a group that has wasted time, was inefficient, and generally produced poor work. Ineffective and destructive groups are characterized by a number of dynamics (Johnson & Johnson, 2000a), such as social loafing, free-riding, group immaturity, uncritically and quickly accepting members' dominant response, and group-think. Such hindering factors are eliminated by carefully structuring the five essential elements of cooperation. Those elements are positive interdependence, face-to-face promotive interaction, individual and group accountability, appropriate use of social skills, and group processing.

Positive Interdependence: We Instead of Me

The first and most important set of competencies needed for cooperative group work is establishing and strengthening positive interdependence. *Positive interdependence* exists when one perceives that one is linked with others in a way so that one cannot succeed unless they do (and vice versa) and/or that one must coordinate one's efforts with the efforts of others to complete a task (Deutsch, 1962; Johnson & Johnson, 1989). Effective groups begin with structuring positive interdependence. Group members have to know that they "sink or swim together," that is, they have two responsibilities: to maximize their own productivity and to maximize the productivity of all other group members. There are two major categories of interdependence: outcome interdependence and means interdependence (Johnson & Johnson, 1989). When persons are in a cooperative or competitive situation, they are oriented toward a desired outcome, end state, goal, or reward. If there is no outcome interdependence (goal and reward interdependence), there is no cooperation or competition. In addition, the means through which the mutual goals or rewards are to be accomplished specify the actions required on the part of group members. Means interdependence includes resource, role, and task interdependence (which are overlapping and not independent from each other).

Positive interdependence has numerous effects on individuals' motivation and productivity, not the least of which is highlight the fact that the efforts of all group members are needed for group success. When members of a group see their efforts as dispensable for the group's success, they may reduce their efforts (Kerr, 1983; Kerr & Bruun, 1983; Sweeney, 1973). When group members perceive their potential contribution to the group as being unique they increase their efforts (Harkins & Petty, 1982). When goal, task, resource, and role interdependence are clearly understood, individuals realize that their efforts are required in order for the group to succeed (i.e. there can be no "free-riders") and that their contributions are often unique.

A series of research studies were conducted to clarify the impact of positive interdependence on achievement. The results indicate that:

1. Group membership in and of itself does not seem sufficient to produce higher achievement and productivity—positive interdependence is also required (Hwong et al., 1993). Knowing that one's performance affects the success of group mates seems to create "responsibility forces" that increase one's efforts to achieve.
2. Interpersonal interaction is insufficient to increase productivity—positive interdependence is also required (Lew et al., 1986a, b; Mesch, Johnson, & Johnson, 1988; Mesch et al., 1986). Individuals achieved higher under positive goal interdependence than when they worked individualistically but had the opportunity to interact with classmates.
3. Goal and reward interdependence seem to be additive (Lew et al., 1986a, b; Mesch, Johnson, & Johnson, 1988; Mesch et al., 1986). While positive goal interdependence is sufficient to produce higher achievement and productivity than individualistic efforts, the combination of goal and reward interdependence is even more effective.
4. Both working to achieve a reward and working to avoid the loss of a reward produced higher achievement than did individualistic efforts (Frank, 1984). There is no significant difference between the working to achieve a reward and working to avoid a loss.
5. Goal interdependence promotes higher achievement and greater productivity than does resource interdependence (Johnson et al., 1991).
6. Resource interdependence by itself may decrease achievement and productivity compared with individualistic efforts (Johnson et al., 1990; Ortiz, Johnson, & Johnson, 1996).
7. The combination of goal and resource interdependence increased achievement more than goal interdependence alone or individualistic efforts (Johnson et al., 1990; Ortiz, Johnson, & Johnson, 1996).
8. Positive interdependence does more than simply motivate individuals to try harder, it facilitates the development of new insights and discoveries through promotive interaction (Gabbert, Johnson, & Johnson, 1986; Johnson & Johnson, 1981; Johnson, Skon, & Johnson, 1980; Skon, Johnson, & Johnson, 1981). Members of cooperative groups use higher-level reasoning strategies more frequently than do individuals working individualistically or competitively.
9. The more complex the procedures involved in interdependence, the longer it will take group members to reach their full levels of productivity (Ortiz, Johnson, & Johnson, 1996). The more complex the group work procedures, the more members have to attend to group work and the less time they have to attend to task work. Once the group work procedures are mastered, however, members concentrate on task work and outperform individuals working alone.

Individual Accountability/Personal Responsibility

The second set of competencies needed for cooperative group work is establishing and strengthening individual and group accountability. *Group accountability* exists when the overall performance of the group is assessed and the results are given back to all group members to compare against a standard of performance. *Individual accountability* exists when the performance of individual students is assessed, the results are given back to the individual and the group, and the member is held responsible by group mates for contributing his or her fair share to the group's success. It is important that the group knows who needs more assistance, support, and encouragement in completing their share of the work. It is also important that group members know they cannot "hitchhike" on the work of others. Group members tend to reduce their contributions to goal achievement when it is difficult to identify members' contributions, there is an increased likelihood of redundant efforts, there is a lack of group cohesiveness, and there is lessened responsibility for the final outcome (Harkins & Petty, 1982; Ingham et al., 1974; Kerr & Bruun, 1981; Latane, Williams & Harkins, 1979; Moede, 1927; Petty et al., 1977; Williams, 1981; Williams, Harkins, & Latane, 1981). The higher the individual accountability, the clearer the contributions of each member, the less members' efforts are redundant, the more every member is responsible for the final outcome, and the more cohesive the group. Under such conditions, the social loafing effect vanishes. The smaller the size of the group, in addition, the greater the individual accountability may be (Messick & Brewer, 1983).

Archer-Kath, Johnson, and Johnson (1994) investigated whether or not positive interdependence and individual accountability are two separate and independent dimensions. They compared the impact of feedback to the learning group as a whole with the individual feedback to each member on achievement, attitudes, and behavior in cooperative learning groups. Individuals received either individual or group feedback in written graph/chart form only on how frequently members engaged in the targeted behaviors. If individual accountability and positive interdependence are unrelated, no differences should be found in perceived positive interdependence between conditions. If they are related, individuals in the individual feedback condition should perceive more positive interdependence than individuals in the group feedback condition. Individual feedback resulted in greater perceptions of cooperation, goal interdependence, and resource interdependence than did group feedback, indicating that positive interdependence and individual accountability are related, and by increasing individual accountability perceived interdependence among group members may also be increased.

Promotive (Face-to-face) Interaction

The third set of competencies needed for cooperative group work is establishing and strengthening promotive interaction among group members. *Promotive interaction* exists when individuals encourage and facilitate each other's efforts to complete tasks and achieve the group's goals. In order to promote each other's success, group members (a) help and assist each other, (b) exchange needed resources such as information and materials, (c) provide each other with feedback, (d) challenge each other's conclusions and reasoning, (e) advocate working harder to achieve the group's goals, (f) influence each other, and (g) act in trusting and trustworthy ways (Johnson & Johnson, 1989). The amount of research documenting the impact of promotive interaction on achievement is too voluminous to review here. Interested readers are referred to Johnson and Johnson (1989).

Social Skills

The fourth set of competencies needed for cooperative group work is appropriately engaging in small group and interpersonal skills. Placing socially unskilled individuals in a group and telling them to cooperate will obviously not be successful. Individuals must be taught the interpersonal and small group skills needed for high-quality cooperation, and be motivated to use them. To coordinate efforts to achieve mutual goals, individuals must master the interpersonal skills of:

(a) getting to know and trust each other;
(b) communicating accurately and unambiguously;
(c) accepting and supporting each other;
(d) resolving conflicts constructively (Johnson, 2000).

Individuals must also master the group skills:

(a) ensuring each member is committed to clear mutual goals that highlight members' interdependence;
(b) ensuring accurate and complete communication among members;
(c) providing leadership and appropriate influence;
(d) flexibly using decision-making procedures that ensure all alternative courses of action receive a fair and complete hearing and each other's reasoning and conclusions are challenged and critically analyzed;
(e) resolving their conflicts constructively (Johnson & Johnson, 2000a).

Interpersonal and small group skills form the basic nexus among individuals, and if individuals are to work together productively and cope with the stresses and strains of doing so, they must have a modicum of these skills.

In their studies on the long-term implementation of cooperation, Marvin Lew and Debra Mesch (Lew et al., 1986a, b; Mesch, Johnson, & Johnson, 1988; Mesch et al., 1986) investigated the impact of a reward contingency for using social skills as well as positive interdependence and a contingency for individual productivity on performance within cooperative groups. In the cooperative skills conditions, individuals were trained weekly in four social skills and each member of a cooperative group was given two bonus points toward the quiz grade if all group members were observed by the teacher to demonstrate three out of four cooperative skills. The results indicated that the combination of positive goal interdependence, an academic contingency for high performance by all group members, and a social skills contingency, promoted the highest achievement.

Archer-Kath, Johnson, and Johnson (1994) trained individuals in the social skills of praising, supporting, asking for information, giving information, asking for help, and giving help. Individuals received either individual or group feedback in written graph/chart form on how frequently members engaged in the targeted behaviors. The researchers found that giving individuals individual feedback on how frequently they engaged in targeted social skills was more effective in increasing individuals' achievement than was group feedback. The more socially skillful individuals are, the more attention teachers pay to teaching and rewarding the use of social skills, and the more individual feedback individuals receive on their use of the skills, the higher the individual performance that can be expected within cooperative groups.

Not only do social skills promote higher productivity, they contribute to building more positive relationships among group members. Putnam et al. (1989) demonstrated that, when individuals were taught social skills, were observed by their superior, and were given individual feedback as to how frequently they engaged in the skills, their relationships became more positive.

Group Processing

The fifth set of competencies needed for cooperative group work is engaging in group processing. In order to achieve, individuals in cooperative groups have to work together effectively. Effective group work is influenced by whether or not groups periodically reflect on how well they are functioning and how they may improve their work processes. A *process* is an identifiable sequence of events taking place over time, and *process goals* refer to the sequence of events instrumental in achieving outcome goals. *Group processing* may be defined as reflecting on a group session to (a) describe what member actions were helpful and unhelpful in achieving the group's goals and ensuring members work together effectively and (b) make decisions about what actions to continue or change.

Yager, Johnson, and Johnson (1985) examined the impact on productivity of (a) cooperative groups in which members discussed how well their group was functioning and how they could improve its effectiveness, (b) cooperative groups without any group processing, and (c) individualistic efforts. The results indicate that the high-, medium-, and low-achieving individuals in the cooperation with group processing condition performed higher on daily achievement, post-instructional achievement, and retention measures than did the individuals in the other two conditions. Individuals in the cooperation without group processing condition, furthermore, achieved higher on all three measures than did the individuals in the individualistic condition.

Putnam et al. (1989) conducted a study in which there were two conditions: cooperative groups with social skills training and group processing and cooperative groups without social skills training and group processing. Forty-eight fifth-grade individuals (32 nonhandicapped and 16 individuals with IQs ranging from 35 to 52) participated in the study. In the cooperative groups with social skills training condition the teacher gave individuals examples of specific cooperative behaviors to engage in, observed how frequently individuals engaged in the skills, gave individuals feedback as to how well they worked together, and had individuals discuss for five minutes how to use the skills more effectively in the future. In the uninstructed cooperative groups condition individuals were placed in cooperative groups and worked together for the same period of time with the same amount of teacher intervention (aimed at the academic lesson and unrelated to working together skillfully). Both nonhandicapped and handicapped individuals were randomly assigned to each condition. They found more positive relationships developed between handicapped and nonhandicapped individuals in the cooperative skills condition and that these positive relationships carried over to post-instructional free-time situations.

Johnson et al. (1990) conducted a study comparing cooperative groups with no processing, cooperative groups with teacher processing (teacher specified cooperative skills to use, observed, and gave whole class feedback as to how well individuals were using the skills), cooperative groups with teacher and individual processing (teacher specified cooperative skills to use, observed, gave whole class feedback as to how well individuals were using the skills, and had groups discuss how well they interacted as a group), and individualistic efforts. Forty-nine high-ability Black American high-school seniors and entering college freshmen at Xavier University participated in the study. A complex computer-assisted problem-solving assignment was given to all individuals. All three cooperative conditions performed higher than did the individualistic condition. The combination of teacher and individual processing resulted in greater problem-solving success than did the other cooperative conditions.

Archer-Kath, Johnson, and Johnson (1994) provided cooperative groups with either individual or group feedback on how frequently members had engaged in targeted social skills. Each group had five minutes at the beginning of each session to discuss how well the group was functioning and what could be done to improve the group's effectiveness. Group processing with individual feedback was more effective than was group processing with whole group feedback in increasing individuals' (a) achievement motivation, actual achievement, uniformity of achievement among group members, and influence toward higher achievement within cooperative groups, (b) positive relationships among group members and between individuals and the teacher, and (c) self-esteem and positive attitudes toward the subject area.

The results of these studies indicated that engaging in group processing clarifies and improves the effectiveness of the members in contributing to the achievement of the group's goals, especially when specific social skills are targeted and individuals receive individual feedback as to how frequently and how well they engaged in the skills.

ENHANCING VARIABLES: TRUST AND CONFLICT

During the 1950s and 1960s, Deutsch (1962, 1973) researched two aspects of the internal dynamics of cooperative groups that potentially enhanced outcomes: trust and conflict.

Trust

The sixth set of competencies needed for cooperative group work is establishing and maintaining a high level of trust. Trust includes:

(a) the awareness that beneficial or harmful consequences could result from one's actions;
(b) realization that others have the power to determine the consequences of one's actions;
(c) the awareness that the harmful consequences are more serious than are the beneficial consequences;
(d) confidence that the others will behave in ways that ensure beneficial consequences for oneself (Deutsch, 1958, 1960, 1962).

Interpersonal trust is built through placing one's consequences in the control of others and having one's confidence in the others confirmed. Interpersonal trust is destroyed through placing one's consequences in the hands of others and having one's confidence in the others disconfirmed through their behaving in ways that ensure harmful consequences for oneself.

Trust tends to be developed and maintained in cooperative situations and it tends to be absent and destroyed in competitive and individualistic situations (Deutsch, 1958, 1960, 1962; Johnson, 1971, 1974; Johnson & Noonan, 1972).

Trust is composed of two sets of behaviors. *Trusting* behavior is the willingness to risk beneficial or harmful consequences by making oneself vulnerable to another person. *Trustworthy* behavior is the willingness to respond to another person's risk-taking in a way that ensures that the other person will experience beneficial consequences. In order to establish trust, two or more people must be trustworthy and trusting. The greater the trust among group members, the more effective their cooperative efforts tend to be (Deutsch, 1962; Johnson, 2000; Johnson & Noonan, 1972).

Conflict

The seventh set of competencies needed for cooperative group work is resolving conflicts constructively. Conflict within cooperative groups, when managed constructively, enhances the effectiveness of cooperative efforts (Deutsch, 1973; Johnson & Johnson, 1989). There are two types of conflict that occur frequently and regularly within cooperative groups—constructive controversy and conflict of interests (Johnson & Johnson, 1995a, b).

CONSTRUCTIVE CONTROVERSY

Constructive controversy exists when group members have different information, perceptions, opinions, reasoning processes, theories, and conclusions, and they must reach agreement (Johnson & Johnson, 1995b). When the group is faced with a problem to be solved or a decision to be made, even if it is about how to proceed to achieve the group's goals, each alternative course of action is assigned to a subgroup. Members then (a) prepare the best case possible for their assigned position, (b) make a persuasive presentation of their position, (c) engage in an open discussion in which they continue to advocate their position, refute the other alternative courses of action, and rebut attacks on their position, (d) drop all advocacy and view the issue from all perspectives, and (e) achieve consensus as to the course of action to adopt based on the best reasoned judgments of all group members.

When controversies arise, they may be dealt with constructively or destructively, depending on how they are managed and the level of interpersonal and small group skills of the participants. When managed constructively, controversy promotes uncertainty about the correctness of one's views, an active search for more information, a reconceptualization of one's knowledge and conclusions, and, consequently, greater mastery and retention of the material being discussed and a more reasoned judgment on the issue being considered. Individuals working alone in competitive and individualistic situations do not have the opportunity for such a process and, therefore, their productivity, quality of decision making, and achievement suffer (Johnson & Johnson, 1995b).

Compared with concurrence-seeking, debate, and individualistic efforts, controversy results in greater mastery and retention of the subject matter, higher-quality problem solving, greater creativity in thinking, greater motivation to learn more about the topic, more productive exchange of expertise among group members, greater task involvement, more positive relationships among group members, more accurate perspective taking, and higher self-esteem. In addition, individuals enjoy it more (Johnson & Johnson, 1995b).

Controversies tend to be constructive when the situational context is cooperative, group members are heterogeneous, information and expertise is distributed within the group, members have the necessary conflict skills, and the canons of rational argumentation are followed.

INTEGRATIVE NEGOTIATION AND PEER MEDIATION

A *conflict of interests* occurs when the actions of one person striving to achieve his or her goal interfere with and obstruct the actions of another person striving to achieve his or her goal (Johnson & Johnson, 1995a, 2000b). Within the ongoing relationships of a group, conflicts of interests are resolved constructively when group members (a) negotiate integrative agreements and (b) mediate the conflicts among their group mates. Group members negotiate integrative agreements by (a) describing what they want, (b) describing how they feel, (c) describing the reasons for their wants and feelings, (d) taking the perspective of the opposing member, (e) inventing several optional agreements that would maximize joint benefits, and (f) selecting the agreement that seems most effective (Johnson & Johnson, 1995a). When group members use integrative negotiations and peer mediation, group productivity is considerably enhanced.

When group members are unable to negotiate an agreement, other group members may wish to mediate. A *mediator* is a neutral person who helps two or more people resolve their conflict, usually by negotiating an integrative agreement. Mediation consists of four steps (Johnson & Johnson, 1995a): (a) ending hostilities, (b) ensuring disputants are committed to the mediation process, (c) helping disputants successfully negotiate with each other, and (d) formalizing the agreement into a contract.

A meta-analysis of the studies on teaching children and adolescents to use the integrative negotiation and peer mediation procedures has recently been completed (Johnson & Johnson, 2000b). Individuals who received training mastered the integrative negotiation and peer mediation procedures, maintained that mastery months after the training had ended, applied the learned procedures to actual conflicts in classroom, school, and family settings, developed more positive attitudes toward conflict, and generally resolved the conflicts in their lives more constructively.

CONCLUSIONS

The application of social interdependence theory and research to cooperative group work is one of the most successful and widespread applications of social psychology. The theory provides a conceptual framework from which practical procedures that individuals may use to promote cooperative group work may be developed. The power of cooperative group work comes from its foundation on a profound and strategic theory, the substantial research validating its effectiveness, and the practical procedures that have been developed.

Over the past 100 years researchers have focused on such diverse outcomes as productivity, achievement, higher-level reasoning, retention, quality of decision making and problem solving, creativity, achievement motivation, intrinsic motivation, transfer of learning, interpersonal attraction, social support, friendships, valuing differences, self-esteem, social competencies, psychological health, moral reasoning, and many others. These numerous outcomes may be subsumed within three broad categories: effort to achieve, positive interpersonal relationships, and psychological health. Cooperative efforts, compared with competitive and individualistic ones, tend to result in higher levels of these outcomes. This is true when the studies compared group and individual productivity, and it is true when the studies compared individual performance of group members with the performance of individuals working alone competitively or individualistically.

In order to capitalize on the potential effects of cooperation, group members must be skilled in establishing strong positive interdependence, individual accountability, promotive interaction, appropriate use of social skills, and group processing. In addition, group members must be able to establish and maintain a high level of trust and resolve conflicts constructively. Two of the most important types of conflicts inherent in group work are constructive controversy and conflicts of interests.

Finally, the research on social interdependence has an external validity and a generalizability rarely found in the social sciences. The more variations in places, people, and procedures the research can withstand and still yield the same findings, the more externally valid the conclusions. The research has been conducted in 10 different historical decades. Research participants have varied as to age, gender, economic class, nationality, and cultural background. A wide variety of research tasks, ways of structuring the types of social interdependence, and measures of the dependent variables have been used. The research has been conducted by many different researchers with markedly different theoretical and practical orientations working in different settings and even in different countries. The diversity of participants, settings, age levels, and operationalizations of social interdependence and the dependent variables give this work a validity and a generalizability rarely found in the educational literature.

REFERENCES

Archer-Kath, J., Johnson, D. W., & Johnson, R. (1994). Individual versus group feedback in cooperative groups. *Journal of Social Psychology, 134*, 681–694.

Crandall, J. (1982). Social interest, extreme response style, and implications for adjustment. *Journal of Research in Personality, 16*, 82–89.

Deutsch, M. (1949). A theory of cooperation and competition. *Human Relations, 2*, 129–152.

Deutsch, M. (1958). Trust and suspicion. *Journal of Conflict Resolution, 2*, 265–279.

Deutsch, M. (1960). The effects of motivational orientation upon trust and suspicion. *Human Relations, 13*, 123–139.

Deutsch, M. (1962). Cooperation and trust: some theoretical notes. In M. R. Jones (ed.), *Nebraska Symposium on Motivation* (pp. 275–319). Lincoln: University of Nebraska Press.

Deutsch, M. (1973). *The Resolution of Conflict*. New Haven, Conn.: Yale University Press.

Frank, M. (1984). A comparison between an individual and group goal structure contingency that differed in the behavioral contingency and performance–outcome components (Doctoral dissertation, University of Minnesota). *Dissertation Abstracts International, 45*/05, 1341-A.

Gabbert, B., Johnson, D., & Johnson, R. (1986). Cooperative learning, group-to-individual transfer, process gain and the acquisition of cognitive reasoning strategies. *Journal of Psychology, 120*(3), 265–278.

Hagman, J. & Hayes, J. (1986). Cooperative learning: effects of task, reward, and group size on individual achievement (Technical Report 704). Boise, Idaho: Scientific Coordination Office, US Army Research Institute for the Behavioral and Social Sciences (ERIC Document Reproduction Service No. ED 278 720).

Harkins, S. G. & Petty, R. E. (1982). The effects of task difficulty and task uniqueness on social loafing. *Journal of Personality and Social Psychology, 43*, 1214–1229.

Hayes, L. (1976). The use of group contingencies for behavioral control: a review. *Psychological Bulletin, 83*, 628–648.

Hwong, N., Caswell, A., Johnson, D. W., & Johnson, R. (1993). Effects of cooperative and individualistic learning on prospective elementary teachers' music achievement and attitudes. *Journal of Social Psychology, 133*, 53–64.

Ingham, A., Levinger, G., Graves, J., & Peckham, V. (1974). The Ringelmann effect: studies of group size and group performance. *Journal of Personality and Social Psychology, 10*, 371–384.

James, N. & Johnson, D. W. (1983). The relationship between attitudes toward social interdependence and psychological health within three criminal populations. *Journal of Abnormal and Social Psychology, 121*, 131–143.

James, S. & Johnson, D. W. (1988). Social interdependence, psychological adjustment, orientation toward negative life stress, and quality of second marriage. *Journal of Social Psychology, 128*(3), 287–304.

Jensen, M., Johnson, D. W., & Johnson, R. (in press). Impact of positive interdependence during electronic quizzes on discourse and achievement. *Journal of Educational Research.*

Johnson, D. W. (1971). Role reversal: a summary and review of the research. *International Journal of Group Tensions, 1*, 318–334.

Johnson, D. W. (1974). Communication and the inducement of cooperative behavior in conflicts: a critical review. *Speech Monographs, 41*, 64–78.

Johnson, D. W. (2000). *Reaching Out: Interpersonal Effectiveness and Self-actualization* (7th edn). Boston: Allyn & Bacon.

Johnson, D. W. & Johnson, F. (2000a). *Joining Together: Group Theory and Group Skills* (7th edn). Boston: Allyn & Bacon.

Johnson, D. W. & Johnson, R. (1981). Effects of cooperative and individualistic learning experiences on interethnic interaction. *Journal of Educational Psychology, 73*(3), 454–459.

Johnson, D. W. & Johnson, R. (1989). *Cooperation and Competition: Theory and Research.* Edina, Minn.: Interaction Book Company.

Johnson, D. W. & Johnson, R. (1995a). *Teaching Students to be Peacemakers.* Edina, Minn.: Interaction Book Company.

Johnson, D. W. & Johnson, R. (1995b). *Creative Controversy: Intellectual Challenge in the Classroom.* Edina, Minn.: Interaction Book Company.

Johnson, D. W. & Johnson, R. (2000b). Teaching students to be peacemakers: a meta-analysis. Paper presented at the Convention of the Society for the Psychological Study of Social Issues, Minneapolis, June.

Johnson, D. W., Johnson, R., & Krotee, M. (1986). The relationship between social interdependence and psychological health within the 1980 United States Olympic ice hockey team. *Journal of Psychology, 120*, 279–292.

Johnson, D. W., Johnson, R., Ortiz, A., & Stanne, M. (1991). Impact of positive goal and resource interdependence on achievement, interaction, and attitudes. *Journal of General Psychology, 118*(4), 341–347.

Johnson, D. W., Johnson, R., Stanne, M., & Garibaldi, A. (1990). Impact of group processing on achievement in cooperative groups. *Journal of Social Psychology, 130*, 507–516.

Johnson, D. W. & Noonan, P. (1972). Effects of acceptance and reciprocation of self-disclosures on the development of trust. *Journal of Counseling Psychology, 19*(5), 411–416.

Johnson, D. W. & Norem-Hebeisen, A. (1977). Attitudes toward interdependence among persons and psychological health. *Psychological Reports, 40*, 843–850.

Johnson, D. W., Skon, L., & Johnson, R. (1980). Effects of cooperative, competitive, and individualistic conditions on children's problem-solving performance. *American Educational Research Journal, 17*(1), 83–94.

Kerr, N. (1983). The dispensability of member effort and group motivation losses: free-rider effects. *Journal of Personality and Social Psychology, 44*, 78–94.

Kerr, N. & Bruun, S. (1981). Ringelmann revisited: alternative explanations for the social loafing effect. *Personality and Social Psychology Bulletin, 7*, 224–231.

Kerr, N. & Bruun, S. (1983). The dispensability of member effort and group motivation losses: free-rider effects. *Journal of Personality and Social Psychology, 44*, 78–94.

Latane, B., Williams, K., & Harkins, S. (1979). Many hands make light the work: the causes and consequences of social loafing. *Journal of Personality and Social Psychology, 37*, 822–832.

Lew, M., Mesch, D., Johnson, D. W., & Johnson, R. (1986a). Positive interdependence, academic and collaborative-skills group contingencies and isolated students. *American Educational Research Journal, 23*, 476–488.

Lew, M., Mesch, D., Johnson, D. W., & Johnson, R. (1986b). Components of cooperative learning: effects of collaborative skills and academic group contingencies on achievement and mainstreaming. *Contemporary Educational Psychology, 11*, 229–239.

Mesch, D., Johnson, D. W., & Johnson, R. (1988). Impact of positive interdependence and academic group contingencies on achievement. *Journal of Social Psychology, 128*, 345–352.

Mesch, D., Lew, M., Johnson, D. W., & Johnson, R. (1986). Isolated teenagers, cooperative learning and the training of social skills. *Journal of Psychology, 120*, 323–334.

Messick, D. & Brewer, M. (1983). Solving social dilemmas: a review. In L. Wheeler & P. Shaver (eds), *Review of Personality and Social Psychology* (Vol. 4, pp. 11–44). Newbury Park, Calif.: Sage Publications.

Moede, W. (1927). Die Richtlinien der Leistungs-Psychologie. *Industrielle Psychotechnik, 4*, 193–207.

Norem-Hebeisen, A. & Johnson, D. W. (1981). Relationships between cooperative, competitive, and individualistic attitudes and differentiated aspects of self-esteem. *Journal of Personality, 49*, 415–425.

Norem-Hebeisen, A., Johnson, D. W., Anderson, D., & Johnson, R. (1984). Predictors and concomitants of changes in drug use patterns among teenagers. *Journal of Social Psychology, 124*, 43–50.

Ortiz, A., Johnson, D. W., & Johnson, R. (1996). The effect of positive goal and resource interdependence on individual performance. *Journal of Social Psychology, 136*(2), 243–249.

Petty, R., Harkins, S., Williams, K., & Latane, B. (1977). The effects of group size on cognitive effort and evaluation. *Personality and Social Psychology Bulletin, 3*, 575–578.

Putnam, J., Rynders, J., Johnson, R., & Johnson, D. W. (1989). Collaborative skill instruction for promoting positive interactions between mentally handicapped and nonhandicapped children. *Exceptional Children, 55*(6), 550–557.

Skon, L., Johnson, D., & Johnson, R. (1981). Cooperative peer interaction versus individual competition and individualistic efforts: effects on the acquisition of cognitive reasoning strategies. *Journal of Educational Psychology, 73*(1), 83–92.

Sweeney, J. (1973). An experimental investigation of the free-rider problem. *Social Science Research, 2*, 277–292.

Tjosvold, D. (1986). *Working Together to Get Things Done*. Lexington, Mass.: D. C. Heath.

Williams, K. (1981). The effects of group cohesiveness on social loafing. Paper presented at the annual meeting of the Midwestern Psychological Association, Detroit.

Williams, K., Harkins, S., & Latane, B. (1981). Identifiability as a deterrent to social loafing: two cheering experiments. *Journal of Personality and Social Psychology, 40*, 303–311.

Yager, S., Johnson, D., & Johnson, R. (1985). Oral discussion, group-to-individual transfer, and achievement in cooperative learning groups. *Journal of Educational Psychology, 77*(1), 60–66.

Section III

WORK GROUPS

10

TEAM-BASED ORGANIZATION

CREATING AN ENVIRONMENT FOR TEAM SUCCESS

Cheryl L. Harris and Michael M. Beyerlein

Team-based organization (TBO) shifts attention from teams to their context and integration. This chapter reviews the essential components of TBOs. Although redesign of a traditional organization to a TBO is an expensive and risky undertaking, attending to the key components ought to increase the probability of success in using teams as a mechanism for achieving strategic goals of the business. The claims below are based on a review of a small literature and projects at the Center for the Study of Work Teams including: 610 interviews with team members and leaders, 28 conferences on teams for 16,000 participants from 350 organizations over 13 years, fieldwork with the steering committees in TBOs, and interviews of 21 recognized experts. The result is thus an integration of findings from the Center's work, the experts, and the several scholars who have published in the area, particularly Susan Mohrman of the Center for Effective Organizations.

A TBO results from a desire to organize work in a way that formally optimizes collaborative capability. There is recognition that teams enable line workers, support workers, and managers to be more effective in their work. However, there is also recognition that the effectiveness is limited unless the environment or context of the organization surrounding those teams is aligned with them. Many teams fail to achieve expected results, because the context contradicts, abandons, or undermines team functioning. The TBO is designed to address that problem.

The last two decades ushered in a much more complex business environment, causing two trends in organizations: a need for speed and flexibility, and increased use of teams to help achieve that. Focusing on creating teams alone provided limited success. Recently, focus shifted to the context around teams. In a study of 25 knowledge work teams in four companies, the "team context appeared to be the overwhelming determinant of whether a team functioned effectively in accomplishing its goals" (Mohrman, Cohen, & Mohrman, 1995, p. 34).

When teams are formed without heed to the organizational context, they tend to become isolated and cut off from the rest of the organization. The isolated team becomes akin to a disease in the body; the larger organization acts as an immune system (Pinchot, 1985) doing

International Handbook of Organizational Teamwork and Cooperative Working. Edited by M. A. West, D. Tjosvold, and K. G. Smith.

whatever it can to expel the disease. "When teams are introduced as an isolated practice, they fail. My gut feeling is most are introduced in isolation.... And time and time again teams fall short on their promise because companies don't know how to make them work together with other teams" (Dumaine, 1994, p. 92).

The term "team-based organization" (TBO) was coined to describe the new type of organization theorized to support teams. TBO is an organization that uses teams as the core performing units, and the organization is designed to support teams. The logic of the organization shifts from individual-oriented to team-oriented, and a dual focus on both the team and the larger context of the team is required (Mohrman, Cohen, & Mohrman, 1995). One criticism of the term TBO is that some see it as implying teams as an end, not a means to an end. Another is that TBO implies long-term and static organizations, which simply does not fit the current business environment of increasing complexity and change (Harris & Steed, 2001). Because of these negative connotations, many have shied away from the term TBO. However, the practices associated with TBO remain in place.

We suggest that a fully realized redesign effort ultimately produces a TBO. Achieving TBO is the ideal. However, that term connotes an ending point. Once people perceive (correctly or incorrectly) that the ending point is met, the energy around the initiative often wanes. As energy diminishes, the organization tends to go back to bad habits, saying, "TBO—we've done that, and it didn't work for us." In reality, the journey never ends, and the effort must be sustained indefinitely. Accordingly, the term "team-based organizing" (TBO*ing*) represents continuous improvement and continuous reinvention. The TBO*ing* approach and the historically dominant approach that focuses on the individual as the unit of accountability, leadership, and support are radically different!

The primary goal of this chapter is to explore the answer to the question, "what is TBO*ing*?" Since each organization is unique, there is no step-by-step list to follow. Instead, we will share some of our general findings in an effort to describe TBO*ing*.

WHAT IS TEAM-BASED ORGANIZING?

"Team" is the core building block of the team-based organization (TBO). However, focusing solely on the team is not enough to ensure team effectiveness. The crucial point to be made in team-based organizing (TBO*ing)* is the focus on the organization. The key tenets to our definition of TBO*ing* are:

- Teams are the basic units of accountability and work.
- Only use teams when teams are appropriate.
- Teams lead teams.
- Use an array of teams.
- Recognize that it is a never-ending, continuous process.
- Design in flexibility for adaptability.
- Design organization to support teams.
- Hold it all together with alignment.
- Organization leaders must have TBO-compatible philosophy.
- It requires intentional effort.

Each of these tenets is briefly reviewed below.

Teams are the Basic Units of Accountability and Work

This is the most widely accepted tenet of research on the topic of TBO, and the major element that distinguishes TBOs from other organizations. While TBO*ing* often incorporates elements from other initiatives (e.g. total quality management, business process reengineering, and many others), having teams as the basic work unit sets TBO apart from other initiatives. TBOs and organizations that use teams are very different. In a TBO, the organization must be redesigned to support the work of teams. An organization that simply uses teams for special purposes in parallel to a traditional hierarchical structure is not a TBO (Mohrman, Cohen, & Mohrman, 1995). TBOs use teams to perform the core work of the organization (Mohrman, Cohen, & Mohrman, 1995; Mohrman & Mohrman, 1997; Shonk, 1997). In a TBO, teams are responsible for doing the planning, decision making, and implementation of the work (Shonk, 1997).

Transforming a work group to a team or an organization to a TBO represents decisions that are subject to the criterion of cost/benefit analysis. There is a cost and there is a risk that the transformational effort will fail. Costs include time invested in training, lost production time during reorganization, loss of knowledge sets when supervisors or middle managers are laid off or reassigned, etc. Benefits include increased employee commitment, quick response to customers, reduced error rates, and reduced absenteeism. But the investment and risk are only worthwhile if they fit the nature of the work and the strategic plan of the top management group. The strategic plan dictates the design needed to deliver a given set of products or services to customers in a way that generates a profit.

Smolek, Hoffman, and Moran (1999) argue that the structure of the design must include some essential features for teams to be the right choice. The features include:

1. Clarity of purpose so the team knows "why are we here?";
2. Appropriate measures of performance, both qualitative and quantitative, that are aligned with the organization's goals;
3. Clearly defined boundaries that identify the team's scope, responsibilities, authority, and resources;
4. Work processes that require interdependence of the team's members in performing production tasks, but also in making decisions, getting information, and generating feedback.

We agree that features like this are prerequisite to effective teaming; the features are either in place or are established as early phases of the transformation to a TBO. Smolek, Hoffman, and Moran (1999) offer the example of MotorCo (a pseudonym for a real company) where the top management groups of the nine plants were charged with transforming to work team structures to increase competitiveness in the difficult market of electric motor production. After seven months of design work, the plants were ready to implement the transformation. Initial results were mixed, but outstanding teams exceeded expectations and it became clear that investing in people and organization had a larger potential payoff than investing in equipment.

Teams must not become the new silos in an organization. So, while the core performing unit is the team, attention must be focused on business unit and above levels of performance and on promoting integration among teams.

Only Use Teams when Teams are Appropriate

While the core work unit of the TBO is the team, not every person in the organization necessarily belongs on a team. This is a common myth that must be debunked. Teams should only be used when teams are appropriate. Some tasks simply are not appropriate for a team. In this case, a team should not be launched. In the case that an individual is more appropriate for the task, that individual still must learn how to deal with teams in the organization, as the primary organizing feature is the team. Molecular structure may represent an appropriate analogy: individuals act as atoms which combine into teams at the molecular level which mix as business units in compounds to form the chemistry of organizations. There is value in focusing on any of the three levels, but practical value usually emerges from the mixture of new compounds.

In a TBO, the natural inclination should be to put a team on a task. The goal is to maximize the effectiveness of teams, when a team is appropriate. However, before assuming a team is the best structure for accomplishing the task, the work itself has to be analyzed to see if it is amenable to a team structure. A team is a complex solution inappropriate for simple problems; applying a team to a task that individuals can accomplish wastes resources, particularly time. Teams are only appropriate when the work requires the extra investment. It is important to identify collective work, and create teams around that work. The work has to require interdependent effort by multiple people in order for a team structure to emerge and leverage resources.

Teams Lead Teams

Putting the workforce in teams is not enough for successful TBO*ing*. Teams must cascade down throughout the organization, with teams leading teams leading teams. Having teams at all levels models and reinforces the team concept (Mohrman, Cohen, & Mohrman, 1995). The top management group must become a team for three reasons:

(a) building tacit understanding of teaming, so top management group members can recognize challenges and appreciate value added from teaming;
(b) leading the TBO*ing* change effort by modeling it;
(c) aligning support systems top management group members control.

In many organizations the top management group remains relatively unchanged while pushing the rest of the organization to change—a formula for failure. An effective top management group that can function as a team not only supports TBO*ing*, but also increases market success (Mathews, 1996).

Use an Array of Teams

Some believe that using a TBO implies the use of long-term, permanent work teams. We suggest that, as long as teams are performing the core work of the organization, any type of team may be used. For example, project teams are becoming a prevalent work structure in technologically oriented organizations. We would include these project-team-based organizations under the TBO umbrella.

A TBO uses a variety of team types (e.g. work teams, management teams, task teams, and project teams) to meet the needs of each situation. The type of team varies as the work varies—different types of teams are needed for different types of work. TBO can accommodate both permanent and temporary teams. Finally, as discussed in the previous section, management teams are important as well.

Recognize that it Is a Never-ending, Continuous Process

The question "is your organization a TBO?" is a difficult one to answer. The question presumes a dichotomous relationship between TBO and traditional, individually oriented organizations. In reality, organizations fall on a continuum of progress toward the elusive TBO ideal, so they have degrees of TBO. If we look at TBO as the ideal target, then TBO*ing* is the process of moving toward that target. Reframed as a process instead of an end, TBO*ing* is better understood as the continuous improvement process that it is. Too often organizations chase the TBO goal, and then either decide it is too difficult to achieve, or think they have achieved it, rest on their laurels, and immediately start a decline. TBO*ing* suggests that the journey is never over, and the organization must constantly strive to improve in terms of TBO*ing* and its resulting adaptability in order to succeed.

The catchphrase in the 1980s was "reinvention"; today it must be "continuous invention." The change process must be a continuous one to constantly adapt to environmental demands. A major transformation like TBO must also be viewed as a continuous process. The principles of continuous improvement seem to act at least as metaphors, if not as actual tools for change. The TBO initiative builds collaborative capability through education and redesign of the organization that takes many years. There is periodic renewal based on data from regular assessment of the change initiative, the need to reenergize the initiative at critical points, and the continuous need to provide cost/benefit data to the strategic decision makers who have the power to sustain the initiative or starve it.

One manufacturing plant was designed as a TBO from its conception in 1987. Five years later, the emphasis on TBO*ing* was dropped because workload required such a rapid increase in the number of employees in a short period (from 600 to about 2000 over two years) that the systems in place for teams could not be maintained. For example, the use of existing teams as assessors in assessment center processes for selecting new team members was replaced by traditional HR processes for selection. Five years later in response to union demands and a new corporate emphasis on people, a new steering team was formed to plan transformation back to a TBO. Three years after that when a rapid drop in business demand occurred as a result of the bursting technology bubble and the terrorist attacks on September 11, 2001, top management again abandoned teaming and initiated layoffs of 40 percent of the employees. Nine months later, under significant pressure from a new vice president and after reorganization to a project-based matrix organization, the team initiative was again brought to the top of the priority list.

Design in Flexibility for Adaptability

Flexibility is a key effectiveness factor in TBO*ing*, as flexibility throughout the organization must be designed to meet the needs of the fluid business environment. Flexibility of structures, systems, and individuals is crucial for adaptability. To meet the needs of the work and the environment, the organization must be flexible enough to launch different types of teams quickly. The systems of the organization also need to be flexible to deal with these various types of teams and individual and team structures. If the work of the organization requires different team types, then flexibility of systems would become more crucial than for an organization with fairly homogeneous tasks. Individuals within the TBO must also be flexible. They must be willing to make a change, and willing to adapt to the demands on them at any given time or over the long term. This adaptability enhances the organization's ability to meet the needs of changing external circumstances.

The continuous development of the TBO initiative enables the steering team to base progress on many small steps rather than one grand change. As a result, risk is reduced and the ability to adapt the initiative to changing business conditions is possible. The design remains reconfigurable. As with many management decisions, getting started with a modest plan is more effective than waiting until a perfect plan has been developed. Incremental change allows for adjustments along the path toward the goal state. One example involves the radical change at a national bank.

Devane (in press) described the transformation of the Land Bank of South Africa into a TBO under the dynamic leadership of its new president. The intent was to create an adaptive organization, so "the formal design of the organizational structure was never considered 'done.'" This contrasted with prior change experience for the bank, which was "cast in concrete for eight to 20 years." Through empowerment and education, branches of the bank could be redesigned as their members felt the need.

At Hewlett-Packard and other companies whose industries are subject to rapid technological change and short product life cycles, employees must be closely in touch with customers, so quick decisions can be made to facilitate mass customization. Employees must be both motivated and organized to help with the transformation to an organizational design that can be that responsive (Zell, 1997). At the Roseville plant, the HP design team created self-managing teams with "the necessary power, knowledge, authority, and information to make decisions on their own" (p. 137). They achieved alignment among the teams and the rest of the organization through use of the "Bull's-Eye" diagram, which placed customers and values in the center surrounded by concentric circles for the business system, the structural system, the support system, and finally the people system. The latter had the most room for improvement. At the Roseville plant, the redesign work was fairly straightforward, but at the Santa Clara plant, the "structure had to be completely dismantled before a business strategy could be established."

Design Organization to Support Teams

Team-based organizing is not about teams. It is about the organization. Most publications and most examples focus on individual teams. The leap from team to team-based system of work is as large as the leap from individual work to teamwork. Redesign to a TBO demands redesign of the organization as a whole. The environment the teams work in is critical to their performance level, so redesigning the whole makes effectiveness possible at the lower level (Beyerlein & Harris, in press).

TBO applies to organizations of all sizes. When we say "organization," we mean the site or department level. Preferably, the entire site would be transformed in a TBO*ing* effort.

However, a full redesign at the corporate level is rare, as the size of the organization makes transformative change difficult to manage.

Hold it All Together with Alignment

Alignment is the foundational principle in our definition of TBO. In order to be successful, alignment must occur externally and internally in the organization. Externally, the organization must align with stakeholders, customers, suppliers, competitors, and partners. Internally, alignment must occur across: (a) multiple change initiatives; (b) deployment of strategy, mission, vision, and values; (c) support systems (with each other and with team needs); and (d) teams forming lateral relationships.

As with any organization design, organizational structure, systems, and culture should be aligned with each other. Therefore, if the organization is comprised of teams, the organization context and systems must be congruent with teams. In studies of team failures (Beyerlein et al., 1997; Mohrman & Tenkasi, 1997), the key factor that emerged was alignment of support systems with work teams. Beyerlein et al. suggested that more than 50 percent of the failure of teams to achieve expected gains was due to lack of alignment. Mohrman and Tenkasi suggested 90 percent of the failures were due to context factors and specified support systems as the key. Lack of alignment between support systems creates contextual inconsistencies that send mixed messages to team members (e.g. rewards based exclusively on individual achievement when managers are saying "work as a team") or that undermine performance as an integrated team (e.g. information systems that prevent access to work-relevant material by anyone but the team's formal manager). Mohrman (Mohrman, Cohen, & Mohrman, 1995) suggests that the alignment issue will only become salient with experience in TBO*ing*—manager awareness shifts from surface features to deeper structure as understanding of the new design grows.

One of the most critical forms of alignment is the TBO*ing* effort with business strategy. If the motivation for TBO*ing* does not directly relate to business reasons, then the initiative is doomed to failure. The investment required for successful TBO*ing* is large and long term, and a significant expectation for business improvement must be pursued in order to build and maintain the momentum of the redesign effort.

Strategic decision makers at the top of the organization base many decisions on financial information and financial goals (often short-term goals). Work teams and TBO*ing* provide a number of benefits, but sometimes the mechanisms are not in place for valuing those benefits in financial terms. Kennedy describes a system for using management accounting concepts and team effectives and support system alignment data for providing such data to top management (Kennedy, 2002). Plants for such companies as Shell, Raytheon, and Colgate, and departments at First American Financial have been testing the model. The initial goal was to provide feedback to the top management group about the success of teams, so strategic decision making would sustain the initiative. More recently, the idea of building an innovation culture has been added to the project, since the dollar value of team process improvements is captured and aggregated at several levels.

Jones and Moffett (1999) emphasize the alignment of the team's strategy with the organization's strategy as a way of focusing on business results. They call this "line of sight" and argue that it must be clear; that is, team members need enough knowledge of the business strategy to clearly see how to align their decisions with it. Two examples they present illustrate this alignment. At Xerox, the corporate document called "Vision 2000" shared the corporate goal and the competitive pressures that strategy targeted. When teams needed to upgrade their technical skills because of a product transformation to digital equipment, the teams' goals became clear and the measurement system was adapted to capture the change.

At Electronic Components (a fictional name for a real company), teams worked to solve productivity problems that impacted bottom-line performance. Focusing on the reduction of defects enabled the teams to cut cycle time, reduce overtime, and improve on-time delivery to the customer. This improved team performance measures and the company's profits. The use of theory of constraints (TOC) through total preventive maintenance (TPM) teams at many semiconductor plants, including Harris Semiconductor (Rose, Gilmore, & Odom, 1998), formalizes the process for identifying defects in process that act as bottlenecks to production flow. The general pattern is for the teams to collect and analyze data to identify the point in a complex set of production steps that is acting as the greatest constraint, such as the slowest machine or the point where most breakdowns occur. The teams then fix the problem or get help to do so before moving on to the next slowest step. The result is speeded production and greater efficiency in the process.

Organization Leaders Must Have TBO-Compatible Philosophy

Although leadership represents a support system and is treated in that section of this chapter, it deserves notice here, because it is the only system that is responsible for changing the systems. It is also one of the hardest systems to change. Organization change starts with self-change. If management does not change, it stifles the rest of the initiative. Moran (1996) discovered that 77 percent of team initiatives failed due to lack of management support.

Organization leaders advocate TBO through words and actions, which are indicative of their management philosophy. First, the management philosophy must be one of involvement. The organization is built on the principle that people have a right to be involved in matters that affect them. In return, people will make decisions in the best interest of the organization because of awareness of mutual benefit. Second, management development must be built around the team concept, focusing on a collaborative, facilitative, development role. Part of this includes redefining the ego role to become less controlling. Top management in the business unit (as well as the other levels of management) must have announced and demonstrated commitment to the team concept in order for it to succeed.

Implementation Requires Intentional Effort

Creating an environment where teams can thrive does not happen by chance, but comes through time, effort, and commitment. Teams and the larger organization must give some careful thought to what is needed to support teams. These reflective activities must occur regularly. The most important points must be supported by systems that reinforce their occurrence (Mohrman, Cohen, & Mohrman, 1995).

TBO is a decision, just like personal health is a decision. Unless one makes a decision to establish the practices that generate and maintain health and fitness, a gradual deterioration occurs and achievable performance goals become more and more humble. High performance levels in an organization that relies on teams require that decision makers commit to the transformation effort that is necessary in creating a TBO. It starts with a decision.

The manufacturing plant example earlier in the chapter represented a TBO*ing* effort that has already covered 15 years and may have 15 more to reach a mature state. Literature on teams published in the 1990s suggested the transformation typically took 6–11 years. Most efforts are not so complete; few organizations make the investment to actually create a fully developed TBO. Many organizations prefer to stop part way along the journey. For example, one meat packing company is only interested in having self-directed work teams embedded within an otherwise traditional hierarchy.

COMPONENTS OF TEAM-BASED ORGANIZING

The Organizational "Road Map"

In this section, we will delve further into the details of TBO*ing*. The components are organized using a theoretical "road map" of an organization. This "road map" could be a model for any organization using any type of work. It is an alignment model, with congruent design as the goal. In a TBO, teams would carry out the majority of work, which assumes that the work is amenable to teams. We will use it as a road map for sharing themes related specifically to TBO. How does the organization, including culture, systems, and structure, have to change from the traditional design in order to support teams to maximize effectiveness? We will explore this in the rest of the chapter.

The Work

The work is at the center of the organizational "road map," because the ultimate objective of the organization is to accomplish its task—whether the work is production, service, or new product development. The organizational pieces—culture, structure, and systems—must create a bridge of alignment between the work and the environment. While the characteristics of the work in most situations are fairly set, the task can be reframed through work process redesign (Dalton, 1998). The following points characterize TBO work.

INTERDEPENDENT WORK

In a TBO, teams should be created around tasks that are appropriate to teams. Appropriate team tasks require interdependence (Mohrman, Cohen, & Mohrman, 1995; Saavedra, Earley, & van Dyne, 1993). This interdependence requires the integration of the knowledge and work of different individuals. In other words, simple, single-function tasks, such as turning a screw to complete a roller skate, would be less appropriate for a team than assembly and inspection of an entire roller skate. In a TBO, teams are created based on their interdependencies. In teams, members depend on each other to achieve work goals.

The interdependencies of the work are often identified through process analysis (Dalton, 1998).

WHOLE PIECE OF WORK

In a TBO, the whole organization is designed to create units comprised of the various skills and experiences necessary to do a whole piece of the business (Mohrman, Cohen, & Mohrman, 1995). These units are then given responsibility and accountability for their part of the business. When the overall task is too complex for a single team (e.g. building an airplane), then the work of the team represents a complete piece of the larger project, e.g. the paint team handling the entire exterior of the plane rather than breaking it into tail section, wings, or fuselage for separate work groups, resulting in the work having less segmentation (Goodman, Devadas, & Hughson, 1988; Lawler, 1990). Because teams are organized around whole pieces of work, the organization becomes more process than product focused (Harris & Steed, 2001). An important result of cross-functional teams looking at a whole piece of work is that the individuals begin to see themselves as customers and suppliers, a mentality that cascades throughout the internal and external supply chains.

INCREASE IN LATERAL WORK

In a traditional organization, much of the work is accomplished vertically. If a person has a problem, he or she goes to the boss, who sends it to the next boss, and so on, until the appropriate functional silo is able to answer the question. Instead, since TBO*ing* organizations are organized into teams conducting whole pieces of work, they have many more lateral work opportunities, decreasing the amount of time that decisions have to go up and down the hierarchy and reducing the isolation caused by chimney structures or silos. The teams are empowered to make many decisions themselves. The results are faster and higher-quality decisions. In addition to lateral work within the team, successful TBO*ing* requires integration among teams, causing even more lateral work. The members readily reach out across functional and project boundaries to gather information or coordinate flow of work.

BROADER SKILL SETS

Because of the more holistic nature of work in teams, broader skills are required. Jobs are enlarged to include planning, control, and coordination, instead of just doing the work.

CHANGES IN ROLE DIFFERENTIATION AND COMMUNICATION

It is a myth that all team members must be cross-trained. Instead, specialists in a team must learn enough about the other specialties to be able to communicate with them (Klein, 1993). In fact, a moderate degree of role differentiation is required. If each person has exactly the expertise and experiences, what is the point in putting them together in a team? It is this diversity that makes a team strong. As a result of the improved decisions, individuals learn that it is valuable to see another point of view (Harris & Steed, 2001).

APPROPRIATENESS OF THE WORK FOR TEAMING

The nature of work is not completely a given in each organization. If work is not amenable to teams, then perhaps it should be. Are there opportunities for increased collaboration? How can this occur? Work process redesign facilitates this process. Not all work is teamwork, but some work that looks like individual work can be redesigned to be teamwork, and is better as a result. Not everyone in a TBO has to be in a team, and team members usually spend a significant proportion of their time working individually.

Work teams and TBOs are not appropriate for all situations. First, their success depends on sustained support and investment that are not always available. Second, the work may not always require a team approach or seem to. For example, sales may be handled in the field by individuals working alone, if the products are not complex or dependent on service. When complexity of a product requires input from people with a variety of types of expertise or tailoring by engineering before manufacture or extensive service support, such as enterprise resource planning software, a sales team approach will be far more effective. One microwave antenna manufacturer made this change and found customers were much more satisfied—they worked with a stable group who had the expertise to provide high-quality service, so relationships evolved that facilitated the work. Successful execution of the work must drive the decision to use a team approach.

Even when teams are adopted and a TBO infrastructure surrounds them, not all members of the organization need to work in teams. Also, team members usually spend a significant proportion of their time working individually, moving back and forth between the group interaction and the solo role where concentration may be enhanced.

THE CHANGING NATURE OF WORK

The nature of work has been changing in recent years in a number of ways. For example, the work simplification approach that developed out of the Taylorist tradition has been giving way to job enlargement and enrichment—increasing responsibilities in both vertical and horizontal directions. The design trend has led to a shift from emphasis on the use of job descriptions toward use of job roles. Those new roles include a shift in attention for frontline employees for simple job duties to the welfare of the entire organization. Such changes seem to align with the shift toward a greater emphasis on knowledge work and a more educated body of employees, as well as the increasing dependence of strategic advantage on the optimal use of all the intelligence in an organization. TBO provides a natural fit with these changes and capitalizes on the options they provide.

Automation, cell-based clustering of people and machines, just-in-time procedures, total quality management, product and materials changes, and other influences have contributed to changes in job design. Job design aims at two goals: employee motivation and efficient use of resources, including work flow. There are many ways to design most jobs and clusters of jobs. The choice of design must align with the organization's strategy. Traditional approaches to job design tend to focus on efficiency; psychological approaches focus on motivation. TBO*ing* needs to focus on both within the framework of the mission-based strategy. Intelligent effort by individuals must be leveraged by appropriate collaboration and smooth work flow. Since TBO*ing* attempts to be comprehensive in its examination of work infrastructure, it provides an opportunity for a more complete approach to job design.

The Environment

Trends in today's environment include globalization, a fast pace of change, increased complexity, permeable organizational boundaries, and rapid technology change. A central principle of organizational design is matching the logic of organization to the environment and to the work or task to be accomplished (Dijksterhuis & van den Bosch, 1999). Traditional command-and-control organizations were appropriate for their time, when the environment was simpler and more stable, the work more segmented, and employees less educated. However, command and control is structurally maladaptive, given today's environment. At present, the environment calls for organizations that meet the six Fs—flat, fast, flexible, fun, focused, and "fatherless" (referring to the employment contract that is no longer paternalistic, but rather requires individuals to develop themselves) (cf. Crawford & Brungardt, 1999). To fit this complex environment, organizations must "complexify." The complexity of the environment must be matched by the complexity of the organization's design. TBO*ing* is one method of decentralizing knowing and decision making to promote the six Fs. The old cliché rings true—"all of us are smarter than any of us!"

The current environment demands adaptability. Adaptable organizations are flexible organizations with reorganization ability. Adaptability requires both awareness of the environment and the capability to change internally to meet the challenges of the environment. This need for constant environmental awareness calls for continuous links to the environment. TBO*ing* builds in adaptability by creating a few broad rules (Brown & Eisenhardt, 1998), then facilitating self-design by the teams. Teams are in touch with customers and suppliers and can make rapid adjustments when changes occur in the market place. The bottom level is the most adaptable level within the organization (Baskin, 2001). Stifling the bottom through rigid control reduces adaptability, whereas supporting it increases adaptability. Part of remaining adaptable includes connecting beyond the traditional walls of the organization to multiple organizations. The number, quality, and malleability of those connections add up to the viability of the organization. TBO*ing* enables this to occur.

At Lockheed Martin Electronics and Missiles in Orlando, Florida, integrated product teams (IPTs) bring together multiple disciplines on the production floor. In addition, customers and suppliers participate in these teams (http://www.bmpcoe.org/bestpractices/external/lmem/lmem_39.html). The teams represent one of the ways that Lockheed Martin builds bridges in the supply chain or value chain. Other mechanisms for involving suppliers include strategic alliances, teaming directly with suppliers, design of materials flow, and joint supply purchases. Building mutually advantageous relationships with suppliers is considered a best practice, meaning that it sets a standard of practice with the goal of all participating organizations forming an integrated process partly based on mandatory membership of suppliers on the IPTs.

Organizational Culture

Most scholars view organizational culture as a pattern of shared organizational values, basic underlying assumptions, and informal norms that guide the way work is accomplished in an organization (e.g. Ott, 1989). This approach assumes that a shared cognitive framework creates a social glue that holds people together in an organization. Hofstede and Neuijen (1990) argue that such a view may be more appropriate for thinking about national cultures. They emphasize shared practices as the glue in work organizations that enables coordination of activity. They state that "most authors will probably agree on the following characteristics of the organizational/corporate culture construct: it is (1) holistic, (2) historically determined, (3) related to anthropological concepts, (4) socially constructed, (5) soft, and (6) difficult to change."

The focus on practice was reinforced by the work of Brown and Duguid (2000) in their study of the idiosyncrasies of practice. They found that policy, principles, and engineered processes were generic only because they were propagated at a level above practice. The situational nature of practice requires local adjustments on machines, in relationships, and in interpretation of information. Coordination of activity among employees then depends on the way practice occurs. Hofstede and Neuijen (1990) indicate that practices may be referred to as "conventions," "customs," "habits," "mores," "traditions," or "usages." Since practices are learned at work, the opportunity to change organizational culture seems to improve when education and design of the work environment recognize and support certain practices and sharing of practices. Culture change at the higher level of values, beliefs, and assumptions remains a worthwhile goal that provides the socio-cognitive infrastructure for establishing overall alignment for activities within the organization but one that requires long-term investment through education, reward, modeling, and selection. Tailoring processes to fit the practice level requires some discretion and authority. These are provided through empowerment and self-management. The addition of teaming creates an environment where small clusters of people may work together within an environment that facilitates use of collaboration in problem solving. Subcultures and nested cultures are likely to arise in such settings where sharing is more intense at the local level. The culture in a TBO is very different than in a traditional organization. Some of the assumptions of the TBO culture are explored below.

DECISION MAKING WHERE THE WORK IS DONE

Because the employees actually doing the work have the most expertise about that work, it makes sense to push decision making down to these workers. In a traditional organization, the decision is passed upward to someone who may not have the relevant expertise to make the decision. As a result of decision making being pushed down to lower levels, work is coordinated and controlled at local levels as well. Day-to-day operational decisions are made lower in the organization. Responsibility, authority, and autonomy are pushed to the team level to support decision making (Harris & Steed, 2001).

TEAMS MAKE DECISIONS, WHEN APPROPRIATE

When crucial decisions require multiple types of expertise, the team makes the decisions. However, a delicate balance exists between individual decision making and willingness to involve others. Excess in either direction creates dysfunction. If all decisions become team decisions, then decision making becomes an arduous, frustrating, and time-consuming process. If too many decisions become individual decisions, then the trust and cohesiveness of the team dissipate. Also, sometimes decisions must be escalated to a higher level in the organization. It is important to work with teams to determine which types of decisions are team decisions, and which are not.

ENGAGEMENT OF EMPLOYEES LEADS TO INCREASED COMMITMENT

A foundational principle of effective TBO*ing* is the engagement of all employees in the work process. Employees also must be engaged in the design and change process. People are engaged well beyond traditional workplace norms. Employees are invited into decision making and ownership of outcomes. The increased engagement leads to greater ownership and commitment. It also mitigates the negative impact of stress (Maslach & Leiter, 1997). Because of the increased participation, everyone has a shared stake in the output. The responsibility for the health of the organization is shared much more evenly across the organization. It is not just top management's job to figure it out.

Organizational Structure

In a TBO, work is done collaboratively in a team structure. Teams are the basic performing unit, the formal organizing unit, of the organization. Some of the characteristics of structure in a TBO are explored below.

A VARIETY OF TEAM TYPES SUPPORTS DIFFERENT TYPES OF WORK

Because flexibility and adaptability are so important to meeting the demands of the ever-changing business environment, organizational structure of a TBO must be able to flex and change as well. Because of the different needs, many different types of teams exist.

Teams can be temporary or permanent, single function or multifunctional, inside one organization or across several, and have co-located or distributed membership. Cohen and Bailey (1997) identified four types of teams in their review of empirical team studies published from 1990 to 1996. Work teams are long-term and fairly stable teams that are responsible for producing goods or services. Parallel teams are short-term teams with limited authority (usually with recommendation power only) that exist in parallel to existing organizational structure. Project teams are short-term teams with a specific goal or objective that is completed, and then the team is disbanded. Project teams usually are cross-functional. Finally, management teams are long-term teams of managers that coordinate, integrate, and provide direction to other teams.

In order to avoid making teams the new silos, integration mechanisms among teams are necessary. One way to do this is via boundary workers, where team members are members of more than one team (Harris & Steed, 2001). Integration teams can also be created where representatives from several teams work together (Mohrman, Tenkasi, & Mohrman, 2000). This is especially important when the work between teams is highly interdependent (e.g. building an airplane).

TEAMS VARY IN THEIR LEVEL OF EMPOWERMENT

Just as a TBO contains various types of teams, teams vary in their level of empowerment. Different types of tasks may call for different levels of empowerment. Ray and Bronstein

(1995) describe a continuum of group structures as follows:

- Type I: Leader centered/leader focused
- Type II: Leader centered/function focused
- Type III: Leader centered/integrated-task focused
- Type IV: Self-led/time and task focused
- Type V: Self-led/task focused

As levels of competency and accompanying empowerment increase, the team becomes more able to make decisions and act on its own, without reliance on a manager or supervisor.

TEAMS ORGANIZE AROUND PROCESS OR PRODUCT

In a TBO, teams are organized around processes, products, or customers in order to maximize the use of cross-functional teams that bring diverse experience and expertise together. Because of the process or product focus, the TBO has a more lateral focus to work as opposed to a vertical silo focus (Harris & Steed, 2001).

TEAMS LEADING TEAMS IN A FLAT HIERARCHY

As mentioned previously, an important defining characteristic of TBO is that teams lead teams. In other words, it is not just the workforce that is in teams; the management is organized in teams as well (Mohrman, Tenkasi, & Mohrman, 2000). TBOs represent a flatter organization than the traditional, individually focused organization. Flat reporting relationships mean less hierarchy, and communication goes across the organization instead of exclusively up one chain and down the other, increasing the speed of communication. However, "flat" does not mean an absence of hierarchy. The organizational structure looks like a flat hierarchy of layers of teams leading teams.

NOT EVERYONE HAS TO BE IN A TEAM

Contrary to popular myth, not everyone in a TBO*ing* organization must belong to a formal team. Some tasks exist that may be more appropriate to an individual. In contrast to an individually oriented organization where an individual is immediately put on a task, the immediate reaction in a TBO is to put a team on it. However, that does not mean that everyone necessarily has to be on a team. Often individuals in specialized roles or with rare knowledge become contract workers to the teams rather than official members of lots of teams.

TBO UNIT OFTEN MUST INTERFACE WITH TRADITIONAL CORPORATE ENTITY

Unfortunately, not every part of every organization will be a TBO. Since TBO is a fairly new organizational form, TBO*ing* organizations are rare. A challenge occurs when the TBO unit interfaces with other entities that are more accustomed to dealing with traditional systems.

This dichotomy can occur between the TBO*ing* business unit and suppliers, customers, and even different parts of the broader organization. Enterprise systems built at the corporate level often pose a challenge for business units attempting new ways of working. This reality must be addressed in the organizational change, and mechanisms put in place to deal with the dichotomy.

Organizational Systems

Team-based support systems are enablers of a healthy team environment. The idea of changing the environment (infrastructure and culture) of teams is overwhelming when looked at from a broad perspective. The term "support system" is used to further define the organizational surroundings. A support system is "part of the organizational infrastructure that facilitates carrying out the processes necessary to do the work; to manage, control, coordinate, and improve it; and to manage the people who are doing it" (Mohrman, Cohen, & Mohrman, 1995, p. 302). For optimal success, organizational support systems must be aligned with the organizational design and the type of work being done. Therefore, if a team is chosen as the basis of organizational design, presumably because the work requires a team, then the organizational support systems must be team-based. The whole array of support systems should also be viewed as a system. When individual support systems conflict with each other, quality of support drops, and team performance drops with it.

For TBOs to be effective, they must have a comprehensive and complementary set of support systems that guide teams to meet organizational and business unit goals (Mohrman, Cohen, & Mohrman, 1995). To the degree that the teams lack support systems aligned with their needs, they will fall short of performance possibilities. Leaders and designers need to consider all these parts of the organizational context when making a change to teams. They will be disappointed to the extent that they consider only the within-team aspects.

TRADITIONAL VERSUS TEAM-BASED SUPPORT SYSTEMS

In general, support systems in a traditional organization are focused on individual performance. In a TBO, support systems must be modified and created to facilitate team performance. In a traditional organization, systems are controlled by management, are strongly linked to the chain of command, and promote stability and uniformity. In contrast, TBO support systems promote flexibility, continuous adjustment, and are self-managed (Mohrman, Cohen, & Mohrman, 1995).

FLEXIBILITY OF SUPPORT SYSTEMS

Support systems must be flexible to deal with changes in the external environment. Much attention has been paid lately to the increasing rate of change and complexity in our ever-global world environment. Organizations must be able to deal quickly with, and even think ahead of, changes in the environment. Because changes occur so often, support systems must also be able to flex with the needs of the environment. TBOs are much more flexible organizations than traditional organizations, and better able to meet the needs of the changing environment. In turn, teams must be supported by more flexible systems than the norm.

Support systems must be flexible to deal with various team types, as well as individual and teamwork. Different types of tasks require different kinds of teams (e.g. management team, project team, work team, parallel team, cross-functional team, or integration team). In fact, some tasks may require an individual instead of a team. Since organizational support systems need to be aligned with the organizational design for optimization, support systems need to be flexible to accommodate various team types and individual work. Support systems should create an umbrella so the organization can remain a cohesive whole, yet be flexible to meet the needs of various teams and individuals under the umbrella of support.

LIST OF SUPPORT SYSTEMS

Support systems can be defined in many different ways. The list below comes from five years of research on team-based support systems (Beyerlein & Harris, in press). After the list, some general findings about how some of the support systems look in a TBO are described. For definitions of the support systems and supporting references, see Table 10.1.

- Leadership, including executive leaders, direct supervision, team leaders, and team members/shared leadership
- Organization and team design
- Performance management, including goal setting, performance measurement, performance feedback, rewards, and recognition
- Financial and resource allocation
- Learning, including communication, information, knowledge management, and training
- Physical workspace and tools
- Change and renewal
- Integration, including between-teams integration, teams and systems integration, and change initiatives integration
- Creativity and innovation

In a TBO, teams are organized around deliverables of some kind, and have shared objectives. Teams set and monitor their own team goals, and are appraised as a team, ensuring team accountability for the work. Ideally, teams are able to set up their own goals, ensuring commitment to the goals. Teams measure team performance themselves and have their own measures that align with organizational measures. Importantly, all team members understand how measures relate to daily performance. Finally, while measures can occur at the team level, it is critical that they also take place at the business unit level, to ensure that measurements are aligned to business level results.

In terms of information, communication, and learning, a sign of a successful TBO is greater information sharing all around (including upward and downward communication), where everyone throughout the organization knows what is going on. Because of the flatness and complexity of the organizational structure, TBOs have more complex communication networks and decision-making patterns. Often TBOs have a higher level of technology in order to facilitate greater sharing of information. TBOs place a greater emphasis on training and development, and are better learning organizations, because they design in learning through the sharing of lessons learned and lateral and horizontal interactions among team members and across teams.

Table 10.1 Team-based support systems

Support system category	Support system	Team-based definition	References
Leadership	Executive leaders	Formal and informal processes that top leaders use to create leadership conducive to teamwork	Beyerlein & Harris (in press) Hall (1998) Leader's roles—Sundstrom and associates (1999)
	Direct supervision	Formal and informal processes that direct supervisors use to create leadership conducive to teamwork	Beyerlein & Harris (in press) Hall (1998) Leader's roles—Sundstrom and associates (1999)
	Team leaders	Formal and informal processes that team leaders use to create leadership conducive to teamwork	Beyerlein & Harris (in press) Leader's roles—Sundstrom and associates (1999)
	Team members/shared leadership	Formal and informal processes that team members use to create leadership conducive to teamwork	Beyerlein & Harris (in press)
Design	Organization design	Methods of looking at the organization as a whole and determining appropriate places for teams, and supporting them through support system design and culture work	Beyerlein & Harris (in press) Group design—Hall (1998) Team structure—Sundstrom and associates (1999)
	Team design	At the team level, making sure the team has the inputs it needs to get the work done	Beyerlein & Harris (in press) Team structure—Sundstrom and associates (1999)
Performance management	Goal-setting system	Methods of establishing aligned goals (e.g. goals, priorities, and tasks)	Beyerlein & Harris (in press) Direction setting—Mohrman, Cohen, & Mohrman (1995)
	Performance measurement system	Methods of identifying and measuring appropriate performance	Beyerlein & Harris (in press) Defining performance—Hall (1998) Defining performance—Mohrman, Cohen, & Mohrman (1995) Measurement and feedback—Sundstrom and associates (1999)

	Performance feedback system	Methods (formal and informal) of reviewing and appraising appropriate performance and other desired behaviors associated with performance	Beyerlein & Harris (in press) Performance appraisal—Hall (1998) Reviewing performance—Mohrman, Cohen, & Mohrman (1995) Measurement and feedback—Sundstrom and associates (1999)
	Reward system	Methods of rewarding performance and other desired behaviors (individual, team, business unit levels of performance)	Beyerlein & Harris (in press) Hall (1998) Rewarding performance—Mohrman, Cohen, & Mohrman (1995)
	Recognition system	Methods recognizing, formally and informally, performance and other desired behaviors (individual, team, business unit levels of performance)	Beyerlein & Harris (in press)
Financial	Financial system	Creating financial systems to support teams, including the accounting and reporting systems	Beyerlein & Harris (in press)
	Resource allocation system	Processes for ensuring that teams get the resources they need to get the work done	Beyerlein & Harris (in press)
Learning (formal and informal)	Communication system	Methods for communication throughout the organization	Beyerlein & Harris (in press) Mohrman, Cohen, & Mohrman (1995) Communication technology—Sundstrom and associates (1999)
	Information system	Methods for teams to get the information it needs to perform effectively (access and sharing, e.g. common databases, goals, and priorities)	Beyerlein & Harris (in press) Hall (1998) Information technology—Mohrman, Cohen, & Mohrman (1995) Sundstrom and associates (1999)
	Knowledge management system	Processes for acquiring, organizing, sharing, utilizing knowledge	Beyerlein & Harris (in press)

(*continues overleaf*)

Table 10.1 *(continued)*

Support system category	Support system	Team-based definition	References
	Training system	Methods for teams and individuals to identify and get the skills needed to perform (e.g. interpersonal skills training, and business skills training)	Beyerlein & Harris (in press) Hall (1998) Developing performance—Mohrman, Cohen, & Mohrman (1995) Sundstrom and associates (1999)
Selection system	Selection system	Processes for bringing new and transferred employees with the right skills into the right teams	Beyerlein & Harris (in press) Team staffing—Sundstrom and associates (1999)
Physical workspace and tools	Physical workspace and tools	The actual space in which the team works. If it is a virtual team, then the "space" created by technology (e.g. budgets, tools, and computers)	Beyerlein & Harris (in press) Facility—Sundstrom and associates (1999)
Change and renewal	Renewal system	Methods for periodically reevaluating and changing organizational design and systems, when necessary	Beyerlein & Harris (in press)
Integration	Between-teams integration	Methods for ensuring that teams do not become the new silos, and instead are pieces of an integrated whole (e.g. informal integration, formal leadership roles, and policies)	Beyerlein & Harris (in press)
	Change initiatives integration	Methods for ensuring that multiple change initiatives are aligned in terms of complementary content and sequence	Beyerlein & Harris (in press)
Creativity and innovation	Creativity and innovation system	Methods for ensuring that creativity and innovation are built into the system	Beyerlein & Harris (in press)

In a TBO, there is a shift from individual to team-based accountability. This accountability is designed into the organization. This means that any team in the organization can hold any other team accountable for not doing their work or creating problems for them. Because accountability at the team level is designed into the organization, the hierarchy of control and accountabilities becomes clearer, which is contrary to the popular myth that TBOs not only reduce control of the work, but that control and accountability lines become fuzzy. Control increases because of peer pressure—concertive control (Barker, 1995).

In a TBO, formal managers and leaders do not play traditional oversight roles. Instead, they become participative partners with employees—working with and through them, rather than over them—facilitating a philosophy that employees want to do the right thing for the organization, and tapping the expertise of team members in an environment that is too complex for one person to make good decisions. In a TBO, there is a different role definition of who does what kinds of activities—oversight tasks of traditional managers become the responsibility of the team, leaving the manager free to do more strategic work. Managers have responsibility for cultivating an environment of involvement where everyone is engaged or invited to engage in the business, a supportive environment where participation is the rule, and where everyone's voice counts. Because of this environment and the increased communications and interaction it brings, top management becomes more aware of the needs, values, and concerns of employees. Formal leaders have to develop facilitative leadership styles, and become less directive with an emphasis on coaching and facilitation. The role of formal leaders is to enable, inspire, and guide the teams.

CONCLUSION

In this chapter, we shared a descriptive overview of TBO*ing*. In summary, the key tenets of TBO*ing* are reviewed here. The team replaces the individual as the unit of work, of assessment, and to some extent, of reward. There are a variety of team designs and the chosen design should match the work situation. However, multiple designs should be combined into an array of interdependent and intact social/work systems—whether temporary or permanent, co-located or distributed, single function or multifunctional. In most organizations using teams, the structure at the management levels does not change; in a TBO, managers also work in teams. The rest of the organization surrounding the working teams must be organized to support them. That depends on aligning support functions with team needs. This all represents a radical change from traditional design. It requires substantial investment and intentional effort.

A big problem when discussing TBO*ing* is the lack of a common language. In a recent interview study of individuals with knowledge in the area, only 70 percent used the term "TBO" (Harris & Steed, 2001), and of these, many did not use the term consistently. Some similar terms include:

- High-performance work organizations
- Self-managing work teams
- Flexible, lateral organization
- Socio-technical systems
- New design plants
- Self-managing organizations

- Collaborative work systems
- Project-based organization

The majority of participants indicated that they tended to use whatever terminology was preferred by the customer organization. The bottom line is that anyone using TBO language must be careful to educate and create a shared meaning among the people using it.

TBO is only one approach to designing organizations to achieve strategic objectives, and it is not the right choice for every organization. TBO*ing* takes more time, effort, and investment than working individually. TBO*ing* is an expensive advanced social technology that requires commitment and resources to succeed, but, when done well, the social and financial benefits are tremendous. We believe that those who are successfully implementing this advanced social technology have a competitive advantage in a complex business environment. Further research will articulate the benefits, as well as the key critical success factors, for TBOs.

ACKNOWLEDGEMENTS

Thanks to the Center for Creative Leadership for supporting the interview study of experts in TBO. Special acknowledgement goes to colleagues Judith Steed and Gina Hernez-Broome for their help conceptualizing the study. Thanks to David Loring for supporting the idea. Special appreciation goes to the interview participants who gave from one to four hours of their busy schedule to share their thoughts on this exciting topic. Thank you!

REFERENCES

Barker, J. R. (1995). Communal–rational authority as the basis of leadership for self-managing teams. In M. Beyerlein, D. Johnson, & S. Beyerlein (eds), *Advances in Interdisciplinary Studies of Work Teams*, Vol. 3, *Team Leadership*. Greenwich, Conn.: JAI Press.

Baskin, K. (2001). What your body would tell you if it could talk. Keynote presentation, *Collaborative Work Systems Symposium*, University of North Texas, May 23–25, Denton, Tex.

Beyerlein, M., Hall, C., Harris, C., & Beyerlein, S. (1997). The failure of transformation to teams. *Proceedings of the International Conference on Work Teams*, Dallas, pp. 57–62.

Beyerlein, M. M. & Harris, C. L. (in press). Critical success factors in team-based organizing: a top ten list. In M. Beyerlein, C. McGee, G. Klein, J. Nemiro, & L. Broedling (eds), *The Collaborative Work Systems Fieldbook: Strategies, Tools & Techniques*. San Francisco: Jossey-Bass.

Brown, J. S. & Duguid, P. (2000). *The Social Life of Information*. Cambridge, Mass.: Harvard Business School Press.

Brown, S. L. & Eisenhardt, K. M. (1998). *Competing on the Edge: Strategy as Structured Chaos*. Cambridge, Mass.: Harvard Business School.

Cohen, S. & Bailey, D. (1997). What makes teams work: group effectiveness research from the shop floor to the executive suite. *Journal of Management, 23*, 239–290.

Crawford, C. B. & Brungardt, C. L. (1999). Building the corporate revolution: real empowerment through risk leadership. *Proceedings of the Annual Meeting of the International Leadership Association*, Atlanta, Ga, http://www.academy.umd.edu/ila/1999proceedings/crawford.htm

Dalton, G. L. (1998). The collective stretch. *Management Review, 87*(11), 54–60.

Devane, T. (in press). Big change fast: a case study in transformation from a traditional organization to a team-based organization. In J. Nemiro, G. Klein, C. McGee, & M. Beyerlein (eds), *The Collaborative Work System Casebook*. San Francisco: Jossey-Bass/Pfeiffer.

Dijksterhuis, M. S. & van den Bosch, F. (1999). Where do new organizational forms come from? Management logics as a source of coevolution. *Organization Science, 10*(5), 569–583.

Dumaine, B. (1994). The trouble with teams. *Fortune*, 5 September, pp. 86–92.
Goodman, P. S., Devadas, S., & Hughson, T. L. (1988). Groups and productivity: analyzing the effectiveness of self-managing teams. In J. P. Campbell, R. J. Campbell, & associates (eds), *Productivity in Organizations* (pp. 295–327). San Francisco: Jossey-Bass.
Harris, C. L. & Steed, J. (2001). *Team-based Organizations: Crafting the Organizational Context for Team Success.* Colloquium presented at the Center for Creative Leadership, Colorado Springs, Colorado.
Hofstede, G. & Neuijen, B. (1990). Measuring organizational cultures: a qualitative and quantitative study across twenty cases. *Administrative Science Quarterly, 35*(2), 286–317.
Jones, S. & Moffett, R. G., III (1999). Measurement and feedback systems for teams. In E. Sundstrom (ed.), *Supporting Work Team Effectiveness: Best Management Practices for Fostering High Performance*. San Francisco: Jossey-Bass.
Kennedy, F. (2002). Managing a team-based organization: a proposed strategic model. In M. M. Beyerlein, D. A. Johnson, & S. T. Beyerlein (eds), *Team-based Organizing*. Oxford: JAI/Elsevier.
Klein, J. A. (1993). Maintaining expertise in multi-skilled teams. In M. Beyerlein, D. Johnson, & S. Beyerlein (eds), *Advances in Interdisciplinary Studies of Work Teams*, Vol. 1, *Theories of Self-Managing Work Teams* (pp. 145–166). Greenwich, Conn.: JAI Press.
Lawler, E. E., III (1990). The new plant revolution revisited. *Organizational Dynamics, 19*(2), 5–14.
Maslach, C. & Leiter, M. P. (1997). *The Truth about Burnout: How Organizations Cause Personal Stress and What to Do about It.* San Francisco: Jossey-Bass.
Mathews, L. L. (1996). Top management groups: the relationships among member characteristics, group processes, business environments, and organizational performance. Dissertation, University of North Texas, Denton.
Mohrman, S. A., Cohen, S. G., & Mohrman, A. M. Jr (1995). *Designing Team-based Organizations: New Forms for Knowledge Work.* San Francisco: Jossey-Bass.
Mohrman, S. A. & Mohrman, A. M. Jr (1997). *Designing and Leading Team-based Organizations: A Workbook for Organizational Self-design.* San Francisco: Jossey-Bass.
Mohrman, S. A. & Tenkasi, R. (1997). Patterns of cross-functional work: behaviors and benefits. Paper presented at the University of North Texas Symposium on Work Teams, Dallas, Tex.
Mohrman, S. A., Tenkasi, R. V., & Mohrman, A. M. Jr (2000). Learning and knowledge management in team-based new product development organizations. In M. M. Beyerlein, D. A. Johnson, & S. T. Beyerlein (eds), *Advances in Interdisciplinary Studies of Work Teams* (Vol. 5, pp. 63–88). Amsterdam: JAI Press.
Moran, L. (1996). *Keeping Teams on Track: What to Do When the Going Gets Rough.* New York: McGraw-Hill.
Ott, S. J. (1989). *The Organizational Culture Perspective*. Florence, Ky: Brooks/Cole.
Pinchot, G., III (1985). *Intrapreneuring: Why You Don't Have to Leave the Corporation to Become an Entrepreneur*. New York: Harper & Row.
Ray, D. & Bronstein, H. (1995). *Teaming up: Making the Transition to a Self-directed, Team-based Organization*. New York: McGraw-Hill.
Rose, E., Gilmore, S., & Odom, R. D. (1998). Organizational transformation for effectively implementing a team-based culture. In S. D. Jones & M. M. Beyerlein (eds), *Developing High-performance Work Teams*. Alexandria, Va: ASTD Publications.
Saavedra, R., Earley, R. C., & van Dyne, L. (1993). Complex interdependence in task-performing groups. *Journal of Applied Psychology, 78*: 61–72.
Shonk, J. H. (1997). *Team-based Organizations: Developing a Successful Team Environment*. Homewood, Ill.: Business One Irwin.
Smolek, J., Hoffman, D., & Moran, L. (1999). Organizing teams for success. In E. Sundstrom (ed.), *Supporting Work Team Effectiveness: Best Management Practices for Fostering High Performance*. San Francisco: Jossey-Bass.
Sundstrom, E. & associates (1999). *Supporting Work Team Effectiveness: Best Management Practices for Fostering High Performance.* San Francisco: Jossey-Bass.
Zell, D. (1997). *Changing by Design: Organizational Innovation at Hewlett-Packard.* Ithaca, NY: ILR Press.

11

TEAM DECISION MAKING IN ORGANIZATIONS

Mary Ann Glynn and Pamela S. Barr

Today, organizations operate in fast-paced, pluralistic, complex, and uncertain environments; to keep pace, they increasingly use teams to make decisions (Hollenbeck et al., 1995). There is good reason for doing so. A robust tradition of research offers ample testimony to the fact that, on average, teams tend to make better quality and more accurate decisions than individuals (e.g. Gruenfeld et al., 1996; Hollenbeck et al., 1995, 1998). As a set of individuals, teams have the potential for incorporating more breadth and depth of expertise, defined as the "allocation of critical information (cues) about the decision to individuals in the team and knowledge of how that information should be used to reach decisions" (Hollenbeck et al., 1995, p. 295).

And yet, in spite of the consensus about the effectiveness of team decision making, there is still vigorous debate as to the processes whereby this happens. Although researchers have demonstrated the link between decision-making outcomes and a host of team variables, they have tended to focus on more visible and measurable features of teams including, but not limited to, variables such as hierarchical relationships, demography (i.e. heterogeneity/homogeneity of membership) (e.g. Gruenfeld et al., 1996; Hambrick & Mason, 1984; Hollenbeck et al., 1995, 1998), and/or the mapping of interaction patterns of communications and information processing (e.g. Bunderson & Sutcliffe, 2002). The very concept of "team as decision maker" is left unspecified. Although there has been debate as to whether it is appropriately modeled as a latent construct or an interpretive metaphor (Klimoski & Mohammed, 1994), the emerging literature on supraindividual cognition, and the plethora of terms such as "collective mind" (Fiol, 1994; Weick & Roberts, 1993), "organizational mind" (Sandelands & Stablein, 1987), and "group mind" (Wegner, 1987), seem to suggest a resolution: team cognition underlies decision making in organizations. We take this as our starting point in this chapter.

Our goal is to add to the conversation on how teams cognate in the process of organizational decision making. A cognitive perspective on business decision making focuses on problem framing, information processing, and issue interpretation; essentially, it involves "sensemaking" (Weick, 1995) at the team level, an implicitly higher level of abstraction

International Handbook of Organizational Teamwork and Cooperative Working. Edited by
M. A. West, D. Tjosvold, and K. G. Smith.

than that of the individual level of analysis. As a result, our inquiry begins with a consideration of defining both the appropriate level of analysis and the appropriate mechanisms of transfer, from the micro-level of individual cognition to the more macro-level of team cognition. We accept the received wisdom that, on average, teams tend to make better decisions than individuals; our focus is on the role of "team cognition" or "team mental model" (Klimoski & Mohammed, 1994) in linking processes and outcomes of decision making in organizations. We conclude with implications for future theorizing and research.

This chapter is organized as follows. Initially, we discuss multilevel models of teams as decision-making entities. Next, we apply these models to an examination of team decision making within a particularly critical work context, that of strategic decision making; more specifically, we focus on how top management teams make decisions. In this context, we examine processes and outcomes in team decision making. Finally, we end with ideas on a future agenda for theory and practice on team decision making.

CONCEPTUALIZING TEAMS AS DECISION-MAKING ENTITIES: A MULTILEVEL PERSPECTIVE

An inquiry into team decision making necessarily begins with a model of teams as decision makers. We adopt the lucid definition offered by March (1994, p. 104): "A team is a theoretical construct, a collection of individuals with problems of uncertainty but without conflict of interest or identities." To explicate how teams make decisions, Klimoski and Mohamed (1994, p. 403) observe that "group mind"-like constructs, or, in their terminology, "team mental models," have been advanced to explain variance in team decision making in organizations and, in particular, strategic decision making.

A cognitive approach to team decision making focuses on sensemaking (Weick, 1995), a process whereby individual team members pose a question to themselves along the lines of "What is it that is going on here?" (Goffman, 1974). The answer determines the nature of decision making, the problem(s) to be addressed, the mode of engagement, and the generation of solution(s). Making sense of a dilemma, decision, or situation permits the team to act in some rational manner; thus, meaning or sensemaking is a primary driver of team decisions. The meanings attached to decisions or situations have been variously labeled as frames (Bateson, 1972; Goffman, 1974), enactments (Weick, 1979), schema (Walsh, 1995), or interpretations (Fiol, 1994). At their core, these various terms used to describe cognition involve an understanding of causal maps (antecedents and effects), as well as the stimuli, actions, and consequences that attend decisions (Barr, Stimpert, & Huff, 1992). As Klimoski and Mohamed (1994) note, extending cognition to the team (or collective) level invites a consideration of how micro-level individual constructs such as schema, script, perceptual frame, or mental model can usefully and veridically apply to the macro-level of the team as a decision-making unit.

Although mechanisms for relating individual and team level cognition in decision making are recognized, models of how these transference processes operate are relatively scarce. As in Glynn (1996), we can identify three sets of mechanisms for articulating this micro–macro linkage between a team and its individual members:

1. *Aggregation effects*, whereby team members' individual cognitions aggregate to become those of the team;

2. *Cross-level effects*, whereby individual members' cognitions are shared through team interactions, transformed, codified, and understood (by members) to become those of the team;
3. *Distributed effects*, whereby team decision-making cognition exists in the patterned thoughts and actions in which team members interact and engage with each other but such cognitions are not the sole province of individuals.

Each of these mechanisms of team cognition is built upon a different set of theoretical premises; the models are summarized in Table 11.1.

Aggregation Model of Team Cognition

Existing models of team decision making tend to be predicated largely upon an aggregate movement between levels of analysis (Glynn, 1996; Rousseau, 1985): decision making at the collective level is modeled as the summation or accumulation of individual proclivities for action. In other words, theoretical models tend to depict decision making as originating within individuals, accumulating within dyads or subgroups, and then, depending upon the size of its membership, aggregating to the team level. Measures of central tendency (frequency counts; means) and dispersion (deviations; heterogeneity) operationalize aggregation models. Modeled as an aggregation, team cognition is simply the accumulation of its members' individual mental models. Although an aggregation model affords a rather straightforward assessment of team cognition, it does not capture the multiplicity or diversity of its members' individual models, nor does it recognize how a team mental model may exist apart from those of its members.

A good illustration of this model is advanced by Hollenbeck et al. (1995) in their "multilevel theory of team decision making." According to these authors, the accuracy of team-level decision making is a function of decision-making variables at lower levels of analysis; they summarize:

> Briefly . . . team decision-making accuracy is determined by constructs that occur at one of four levels: team, dyad, individual, and decision. The theory identifies the most critical variable at each of the three lower levels and *then aggregates these variables at the team level* (Hollenbeck et al., 1998, p. 270, emphasis added).

In this model, the core constructs of decision informity, individual validity, and dyadic sensitivity are modeled at both more micro-levels—the decision, the individual, and the dyadic pair, respectively—as well as that of the team as a whole. Subsequent empirical research has tended to validate this model, demonstrating that these core constructs, at both lower and higher (team) levels of analysis, function to significantly affect team-level decision-making accuracy (Hollenbeck et al., 1998).

An aggregation model is also evident in Bougon, Weick, and Binkhorst's (1977) model of the collective map of orchestral members operationalized as the "simple average of the individuals' maps" (Walsh, Henderson, & Deighton, 1988, p. 195). These and other studies point to the appropriateness of a multilevel approach; an aggregation model of team decision making is perhaps the most parsimonious type in this category. Essentially it emphasizes the composition or structure of a team, as reflected in the patterning of individual attributes, over the processes that attend decision making, such as communication and negotiation.

Table 11.1 Multilevel models of team cognition

Type of model	Key theoretical assumptions	Exemplars	Advantages of model	Limitations of model
Aggregation Model	Mental models of individual team members aggregate to the team level. Team mental model is defined in terms of the accumulation (or summary or average) of its membership. Team cognition is a function of individual capabilities and differences	"Multilevel theory of team decision making" (Hollenbeck et al., 1995, 1998); "Collective Map" (Bougon, Weick, & Binkhorst, 1977)	Theoretically parsimonious; relatively easy to operationalize and measure. Changes in team cognition to enable decision making are achieved through personnel changes and flows	Limited application and generalizability. Theoretically, a team is constrained to be no better than the sum (aggregation) of its component parts (individual members); content of mental models is emphasized over other features, e.g. form, organization, complexity
Cross-level model	Team members' mental models are transferred and encoded to become those of the team. Teams with better process dynamics (interaction patterns; communications, etc.) will tend to develop better models	"Negotiated Beliefs" (Walsh, Henderson, & Deighton, 1988)	Captures the role of team dynamics and mechanisms of information exchange	More difficult and complex to measure; requires a process perspective and methodology. Interventions to enable more effective decision making focus on team dynamics and processes of communications, interaction, socialization, diffusion, institutionalization, and politics, etc.
Distributed model	Team mental model is embedded in the team's systems, routines, norms, symbols, culture, and language. Mental models are more developed to the extent that they encode information that is rich, complex, and isomorphic with needs	"Collective Mind" (Weick & Roberts, 1993; Crowston & Kammerer, 1998; Brockman & Anthony, 1998)	Most veridical assessment of collective cognition at the team level. Team cognition can supersede that of its individual members, either alone or in the aggregate. Decision-making processes shape, and are shaped by, the team's transactive memory (Wegner, 1987)	Least transparent; can be difficult to measure and observe because of the need to capture cognitive and behavioral interaction patterns of team

Although an aggregation model has the advantages of theoretical clarity and operational ease (i.e. assessing central tendencies and variations across individuals), it, like any model, has inherent limitations. Critically, it does not take into account the influences of team dynamics, powerful actors, or environmental context, in crafting how individual cognitions aggregate to become a collective perspective; this issue is addressed more directly in both the cross-level and distributed models of team cognition.

Cross-level Model of Team Cognition

This approach focuses on the upward-oriented and downward-oriented transference between an individual's mental model and that of the team in a decision-making situation. The diffusion of ideas, knowledge, schema, and cognitive maps that enable the flow of decision-making resources is achieved through the conduct of team interactions; further, any shared or consensual mental models are codified and institutionalized in the collective memory of the team, memorialized in decision-making routines, rituals, habits, and practices to become a team-level cognitive construct. In turn, socialization, membership interactions, and team dynamics transfer team understandings and scripted decision-making styles to members, particularly new ones.

A cross-level approach to understanding team cognition focuses at the intersubjective level, capturing the criticality of group processes, interactions, and communications that harvest information from individual members. Team cognition benefits from a culture that permits and encourages diversity in thinking and decision-making styles as well as norms and practices of discussion to process a variety of perspectives. Such diversity in individual members' cognition may either converge to become a shared mental model for decision making or become negotiated through political processes of influence. This is the case for the model of team cognition as a "negotiated belief structure" (Walsh & Fahey, 1986; Walsh, Henderson, & Deighton, 1988). To summarize the approach embedded in a cross-level perspective on team cognition, Walsh (1995, p. 291) offers the following assessment:

> A number of writers examined the work on individual knowledge structures and concluded that when a group of individuals is brought together, each with their own knowledge structure, about a particular information environment, some kind of emergent collective knowledge structure is likely to exist. . . . The key challenge in considering knowledge structures at the supra-individual level of analysis is to account for the role of social processes in the acquisition, retention and retrieval of information.

Walsh (1995, p. 291) notes that this model has been labeled with a variety of terms, including collective cognitive map (Axelrod, 1976), team mental model (Klimoski & Mohammed, 1994), collective cognition (Langfield-Smith, 1992), hypermap (Bryant, 1983), intersubjectivity (Eden et al., 1981), dominant logic (Prahalad & Bettis, 1986), or collectively produced frames of reference (Bettenhausen & Murnighan, 1985). The contrast between this cross-level model and the aggregation model (discussed previously) is noted by Walsh, Henderson, and Deighton (1988, p. 207), as follows:

> Decisions reflect the schemata employed in the decision making process. It is not just a simple aggregation of schemata, however, but the selectively employed schemata which structure decision environments that are important . . . . We . . . need to investigate how political processes

> interact with a group's schematic endowment to affect performance in discrete stages of decision making (i.e. problem definition, alternative generation, alternative evaluation, decision choice, and decision implementation).

A cross-level model thus overcomes one of the restrictions of the aggregation model, by explicitly incorporating the role of team dynamics in forging team cognition. Team interaction, communication, socialization, politics, and other dynamic processes work to shape individuals' cognitions into those of the team that are then applied to making decisions. However, like the aggregation model, a cross-level model still emphasizes the individual level of analysis; a perspective that focuses entirely on the team level, apart from the individual level of analysis, is found in the distributed model of team cognition, to which we now turn.

Distributed Model of Team Cognition

Rather than the transference of mental models that is the focus of a cross-level approach, a distributed model focuses on how team cognition emerges from, and resides in, the patterned interactions of its members (Brown & Dugoid, 1991; Lave & Wenger, 1991) apart from the individual decision makers. The emphasis here is on the team itself and the extent to which it embeds specific models of decision making for the team. The team's cognition exists independent of individual members and is, instead, located or distributed within the structural (roles) and symbolic (language) properties of the team; the focus is on the patterning and dynamism of team interactions and behaviors rather than on individual members' minds (Weick & Roberts, 1993). Cognition is thus "situated" within the team and its decision-making context (Brown & Dugoid, 1991; Lave & Wenger, 1991). This model focuses on how team cognition consists of a set of intersubjectively shared set of meanings that is sustained through the interactions of team members.

A distributed model of team cognition in decision making centers on the creation of meaning, the social construction of reality, and the development of culture, symbolism, and social patterns that exist at a level of abstraction higher than that of individual team members (e.g. Walsh & Ungson, 1991; Weick, 1979). The team consists of interlocked, formalized, and routinized modes of thinking and action that drive decision making. Thus, a team may know more—and make better decisions—than its individual members, either individually or collectively.

> A key implication of distributed cognition is that a group performing a cognitive task may have cognitive properties that differ from the cognitive properties of any individual in the group. . . . The cognitive properties of the groups are produced by interactions internal to individuals and external to individuals (Thompson & Fine, 1999).

A distributed model of team cognition focuses on the embodiment of knowledge, information, and expertise within the team and, in turn, its role in decision making. A collective mind can emerge from the collective interaction of team members (Weick & Roberts, 1993). Through their interactions, undertaken to develop an understanding and framing of the focal decision, team members develop a more universal or consensual (Fiol, 1994) sense of what makes sense.

Given its location at the team level, preserving what the team knows is key; thus, a transactive memory is critical and "... not traceable to any of the individuals alone, nor can it be found somewhere 'between' individuals. Rather, it is a property of the group" (Wegner, 1987, p. 191). Transactive memory is defined as "a group memory system that details the expertise possessed by group members along with an awareness of who knows what within the group" (Rulke & Rau, 2000, p. 373). Of particular relevance for team decision making, transactive memory systems "should be particularly well developed in intimate relationships in which people share responsibilities, engage in many conversations about different topics, and make joint decisions" (Hollingshead, 1998, p. 659).

Summary: Models of Team Cognition

In the preceding sections, we have outlined three different approaches to modeling team cognition: as the aggregate of individual members' cognition, as the cross-level interaction between individual and collective cognition, and finally as a distributed property of the team as a whole. These three different models have different implications for the way we conceptualize team decision making in organizations.

In our consideration of these variations on team cognition, we chose to focus on strategic decision-making teams, typically those incorporating the organization's top management team (TMT). Our reasons for doing so are multiple. First, these teams make decisions that have not only consequences for the teams themselves but also for the organization. By focusing on organizational outcomes, we heed Klimoski and Mohammed's (1994, p. 428) admonition that, "In the area of strategic decision making, team mental models most likely have their greatest impact, not on the decision phase, but the implementation phase." Thus, examining strategic decision-making teams allowed our central construct of team mental models the greatest transparency. Second, TMTs are the primary focus of much of the organizational literature on management teams. Bunderson and Sutcliffe (2002), in their review of the literature, identified 15 studies published since 1989 that focused on the composition and outcomes of decision making in TMTs. Finally, strategic decision-making teams satisfy a number of the environmental conditions that make the development of collective mind operative and beneficial (Weick & Roberts, 1993): the need for high reliability decisions, nonroutine decisions, and interactive complexity in decision making. We turn now to an examination of how different models of team cognition (aggregation; cross-level; distributed) affect how we research strategic decision making in TMTs.

TEAM COGNITION IN CONTEXT: STRATEGIC DECISION MAKING

When we think of organizational teamwork, one of the most visible teams in organizations is the TMT, which is typically responsible for strategic decision making in the firm. Many studies in the organizational literature seek to investigate how the characteristics and processes of the strategic decision-making team affect the actions and outcomes of the organization (see Bunderson & Sutcliffe (2002) for an overview of the relevant literature). Perhaps strategic decisions have attracted such attention because of their inherent intrigue, dealing as they do with complexity, uncertainty, and consequence in a changing organizational environment. We acknowledge, however, that team decision making in organizations is obviously not limited to organizational elites; often project managers or work teams have decision-making authority to conceive and implement organizational actions. However, for the sake of focus and parsimony, we limit our scope to the TMT level.

We find that March's (1994) two key approaches to decision making reflect the logic that underlies the three conceptualizations of team cognition discussed in the prior section of this chapter. In March's (1994, p. 103) portrayal, individual decision makers can be intendedly rational actors who search for preferred alternatives in a world of limited knowledge and use the logic of consequence. Moving to decision making at the level of the team, a focus on preferred outcomes as a primary driver of the decision-making process suggests that team decisions are an outcome of interactive patterns of communication whereby the team negotiates and enacts a team-level understanding of preferred outcome, and how to reach that outcome. These patterns of communication, negotiation, and enactment are the very processes that are associated with cross-level and distributed models of team cognition.

March (1994, p. 103) also depicts how individual decision makers can be "rule followers," matching appropriate behavior to situations in an attempt to fulfill their identities; in this case, decision making is guided by the logic of appropriateness. Again, moving to team-level decision making, this correspondence between identity and decision rules depends less on team-level processes that craft a shared preference for an outcome (as in an "intendedly rational" approach), and instead, focuses on those individual features that lend identity characteristics to the teams, such as the homogeneity or heterogeneity of compositional characteristics (e.g. functional background, age, gender, tenure). The assumed tight coupling between decision makers' identity and their decision preferences shifts attention toward a team's identity, operationalized in terms of central tendency or dispersion of member characteristics, an approach that reflects an aggregation model of team cognition.

Thus, we observe that both types of decision makers March (1994) identifies—intendedly rational actors and rule-bound role players—reflect cognitive guidance systems (or forms of logic) that embed particular models of decision making. In the following discussion, we shall see how assumptions about these forms of logic in team mental models seem to imply a particular cognitively based logical system of team decision making.

Equipped with March's (1994) insights, we approach the literature to highlight, in depth, a few significant pieces that speak to the interface between team cognition and strategic decision making. Our reading of the critical works led us to observe that, over time, there seemed to be an evolution in theorizing from a focus on team composition and the aggregation of individual TMT member characteristics, to a focus on higher levels of abstraction, embedding more complex processes of team dynamics, information processing, and communication/interaction patterns. It is this historical trajectory, with its movement from more simple to more complex, to a shift in focal level of analysis from individual to collective, that we seek to map. We focus on a few influential pieces to distill significant themes that incorporate different models of team cognition in the study of TMT strategic decision making. We organize our discussion by the three models identified earlier—aggregation, cross-level, and distributed.

TMT Strategic Decision Making as an Aggregation of Member Attributes

In examining the extant literature, it quickly became apparent that much of the debate in this stream of research turns on the advantages and disadvantages of diversity in the composition of the TMT. Investigations into the conceptualization and measurability of a variety of team characteristics have propelled advances in the arena of strategic decision making and mapped their effects on team processes and organizational outcomes.

An inquiry into TMT strategic decision making begins with the influential work of Hambrick and Mason (1984) who theorized that the composition of the executive team would affect the performance outcomes of the organization. Counterposing their ideas against views of strategic processes as "flows of information and decisions, detached from the people involved" (p. 193), they directed attention away from institutional procedures and, instead, toward individual decision makers. Their model construed a profile of the TMT in terms of the composition of the characteristics of team members. The authors defended their approach by reasoning that "If strategic choices have a large behavioral component, then to some extent they reflect the idiosyncrasies of decision makers" (p. 195). To Hambrick and Mason (1984), understanding not only the chief executive but the "entire team increases the potential strength of the theory to predict, because the chief executive shares tasks and, to some extent, power with other team members" (p. 196).

Hambrick and Mason (1984) focused on the role of TMT demographics as a proxy for cognitive attributes. In particular, they emphasized how diversity in team members' age, education, socio-economic roots, functional background, financial position, organizational and team tenure influenced outcomes. The basic model is one that mirror's Ashby's (1952) notion of requisite variety in that the complexity of the decision-making environment should be mirrored in the complexity of the decision-making team. Team processes were not theorized directly, but rather presumed as a latent dynamic that glosses over members' diversity so as to yield rational and coherent decisions. The one team-level variable they consider is heterogeneity, or the amount of dispersion of TMT demography. Building on prior group research, they proposed, for instance, "Homogeneous top management teams will make strategic decisions more quickly than will heterogeneous ones" (p. 203).

Writing at a time when "[n]o such research centering on characteristics of entire top management teams is known to the authors" (p. 196), Hambrick and Mason (1984) articulated a perspective that is essentially an aggregation model. In their conceptualization of the link between team characteristics and strategic outcomes, they propose that a team's mental model is a reflection of the central tendencies of its individual members, assessed through counts or averages of the numbers of executives in one demographic category or another. Focusing on the upper echelon characteristic of functional background, for instance, they write:

> ... assume that two firms each have chief executives whose primary functional backgrounds are in production. In Firm A, three of four other key executives also rose primarily through production-oriented careers, even though they now are serving in nonproduction or generalist roles. In Firm B, the mix of executive backgrounds is more balanced and typical—one from production, one from sales, one from engineering, and one from accounting. Knowledge about the *central tendencies* of the entire top management team improves one's confidence in any predictions about the two firms' strategies. Moreover, the study of an entire team has the added advantage of allowing inquiry into dispersion characteristics, such as homogeneity and balance (Hambrick & Mason, 1984, pp. 196–197, emphasis added).

The focus on decision makers' attributes is predicated upon what March (1994) calls "rule-following," whereby individuals follow rules consistent with their salient identities. Identities are social constructions that relate the decision maker to organizational rules, structures, norms, and institutionalized practices that control decision making by indicating appropriateness. As March explains:

> The logic of appropriateness is tied to the concept of identity. An identity is a conception of self organized into rules for matching action to situations.... When an executive is enjoined to "act like a decision maker," he or she is encouraged to apply a logic of appropriateness to a conception of identity.
>
> Individuals describe themselves in terms of their occupational, group, familial, ethnic, national, and religious identities. Identities are both constructed by individuals and imposed upon them (March, 1994, pp. 62–63).

The logic of appropriateness is operative in an aggregation model of TMT strategic decision making. Doing what is expected of a "good accountant" is what is captured and highlighted in those studies examining the functional composition and diversity of the TMT. The conundrum of TMT functional diversity—that breadth of expertise and perspective is purchased at the expense of team consensus and expedient communication—is consistent with the notion that individuals act in ways that are normatively appropriate with their occupational identity, but in ways that may not be appropriate (or even comprehensible) to those bound by the rules of other occupational identities. Team members with different functional backgrounds thus may claim different logics as the basis for appropriate, credible, and legitimate decisions.

A TMT strategic decision-making model that is based on an aggregation model of team cognition thus capitalizes on both its strengths (particularly in terms of diversity of knowledge, perspective, and experience) and weaknesses, as team members literally occupy different "thought worlds" (Dougherty, 1992) whereby sensemaking (Weick, 1995) is an individual and not a collective (team) level process. With newer methodologies that tap into cognition more directly (than proxy measures such as demographics) and alternative models that incorporate team dynamics more directly (implicating a cross-level approach to team decision making), the field has begun to shift in its approach to modeling TMT strategic decision making so as to allow for the interaction between individual cognition and team processes of dialog, influence, and politics. Keck (1997, p. 144) observes:

> Evidence is emerging (notably Smith et al., 1994) that the relationship among team structure, team process, and firm performance may be much more complex than originally modeled or assumed in previous work. According to Smith et al. (1994), there are three competing models of the effects of team structure on firm performance: 1) the demography model based on the direct effect of team structure on performance, 2) the process model based on the direct effect of team process above and beyond the direct effect of team structure, and 3) the model of team processes as intervening variables.

The influence of Hambrick and Mason's (1984) "general model" (p. 203) cannot be overstated; their ideas set into motion a generation of researchers attempting to map upper echelon characteristics to firms' strategic outcomes that persists to the present. However, a different model of team cognition was emerging.

TMT Strategic Decision Making from a Cross-level Perspective

Partly to overcome some of the conceptual and methodological limitations embedded in an aggregation model of team cognition in strategic decision making, researchers began to focus on explicating the implicit links in the aggregation model, teasing out the implicit processes relating individuals' demographic attributes to decision and organizational outcomes. Kilduff, Angelmar, and Mehra (2000, p. 32) offer this insight:

> According to Hambrick et al. (1996, page 66), the heterogeneous team has a broad potential behavioral repertoire and is able to "conceive and launch actions on many fronts." From this perspective, demographic heterogeneity may well complement rather than determine cognitive heterogeneity . . . teams heterogeneous on demographic variables may be better able to build on the diverse experience base of the team to validate diverse cognitions, and thus take advantage of innovative suggestions.

The links implicit in the Hambrick and Mason (1984) model, connecting team demography, team process, and firm performance outcomes, were studied more explicitly by Smith et al. (1994) in their widely cited work. In their research, they examined 53 high-technology firms to investigate the roles of team demography and team process in explicating performance (as noted in the Keck (1997) quote above). They empirically examined three models. The first, a demography model, relating TMT member attributes directly to firm performance, is consistent with the aggregation model of Hambrick and Mason (1984), outlined above. The second, a process model, integrating ideas from social psychology, shifts from individual characteristics (of the demography model) to team interactive dynamics, particularly social integration and communication, in terms of both their formality and frequency. The explanatory power of these process factors is examined for their effects above and beyond those of demography. Finally, Smith and his colleagues (1994) investigate a third model, which posits that team process is a mediator between team demography and firm performance. They summarize their results as follows:

> Overall, there was partial support for the intervening model, in which process is a mediator of the relationship between demography and performance, and the process model, in which demography and process variables each affect performance separately. Little support was found for the argument underlying the demography model, in which demography rather than process affects performance (Smith et al., 1994, p. 431).

Their findings attest to the feasibility of a cross-level model of team cognition in strategic decision making; their results speak to the role of team processes in relating the attributes of team members to organizational performance. Although Smith and colleagues (1994) found significant main effects for the demographic variables of tenure, experience, education, and background, an aggregation framework modeling team characteristics in terms of centrality or dispersion of these individual factors underspecifies the relationship between team decision making and organizational performance. In other words, what individual team members bring to the table, by way of personal experience and perspective, as represented in demographic variables, does matter; however, how these individual proclivities are processed within the team adds to their effects on outcomes. Thus, by demonstrating the contribution of team process, above and beyond demography, Smith and colleagues (1994) offer evidence in support of a cross-level model of team decision making.

Given their demonstration that process affects performance, the question then becomes: why? In an extension of this work, Knight et al. (1999) scrutinize more closely the link between team demography and team process. Using data from 76 high-technology firms in the United States and Ireland, Knight and colleagues found that TMT diversity in demography (function, age, education, employment tenure) exerted significant main effects on strategic consensus, but that "the overall fit of the model was not strong. Adding two intervening group process variables, interpersonal conflict and agreement-seeking, to the model greatly improved the overall relationship with strategic consensus" (Knight et al., 1999, p. 445). Thus, beyond the earlier effects found for organizational performance, these researchers demonstrated that group processes similarly played a significant role in influencing team demography to affect team cognition. Further, Simons, Pelled, and Smith (1999, p. 670) support this reasoning in their study. They report: "Our data revealed that debate increased the tendency for diversity to enhance TMT performance. Further, debate—by diversity—interactive effects were strongest for more job-related forms of diversity. Decision comprehensiveness partially mediated these interactive effects." Finally, we note that Ken A. Smith and Ken G. Smith, along with their colleagues, have extensively investigated the effects of demography and process; across several studies, their results support a significant role for team processes in team decision making, thus indicating that a cross-level model that interacts individual cognition with team dynamics is a viable one.

These studies of TMT strategic decision making that incorporate process variables imply that decision makers may not always follow blindly the normative rules associated with their identities. This may be because individual identities are not salient, a notion that has not been tested yet in this literature. Alternatively, however, they do suggest that process variables, particularly those that focus on forging agreement and information sharing among diverse team members, may function either by creating a "team" identity, with a logic of appropriateness that supersedes those of individual members, or by invoking a logic of consequence that focuses not so much on shared identity as shared goal. Both imply different types of decision makers—rational actor versus role actor (March, 1994)—and a different sense of what is shared or held in common by the team, perhaps "partaking in an agreement," with its implications of team consensus or acceptance (Thompson & Fine, 1999). Thus, cross-level models have been effective in illuminating how different assumptions about the bases of decision making—identity and/or rationality—may independently or jointly be embedded in a particular theoretical or empirical approach. Moreover, the cross-level model hints at the emergence of the next perspective in the evolution of team decision making: that at the collective or distributed level.

TMT Strategic Decision Making as Collective Mind

In some ways, this model of team decision making seems to circle back to the original observation that prompted Hambrick and Mason's (1984) work: the criticality of institutionalized flows, patterns, and procedures in the distribution of information and in decision making. It was the lack of agency in this perspective that motivated them to theorize about the role of individual TMT characteristics. Two decades ago, the role of cognition and individual agency in organizing and directing these flows was notably absent; this is no longer so. Current perspectives on TMT decision making, perhaps because of their interest in promoting agency, have minimized the impact of "institutionalized flows, patterns, and procedures." The notion of "collective mind" in team decision making marries the agency, represented by individual level cognition, to the patterns and practices that define "team" and influence decision making by the team.

Weick and Roberts (1993, p. 360) define what is meant by the construct of "collective mind":

> The word "collective," unlike the words "group" or "organization," refers to individuals who act as if they are a group. People who act as if they are a group interrelate their actions with more or less care, and focusing on the way this interrelating is done reveals collective mental processes that differ in their degree of development. Our focus is at once on the individual and the collective, since only individuals can contribute to a collective mind, but a collective mind is distinct from an individual mind because it inheres in the pattern of interrelated activities among many people.

They contend that the "[c]ollective mind is manifest when individuals construct mutually shared fields" (Weick & Roberts, 1993, p. 365). Collective mind springs from individuals' thoughtful contributions, enriched representation of a collective to which their actions connect them, and interrelate and subordinate them; conversely, limitations or deficiencies in individuals' representations of the process and their subordination to team goals can limit the value of their contributions to collective mind (Crowston & Kammerer, 1998, p. 204).

This notion of team cognition is still emergent and has not yet been applied empirically to decision making in TMTs. However, there is much to recommend it. First, a number of the environmental conditions that make the development of collective mind operative and beneficial (Weick & Roberts, 1993) characterize the nature of strategic decision making; as indicated earlier, these include a need for high reliability (and error-free) decisions; nonroutine decisions; and interactive complexity in decision making. Second, the types of interpersonal interactions that reflect the application of a model of collective mind to team decision making—representation of different areas of expertise or knowledge, subordination of personal goals in favor of the attainment of team goals, and heedful interrelating, i.e. the process of keying off other team members—are similar to what one would expect in TMT strategic decision making. Most TMTs are composed of top executives who represent the various functional and/or divisional activities of the firm; the expectation is that the decision outputs will represent what is good for the company and not solely what is in the best interest of individual team members.

Perhaps because it is somewhat antithetical to the American cultural identity of individuated, differentiate self—as well as stereotypes about TMTs as heroic, independent, and insubordinate decision makers—a collective mind model of TMT decision making is not as prevalent as the aggregation or cross-level models. However, the coemergence of new organizational forms that emphasize structures that are more flat, flexible, and networked and strategies that make use of intraorganizational as well as interorganizational networks and alliances to create competitive advantage has had the result of making organizations more interconnected and team-based. We believe that the notion of team cognition at this higher level of abstraction will find wider applicability, consistent with the observations of Brockman and Anthony (1998, p. 210):

> In the strategy context, a collective mind is particularly valuable in helping to surface tacit considerations. For instance, during strategy formulation, the heedful interrelating should help explicate tacit dimensions inherent in the strategic visioning process. During strategy formulation, more strategic alternatives should be identified and then be open for evaluation before becoming strategic objectives. Even for strategy implementation, interrelating may help surface previous experiences of the TMT members that can then be evaluated by the team as alternatives.

Modeling team cognition as collective mind in the process of TMT strategic decision making offers the potential of reconciling several dilemmas in the extant literature. First, it allows researchers to consider the problem of accounting for a persistent firm-level "dominant logic" (Prahalad & Bettis, 1986), even under conditions of TMT change and personnel flows. A view of team cognition as "collective mind" draws attention to how such logic may exist apart from individual members and remain relatively inert over time; thus, it becomes less dependent on the particular attributes of TMT members and more reliant on how such logic is distributed within the substrata of the TMT's institutionalized structural, cultural, and political systems. Second, a collective mind perspective shifts researcher focus away from mapping the functional/demographic diversity of TMT members (an aggregation approach) or the political processes of team influence (a cross-level approach) and toward a fuller integration of the role of team cognition in decision making. Collective mind acknowledges how a diverse set of individual views can contribute to, and be represented in, a team perspective; however, its notion of heedful interrelating offers a counterpoint to explanations that are mired in politics and influence peddling among TMT members. Thus, it allows for variations in TMT strategic decision making and effectiveness without resorting to theorizing about demographic aggregation or building models of upward and downward political and social influence. We offer some extensions on these ideas and how they may build an agenda for future work on team decision making in organizations in our conclusions.

CONCLUSIONS

In this chapter we have identified three models of team-based cognition (aggregation; cross-level; distributed), and related each to specific perspectives on TMT strategic decision making published in the literature. While all three models have their merit and offer explanatory power, we suggest that the notion of distributed cognition and the collective mind offers a promising direction for future research on team decision making. We base this conclusion on several observations.

First, in neither the aggregation nor the cross-level models is the development of the team as intertwined with the team cognition at the collective level. Because the collective mind is "located" in the team process of interrelating (Weick & Roberts, 1993), the development of mind is tightly coupled to the development of group. To create high reliability (or error-free) environments, both mind and team must be mature in their development: "both interrelating and intimacy develop jointly" (Weick & Roberts, 1993, p. 374).

The problems of decoupling the development of mind from collective can be seen in the off-diagonals of Table 11.2, which is derived from Weick and Roberts's (1993, pp. 374–376) discussions. To develop mind without team is to have a shallow and often fleeting pattern of heedful, appropriate, and intelligent team interrelating; its effectiveness may be limited to those types of teams that quickly develop and evaporate, such as ad hoc project teams that assemble to produce films or television shows (e.g. Faulkner & Anderson, 1987; Peters, 1992). Conversely, to develop the collective (team) without an intelligent, heedful mind is to invite dysfunctionality in organizational outcomes, including low reliability, incomprehensibility, and illegitimacy; failure and disaster may result. It is associated with the narrowness and inaccuracies consonant with groupthink in decision making (Janis, 1982).

As suggested in the language of the label itself—"collective mind"—collective and mind become an effective unit when both are well developed. Thus, it is through individuals' contributions, internal representations of the team, and subordination to the goals of the

Table 11.2 Collective mind and group development

	Developed collective mind	Undeveloped collective mind
Developed group	• Interrelating and intimacy develop jointly • Heedful interrelating • Contributions made thoughtfully • Representations are constructed carefully and appreciated by others • High reliability and error reduction Illustrations: Flight operations on aircraft carriers (Weick & Roberts, 1993); teams of software requirements analysts (Crowston & Kammerer, 1998); strategic planning teams (Brockmann & Anthony, 1998)	• Subordination to a system that is envisaged carelessly; overestimation of group's power, morality, and invulnerability • Contributions are made thoughtlessly; self-censorship of deviations, doubts, and counterarguments • Representations are careless; members maintain the false assumption that silence means consent • Heedless interrelating • Comprehension declines • Disasters result Illustrations: Groupthink (Janis, 1982); cults (Galanter, 1989); interactions at NASA prior to the *Challenger* disaster (Starbuck & Milliken, 1988); ethnocentric research groups (Weick, 1979)
Undeveloped group	• Nondisclosive intimacy stressing coordination of action over alignment of cognitions, mutual respect over agreement, trust over empathy, diversity over homogeneity, loose over tight coupling, and strategic communication over unrestricted candor (Eisenberg, 1990) • Shared values, openness, and disclosure are not fully developed • Heedful contributing (e.g. loose coupling, diversity, strategic communication) • Heedful representing (e.g. mutual respect, coordination of action) • Heedful subordination (e.g. trust) Illustrations: Ad hoc project teams (Faulkner & Anderson, 1987; Peters, 1992); temporary systems—in aircraft cockpits (Ginnett, 1990); jazz improvisation (Eisenberg, 1990); in response to crises (Rochlin, 1989) or in high-velocity environments (Eisenhardt, 1989)	

Note: Table is adopted from Weick and Roberts (1993, pp. 374–376).

team that mind is realized and individuals and team become indistinguishable. It is through this connection of heedful interrelating among members of the team that the collective mind becomes functional, transparent, and manifest. As Weick and Roberts (1993, p. 374) explain:

> For the collective mind, the connections that matter are those that link distributed activities, and the ways those connections are accomplished embody much of what we have come to mean by the word "mind." The ways people connect their activities make conduct mindful.

Understanding team cognition as collective mind affords a different perspective on decision-making models as well. The logic of consequence, embedded in the rational actor model of decision making (March, 1994), suggests that, to be effective, the collective mind must represent a commonly held goal to which individuals contribute intelligence and subordinate their personal goals. The logic of appropriateness, embedded in rule-following actors, similarly suggests that individual identities must be subordinated to the collective identity, and new rules of appropriateness need to emerge to guide decision making.

The implications for strategic decision making of a model of team cognition as collective mind depart from that of a cross-level model of team cognition in two important ways. First, a collective mind necessitates the *subordination* of both goals and identities of individuals; a cross-level model necessitates *integration* of individual goals and identities with those of the team. That is, in cross-level models, team processes such as information sharing, consensus seeking, team maintenance, and effective communication encourage the disclosure of individual proclivities and the discovery of overlapping (shared) goals and identities. By contrast, a collective model shifts attention from individual attributes to the distributed patterning of these across the team. The individual becomes less identifiable and the mind of the team exists apart from the individuals; individuals' role is not necessarily to share but to interrelate heedfully, thoughtfully, and carefully.

Our overview of team cognition, in the context of strategic decision making in organizations, offers new perspectives on how we can forge more cooperative behavior within organizations. In this chapter, we have considered three primary avenues: through the aggregation of individual attributes, through the processes of upward and/or downward influence, or through the processes of heedful interrelating that converge a collective mind from distributed cognition. We suggest that, whether building from team members' individual attributes, from interactive team processes that share information and forge agreement on goals and preferences, or from a collective thrust that relates individuals to relate intelligently, teams become effective as decision makers when a perspective on the collective emerges. Informed by these perspectives, future research will hopefully expand on these models and afford richer descriptions on the role of team cognition in decision making.

REFERENCES

Ashby, W. R. (1952). *A Design for a Brain*. New York: Wiley.

Axelrod, R. (1976). *The Structure of Decision*. Princeton: Princeton University Press.

Barr, P. S., Stimpert, J. L., & Huff, A. S. (1992). Cognitive change, strategic action, and organizational renewal. *Strategic Management Journal, 13*, 15–36.

Bateson, G. (1972). *Steps to an Ecology of Mind.* New York: Ballantine Books.
Bettenhausen, E. & Murnighan, J. K. (1985). The emergence of norms in competitive decision making groups. *Administrative Science Quarterly, 20*, 350–372.
Bougon, M., Weick, K., & Binkhorst, D. (1977). Cognition in organizations: an analysis of the Utrecht Jazz Orchestra. *Administrative Science Quarterly, 22*, 606–639.
Brockman, E. P. & Anthony, W. P. (1998). The influence of tacit knowledge and collective mind on strategic planning. *Journal of Managerial Issues, 10*, 204–222.
Brown, J. S. & Dugoid, P. (1991). Organizational learning and communities-of-practice: toward a unified view of working, learning, and innovation. *Organization Science, 2*, 40–57.
Bryant, J. (1983). Hypermaps: a representation of perceptions in conflicts. *Omega, 11*, 575–586.
Bunderson, J. S. & Sutcliffe, K. (2002). Comparing alternative conceptualizations of functional diversity in management teams: process and performance effects. *Academy of Management Journal, 45*, 875–893.
Crowston, K. & Kammerer, E. E. (1998). Coordination and collective mind in software requirements development. *IBM Systems Journal, 37*, 227–245.
Dougherty, D. (1992). Interpretive barriers to successful product innovation in large firms. *Organization Science, 3*, 179–202.
Eden, C., Jones, S., Sims, D., & Smithin, T. (1981). The intersubjectivity of issues of intersubjectivity. *Journal of Management Studies, 18*, 37–47.
Eisenberg, E. (1990). Jamming: transcendence through organizing. *Communication Research, 17*, 139–164.
Eisenhardt, K. M. (1989). Building theories from case study research. *Academy of Management Review, 14*, 532–550.
Faulkner, R. R. & Anderson, A. B. (1987). Short-term projects and emergent careers: evidence from Hollywood. *American Journal of Sociology, 92*, 879–909.
Fiol, C. M. (1994). Consensus, diversity, and learning in organizations. *Organization Science, 5*, 403–420.
Galanter, M. (1989). *Cults.* New York: Oxford University Press.
Ginnett, R. C. (1990). Airline cockpit crew. In J. Richard Hackman (ed.), *Groups That Work (and Those That Don't)* (pp. 427–448). San Francisco: Jossey-Bass.
Glynn, M. A. (1996). Innovative genius: a framework for relating individual and organizational intelligences. *Academy of Management Review, 4*, 1081–1111.
Goffman, E. (1974). *Frame Analysis.* Cambridge, Mass.: Harvard University Press.
Gruenfeld, D. H., Mannix, E. A., Williams, K. Y., & Neale, M. A. (1996). Group composition and decision making: how member familiarity and information distribution affect process and performance. *Organizational Behavior and Human Decision Processes, 67*, 1–15.
Hambrick, D. C. & Mason, P. A. (1984). Upper echelons: the organization as a reflection of its top managers. *Academy of Management Review, 9*, 193–206.
Hollenbeck, J. R., Ilgen, D. R., LePine, J. A., Colquitt, J. A., & Hedlund, J. (1998). Extending the multilevel theory of team decision making: effects of feedback and experience in hierarchical teams. *Academy of Management Journal, 41*, 269–282.
Hollenbeck, J. R., Ilgen, D. R., Sego, D., Hedlund, J., Major, D. A., & Phillips, J. (1995). The multilevel theory of team decision-making: decision performance in teams incorporating distributed expertise. *Journal of Applied Psychology, 80*, 292–316.
Hollingshead, A. B. (1998). Retrieval processes in transactive memory systems. *Journal of Personality and Social Psychology, 74*, 659–671.
Janis, I. (1982). *Groupthink* (2nd edn). Boston: Houghton-Mifflin.
Keck, S. (1997). Top management team structure: differential effects by environmental context. *Organization Science, 8*, 143–156.
Kilduff, M., Angelmar, R., & Mehra, A. (2000). Top management-team diversity and firm performance: examining the role of cognitions. *Organization Science, 11*, 21–34.
Klimoski, R. & Mohammed, S. (1994). Team mental model: construct or metaphor. *Journal of Management, 20*, 403–437.
Knight, D., Pearce, C. L., Smith, K. G., Olian, J. D., Sims, H. P., Smith, K. A., & Flood, P. (1999). Top management team diversity, group process, and strategic consensus. *Strategic Management Journal, 20*, 445–465.

Langfield-Smith, K. (1992). Exploring the need for a shared cognitive map. *Journal of Management Studies, 29*, 349–368.
Lave, J. & Wenger, E. (1991). *Situated Learning*. Cambridge, England: Cambridge University Press.
March, James G. (1994). *A Primer on Decision Making*. New York: Free Press.
Peters, T. (1992). *Liberation Management*. New York: Knopf.
Prahalad, C. K. & Bettis, R. A. (1986). The dominant logic: a new linkage between diversity and performance. *Strategic Management Journal, 7*, 485–501.
Rochlin, G. I. (1989). Organizational self-design is a crisis-avoidance strategy: US naval flight operations as a case study. *Industrial Crisis Quarterly, 3*, 159–176.
Rousseau, D. M. (1985). Issues of level in organizational research. In B. M. Staw & L. L. Cummings (eds), *Research in Organizational Behavior* (Vol. 17, pp. 1–37). Greenwich, Conn.: JAI Press.
Rulke, D. L. & Rau, D. (2000). Investigating the encoding process of transactive memory development in group training. *Group & Organization Management, 25*, 373–396.
Sandelands, L. E. & Stablein, R. (1987). The concept of organization mind. In S. Bacharach & N. DiTomaso (eds), *Research in the Sociology of Organizations* (Vol. 5, pp. 135–161). Greenwich, Conn.: JAI Press.
Simons, T., Pelled, L. H., & Smith, K. A. (1999). Making use of difference: diversity, debate, and decision comprehensiveness in top management teams. *Academy of Management Journal, 42*, 662–673.
Smith, K. G., Smith, K. A., Olian, J. D., Sims, H. P., O'Bannon, D. P., & Scully, J. A. (1994). Top management team demography and process: the role of social integration and communication. *Administrative Science Quarterly, 39*, 412–438.
Starbuck, W. H. & Milliken, F. J. (1988). Challenger: fine-tuning the odds until something breaks. *Journal of Management Studies, 25*, 319–340.
Thompson, L. & Fine, G. A. (1999). Socially shared cognition, affect, and behavior: a review and integration. *Personality & Social Psychology Review, 3*, 278–304.
Walsh, J. P. (1995). Managerial and organizational cognition: notes from a trip down memory lane. *Organization Science, 6*, 280–320.
Walsh, J. P. & Fahey, L. (1986). The role of negotiated belief structures in strategy making. *Journal of Management, 12*, 325–338.
Walsh, J. P., Henderson, C. M., & Deighton, J. (1988). Negotiated belief structures and decision performance: an empirical investigation. *Organizational Behavior and Human Decision Processes, 42*, 194–216.
Walsh, J. P. & Ungson, G. R. (1991). Organizational memory. *Academy of Management Review, 16*, 57–91.
Wegner, D. M. (1987). Transactive memory: a contemporary analysis of group mind. In B. Mullen & G. R. Goethals (eds), *Theories of Group Behavior* (pp. 185–208). NewYork: Springer.
Weick, K. E. (1979). *The Social Psychology of Organizing* (2nd edn). New York: McGraw-Hill, Inc.
Weick, K. E. (1995). *Sensemaking in Organizations*. Thousand Oaks, Calif.: Sage Publications.
Weick, K. E. & Roberts, K. (1993). Collective mind in organizations: heedful interrelating on flight decks. *Administrative Science Quarterly*, 38, 357.

12

POWER IN GROUPS AND ORGANIZATIONS

Peter T. Coleman and Maxim Voronov

This is a chapter about power in groups and organizations. In the following pages, we suggest that the analysis and exploration of the complexities of organizational power by managers and workers are both necessary and useful. We begin by discussing three of the prominent theoretical perspectives on power from the literatures of social and organizational psychology and critical management studies. We then outline some of the dilemmas and challenges faced by executives, managers, and workers around empowerment, disempowerment, and organizational democracy. Then, building on the seminal works of Follet, Deutsch, Tjosvold, Clegg, Mumby, and others, we offer a framework of organizational power which views power as a multifaceted phenomenon; as thoughts, words, and deeds which are both embedded within and determining of a complex network of relations, structures, and meaning-making processes at different levels of organizational and community life. Such a framework enables us to understand the relational aspects of power and authority within the context of the macro structures and ideologies that give them meaning. It can also help identify those domains in organizations where the potential for sharing cooperative power is, in fact, not disempowering, but genuinely empowering for all concerned. The chapter concludes with a set of practical recommendations for managers that emphasize the benefits of multiple emancipatory initiatives within organizations when implemented with respect to the paradoxes of power.

THEORETICAL PERSPECTIVES ON POWER: CONTROLLING, COOPERATIVE, AND CRITICAL

Power, like other essential organizational phenomena, has been studied through the years from a variety of theoretical perspectives. Each approach has contributed to our understanding of power and influence in organizations; however, each is aspectual, focusing on particular aspects of power at the expense of our understanding of others. Below, we summarize the three primary paradigms of power: controlling, cooperative, and critical.

International Handbook of Organizational Teamwork and Cooperative Working. Edited by M. A. West, D. Tjosvold, and K. G. Smith.

Power-as-control

Morgan (1997) claims that many organizational theorists derive their thinking on power from the definition of power offered by American political scientist Robert Dahl. Dahl (1968) proposed that power involves "an ability to get another person to do something that he or she would not otherwise have done" (p. 158). This ability is often linked with the capacity to overcome the resistance of the other. This type of definition has been influential with many eminent social theorists and researchers, past (Cartwright, 1959; Dahl, 1957; French & Raven, 1959; Lasswell & Kaplan, 1950; Weber, 1947) and present (Hinkin & Schriesheim, 1989; Kipnis, 1976; Mossholder et al., 1998; Pfeffer, 1981; Rahim, 1989; Raven, Schwarzwald, & Koslowsky, 1998; Schriesheim, Hinkin, & Podsakoff, 1991). Power, from this perspective, is seen as a special kind of influence of A over B. This emphasizes the controlling and potentially coercive aspects of person-centered power (A) and views it as both a mechanism for maintaining order and authority and, when abused, a problem to be contained. As such, this perspective is consistent with the technical, mechanistic, and unilateral approaches to organizational life epitomized by Taylor's methods of scientific management.

The study of power-as-control has been immensely important. First, the need for management to maintain a reasonable degree of order and efficiency in organizations is obvious. Furthermore, under certain conditions even coercive power can be a necessary or practical tool. For example, when in conflict with unjust and unresponsive others, or in situations where subordinates are hostile or unmotivated to comply with reasonable demands. In addition, the prevalence in organizations of destructive forms of controlling power through the use of humiliation, fear tactics, and oppression has warranted the need to better comprehend and thereby deter such practices. This approach to the study of power has also led to important advances in the measurement of individual differences such as authoritarianism (Adorno et al., 1950), Machiavellianism (Christie & Geis, 1970), and social dominance orientation (Sidanious & Pratto, 1999), as well as a useful typology of the resources of power often used when asserting power over others (French & Raven, 1959).

Nevertheless, useful as the power-as-control perspective may be, it is limited, conceptually and practically, and ultimately neglects other important aspects of power. Like all theories of power, this perspective contains a set of underlying assumptions and values about the nature of power, the nature of people, and the nature of power relations that limit its applicability (Coleman & Tjosvold, 2000). These include:

1. There is a limited amount of power that exists in any relationship; therefore the more power A has the less power available for B.
2. People use what power they have to increase their power.
3. Power relations are unidirectional; power is located in A and moves from A to B.
4. Due to the scarcity of power as a resource, power relations are intrinsically competitive.
5. Control of another through coercion is the essence of power.

These assumptions, however valid at times, define only a limited view of power.

In practice, a predominantly controlling approach to power is likely to have harmful consequences, producing alienation and resistance in those subjected to the power (Deutsch, 1973). This, in turn, limits the powerholder's ability to use other types of power that are based on trust (such as normative, expert, referent, and reward power), and increases the need for continuous scrutiny and control of subordinates. If the goal of the powerholder is to achieve compliance *and* commitment from her or his subordinates, then reliance on a "power over" strategy will prove to be costly as well as largely ineffective.

Power through Cooperation

Mary Parker Follett, writing in the 1920s, offered a different perspective on power. Follett argued that even though power in organizations was usually conceived of as "power-over" others, it would also be possible to develop the conception of "power-with" others. She envisioned this type of power as jointly developed, coactive and noncoercive (see Follett, 1973). Cooperative power, then, is that type of power that brings about constructive outcomes for all. It motivates people to search out each other's abilities and to appreciate their contributions, to negotiate and influence each other to exchange resources that will help them both be more productive, and to encourage each other to develop and enhance their valued abilities. In fact, Follett suggested that one of the most effective ways to limit the use of coercive power strategies was to develop the idea, the capacity, and the conditions that foster cooperative power. As such, she was able to rise above the dualistic power struggles between labor and management that had threatened the survival of many organizations during her time. She did so by encouraging both groups to see the value of working together to improve their mutual situation. This was Follett's attempt to temper scientific management practices with her own "science of the situation," where labor and management collaborated to define acceptable rates of productivity and social justice (Boje & Rosile, 2001). Thus, cooperative power was consistent with the values and intentions of the emerging human relations school of management.

The empirical research on cooperation and power, although not abundant, has largely supported Follett's propositions. In a series of studies on power and goal interdependence (Tjosvold, 1981, 1985a, b; Tjosvold, Johnson, & Johnson, 1984), researchers found that differences in goal interdependence (task, reward, and outcome goals) affected the likelihood of the constructive use of power between high- and low-power persons. Cooperative goals, when compared to competitive and independent goals, were found to induce "higher expectations of assistance, more assistance, greater support, more persuasion and less coercion and more trusting and friendly attitudes" between superiors and subordinates (Tjosvold, 1997, p. 297). Similar effects have been found with members of top management teams. In a recent study with 378 executives from 105 organizations in China, perceived cooperative goals were found to reinforce mutually enhancing interactions and promote team recognition of abilities, which in turn resulted in a strategic advantage for the company (Tjosvold, Chen, & Liu, 2001). Coleman (in press) found that people with both chronic and primed cooperative cognitive orientations to power were more willing to share resources and involve others in decision-making processes than those with competitive orientations. In another experiment, powerholders who were led to believe that power was expandable in a given context (compared to a limited and thus competitive resource) developed cooperative relationships and provided support and resources to their subordinates, especially when employees lacked the ability rather than the motivation to perform well (Tjosvold, Coleman, & Sun, in press). These studies support the assertion that, under cooperative conditions, people want others to perform effectively and use their joint resources to enhance each other's power and promote common objectives.

The underlying values and assumptions of cooperative power are in contrast to those of power-as-control. These include:

1. It is possible to create power and enhance everyone's situation through mutually cooperative efforts.
2. Under certain conditions, people will share their power with others.
3. Power relations are bidirectional and mutually interdependent.
4. Often, promotively interdependent goals exist between A and B, as does the opportunity for mutually satisfying outcomes to be achieved.
5. People's power can be positively affected by harmonious relations with others and through their openness to the influence of others (Coleman & Tjosvold, 2000).

Again, these assumptions define the boundaries and limitations of this perspective.

The cooperative perspective on power has not gone without criticism. From the realist camp, concerns have been voiced that this view of power offers us a well-intentioned pipe dream, an idealistic vision of something ultimately unattainable. Given the ruthless jungle of the marketplace and of most organizational environments, they argue, the possibilities for mutual enhancement through cooperative power are severely limited. Even under the best circumstances, mutual power enhancement is a fragile process, highly susceptible to suspicion and ruptures in trust between the parties. And at their extreme, cooperative and participatory processes can be pathological, leading to inefficiency, irresponsible leadership practices, chronic consensus seeking, and nepotism (see Deutsch, 1985, for an extensive discussion of the problems of cooperation and equality).

However, it is the critical theorists and postmodernists that deliver the most scathing critique of the cooperative approach to power (see Alvesson & Willmott, 1992a, b; Boje & Rosile, 2001; Townley, 1993). They raise four primary concerns. First, they argue that the power achieved through cooperative and participatory practices by those in low power in organizations is restricted to those practices that are instrumental to the enhanced achievement of organizational goals, which subordinates do not participate in determining, and the improvement of organizational performance. Thus, these practices restrict the experiences of autonomy and opportunities for development that would result in a genuine sense of empowerment for these individuals (see, for example, Barker, 1993; Ezzamel & Willmott, 1998; Ezzamel, Willmott, & Worthington, 2001). Second, because of the persuasiveness of the empowerment ideologies used to justify cooperative and participatory management practices, employees often abandon the need to critically reflect on and challenge the many injustices and inequities (such as sexual and racial discrimination) which pervade most organizations. This notion was preceded by Marx's concern over the development of a false consciousness among workers (Marx, 1844). In other words, emphasizing micro-level cooperative practices in organizations can often mask the pressing need for macro-level reform (see Barker, 1993; Mumby & Stohl, 1991).

Third, some critics contend that the well-intended human relations and participative management initiatives often become appropriated by management and used as subtle forms of control. For example, Mumby and Stohl (1991) demonstrated how team-based work designs can construct the illusion of worker autonomy and draw the workers' attention away from the structure imposed on them by the management. As the structure becomes a given, conflicts among workers begin to be perceived by them as merely interpersonal ones and unrelated to management's policies and objectives. Norms are then established to govern each worker's obligations toward the team, and efforts are undertaken to enforce those norms, instead of reflecting upon and possibly questioning the agenda dictated from above. Thus, rather than offering workers more autonomy and discretion, such cooperative team-based work arrangements often result in more intensive monitoring than would have been possible under the traditional work arrangements. Instead of freeing workers from traditional vertical monitoring, improved management information systems have strengthened vertical control, and the new team-based arrangements add horizontal peer monitoring (Sewell, 1998; Sewell & Wilkinson, 1992), which can be a great deal more intrusive, coercive, and abusive than the traditional work processes (Barker, 1993, 1999). Finally, the critical and postmodern theorists argue, the overemphasis on the A to B relational power processes of both the controlling and cooperative perspectives tends to decontextualize the theoretical discussion of power, which is often largely predetermined by the historical and normative context of communications and meaning-making typically controlled by elites in organizations (Alvesson & Willmott, 1992a).

Critical Perspectives on Power

Critical management studies (CMS) have sought to challenge the assumption that management is a neutral and value-free activity concerned with attaining the instrumental goals of organizations that serve a common good. Reynolds (1998, p. 190) writes:

> Managing is not a neutral or disinterested activity. The socially intrusive nature of managing means involvement in and having effects on the lives of others and on their future and the future conditions of wider society. The essential stuff of management is the construction of particular power relations through which these processes are instigated and maintained.

Although mainstream humanist approaches to management also aspire to foster fairer organizational practices, they generally focus on curbing more blatant abuses and do not question the taken-for-granted assumptions of management. CMS is concerned with the "questioning of taken-for-granteds, both about practice and its social and institutional context. . . . Identifying and questioning both purposes, and conflicts of power and interest" (Reynolds, 1998, p. 192). It aims to expose and reform the mundane and frequently unnoticed practices that privilege some groups (and individuals) at the expense of others (e.g. how many seemingly neutral aspects of engineering work tend to privilege men over women; see Fletcher, 1999).

CMS's critique targets not only managers (and others who create and sustain the kind of practices that CMS seeks to expose and reform) but also many mainstream management research projects. Critical researchers have pointed out that mainstream management research tends to take the managerial or pro-elite point of view. The aim of mainstream research is to help managers and elites attain their goals, such as overcoming resistance to change or more readily attaining maximum productivity. Employees' needs are considered solely from an instrumental perspective. Furthermore, mainstream organizational scholars are criticized for assuming the privileged position of "objective" and disinterested purveyors of pure knowledge while in reality manufacturing knowledge that is political and serves those at the top of the hierarchy.

CMS has taken seriously the role of language in shaping and maintaining social reality. Language is not viewed as a transparent or neutral carrier of meaning. In other words, language does not merely represent reality out there but constitutes what we take to be reality out there and opens and constrains the ways in which we act upon this reality (Gergen, 1992). CMS also contends that an orderly reality is not natural but is a result of power plays that suppress the inherent contradictions, inconsistencies, and conflicts of interest in organizations. Power is embedded within the organizational structure, and mundane and taken-for-granted organizational practices both express and reproduce this power structure.

When organization is viewed as a conversation (Ford, 1999), or a story (Boje, 1991, 1995), the critical question is: whose story? Wallemacq and Sims (1998) write: "Storytelling is not a universal privilege. A key indicator of power in organizations is who has the right to tell stories" (p. 123). Although the conversation that constitutes organization includes many voices, some voices are louder than others. Voices compete for dominance for the right—the privilege—to frame the organizational reality for others and to define meaning for all (Salzer-Mörling, 1998; Wallemacq & Sims, 1998).

Clegg (1989) uses the pool-table metaphor to illustrate the difference between conventional theories of power and ones proposed by critical and postmodern theorists. The former conceptualizes the players A and B playing on a carefully calibrated table, where neither party has an advantage (for example, A over B or A with B). The latter assume that the playing field is uneven. Players find themselves thrown into a game in which the playing field has been skewed to the benefit of one of the parties, and this privilege makes it easier for that party to accomplish its goals. In this view power does not reside solely within the A–B relation. Instead, the two are embedded within a predefined set of rules and meanings that have been fixed. That is not to exclude the possibility that social actors may be invested in maintaining the existing power relations (see Potter, 1996; Wetherell & Potter, 1992, for related discussions). Thus, as reality is not a given but is continuously constructed and reconstructed, so too are power relations, which cannot be separated from reality construction. As Tsoukas (2000) writes, "social reality is causally independent of actors (hence realists have a point) and, at the same time, what social reality is depends on how it has been historically defined, the cultural meanings and distinctions which have made this reality as opposed to that reality (hence constructivists also have a point)" (p. 531). Since it is argued that meanings do not inhere in situations but are assigned to them, as things are defined and assigned meaning, some people find themselves in positions of power, while others find themselves subordinated (Mumby & Stohl, 1991). Power then is not only a personal or a relational variable. More dramatically, it emerges as meanings are defined.

As the meaning of such things as what constitutes historical "fact," or the standards of fairness and value become fixed, alternative meanings and possibilities are suppressed. Mumby and Stohl (1991) described the case of a male secretary who was ostracized in his organization because he violated the notions of what it meant to be a secretary (i.e. necessarily a woman) and what it meant to be a man (i.e. necessarily an executive). Thus, a male secretary becomes an "impossibility" in such a setting because the meanings associated with "masculinity" and with the profession of "secretary" become fixed, and are seen as mutually exclusive (Mumby & Stohl, 1991).

Organizations oftentimes suffer from narrowly fixed meanings of "how work should be done," which privileges some groups in relation to others. For instance, engineering firms tend to value problem solving a great deal more than problem prevention (e.g. Fletcher, 1999; Wright, 1996). These are stereotypically masculine ways of conducting work. Yet all that such practices accomplish is a constant operation in a crisis mode. At the same time the value of relational practices, such as organizational citizenship behaviors (OCBs), is overlooked (Fletcher, 1999). Performance tends to be assessed indirectly by measuring commitment, as expressed in willingness to work long hours and to put work above family, a masculine trait (Bailyn, 1993a, b; Eaton & Bailyn, 1999; van Maanen & Kunda, 1989). While penalizing many employees (female and male), who may need greater flexibility of work schedules in order to better meet their many obligations, this rigid insistence on long hours does not benefit organizations (Bailyn, 1993a, b).

Like the two previously discussed power paradigms, CMS has not escaped its share of criticism. Whereas mainstream management research has been accused of taking the managerial perspective and of failing to address the needs of those with less power, CMS has tended to marginalize managerial interests. Both critical theory and postmodernism tend to take the workers' point of view and to portray the needs of managers as illegitimate. Another criticism frequently directed at CMS is its intellectualism and apparent impracticality (Alvesson & Willmott, 1992a, b). It appears to see power and oppression everywhere, yet seems unable to locate it anywhere in particular. This leaves managers with a clear sense of the negative impact of current organizational arrangements, but with little sense of how to begin to create alternatives.

Nord and Jermier (1992) have pointed out that many managers find critical social science appealing. What has been neglected is that non-elites are not the only ones who are oppressed by the prevalent power arrangements. As Alvesson and Willmott (1992a) note, "Caught between contradictory demands and pressures, they [managers] experience ethical problems, they run the risk of dismissal, they are 'victims' as well as perpetrators of discourses and practices that unnecessarily constrain their ways of thinking and acting" (p. 7). McCabe (2000, 2002), for instance, offers two intensive case studies of an automotive plant and an insurance company, respectively, to show that not only do the managers exercise or attempt to exercise power over others, but that often their own identities are also constructed and constrained by these power relations. Thus, those with relatively higher power should not be viewed as exempt from the operations and consequences of power (see also Alvesson, 2002, Chapter 5, for a related discussion of leadership).

However, as a result of its frequently hostile tone and abstract and inaccessible language, CMS often appears irrelevant to managers. They often do not find it interesting, because it does not appear to be interested in them. If CMS is to be heard, it must adopt a more compassionate approach and seek to liberate all groups of people from oppressive social arrangements, rather than privileging the "underdog" (workers) while creating a new one (management). Furthermore, in keeping with its democratic ideals, CMS must learn to communicate its concepts in a clear and less intellectualized manner and to demonstrate its practical relevance to a wider audience.

Two Powers?

In reviewing the three perspectives on power, it becomes evident that there is much greater similarity between the power-as-control and cooperative power perspectives than between either of these perspectives and the critical one. The first two camps view power as relational, while the critical camp views relationships as embedded within and expressive of systems of meaning-making. Even the ontological and epistemological assumptions of these researchers and methodologies used are quite different. We suggest that rather than deciding which group is "right" or "wrong," it may be more instructive to recognize that conventional (i.e. power as control and co-power) and critical researchers speak of different things when discussing power. We offer the distinction between *primary* and *secondary* power as a heuristic to illuminate that distinction.

Primary power refers to the socio-historical process of reality construction. This is the process by which our sense of reality, as we know it, is constructed. As Chia (2000, p. 513) writes,

> Social objects and phenomena such as "the organization", "the economy", "the market" or even "stakeholders" or "the weather", do not have a straightforward and unproblematic existence independent of our discursively-shaped understandings. Instead, they have to be forcibly carved out of the undifferentiated flux of raw experience and conceptually fixed and labeled so that they can become the common currency for communicational exchanges. Modern social reality, with its all-too-familiar features, has to be continually constructed and sustained through such aggregative discursive acts of reality-construction.

Thus, primary power defines the domain. A manager is able to give orders and to expect them to be followed because the role of a manager has been historically constructed so as to include notions of order giving. It is important to recognize that the various sources of power (e.g. French & Raven, 1959) are not concrete but socially constructed. "Legitimacy," for example, is not objective but is created through management of meaning, and thus legitimacy requires power to be demonstrated (Hardy & Phillips, 1998). Only once the domain has been defined does it become possible for power as conceived of in conventional theories to be exercised (Hardy, Palmer, & Phillips, 2000).

Secondary power refers to the exercise of power in the conventional sense—the ability to get one's goals met. This can take a coercive or positive form. However, it involves working in a domain that has already been largely defined. Thus, the various strategies that managers may use to obtain their employees' compliance or commitment would constitute secondary power. The manager indeed has a choice whether to attempt to sell her or his ideas to the employees or to force them to obey. However, it is primary power that has made entertaining the options possible.

The two forms of power then are interconnected. Primary power opens and constrains the possibilities for exercising secondary power. Secondary power can be seen as expressing and reproducing the primary power relations. Individuals' identities are constituted by primary power, and these identities determine how much secondary power these individuals can exercise. However, secondary power can also contribute to transforming primary power. Revolutions or hostile takeovers are dramatic examples of secondary power being used in an attempt to transform primary power.

However, it is secondary power that most easily lends itself to the most popular management research methods, such as surveys and experiments. These methods carry a set of epistemological assumptions: there is an a priori social reality that is independent of the researchers' methodology; research uncovers, rather than constructs, reality; theory is a mirror, which putatively reflects the reality out there. Thus, both power-as-control and cooperative power researchers have focused on secondary power. The processes by which secondary power is exercised are crucial to understand. However, it is also important to better understand the operation of primary power.

Critical researchers have to a great extent concentrated on primary power, which is better investigated by methods that carry a different set of epistemological assumptions: the world out there cannot be separated from the research process; researchers are a part of the phenomena that they are investigating and as a result the research process constructs rather than uncovers reality; theory is better viewed as a lens, rather than as a mirror, and should be evaluated not on how accurately it represents the world out there but on what kind of insights it offers and what possibilities for action it opens up. Thus, most of CMS research uses ethnographies and case studies to collect data.

The primary/secondary power distinction helps us recontextualize conventional and critical research on power in a more productive way, such that the merits of each can be appreciated.

The Paradoxes of Emancipation

A serious limitation of many organizational approaches to empowerment, democratization, and emancipation is their rather one-sided view of power-sharing as unquestionably "good." When implemented, these initiatives often have unintended, paradoxical effects and consequences. Costs to the emancipated individuals and groups as well as to the organizations and the larger society must be measured along with the gains (Alvesson & Willmott, 1992b; Deutsch, 1985). Thus, the following paradoxes of emancipation should be thoroughly considered when these practices are applied in organizational change initiatives.

First, it must be recognized that emancipation can be anxiety-provoking for many individuals. Alvesson and Willmott (1992b) write, "A critical questioning of beliefs and values might not only facilitate more rational thinking, recognition and clarification of neglected needs, ideas about fairness, and so on, but, in doing so, may estrange the individual from the tradition that has formed his or her very subjectivity" (p. 447). Thus, emancipation may result in a profound sense of identity loss, confusion, general distrust, and depression (Fay, 1987). Others have suggested that the disempowered, when made to recognize their oppressed state, feel a deep sense of humiliation and resentment toward those who brought on such recognition (see Lindner, 2001). These difficult psychological experiences serve to exacerbate the more mundane anxieties associated with the fear of change, leading to an increased investment in the status quo (see Schein, 1993, for a related discussion).

Emancipation can also negatively affect organizational efficiency and productivity—at least temporarily—as individuals begin to question and challenge the duties, roles, and expectations previously taken for granted. This questioning can lead to a sense of ambivalence, role confusion, and inefficient performance. Management may in turn penalize these employees, leading to further disruptions of work. In addition, the implementation of more inclusive decision-making practices and decentralization of authority may increase the time it takes to make important decisions (Coleman, 2002; Whyte & Blasi, 1982) and negatively impact the organization's bottom line. Thus, increasing the ecological consciousness, level of participation, and free choice of employees, although beneficial, could ultimately result in bankruptcy and unemployment (Alvesson & Willmott, 1992b).

Another potential trap of emancipatory practices is that even if they begin by opening up understanding and encouraging reflection on taken-for-granteds, they can end up locking people into another form of fixed, unreflective thinking (Alvesson, 1996). For instance, one of the main arguments of CMS is that those in the lower echelons of the hierarchy are often "duped" by those at the top into believing that they are empowered, while in reality still being controlled from above through ideology. However, there remains a possibility that in trying to relieve the oppressed of their false consciousness, CMS is merely replacing one ideology with another. How does a CMS-inspired scientist or practitioner make people who think they are empowered realize that they are not? Does s/he not still bring this knowledge "from above"? Following its own ideals, then, CMS must refrain from "telling people what to do," while at the same time attempting to alter the apparently natural way that people have been "doing things"—sometimes all their lives.

Furthermore, when focusing on the oppressive nature of dominant ideologies, structures, and practices, it is sometimes easy to overlook the "loopholes" in the operations of power that are available to those in low power. These are microemancipatory processes "in which attention is focused on concrete activities, forms, and techniques that offer themselves not only as means of control, but also as vehicles for liberation" (Alvesson & Willmott, 1992b, p. 446). Sometimes, managerial initiatives aimed at increasing cultural control "trigger suspicion, resistance, and critical reflections" (Alvesson & Willmott, 1992b, p. 446; see also Collinson, 1994). These initiatives, then, have the paradoxical effect of fostering the opposite of their objectives. For example, a number of scholars (e.g. Collinson, 1994; Ezzamel, Willmott, & Worthington, 2001; Knights & McCabe, 2000) have documented how workers can and often do resist management's initiatives designed to increase their control over workers.

Finally, it is crucial to also examine what drives the empowerment initiatives themselves. Many of the "new" approaches to management, such as just-in-time and total quality management, are, again, frequently driven by an economic, rather than emancipatory agenda. Although both concerns are certainly legitimate, the two should not be confused, and "empowerment" should not become a marketing ploy for selling a new financial strategy to employees, for as several researchers have shown, employees tend to be better at sensing the true agenda than managers think (Collinson, 1994; Covaleski et al., 1998; Ezzamel, Willmott, & Worthington, 2001; Knights & McCabe, 2000; McCabe, 2000).

The preceding cautions are not intended to dismantle the emancipatory and empowerment agenda of organizational scholars and practitioners. Instead, the aim is to encourage critical examination on the part of such initiatives, so they can better avoid the pitfalls that have characterized much of mainstream organizational research and practice (Alvesson, 1996). In practice, however, this is a demanding task. As Deutsch (1985, p. 244) writes,

> I am further persuaded that even the nearest thing to common visions of an earthly utopia—a small, well-functioning, worldly, cooperative, egalitarian community—has to work hard and thoughtfully on a continuing basis to preserve its democracy, cooperativeness and egalitarianism as well as to survive. The inherent tendency of such communities is to break down; it takes sustained effort to prevent this from happening.

A CRITICAL–POSTMODERN FRAMEWORK OF ORGANIZATIONAL POWER

In this section, we present a brief overview of our framework of organizational power that builds on the controlling, cooperative, and critical perspectives in a manner that is mindful of the multifaceted and paradoxical nature of power and emancipation. The objective of such an approach is to offer a more comprehensive view of organizational power that is also concrete, useful, and applicable to organizational phenomena. The framework centers on an image of *power as exercised within a complex and contradictory network of*

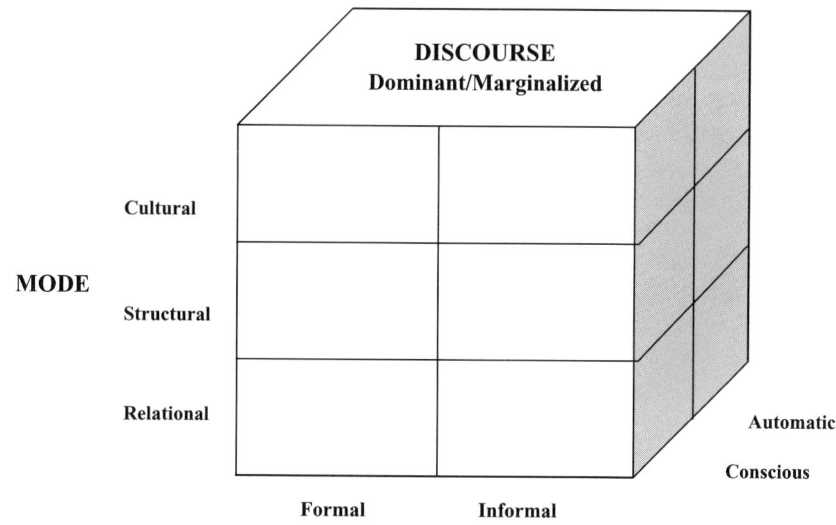

Figure 12.1 A critical–postmodern framework of organizational power

relations, structures, and meaning-making processes at different levels of organizational and community life. It prioritizes the construction and management of meaning and ideology as a central mechanism of power (by defining what is good, normal, ideal, deviant, etc.), but heeds the important roles that structural and relational variables also play. The framework acknowledges both the destructive and constructive potentialities inherent in the exercise of power, but can help to identify targeted and concrete opportunities for democratization, emancipation, and constructive change in organizational–community systems.

Dimensions of the Framework

We begin by articulating the four dimensions of our critical–postmodern framework of organizational power (CFOP): multimodal analysis, formal/informal activities, conscious/automatic activities, and oppositional discourses (ideologies and practices; see Figure 12.1). Each of these dimensions could be considered "meta-theoretical" because of their usefulness in enhancing the understanding of phenomena across different theoretical orientations.

MULTIMODAL ANALYSIS

A variety of scholars interested in the study of power in social systems have approached it from a multimodal perspective (see Alvesson & Willmott, 1992b; Boje & Rosile, 2001; Clegg, 1989; Deutsch, 1973; Foucault, 1980; Marshak, 1998). Each of these approaches has differed, but all have argued for the value of conceptualizing complex power dynamics through different modes in social systems, as well as understanding the relationships between the modes.

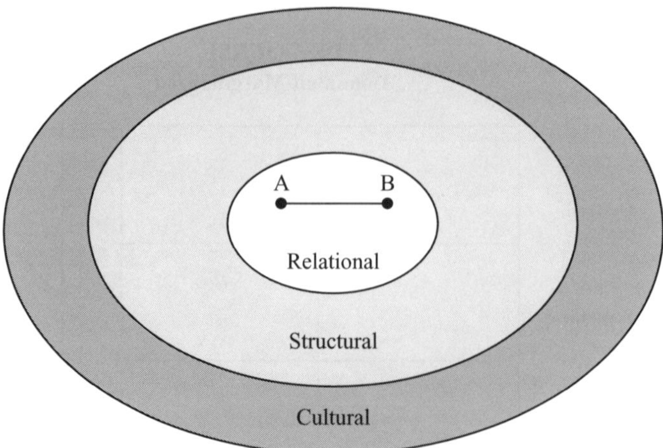

Figure 12.2 Nested levels of organizational power

The CFOP conceptualizes power in organizations through three nested modes: the relational, the structural, and the cultural (see Figure 12.2). Each mode can be affected by and can affect variables in the other modes, but each mode differs to the degree that it is associated with primary vs secondary power.

Power in the *relational* mode considers those factors and dynamics between people and between groups of people at the most micro-level of work and interaction. This can include all nature of interactive exchanges and behaviors including verbal and nonverbal communication, the management of conflict, and interpersonal or intergroup attempts at control, countercontrol, and resistance. This is power as conceptualized by many power-as-control and cooperative power scholars and corresponds to our notion of secondary power.

Power in the *structural* mode is concerned with macro-level systems of strategy, technology, work and organization design, decision making, reward, and punishment. Power in this mode is a mixture of primary and secondary power, in that it reproduces primary power relations, but changes in a system through this mode (including changes in rules, policies, procedures, goals, and incentives) can directly affect the character of the interactions in the relational mode.

Finally, power in the *cultural* mode considers those taken-for-granted aspects of organizational life: assumptions, ideologies, habits, and practices, which construct, express, and challenge the status quo of power in the system. These processes are pervasive, operating at both micro- and macro-levels, and correspond directly to primary power.

Thus, the power and authority relations between a manager and his/her subordinate will be affected by their unique relational dynamics (for example, the flexibility, temperament, and inducibility of each party in relation to the other), which are to some degree shaped by contextual structures (cooperative goals and incentives, labor/management policies, decentralized decision-making designs), which are largely determined by the taken-for-granted meaning of such structures and relations in that organization (employees who are not "team-players" are problematic, strike-busters are scabs, women managers should be empathetic, etc.).

FORMAL/INFORMAL ACTIVITIES

Over the past few decades, there has been a trend in organizational life toward more egalitarian and inclusive structures and policies (Burke, 1986). For example, many organizations have attempted to decentralize authority and power and promote more delegation and participative decision making. Similarly, there has been an ongoing attempt in organizations to implement diversity programs in order to meet EEOC regulatory standards and be more respectful and responsive to an increasingly diverse and "globalized" workforce and marketplace. However, many of these initiatives fail.

Current research on organizational citizenship behaviors (Organ & Bateman, 1991) and emotional labor (van Maanen & Kunda, 1989) has shed light on some of the obstacles these democracy and diversity initiatives face. This work has highlighted the central importance of *informal* or "extra-role" organizational practices for understanding and changing organizational processes and performance. Moghaddam (1997) contends that, despite the implementation of new decentralized and inclusive formal policies and structures, informal organizational practices often remain unaffected and ultimately hinder the desired changes in organizational culture.

Understanding the mechanisms through which these informal processes are sustained and affect power relations and intergroup dynamics can be extremely beneficial to executives, managers, and workers alike. Such an understanding can help shed light on:

(a) the nature and value of the system's resistance to the implementation of new policies;
(b) how their own actions may inadvertently perpetuate these undesirable informal practices;
(c) how informal practices sometimes benefit certain identity groups (e.g. racial or ethnic groups) over others and cause tension in the system;
(d) how they can become more effective in implementing desired systemic changes.

CONSCIOUS/AUTOMATIC ACTIVITIES

Contemporary research on social cognition has indicated that there are important forms of thought and action that are not under our control in that they are autonomous and detached from our will and intentions (Bargh, 1996). These thoughts and actions are believed to have been made cognitively accessible from previous experiences, and to be triggered by stimuli in the environment. For instance, stereotypes of low-power social groups (women, the elderly, ethnic minorities, etc.) have been shown to become active automatically in response to the perception of a group's distinct physical features in an individual (Fiske, 1993). In fact, there are very few research phenomena in mainstream social psychology that have not been shown to occur at least partially automatically (Bargh, 1996). Typically, however, these phenomena are considered to be affected by a combination of conscious and automatic processing. Current research on stereotyping (see Devine, 1989; Operario & Fiske, 2001), intergroup bias (Dovidio, Kawakami, & Beach; 2001), attitudes and persuasion (Chaiken, Giner-Sorolla, & Chen, 1996), and even the management of death-related anxieties (Pyszczynski, Greenberg, & Solomon, 1999) offer such dual-process theories. Thus, when analyzing the exercise of power in organizations, we must consider the role of both conscious and automatic processes in maintaining the status quo and creating change.

OPPOSITIONAL DISCOURSES

We use the term *discourse* to refer to all processes of meaning-making in organizations, which are typically accomplished through self-reflection and interpersonal communication between people. Power operates through discourse by framing the reality of organizational members in particular ways. Before reality can be acted upon, it has to be defined, and power manifests itself—perhaps most dramatically—in being able to define things (Alvesson, 1996), for certain definitions invite or even demand particular actions. For example, the emphasis on "teamwork" is becoming widespread in contemporary organizations. Although this notion is a social construction, it is often assumed to be a given, natural and unproblematic. The reification of teamwork can obscure the systemic nature of power by emphasizing power at the relational level and encouraging power negotiations to occur between individual actors within the team (Mumby & Stohl, 1991). Group norms start emerging, certain individuals assume leadership, and team-based sanctioning mechanisms develop only after the reification of the notion that "teamwork is the way we do work here" has made such activities possible.

We will address two of the many aspects of discourse: ideology and what we call organizational power practices (OPPs). Ideologies are various competing metanarratives that provide the frames of reference that individuals use to interpret reality. An example of such competing ideologies is what Sidanius and Pratto (1999) call "legitimizing myths." These can be hierarchy-enhancing (e.g. racism, sexism, meritocracy) or functioning to reproduce inequalities and hierarchies, or hierarchy-attenuating (e.g. civil rights, feminism, egalitarianism) or functioning to promote equality and to flatten the various hierarchies.

The other aspect of discourse, the OPPs, operate in ways that are automatic and virtually imperceptible. This refers to mundane and taken-for-granted social practices, such as rules of politeness, the way work is routinely done, and so on, that appear neutral and natural but in fact systematically reproduce hierarchies based on gender, race, sexual orientation, and so forth. These practices will be discussed in greater detail below.

Organizational cultures are often portrayed as monolithic and uniform systems of values, beliefs, attitudes, and practices. However, such coherence and integration are not natural but instead result from the suppression of alternative discourses, "where the managerial monologue seems to orchestrate the polyphony into one coherent voice . . . a process of homogenization of meanings" (Salzer-Mörling, 1998, p. 117; see also Alvesson, 1996). The process by which conflicting interests and contradictory values, beliefs, attitudes, and practices are suppressed and the illusion of consensus is produced is referred to as *discursive closure* (Alvesson & Deetz, 2000). Because ideological control is usually approached from an instrumental perspective—it is a much more efficient mode of controlling organizations than direct supervision (Deetz, Tracy, & Simpson, 2000)—discursive closure is not only common, but is often seen as desirable.

There are multiple reasons why this type of ideological control in organizations is problematic. First, it should be questioned on ethical grounds. Controlling another human being's subjectivity is perhaps more abusive than direct coercion. Here employees end up controlling themselves on behalf of management, as was suggested in the critique of the phenomena of work teams above (see also Deetz, 1995; Deetz, Tracy, & Simpson, 2000). Second, it can have detrimental long-term effects on organizational well-being. Homogenization of meanings facilitates managerial control and reduces blatant conflicts, but it does little for organizational performance. There appears to be increasing evidence for Kenneth Gergen's assertion that "if everything is running smoothly, the organization is in trouble" (1992, p. 223). Discursive closure achieves control at the expense of effective decision making, as dramatically illustrated by such fiascoes as the Bay of Pigs invasion (Janis, 1983) or the Watergate scandal (Deetz, Tracy, & Simpson, 2000). As organizations are becoming increasingly diverse, many of them find it tempting to continue "doing business as usual," or to use minorities and women to break into new markets instead of allowing diversity to change the organizational culture and work process (Thomas & Ely, 1996). As a result, such organizations fail to reap the benefits of diversity.

The final point against discursive closure is the practical impossibility of attaining a complete homogenization of meaning. As discussed before, every attempt at increased control can also facilitate resistance. Oppositional discourses may become marginalized, dormant, or temporarily silenced, but never die. The suppressed voices can find outlet in ways that are detrimental to an organization's goals. For instance, Collinson (1994) shows how workers at an assembly plant resisted management's attempts at ideological control through various subversive activities, such as using work time and equipment to produce products (car parts, sleds for their children) for their own use (for other examples, see Ezzamel, Willmott, & Worthington, 2001; Knights & McCabe, 2000).

Because ideological control tends to present certain values, interests, and practices as "common sense," those that do not endorse such values, interests, and practices come to be perceived as problematic and become marginalized by the dominant groups. Over time, polarized identities are created and sustained on both sides of these differences (Sampson, 1993a, b), often leading to protracted social conflicts between groups.

Putting it All Together

The four dimensions of the CFOP are presented in Table 12.1. To illustrate the four dimensions of power that comprise the framework, we present a brief analysis of a research workgroup in which we both participate. The workgroup conducts research on conflict resolution and power and consists of one professor, four doctoral students, and seven master's students. The group meets weekly for two hours to plan, review, and present research conducted by its members. Formally, it is designed to facilitate cooperative, team-based work, with positively interdependent tasks and goals. However, in practice the group members have a combination of competitive, cooperative, and independent goals. The data in Table 12.1 were collected using detailed observations of group meetings for two weeks and conducting interviews with several members.

Table 12.1 presents some examples from the research group to illustrate the different dimensions of the CFOP. Space limitations do not permit us to discuss examples of all the dimensions in detail. Since this chapter has emphasized the importance of the cultural mode, we will briefly discuss the examples that illustrate that dimension.

The cultural mode focuses on seemingly "normal" activities and seeks to understand how they function to construct and reproduce a certain version of reality that privileges some people at the expense of others. Looking at the top-right four cells, we observe that the group favors theoretical arguments over personal experiences as a strategy for contributing to the group (dominant/conscious/formal cell). In other words, members who are best able to use

Table 12.1 Twenty-four types of organizational power

Oppositional Discourses		Mode					
		Relational		Structural		Cultural	
		Formal	Informal	Formal	Informal	Formal	Informal
Dominant	Conscious	Professor establishes a vision for the research	Professor offers general academic advice to students	Inclusion of MA and Ph.D. students in workgroup	Professor encourages teamwork	Privileging theory over personal experience to make a point	Using intellectualized language
Dominant	Automatic	Connecting world affairs to research	Expressing concern for members who are ill	Professor opens and closes each meeting	Evaluation of fellow student's work	Professor summarizes and integrates conflicting strands of discussions	Ph.D. students interrupting others when speaking
Marginal	Conscious	Students offering a marginalized theoretical interpretation (e.g. post-modern)	Students inviting professor to informal get-togethers	MA students initiating a project	Students expressing contrary opinions of the work to other students in hallway	Offering a personal experience to make a point	MA students changing the topic in the group
Marginal	Automatic	Cognitively disengaging (doodling) when in dis-agreement with speaker	Students chronically arriving late to meetings	Students meeting in-dependently with other students to initiate new projects	Students sharing concerns with each other re the work—independent of professor	Students presenting their work with air of confidence and inde-pendence	MA students interrupting others when speaking

their knowledge of various theories to support their arguments—usually the professor and doctoral students—are more likely to be heard and to influence the direction of discussions. This is understandable in an academic research setting; however it is important to recognize that this practice tends to neglect the considerable value of the practical insight brought to the group by the experienced practitioners in the group. As such, psychological jargon and social science concepts are preferred over personal rumination (dominant/conscious/informal). Again, given their academic training, the professor and doctoral students in the group are more likely to be able to use this type of language than the master's students.

When seeking to move the discussion forward, the professor sometimes integrates conflicting points made by several students into a coherent narrative (dominant/automatic/formal), which allows him to move the discussion in his desired direction. Due to their relatively privileged position in the group, the doctoral students tend to interrupt the other students when speaking more than the master's students (dominant/automatic/informal).

Both of these practices have a negative impact on the MA student-practitioner's experience of autonomy and ability to contribute to the research.

As argued above, there are always oppositional discourses that can be more or less audible. Looking at the bottom-right four cells, we note the marginalized discourses in our group. Personal experience is not valued as highly as theory and research to make points (marginal/conscious/formal). Attempts at switching discussion topics made by master's students are rarely successful (marginal/conscious/informal). It is relatively uncommon for students who report the progress of their research not to seek reassurance from the professor. They typically make eye contact with him, leave pauses in sentences for him to fill in information, and so on. However, on occasion an elite member of the Ph.D. group may present his or her work with a greater sense of independence and confidence (marginal/automatic/formal). As common as interrupting by doctoral students may be, it is highly uncommon for master's students to interrupt others (marginal/automatic/informal).

Putting the examples together, it becomes apparent that despite the cooperative, team-based structure of the group there is a clear hierarchy and a dominant culture within the research group. We are not suggesting that finding a hierarchy in the research group is unexpected or undesirable. Given the normative expectation at universities, the resulting hierarchy and culture would be considered "legitimate." However, it is *where* and *how* the hierarchy manifests, is maintained, and the consequences of such a culture that are of interest. Our analysis allowed us to observe how practices that appeared harmless on the surface, positioned the professor at the top of the hierarchy and claimed a privileged spot for the doctoral students and the academically trained at the expense of the master's students and practitioners in the group. This arrangement, although typical of university settings, was having unintended consequences for our work; shutting down some of the valuable insights from practice that could inform our research. Of course, explicitly identifying these processes, on this or other hierarchies of difference (such as those based on race, gender, sexual orientation, nationality, class, etc.), can come at some costs to the efficient functioning of the group.

Practical Implications

We began this chapter with an image of power as a multifaceted phenomenon exercised within a complex and contradictory network of relations, structures, and meaning-making processes at different levels of organizational and community life. Thus, any practical implications emerging from our discussion must address the same degree of complexity, contradiction, and scope. We support the position that it is insufficient to conduct meaningful organizational change solely at the relational level (Boje & Rosile, 2001) or at either one of the more macro-levels (Deetz, Tracy, & Simpson, 2000; Moghaddam, 1997). Instead, we advocate a program of *multiple emancipatory initiatives*, in which different groups of stakeholders at different levels attempt separate initiatives. These initiatives may combine controlling, cooperative, and critical activities, and can serve as a safeguard against institutionalizing new interests at the expense of others. Ideally, a plurality of actions helps ensure representation and voice for all stakeholders, including consumers, workers, investors, suppliers, host communities, the general society, and the world ecological community (Deetz, 1995). Social responsibility and consideration of the stakeholders' well-being is not only the "right" thing to do but is also important for the long-term economic sustainability of the organization.

In service of such a program, we offer the CFOP (see Figure 12.1 and Table 12.1) as an analytic and diagnostic tool for use in identifying organization-specific patterns and tendencies around power, dominance, and change. However, like any diagnostic tool, the CFOP has the potential to be abused by members of both dominant and marginalized groups. Thus, we recommend that it be utilized through a process of participatory action research (PAR). PAR is a methodology that places social transformation and empowerment at the center of the research process (Brydon-Miller, 1997; Lykes, 1997). Originating from Kurt Lewin's action research methodology (Lewin, 1946), and the emancipatory work of Paulo Freire (1970), Marxists (Oquist, 1978), feminists (Maguire, 1987), and various critical theorists (Comstock & Fox, 1993; Habermas, 1971), PAR attempts to achieve positive social change by addressing the concerns of all stakeholders, which includes the fundamental causes of oppression. It is "at once a process of research, education, and action to which all participants contribute their unique skills and knowledge and through which all participants learn and are transformed" (Brydon-Miller, 1997, p. 661). When combined with the CFOP, PAR can facilitate an increase in awareness around power and dominance and an openness to learning and influence for all members of the organization.

However, we again stress that any emancipatory initiative must be implemented with an understanding of the paradoxical nature of such initiatives. This requires recognition of the merits and the trade-offs of both sides of emancipation. The needs for stability, adaptability, and reform cannot be seen as mutually exclusive, but must be recognized as part of a dynamic whole. In other words, *a key to fostering constructive change processes in organizations is in managing these basic tensions and reframing them in a manner that influences their direction*. These processes will need to respond to resistance (closed mind-sets, vested interests, practices, structures, identities, etc.), but do so in a more balanced manner. Thus we must look for approaches that seek sufficient control *and* equal participation, that meet short-term *and* long-term objectives, and that create value for laborers *and* managers alike. Morgan (1997) suggests that this can be achieved through the creation of *new contexts* based on *new understandings* of paradox and *new actions*. He contends that the fact that these tensions are perceived as contradictory in the first place is germane to the problem. Thus, we need to develop new contexts and approaches that reframe the tensions between control and emancipation as natural and complementary, and respond to them with new actions (experiments, prototypes) which enable stakeholders to manage the tensions constructively.

The following are some examples of the types of initiatives that can be undertaken by separate groups of stakeholders within the relational, structural, and cultural modes of the organization to mobilize a program of multiple emancipatory initiatives.

Relational Initiatives

Tjosvold, Andrews, and Struthers (1991) provided a series of recommendations for establishing strong cooperative links and constructive power relations in organizations by developing: (a) a common direction and vision, (b) mutual tasks, (c) assessment of joint productivity, (d) shared rewards contingent upon success, (e) complementary responsibilities and roles that require collaboration, and (f) team identity and supportive culture (p. 297). Coleman and Tjosvold (2000) added: (g) mutual recognition and appreciation of each other's strengths, (h) reciprocal exchange of resources, (i) openness to development and learning, and ideally (j) a shared value base that emphasizes human dignity, human equality, nonviolence, reciprocity, respect of diverse others, and a common good (Deutsch, 2000; Rawls, 1996). These are primarily structural and cultural interventions aimed at fostering promotively interdependent relations. Training in the knowledge, attitudes, and skills necessary for cooperative work and constructive conflict resolution are also basic to promoting positive relational dynamics. These activities can create the conditions and capacities for cooperative power to develop where people want others to perform effectively and use their joint resources to promote common objectives. However, concerns over the disempowering effects of relational strategies must be addressed through additional co-power initiatives within the structural and cultural modes.

Structural Initiatives

Boje and Rosile (2001) proposed two major democratization initiatives within the structural mode. Based on the works of Mary Parker Follett (1973) and Stuart Clegg (1989), they advocate co-power reforms in both corporate governance and at the organization–community interface (see also Deutsch's (1985) discussion of worker capitalism and worker-owned collectives). First, they recommend cooperative forms of joint democratic governance for management and labor. They write (p. 68):

> Follett, however, favored workers' councils, including direct representation of workers on boards of directors and departments and the training of workers in the financial affairs of the entire firm. The cooperative and guild movements also stressed worker participation in the governance of the whole firm; employees were to become co-owners of production, not just design participants. Empowerment through co-ownership is not the same as empowerment through participative approaches to work design that afford more team participation or worker control over the pace and layout of work.

Second, Boje and Rosile (2001) cite the value of the current charter movement, a grassroots movement to return control of local corporate charters back to the communities in which they are situated. This is an attempt to make corporations in this age of globalization more accountable for "spreading mass poverty, environmental devastation, and social disintegration . . . weakening our capacity for constructive social and cultural innovation" (Korten, 1995, p. 268). They argue for a movement to firms that are locally controlled and accountable to emphasize the need for corporations to serve public and ecological well-being. They envision a global system of localized economies that celebrate and support local diversity, which ultimately enriches the whole. Both of these initiatives—corporate governance and corporate charter movements—situate the mechanisms of co-power within the macro-structural mode where their effects are profound and lasting.

Cultural Initiatives

Emancipatory initiatives targeted at organizational culture are the most central to our framework, for it is within this mode that meaning, status, and dominance are constructed, maintained, and ultimately challenged. Although it is often difficult to determine how or where to intervene in a mode as pervasive and mercurial as culture, we suggest three methods: through the identification and discussion of organizational power practices (OPPs), through training in critical reflection, and by creating a climate which values oppositional and marginalized voices.

IDENTIFYING AND EXPLORING ORGANIZATIONAL POWER PRACTICES

Not knowing whether or when to smile, to laugh out loud, or to nod in solemn agreement in a meeting can adversely affect one's status within that group. We call this type of taken-for-granted practice *organizational power practices* (*OPPs*) because they can serve to privilege some individuals in relation to others along important dimensions of difference. To be sure, it can be argued that all aspects of organizational behavior are to some extent structured by and reproduce power relations (Alvesson, 1996; Townley, 1993)—including the organizational members' emotional experience of work (see Hancock & Tyler, 2001, Chapter 5, for a review). However, because it is impossible and impractical to identify the many ways in which every action is connected to power, we offer OPPs as an analytic concept through which to better understand power relations. In other words, OPPs can help us to determine which social practices are most essential to power relations in a given context. Thus, *OPPs are the social practices that are most relevant to operations of power in a given context*. We offer several "rules of thumb" about OPPs.

Point 1: OPPs are group-specific; what is an OPP within a certain group may not be an OPP within another. For example, Collinson (1994) described a case where, in the spirit of a corporate culture campaign, management sought to de-emphasize hierarchy by encouraging workers to call managers by their first names. Thus, calling a manager by his/her first name was a hierarchy-attenuating OPP from management's perspective. However, the workers were determined to resist the corporate culture initiative, which they perceived as a management trick designed to increase productivity, and in order to do so sought to distance themselves from management. Thus, from the workers' perspective addressing a manager by his/her first name did not constitute an effective OPP.

We can see here how the social practices within the cultural mode can resist attempts at reform within the relational and structural modes. Managers' OPPs are attempts at creating a new organizational structure (structural mode), which is more in keeping with the ideology of "flat organizations" (cultural level). The workers' refusal to perform such OPPs prevents the desired structure from taking shape and fuels the oppositional discourse, such as "No, we are not all equal here."

Point 2: OPPs can be conscious or automatic. Sometimes people are conscious of the OPPs in a given system or subsystem and try to perform them. For example, the various subversive activities in which the workers in Collinson's (1994) study engaged were for the most part performed deliberately and intentionally. However, many—if not most—OPPs are automatic and do not require much thought. OPPs are learned by living in a system and observing others perform OPPs that eventually become part of an individual's repertoire to be used in appropriate situations. People are usually efficient in reading the power relations in a particular context and acting as the situation demands. For instance, at a meeting we usually know whether or not and when to speak up and how to do it. Some people will not speak at all. Other people may interrupt others, while others patiently wait for their turn to speak.

Point 3: OPPs can enhance current power relations or subvert the power structure—sometimes simultaneously. Since most mundane practices are somehow linked to power, when engaging in any behavior that is seen as appropriate to one's position (e.g. superior giving a subordinate advice and the subordinate receiving it), the status quo of power is maintained. However, some attempts at control from above backfire and stimulate awareness and resistance on the part of those below. Those with less power may then develop OPPs that revolve around subverting managerial control (Collinson, 1994). On the other hand, resistance can also reproduce the status quo. In Collinson's (1994) study the workers voluntarily distanced themselves from management and thwarted the potential for genuine improvement in their conditions through obtaining more information about the decision-making processes and attempting to influence them.

Point 4: An individual's OPPs depend on her or his status relative to others in a particular group. Fletcher (1999) discusses how in the engineering firm that she studied more "masculine" and aggressive patterns of behavior were valued. However, women who attempted to act "more masculine" in order to fit in were frequently informally sanctioned for not acting "feminine enough." Thus, different roles and statuses carry with them particular OPPs, and successful performance of OPPs is conditional upon the individuals' correct reading of their particular roles and statuses in any given interaction (Hardy, Palmer, & Phillips, 2000; Voronov & Coleman, 2001).

Point 5: The category of interest will drive which OPPs are noted and investigated. Power hierarchies are often constructed around a wide range of social categories, such as gender, race, sexual orientation, and so on. Thus, which social practices are construed as OPPs will depend on the kind of power hierarchy one seeks to investigate. For example, when trying to uncover gender inequities in an organization, one may note the privileging of more masculine behaviors in a given situation (e.g. Fletcher, 1999). The OPPs here then would be the taken-for-granted social practices that construct and reproduce a gender hierarchy.

To sum up, OPPs are an analytic tool that allows us to see the links between the social practices within the cultural mode and the relational and structural modes. OPPs emphasize the importance of the informal and taken-for-granted social practices for the maintenance of the status quo of power. Thus, a successful culture change demands more than formal restructuring; the informal practices and communication must also express the new vision (Deetz, Tracy, & Simpson, 2000).

TRAINING AND SUPPORTING CRITICAL REFLECTION

Many human resource training programs utilize self-reflection as a mechanism to increase awareness of personal beliefs, values, attitudes, problem-solving strategies, and other behavioral tendencies. However, very few such programs include *critical reflection* as an integral part of their curriculum. Critical reflection is distinct from self-reflection in four ways:

1. It is principally concerned with developing the capacity to question "common sense" assumptions.
2. Its focus is social, political, and historical rather than individual.
3. It pays particular attention to the analysis of power relations, hierarchies, and privilege.
4. It is concerned with emancipation and, as such, is ideological (Reynolds, 1998).

The ability to critically reflect is essential for all members of contemporary organizations. We understand that all employees may not be in the position to act upon the system to make it reflect critical–postmodern ideals. However, having learned to engage in critical reflection, they may be more likely to seize the available opportunities to change aspects of organizational functioning toward a more inclusive and democratic end—given the practical and political limitations that they face. The idea of OPPs can be particularly useful for such critical reflection training, because it offers a way to see the operations of power more concretely and without falling into the trap of many CMS writings where dominance is thought to be everywhere but cannot be identified anywhere.

FOSTERING A CLIMATE FAVORABLE TO MARGINALIZED VOICES

Engaging in participatory action research on OPPs and offering training in critical reflection can go a long way in assessing the value and consequences of the dominant system of power in any organization. However, we have repeatedly emphasized the need to be mindful of the costs and consequences of such emancipatory initiatives, as well as the reactive tendencies to close out previously privileged discourses. Thus, we recommend viewing emancipation not as an outcome, but as an ongoing process of critical reflection, exploration, and restructuring. A commitment to a process of questioning the taken-for-granteds in any organization can help establish a climate where all voices are valued and where the true value of diversity can flourish.

REFERENCES

Adorno, T. W., Frenkel-Brunswick, E., Levinson, D. J., & Sanford, R. N. (1950). *The Authoritarian Personality*. New York: Harper and Brothers.

Alvesson, M. (1996). *Communication, Power and Organization.* Berlin: Walter de Gruyter.

Alvesson, M. (2002). *Understanding Organizational Culture.* London: Sage.

Alvesson, M. & Deetz, S. (2000). *Doing Critical Management Research.* London: Sage.

Alvesson, M. & Willmott, H. (1992a). Critical theory and management studies: an introduction. In M. Alvesson & H. Willmott (eds), *Critical Management Studies* (pp. 1– 20). London: Sage.

Alvesson, M. & Willmott, H. (1992b). On the idea of emancipation in management and organization studies. *Academy of Management Review, 17*, 432–464.

Bailyn, L. (1993a). *Breaking the Mold: Women, Men, and Time in the New Corporate World.* New York: The Free Press.

Bailyn, L. (1993b). Patterned chaos in human resource management. *Sloan Management Review*, Winter, pp. 77–83.

Bargh, J. A. (1996). Automaticity in social psychology. In E. T. Higgins & A. W. Kruglanski (eds), *Social Psychology: Handbook of Basic Principles*. New York: Guilford Press.

Barker, J. R. (1993). Tightening the iron cage: concertive control in self-managing teams. *Administrative Science Quarterly, 38*, 408–437.

Barker, J. R. (1999). *The Discipline of Teamwork: Participation and Concertive Control.* Thousand Oaks, Calif.: Sage.

Boje, D. M. (1991). The storytelling organization: a study of story performance in an office-supply firm. *Administrative Science Quarterly, 36*, 106–126.

Boje, D. M. (1995). Stories of the storytelling organization: a postmodern analysis of Dysney as a "Tamara-Land". *Academy of Management Journal, 38*, 997–1035.

Boje, D. M. & Rosile, G. A. (2001). Where's the power in the empowerment? Answers from Follett and Clegg. *The Journal of Applied Behavioral Science, 37*, 90–117.

Brydon-Miller, M. (1997). Participatory action research: psychology and social change. *Journal of Social Issues, 53*(4), 657–666.
Burke, W. W. (1986). Leadership as empowering others. In S. Srivastra & associates (eds), *Executive Power: How Executives Influence People and Organizations*. San Francisco: Jossey-Bass.
Cartwright, D. (1959). *Studies in Social Power*. Ann Arbor, Mich.: Institute for Social Research.
Chaiken, S., Giner-Sorolla, R., & Chen, S. (1996). Beyond accuracy: defense and impression motives in heuristic and systematic information processing. In P. M. Goldwitzer & J. A. Bargh (eds), *The Psychology of Action: Linking Cognition and Motivation to Behavior* (pp. 553–587). New York: Guilford Press.
Chia, R. (2000). Discourse analysis as organizational analysis. *Organization, 7*, 513–518.
Christie, R. & Geis, F. L. (1970). *Studies in Machiavellianism*. New York: Academic Press.
Clegg, S. (1989). *Frameworks of Power.* Thousand Oaks, Calif.: Sage.
Coleman, P. T. (2002). Change, paradox, complexity and meaning: a meta-framework for working seemingly intractable conflict. Working Paper, The International Center for Cooperation and Conflict Resolution, Teachers College, Columbia University.
Coleman, P. T. (in press). Implicit power theories: impact on perceptions of power and power sharing decisions. *Journal of Applied Social Psychology.*
Coleman, P. T. & Tjosvold, D. (2000). Positive power: mapping the dimensions of constructive power relations. Unpublished manuscript.
Collinson, D. (1994). Strategies of resistance: power, knowledge and subjectivity in the workplace. In J. M. Jermier, D. Knights, & W. R. Nord (eds), *Resistance and Power in Organizations* (pp. 25–68). London: Routledge.
Comstock, D. & Fox, R. (1993). Participatory research as critical theory: the North Bonneville, USA experience. In P. Park, M. Brydon-Miller, B. Hall, & T. Jackson (eds), *Voices of Change: Participatory Research in the United Sates and Canada*. Westport, Conn.: Bergin and Garvey Press.
Covaleski, M. A., Dirsmith, M. W., Heian, J. B., & Samuel, S. (1998). The calculated and the avowed: techniques of discipline and struggles over identity in Big Six public accounting firms. *Administrative Science Quarterly, 43*, 293–327.
Dahl, R. P. (1957). The concept of power. *Behavioral Science, 2*, 201–218.
Dahl, R. P. (1968). Power. In D. L. Sills (ed.), *International Encyclopedia of the Social Sciences* (Vol. 12). New York: Macmillan.
Deetz, S. (1995). *Transforming Communication, Transforming Business: Building Responsive and Responsible Workplaces.* Cresskill, NJ: Hampton Press, Inc.
Deetz, S., Tracy, S. J., & Simpson, J. L. (2000). *Leading Organizations through Transition: Communication and Cultural Change.* Thousand Oaks, Calif.: Sage.
Deutsch, M. (1973). *The Resolution of Conflict*. New Haven, Conn.: Yale University Press.
Deutsch, M. (1985). *Distributive Justice: A Social–Psychological Perspective*. New Haven, Conn.: Yale University Press.
Deutsch, M. (2000). Justice and conflict. In Morton Deutsch & Peter T. Coleman (eds), *The Handbook of Conflict Resolution: Theory and Practice* (pp. 41–64). San Francisco: Jossey-Bass.
Devine, P. G. (1989). Stereotypes and prejudice: their automatic and controlled components. *Journal of Personality and Social Psychology, 56*, 5–18.
Dovidio, J. F., Kawakami, K., & Beach, A. (2001). Reducing intergroup bias: the benefits of recategorization. In R. Brown & S. Gaertner (eds), *Blackwell Handbook of Social Psychology: Intergroup Processes* (pp. 22–44). Malden, Mass.: Blackwell Publishers.
Eaton, S. C. & Bailyn, L. (1999). Work and life strategies of professionals in biotechnology firms. *The Annals of the American Academy of Political and Social Science, 562*, 159–173.
Ezzamel, M. & Willmott, H. (1998). Accounting for teamwork: a critical study of group-based systems of organizational control. *Administrative Science Quarterly, 43*, 358–396.
Ezzamel, M. Willmott, H., & Worthington, F. (2001). Power, control and resistance in "The factory that time forgot". *Journal of Management Studies, 38*, 1053–1079.
Fay, B. (1987). *Critical Social Science.* Cambridge, UK: Polity Press.
Fiske, Susan T. (1993). Social cognition and social perception. *Annual Review of Psychology, 44*, 155–194.

Fletcher, J. (1999). *Disappearing Acts: Gender, Power, and Relational Practice at Work.* Cambridge, Mass.: The MIT Press.

Follett, M. P. (1973). Power. In E. M. Fox & L. Urwick (eds), *Dynamic Administration: The Collected Papers of Mary Parker Follett* (pp. 66–87). London: Pitman.

Ford, J. D. (1999). Organizational change as shifting conversations. *Journal of Organizational Change Management, 12*, 480–500.

Foucault, M. (1980). *Power/knowledge.* New York: Pantheon.

Freire, P. (1970). *Pedagogy of the Oppressed.* New York: Seabury Press.

French, J. R. P., Jr & Raven, B. (1959). The bases of social power. In D. Cartwright (ed.), *Studies in Social Power*, (pp. 150–167). Ann Arbor: University of Michigan Press.

Gergen, K. J. (1992). Organization theory in the postmodern era. In M. Reed & M. Hughes (eds), *Rethinking Organization: New Directions in Organization Theory and Analysis* (pp. 207–226). London: Sage.

Habermas, J. (1971). *Knowledge and Human Interests.* Boston: Beacon.

Hancock, P. & Tyler, M. (2001). *Work, Postmodernism and Organization: A Critical Introduction.* London: Sage.

Hardy, C., Palmer, I., & Phillips, N. (2000). Discourse as a strategic resource. *Human Relations, 53*, 1227–1248.

Hardy, C. & Phillips, N. (1998). Strategies of engagement: lessons from the critical examination of collaboration and conflict in an organizational domain. *Organization Science, 9*, 217–230.

Hinkin, T. R. & Schriesheim, C. A. (1989). Development and application of new scales to measure the French and Raven (1959) bases of power. *Journal of Applied Psychology, 74*, 561–587.

Janis, I. L. (1983). Groupthink. In J. R. Hackman, E. E. Lawler, & L. W. Porter (eds), *Perspectives on Behavior in Organizations* (2nd edn, pp. 378–384). New York: McGraw-Hill.

Kipnis, D. (1976), *The Powerholders.* Chicago: University of Chicago Press.

Knights, D. & McCabe, D. (2000). Bewitched, bothered and bewildered: the meaning and experience of teamworking for employees in an automobile company. *Human Relations, 53*, 1481–1517.

Korten, D. C. (1995). *When Corporations Rule the World.* San Francisco: Berrett-Koehler.

Lasswell, H. D. & Kaplan, A. (1950). *Power and Society.* New Haven, Conn.: Yale University Press.

Lewin, K. (1946). Action research and minority problems. *Journal of Social Issue, 2*(4), 34–46.

Lewin, K. (1947). Frontiers in group dynamics. *Human Relations, 1*, 5–41.

Lindner, E. (2001). Humiliation and the human condition: mapping a minefield. *Human Rights Review, 2*(2), 46–63.

Lykes, M. B. (1997). Activist participatory research among the Maya of Guatemala: constructing meanings from situated knowledge. *Journal of Social Issues, 53*(4), 725–746.

McCabe, D. (2000). Factory innovations and management machinations: the productive and repressive relations of power. *Journal of Management Studies, 37*, 931–953.

McCabe, D. (2002). "Waiting for dead men's shoes": towards a cultural understanding of management innovation. *Human Relations, 55*, 505–536.

Maguire, P. (1987). *Doing Participatory Research: A Feminist Approach.* Amherst, Mass.: Center for International Education, University of Massachusetts.

Marshak, R. J. (1998). A discourse on discourse: redeeming the meaning of talk. In D. Grant, T. Keenoy, & C. Oswick (eds), *Discourse and Organization* (pp. 15–30). Thousand Oaks, Calif.: Sage.

Marx, K. (1844). *Critique of the Hegelian Philosophy of Right.* Deutsche–französische Jahrbücher.

Moghaddam, F. M. (1997). Change and continuity in organizations: assessing intergroup relations. In C. S. Granrose & S. Oskamp (eds), *Cross-cultural Workgroups* (pp. 36–58). Thousand Oaks, Calif.: Sage.

Morgan, G. (1997). *Images of Organization* (2nd edn). London: Sage.

Mossholder, K. W., Bennett, N., Kemery, E. R., & Wesolowski, M. A. (1998). Relationships between bases of power and work reactions: the mediational role of procedural justice. *Journal of Management, 24*(4), 533–552.

Mumby, D. K. & Stohl, C. (1991). Power and discourse in organization studies: absence and the dialectic of control. *Discourse and Society, 2*, 313–332.

Nord, W. R. & Jermier, J. M. (1992). Critical social science for managers? Promising and perverse possibilities. In M. Alvesson & H. Willmott (eds), *Critical Management Studies* (pp. 202–222). London: Sage.

Operario, D. & Fiske, S. T. (2001). Stereotypes: content, structures, processes, and context. In R. Brown & S. Gaertner (eds), *Blackwell Handbook of Social Psychology: Intergroup Processes* (pp. 22–44). Malden, Mass.: Blackwell Publishers.

Oquist, P. (1978). The epistemology of action research. *Acta Sociologica, 21*(2), 143–163.

Organ, D. W. & Bateman, T. S. (1991). *Organizational Behavior* (4th edn). Boston: Irwin.

Pfeffer, J. (1981). *Power in Organizations*. Marshfield, Mass.: Pitman.

Potter, J. (1996). *Representing Reality: Discourse, Rhetoric and Social Construction*. Thousand Oaks, Calif.: Sage.

Pyszczynski, T., Greenberg, J., & Solomon, S. (1999). A dual-process model of defense against conscious and unconscious death-related thoughts: an extension of terror management theory. *Psychological Review, 106*(4), 835–845.

Rahim, M. A. (1989). Relationships of leader power to compliance and satisfaction with supervision: evidence from a national sample of managers. *Journal of Management, 15*, 545–556.

Raven, B. H., Schwarzwald, J., & Koslowsky, M. (1998). Conceptualizing and measuring a power/interaction model of interpersonal influence. *Journal of Applied Social Psychology, 28*(4), 307–332.

Rawls, J. (1996). *Political Liberalism*. New York: Columbia University Press.

Reynolds, M. (1998). Reflection and critical reflection in management learning. *Management Learning, 29*, 183–200.

Salzer-Mörling, M. (1998). As God created the Earth ... A saga that makes sense? In D. Grant, T. Keenoy, & C. Oswick (eds), *Discourse and Organization* (pp. 104–118). Thousand Oaks, Calif.: Sage.

Sampson, E. E. (1993a). *Celebrating the Other: A Dialogic Account of Human Nature*. Boulder, Colo.: Westview Press.

Sampson, E. E. (1993b). Identity politics: challenges to psychology's understanding. *American Psychologist, 48*, 1219–1230.

Schein, E. H. (1993). How can organizations learn faster? The challenge of entering the green room. *Sloan Management Review*, Winter, 85–92.

Schriesheim, C. A., Hinkin, T. R., & Podsakoff, P. M. (1991). Can ipsative and single-item measures produce erroneous results in field studies of French and Raven's (1959) bases of power? An empirical investigation. *Journal of Applied Psychology, 76*, 106–114.

Sewell, G. (1998). The discipline of teams: the control of team-based industrial work through electronic and peer surveillance. *Administrative Science Quarterly, 43*, 397–428.

Sewell, G. & Wilkinson, B. (1992). "Someone to watch over me": surveillance, discipline and the just-in-time labour process. *Sociology, 26*, 271–289.

Sidanius, J. & Pratto, F. (1999). *Social Dominance*. Cambridge University Press.

Thomas, D. A. & Ely, R. J. (1996). Making differences matter: a new paradigm for managing diversity. *Harvard Business Review*, September–October, 79–90.

Tjosvold, D. (1981). Unequal power relationships within a cooperative or competitive context. *Journal of Applied Social Psychology, 11*, 137–150.

Tjosvold, D. (1985a). The effects of attribution and social context on superiors' influence and interaction with low performing subordinates. *Personnel Psychology, 38*, 361–376.

Tjosvold, D. (1985b). Power and social context in superior–subordinate interaction. *Organizational Behavior and Human Decision Processes, 35*, 281–293.

Tjosvold, D. (1997). The leadership relationship in Hong Kong: power, interdependence and controversy. In K. Leung, U. Kim, S. Yamaguchi, & Y. Kashima (eds), *Progress in Asian Social Psychology* (Vol. 1). New York: Wiley.

Tjosvold, D., Andrews, I. R., & Struthers, J. T. (1991). Power and interdependence in workgroups. *Group and Organization Studies, 16*(3), 285–299.

Tjosvold, D., Chen, G., & Liu, C. H. (2001). Interdependence, mutual enhancement and strategic advantage: top management teams in China. Paper, Social Interdependence Theory Conference, July, Minneapolis.

Tjosvold, D., Coleman, P. T., & Sun, H. (in press). Effects of power concepts on using power to affect performance in China. *Group Dynamics: Theory, Research, and practice*.

Tjosvold, D., Johnson, D. W., & Johnson, R. T. (1984). Influence strategy, perspective-taking, and relationships between high and low power individuals in cooperative and competitive contexts. *Journal of Psychology, 116*, 187–202.

Townley, B. (1993). Foucault, power/knowledge, and its relevance for human resource management. *Academy of Management Review, 18*, 518–545.

Tsoukas, H. (2000). False dilemmas in organization theory: realism or social constructivism? *Organization, 7*, 531–535.

Van Maanen, J., & Kunda, G. (1989). "Real feelings": emotional expression and organizational culture. In L. L. Cummings & B. M. Staw (eds), *Research in Organizational Behavior* (pp. 43–103). Greenwich, Conn.: JAI Press.

Voronov, M. & Coleman, P. T. (2001). Expanding the horizons of organizational discourse: social reductions, gender, and power in technical fields. Manuscript under review.

Wallemacq, A. & Sims, D. (1998). The struggle with sense. In D. Grant, T. Keenoy, & C. Oswick (eds), *Discourse and Organization* (pp. 119–133). Thousand Oaks, Calif.: Sage.

Weber, M. (1947). *The Theory of Social and Economic Organization*. New York: Oxford University Press.

Wetherell, M. & Potter, J. (1992). *Mapping the Language of Racism: Discourse and the Legitimation of Exploitation.* New York: Columbia University Press.

Whyte, F. W. & Blasi, J. R. (1982). Worker ownership, participation and control: toward a theoretical model. *Policy Sciences, 4*, 137–163.

Wright, R. (1996). The occupational masculinity of computing. In C. Cheng (ed.), *Masculinities in Organizations* (pp. 77–96). Thousand Oaks, Calif.: Sage.

13

MANAGING THE RISK OF LEARNING

PSYCHOLOGICAL SAFETY IN WORK TEAMS

Amy C. Edmondson

INTRODUCTION

This chapter explores how members of organizational work teams can overcome the interpersonal risks they face every day at work, to help themselves, their teams, and their organizations to learn. Over the past few years I have been developing a model of learning in the work group setting that stems from the underlying premise that people are (both conscious and unconscious) impression managers—reluctant to engage in behaviors that could threaten the image others hold of them. Although few of us are without concern about others' impressions, our immediate social context can mitigate—or exacerbate—the reluctance to relax our guard. In field studies in several organizational contexts, I have found enormous differences across teams in people's willingness to engage in behavior for which the outcomes are both uncertain and potentially harmful to their image.

An extensive literature on organizational culture examines how norms, values, and beliefs arise in organizations to reduce the anxiety people feel confronting ambiguity and uncertainty (Schein, 1985). In times of significant organizational or environmental change the potential for anxiety is increased because people must take action without knowing whether things will work out as expected. Organizational culture, for all its complexity, cannot fully mitigate the anxiety and uncertainty that accompany novel behaviors or activities. For example, a team launching a new product targeted for unfamiliar customers faces unavoidable technical and business risk. This can provoke feelings of anxiety in the team, but these risks can be minimized by formal risk assessment methods and explicit discussion. At the same time, all individuals in organizations constantly face more subtle interpersonal risks that provoke anxiety and yet tend to remain tacit and undiscussed.

Some years ago I became intrigued by the small risks people face every day at work, when interacting with others and facing change, uncertainty, or ambiguity. To take action in such situations involves learning behavior, including asking questions, seeking help, experimenting with unproven actions, or seeking feedback. Although these activities are associated with such desired outcomes as innovation and performance (e.g. Edmondson, 1999; West, 2000),

International Handbook of Organizational Teamwork and Cooperative Working. Edited by
M. A. West, D. Tjosvold, and K. G. Smith.

engaging in them carries a risk for the individual of being seen as ignorant, incompetent, or perhaps just disruptive. Most people feel a need to manage this risk to minimize harm to their image, especially in the workplace and especially in the presence of those who formally evaluate them. This is both instrumental (promotions and other valued rewards may be dependent on impressions held by bosses and others) and socio-emotional (we prefer others' approval rather than disapproval). One solution to minimizing risk to one's image is simply to avoid engaging in interpersonal behaviors for which outcomes are uncertain. The problem with this solution is that it precludes learning. Another solution—to create conditions in which perceived interpersonal risk is reasonably low—is explored in this chapter.

Most people in organizations are being evaluated—whether frequently or infrequently, overtly or implicitly—in an ongoing way. The presence of others with more power or status makes the threat of evaluation especially salient, but it by no means disappears in the presence of peers and subordinates. This salience of evaluation in organizations intensifies the problem of image risk that people also confront in everyday lives (de Cremer, Snyder, & Dewitte, 2001; Snyder, 1974; Turnley & Bolino, 2001). Here I posit four specific risks to image that people face at work: being seen as ignorant, incompetent, negative, or disruptive. Each is triggered by particular behaviors through which individuals and groups learn.

First, when individuals ask questions or seek information, they run the risk of being seen as ignorant. Most of us can think of a time when we hesitated to ask a question because it seemed that no one else was asking, or perhaps we believed that the information was something we were expected to know already.

Second, when admitting (or simply calling attention to) mistakes, asking for help, or accepting the high probability of failure that comes with experimenting, people risk being seen as incompetent, whether in a narrow, particular domain, or more broadly. Reluctance to take such *interpersonal* risks can create *physical* risks in high-risk industries such as nuclear power, where admitting mistakes and asking for help may be essential for avoiding catastrophe (Carroll, 1998; Weick & Roberts, 1993). Similarly, this phenomenon is particularly troubling in organizations where lives are at stake, such as in hospitals. Reluctance to report mistakes in the health care setting is widely reported (e.g. Leape et al., 1991). Although this silence limits the ability of hospitals as organizations to improve through collective learning from mistakes, a goal most health care professionals would heartily endorse, the perceived need for impression management to protect one's professional image is extremely high in medicine.

Third, to learn and improve—as individuals and collectives—it is essential to reflect critically on current and past performance. The risk of being seen as negative often stops people from delivering critical assessments of a group or individual's performance, which limits the thoroughness and accuracy of collective reflection (Edmondson, 2002). Moreover, people strive to maintain their own and others' face, a tendency that inhibits sharing negative feedback. It is well known that bad news rarely travels well *up* the hierarchy, such that in the presence of supervisors and bosses, the risk of being seen as negative has been shown to be more acute than it might otherwise be (Reed, 1962).

Fourth, to avoid disrupting or imposing upon others' time and goodwill, people will avoid seeking feedback, information, or help (Brown, 1990). In particular, individuals are often reluctant to seek feedback about their performance. Despite the gains that can be obtained from feedback (Ashford & Cummings, 1983), many fail to take advantage of the opportunity. Although this can be driven by avoidance of the possibility of hearing something we do not want to hear, it also stems from a wish not to be seen as lacking in self-sufficiency, or as intrusive.

I have used the term "psychological safety" (Edmondson, 1999, 2002) to capture the degree to which people perceive their work environment as conducive to taking these interpersonal risks. In psychologically safe environments, people believe that if they make a mistake others will not penalize them or think less of them for it. They also believe that others will not resent or penalize them for asking for help, information, or feedback. This belief fosters the confidence to take the risks described above and thereby to gain from the associated benefits of learning.

I argue that creating conditions of psychological safety is essential to laying a foundation for effective learning in organizations. I further propose that structuring a collective learning process at the team or group level is a second critical element for effective organizational learning, and that a compelling goal is necessary for motivating this collective learning process. Although human beings are endowed with both desire and ability for learning, collections of interdependent individuals, whether small groups or large organizations, do not learn automatically. Not only does interpersonal risk inhibit some of the necessary behaviors, but organizational routines tend to endure and have a permanence of their own, independent of the actors who engage in them (Gersick & Hackman, 1990; Levitt & March, 1988). Moreover, traditions and beliefs about the appropriateness of the status quo inhibit learning and change (Levitt & March, 1988). Thus, an important aim of this chapter is to describe a collective learning process I observed taking place in similar ways across different contexts in a number of organizational work teams I have studied over the past few years. Teams are defined as work groups that exist within the context of a larger organization, have clearly defined membership, and share responsibility for a team product or service (Alderfer, 1987; Hackman, 1987).

In what follows, I describe the construct of psychological safety, the process of team learning, the role of the team leader, and how these constructs are related—drawing from my own and others' research. I first discuss psychological safety and how it differs from the related notion of interpersonal trust, and then describe team learning as an iterative process of action and reflection. I argue that compelling goals are necessary to motivate this deliberate, effortful process, and that psychological safety enhances the power of such goals. Without a goal, there is no clear direction to drive toward and no motivation to do so. However, without psychological safety, the risks of engaging wholeheartedly in this learning process are simply too great. The team leader can shape and strengthen the collective learning process both directly and indirectly by fostering psychological safety, and, in turn, setting goals. This chapter thus introduces a new theoretical model, depicted in Figure 13.1, in which psychological safety moderates the positive relationship between learning goals and

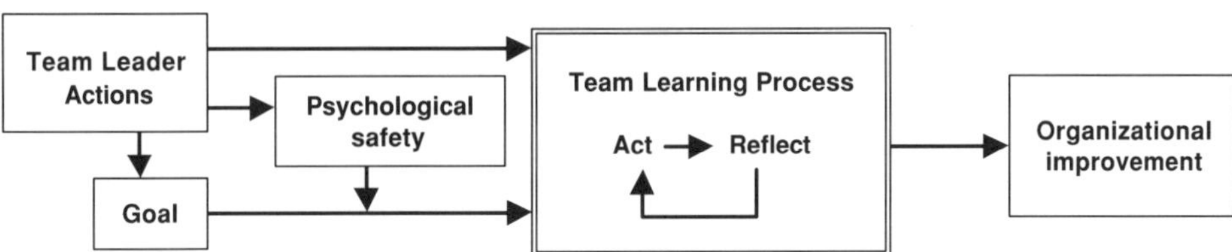

Figure 13.1 Model of team learning process

effortful learning behavior to accomplish them. I conclude with implications for future research and practice.

PSYCHOLOGICAL SAFETY: A COGNITIVE GROUP-LEVEL CONSTRUCT

Psychological safety describes individuals' perceptions about the consequences of interpersonal risks in their work environment. It consists of taken-for-granted beliefs about how others will respond when one puts oneself on the line, such as by asking a question, seeking feedback, reporting a mistake, or proposing a new idea. I argue that individuals engage in a kind of tacit calculus at micro-behavioral decision points, in which they assess the interpersonal risk associated with a given behavior (Edmondson, 1999). In this tacit process, one weighs the potential action against the particular interpersonal climate, as in "If I do this here, will I be hurt, embarrassed, or criticized?" A negative answer to this tacit question allows the actor to proceed. In this way, an action that might be unthinkable in one work group can be readily taken in another, due to different beliefs about probable interpersonal consequences.

The construct of psychological safety has roots in early research on organizational change, in which Schein and Bennis (1965) discussed the need to create psychological safety for individuals if they are to feel secure and capable of changing. More recently, Schein (1985) argued that psychological safety helps people overcome the defensiveness, or "learning anxiety," that occurs when people are presented with data that disconfirm their expectations or hopes, which can thwart productive learning behavior. However necessary the need for a comfortable learning environment, psychological safety does not imply a cozy environment in which people are necessarily close friends, nor does it suggest an absence of pressure or problems. Team psychological safety is distinct from group cohesiveness, as research has shown that cohesiveness can reduce willingness to disagree and challenge others' views, such as in the phenomenon of groupthink (Janis, 1982)—implying a lack of interpersonal risk-taking. Psychological safety describes a climate in which the focus can be on productive discussion that enables early prevention of problems and the accomplishment of shared goals because people are less likely to focus on self-protection.

Psychological Safety Versus Trust

The importance of trust in groups and organizations has long been noted by researchers (Kramer, 1999). Trust, defined as the expectation that others' future actions will be favorable to one's interests, makes one willing to be vulnerable to those actions (Mayer, Davis, & Schoorman, 1995; Robinson, 1996). The nature of this vulnerability is more narrowly defined for psychological safety than for trust. The concepts of psychological safety and trust have much in common; they both describe intrapsychic states involving perceptions of risk or vulnerability, as well as making choices to minimize negative consequences, and, as explored below, both have potential positive consequences for work groups and organizations. This section describes conceptual differences between these related constructs, to argue that they are complementary but distinct interpersonal beliefs. Three elements of psychological safety are described to distinguish it from trust—the timeframe, the object of focus, and level of analysis.

TEMPORAL IMMEDIACY

The tacit calculus inherent in perceptions of psychological safety considers the very short-term interpersonal consequences one expects from engaging in a specific action. For example, a nurse facing the decision of whether to ask a physician in the unit about a medication dosage she suspects is erroneous may be so focused on the potential immediate consequences of asking this question, such as being scolded and humiliated for being ignorant, that she temporarily discounts the longer-term consequence of *not* speaking up—that is, the harm that may be caused to a patient. Although the differential weighting of consequences in this example is clearly not rational, I have heard countless similar stories in field studies in markedly different organizational contexts. For example, nurses in one of several hospital teams in a study of medication error, after embarrassing past encounters with the nurse manager, were inclined to avoid speaking up about mistakes for fear of getting "put on trial," thereby unwittingly discounting the longer-term consequences of silence for patients and for the team (Edmondson, 1996). The construct of trust, in contrast, pertains to anticipated consequences across a wide temporal range, including the relatively distant future.

FOCUS ON "SELF" VERSUS "OTHER"

Trust involves giving others the benefit of the doubt—indicating a focus on *others'* potential actions or trustworthiness. In contrast, in discussing psychological safety, the question is whether others will give *you* the benefit of the doubt when, for instance, you have made a mistake or asked an apparently stupid question. For example, a member of a production team I studied in a manufacturing company reported, "I don't have to wear a mask in this team . . . it's easy to be myself." When people describe their situation at work in this way, they are revealing a sense of psychological safety, a sense of comfort expressing their true selves. The focus is internal, in contrast to the focus on others' future actions implicit in the construct of trust.

LEVELS OF ANALYSIS

An individual's sense of psychological safety in the workplace is likely to be shaped by ongoing interpersonal interactions among close coworkers. Although words and actions of top management may contribute to perceptions of psychological safety (e.g. Detert, 2002), as might individual differences in temperament (Tynan, 1999), the most salient influence is the perceptions of those individuals with whom an individual works most closely. Because psychological safety describes beliefs about interpersonal interaction, those interactions that are best situated to affect these beliefs are contained within a local work group or team. Moreover, members of teams tend to hold similar perceptions about psychological safety—that is, about "the way things are around here"—because they are subject to the same set of objective influences (for example, in having a common manager or a similar level of access to organizational resources), as well as because many of their beliefs develop out of shared experiences. Thus, team members of a nurse who reported being "made to feel like a two year old" when reporting a drug error independently reported similar feelings of discomfort about speaking up, for example commenting that "nurses are blamed for mistakes" and "[if you make a mistake here,] doctors bite your head off." These nurses, either from personal or vicarious experience, came to the conclusion that, on their team, reporting mistakes was interpersonally penalized. Consistent with this line of reasoning, in two studies I have found significant variance in psychological safety at the group level of analysis (Edmondson, 1996, 1999). In contrast, trust pertains primarily to a dyadic relationship, even if that dyad is sometimes conceptualized as consisting of large entities.

Others have studied both interpersonal trust and psychological safety; for example, in a recent study, May, Gilson, and Harter (1999) showed that coworker trust had a significant positive effect on psychological safety. Kahn (1990) found that "interpersonal relationships [in an architecture firm he studied] promoted psychological safety when they were supportive and trusting." Informants in his study felt free to share ideas and concepts about designs when they believed that any criticism would be constructive rather than destructive. The belief that others see one as competent (an aspect of respect) is particularly salient in this context; those who feel that their capability is in question are more likely to feel judged or monitored and thus may keep their opinions to themselves for fear of harming their reputation (Edmondson & Moingeon, 1998). In sum, if relationships within a group are characterized by trust and respect, individuals are likely to believe they will be given the benefit of the doubt—a defining characteristic of psychological safety.

Outcomes of Psychological Safety

Psychological safety can increase the chances of effortful, interpersonally risky, learning behavior, such as help seeking, experimentation, and discussion of error. Empirical support for this was found in the manufacturing company study, referenced earlier, in which I collected both qualitative and quantitative data on 51 teams of four types (management, new product development, staff services, and production) (Edmondson, 1999). These data were analyzed to show that psychological safety promoted team learning, which in turn facilitated team performance in teams throughout the organizational hierarchy.

In a more recent field study of 16 operating room teams learning to use an innovative (and extremely challenging) new technology for minimally invasive cardiac surgery, Edmondson, Bohmer, and Pisano (2000) found that psychological safety allowed nonsurgeons to speak up—despite facing long-standing status barriers—with observations, questions, or concerns about the new technology. Established hierarchical roles and routines in the operating were renegotiated to allow the technology to be implemented successfully (Edmondson, Bohmer, & Pisano, 2001). Rather than only waiting for the chief surgeon to issue commands, all team members (nurses, perfusionists, and anesthesiologists) had to speak up about and act upon crucial information from each other. Teams that were able to establish a degree of psychological safety were better able to renegotiate the ingrained hierarchy within the surgical team, and speaking up was a predictor of successful implementation of the technology. One of the successful implementers, for example, reported team members speaking up, even if it meant correcting a superior. One scrub nurse volunteered a story about her own error and how her junior, a circulating nurse, pointed it out to her:

> We all have to share the knowledge. For example, in the last case, we needed to reinsert a guidewire and I grabbed the wrong wire and I didn't recognize it at first. And my circulating nurse said, "Sue, you grabbed the wrong wire." This shows how much the different roles don't matter. We all have to know about everything. You have to work as a team.

In contrast, unsuccessful implementers reported great difficulty in doing this. For example, a nurse in one hospital explained that it was difficult to speak up when she suspected that something might be wrong:

> I'd tell the adjunct. Or, I might whisper to the anesthesiologist, "does it look like [the clamp] migrated?" In fact I've seen that happen. It drives me crazy. They are talking about it—the adjunct is whispering to the anesthesiologist, "It looks like it moved" or "There is a leak in the ASD" or something, and I'm saying "You've got to tell him! Why don't you tell him?" But they're not used to saying anything. They are afraid to speak out. But for this procedure you have to say stuff.

Research has also found that psychological safety can stimulate innovation. For example, West and Anderson (1996) studied top management teams in British hospitals and found that organizational support for innovation enabled both "participative safety" and participation, which led to proposing more innovations. In other studies, participative safety allowed teams both to generate and integrate innovations into practice (D'Andrea-O'Brien & Buono, 1996). Similarly, in the study of cardiac surgery teams, teams with greater psychological safety were also more likely to engage in process innovation—another factor associated with successful implementation of the technology in their hospitals (Edmondson, Bohmer, & Pisano, 2000, 2001).

Removing the fear of speaking up can promote innovation by freeing people up to suggest novel or unorthodox ideas. For example, in one of the cardiac surgery teams we studied, where unobtrusive measures revealed the presence of psychological safety (see Edmondson, Bohmer, & Pisano, 2001), a nurse spontaneously suggested solving a particular problem experienced in the new technology by using a long-forgotten piece of equipment—a clamp nicknamed the "iron intern." The nurse's brainstorm ultimately became a part of that team's routine. This kind of creative innovation can be contrasted with the views of members of other teams. For example, an anesthesiologist in an operating room team lacking psychological safety told the researchers that, although team members saw opportunities for change and experimentation, "It is best not to stick your neck out. Innovation is tolerated at best." The latter team ranked among the least successful implementers of the new technology, while the former was one of the most successful.

THE COLLECTIVE LEARNING PROCESS IN TEAMS

Mitigating the inherent risks of speaking up through psychological safety is only part of enabling teams to learn. Learning as a team also requires coordination and some degree of structure, to ensure that insights are gained from members' collective experience and also used to guide subsequent action. Individual learning is thought of as an iterative process in which actions are taken, reflected upon, and modified in an ongoing way (Kolb, 1984; Schön, 1984). This iterative process does not happen automatically in a team (Edmondson, Bohmer, & Pisano, 2001; West, 2000). This section describes the somewhat structured process through which teams learn and then discusses factors that contribute to this process, again drawing from three field studies to illustrate these factors.

Collective Learning as an Iterative Process

First, organizational learning researchers have described the need for reflection-in-action, or "double-loop learning" (Argyris & Schön, 1978), for effective organizational adaptation. Reflection-in-action is the critical examination of a process, such that it can be subsequently adjusted according to new data and knowledge. One component of reflection-in-action is analogic thinking (Hargadon, 1998). Analogic thinking—merging diverse pools of knowledge and integrating past and present experiences—is a learning strategy particularly relevant to new product development teams and others that are confronted with a learning challenge.

The team learning process consists of iterative cycles of action, reflection, and adjustment. What is being learned, made more effective, or disseminated are routines for conducting work that accomplishes goals. Although some organizational routines are simple and carried out by one person, most require coordinated action from multiple people. The knowledge needed to carry out these routines is stored in many different forms and locations, including procedure manuals, physical equipment and layout, and individual minds. Through repeated action and reflection, teams access this knowledge and learn how to best use it. In developing this conceptualization of team learning, I draw both from the literature (e.g. West, 2000) and from empirical evidence. In particular in studying cardiac surgery teams, those that successfully implemented a new technology in their hospitals tended to engage in a qualitatively different process—one characterized by iterative trial and reflection—than unsuccessful teams (Edmondson, Bohmer, & Pisano, 2001).

West (2000) stated that reflexive learning teams possess self-awareness and the *agency* to enable change. Periods of reflection in teams are structured around the questions: "What are we learning? What can we do better? What should we change?" and are followed by planning and implementation, or action. Some teams engage in reflection on a daily basis; others reflect at a natural break in the project, such as at "half-time" for sports teams (Katz, 2001); still others reflect when a project is completed, as in the "after action reviews" conducted by the US Army following military exercises (Garvin, 2000). The chronological midpoint of a project is a crucial time for reflection and change; anticipating "half-time" allows team members to work toward mini-deadlines and makes long-term projects approachable (Gersick, 1988). Furthermore, resolution is more easily obtained if it occurs "in the moment" because fidelity to data is likely to be greater.

Team reflection does not necessarily indicate extensive sessions to thoroughly analyze team process or performance, but instead can be quick and pragmatic. For example, a production team responsible for technical support in the manufacturing company included short daily meetings to check on team progress. Observing one of these meetings, I was struck by the quick task-focused updates, in which members described problems or solutions that had arisen within the past day or two, and others asked questions and offered suggestions. For example, after one member described "printer problems with those labels" and asked, "Who can we ask for help?" another member responded "How about asking the vendors who make the labels? They probably know how to fix it," and the team leader offered to make a phone call—closing the loop and dealing with the problem before it escalated in magnitude. Knowing that they would have a chance to reflect on triumphs and worries, the daily check-in contributed to this team's success within the organization.

For other teams it may be more appropriate to wait for outcomes to be available before reflecting on the team process. In a study of design firm teams, for example, Busby (1999) found that periods of collective retrospection after project completion produced cognitive and (to a lesser extent) behavioral learning. Increases in shared understanding (cognitive learning) were the most trenchant outcomes of these more extensive reflective sessions, and this shared understanding allowed team members to act and reflect in a coordinated manner.

Summary of the Team Learning Process

Across varying forms of team reflection (which differ in the frequency at which it occurs, at what point(s) in the project it happens, and what its outcomes might be) are some common themes: collaborating, making changes (whether mid-course or for subsequent projects), and expecting to encounter problems that will require changes. Reflection-in-action can lead to increased success in new technology implementation (Edmondson, Bohmer, & Pisano, 2001) and in product development. Reporting on a study of learning in new product development teams, Lynn et al. (1998, p. 8) concluded, "The key to developing really new products successfully is the degree to which teams are able to learn from prior steps—frequently in unpredictable ways—and act on that information."

LEARNING GOALS

Learning behavior is effortful. Something must motivate individuals to exert the effort to engage in learning behavior and drive groups to adopt the discipline to enact a collective learning process. A compelling shared goal motivates teams by establishing positive pressure or stress. A compelling goal for learning is one that is both meaningful (achieving it would in some way help the team or the organization accomplish something of generally agreed upon value) and sufficiently challenging to incur some doubt about its feasibility—but not so much doubt as to evoke feelings of helplessness (Csikszentmihalyi, 1994; Locke, 2001). For example, surgeon leaders of the more successful teams presented the new technology as an opportunity to help patients (by dramatically reducing the size of the surgical wound) and also stressed the difficulty of the challenge, explaining that it would require everyone on the team's active participation to pull it off. This emphasis on the goal and on the outcomes of their effort helped the team go through the arduous learning process.

The motivational power of goals is well established in the literature (Locke, 2001). Research has also shown that goal interdependence enables efficiency in group problem solving (Tjosvold, 1990), a kind of learning behavior. Other research (Frink & Ferris, 1998) suggests that goal setting and the effort invested in reaching goals are positively correlated to perceptions of accountability and performance evaluation. Goals also keep a team "on track" by establishing a benchmark against which its members can measure progress.

The Role of Shared Goals in Team Learning

Goals must be reasonably well defined and understood by all team members to foster reflection-in-action. For example, in a study of geographically dispersed product development teams (Sole & Edmondson, 2002), one team was working to develop a radical new material for a large Asian manufacturer. Distant team members had had no direct contact with this customer yet needed to understand its market strategy to estimate the longer-term commitment required for the team and its company. Other team members were located near the customer site and seemed to be in a good position to have the necessary information. After waiting for some time for the requested information, the distant team members' frustrations escalated:

> [We thought] our colleagues weren't putting priority and effort into it, when actually [we later learned] there was a void with the customer being able to articulate that themselves.

An intermediary familiar with both companies became involved and through his probing discovered that the customer itself had not yet established sales, marketing, or distribution plans, nor identified people responsible for these activities. A research scientist on the dispersed development team described this realization as an "ah-ha" moment:

> That was probably one of the biggest issues, because the customer themselves, for the longest time, didn't have their own strategy clear and *we didn't know it*.

The distant team members had made two assumptions: first that a *shared* team goal existed and second that the team members in contact with the customer had data relevant to achieving that goal. From these assumptions came attributions of noncompliance, leading to negative emotions within the team. Through better articulation of the team's shared goals (which would begin to suggest strategies for obtaining the information needed to achieve them), this miscommunication would have been less likely to happen. In fact, the act of goal setting can be as or more important than the goal itself, because it creates shared understanding of the team's task and suggests implications for how to work together.

Psychological Safety as a Moderator

Social psychologists have investigated relationships between objective goals and intrapsychic and interpersonal states in a group. For example, Dirks (1999) showed that trust moderates the relationship between goals and performance: when there is a low level of trust in a group, contributions of group members were limited to achieving personal rather than cooperative goals. This can inhibit group-level learning and get in the way of accomplishing a desired organizational change (Edmondson & Woolley, 2003). Similarly, in this chapter I propose that psychological safety moderates the positive relationship between a compelling goal and team learning. When psychological safety is high, this relationship is likely to be strong; when it is low, the motivating effects of goals are inhibited, as, despite the desire to learn, interpersonal risk may inhibit the necessary behavior. This hypothesis is consistent with existing theories of task motivation which maintain that behavior and performance are driven by needs, goals, and rewards (Dirks, 1999; Kanfer, 1990). Consistent with this, Figure 13.1 presented learning as motivated by goals, not by psychological safety itself. Psychological safety, when present, may enhance the motivating effects of goals on behavior, just as trust has been shown to moderate the effects of task (cognitive) conflict on relationship (affective) conflict (Simons & Peterson, 2000). In this study, trust reduced the likelihood of relationship conflict in top management teams, such that task conflict (productive disagreement over the content of one's decisions and ideas that deepen cognitive understanding of the problem) was able to help the team produce better solutions. Termed "creative abrasion" by Leonard-Barton (1995), task conflict thus may have to exist within a cushion of psychological safety to enable a learning climate of discussion, innovation, and productive group thinking. Otherwise such conflict is destructive—characterized by aggression, harsh language, and the threat of humiliation in front of others. Similarly, Barsade and her colleagues (2001) found that psychological safety moderates the effect of conflict on anger. Psychological safety allows groups to set high goals and work toward them through cycles of learning and collaboration.

In this way, psychological safety allows the interpersonal risks of learning to be mitigated. It has very real consequences for the way learning occurs—or fails to occur—in work teams of all kinds, and thus organizations. As depicted in Figure 13.1, team leader actions are predicted to influence goals, psychological safety, and the team learning process, while psychological safety moderates the relationship between a compelling team goal and a team learning process—enhancing or inhibiting the effect of goals on team learning.

THE ROLE OF TEAM LEADERS IN PSYCHOLOGICAL SAFETY, LEARNING PROCESS, AND GOALS

Factors that shape the team learning process include power relationships and how team leaders manage them. Above, I argued that psychological safety facilitates freedom and openness to engage in the interpersonally risky behaviors needed for learning, and also, perhaps paradoxically, that an effective team learning process is structured and guided, through deliberate action (West, 2000). Managing this apparent tension is the job of a team leader. Further, team leaders help to articulate or highlight a shared goal for the team.

The actions and attitudes of the team leader are thus important determinants of the team learning process. First, team leaders are a critical influence on psychological safety; second, they can deliberately work to structure a learning process, and third, team leaders play a role in shaping, or at least communicating, the team's goal. In this section, I develop implications for team leaders related to managing all three elements of team learning.

Creating Psychological Safety

Team leaders have a powerful effect on psychological safety. Researchers have shown that team members are particularly aware of the behavior of the leader (Tyler & Lind, 1992), and leaders' responses to events and behaviors influence (in a way either beneficial or detrimental to the group) other members' perceptions of appropriate and safe behavior (Winter, Sarros, & Tanewski, 1997). Leaders can create environments for learning by acting in ways that promote psychological safety. Autocratic behavior, inaccessibility, or a failure to acknowledge vulnerability all can contribute to team members' reluctance to incur the interpersonal risks of learning behavior (Edmondson, 1996; Edmondson, Bohmer, & Pisano, 2001). And, when team leaders are selected solely on the basis of technical expertise, such as skill and knowledge about a topic, they may lack the interpersonal skills necessary to seek others' input, invite feedback and ideas, and create an interpersonal climate in which others are willing to speak up with ideas and concerns.

ACCESSIBILITY

Leaders encourage team members to learn together by being accessible and personally involved. In one of the cardiac surgery teams that promoted organizational learning (in the form of successfully implementing the challenging new technology), an operating room nurse implicitly made this association by describing the surgeon leading her team as "very accessible. He's in his office, always just two seconds away. He can always take five minutes to explain something, and he never makes you feel stupid." In striking contrast, the surgeon in one of the less successful teams requested that nonphysician team members go through his residents (junior physicians who are still in training) rather than speak to him directly. Through their behaviors, these two surgeons conveyed very different messages to their teams. The first surgeon increased the likelihood that people would come to him with questions or problems, and, more importantly, would speak up quickly and openly in the operating room, with questions and observations, while the other surgeon made this more difficult (Edmondson, Bohmer, & Pisano, 2001).

ACKNOWLEDGING FALLIBILITY

To create psychological safety, team leaders also can demonstrate tolerance of failure, such as by acknowledging one's own fallibility, taking interpersonal risks, and religiously avoiding punishing others for well-intentioned risks that backfire. Self-disclosure by team leaders is one way to do this (Gabarro, 1987). For example, one surgeon team leader repeatedly told his team: "I need to hear from you because I'm likely to miss things." The repetition of this phrase was as important as its meaning: people tend not to hear—or not to believe—a message that contradicts old norms when they hear it only once. Soliciting feedback suggests to others that their opinion is respected; it may also contribute to establishing a norm of active participation.

Other vivid examples of purposefully refraining from penalizing failure exist in the management literature. For example, Brand (1998) reiterates the tale of how innovation at 3M was fostered by a culture of leaders and management tolerant of mistakes: the adhesive used in the now ubiquitous Post-it notes was the botched version of another product development project. The motto of product-design firm IDEO is "Fail often, so you'll succeed sooner" (Katz, 2001, p. 61). Similarly, Cannon and Edmondson (2001) describe the "Mistake of the Month" ritual at a public relations firm, in which certain meetings opened with a review of mistakes—a lighthearted way to acknowledge the learning value in mistakes, and even for building a sense of community.

PSYCHOLOGICAL SAFETY VERSUS ACCOUNTABILITY

In supporting a climate of psychological safety, are leaders sacrificing team member accountability? I argue that this is a false trade-off. First, it is inaccurate to equate psychological safety with the removal of consequences for lack of performance. My research suggests that skilled team leaders can reward excellence, sanction poor performance, and at the same time embrace the imperfection and error that are inevitable under conditions of uncertainty and change. Psychological safety is nurtured without sending the message that "anything goes." In this way, team leaders and other immediate supervisors of work must communicate clear expectations about performance and accountability, without communicating that they are closed to, or unwilling to hear, bad news. Psychological safety means no one will be punished or humiliated for errors, questions, or requests for help, in the service of reaching ambitious performance goals. To make this work, team leaders must inspire team members to embrace error and deal with failure in a productive manner. This balancing act may be difficult to enact without some natural leadership ability or training, or may require excellent interpersonal skills, and perhaps even humor (Filipowicz, 2002).

Managing Process

To encourage learning, the leader must impose structure on the team to ensure that reflection follows action and that changes are both suggested and implemented accordingly (Edmondson, 2002). This structured learning process will benefit from the leader's explicit request for input from the team. Team and organizational-level learning both necessarily depend on individually held knowledge, and there is a large body of valuable, untapped knowledge within the organization (Macdonald, 1995). Leaders must seek out this internal knowledge especially from lower-status team members (such as nurses and technicians in the context of the cardiac surgery operating room) who might otherwise be reluctant to speak. Team leaders can play a role in drawing members' thoughts out by setting up reflective sessions where task and time pressures are temporarily removed.

POWER

Leaders can manage power from both directions, first by empowering those in lower-power positions to speak up and second by minimizing the domineering tendencies of higher-power individuals. For example, in a qualitative study of four production teams in a manufacturing company, Brooks (1994) described one in which the leader, Dave, used his position as an engineer as an advantage over lower-status technicians in the team. Dave and another engineer dominated meetings and regularly belittled their teammates' contributions. The leader's style so swayed the group that Brooks characterized them as the "lost team," unable to set goals or make any real efforts to achieve them. Dominant individuals like Dave can be useful in prompting team reflection but should not be allowed to dictate the form of subsequent action (Wageman & Mannix, 1998). Power differences can and must be managed to enhance team learning and performance. Suppressing the input of team members reduces opportunities for learning, with such consequences as less robust data or poorly articulated, constructed, and executed projects.

Research on power differentials explains such scenarios as the relative presence or potency of power in a group influences willingness to participate and the type of knowledge produced (Brooks, 1994; Dirks, 1999; Lee et al., 2001). Other research suggests that fear (on an individual or organizational level) impedes collective learning by marring what Rifkin and Fulop (1997) term a "learning space." Fear in people holding subordinate positions within the team causes concealment of one's identity, blocking "mutual self-disclosure" (Rifkin & Fulop, 1997) and hindering the process of team learning. Psychological safety, however, can counteract the debilitating forces of power.

STRUCTURING A PROCESS

The second way leaders contribute to structuring the learning process is by guiding the team through preparation and early, sometimes experimental, efforts. The challenge of learning behaviors such as talking about errors, experimenting, and learning how to gather data from varied sources is affected by team composition. Knowledge differences, credentials, length of tenure, gender, and rank within the organization can threaten collective learning, yet many teams are successful learners in spite of these inequalities. Leaders can help this come about: in addition to building psychological safety, they can lead training and practice sessions, use direct, actionable language, and articulate norms for working together. Vignettes from several field studies illustrate these aspects of the team learning process.

STRUCTURE VERSUS INNOVATION

At first glance it may seem that leaders must sacrifice innovation by imposing the structure of a learning process. On the one hand, ensuring that action and reflection occur in a timely and productive way requires the imposition of structure, schedule, and guidance. On the other hand, this process not only allows spontaneity, creativity, and process innovation, it can promote it (West, 2000). Enabling innovation thus may require being flexible while imposing structure, another skillful balancing act that involves prodding the team to reflect, while remaining open to what transpires in the reflection process.

Setting Team Goals

IMPOSING VERSUS PARTICIPATING

The leader's role in setting team goals also involves a tension between setting direction unilaterally and allowing group participation in shaping goals. Clear, compelling goals are considered an essential prerequisite for team effectiveness (Hackman, 1987), and imposing a goal from above is often considered effective practice. This imposition can come at the cost of valuable input from members who may know more about certain facets of the team's work than the leader does. One factor driving this balance is the role a given team plays in executing the organization's strategy. If a team's job is defined by organizational imperatives, its specific goals may be set by senior management but perhaps further developed by the team leader and team members. An externally imposed goal may also be required if a team's work must be integrated with the work of other teams. This integration can either be planned in advance, when enough is known to do so, or coordinated through interaction across team boundaries throughout different teams' progress on their tasks. In this model, a network of teams in the organization shares knowledge and works cooperatively toward organizational goals in an iterative learning process. For most teams, team members' input is more important and more useful for figuring out how goals will be achieved rather than what the goals are—that is, input is directed into means not ends (Hackman, 1987). Finally, effective goals for learning must balance radical ("stretch") and incremental (finite, foothold) goals to measure progress along the way to achieving goals that seem ambitious if not impossible to achieve at the outset.

IMPLICATIONS FOR THEORY AND PRACTICE

The model presented in this chapter extends previous theory on team learning by introducing the role of a compelling goal that is both meaningful and challenging as a driver of the team learning process, and by arguing that psychological safety moderates this relationship. I draw from the literature and from several field studies to illustrate and demonstrate the plausibility of relationships in the model. These examples are by no means offered as conclusive evidence of the hypothesized relationships, however, and empirical research is needed to test and extend the model depicted in Figure 13.1.

The Role of Psychological Safety in Team Learning

Field studies in various settings—health care delivery, product development, production, and management—suggest that, in situations where collaboration is critical to learning, certain conditions must be present for teams to learn and to work together effectively—especially psychological safety and (not unrelated) an open, coaching-oriented team leader. The construct and effects of psychological safety have growing support in the literature (e.g. Barsade, Gibson, & Putzel, 2001; Edmondson, 1999, 2002; Kahn, 1990); however, further research is needed to build on the studies referenced above.

IMPLICATIONS OF PSYCHOLOGICAL SAFETY AS A MODERATOR

Previously, I have discussed psychological safety as a mechanism that translates supportive inputs into outcomes (Edmondson, 1999). This conceptualization makes sense, given inputs that directly help build psychological safety, but it is incomplete in that it bypasses the issue of motivation. The model presented in this chapter thus may be more accurate and complete. Proposing psychological safety as a moderator is meant to help explain the differential impact of goals on outcomes and why teams learn and improve at varying rates. These propositions are offered to encourage additional work to support a new theory of work motivation in teams, with a focus on motivators and detractors.

PSYCHOLOGICAL SAFETY'S LIMITATIONS

Psychological safety is an explanatory construct—a set of intangible interpersonal beliefs and predictions—rather than a managerial lever or action. There are actions leaders can take to build psychological safety, as discussed above, but psychological safety cannot be mandated or altered directly. In this sense, theory and practice related to psychological safety must be advanced by research that investigates effects of leader behavior and other organizational factors on psychological safety and on more tangible outcomes related to performance and job satisfaction.

Research on explanatory constructs like trust and psychological safety (both intrapsychic states) has a particular burden: to be relevant to practitioners the concepts must be unpacked into specific, actionable steps and they must be related to other critical variables such as goals and task design. Such research must balance the development of theoretical bodies of knowledge and the investigation of "real world" problems (King, Keohane, & Verba, 1994).

Implications for Practice

A few practical suggestions can be gleaned from the ideas and studies reviewed in this chapter. First, we can return to a suggestion raised by Peter Senge (1990) in his influential book on organizational learning, where he argued that managers lack, yet need, management "practice fields," where they can participate together in simulated experiences, make and learn from mistakes without actual harm to the organization, and conduct experiments.

PRACTICE FIELDS

Leaders of teams can orchestrate explicit sessions for off-line "practice," in which the team is able to learn from simulated experiences or from thought experiments, without risk of harming their real work. Six of the eight successful cardiac surgery teams we studied used a form of this technique, by engaging in a thorough team practice session, in the form of a dry run, while six of the eight unsuccessful teams did not engage in a dry run. In these explicit practice sessions, team members walked through the procedure in "real time," discussing what moves each person would be making if a real patient had been present. Through this kind of off-line practice, the teams were able to anticipate technical problems that might arise during surgery and also to get comfortable in new interpersonal roles and relationships (Edmondson, Bohmer, & Pisano, 2001). Similarly, other recent research found that leader briefings and team training influenced mental model accuracy and were integral to team performance in new environments (Marks, Zaccaro, & Mathieu, 2000). Practice fields are also likely to foster psychological safety, not only because real financial or medical consequences are removed, but because they convey to the members of the team that learning is important and that getting it right the first time is understood to not always be possible. Team leaders are most often in a position to suggest and implement practice fields as a tool in promoting team learning.

DIRECT LANGUAGE

In addition to setting a context for learning that encourages participation from all members, using direct, actionable language also contributes to an effective learning process (Argyris, 1993). Teams cannot afford to shirk critiques—the risk of sounding negative, criticizing the boss, or making the company appear fallible. For example, management teams often face strategic decisions in which they must reflect on the company's current situation and suggest changes. The challenge in such discussions is to be objective and blunt about problems and about what is not working. In many such team discussions, however, the language is anything but direct and clear. For example, a top management team I studied engaged in a series of meetings for the explicit purpose of developing a new strategy. In these conversations, I observed a persistent pattern of using metaphor to evade stating a critical assessment of the team's progress. To illustrate, one member commented,

> Listening to Bob talk about the ship, I'd like to explore the difference between the metaphor of the ship and how the rudder gets turned and when, in contrast to a flotilla, where there's lots of little rudders and we're trying to orchestrate the flotilla. I think this contrast is important. At one level, we talk about this ship and all the complexities of trying to determine not only

its direction but also how to operationalize the ship in total to get to a certain place, versus allowing a certain degree of freedom that the flotilla analogy evokes.

Although metaphors such as this can provoke new ideas and creativity, they can also obscure the real issues and preclude direct or contentious discussion. In this team, members rarely inquired to clarify the meaning of each other's words, or to seek to identify areas of disagreement. The team continued to discuss the company and its situation abstractly in this way, avoiding disagreement and postponing resolution of the self-assessment process, and members tended not to challenge each other's abstract language. By the end of six months, little progress and no decisions had been made. The team's abstract ruminations did not translate easily into action (Edmondson, 2002).

NORMS

Finally, team leaders and members can explicitly seek to define objectives and agreed upon norms for how to work toward them. For example, in the study of geographically dispersed product development teams cited above, we found some teams establishing clear norms for working together and an explicit process for learning from each other (Sole & Edmondson, 2002). One team held weekly "virtual" meetings via telephone to share recently collected data. In contrast, another team had no established routine for collecting and distributing information, ultimately contributing to mistrust and frustration in the team. Another way in which the first team encouraged collective learning was by being explicit about goals and taking inventory of members' capacities and strengths—and weaknesses—what they *needed* to know. Based on the results of this informal inventory, the team exercised flexibility and brought in someone not officially on the team to fill gaps in their knowledge and expertise.

Similarly, differences in technology implementation success in the cardiac surgery study could be accounted for in part by how the team leader framed the learning challenge. Successful implementers viewed technology implementation as a team learning project; unsuccessful implementers viewed it as a technical challenge. These different frames led to different norms for team member interaction, which ultimately allowed or disallowed a structured team learning process of testing, reflecting, and modifying the procedure, in an ongoing, participative way.

CONCLUSION

This chapter has drawn from teams in many contexts to model the collective learning process in teams. One the one hand, these teams may seem too diverse to allow useful comparisons and to develop general insights. The challenges encountered on the factory floor, in the operating room, and around the glass-topped tables in a management team's conference room differ substantively. On the other hand, all of the teams studied—whether geographically dispersed product development teams or co-located nursing teams—struggled with the need for learning and all struggled with issues of power, trust, and psychological safety. In each, it appeared that team leaders were in positions to play a critical role in shaping the learning process. The model and guidelines presented above provide team leaders with a supportive framework for understanding and responding to the dynamics of the collective learning process.

Team leaders can be seen to occupy an increasingly sophisticated and challenging role, especially when they lead teams that need to learn. These leaders, found throughout the organization, must continually clarify the meaning and importance of the team's goal, make sure that goal is serving the organization's strategic aims, and remain open to input from other team members about ways in which the goal must be modified to meet new changes in the team's environment. This means setting challenging goals and specific direction without engaging in authoritarian action that stifles participation. It means allowing team members the latitude for innovation while providing the structure needed for learning. To do this, I argue, requires enough structure to ensure inclusiveness and teamwork without restricting the spontaneity and creativity that can produce unexpected synergies—structure without rigidity. It means creating a climate of psychological safety that allows people to feel safe taking risks, while also setting high standards that require enormous effort and preclude settling into a comfort zone—safety without complacency.

ACKNOWLEDGEMENTS

The research described in this chapter was supported by the Division of Research at Harvard Business School. The chapter benefited from the superb research assistance of Laura Feldman, and helpful comments and suggestions from Michael West improved the text immensely.

REFERENCES

Alderfer, C. P. (1987). An intergroup perspective on organizational behavior. In J. W. Lorsch (ed.), *Handbook of Organizational Behavior*. Englewood Cliffs, NJ: Prentice-Hall.

Argyris, C. (1993). *Knowledge for Action: A Guide to Overcoming Barriers to Organizational Change*. San Francisco: Jossey-Bass.

Argyris, C. & Schön, D. (1978). *Organizational Learning: A Theory of Action Perspective*. Reading, Mass.: Addison-Wesley.

Ashford, S. J. & Cummings, L. L. (1983). Feedback as an individual resource: personal strategies of creating information. *Organizational Behavior and Human Performance, 32*, 370–398.

Barsade, S. G., Gibson, D. E., & Putzel, R. (2001). *To Be Angry or Not to Be Angry in Groups: Examining the Question*. Washington, DC: Academy of Management.

Brand, A. (1998). Knowledge management and innovation at 3M. *Journal of Knowledge Management, 2*(1), 17–22.

Brooks, A. K. (1994). Power and the production of knowledge: collective team learning in work organizations. *Human Resource Development Quarterly, 5*(3), 213–235.

Brown, R. (1990). Politeness theory: exemplar and exemplary. In I. Rock (ed.), *The Legacy of Solomon Asch: Essays in Cognition and Social Psychology* (pp. 23–37). Hillsdale, NJ: Lawrence Erlbaum Associates.

Busby, J. S. (1999). The effectiveness of collective retrospection as a mechanism of organizational learning. *Journal of Applied Behavioral Sciences, 31*(1), 109–129.

Cannon, M. D. & Edmondson, A. C. (2001). Confronting failure: antecedents and consequences of shared beliefs about failure in organizational work groups. *Journal of Organizational Behavior, 22*, 161–177.

Carroll, J. S. (1998). Organizational learning activities in high-hazard industries: the logics underlying self-analysis. *Journal of Management Studies, 35*(6), 699–717.

Csikszentmihalyi, M. (1994). *Flow: The Psychology of Optimal Experience*. New York: Simon and Schuster.

D'Andrea-O'Brien, C. & Buono, A. F. (1996). Building effective learning teams: lessons from the field. *S.A.M. Advanced Management Journal, 61*(3), 4–10.

De Cremer, D., Snyder, M., & Dewitte, S. (2001). "The less I trust, the less I contribute (or not)?" The effects of trust, accountability and self-monitoring in social dilemmas. *European Journal of Social Psychology, 31*, 93–107.

Detert, J. R. (2002). Speaking up at Hi-Co. Harvard Business School Working Paper.

Dirks, K. T. (1999). The effects of interpersonal trust on work group performance. *Journal of Applied Psychology, 84*(3), 445–455.

Edmondson, A. (1996). Learning from mistakes is easier said than done: group and organizational influences on the detection and correction of human error. *Journal of Applied Behavioral Sciences, 32*(1), 5–32.

Edmondson, A. (1999). Psychological safety and learning behavior in work teams. *Administrative Science Quarterly, 44*, 350–383.

Edmondson, A. (2002). The local and variegated nature of learning in organizations: a group-level perspective. *Organization Science, 13*(2), 128–146.

Edmondson, A., Bohmer, R. M. J., & Pisano, G. (2000). Learning new technical and interpersonal routines in operating room teams: the case of minimally invasive cardiac surgery. In B. Mannix, M. Neale, & T. Griffith (eds), *Research on Groups and Teams* (pp. 29–51). Greenwich, Conn.: JAI Press.

Edmondson, A., Bohmer, R. M. J., & Pisano, G. (2001). Disrupted routines. *Administrative Science Quarterly, 46*(4), 685–716.

Edmondson, A. C. & Moingeon, B. (1998). From organizational learning to the learning organization. *Management Learning, 29*(1), 5–20.

Edmondson, A. C. & Woolley, A. (2003). Understanding outcomes of organizational learning interventions. In M. Easterby-Smith et al. (eds), *International Handbook on Organizational Learning and Knowledge Management*. London: Blackwell.

Filipowicz, A. (2002). The impact of humor on performance in task-based interactions: a theoretical model. Harvard University Working Paper.

Frink, D. D. & Ferris, G. R. (1998). Accountability, impression management, and goal setting in the performance evaluation process. *Human Relations, 51*(10), 1259–1283.

Gabarro, J. J. (1987). The development of working relationships. In J. Lorsch (ed.), *Handbook of Organizational Behavior* (pp. 172–189). Englewood Cliffs, NJ: Prentice-Hall.

Garvin, D. A. (2000). *Learning in Action*. Boston: Harvard Business School Press.

Gersick, C. J. G. (1988). Time and transition in work teams: toward a new model of group development. *Academy of Management Journal, 31*, 9–41.

Gersick, C. J. G. & Hackman, J. R. (1990). Habitual routines in task-performing teams. *Organizational Behavior and Human Decision Processes, 47*, 65–97.

Hackman, J. R. (1987). The design of work teams. In J. Lorsch (ed.), *Handbook of Organizational Behavior* (pp. 315–342). Englewood Cliffs, NJ: Prentice-Hall.

Hargadon, A. B. (1998). Firms as knowledge brokers: lessons in pursuing continuous innovation. *California Management Review, 40*(3), 209–227.

Janis, I. L. (1982). *Groupthink: Psychological Studies of Policy Decisions and Fiascos*. Boston: Houghton Mifflin.

Kahn, W. A. (1990). Psychological conditions of personal engagement and disengagement at work. *Academy of Management Journal, 33*(4), 692–724.

Kanfer, R. (1990). Motivation theory and industrial and organizational psychology. In M. D. Dunnette & L. M. Hough (eds), *Handbook of Industrial and Organizational Psychology* (Vol. 1, p. 755). Palo Alto, Calif.: Consulting Psychologists Press, Inc.

Katz, N. (2001). Sports teams as a model for workplace teams: lessons and liabilities. *Academy of Management Executive, 15*(3), 56–67.

King, G., Keohane, R., & Verba, S. (1994). *Designing Social Inquiry*. Princeton, NJ: Princeton University Press.

Kolb, D. A. (1984). *Experiential Learning: Experience as the Source of Learning and Development*. Englewood-Cliffs, NJ: Prentice-Hall.

Kramer, R. M. (1999). Trust and distrust in organizations: emerging perspectives, enduring questions. *Annual Review of Psychology, 50*, 569–598.
Leape, L. L., Brennan, T. A., Laird, N., Lawthers, A. G., Localio, A. R., Barnes, B. A., Hebert, L., Newhouse, J. P., Weiler, P. C., & Hiatt, H. (1991). The nature of adverse events in hospitalized patients: results of the Harvard Medical Practice Study II. *New England Journal of Medicine, 324*, 377–384.
Lee, F., Edmondson, A., Thomke, S., & Worline, M. (2001). Promoting experimentation in organizational knowledge creation: effects of status, values and rewards. Manuscript under review.
Leonard-Barton, D. (1995). *Wellsprings of Knowledge: Building and Sustaining the Sources of Innovation*. Boston: Harvard Business School Press.
Levitt, B. & March, J. G. (1988). Organizational learning. *Annual Review of Sociology, 14*, 319–340.
Locke, E. A. (2001). Motivation by goal setting. In R. T. Golembiewski (ed.), *Handbook of Organizational Behavior* (pp. 43–56). New York: Marcel Dekker, Inc.
Lynn, G. S., Mazzuca, M., Morone, J. G., & Paulson, A. S. (1998). Learning is the critical success factor in developing truly new products. *Research Technology Management, 41*(3), 45–51.
Macdonald, S. (1995). Learning to change: an information perspective on learning in the organization. *Organization Science, 6*, 557–568.
Marks, M. A., Zaccaro, S., & Mathieu, J. E. (2000). Performance implications of leader briefings and team-interaction training for team adaptation to novel environments. *Journal of Applied Psychology, 85*(6), 971–986.
May, D. R., Gilson, R. L., & Harter, L. (1999). Engaging the human spirit at work: exploring the psychological conditions of meaningfulness, safety and availability. Chicago, Ill., National Meeting of the Academy of Management.
Mayer, R. C., Davis, J. H., & Schoorman, F. D. (1995). An integrative model of organizational trust. *Academy of Management Review, 20*(3), 709–734.
Reed, W. H. (1962). Upward communication in industrial hierarchies. *Human Relations, 15*, 3–15.
Rifkin, L. F. & Fulop, W. D. (1997). Representing fear in learning in organizations. *Management Learning, 28*(1), 45–63.
Robinson, S. L. (1996). Trust and breach of the psychological contract. *Administrative Science Quarterly, 41*(4), 574–599.
Schein, E. H. (1985). *Organizational Culture and Leadership*. San Francisco: Jossey-Bass.
Schein, E. H. & Bennis, W. (1965). *Personal and Organizational Change through Group Methods*. New York: Wiley.
Schön, D. (1984). *The Reflective Practitioner*. New York: Basic Books.
Senge, P. (1990). *The Fifth Discipline: The Art and Practice of the Learning Organization*. New York: Doubleday.
Simons, T. L. & Peterson, R. S. (2000). Task conflict and relationship conflict in top management teams: the pivotal role of intra-group trust. *Journal of Applied Psychology, 85*(1), 102–111.
Snyder, M. (1974). Self-monitoring of expressive behavior. *Journal of Personality and Social Psychology, 30*(4), 526–537.
Sole, D. & Edmondson, A. (2002). Bridging knowledge gaps: learning in geographically dispersed cross-functional development teams. In N. Bontis & C. W. Choo (eds), *The Strategic Management of Intellectual Capital and Organizational Knowledge: A Collection of Readings* (pp. 587–604). New York: Oxford University Press.
Tjosvold, D. (1990). Making technological innovations work. *Human Resources, 43*, 1117–1131.
Turnley, W. H. & Bolino, M. C. (2001). Achieving desired images while avoiding undesired images: exploring the role of self-monitoring in impression management. *Journal of Applied Psychology, 86*(2), 351–360.
Tyler, T. R. & Lind, E. A. (1992). A relational model of authority in groups. In M. Zanna (ed.), *Advances in Experimental Psychology*. New York: Academy.
Tynan, R. (1999). The impact of threat sensitivity and face giving on upward communication. Paper presented at the Academy of Management Conference, Chicago, Ill.
Wageman, R. & Mannix, E. A. (eds) (1998). *Uses and Misuses of Power in Task-performing Teams. Power and Influence in Organizations*. Thousand Oaks, Calif.: Sage.
Weick, K. E. & Roberts, K. H. (1993). Collective mind in organizations: heedful interrelating on flight decks. *Administrative Science Quarterly, 38*, 357–381.

West, M. A. (2000). Reflexivity, revolution, and innovation in work teams. In M. M. Beyerlein, D. A. Johnson, & S. T. Beyerlein (eds), *Advances in Interdisciplinary Studies of Work Teams* (Vol. 5, pp. 1–29). Greenwich, Conn.: JAI Press.

West, M. & Anderson, M. (1996). Innovations in top management teams. *Journal of Applied Psychology, 31*(6), 680–693.

Winter, R. P., Sarros, J. C., & Tanewski, G. A. (1997). Reframing managers' control orientations and practices: a proposed organizational learning framework. *The International Journal of Organizational Analysis, 5*(1), 9–24.

14

MANAGING WORKFORCE DIVERSITY TO ENHANCE COOPERATION IN ORGANIZATIONS

Aparna Joshi and Susan E. Jackson

INTRODUCTION

The growing sophistication of research on diversity in organizations parallels the evolution of organizations into increasingly complex and dynamic forms. More than a decade ago, Miles and Snow (1986) described a futuristic network organization characterized by constantly evolving inter-team linkages that allow organizations to quickly respond to technological and market changes, and thereby improve their chances of survival. Today, we witness widespread implementation of such team-based organizational forms (Hackman, 1999).

As teams interact with other teams, the organizational context in which teams operate can create opportunities as well as pose challenges for team functioning. In this chapter, we consider how the demographic characteristics of the organizational context influences teamwork and so attempt to contribute to the academic discourse on diversity in two ways. First, we draw attention to the intrinsic value of diversity in relation to a team's external relationships. To meet organizational goals, each team must be effective in terms of its internal functioning. In addition, each team must effectively manage its relationships with other teams and individuals in the organization. Through their relationships, team members may gain access to needed resources and exert influence that is beneficial to the team and its individual members. Past research, grounded in social psychological theory, has focused on the negative relationship between team diversity and internal team processes such as team cooperation. We recognize that an additional component of team functioning is relationships *between* teams. Based on social psychological theory, we argue that diversity in teams will be manifested in cooperative behaviors between teams in organizations.

A second contribution of this chapter is to provide a framework for understanding how the demographic composition of organizations influences the relationships between and within teams. Building upon social identity theory as well as social network theory, we argue that

International Handbook of Organizational Teamwork and Cooperative Working. Edited by M. A. West, D. Tjosvold, and K. G. Smith.

cooperation within and between teams is a function of the demographic distinctiveness of team members in relation to the immediate environment. By recognizing organizational level demography as a contextual influence on the outcomes of team diversity, we draw workplace diversity research into the realm of cross-level theory and methodology. Based on an ongoing research study involving several hundred service teams, we also provide empirical support for our theoretical framework and make suggestions for future research and practice.

This chapter is primarily organized into four sections. Past research on team functioning has found that the diversity present in teams has important implications for how team members behave toward each other, as well as for the team's overall performance. In the first section, we begin by considering the implication of team diversity for cooperative behaviors within teams. Next, in the second section we extend existing research and theory to describe how team diversity is likely to influence external team relationships and cooperation between teams. Our review and extension of the literature suggest that diversity can have paradoxical consequences in organizations. On the one hand, diverse work teams may experience lower levels of cooperation among team members. On the other hand, diversity within a team may bolster the team's external communication and its ability to cooperate with other teams. In the third section we argue that understanding these paradoxical outcomes of team diversity would be incomplete without an appreciation of the context in which teams function. Specifically, we consider how the degree of diversity present in the broader organization is likely to influence the interpersonal dynamics that arise within and between teams. Using a multi-level approach, we propose that the demography of the organization within which diverse teams operate is an important factor that determines the degree of cooperation within and between diverse work teams. We present results of a recent study that illustrate the importance of considering the demographic context in which teams operate. In the fourth and final section we discuss the theoretical as well as practical implications of our findings.

The Meaning of Work Team Diversity

During the past decade, the term "diversity" has been widely used to refer to the demographic composition of a team. In empirical studies, team diversity is usually measured using the compositional approach (Tsui & Gutek, 2000), which focuses on the distribution of demographic attributes—e.g. age, ethnicity, gender—within teams. Studies of team diversity directly parallel the methods that have been used to study organizational demography, which is a closely related field of study. Researchers studying team diversity and organizational demography both assess the extent to which members of an organizational unit are (dis)similar to each other. Furthermore, both literatures use indices of variation (not central tendency) to assess the composition of organizational units (teams, departments, entire organizations).[1]

In studies of team diversity and organizational demography, numerous attributes have proved to be of interest, including age, gender, ethnicity, length of tenure in the organization, functional specialization, educational background, cultural values, and personality. We refer to these attributes as the *content* of diversity (following Jackson, May, & Whitney, 1995).

[1] In contrast, when personality researchers study team composition, they have more often used measures of central tendency to describe the composition of teams.

Table 14.1 A scheme for categorizing the personal attributes of individuals

	Attributes that are more likely to be task related	Attributes that are more likely to be relationship oriented
Readily detected attributes	Department/unit membership Organizational tenure Formal credentials and titles Education level Memberships in professional associations	Sex Socioeconomic status Age Race Ethnicity Religion Political memberships Nationality Sexual orientation
Underlying attributes	Knowledge and expertise Cognitive skills and abilities Physical skills and abilities	Gender Class identity Attitudes Values Personality Racial/ethnic identity Sexual identity Other social identities

Broadly defined, the content of diversity can be classified as relations oriented and task oriented (Jackson, May, & Whitney, 1995; Milliken & Martins, 1996). Relations-oriented diversity refers to the distribution of attributes that are instrumental in shaping interpersonal relationships, but which typically have no apparent direct implications for task performance. As we use the term here, relations-oriented diversity is similar to what Jehn, Chadwick, and Thatcher (1997) called social-category diversity. As the term suggests, task-oriented diversity refers to the distribution of performance-relevant attributes. In contrast to Jehn, Chadwick, and Thatcher (1997), we do not distinguish between informational diversity and diversity of views about the team's objectives. In our taxonomy, both of these are considered types of task-related diversity. As shown in Table 14.1, many attributes can be readily detected by members of a group, while others are psychological characteristics that become evident as team members become personally acquainted.

A growing literature supports the general proposition that diverse teams function differently from homogeneous teams (for reviews, see Jackson, May, & Whitney, 1995; Milliken & Martins, 1996; Webber & Donahue, 2001; Williams & O'Reilly, 1998). Although the mechanisms through which diversity operates are not yet fully understood, existing theories point to two fundamental explanations—both of which are likely to be true. Sociological explanations assume that social groups compete with each other for material and social resources, creating a situation of conflict rather than cooperation (e.g. Blalock, 1967). Within this perspective, social groups are defined by demographic categories (e.g. based on race, gender, age). Thus, readily detected attributes are the signals that provide information about group membership and determine whether interactions will be characterized by competition or cooperation. In contrast, many psychological explanations emphasize the role of personality, cognition, and values as determinants of behavior. Psychologically oriented researchers who focus on the role of individual differences often assume that attributes such as age, gender, and race are of little theoretical interest—at best, they serve as convenient but weak measures of more relevant underlying attributes such as beliefs and values. Positioned between these two extremes is social identity theory, which assumes that social and psychological processes mutually influence each other. In this chapter, we assume that all of these perspectives can be useful for explaining the behavior of people working in diverse or homogeneous settings, and we draw on multiple theoretical perspectives throughout this chapter.

DIVERSITY AND COOPERATION WITHIN TEAMS

Research on inter-group relations shows that conflict is a common outcome when members of different groups come into contact with each other. By definition, diverse work teams include members who can be identified as belonging to distinct groups. When findings from research on inter-group relations is applied to understanding dynamics within diverse teams, the natural prediction is that diversity in work teams leads to negative outcomes such as disruptive conflict (Guzzo & Shea, 1992).

The most widely used perspective for explaining the negative outcomes of team diversity is social identity theory. According to social identity theory, it is predictable that people will exhibit a favorable bias toward others who are viewed as members of their in-group, and they will view themselves as being in conflict with out-group members (Turner & Haslam, 2001). Within work teams, the categorization of team members into those belonging to an in-group and out-group creates a barrier to cooperative behavior and may even stimulate competitive behavior among members of a team (Brewer, 1995; Lott & Lott, 1965; Sanchez-Mazas, Roux, & Mugny, 1994).

After nearly three decades of research, there is now substantial evidence to demonstrate that simply categorizing someone as a member of the in-group or out-group determines subsequent interactions with that person. In-group members are assumed to have shared interests and goals, and cooperative behavior follows because it is consistent with one's self-interest. Furthermore, readily detected personal attributes such as gender, ethnicity, organizational tenure, and age stimulate perceptions of in-group and out-group membership (Ashforth & Mael, 1989). When members of a work team are similar on these attributes (low diversity), team members are likely to view each other as belonging to the in-group. In a homogeneous team, higher levels of in-group identification result in more cooperative behaviors (Kramer, 1991). In a heterogeneous team, however, the apparent dissimilarity among team members inhibits in-group identification, which translates into low cooperation among team members (Kramer, 1991).

Social identity theory is clear in predicting that social categorization processes are important determinants of cooperation and competition. In addition, there is substantial empirical evidence showing that perceptions of in-group and out-group status can be formed on the basis of minimal information. People need not interact with each other in order to perceive that they share common interests. Simply knowing that another person is similar—e.g. knowing that the person belongs to one's own demographic group—is sufficient to trigger in-group categorization and cooperation (Oakes, Haslam, & Turner, 1994). Furthermore, such categorization is more likely to occur in demographically heterogeneous groups (Stroessner, 1996).

Theory predicts that diversity within a team is likely to result in competitive behavior and conflict. Despite this clear prediction, empirical research has found mixed results. Here we briefly summarize studies relating work team diversity to within-team cooperation. We first consider how diversity on relations-oriented attributes influences team dynamics, and then review studies that examined the effects of diversity on task-related attributes.

Relations-oriented Diversity and Team Functioning

When examining the effects of diversity on team functioning, researchers have used a variety of indicators to assess intra-team dynamics. Although cooperation is seldom measured directly, inferences about the effects of diversity on cooperation can be easily drawn from studies that measure closely related constructs such as conflict and social integration.

GENDER

Studies that have examined the relationship between gender diversity have yielded mixed findings. For example, in a laboratory setting, members of mixed gender groups reported lower levels of "friendliness" and higher levels of conflict in comparison to homogeneous work groups (Alagna, Reddy, & Collins, 1982). In a field setting, Tsui, Egan, and O'Reilly (1992) found that being dissimilar to the group in terms of gender resulted in feelings of lower social integration. Lewis and Gibson (2000) found that gender diversity was associated with lower perceptions of collective efficacy in the group, but the effect was too weak to reach conventional levels of statistical significance. Similarly, nonsignificant findings were reported by Pelled, Eisenhardt, and Xin (1999) in a study of product development teams.

RACE AND ETHNICITY

With regard to racial and ethnic diversity, early research into the consequences of social desegregation within the United States suggested that increasing racial diversity in predominantly white communities led to increased levels of racial conflict (Blalock, 1967; Reed, 1972). Similarly, in a study of work groups developing new processes and electronic products, Pelled, Eisenhardt, and Xin (1999) found that racial diversity was associated with higher levels of emotional conflict in teams. In a laboratory study of student groups, Watson, Kumar, and Michaelson (1993) found that racially diverse groups exhibited lower cooperation compared to homogeneous groups.

AGE

Along with the trend of an aging US workforce has come increased interest in understanding intergenerational relationships within organizations (e.g. see Tsui, Xin, & Egan, 1995). Yet, most studies of age diversity within organizations have focused on top management teams, where age diversity is somewhat limited. Despite the restricted age ranges found in top management teams, there is some support for the predictions made by social identity theory. For example, Knight et al. (1999) found that top management teams with greater age diversity were less likely to engage in agreement-seeking behaviors that could result in reaching strategic consensus. These researchers also found that age diversity was associated with higher levels of interpersonal conflict, although the effect was not statistically significant. Other studies on top management teams have found significant relationships between age diversity and behavioral outcomes that are assumed to result from conflict, such as turnover (Jackson et al., 1991; Wiersema & Bird, 1993). Pelled, Eisenhardt, and Xin (1999) reported a contradictory finding in their study. In work groups with greater age diversity, employees reported experiencing less emotional conflict. To explain this finding, Pelled, Eisenhardt, and Xin (1999) speculated that individuals belonging to a similar age group may form rivalries and compete for the role of team "leader." In summary, as with regard to gender and ethnic diversity, the findings concerning age diversity are not completely consistent.

Task-related Diversity and Intra-team Cooperation

So far the dimensions of diversity that have been discussed are considered relations oriented. Relations-oriented attributes are likely to influence perceptions of in-group and out-group membership in any social setting, even when there is no work task to be performed. By comparison, task-related attributes refer to characteristics that are made salient by the task setting. Two frequently studied task-related attributes are organizational tenure and educational background.

TENURE

Whether due to the implicit knowledge that a person accumulates through experience or to specific on-the-job training, organizational tenure bestows knowledge, skills, and abilities that are job relevant. Furthermore, employees who enter an organization at about the same time will share similar experiences (Pfeffer, 1983) and may develop similar values and patterns of communication (Wagner, Pfeffer, & O'Reilly, 1984). Tenure diversity has often been assessed in studies of top management team composition, but seldom do such studies directly assess cooperation or conflict. Thus there is scant direct evidence concerning tenure diversity as a predictor of cooperation.

Consistent with the predictions of social identity theory, Pelled, Eisenhardt, and Xin (1999) found that teams characterized by greater tenure diversity experience more conflict than teams characterized by less tenure diversity. Knight et al. (1999) also found that tenure diversity was associated with greater interpersonal conflict and less agreement seeking, but in this study the effects of tenure diversity were not statistically significant.

EDUCATIONAL BACKGROUND

Like tenure, educational background bestows skills that are required or useful in one's job. Education may also serve to socialize members of a profession to use a common language, accept a common set of values, and adopt a common world view (Jackson et al., 1991; Jehn, Chadwick & Thatcher, 1997). Like organizational tenure, therefore, educational background is likely to trigger perceptions of in-group or out-group status.

Both the content and amount of education received can serve as signals that trigger social categorization processes. In addition, differences in educational background are likely to be associated with substantively different perspectives about how to approach and solve work-related problems. Although substantive differences in perspective may actually be beneficial to the team's performance on some types of tasks (see Jackson et al., 1991; Jackson, May, & Whitney, 1995), educational diversity is also likely to stimulate conflict and reduce cooperation.

Jehn, Chadwick, and Thatcher (1997) found that that when team members differed in terms of educational background they perceived greater conflict in the group. In a study of a household goods moving firm, Jehn and her colleagues found that greater informational diversity (which could be created by educational differences) in teams was associated with more task conflict (Jehn, Northcraft, & Neale, 1999). In their study of top management teams, Knight et al. (1999) found that educational diversity was associated with lower levels of strategic consensus.

Conclusion

The preceding review of research findings shows a mixed pattern of results. Many studies indicate that teams characterized by relations-oriented and task-related diversity are likely to be less cohesive and experience lower levels of cooperation. The observed effects were weak, however, and in some cases the effects of diversity were not statistically significant.

This mixed pattern of results does not disconfirm social identity theory, however. Proponents of social identity theory recognize that social categorization processes take place in a larger social context. The larger social context, in turn, can attenuate or even reverse the negative effects of social categorization processes (Turner & Haslam, 2001).

For work teams, the larger organizational context serves as the backdrop for perceptions of in-group and out-group status. Just as the physical context can determine whether a person notices and attends to certain visual or auditory cues, the social context may amplify or divert attention to demographic cues. The organizational context also imbues social identities (such as those based on gender or age) with meaning. Later in this chapter, we return to the question of how the organizational context may shape social categorization processes and their consequences for cooperation within teams. Before moving to this discussion, however, we first consider how diversity may influence the degree of cooperation found *between* work teams.

DIVERSITY AND COOPERATION BETWEEN TEAMS

Typically, work teams in organizations need to rely on other teams for resources and support in order to function effectively (Hackman, 1999). In this section, we strive to describe how a team's diversity is likely to shape its relationships with other teams.

Ashforth and Mael (1989) provide insights that aid our understanding of how a team's diversity can influence its external relationships. Following the logic of social identity theory, Ashforth and Mael argued that members of homogeneous teams would be more likely to view themselves as the in-group, and categorize those outside the team as the out-group. In effect, homogeneous teams create perceptual boundaries that bind them together and separate them from others in the external environment. Individuals in homogeneous groups find all their social identification needs satisfied within the team and hence do not feel the need to interact with individuals outside the group. This self-insulating effect is especially strong when members of the team share *several* social identities (Brewer & Miller, 1984). A team of design engineers who were all males of about the same age and from the same ethnic background could be expected to become more insulated from others in the organizations, compared to a group that has more diversity in terms of gender, age, or ethnicity.

Conversely, heterogeneous work teams are less likely to feel bound together as members of the same in-group. Their team boundaries are more permeable and team members are more likely to form in-group relationships with people outside the team (Ancona & Caldwell, 1998; Ashforth & Mael, 1989). Ancona and Caldwell (1992) recognized that team composition could be an important determinant of its external behavior. In particular, they noted the important role that task-related attributes such as tenure and area of specialization could play in determining "boundary spanning" behaviors—that is, interactions outside the team boundary. They did not, however, acknowledge that relations-oriented diversity might also influence a team's external relationships and boundary-spanning behaviors. In this section, we present evidence to support the argument that team diversity promotes the development of effective external relationships. Through this process, team diversity may promote team effectiveness. Here we argue that the social categorization processes that weaken intra-team cohesiveness may enable the team to better leverage resources in its external environment. By examining inter-team relationships as an outcome of team diversity, we add support to the "value in diversity" proposition that some researchers have espoused (Cox, 1993; Jackson, May, & Whitney, 1995).

Relations-oriented Diversity and Cooperation between Teams

In organizations, informal relationships and roles often transcend formal positions and hierarchies. Informal relationships in organizations reflect social identifications with extra-organizational communities such as age groups, racial groups, or gender groups (Ibarra, 1992, 1995).

Members of minority groups often find that it is more difficult to establish beneficial social relationships within their immediate work group due simply to the absence of others who are similar to them. Feelings of isolation are the natural result. To alleviate feelings of isolation, today many US organizations provide support to employee affinity groups (also called network groups or caucuses), which facilitate socializing among members of demographically similar groups (Friedman, 1996). Even when formal organizational practices do not intentionally encourage the formation of such social communities, they may arise naturally as minority members seek to form informal relationships with similar others (e.g. see Blau, 1977). Thus, relations-oriented attributes such as race, age, or gender influence the boundary-spanning activities of team members.

GENDER

Studies on social networks suggest that employees form relationships with each other based on their gender (Ibarra, 1992). In a study of male and female managers in an advertising firm, Ibarra (1992) found that men formed same-gender networks that served both social and instrumental goals. In this study, women also formed same-gender social networks, while their instrumental networks tended to cut across gender lines—perhaps out of necessity. Given the propensity of individuals to form same-gender relationships within an organization, gender diversity in teams may indicate the extent to which team members form same-gender relationships outside the team. Social identity theory predicts that homogeneous teams (i.e. predominantly male or female) are most likely to form impermeable boundaries that bind team members together, while pitting them against members of other teams (the out-group). Thus, while cooperation within the team may be high, the cost of such intra-team cooperation may be reduced cooperation between teams. By comparison, the boundaries of mixed gender teams should be more permeable as both men and women form same-gender relationships outside the team. Such external relationships may be formed on an individual basis and for mostly social reasons; nevertheless, they provide a foundation from which instrumental team cooperation may arise in the future. We could find no published studies that support or refute the role of gender diversity in facilitating cooperation between teams, so our argument here must be considered speculative.

ETHNICITY

Just as gender provides a basis for the development of relationships outside of one's work group, so too does ethnicity. For example, in a study of friendship networks of MBA students, Mehra, Kilduff, and Brass (1998) found that students formed friendships with others from similar ethnic backgrounds. Thus, students who were not members of the majority ethnic group were marginal in the overall friendship network, and tended to form friendships with other minority students.

In anthropological studies of tribal behavior, tribal membership is a social identity that is somewhat similar to ethnicity. Conflict between tribes is a classic and familiar example of inter-group conflict. Such conflict is not inevitable, however. Anthropological studies have found that hostilities between tribes decrease when individuals from one tribe cross over to the "enemy" tribe. Such crossing over occurs when individuals from one tribe marry into another tribe. In these situations, the individual begins to identify with both tribes and over time the conflicts between the two tribes seem to decrease (Levine & Campbell, 1972).

Regarding work teams, we found no studies that examined the relationship between team ethnic diversity and external behavior or inter-team cooperation. Nevertheless, this limited evidence is consistent with our assertion that ethnic diversity within a team is likely to contribute to greater cooperation with other teams.

AGE

Perhaps because people within age cohorts share common experiences, attitudes, and values (Lawrence, 1988), a person's age can act as a cue that triggers social categorization processes and promotes communication among cohort members. In teams of people from a single age cohort, age similarity is likely to promote in-group identification and make it easier for team members to satisfy their social needs within the team. Consistent with this logic, Zenger and Lawrence (1989) found that members of project groups tended to communicate with others outside the group based on age similarity. This study did not consider whether teams that were more age diverse engaged in more external communication overall, but the findings are suggestive. Imagine a team in which all members are from the same age cohort. We have already suggested that members of such a team would have less need to seek friendships outside the team. They may, however, need to establish instrumental relationships. These relationships also may be shaped by age similarity. Because all members of the team are similar, the net effect for the team is likely to be a constrained set of external relationships. Conversely, it seems likely that age diversity within a team should result in a more comprehensive network of communications outside the team.

Task-related Diversity and Cooperation between Teams

Just as relations-oriented diversity may contribute to the development of external social relationships, task-related diversity is likely to contribute to the development of more external relationships. In organizational settings, task-related attributes include tenure, occupational background, and functional experience.

Often in organizations, departmental memberships or shared functional expertise result in common behaviors, languages, and attitudes among employees (Alderfer, 1988; Kramer, 1991). As members within a department or occupational specialty develop into close-knit communities, cooperation between organizational units may decline. Likewise, common tenure or educational background may foster common attitudes and values that lead to close relationships among similar employees.

As we argued above, in homogeneous teams, the shared experiences and backgrounds of team members may result in the team becoming isolated from other teams or even becoming competitive with other teams. On the other hand, the natural tendency to form relationships with others who are similar on a variety of task-related attributes may also serve to create bridges between a diverse team and members of other teams.

TENURE

Employees who enter an organization at the same time often share similar organizational experiences and have similar attitudes and values toward work (Pfeffer, 1983; Wagner, Pfeffer, & O'Reilly, 1989). The importance of tenure-based cohorts may be particularly great in organizations that have undergone periods of substantial change, such as the replacement of the company's founder, an organizational crisis, or a merger. Such events create clear differences in the experiences and perspectives of oldtimers versus newcomers (cf. Jackson & Alvarez, 1992; Moreland & Levine, 2001). Furthermore, if the event had been considered a threat to the organization, it would be accompanied by the development of closer personal relationships among the employees who experienced it (Staw, Sandelands, & Dutton, 1981). Such relationships would endure long after the threat was overcome.

In the study of project engineers conducted by Zenger and Lawrence (1989), engineers who entered the organization at approximately the same time showed higher rates of communication with each other (compared to those who entered at other times) even when they were not members of the same work team. Engineers with similar tenure continued to communicate more with each other about technical issues. Thus, tenure similarity created work-relevant bridges from the team to its external environment.

Ancona and Caldwell (1998) have also argued that tenure diversity in teams is beneficial because it promotes useful boundary-spanning behaviors. In addition to increasing lateral communication among peers in the organization, tenure diversity may increase the team's upward communication. For example, team members with long tenure in the organization may provide avenues of access to upper levels of management. On the other hand, newcomers in the organization may form relationships with other newcomers outside the team and gain access to the latest technical know-how. When teams throughout the organization are linked together through such relationships, the teams may find it relatively easy to recognize their common goals and to cooperate in order to achieve those goals.

EDUCATION AND FUNCTIONAL SPECIALTY

In organizational settings, educational backgrounds and areas of functional specialty tend to be strongly related. And, like tenure, similarity on these attributes serves as a basis for relationship building. As social identity theory predicts, Ancona and Caldwell (1992) found that teams characterized by greater functional diversity formed more external relationships. In a study of top management teams in Japan, Wiersema and Bird (1993) found that educational affiliations determined social interactions across team boundaries.

Conclusion

We have proposed that team diversity is likely to benefit work teams and their individual members by increasing the connections between the team and its external environment. Although there is little research that directly tests this proposition, the findings from several studies are suggestive. Both relations-oriented and task-related diversity create the motivation and the opportunities for team members to develop relationships beyond the team's boundaries. Due to these relationships, inter-team cooperation and communication are likely to be enhanced. Furthermore, these relationships may serve the team's instrumental purposes by giving the team greater access to information and other resources in the external environment.

ORGANIZATION DEMOGRAPHY AS THE CONTEXT FOR COOPERATION

So far, we have argued that the effects of team diversity are not limited to consequences for the internal functioning of teams. Although intra-team dynamics have been the focus of most attention to date, we believe that diversity also shapes inter-team relations. Specifically, we have argued that members of diverse teams are more likely to build external bridges to other individuals and teams. That is, compared to more homogeneous teams, the boundaries of diverse teams are less rigid and more permeable. As a result, we expect diverse teams to have more cooperative relationships with other individuals and other teams in the organization.

In order for team diversity to create this phenomenon of greater inter-team cooperation, however, certain other conditions must be met. A team and its members do not exist in a vacuum; they are embedded within a larger organization. To fully understand the dynamics of diversity and cooperation, these multiple levels of the social environment—individuals, teams, and organizations—must be considered together.

Since 1964, US Equal Employment Opportunity laws have promoted the representation of women and ethnic minorities in US work organizations. Nevertheless, US employers differ greatly in their efforts to promote ethnic and gender diversity as well as the outcomes of these efforts (Cox, 1993). In some organizations, little progress has been made and few women and members of ethnic minority groups are found in the organization. In other organizations, the proportions of women and minorities have increased substantially, but members of these social groups remain clustered within a few departments and occupational groups. Often they remain segregated in lower-status, lower-paying jobs. Finally, in some organizations, equal employment efforts and proactive efforts to manage diversity effectively have created reasonably integrated work settings.

Whereas legal and social pressures have been the impetus for increasing gender and ethnic diversity in the workplace, the other contours of an organization's diversity are more likely to be shaped by normal business processes. For example, economic cycles of growth and contraction create tenure and age cohorts. Business strategies and organizational structures determine the mix of occupational groups in the organization. Labor market conditions and hiring practices determine the mix of educational backgrounds found among employees (as well as their ethnicity and gender), and so on. Regardless of how an organization's demographic composition is created, it provides the context that may either support or inhibit cooperation within and between teams.

In this section, we argue that the demographic make-up of the larger organization creates the opportunities for, or imposes barriers to, the building of cooperative relationships between teams. As we explain next, the probability that inter-team cooperation will arise out of intra-team diversity is greatest when two conditions are present: the organization as a whole is relatively diverse *and* the teams within the organizations also are diverse. A diverse team in a homogeneous organization will not be able to leverage its team diversity. Likewise, a diverse organization that segregates different social groups into homogeneous teams will not be able to leverage its organizational diversity. While social identity theory predicts that diversity in teams is related to conflict and lack of cooperation with the team, based on an extension of this theory, we propose that these negative outcomes can materialize only when the demographic context presents conditions that increase demographic identity-based salience in the team. When individuals find that their demographic traits are distinctive with respect to their immediate environment, identification based on that trait will be heightened (McGuire et al., 1978). Similarly, diversity will support the development of external team relationships only when the demographic setting presents opportunities for such relationships. Members of diverse teams will more readily form external relationships when there is diversity in their immediate setting.

Organizational Demography and Intra-team Cooperation

Within teams, helping and cooperative behavior have been shown to increase along with the degree of interdependence among team members (see Saavedra, Earley, & van Dyne, 1993). Psychologists have argued that feelings of interdependence among members of a team can be created by features of the task itself as well as by rewards that are contingent upon the team's performance. Sociologists, on the other hand, have argued that members of demographically defined social groups are likely to view themselves as interdependent, because social groups compete with each other for scarce resources (Blau, 1977). A combination of these two perspectives has led some to argue that the uncooperative behavior that occurs within demographically diverse teams should be reduced when the task and reward structures promote feelings of interdependence.

We agree that task and reward interdependence may be sufficient to increase cooperation within diverse teams, but these conditions may not be necessary. Feelings of interdependence may also arise in response to perceptions of organizational demography. Just as the composition of a work team is the ground against which self-identifications occur, so is organizational demography the ground against which group identification takes place. When members of a work team view themselves as distinctive compared to others in the organization, team membership becomes a salient identity and intra-team cooperation should follow. Several different combinations of team and organizational demographics can create perceptions of team distinctiveness: for example, a demographically homogeneous team would be distinctive in a demographically diverse organization, while a diverse team would be distinctive in a homogeneous organization. For either team, the contrast between the team's composition and the larger organizational context leads the team to perceive itself as distinctive. Such perceptions of team distinctiveness should increase intra-team cooperation.

Conversely, when a team's demographic composition is similar to that of the larger organization, it is less salient. In such situations, the effects of team composition may be weakened. For demographically homogeneous teams in homogeneous organizations, demographic characteristics are not salient. They do not serve to define the team, and so do not create barriers between team members and their external environment. Similarly, for diverse teams in heterogeneous organizations, demographic cues are not particularly salient. When a team's demographic composition matches the organization demography, its demographic attributes are less likely to determine patterns of cooperative behavior. In other words, we propose that the context of organizational demography moderates the effects of team diversity.

Organizational Demography and Inter-team Cooperation

The preceding section proposed that internal team processes such as team cooperation are influenced by the extent of diversity of the immediate organizational context. These observations are also relevant for relationships between teams.

Organizational policies of recruitment, selection, and promotions often perpetuate segregation based on gender or race (Ely, 1995; Nkomo, 1992; Wharton, 1992). While upper management levels in organizations may be predominantly White or male, minorities and women are often confined to entry levels. These characteristics of organizational demography reinforce identification on the basis of gender and race (Ely, 1995; Nkomo, 1992; Wharton, 1992) as well as the formation of segregated social networks within an organization (Ibarra & Smith-Lovin, 1997). When women and minorities are isolated from social and instrumental exchanges in organizations (Ibarra, 1992, 1995), their lack of access to social capital acts as a barrier to advancement (Friedman & Krackhardt, 1997; Ragins & Sundstrom, 1990). Increasing the representation of women and minorities throughout an organization—increasing the diversity of the organization—is one way to improve their access to social capital (Morrison & von Glinow, 1990). Another way that employers can increase the access to social capital of women and minority employees is by supporting identity network groups (Friedman, 1996). However, the extent to which female and minority network groups can harness the benefits of their solidarity depends on the degree of diversity present throughout the organization. Network groups are likely to be of little value to their members if the network itself is small or if members of the network are marginal in

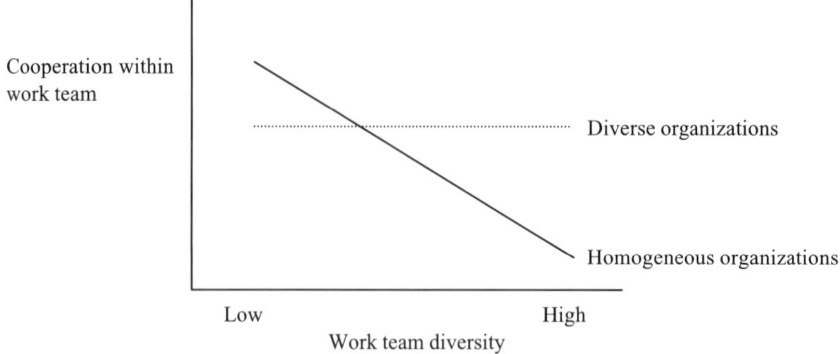

Figure 14.1 Organizational diversity as a moderator of the effect of team diversity on co-operation within the team

the larger organization. Thus, just as organizational demography may moderate the effects of team diversity on intra-team cooperation, so too is it likely to moderate the effects of team diversity on inter-team cooperation.

Figures 14.1 and 14.2 illustrate the moderating role of organizational demography that we have proposed. To date, studies of team diversity have ignored the role of organizational demography. We believe that this omission may account for some of the inconsistent results reported in the literature. An organization's specific demographic contours are likely to determine whether gender diversity or ethnic diversity or tenure diversity, and so on, will be predictive of team processes and outcomes.

Preliminary Empirical Evidence

Research that we have been conducting in a Fortune 500 company provides some initial support for the moderating role of organizational demography proposed in the previous section (for a more detailed description of this study and additional results, see Joshi, 2002). Throughout the past several decades, Company ABC (not its real name) has consistently

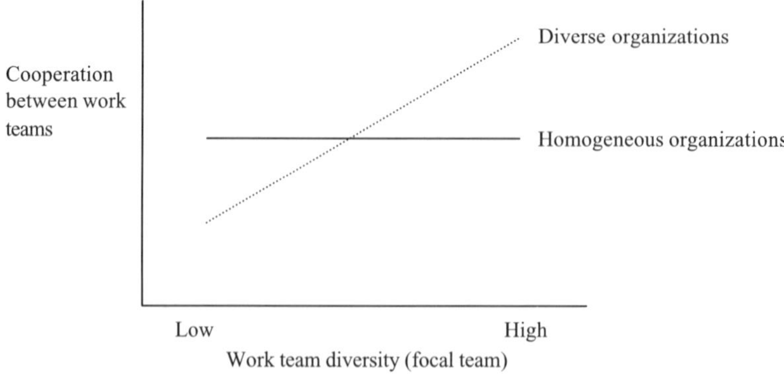

Figure 14.2 The proposed moderating role of organizational demography on the relationship between team diversity and inter-team cooperation

promoted workforce diversity and worked to increase the proportions of women and ethnic minorities. The company's efforts to promote diversity are reflected in staffing practices, performance appraisals, training procedures, and the reward system. For example, all division managers must meet annual targets for the representation of majority and minority males and females in each employee grade level. Targets are determined by studies of the internal labor pool and US census data. In order to ensure that managers meet their staffing targets, performance appraisals assess performance against these targets and the results of these performance appraisals are considered in decisions about promotion and compensation. Diversity training is also provided to develop managerial capabilities for interacting with subordinates and colleagues irrespective of demographic differences.

PARTICIPANTS

The data we present here were collected from employees ($n = 8636$) who worked as members of equipment service teams ($n = 1820$). These service teams were organized into 68 regional divisions. The average regional division employed 133 individuals. For the purpose of this study, we focused on teams with 3 or more individuals ($n = 1401$). The average team size was 5.77 individuals.

TEAM TASK

Service personnel provided technical support to customers. Their services included performing ongoing maintenance, responding to unscheduled calls from customers, and making calls initiated by the company. Team members were highly interdependent in terms of their tasks and outcomes; they discussed calls and assessed their priority in order to establish the material resources and manpower that should be allocated. Performance was measured on the basis of the team's achievement of objective, quantitative goals, and these team performance measures were used as a basis for compensation.

DATA AND ANALYSIS

All data were collected from the organization's archives. We used employee personnel records to obtain information on respondents' demographic attributes such as age, ethnicity, gender, tenure, and educational background. Team performance data were obtained from operational records. Perceptions of intra- and inter-team dynamics were obtained from an employee survey, which was conducted annually by an external vendor.

The data for this study are characterized by multi-level nesting of individuals within teams and teams within service regions. Our analysis used hierarchical linear modeling to examine whether the demography of service regions acted as a moderator of the relationship between team diversity and various consequences.

RESULTS

Unlike many prior studies, we found no main effects of team diversity on employee reports of team processes or objective measures of team performance. Notably, reports of cooperation within teams were unrelated to their gender, ethnic, and age compositions. However, as predicted by the arguments we presented above, adding information about organizational demography revealed a very different picture. In this case, measures of organizational demography captured the composition of the region within which teams were embedded. The demography of the regional-level organization was a significant moderator of the effects of team diversity. The pattern was not exactly as we had predicted, however. Specifically, a positive relationship was found between team gender diversity and intra-team cooperation, but only within regions that were relatively diverse in terms of gender. Furthermore, team gender diversity was positively related to team performance, but again this was true only within regions characterized by relatively high gender diversity. Overall, regions with greater gender diversity at managerial as well as nonmanagerial levels were more cooperative.

When we examined the role of ethnic diversity, we found a slightly different pattern. Again, there was no main effect of team ethnic diversity on reports of team cooperation, nor did we find a significant moderating effect of organizational demography. However, we did find a significant moderating effect of organizational ethnic demography when we examined objective team performance. Ethnically diverse teams working in relatively homogeneous organizations experienced performance deficits relative to the more homogeneous teams. The performance deficit was not evident for ethnically diverse teams working in ethnically diverse organizations. Given the nature of the tasks performed by these teams, this finding is consistent with our predictions. In ethnically homogeneous organizations, the ethnic differences among members of diverse teams become more salient and are more likely to interfere with performance. In ethnically heterogeneous organizations, however, the ethnic identities of team members may be less salient and therefore they create less disruption.

CONCLUSIONS AND DIRECTIONS FOR FUTURE RESEARCH

Work team diversity can have both positive and negative outcomes in organizations. In this chapter we focused on two specific outcomes—intra-team cooperation and inter-team cooperation. Our review and extension of past research suggested that *intra-team* cooperation may be negatively related to team diversity due to social categorization processes. Our conclusion is based on the predictions offered by social identity theory since empirical studies indicate mixed support for this proposition. Based on social identity theory, we also predicted that cooperation *between* teams would be positively associated with diversity. Diverse teams have the opportunity to capitalize on diverse social networks outside the team and enhance performance. We argued that an important consideration while examining both these outcomes of team diversity is the demographic context in which teams function. The representation of women and minorities in the organization as a whole triggers social–psychological processes that are relevant for team functioning. Thus, we proposed that the relationship between team diversity and cooperation within and between teams would be moderated by the organization's demographic context. Our study suggests that this proposition is justified with regard to some of the dimensions of diversity.

Before drawing firm conclusions from the findings presented in the previous section, particular characteristics of the research setting that may limit the generalizability of these findings need to be acknowledged. For example, although the teams of service technicians in this study were interdependent with each other, reliance on external relationships may not be as critical to these teams as it would be for cross-functional teams. Future research may test similar hypotheses in multiple organizational settings and extend the generalizability of the findings. The lack of significant effects of diversity at the team level also calls for some explanation. Company ABC has a long tradition of diversity-related interventions. These practices may have served to neutralize some of the effects of diversity within teams, although such practices apparently did not diminish the desire of employees to seek out similar others elsewhere in the organization. Regardless of the limitations of the study, we believe that the review and findings presented in this chapter make theoretical as well as practical contributions.

Theoretical Implications

Both the theoretical arguments we developed here and our findings from the study described suggest that a cross-level application of social identity theory to research on team diversity may prove fruitful. A theoretical perspective that takes into account the potential cross-level effects of workplace diversity may shed light on the mixed findings of past research. Given that social identification processes are partially driven by the distinctiveness of team members in relation to their immediate organizational environment, the larger social context is an important factor to take into consideration when conducting studies of work teams.

By including inter-team relationships as outcomes of social identification we are also able to reconcile the pessimistic predictions of social identity theory regarding inter-group relations in organizations with the "value in diversity" proposition (Ashforth & Mael, 1989). By developing this external perspective, we hope to stimulate new research on work team diversity. Additional research is needed to determine whether our findings regarding the beneficial effects of organization-wide diversity are replicable, however. Our findings suggest that performance of ethnically and gender-diverse teams is significantly improved when such teams are embedded in a larger social context that is also characterized by ethnic and gender diversity. But in order for these benefits to accrue, organizations may need to proactively engage in practices that ensure organization-wide integration of women and minorities.

Practical Implications

Clearly, the cross-level approach to work team diversity suggested in this chapter also has some practical implications. If an organization's existing HR practices permit the presence of glass ceilings and walls that limit the career opportunities of women and minorities, then it is quite possible that the creation of diverse work teams will not yield the desired performance improvements. Segregation within organizations creates conditions that increase the likelihood of negative outcomes arising from social identification processes (Wharton, 1992). HR policies and practices related to recruitment and career progression can help ensure that the demographic make-up of the entire organization is conducive to the functioning of diverse teams. Practices that create diversity at entry levels but do not support the presence of diversity at higher levels in the organization may be particularly harmful in that they help to set the stage for dysfunctional team processes.

In addition to ensuring that glass ceilings and walls have been eliminated, organizations may also find that it is helpful to support the formation and operation of employee caucus groups. Caucus groups often are implemented in order to create opportunities for women and minorities to access social capital and advance their careers. But caucus groups may also prove beneficial to team functioning. When team members can tap into external relationships that have been formed though caucus group activities, they increase the team's ability to gain information and other resources that may be needed to maximize their team's performance.

Conclusion

Demographic differences within work groups have been typically linked to conflict and lack of cooperation. This chapter proposed that the negative relationship between work team diversity and teamwork or cooperation needs to be revisited. We extended past research to emphasize the positive influence of diversity on cooperation between teams. A discussion of diversity and cooperative behaviors in organizations is incomplete without acknowledging the role of the broader organizational context in shaping these behaviors. This chapter attempted to make a contribution to the understanding of cooperation and teamwork in organizations by suggesting a cross-level approach to studying the outcomes of diversity in work teams.

REFERENCES

Alagna, S., Reddy, D., & Collins, D. (1982). Perceptions of functioning in mixed-sex and male medical training groups. *Journal of Medical Education, 57*, 801–803.

Alderfer, C. (1988). An intergroup perspective on group dynamics. In J. Lorsch (ed.), *Handbook of Organizational Behavior* (pp. 190–222). Englewood Cliffs, NJ: Prentice-Hall.

Ancona, D. G. & Caldwell, D. F. (1992). Bridging the boundary: external activity and performance for organizational teams. *Administrative Science Quarterly, 37*, 634–665.

Ancona, D. G. & Caldwell, D. F. (1998). Rethinking team composition from the outside in. In M. A. Neale & E. A. Mannix (eds), *Research on Managing Groups and Teams* (Vol. 1, pp. 21–37). Stamford, Conn.: JAI Press.

Ashforth, B. & Mael, F. (1989). Social identity theory and the organization. *Academy of Management Review, 14*, 20–39.

Blalock, H. M. (1967). *Toward a Theory of Minority Group Relations*. New York: Wiley.

Blau, P. M. (1977). *Inequality and Heterogeneity: A Primitive Theory of Social Structure*. New York: Free Press.

Brewer, M. B. (1995). Managing diversity: the role of social identities. In S. E. Jackson & M. Ruderman (eds), *Diversity in Work Teams: Research Paradigms for a Changing Workplace* (pp. 47–68). Washington, DC: American Psychological Association.

Brewer, M. & Miller, N. (1984). Beyond the contact hypothesis: theoretical perspectives on desegregation. In N. Miller & M. Brewer (eds), *Groups in Contact: The Psychology of Desegregation* (pp. 281–302). New York: Academic Press.

Cox, T. (1993). *Cultural Diversity in Organizations: Theory, Research and Practice*. San Francisco: Berrett-Koehler Publishers.

Ely, R. J. (1995). The power in demography: women's social constructions of gender identity at work. *Academy of Management Journal, 38*, 589–634.

Friedman, R. (1996). Defining the scope and logic of minority and female network groups: can separation enhance integration? In G. Ferris (ed.), *Research in Personnel and Human Resource Management* (Vol. 14, pp. 307–349). Greenwich, Conn.: JAI.

Friedman, R. A. & Krackhardt, D. (1997). Social capital and career mobility: a structural theory of lower returns to education for Asian employees. *Journal of Applied Behavioral Science, 33*, 316–334.

Guzzo, R. A. & Shea, G. P. (1992). Group performance and intergroup relations in organizations. In M. D. Dunnette & L. M. Hough (eds), *Handbook of Industrial and Organizational Psychology* (2nd edn, Vol. 3, pp. 269–313). Palo Alto, Calif.: Consulting Psychologists Press.

Hackman, R. (1999). Thinking differently about context. In M. A. Neale & E. A. Mannix (eds), *Research on Managing Groups and Teams* (Vol. 2, pp. 233–247). Stamford, Conn.: JAI Press.

Ibarra, H. (1992). Homophily and differential returns: sex differences in network structure and access in an advertising firm. *Administrative Science Quarterly, 37*, 422–447.

Ibarra, H. (1995). Race, opportunity, and diversity of social circles in managerial networks. *Academy of Management Journal, 38*, 673–703.

Ibarra, H. & Smith-Lovin, L. (1997). New directions in social network research on gender and organizational careers. In C. L. Cooper & S. E. Jackson (eds), *Creating Tomorrow's Organizations: A Handbook for Future Research in Organizational Behavior* (pp. 359–384). New York: John Wiley & Sons.

Jackson, S. E. & Alvarez, E. B. (1992). Working through diversity as a strategic imperative. In S. E. Jackson (ed.), *Diversity in the Workplace: Human Resources Initiatives* (pp. 13–35). New York: Guilford Press.

Jackson, S. E., Brett, J. F., Sessa, V. I., Cooper, D. M., Julin, J. A., & Peyronnin, K. (1991). Some differences make a difference: individual dissimilarity and group heterogeneity as correlates of recruitment, promotions, and turnover. *Journal of Applied Psychology, 76*, 675–689.

Jackson, S. E., May, K. E., & Whitney, K. (1995). Understanding the dynamics of diversity in decision-making teams. In R. A. Guzzo & E. Salas (eds), *Team Effectiveness and Decision Making in Organizations* (pp. 204–261). San Francisco: Jossey-Bass.

Jehn, K. A., Chadwick, C., & Thatcher, S. (1997). To agree or not to agree: diversity, conflict, and group outcomes. *International Journal of Conflict Management, 8*, 287–306.

Jehn, K. A., Northcraft, G. B., & Neale, M. A. (1999). Why differences make a difference: a field study in diversity, conflict, and performance in workgroups. *Administrative Science Quarterly, 44*, 741–763.

Joshi, A. (2002). How does context matter? Examining the process and performance outcomes of work team heterogeneity. Doctoral dissertation, Rutgers University, New Jersey.

Knight, D., Pearce, C. L., Smith, K. G., Olian, J. D., Sims, H. P., Smith, K. A., & Flood, P. (1999). Top management team diversity, group process, and strategic consensus. *Strategic Management Journal, 20*, 445–465.

Kramer, R. (1991). Intergroup relations and organizational dilemmas: the role of categorization processes. In L. L. Cummings & B. M. Staw (eds), *Research in Organizational Behavior* (Vol. 13, pp. 191–228). Greenwich, Conn.: JAI Press.

Lawrence, B. S. (1988). New wrinkles in a theory of age: demography, norms, and performance ratings. *Academy of Management Journal, 31*, 309–337.

Levine, R. & Campbell, D. (1972). *Ethnocentrism: Theories of Conflict, Ethnic Attitudes and Group Behavior*. New York: Wiley.

Lewis, K. & Gibson, C. (2000). The efficacy advantage: observing and modeling the relationships between team heterogeneity, group efficacy, and outcomes. Paper presented at the 15th annual meeting of the Society of Industrial and Organizational Psychology, New Orleans, Louisiana.

Lott, A. & Lott, B. (1965). Group cohesiveness as interpersonal interaction: a review of relationships with antecedent and consequent variables. *Psychological Bulletin, 64*, 259–309.

McGuire, W., McGuire, C., Child, P., & Fujioka, T. (1978). Salience of ethnicity in the spontaneous self-concept as a function of one's ethnic distinctiveness in the social environment. *Journal of Personality and Social Psychology, 36*, 511–520.

Mehra, A., Kilduff, M., & Brass, D. (1998). At the margins: a distinctiveness approach to social identity and social networks of underrepresented groups. *Academy of Management Journal, 41*, 441–452.

Miles, R. & Snow, C. (1986). Network organizations: new concepts and new forms. *California Management Review, 28*, 62–73.

Milliken, F. J. & Martins, L. L. (1996). Searching for common threads: understanding the multiple effects of diversity in organizational groups. *Academy of Management Review, 21*, 402–433.

Moreland, R. L. & Levine, J. M. (2001). Socialization in organizations and work groups. In M. E. Turner (ed.), *Groups at Work: Theory and Research* (pp. 69–112). Mahwah, NJ: Lawrence Erlbaum.

Morrison, A. M. & von Glinow, M. A. (1990). Women and minorities in management. *American Psychologist, 45*, 200–208.

Nkomo, S. (1992). The emperor has no clothes: rewriting "race in organizations." *Academy of Management Review, 17*, 487–513.

Oakes, P. J., Haslam, S. A., & Turner, J. C. (1994). *Stereotyping and Social Reality*. Oxford: Blackwell.

Pelled, L. H., Eisenhardt, K. M., & Xin, K. R. (1999). Exploring the black box: an analysis of work group diversity, conflict, and performance. *Administrative Science Quarterly, 44*, 1–28.

Pfeffer, J. (1983). Organizational demography. In B. Staw & L. Cummings (eds), *Research in Organizational Behavior* (Vol. 5, pp. 299–357). Greenwich, Conn.: JAI Press.

Ragins, B. & Sundstrom, E. (1990). Gender and power in organizations: a longitudinal perspective. *Psychological Bulletin, 105*, 51–88.

Reed, J. (1972). Percent black and lynching: a test of Blalock's theory. *Social Forces, 50*, 356–365.

Saavedra, R., Earley, P. C., & van Dyne, L. (1993). Complex interdependence in task-performing groups. *Journal of Applied Psychology, 78*, 61–72.

Sanchez-Mazas, M., Roux, P., & Mugny, G. (1994). When the outgroup becomes the ingroup and when the ingroup becomes the outgroup: xenophobia and social categorization in a resource allocation task. *European Journal of Social Psychology, 24*, 417–423.

Staw, B., Sandelands, L. E., & Dutton, J. E. (1981). Threat–rigidity effects in organizational behavior: a multi-level analysis. *Administrative Science Quarterly,* 28, 582–600.

Stroessner, S. J. (1996). Social categorization by race or sex: effects of perceived non-normalcy on response times. *Social Cognition, 14*, 274–276.

Tsui, A. & Gutek, B. (2000). *Demographic Differences in Organizations*. New York: Lexington Books.

Tsui, A. S., Egan, T. D., & O'Reilly, C. A., III (1992) Being different: relational demography and organizational attachment. *Administrative Science Quarterly, 37*, 549–579.

Tsui, A., Xin, K., & Egan, T. D. (1995). Relational demography: the missing link in vertical dyadic linkage. In S. E. Jackson & M. N. Ruderman (eds), *Diversity in Work Teams: Research Paradigms for a Changing Workplace* (pp. 97–129). Washington: American Psychological Association.

Turner, J. C. & Haslam, S. A. (2001). Social identity, organizations and leadership. In M. Turner (ed.), *Groups at Work: Theory and Research* (pp. 25–65). London: Lawrence Erlbaum.

Wagner, W. G., Pfeffer, J., & O'Reilly, C. A. (1984). Organizational demography and turnover in top-management groups. *Administrative Science Quarterly, 29*, 74–92.

Watson, W. E., Kumar, K., & Michaelsen, L. K. (1993). Cultural diversity's impact on interaction process and performance: comparing homogeneous and diverse task groups. *Academy of Management Journal, 36*, 590–602.

Webber, S. S. & Donahue, L. M. (2001). Impact of highly and less job-related diversity on work group cohesion and performance: a meta-analysis. *Journal of Management, 27*, 141–162.

Wharton, A. (1992). The social construction of gender and race in organizations: a social identity and group mobilization perspective. In P. Tolbert & S. Bacharach (eds), *Research in the Sociology of Organizations* (Vol. 10, pp. 55–84). Greenwich, Conn.: JAI Press.

Wiersema, M. F. & Bird, A. (1993). Organizational demography in Japanese firms: group heterogeneity, industry dissimilarity, and top management team turnover. *Academy of Management Journal, 36*, 996–1025.

Williams, K. & O'Reilly, C. A. (1998). Demography and diversity in organizations: a review of 40 years of research. In B. Staw & L. Cummings (eds), *Research in Organizational Behavior* (Vol. 20, pp. 77–140). Greenwich, Conn.: JAI Press.

Zenger, T. R. & Lawrence, B. S. (1989). Organizational demography: the differential effects of age and tenure distribution on technical communications. *Academy of Management Journal, 32*, 353–376.

15

COOPERATION AND TEAMWORK FOR INNOVATION

Michael A. West and Giles Hirst

INTRODUCTION

Innovations commonly involve changes to an array of processes and are rarely the result of the activity of one individual. Thus for an innovation to be implemented effectively, teamwork and cooperation are essential. We develop a model which uses an input–process–output structure (see Figure 15.1), to examine the factors likely to influence innovation implementation in work groups. This structure segments variables into inputs of teams such as the task the team is required to perform (e.g. provide health care, make landmines, or sell mobile phones), the composition of the group (such as functional, cultural, gender, and age diversity), and the organizational context (e.g. manufacturing, health service, large or small, organic, the demands it places on the team). Group processes mediate the relationships between inputs and outputs and include levels of participation, support for innovation, leadership, and the management of conflict. These processes create climates of, for example, safety and trust or threat and anxiety. The model proposes that team leaders play a crucial role in moderating the effects of organizational and team context upon team processes and thereby upon innovation outputs. Outputs include the number of innovations, magnitude of innovation, radicalness (changes to the status quo), novelty, and effectiveness of innovation in achieving the desired end. We will consider each of these elements of the framework below. But first it is important to define what is meant by innovation.

Innovation is the introduction of new and improved ways of doing things. A fuller, more explicit definition of innovation is "... the intentional introduction and application within a job, work team or organization of ideas, processes, products or procedures which are new to that job, work team or organization and which are designed to benefit the job, the work team or the organization" (West & Farr, 1990). Innovation is restricted to *intentional* attempts to bring about benefits from new changes; these might include economic benefits, personal growth, increased satisfaction, improved group cohesiveness, better organizational communication, as well as productivity and economic gains. Various processes and products may be regarded as innovations. They include technological changes such as new products,

International Handbook of Organizational Teamwork and Cooperative Working. Edited by M. A. West, D. Tjosvold, and K. G. Smith.

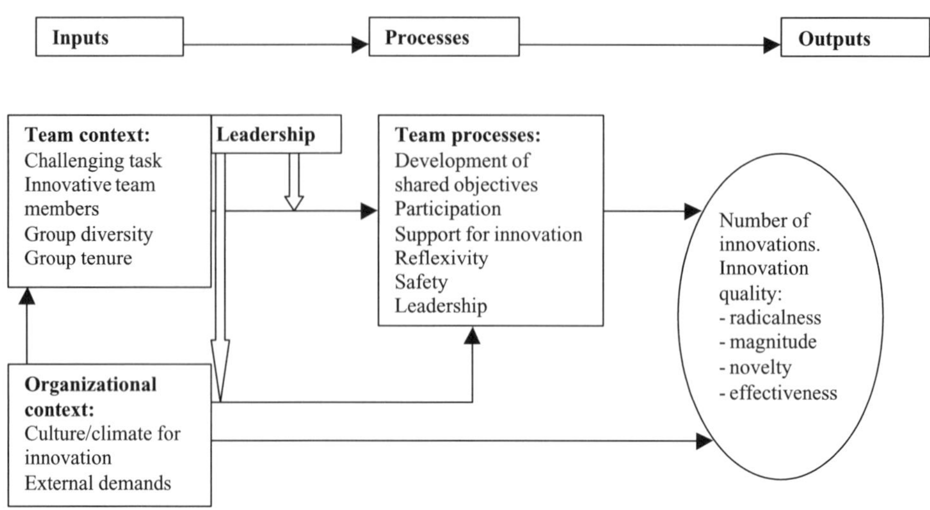

Figure 15.1 An input–process–output model of work group innovation

but may also include new production processes, the introduction of advanced manufacturing technology, or the introduction of new computer support services within an organization. Administrative changes are also regarded as innovations. New human resource management (HRM) strategies, organizational policies on health and safety, or the introduction of teamwork are all examples of administrative innovations within organizations. Innovation implies novelty, but not necessarily absolute novelty (West & Farr, 1990). Innovation encompasses both creative idea generation and idea implementation. What input, process, and output factors related to cooperation and teamwork therefore influence levels and qualities of innovation in work groups? Elsewhere we have examined a broad range of input and process factors (illustrated in Figure 15.1) (see West, 2002). Here we consider those inputs and processes most closely related to concepts of cooperation and teamwork that influence innovation. We begin by examining aspects of team and organizational context: team diversity, team tenure, and organizational climate and culture. In the second part of the chapter we examine how team processes influence levels of team innovation.

TEAM CONTEXT

Group Member Diversity

Are groups composed of very different people (professional background, age, organizational tenure) more innovative than those whose members are similar? This question is prompted by the notion that if people who work together in groups have different backgrounds, personalities, training, skills, experiences, and orientations, they will bring usefully differing perspectives to the group. This divergence of views will create multiple perspectives, disagreement, and conflict. If this informational conflict is processed in the interests of effective decision making and task performance rather than on the basis of motivation to win or prevail, or conflicts of interest, this in turn will generate improved performance and more innovative actions will be the result (De Dreu, 1997; Hoffman & Maier, 1961; Pearce & Ravlin, 1987; Porac & Howard, 1990; Tjosvold, 1985, 1991, 1998).

Of the different classification systems for diversity (e.g. Jackson 1992, 1996; Maznevski, 1994) most differentiate between task-oriented diversity in attributes that are relevant to the person's role or task in the organization (e.g. organizational position and specialized knowledge), and those that are simply inherent in the person and "relations oriented" (e.g. age, gender, ethnicity, social status, and personality) (Maznevski, 1994). Jackson (1992) believes that the effects of diversity on team performance are complex: task-related and relations-oriented diversity have different effects that depend also on the team task. For tasks requiring creativity and a high quality of decision making, Jackson says that "the available evidence supports the conclusion that team [task] diversity is associated with better quality team decision-making" (Jackson, 1996, p. 67), citing evidence provided by Filley, House, and Kerr (1976), Hoffman (1979), McGrath (1984), and Shaw (1981).

The most significant study of innovation in teams to date is a UNESCO-sponsored international effort to determine the factors influencing the scientific performance of 1222 research teams (Andrews, 1979; see also Payne, 1990). Diversity was assessed in six areas: in projects; interdisciplinary orientations; specialities; funding resources; R&D activities; and professional functions. Overall, diversity accounted for 10 per cent of the variance in scientific recognition, R&D effectiveness, and number of publications, suggesting that diversity does influence team innovation.

There is some evidence that heterogeneity in both relations-oriented and task-oriented domains is associated with group innovation, including heterogeneity in personality (Hoffman & Maier, 1961), training background (Pelz, 1956), leadership abilities (Ghiselli & Lodahl, 1958), attitudes (Hoffman, Harburg & Maier, 1962; Willems & Clark, 1971), gender (Wood, 1987), occupational background (Bantel & Jackson, 1989), and education (Smith et al., 1994).

The dominant explanation for the positive effects of diversity on team innovation is that diversity of information, experience, and skills produces more comprehensive and effective decision making. In essence, diversity increases the amount and variety of information accessible for a team's collective problem solving. However, another explanation for the (still debated) effects of task-oriented diversity on team innovation is that functional diversity might influence work group performance as a result of the higher level of external communication which group members initiate, precisely because of their functional diversity (Zenger & Lawrence, 1989). Mohrman, Cohen, and Mohrman (1995) have pointed out that there are likely to be innovation benefits of good linkages between groups and teams and across departments within organizations. The cross-disciplinarity, cross-functionality, and cross-team perspectives that such interactions can produce are likely to generate the kinds of dividends related to innovation that heterogeneity within teams could offer.

In a study of 45 new product teams in five high-technology companies, Ancona and Caldwell (1992) found that when a work group recruited a new member from a functional area in an organization, communication between the team and that area went up dramatically. This would favour innovation through the incorporation of diverse ideas and models gleaned from these different functional areas. Consistent with this, the researchers discovered that the greater the group's functional diversity, the more team members communicated outside the work group's boundaries and the higher ratings of innovation they received from supervisors. The UNESCO research described above also showed that the extent of communication between research teams had strong relationships with scientific recognition of the teams, R&D effectiveness, number of publications, and the applied value of their work. Keller (2001) studied 93 R&D teams. He found that functional diversity increased external communication and thereby enhanced project performance. However, functional diversity also reduced internal communication and cohesiveness. Keller concluded that it is necessary to manage the creative tension between reduced team identification and enhanced organizational integration. Although Keller did not measure whether diversity increased the breadth of team knowledge, his findings illustrate how diversity can impact on both internal and external processes. Further we hypothesize that there are opportunities to advance our understanding of the internal processes by which diversity operates by including measures of team mental models. For example, diversity provides a greater range of knowledge and information as well as differing mental models, i.e. different perspectives and approaches. We propose that divergent mental models and differing social identification, as opposed to diverse information, promote conflict and reduce cohesion.

Although power and status in groups are likely to be associated with innovation in organizations (West, 1987; West & Anderson, 1996), status diversity, in contrast, is likely to threaten integration and safety in the group. The threat occasioned by disagreeing with high-status members is likely to restrict public speculation by lower-status group members. Such status differentials, as much social psychological research has shown, will retard integration because of the barriers to cohesiveness and shared orientation they create. For example, De Dreu (1995) has shown that power and status asymmetries in groups produce hostile interaction patterns in contrast to groups in which there is power balance. Such hostility is clearly likely to inhibit creativity and innovation (West, 2002).

So does diversity predict group innovation? The research evidence suggests that functional or knowledge diversity in the team is associated with innovation. However, when diversity begins to threaten the group's safety and integration (such as status or age diversity) then creativity and innovation implementation will be likely to suffer. Where diversity reduces group members' clarity about and commitment to group objectives, levels of participation (interaction, information-sharing, and shared influence over decision making), task orientation (commitment to quality of task performance), and support for new ideas, then it is likely that innovation attempts will be resisted. Diversity will also be affected by temporal factors, since over time the experience of diversity in a group will be softened into familiarity. We therefore turn to consider how the tenure or age of a work team is likely to affect innovation.

However, the critical influence on how diversity affects group processes, we propose, is leadership within the team. Leaders who effectively integrate diverse perspectives and manage conflict effectively (by, for example, emphasizing shared objectives and vision) are likely to enhance the influence of diversity upon innovation implementation in teams. Leadership processes that inhibit the integration of diverse perspectives (for example by exacerbating conflict between team members) will reduce or nullify the effect of diversity upon group processes and, thereby, team innovation.

Group Tenure

In order to encourage innovation should we try to keep work teams together over time or constantly ensure a change of membership and therefore maintain its diversity? Katz (1982) suggested that project newcomers would increase creativity since they may challenge and thereby improve existing methods and knowledge. He suggested too that the longer groups have been together, the less they communicate with key information sources, scan the environment, and communicate internally within the group and externally. Members of such groups (he proposed) tend to ignore and become increasingly isolated from sources that provide the most critical kinds of feedback, evaluation, and information. This suggests that without changes in membership, groups may become less innovative as time goes by. Indeed some research on diversity in teams (Bantel & Jackson, 1989; Jackson, 1996) suggests that longer tenure might be associated with increasing homogeneity and therefore low levels of innovation. The tenure of a group may result in lower requisite diversity for meeting the demands of the environment as a result of the increasing similarity of group members' attitudes, skills, and experiences through their close association (which symbolic interactionist approaches would suggest is likely).

However, tenure homogeneity has been positively related in some studies to frequency of communication, social integration within the group, and innovation (O'Reilly & Flatt, 1989). This may be because the longer people work together, they more they create a predictable and therefore safer social psychological environment. Such safety may enable the exploration and risk taking necessary for innovation (Edmondson, 1996).

The resolution of these positions may lie not in issues of tenure, diversity, and safety per se, but in the balance between these factors. It may be that tenure, diversity, and psychosocial safety interact in their influence on innovation. Where long tenure leads to high safety this will lead to creativity and innovation, all other things being equal, since it will be safer to take risks and to continually introduce diverse perspectives (see, for example, the discussion on minority influence below and the chapter by Nemeth and Nemeth-Brown, in press). Similarly, individual and group level variables may interact. For example, teams which have worked together for long periods of time may have developed stable norms, understanding of each other's skills, and efficient collaborative approaches. For these teams membership change (either the introduction of new members or their departure) may impact on morale as well as on communication. Conversely, newly formed teams with less crystallized team norms and more fluid work assignments may be more able to adapt to membership changes. Another possibility is that the longer teams work together the more likely they are to develop and apply ways of working that enable them to achieve shared objectives, to implement appropriate participation strategies, and effective communication and decision-making processes, which in turn lead to innovation (West & Anderson, 1996). And leadership processes will play a crucial role in determining whether tenure translates into innovation.

The task a team is required to perform determines to a large extent the level of innovation a team can implement. High levels of autonomy ceded to the group over the performance of its work, interdependence in the work of the team members, and task identity (the team performs a whole task) together will influence the level of innovation. At the same time the characteristics of group members (innovativeness, ability to work in teams, the diversity of skills, perspectives, and knowledge they bring to the task, and the length of time for which the members have worked together) will influence the level of innovation. The reader can consider his or her own team and ponder on the extent to which the task demands innovation. Is the team composed of people who have a propensity to innovate (Bunce & West, 1995, 1996)? And do the team members embody a diversity of knowledge, skills, and perspectives which, when combined, lead to ideas for new and improved ways of working? Are the team members skilled at integrating their perspectives, activities, and knowledge, thus enabling interdependent team working? Have they worked together for a long enough period of time that they are reasonably efficient at decision making and achieving a shared representation of their work and ways of working? And finally, are the leadership processes in the team such that these factors that favour innovation are enhanced? If so, we would argue that the likelihood is that the team has the capacity to be highly innovative, but this capacity can be constrained or enabled by the organization within which the team works in powerful ways. It is to a consideration of the organizational context for team innovation that we turn to next.

ORGANIZATIONAL CONTEXT

How do organizations enable or inhibit team innovation? In this section, we suggest that the culture and the climate of the organization powerfully determine whether teams will attempt to introduce innovation.

Organizational Culture and Climate

Organizations create an ethos or atmosphere within which creativity is either nurtured and blooms in innovation, or is starved of support. Supportive and challenging environments are likely to sustain high levels of creativity (Mumford & Gustafson, 1988; West, 1987), especially those which encourage risk taking and idea generation (Cummings, 1965; Delbecq & Mills, 1985; Ettlie, 1983; Hage & Dewar, 1973; Kanter, 1983; Kimberley & Evanisko, 1981). Employees frequently have ideas for improving their workplaces, work functioning, processes, products, or services (Nicholson & West, 1988; West, 1987), but where climates are characterized by distrust, lack of communication, personal antipathies, limited individual autonomy, and unclear goals, implementation of these ideas is inhibited.

Creative, innovative organizations are those where employees perceive and share an appealing vision of what the organization is trying to achieve—one therefore that is consistent with their values (West & Richter, in press). Innovative organizations have vigorous and mostly enjoyable interactions and debates between employees at all levels about how best to achieve that vision. Conflicts are seen as opportunities to find creative solutions that meet the needs of all parties in the organizations rather than as win–lose situations. And people in such organizations have a high level of autonomy, responsibility, accountability, and power—they are free to make decisions about what to do, when to do it, and who to do it with. Trust, cooperativeness, warmth, and humour are likely to characterize interpersonal and intergroup interactions. There is strong practical support for people's ideas for new and improved products, ways of working, or of managing the organization. Senior managers are more likely than not to encourage and resource innovative ideas, even when they are unsure of their potential value (within safe limits). Such organizations will almost certainly find themselves in uncertain, dynamic, and demanding environments, whether this is due to competition, scarcity of resources, changing markets or legislation, or to global and environmental pressures. After all, that is why innovation has always occurred—humans have adapted their organizations and ways of working to the changing environments they find themselves in.

The leaders of teams will play an important part in buffering team members from the negative effects of organizational climate upon team innovation. A leader who fights for the autonomy of his or her team in an organization that is highly controlling will moderate the effects of organizational culture upon team innovation. Equally, a team leader who dominates the team, whether or not the organizational context is supportive of innovation and team autonomy, will be likely to dramatically reduce the positive influence of a supportive organizational culture upon group processes (such as team member participation in decision making) and thereby levels of team innovation.

Other indicators of culture include the size, age, and structure of the organization. The greater the complexity and more differentiated the organization's structure (in terms of departments, groupings, etc.) the easier it is to cross knowledge boundaries and the greater the number of sources from which innovation can spring. Collaborative idea development across an organization is often cited as a precondition for organizational innovation (Allen, Lee, & Tushman, 1980; Kanter, 1983; Monge, Cozzens, & Contractor, 1992; Zaltman, Duncan, & Holbeck, 1973). There is support for the notion that high centralization is a negative predictor of innovation (Burns & Stalker, 1961; Hage & Aiken, 1967; Shepard, 1967) and Lawrence and Lorsch's (1967) case studies showed that tightly coupled interdepartmental relationships fostered new product development in organizations. However, our research in manufacturing organizations (West et al., 2000) also suggests that centralization may be necessary to ensure innovation implementation. Zaltman, Duncan, and Holbeck (1973) call this the innovation dilemma. Decentralization at local level is necessary for creative ideas to be developed, but centralization may be required for the effective implementation of those ideas in the wider organization. The failure of many organizations to innovate may be a consequence of a failure to recognize this inherent tension.

The resolution of the dilemma may be team-based organizations (Mohrman, Cohen, & Mohrman, 1995). Teams provide the sources for ideas (especially cross-functional teams) while the team-based organization also offers simultaneously centralized and distributed decision-making structures that enable successful innovation. Indeed, the extent of team-based working in organizations appears to be a good predictor of innovation (Agrell & Gustafson, 1996; Mohrman, Cohen, & Mohrman, 1995; West et al., 2000).

What of size and age as cultural indicators? Large organizations have difficulty changing their forms to fit changing environments. Yet organizational size has been a positive predictor of both technological and administrative innovations (Kimberly & Evanisko, 1981). Innovative agility is more a characteristic of smaller organizations (Rogers, 1983; Utterback, 1974). Size may be a surrogate measure of several dimensions associated with innovation such as resources and economies of scale. However, in large organizations, decentralization and specialization are not sufficient to ensure innovation. Integration across groups, departments, and specialisms is also necessary for communication, and sharing of disseminated knowledge, and this requires some centralization or else the sophisticated development of team-based structures. More recent research, examining all 35 US firms that produced microprocessors between 1971 and 1989, showed that smaller organizations were more likely to be the sources of innovation (Wade, 1996). And younger organizations appear to be more innovative, all other things being equal. The longer human social organizations endure, the more embedded become their norms and the more resilient to change become their traditions. Consequently, mature organizations will have difficulty innovating and adapting (Kimberly & Evanisko, 1981; Pierce & Delbecq, 1977). Our data from a 10-year study of 110 UK manufacturing organizations revealed that younger organizations (years since start-up) were likely to innovate in products, production technology, production processes, work organization, and people management (West et al., 2000). Evidence from US studies also suggests younger organizations are the predominant sources of innovation (Wade, 1996).

Amabile's componential model of creativity and innovation (Amabile, 1988, 1997) provides a link between the work environment, individual and team creativity, and organizational innovation. The organizational work environment is conceptualized as having three key characteristics: *organizational motivation to innovate* describes an organization's basic orientation toward innovation, as well as its support for creativity and innovation. *Management practices* include the management at all levels of the organization, but most importantly the level of individual departments and projects. Supervisory encouragement and work group support are two examples of relevant managerial behaviour or practices. *Resources* are related to everything that an organization has available to support creativity at work. Amabile proposes that the higher the concurrent levels of these three aspects of the organizational environment, the more the innovation in organizations. The central statement of the theory is that elements of the work environment will impact individual and team creativity by influencing expertise, task motivation, and creativity skills. The influence of intrinsic task motivation on creativity is considered essential: even though the environment may have an influence on each of the three components, the impact on task motivation is thought to be the most immediate and direct. Furthermore, creativity is seen as a primary source of organizational innovation.

In a study examining whether and how the work environments of highly creative projects differed from the work environments of less creative projects, Amabile and colleagues found that five dimensions consistently differed between high-creativity and low-creativity projects (Amabile et al., 1996). These were challenge, organizational encouragement, work group support, supervisory encouragement, and organizational impediments.

Challenge is regarded as a moderate degree of workload pressure that arises from the urgent, intellectually challenging problem itself (Amabile, 1988; Amabile et al., 1996). The authors carefully distinguish challenge from excessive workload pressure, which is supposed to be negatively related to creativity, and suggest that time pressure may add to the perception of challenge in the work if it is perceived as a concomitant of an important, urgent project. This challenge, in turn, may be positively related to intrinsic motivation and creativity.

Organizational encouragement refers to several aspects within the organization. The first is encouragement of risk taking and idea generation, a valuing of innovation from the highest to the lowest levels of management. The second refers to a fair and supportive evaluation of new ideas; the authors underline this by referring to studies that showed that whereas threatening and highly critical evaluation of new ideas was shown to undermine creativity in laboratory studies, in field research it was shown that supportive, informative evaluation can enhance the intrinsically motivated state that is most conducive to creativity. The third aspect of organizational encouragement focuses on reward and recognition of creativity; in a series of studies, Amabile and colleagues showed that reward perceived as a bonus, a confirmation of one's competence, or a means of enabling one to do better, more interesting work in the future can stimulate creativity, whereas the mere engagement in an activity to obtain a reward can be detrimental towards it (see Amabile et al., 1996). The final aspect refers to the important role of collaborative idea flow across the organization, participative management, and decision making, in the stimulation of creativity.

Work group support indicates the encouragement of activity through the particular work group. The four aspects thought to be relevant for this are team member diversity, mutual openness to ideas, constructive challenging of ideas, and shared commitment to the project; whereas the former two may influence creativity through exposing individuals to a greater variety of unusual ideas, the latter two are thought to increase intrinsic motivation.

Supervisory encouragement stresses the aspects goal clarity, open supervisory interactions, and perceived supervisory or leader support. Whereas goal clarity might have an effect on creativity by providing a clearer problem definition, Amabile et al. argue that open supervisory interactions as well as perceived supervisory support may influence creativity through preventing people from experiencing fear of negative criticism that can undermine the intrinsic motivation necessary for creativity.

In reporting the last of the five factors, organizational impediments, Amabile et al. (1996) refer to a few studies indicating that internal strife, conservatism, and rigid, formal management structures represent obstacles to creativity. The authors suggest that because these factors may be perceived as controlling, their likely negative influence on creativity may evolve from an increase in individual extrinsic motivation (a motivation through external factors but not the task itself) and a corresponding decrease in the intrinsic motivation necessary for creativity. However, research on impediments to creativity, in comparison to research on stimulants of creativity, is still comparatively limited.

In conclusion, therefore, we suggest that the organizational culture or climate provides a context which determines the level of group innovation both directly and via their impact on team inputs and team processes. Clearly the culture will influence the group's task (the amount of autonomy they are given), the group's composition (cross-functional teams are more likely in organic organizations), and group processes (team members are more likely to be supportive of innovation in a culture which recognizes and rewards ideas for new and improved ways of doing things). We cannot treat work teams as isolated islands if we wish to understand creativity and innovation at work. The organizational context plays a powerful part in influencing both the level and type of innovation. But, we shall argue below, the most important factors are the interaction and socio-emotional processes that occur within teams.

TEAM PROCESSES

Task characteristics, group diversity, and organizational context will all influence team processes affecting the development and redevelopment of shared objectives, levels of participation, management of conflict, support for new ideas, and leadership (West, 1990, 1994; West & Anderson, 1996). These processes, if sufficiently integrated (i.e. there are shared objectives, high levels of participation, constructive, cooperative conflict management, high support for innovation, and leadership which enables innovation), will foster creativity and innovation implementation. Moreover, effective group processes will be both sustained by and increase the level of psychosocial safety in the group.

Developing Shared Objectives

In the context of group innovation, clarity of team objectives is likely to facilitate innovation by enabling focused development of new ideas, which can be filtered with greater precision than if team objectives are unclear. Theoretically, clear objectives will only facilitate innovation if team members are committed to the goals of the team since strong goal commitment will be necessary to maintain group member persistence for implementation in the face of resistance among other organizational members. Pinto and Prescott (1987), in a study of 418 project teams, found that a clearly stated mission was the only factor which predicted success at all stages of the innovation process (conception, planning, execution, and termination). Where group members do not share a commitment to a set of objectives (or a vision of the goals of their work) the forces of disintegration created by disagreements (and lack of safety), diversity, and the emotional demands of the innovation process are likely to inhibit innovation.

Participation in Decision Making

Participation leads to a more complete understanding of potential problems, as useful information is shared (Rodgers & Hunter, 1991) leading to the cross-fertilization of ideas, spawning innovation (Mumford & Gustafson, 1988). Kivimaki et al. (2000) found that, based on a sample of 493 employees, participative communication was the strongest predictor of innovation effectiveness out of eight aspects of organizational communication ($r = 0.60$) and of patents produced ($r = 0.19$). The researchers concluded that understanding opposing ideas and information enables employees to see the limitations in their views and incorporate other perspectives, leading to high-quality decision making and innovation. Further high participation in decision making means less resistance to change and therefore greater likelihood of innovations being implemented (Bowers & Seashore, 1966; Coch & French, 1948; Lawler & Hackman, 1969).

Conflict

Many scholars believe that the management of competing perspectives is fundamental to the generation of creativity and innovation (Mumford & Gustafson, 1988; Nemeth & Owens, 1996; Tjosvold, 1998). Such processes are characteristic of task-related conflict (as opposed to conflicts of relationship and process conflict; see De Dreu, 1997). They can arise from a common concern with quality of task performance in relation to shared objectives. Task conflict includes the appraisal of, and constructive challenges to, the group's performance. In essence, team members are more committed to performing their work effectively and excellently than they are either to bland consensus or to personal victory in conflict with other team members over task performance strategies or decision options.

Dean Tjosvold and colleagues (Tjosvold, 1982, 1998; Tjosvold & Field, 1983; Tjosvold & Johnson, 1977; Tjosvold, Wedley, & Field, 1986) have presented cogent arguments and strong supportive evidence that such constructive (task-related) controversy in a cooperative group context improves the quality of decision making and creativity (Tjosvold, 1991). Constructive controversy is characterized by full exploration of opposing opinions and frank analyses of task-related issues. It occurs when decision makers believe they are in a cooperative group context, where mutually beneficial goals are emphasized, rather than in a competitive context where decision makers feel their personal competence is confirmed rather than questioned, and where they perceive processes of mutual influence rather than attempted dominance.

For example, the most effective self-managing teams in a manufacturing plant that Alper and Tjosvold (1993) studied were those which had compatible goals and promoted constructive controversy. The 544 employees who made up the 59 teams completed a questionnaire which probed for information about cooperation, competition, and conflict within the teams. Teams were responsible for activities such as work scheduling, housekeeping, safety, purchasing, accident investigation, and quality. Members of teams which promoted interdependent conflict management (people cooperated to work through their differences), compared to teams with win/lose conflict (where team members tended to engage in a power struggle when they had different views and interests), felt confident that they could deal with differences. Such teams were rated as more productive and innovative by their managers. Apparently, because of this success, members of these teams were committed to working as a team.

Another perspective on conflict and innovation comes from minority influence theory. A number of researchers have shown that minority consistency of arguments over time is likely to lead to change in majority views in groups (Maass & Clark, 1984; Nemeth, 1986; Nemeth & Chiles, 1988; Nemeth & Kwan, 1987; Nemeth & Owens, 1996; Nemeth & Wachtler, 1983) (for an account of this research and an assessment of how it relates to group creativity, see the excellent chapter by Nemeth and Nemeth-Brown, in press).

De Dreu and De Vries (1997) suggest that a homogeneous workforce in which minority dissent is suppressed will reduce creativity, innovation, individuality, and independence (De Dreu & De Vries, 1993; see also Nemeth & Staw, 1989). Disagreement about ideas within a group can be beneficial and some researchers even argue that team task or information-related conflict is valuable, whether or not it occurs in a collaborative context, since it can improve decision making and strategic planning (Cosier & Rose, 1977; Mitroff, Barabba, & Kilmann, 1977; Schweiger, Sandberg, & Rechner, 1989). This is because task-related conflict may lead team members to re-evaluate the status quo and adapt their objectives, strategies, or processes more appropriately to their situation (Coser, 1970; Nemeth & Staw, 1989; Roloff, 1987; Thomas, 1979). However, De Dreu and Weingart (Chapter 8 this volume) suggest that high levels of conflict in teams, regardless of whether the conflict is focused on relationships or task, will inhibit team effectiveness and innovation.

In a study of newly formed postal work teams in the Netherlands, De Dreu and West found that minority dissent did indeed predict team innovation (as rated by the teams' supervisors), but only in teams with high levels of participation (De Dreu & West, 2001). It seems that the social processes in the team necessary for minority dissent to influence the innovation process are characterized by high levels of team member interaction, influence over decision making, and information sharing. This finding has significant implications for our understanding of minority dissent in groups operating in organizational contexts.

Overall, therefore, moderate task-related (as distinct from emotional or interpersonal) conflict and minority dissent in a participative climate will lead to innovation by encouraging debate (requisite diversity) and to consideration of alternative interpretations of information available, leading to integrated and creative solutions.

Support for Innovation

Innovation is more likely to occur in groups where there is support for innovation, and innovative attempts are rewarded rather than punished (Amabile, 1983; Kanter, 1983). Support for innovation is the expectation, approval, and practical support of attempts to introduce new and improved ways of doing things in the work environment (West, 1990). Within groups, new ideas may be routinely rejected or ignored, or attract verbal and practical support. Such group processes powerfully shape individual and group behaviour (for reviews see e.g. Brown, 2000; Hackman, 1992), and those which support innovation will encourage team members to introduce innovations. In a longitudinal study of 27 hospital top management teams, we found that support for innovation was the most powerful predictor of team innovation of any of the group processes so far discussed (Anderson & West, 1998; West & Anderson, 1996).

Reflexivity

Team reflexivity is the extent to which team members collectively reflect upon the team's objectives, strategies, and processes as well as their wider organizations and environments, and adapt them accordingly (West, 1996, p. 559). There are three central elements to the concept of reflexivity—*reflection*, *planning*, and *action or adaptation*. Reflection consists of attention, awareness, monitoring, and evaluation of the object of reflection (West, 2000). Planning is one of the potential consequences of the indeterminacy of reflection, since during this indeterminacy courses of action can be contemplated, intentions formed, plans developed (in more or less detail), and the potential for carrying them out is built up. High reflexivity exists when team planning is characterized by greater detail, inclusiveness of potential problems, hierarchical ordering of plans, and long- as well as short-range planning. More detailed implementation intentions or plans are more likely to lead to innovation implementation (Frese & Zapf, 1993; Gollwitzer, 1996). Indeed the work of Gollwitzer and colleagues suggests that goal-directed behaviour or innovation will be initiated when the team has articulated implementation intentions. This is because planning creates a conceptual readiness for, and guides team members' attention towards, relevant opportunities for action and means to accomplish the team's goal. Action refers to goal-directed behaviours relevant to achieving the desired changes in team objectives, strategies, processes, organizations, or environments identified by the team during the stage of reflection.

Reflexivity can relate to team objectives, strategies, internal processes, development of group psychosocial characteristics, and external relations as well as the external environment. As a consequence of reflexivity, the team's reality is continually renegotiated during team interaction. Understandings negotiated in one exchange between team members may be drawn upon in a variety of ways in order to inform subsequent discussions and offer the possibility of helpful and creative transformations and meanings (Bouwen & Fry, 1996). Research with BBC television programme production teams, whose work fundamentally requires creativity and innovation, provides support for these propositions (Carter & West, 1998). Dunbar (1996) studied four renowned science laboratories tracing the processes underlying scientific discoveries and found that scientific breakthroughs tended to occur when groups reflected on potential causes for negative or inconsistent findings. The findings mirror West's studies of team reflexivity. Reflection was more effective if it occurred in teams, as individuals tended to discount anomalous findings. Secondly, reflection stimulated the reframing of cognitive representations of tasks and questioning of commonly held assumptions, leading to the proposal of alternative, novel, and innovative approaches.

Group Psychosocial Safety

Group psychosocial safety refers to shared understandings, unconscious group processes, group cognitive style, and group emotional tone (Cohen & Bailey, 1997). Examples include norms, cohesiveness, team mental models (members share an understanding of the nature of the group's task, its task processes, how team members are required to work together, and the organizational context), and group affect. In groups with high levels of psychosocial safety, it is suggested, there will be high creativity. Creative ideas arise out of individual cognitive processes and, though group members may interact in ways which offer cognitive stimulation via diversity, creative ideas are produced as a result of individual cognitions. Evidence suggests that, in general, creative cognitions occur when individuals are free from pressure, feel safe, and experience relatively positive affect (Claxton, 1997, 1998). Moreover, psychological threats to face or identity are also associated with more rigid thinking (Cowen, 1952). Time pressure can also increase rigidity of thinking on work-related tasks such as selection decisions (Kruglansky & Freund, 1983). Another example of stress inhibiting the flexibility of responses is offered by Wright (1954), who asked people to respond to Rorschach inkblot tests. Half of the people were hospital patients awaiting an operation and half were "controls". The former gave more stereotyped responses, and were less fluent and creative in completing similes (e.g. "as interesting as..."), indicating the effects of stress or threat upon their capacity to generate creative responses.

Jehn (1995) found that norms reflecting the acceptance of conflict within a group, promoting an open and constructive atmosphere for group discussion, enhanced the positive effect of task-based conflict on individual and team performance for 79 work groups and 75 management groups. Members of high performing groups were not afraid to express their ideas and opinions. Such a finding further reinforces the notion that safety may be an important factor in idea generation or creativity.

Edmondson (1996) found major differences between newly formed intensive care nursing teams in their management of medication errors. In some groups, members openly acknowledged and discussed their medication errors (giving too much or too little of a drug, or administering the wrong drug) and discussed ways to avoid their occurrence. In others, members kept information about errors to themselves. Learning about the causes of these errors, as a team, and devising innovations to prevent future errors, were only possible in groups of the former type. Edmondson gives an example of how, in one learning-oriented team, discussion of a recent error led to innovation in equipment. An intravenous medication pump was identified as a source of consistent errors and so was replaced by a different type of pump. She also gives the example of how failure to discuss errors and generate innovations led to costly failure in the Hubble telescope development project. In particular, Edmondson (1996, 1999) argues that learning and innovation will only take place where group members trust other members' intentions. This manifests in a group level belief that well-intentioned action will not lead to punishment or rejection by the team, which Edmondson calls "team safety": "The term is meant to suggest a realistic, learning oriented attitude about effort, error and change—not to imply a careless sense of permissiveness, nor an unrelentingly positive affect. Safety is not the same as comfort; in contrast, it is predicted to facilitate risk" (Edmondson, 1999, p. 14).

LEADERSHIP

Leaders of groups can seek ideas and support their implementation among members; leaders may promote only their own ideas; or leaders may resist change and innovation from any source. The leader, by definition, exerts powerful social influences on the group or team, and therefore affects team performance (Beyerlein, Johnson, & Beyerlein, 1996; Brewer,

Wilson, & Beck, 1994; Komaki, Desselles, & Bowman, 1989). For example, research in Canadian manufacturing organizations reveals that CEOs' ages, flexibility, and perseverance are all positively related to the adoption of technological innovation in their organizations (Kitchell, 1997). We propose that leadership processes moderate the effects of inputs (team and organizational contexts) upon team processes and thereby affect the level and quality (magnitude, radicalness, and novelty) of the innovation (see Figure 15.1).

In any discussion of team leadership it is important to acknowledge that leadership processes are not necessarily invested in one person in a team. In most work teams there is a single and clearly defined team leader or manager and his or her style and behaviour had a considerable influence in moderating the relationships between inputs and processes. But leadership processes can be distributed such that more than one or all team members take on leadership roles at various points in the team's activities. Consider, for example, the breast cancer care team responsible for diagnosis, surgery, and postoperative treatment of patients. At various points the oncologist, surgeon, and breast care nurse are likely to (and it is appropriate that they should) take leadership roles in the team (Haward et al., 2002).

Recent theories of leadership depict two dominant styles: transformational and transactional. Transactional leaders focus on transactions, exchanges, contingent rewards, and punishments to change team members' behaviour (see Schriesheim & Kerr, 1977; Yammarino, 1996; Yukl, 1994). This style reflects an emphasis on the relationship between task-oriented leader behaviour and effective group member performance. Transformational leaders influence group members by encouraging them to transform their views of themselves and their work. They rely on charisma and the ability to conjure inspiring visions of the future (e.g. Bass, 1990; Burns, 1978; House & Shamir, 1993). Such leaders use emotional or ideological appeals to change the behaviour of the group, moving them from self-interest in work values to consideration of the whole group and organization. Although the reader may be tempted to the conclusion that only the transformational style will produce innovation, it is likely that both of these styles will influence creativity and innovation by moderating the relationship between inputs and processes. Inspiration or reward could lead to individual propensity to innovate being translated into innovation implementation. Rewards used by the leader will influence group creativity and innovation where these rewards are directed towards encouraging individual and group innovation, such as performance-related pay for new product development successes.

Team leadership studies (cf. Barry, 1991; Kim, Min, & Cha, 1999; McCall, 1988) have adopted role-based approaches to measure the specific leadership behaviours that team leaders perform in order to facilitate and direct teamwork. The basic premise of these studies is that team leaders must be competent at performing a diverse array of leadership activities. The most comprehensive framework was developed by McCall (1988) and recently reported and tested by Hoojberg and Choi (2000). This framework is based on the competing values theory that leaders must grapple with very different roles, which can be categorized within the quadrant of internal versus external as well interpersonal versus personal. The most striking finding of Hoojberg and Choi's (2000) research is that there are systematic differences in the structure of these roles depending on which stakeholder's perspective is assessed. More parsimonious frameworks tend to highlight the extent to which leaders foster teamwork, organize and direct project work, manage relationships with external stakeholders, and stimulate creativity and innovation. Barry (1991) conducted a detailed qualitative study of engineering and product development teams and identified four leadership roles that are critical to ensuring teams tackle the challenges of R&D work. Yukl (2002) refined this taxonomy, drawing upon empirical studies of knowledge work teams, to identify four roles: boundary spanning, facilitative leadership, innovation-stimulating leadership, and task management. We describe the four roles and summarize empirical support for each below.

- Leadership boundary spanning involves the management of external relationships, including coordinating tasks, negotiating resources and goals with stakeholders as well as scanning for information and ideas. Waldman and Atwater (1994) conducted a study of 40 R&D project teams; they found, out of a range of leadership behaviours examined (including transformation leadership and goal-setting behaviour), that boundary spanning (in particular championing the project) was the strongest predictor ($r = 0.22$) of research managers' ratings of project performance.

- Facilitative leadership refers to whether the leader encourages an atmosphere conducive to teamwork, ensuring team interactions are equitable and safe, encouraging participation, sharing of ideas, and open discussion of different perspectives. Kim, Min, and Cha (1999) surveyed 87 R&D teams in six Korean organizations; they found that the leader's performance of the team builder role was a significant predictor of team ratings of performance.

- A leader who acts as an innovator envisions project opportunities and new approaches by questioning team assumptions and challenging the status quo. Keller (1992) found that leaders who questioned approaches and suggested innovative ways of performing tasks were more likely to lead effective teams. Likewise Kim, Min, and Cha (1999) found that the leader's technical problem-solving ability, in particular appraisal of problems and identification of new ideas, was significantly correlated with project performance ($r = 0.35$).

- Directive leaders drive structured and ordered performance of project work by communicating instructions, setting priorities, deadlines, and standards. Yukl, Wall, and Lepsinger (1990) found that leaders who clarified tasks, communicated instructions, set priorities, deadlines, and standards, were most effective. Based on a sample of 296 groups, Kim and Yukl (1995) found, from a comprehensive list of managerial activities, planning and organizing were the strongest predictors of subordinate ratings of leadership effectiveness. Clear direction setting enables the focused development of ideas which can be assessed with greater precision than if team members are unclear (West & Anderson, 1996).

Of the four roles described, three pertain to leadership activities directed towards stimulating and managing cooperation within the team, whereas the fourth role, leadership boundary spanning, measures the extent to which the leader manages team relationships and coordination with the external environment. Thus while the nature and content of the roles differ, all roles require leader actions to stimulate and direct cooperation between individuals/groups to perform effectively and develop innovations.

Knorr et al. (1979) found that the team leader's professional status, ability to plan and coordinate activities, integrate the team, and encourage career promotion predicted the climate for innovation in the team as well as its overall performance. McDonough and Barczak (1992) examined the relationships between a leader's cognitive problem-solving style and the team's cognitive problem-solving style in product development teams. Cognitive problem-solving style was characterized as either adaptive (conforms to commonly accepted procedures) or innovative (searches for novel solutions). When the technology they were required to use was familiar to the team, the leader's style was unimportant. However, when the technology was unfamiliar, teams whose leaders had an innovative cognitive style developed new products faster than other teams. For product innovation in familiar situations, it seems leaders can withdraw from the team, but when the situation is unfamiliar, a non-conforming leader enables the team to consider a variety of options.

No discussion of leadership in social or industrial/organizational (I/O) psychology should neglect the impressive programme of work carried out by Norman Maier and his colleagues in the 1960s and 1970s. Maier (1970) conducted a series of experiments with (mostly student) groups exploring the influence of different leadership styles on problem solving and creativity. The results suggested that the leader should encourage "problem mindedness" in groups on the basis that exploring the problem fully is the best way of eventually generating a rich vein of solution options. The leader can delay a group's criticism of an idea by asking for alternative contributions and should use his or her power to protect individuals with minority views, so that their opinions can be heard (Maier & Solem, 1962; see also Osborn, 1957). Maier (1970) argued that leaders should delay offering their opinions as long as possible, since propositions from leaders are often given undue weight and tend either to be too hastily accepted or rejected, rather than properly evaluated, a finding since replicated in a variety of applied studies. Maier (1970) concludes that leaders should function as "the group's central nervous system": receive information, facilitate communication, relay messages, and integrate responses—in short, integrate the group. The leader must be receptive to information, but not impose solutions. The leader should be aware of group processes; listen in order to understand rather than to appraise or refute; assume responsibility for accurate communication; be sensitive to unexpressed feelings; protect minority views; keep the discussion moving; and develop skills in summarizing (Maier, 1970).

Leadership processes have a considerable influence in determining whether the inputs (such as team task, team member characteristics, organizational culture and climate, and demands on the team) are translated into group processes that support innovation implementation or smother both creativity and innovation. In this chapter we have proposed that they play a major role in moderating the relationship between input variables and group processes, and thereby innovation implementation. Generally, leadership is a topic that has been neglected in the study of group creativity and innovation since Maier's seminal work. As we move into an era when the imperatives for innovation in organizations are intense, it is important that social and I/O psychologists stretch their research to achieve a better understanding of how leaders influence creativity and innovation in teams.

CONCLUSIONS

Based upon the premise that cooperation and teamwork are fundamental for innovation, we developed an input–process–output framework examining how measures of teamwork, as well as factors impacting on teamwork, influence innovation. The inputs included team composition and organizational context. We identified a range of team processes including clarity of objectives, participation, and the climate supporting innovation. Thirdly, we proposed that leadership moderated the relationship between inputs and outputs.

Guided by this framework, we conducted a review of relevant literatures. The following themes emerged from this review. Task-oriented diversity acts as a double-edged sword, reducing cooperation and cohesion while providing teams with a greater range of perspectives, information as well as links to the external environment. Organizational contextual factors such as age and size and structural factors such as centralization influence team processes as well as team innovation. Leaders play a key role in buffering the team from the pernicious effects, or enhancing in the team the nurturing effects, of organizational culture. Team leaders also can ensure that team member and task characteristics influence group processes in a way that leads to rather than inhibits innovation. The relationship between team processes and innovation tends to be strong and positive. Although the nature of these processes varies considerably, virtually all include some measure of cooperative task performance, interaction, or social support processes within the group. Cooperation is core to team innovation.

While research has highlighted the importance of teamwork and cooperation, much of this research has adopted a static perspective (Marks, Mathieu, & Zacarro, 2001). Few studies take into account temporal factors which may change across a project's life cycle and a team's development. Punctuated equilibrium theory (cf. Gersick, 1988) predicts that teams have stable and relatively fixed routines and norms which are punctuated by radical change. More traditional theoretical orientations, which adopt stage-based models of teamwork (cf. Tuckman, 1965), suggest that these norms develop over time and after conflicts within teams; groups go through an ordered series of phases. One perspective (e.g. Marks, Mathieu, & Zacarro, 2001) to emerge is that there are times when irrespective of a project's progress or the stages of a team's development high levels of cooperation and teamwork are critical. Periods when high levels of project obstacles are encountered may necessitate intense cooperation and commitment. Failure to perform during these periods of high stress may have a disastrous effect on team performance and innovation. Based on similar assumptions but a different categorization system, Marks, Mathieu, and Zacarro (2001) contrast transition (i.e. periods of time when teams are evaluating or planning actions to attain goals) and action phases (periods when teams are performing activities leading to goal attainment). In essence the authors assert that different processes are important during action as opposed to transition phases. For example, mission analysis and the development of shared objectives are essential during transition phases, whereas during the action phases coordination and cooperation are essential. On the basis of these observations we believe that research in this area should track team development and team innovation in order that we can better understand these dynamic relationships. Sustained high levels of innovation are unlikely, and possibly counterproductive, in any team. Understanding when and how cooperation enables team innovation and when and how team innovation is helpful for effectiveness is important in future research.

For creativity and innovation implementation to emerge from group functioning over time—for groups to be sparkling fountains of ideas and changes—the context must be demanding but there must be strong group integration processes, good leadership, and a high level of intragroup safety. This requires that members have the integration abilities to work effectively in teams; and that they develop a safe psychosocial climate and appropriate group processes (clarifying objectives, encouraging participation, constructive controversy, reflexivity, and support for innovation). Such conditions are likely to produce high levels of group innovation, but crucially, too, the well-being which is a consequence of effective human interaction in challenging and supportive environments.

REFERENCES

Agrell, A. & Gustafson, R. (1996). Innovation and creativity in work groups. In M. A. West (ed.), *The Handbook of Work Group Psychology* (pp. 317–344). Chichester: Wiley.

Allen, T. J., Lee, D. M., & Tushman, M. L. (1980). R&D performance as a function of internal communication, project management, and the nature of work. *IEEE Transactions, 27*, 2–12.

Alper, S. & Tjosvold, D. (1993). Cooperation theory and self-managing teams on the manufacturing floor. Paper presented at the International Association for Conflict Management, Eugene, Ore.

Amabile, T. M. (1983). The social psychology of creativity: a componential conceptualization. *Journal of Personality and Social Psychology, 45*, 357–376.

Amabile, T. M. (1988). A model of creativity and innovation in organizations. In B. M. Staw & L. L. Cummings (eds), *Research in Organizational Behavior* (Vol. 10, pp. 123–167). Greenwich, Conn.: JAI Press.

Amabile, T. M. (1997). Motivating creativity in organizations: on doing what you love and loving what you do. *California Management Review, 40*(1), 39–58.

Amabile, T. M., Conti, R., Coon, H., Lazenby, J., & Herron, M. (1996). Assessing the work environment for creativity. *Academy of Management Journal, 39*, 1154–1184.

Ancona, D. F. & Caldwell, D. F. (1992). Bridging the boundary: external activity and performance in organisational teams. *Administrative Science Quarterly, 37*, 634–665.

Anderson, N. & West, M. A. (1998). Measuring climate for work group innovation: development and validation of the Team Climate Inventory. *Journal of Organizational Behavior, 19*, 235–258.

Andrews, F. M. (ed.) (1979). *Scientific Productivity*. Cambridge: Cambridge University Press.

Bantel, K. A. & Jackson, S. E. (1989). Top management and innovations in banking: does the demography of the top team make a difference? *Strategic Management Journal, 10*, 107–124.

Barry, D. (1991). Managing the boss-less team: lessons in distributed leadership. *Organizational Dynamics*, Summer, 31–47.

Bass, B. M. (1990). *Bass and Stogdill's Handbook of Leadership* (3rd edn). New York: Free Press.

Beyerlein, M. M., Johnson, D. A., & Beyerlein, S. T. (eds) (1996). *Advances in the Interdisciplinary Study of Work Teams* (Vol. 2) *Knowledge Work in Teams*. London: JAI Press.

Bouwen, R. & Fry, R. (1996). Facilitating group development: interventions for a relational and contextual construction. In M. A. West (ed.), *The Handbook of Work Group Psychology* (pp. 531–552). Chichester: Wiley.

Bowers, D. G. & Seashore, S. E. (1966). Predicting organizational effectiveness with a four-factor theory of leadership. *Administrative Science Quarterly, 11*, 238–263.

Brewer, N., Wilson, C., & Beck, K. (1994). Supervisory behaviour and team performance amongst police patrol sergeants. *Journal of Occupational and Organizational Psychology, 67*, 69–78.

Brown, R. J. (2000). *Group Processes: Dynamics within and between Groups*. London: Blackwell.

Bunce, D. & West, M. A. (1995). Changing work environments: innovative coping responses to occupational stress. *Work and Stress, 8*, 319–331.

Bunce, D. & West, M. A. (1996). Stress management and innovation interventions at work. *Human Relations, 49*, 209–232.

Burns, J. M. (1978). *Leadership*. New York: Harper & Row.

Burns, T. & Stalker, G. M. (1961). *The Management of Innovation*. London: Tavistock.

Carter, S. M. & West, M. A. (1998). Reflexivity, effectiveness and mental health in BBC-TV production teams. *Small Group Research, 5*, 583–601.

Claxton, G. L. (1997). *Hare Brain, Tortoise Mind: Why Intelligence Increases When You Think Less*. London: Fourth Estate.

Claxton, G. L. (1998). Knowing without knowing why: investigating human intuition. *The Psychologist, 11*, 217–220.

Coch, L. & French, J. R. (1948). Overcoming resistance to change. *Human Relations, 1*, 512–532.
Cohen, S. G. & Bailey, D. E. (1997). What makes teams work: group effectiveness research from the shop floor to the executive suite. *Journal of Management, 23*, 239–290.
Coser, L. A. (1970). *Continuities in the Study of Social Conflict.* New York: Free Press.
Cosier, R. & Rose, G. (1977). Cognitive conflict and goal conflict effects on task performance. *Organizational Behavior and Human Performance, 19*, 378–391.
Cowen, E. L. (1952). The influence of varying degrees of psychological stress on problem-solving rigidity. *Journal of Abnormal and Social Psychology, 47*, 420–424.
Cummings, L. L. (1965). Organizational climates for creativity. *Journal of the Academy of Management, 3*, 220–227.
De Dreu, C. K. W. (1995). Coercive power and concession making in bilateral negotiation. *Journal of Conflict Resolution, 39*, 646–670.
De Dreu, C. K. W. (1997). Productive conflict: the importance of conflict management and conflict issue. In C. K. W. De Dreu & E. van de Vliert (eds), *Using Conflict in Organizations* (pp. 9–22). London: Sage.
De Dreu, C. K. W. & De Vries, N. K. (1993). Numerical support, information processing, and attitude to change. *European Journal of Social Psychology, 23*, 647–662.
De Dreu, C. K. W. & De Vries, N. K. (1997). Minority dissent in organizations. In C. K. W. De Dreu & E. Van De Vliert (eds), *Using Conflict in Organizations* (pp. 72–86). London: Sage.
De Dreu, C. K. W. & West, M. A. (2001). Minority dissent and team innovation: the importance of participation in decision-making. *Journal of Applied Psychology, 68*, 1191–1201.
Delbecq, A. L. & Mills, P. K. (1985). Managerial practices that enhance innovation. *Organizational Dynamics, 14*, 24–34.
Dunbar, K. (1996). How scientists really reason: scientific reasoning in real-world laboratories. In R. J. Sternberg & J. E. Davidson (eds), *The Nature of Insight* (pp. 365–395). Cambridge, Mass.: MIT Press.
Edmondson, A. C. (1996). Learning from mistakes is easier said than done: group and organizational influences on the detection and correction of human error. *Journal of Applied Behavioral Science, 32*, 5–28.
Edmondson, A. C. (1999). Psychological safety and learning behavior in work teams. *Administrative Science Quarterly, 44*, 350–383.
Ettlie, J. E. (1983). Organizational policy and innovation among suppliers to the food-processing sector. *Academy of Management Journal, 26*, 27–44.
Filley, A. C., House, R. J., & Kerr, S. (1976). *Managerial Process and Organizational Behavior.* Glenview, Ill.: Scott Foresman.
Frese, M. & Zapf, D. (1993). Action as the core of work psychology: a German approach. In H. C. Triandis, M. D. Dunnette, & L. M. Hough (eds), *Handbook of Industrial and Organizational Psychology* (2nd edn, Vol. 4, pp. 271–340). Palo Alto, Calif.: Consulting Psychologists Press.
Gersick, C. J. G. (1988). Time and transition in work teams: toward a new model of group development. *Academy of Management Journal, 31*(1), 9–41.
Ghiselli, E. E. & Lodahl, T. M. (1958). Patterns of managerial traits and group effectiveness. *Journal of Abnormal and Social Psychology, 57*, 61–66.
Gollwitzer, P. M. (1996). The volitional benefits of planning. In P. M. Gollwitzer & J. A. Bargh (eds), *The Psychology of Action: Linking Cognition and Motivation to Behaviour* (pp. 287–312). New York: Guilford Press.
Hackman, J. R. (1992). Group influences on individuals in organisations. In M. D. Dunnette & L. M. Hough (eds), *Handbook of Industrial and Organizational Psychology* (Vol. 3). Palo Alto, Calif.: Consulting Psychologists Press.
Hage, J. & Aiken, M. (1967). *Social Change in Complex Organizations.* New York: Random House.
Hage, J. & Dewar, R. (1973). Elite values versus organizational structure in predicting innovation. *Administrative Science, 18*, 279–290.
Haward, B., Amir, Z., Borrill, C. S., Dawson, J. F., Sainsbury, R., Scully, J., & West, M. A. (2002). Breast cancer teams: the impact of constitution, new cancer workload, and methods of operation on their effectiveness. Unpublished paper, Leeds, UK: Epidemiology and Health Services Research, University of Leeds.

Hoffman, L. R. (1979). Applying experimental research on group problem solving to organizations. *Journal of Abnormal and Social Psychology, 58*, 27–32.

Hoffman, L. R., Harburg, E., & Maier, N. R. F. (1962). Differences and disagreement as factors in creative group problem solving. *Journal of Abnormal and Social Psychology, 64*, 206–214.

Hoffman, L. R. & Maier, N. R. F. (1961). Sex differences, sex composition, and group problem-solving. *Journal of Abnormal and Social Psychology, 63*, 453–456.

Hoojberg, R. & Choi, J. (2000). Which leadership roles matter to whom? An examination of rater effects on perceptions of effectiveness. *Leadership Quarterly, 11*(3), 341–364.

House, R. J. & Shamir, B. (1993). Toward the integration of transformational, charismatic, and visionary theories. In M. M. Chemers & R. Ayman (eds), *Leadership Theory and Research: Perspectives and Directions* (pp. 81–107). San Diego, Calif.: Academic Press.

Jackson, S. E. (1992). Consequences of group composition for the interpersonal dynamics of strategic issue processing. *Advances in Strategic Management, 8*, 345–382.

Jackson, S. E. (1996). The consequences of diversity in multidisciplinary work teams. In M. A. West (ed.), *Handbook of Work Group Psychology* (pp. 53–75). Chichester: Wiley.

Jehn, K. A. (1995). A multimethod examination of the benefits and detriments of intragroup conflict. *Administrative Science Quarterly, 40*, 256–282.

Kanter, R. M. (1983). *The Change Masters: Corporate Entrepreneurs at Work*. New York: Simon & Schuster.

Katz, R. (1982). The effects of group longevity on project communication and performance. *Administrative Science Quarterly, 27*, 81–104.

Keller, R. T. (1992). Transformational leadership and the performance of research and development research groups. *Journal of Management, 18*(3), 489–501.

Keller, R. T. (2001). Cross-functional project groups in research and new product development: diversity, communications, job stress and outcomes. *Academy of Management Journal, 44*(3), 547–555.

Kim, H. & Yukl, G. (1995) Relationships of managerial effectiveness and advancement to self-reported leadership–reported leadership behaviors from the multiple-linkage model. *Leadership Quarterly, 6*(3), 361–377.

Kim, Y., Min, B., & Cha, J. (1999). The roles of R&D team leaders in Korea: a contingent approach. *R&D Management, 29*(2), 153–165.

Kimberley, J. R. & Evanisko, M. J. (1981). Organizational innovation: the influence of individual, organizational and contextual factors on hospital adoption of technological and administrative innovations. *Academy of Management Journal, 24*, 689–713.

Kitchell, S. (1997). CEO characteristics and technological innovativeness: a Canadian perspective. *Canadian Journal of Administrative Sciences, 14*, 111–125.

Kivimaki, M., Lansisalmi, H., Elovainio, M., Heikkila, A., Lindstrom, K., Harisalo, R., Sipila, K., & Puolimatka, L. (2000). Communication as a determinant of organizational innovation. *R&D Management, 30*(1), 33–42.

Knorr, K. D., Mittermeir, R., Aichholzer, G., & Waller, G. (1979). Leadership and group performance: a positive relationship in academic research units. In F. M. Andrews (ed.), *Scientific Productivity* (pp. 95–117). Cambridge: Cambridge University Press.

Komaki, J. L., Desselles, M. L., & Bowman, E. D. (1989). Definitely not a breeze: extending an operant model of effective supervision to teams. *Journal of Applied Psychology, 74*, 522–529.

Kruglansky, A. W. & Freund, T. (1983). The freezing and unfreezing of lay influences: effects on impressional primacy, ethnic stereotyping and numerical anchoring. *Journal of Experimental Social Psychology, 12*, 448–468.

Lawler, E. E., III & Hackman, J. R. (1969). Impact of employee participation in the development of pay incentive plans: a field experiment. *Journal of Applied Psychology, 53*, 467–471.

Lawrence, P. R. & Lorsch, J. W. (1967). *Organization and Environment: Managing Differentiation and Integration*. Boston: Harvard Business School.

Maass, A. & Clark, R. D. (1984). Hidden impacts of minorities: fifty years of minority influence research. *Psychological Bulletin, 95*, 428–450.

McCall, M. W., Jr (1988). Developing leadership. In J. L. Galbraith, E. E. Lawler, III, & associates (eds), *Organizing for the Future: The New Logic for Managing Complex Organizations* (pp. 256–284). Jossey-Bass Series.

McDonough, E. F., III & Barczak, G. (1992). The effects of cognitive problem-solving orientation and technological familiarity on faster new product development. *Journal of Product Innovation Management, 9*, 44–52.
McGrath, J. E. (1984). *Groups, Interaction and Performance*. Englewood Cliffs, NJ: Prentice-Hall.
Maier, N. R. (1970). *Problem Solving and Creativity: In Individuals and Groups*. Monterey, Calif.: Brooks Cole.
Maier, N. R. & Solem, A. R. (1962). Improving solutions by turning choice situations into problems. *Personnel Psychology, 15*, 151–157.
Marks, M. A., Mathieu, J. E., & Zaccaro, S. E. (2001). A temporally based framework and taxonomy of team processes. *Academy of Management Review, 26*(3), 356–376.
Maznevski, M. L. (1994). Understanding our differences: performance in decision-making groups with diverse members. *Human Relations, 47*, 531–552.
Mitroff, J., Barabba, N., & Kilmann, R. (1977). The application of behaviour and philosophical technologies to strategic planning: a case study of a large federal agency. *Management Studies, 24*, 44–58.
Mohrman, S. A., Cohen, S. G., & Mohrman, A. M. (1995). *Designing Team-based Organizations: New Forms for Knowledge Work*. San Francisco: Jossey-Bass.
Monge, P. R., Cozzens, M. D., & Contractor, N. S. (1992). Communication and motivational predictors of the dynamics of organizational innovation. *Organizational Science, 3*, 250–274.
Mumford, M. D. & Gustafson, S. B. (1988). Creativity syndrome: integration, application and innovation. *Psychological Bulletin, 103*, 27–43.
Nemeth, C. (1986). Differential contributions of majority and minority influence. *Psychological Review, 93*, 23–32.
Nemeth, C. & Chiles, C. (1988). Modelling courage: the role of dissent in fostering independence. *European Journal of Social Psychology, 18*, 275–280.
Nemeth, C. & Kwan, J. (1987). Minority influence, divergent thinking and the detection of correct solutions. *Journal of Applied Social Psychology, 9*, 788–799.
Nemeth, C. & Nemeth-Brown, B. (in press). Better than individuals? The potential benefits of dissent and diversity for group creativity. In P. Paulus & B. Nijstad (eds), *Group Creativity*. New York: Oxford University Press.
Nemeth, C. & Owens, P. (1996). Making work groups more effective: the value of minority dissent. In M. A. West (ed.), *Handbook of Work Group Psychology* (pp. 125–142). Chichester: Wiley.
Nemeth, C. & Staw, B. M. (1989). The trade offs of social control and innovation within groups and organizations. In L. Berkowitz (ed.), *Advances in Experimental Social Psychology* (pp. 175–210). New York: Academic Press.
Nemeth, C. J. & Wachtler, J. (1983). Creative problem solving as a result of majority vs minority influence. *European Journal of Social Psychology, 13*, 45–55.
Nicholson, N. & West, M. A. (1988). *Managerial Job Change: Men and Women in Transition*. Cambridge: Cambridge University Press.
O'Reilly, C. A. & Flatt, S. F. (1989). Executive team demography, organizational innovation, and firm performance. Paper presented at the Academy of Management Conference, Washington, DC.
Osborn, A. F. (1957). *Applied Imagination*. New York: Scribner's.
Payne, R. L. (1990). The effectiveness of research teams: a review. In M. A. West & J. L. Farr (eds), *Innovation and Creativity at Work: Psychological and Organizational Strategies* (pp. 101–122). Chichester: Wiley.
Pearce, J. A. & Ravlin, E. C. (1987). The design and activation of self-regulating work groups. *Human Relations, 40*, 751–782.
Pelz, D. C. (1956). Some social factors related to performance in a research organization. *Administrative Science Quarterly, 1*, 310–325.
Pierce, J. L. & Delbecq, A. (1977). Organizational structure, individual attitude and innovation. *Academy of Management Review, 2*, 27–33.
Pinto, J. K. & Prescott, J. E. (1987). Changes in critical success factor importance over the life of a project. *Academy of Management Proceedings*, New Orleans, 328–332.
Porac, J. F. & Howard, H. (1990). Taxonomic mental models in competitor definition. *Academy of Management Review, 2*, 224–240.

Rodgers, R. & Hunter, J. E. (1991). Impact of management by objectives on organizational productivity. *Journal of Applied Psychology, 76*(2), 322–336.
Rogers, E. M. (1983). *Diffusion of Innovations* (3rd edn). New York: Free Press.
Roloff, M. E. (1987). Communication and conflict. In C. R. Berger & S. H. Chaffee (eds), *Handbook of Communication Science* (pp. 484–534). Newbury Park, Calif.: Sage.
Schriesheim, C. A. & Kerr, S. (1977). Theories and measures of leadership: a critical appraisal of current and future directions. In J. G. Hunt & L. L. Larson (eds), *Leadership: The Cutting Edge* (pp. 9–45). Carbondale, Ill.: Southern Illinois University Press.
Schweiger, D., Sandberg, W., & Rechner, P. (1989). Experimental effects of dialectical inquiry, devil's advocacy, and other consensus approaches to strategic decision making. *Academy of Management Journal, 32*, 745–772.
Shaw, M. E. (1981). *Group Dynamics: The Psychology of Small Group Behavior*. New York: McGraw-Hill.
Shepard, H. A. (1967). Innovation-resisting and innovation-producing organizations. *Journal of Business, 40*, 470–477.
Smith, K. G., Smith, K. A., Olian, J. D., Sims, H. P. Jr, O'Brannon, D. P., & Scully, J. A. (1994). Top management team demography and process. The role of social integration and communication. *Administrative Science Quarterly, 39*, 412–438.
Thomas, K. W. (1979). Organizational conflict. In S. Kerr (ed.), *Organizational Behaviour* (pp. 151–184). Columbus, Ohio: Grid Publishing.
Tjosvold, D. (1982). Effects of approach to controversy on superiors' incorporation of subordinates' information in decision making. *Journal of Applied Psychology, 67*, 189–193.
Tjosvold, D. (1985). Implications of controversy research for management. *Journal of Management, 11*, 21–37.
Tjosvold, D. (1991). *Team Organization: An Enduring Competitive Advantage*. Chichester: Wiley.
Tjosvold, D. (1998). Co-operative and competitive goal approaches to conflict: accomplishments and challenges. *Applied Psychology: An International Review, 47*, 285–342.
Tjosvold, D. & Field, R. H. G. (1983). Effects of social context on consensus and majority vote decision making. *Academy of Management Journal, 26*, 500–506.
Tjosvold, D. & Johnson, D. W. (1977). The effects of controversy on cognitive perspective-taking. *Journal of Education Psychology, 69*, 679–685.
Tjosvold, D., Wedley, W. C., & Field, R. H. G. (1986). Constructive controversy, the Vroom–Yetton Model, and managerial decision-making. *Journal of Occupational Behaviour, 7*, 125–138.
Tuckman, Bruce W. (1965). Developmental sequence in small groups. *Psychological Bulletin, 63*, 384–399.
Utterback, J. M. (1974). Innovation in industry and the diffusion of technology. *Science, 183*, 620–626.
Wade, J. (1996). A community level analysis of sources and rates of technological variation in the microprocessor market. *Academy of Management Journal, 39*, 1218–1244.
Waldman, D. A. & Atwater, L. E. (1994). The nature of effective leadership and championing processes at different levels in a R&D hierarchy. *The Journal of High Technology Management Research, 5*(2), 233–245.
West, M. A. (1987). Role innovation in the world of work. *British Journal of Social Psychology, 26*, 305–315.
West, M. A. (1990). The social psychology of innovation in groups. In M. A. West & J. L. Farr (eds), *Innovation and Creativity at Work: Psychological and Organizational Strategies* (pp. 309–333). Chichester: Wiley.
West, M. A. (1994). *Effective Teamwork*. Leicester: British Psychological Society.
West, M. A. (1996). Reflexivity and work group effectiveness: a conceptual integration. In M. A. West (ed.), *Handbook of Work Group Psychology* (pp. 555–579). Chichester: Wiley.
West, M. A. (2000). Reflexivity, revolution, and innovation in work teams. In M. M. Beyerlein, D. A. Johnson, & S. T. Beyerlein (eds), *Advances in Interdisciplinary Studies of Work Teams: Product Development Teams* (pp. 1–29). Stamford, Conn.: JAI Press.
West, M. A. (2002). Sparkling fountains or stagnant ponds: an integrative model of creativity and innovation implementation in work groups. *Applied Psychology: An International Review, 51*, 355–424.

West, M. A. & Anderson, N. (1992). Innovation, cultural values and the management of change in British hospitals. *Work and Stress, 6*, 293–310.

West, M. A. & Anderson, N. (1996). Innovation in top management teams. *Journal of Applied Psychology, 81*, 680–693.

West, M. A. & Farr, J. L. (1990). Innovation at work. In M. A. West & J. L. Farr (eds), *Innovation and Creativity at Work: Psychological and Organizational Strategies* (pp. 3–13). Chichester: Wiley.

West, M. A. & Richter, A. (in press). Climates and cultures for innovation and creativity at work. In C. Ford (ed.), *Handbook of Organizational Creativity*. London: Sage.

West, M. A., Patterson, M., Pillinger, T., & Nickell, S. (2000). Innovation and change in manufacturing. Working paper, Aston Business School, Aston University, Birmingham, UK.

Willems, E. P. & Clark, R. D., III (1971). Shift toward risk and heterogeneity of groups. *Journal of Experimental and Social Psychology, 7*, 302–312.

Wood, W. (1987). Meta-analytic review of sex differences in group performance. *Psychological Bulletin, 102*, 53–71.

Wright, M. (1954). A study of anxiety in a general hospital setting. *Canadian Journal of Psychology, 8*, 195–203.

Yammarino, F. J. (1996). Group leadership: a levels of analysis perspective. In M. A. West (ed.), *Handbook of Work Group Psychology* (pp. 189–224). Chichester: Wiley.

Yukl, G. A. (1994). *Leadership in Organizations*. Englewood Cliffs, NJ: Prentice-Hall.

Yukl, G. A. (2002). *Leadership in Organizations* (5th edn). New Jersey: Prentice-Hall.

Yukl, G. A., Wall, S., & Lepsinger, R. (1990). Preliminary report on validation of the Managerial Practices Survey. In K. E. Clark & M. B. Clark (eds), *Measures of Leadership*. New Jersey: Leadership Library of America.

Zaltman, G., Duncan, R., & Holbeck, J. (1973). *Innovations and Organizations*. London: Wiley.

Zenger, T. R. & Lawrence, B. S. (1989). Organizational demography: the differential effects of age and tenure distributions on technical communication. *Academy of Management Journal, 32*, 353–376.

16

SKILL ACQUISITION AND THE DEVELOPMENT OF A TEAM MENTAL MODEL

AN INTEGRATIVE APPROACH TO ANALYSING ORGANIZATIONAL TEAMS, TASK, AND CONTEXT

Janice Langan-Fox

TEAMWORK AND THE NEEDS OF TEAMS IN ORGANIZATIONS

The Problem with Teams

As commercial environments become increasingly competitive, organizations are searching for new methods to improve workforce productivity. As well as becoming more competitive, workplaces are becoming knowledge-intensive, requiring a wider skill base, and continual training upgrades. In this scenario, workers in knowledge-intensive professions may find it increasingly more difficult to keep up to date. To meet these challenges organizations are employing teams that can pool resources and skills (Coates, 1996; Jacobs & James, 1994; Kozlowski, 1995; Magney, 1995; Marchington et al., 1994), the idea being that, collectively, the team will have more knowledge than any one individual member and that through team member interaction, performance will be greater than any individual part. However, untrained teams often find themselves operating in a new environment of asynchronous communication, new communication technologies, such as email, groupware, and teleconferencing, and new social and increased organizational pressures (Langan-Fox, 2001a, b; Langan-Fox, Code, & Langfield-Smith, 2000). This environment poses new opportunities and challenges that need to be considered in order to maximize a team's efficiency. So-called "high performance teams" have been offered as a central vehicle for achieving innovation (West, 1997). Some of the distinguishing features of "expert" teams are coordinated action, mutual understanding, high commitment, role differentiation, and shared goals (Marchington et al., 1994).

International Handbook of Organizational Teamwork and Cooperative Working. Edited by M. A. West, D. Tjosvold, and K. G. Smith.

There are many instances where teams are not living up to expectations (Kozlowski, 1995; West, 1997). Teams may inadequately coordinate their actions; fail to share key knowledge; be poorly constructed and trained; have a lack of role clarity; or experience disputes over processes and ideas. A greater theoretical understanding needs to be developed of what facilitates high performance teams and how this can be developed and trained in other teams. Unfortunately, little is known about the human resource systems necessary for the management and support of team-based work, and findings from past research are not readily transferable to organizational teams in general (Coates, 1996; Jacobs & James, 1994; Kozlowski, 1995; McClough et al., 1998; Magney, 1995; Marchington et al., 1994).

Unlike laboratory teams, organizational teams have:

(a) ongoing rather than temporary status;
(b) tasks that are complex and evolving, not simple or set;
(c) task allocators who are managers not university staff or students;
(d) team members who typically do not have a university education;
(e) members who bring a history of organizational experience with them to the team;
(f) tasks which can be impacted by a range of factors singly, or together;
(g) outcomes and processes which affect organizational profitability and take-home pay of team members.

NEED FOR AN ANALYTIC FRAMEWORK

To facilitate the analysis of expert teams, a framework is required that facilitates several organizational needs. The design of training programmes could be guided by such a framework in determining team skill shortages. Career coaching could provide feedback to employees on their relative strengths and weaknesses in team-based domains, and suggestions for how skills can be improved. It could inform infrastructure support through providing communication technologies that enable teams to better communicate, or set up incentive schemes that reward team-based responsibility. Selection at the point of recruitment and at the level of allocation of employees to teams could be guided by such a model by making transparent employees' ability to operate in teams and their team-operated style.

If, as is argued, teams are attempting to find solutions to problems in complex environments with a skill shortfall in team training, a conceptual framework for investigating the acquisition and development of all those variables necessary for team efficiency and smooth working would be helpful. In recent times, authors have suggested that a "team mental model" is important for understanding the dynamics and difficulties of teams (see e.g. Langan-Fox, Code, & Langfield-Smith, 2000). A team mental model would be useful for: problem diagnosis; identifying differences in the mental models of team members; team development; analysing team member relationships; and evaluating team success. As people learn about a new system of relationships (a team), or about operating in a team to solve a particular task, their mental models of that system of knowledge and relationships (e.g. team and task) changes, adapts, and develops.

Knowledge about people in a team, a task, and those features of the task which intersect with the organizational environment might always be in a state of growth and development as compared to the mental model of, say, a telecommunications system, which can reach "expert" level: the person "knows" all there is to know about the operation of the system. This is because contemporary organizations are dynamic and changing, as are the people, roles, and environments of that organization (Clegg, 1994; Langan-Fox, 2001a, b; Langan-Fox et al., 2002b). Thus any one individual is constantly in a state of learning as knowledge and experience are incorporated into an existing team mental model, the individual evaluates that knowledge and realigns his/her understanding of the situation, and adjusts his/her behaviour as a consequence of that new information in a cycle commonly found in cybernetic models of self-regulation (see e.g. Carver & Scheier, 1982). The process can also be described as one of skill acquisition. From the point of formation, teams are acquiring skills and as they come to acquire more experience and develop their knowledge, move from being a "novice" team member to an "expert" team member. These concepts will be explored later in this chapter.

The Utility and Definition of the Team Mental Model Construct

In terms of utility, the team mental model construct (hereinafter referred to as TMM) is useful because of its comprehensiveness. It could be described as a "grand landscape" variable. Its potential is as a summary variable: it can consist of the whole picture or snapshot of the situation as it currently stands. In terms of structure or architecture, it can comprise networks or webs of relationships among and between relevant variables consisting of any factors that team members think are vital to ensuring team success. Like organizational culture, the TMM construct is dynamic: it is capable of capturing the more "invisible" or hidden (micro) elements affecting team performance, especially as regards relationships but also general and unique (macro) factors of the organizational environment. Langan-Fox, Code, and Langfield-Smith (2000) list the sort of factors that can be elicited from teams. The construct is more complex than many other organizational variables such as "team performance" (see e.g. Robins, Pattison, & Langan-Fox, 1995), which might consist of some unitary form of output, e.g. solutions found, number of "widgets" produced.

TMM Construct

GENERAL DEFINITIONS

The social cognition literature acknowledges the notion that mental processes can be understood at the group level of analysis (Klimoski & Mohammed, 1994). Advocates of shared cognition suggest that in order to work together successfully, individuals must perceive, encode, store, and retrieve information in a parallel manner (Cannon-Bowers et al., 1995; Converse, Cannon-Bowers, & Salas, 1991; Duffy, 1992). That is, they must hold a "shared mental model" which can be described as the extent to which a group (or dyad) of individuals possess a similar cognitive representation of some situation, phenomenon, or activity (Cannon-Bowers et al., 1995). One aspect of this shared mental model might include, for example, a shared understanding of how the group operates as a system. Another aspect might include a shared understanding of the nature of the problem facing the group (Duffy, 1992). It should be noted, though, that the notion of a "shared mental model" is distinct from the notion of a "team mental model", in that the latter refers to what is shared among the members of a team as a collectivity, not shared cognition among dyads of individuals, which the former phrase allows for (Klimoski & Mohammed, 1994). Shared mental models can roughly be defined as common mental understandings of a particular domain between two or more people, where such understandings are mutually recognized by the other person. Shared mental model theorists imply that common mental models will invariably lead to improved team performance, although this view needs to be substantially qualified to situation and task (Levesque, Wilson, & Wholey, 2001). TMMs are more prescriptive. TMMs are conceptually broader and prescriptively less confined than shared mental models. They describe, define, and measure the individual mental models of members for a team-relevant domain, how these individual mental models interact, and what commonalities, differences, and conflicts exist. The TMM construct allows for a better understanding of a team's shared mental understanding and how the individual mental models of team members interact to effect team efficiency. Alternatively, TMMs prescribe coalitions of TMMs that lead to complementary understandings, which may sometimes be shared, but are at other times reflecting role differentiation.

The relationship of TMMs to shared mental models is similar to the concept of team to group. Teams are about member interdependence, role differentiation, and shared goals, whereas groups may or may not have these characteristics. Teams are in some sense prescriptive (often in terms of roles) of how individuals need to interact to be truly cooperating towards a shared goal. Likewise, TMMs are concerned with what coalition of individual mental models leads to effective team performance which may not involve shared mental models. Related to this understanding of TMMs is the notion of complementarity, which suggests that expert TMMs are dependent on the *right* combination of individual mental models, incorporating specialization and shared understanding. Such a perspective would define expert TMMs pragmatically and view them as context-dependent in regard to the organization, the task, and the team members.

DISTINCTION FROM MENTAL MODELS

TMMs theoretically presume the existence of individual mental models. TMMs by definition are concerned with the interaction of team members' individual mental models, and congruence, complementarity, similarity, and acknowledgement of individual mental models are at the essence of any conception of TMMs. These features explain the TMM in terms of a dynamic emergent property of the interactions and relationships of the team members' individual mental models. Specifically, TMMs relate to individual mental models of team processes, representations of other team members, and the individual tasks completed by team members (Langan-Fox, Code, & Langfield-Smith, 2000). TMMs are concerned with only a portion of an individual's mental model, that which has relevance to the goals and tasks of the team. Thus, there needs to be a clear distinction between team and individual mental models. TMMs are not held by any one individual but are some form of aggregation, abstraction, or team functional capacity. TMMs need to be clearly differentiated from an individual's mental model of a team and from an individual's mental model of how to collaborate and effectively work in a team.

MULTIPLE MENTAL MODELS

Would it be more efficient to attempt to capture the multiple mental models of individuals? For instance, of the team, the task, the environment, and so on? It is debatable whether team members will hold several different mental models for team functioning (see e.g. Cannon-Bowers et al., 1995; Duffy, 1992). However, it is probably not possible nor desirable to construct mental models of all of these, for instance to capture separate mental models for "equipment" and "task". But we do acknowledge that there exist alternative views about the number of mental models held by a single person and whether multiple mental models should be captured (see e.g. Olson & Biolsi, 1991). If we were to attempt to capture separate, multiple mental models from team members, some degree of artificiality may well arise. As described elsewhere (Langan-Fox, Code, & Langfield-Smith, 2000), the semantic features of a mental model are contained in various associative networks in a hierarchical fashion which might be accessed separately, for instance the role functions of individual team members. But, in the mind of the person, such separation may not exist. What gain, then, is secured by accessing sub-mental models? Although there may be some advantage in securing sub-mental models, for instance in the case of diagnosing causal attributes of an industrial accident, for parsimony and efficiency, there is benefit in gleaning a single mental model from an individual because the essential features of the model are crystallized in a coherent way. Perhaps the overriding issue could be to capture accurate mental models on a regular basis from all those individuals involved in the team task.

PAST FRAMEWORKS OF TMMs

For the purpose of constructing a theoretical framework, an important question is the content of the TMM. Several authors have proposed that there may be multiple mental models of team functioning. Glickman et al. (1987) found that two separate tracks of behaviour evolve during team training. The "taskwork" track involves skills that are related to the execution of the task and/or mission (e.g. operating equipment, following procedures) and a second track, the "teamwork" track, involves skills that are related to functioning effectively as a team member. Thus, it could be hypothesized that mental models of both the task and team will be required. Similarly, Converse, Cannon-Bowers, and Salas (1991) proposed a framework of a hierarchical mental model of team functioning. At the highest (and most abstract) level of the framework is a model of the external environment in which the team functions. Clustered within that model is a model of the team environment in which information about team norms is stored. Within the team environment model are team models (e.g. models of teammate behaviour, abilities, and personal characteristics) and task models (e.g. models of the team goal, task structure, teammates' tasks, and the individual's own task). In later publications, Cannon-Bowers and colleagues (Cannon-Bowers, Salas, & Converse, 1993; Orasanu & Salas, 1993; Rouse, Cannon-Bowers, & Salas, 1992) argued that mental models of team functioning are likely to be composed of models of the task, equipment, team, and team interaction. To support this argument, the authors provided an example of the multiple knowledge structures required by team operators in a Navy tactical decision task. In addition, they argued that the exact content of what must be shared/compatible among team members within each of the models (team, task, team interaction, equipment) is most likely to be task dependent. For instance, they suggested that the team model would be less important for relatively proceduralized tasks but more important for dynamic tasks which require a high level of flexibility and adaptability. It could also be argued that equipment models would be more important in highly specific technical tasks (such as air traffic control or nuclear plant monitoring) rather than in organizational team problem-solving tasks.

An examination of the literature reveals that there are a number of taxonomies of teamwork (see e.g. Brannick et al., 1995; Cannon-Bowers et al., 1995; Morgan et al., 1986; Prince & Salas, 1989) but comparatively fewer frameworks or taxonomies of mental models for teamwork. Furthermore, of the TMM frameworks that have been proposed, these have not been geared towards TMMs for teamwork, but rather, TMMs of task procedures in a particular team context (e.g. the cockpit). Much work needs to be done on team mental models in civilian organizational environments where the product of teamwork results not just in better coordination of activities, but, for example, the number of units produced or sold. In other words, the influence of the "customer", absent in laboratory and military team research, has an impact in the real world of organizations. Besides this, TMM research in organizations is scarce.

Problems with the TMM Construct

However, in order to utilize the concept of TMMs fully for the purpose of maximizing expert teams, several theoretical and methodological issues need to be addressed. Several reviews in the area of shared cognition and TMMs in particular have noted the challenges developing the area (Cannon-Bowers & Salas, 2001; Klimoski & Mohammed, 1994). In particular there is the mutually interdependent problem that the theoretical construct of TMMs is dependent on how it is measured, but useful measures cannot be designed until the construct is better defined. There is a risk present that any attempt to develop and improve the concept of TMMs leads to the risk of further fracturing the current understanding that has developed in the field. Another challenge is making theoretical ideas practical enough that translate into productivity and work satisfaction improvements. These issues will be further discussed and the recommendation made that TMMs become more aligned with the applied needs for developing expert teams.

CHAPTER AIMS

In order to meet the challenges mentioned above, this chapter will elaborate on the potential of using the TMM construct in conjunction with a three-phase theory of skill acquisition to better understand team interaction and processes (see e.g. Langan-Fox, Code, & Edlund, 1998; Langan-Fox, Waycott, & Galna, 1997). By incorporating the TMM concept within a skill acquisition framework, a better understanding may be attained of the developmental nature of TMMs; the properties of TMMs will be apparent, and how they may be supported to speed up the developmental process from novice to expert team.

The current work presents a model which describes the factors likely to affect the acquisition and development of TMMs in organizations: the effects of team, task, processes, and context can be utilized in theory-building in the area of teamwork and mental models and as a framework for designing and investigating research, training, and practice in organizational teams. The article focuses on findings which suggest that more work is required to make the TMM concept of value to people in the field attempting to improve team performance. Thus, the current work aims to explicate the concept and show how it can be reconceptualized to be of applied utility. In order to do this, the concept will first be discussed from a historical, comparative, analytic, and pragmatic perspective, drawing out pertinent theoretical and methodological issues. After a working concept has been defined, the literature will be integrated with that of skill acquisition to highlight the developmental nature of TMMs, and allow for cross-fertilization of the already sophisticated theoretical ideas present in the skill acquisition field. Finally, growing out of the developmental perspective of TMMs that is a consequence of the skill acquisition approach, applied considerations will be discussed.

THE DEVELOPMENT OF EFFECTIVE TEAMS

TMM Attributes

TMMs and teamwork in general are developed over time through extensive interaction. High performance teams do not generally form themselves but are developed through a range of factors such as organizational support, communication opportunities, and appropriate role allocation. Teams are in a continuous state of development or learning, as they face new tasks, members change, and understandings grow (see e.g. Langan-Fox et al., 2002b).

Thus the concept of TMM is multifaceted and complex. It is made more complicated by the fact that various researchers have defined, measured, and utilized TMMs in different ways (Klimoski & Mohammed, 1994). In some respects the domain TMMs occupy and the utility it provides is dependent on how broadly it is defined. Thus, it would be beneficial to draw out the different attributes of possible definitions of TMMs in order to decide how best to define the construct.

With appropriate support, fluent teams can emerge where cooperation and coordination of activities occur. These variables are crucial in understanding how expert teams arise.

COOPERATION

Cooperation, the "shared effort by individuals, groups, or political units for common economic, political, or social benefit" (Encarta, 2001), implies goodwill between involved parties but may simply be a function of mutual benefit. Such a concept goes to the essence of teams. As stated in the foregoing, people work in teams because there is a belief by team creators that teams will produce output that is in some way superior than if the individuals were to act alone. This may be in the form of higher creativity, improved efficiency, or increased, higher-quality output. Cooperation and interdependence discriminate teams from groups, which is suggestive of the team's potential to transform organizational effectiveness.

Cooperation is a component of a TMM (Jones & George, 1998). Team members have conceptions of team climate; how much support can be expected from other team members; how coordinated and fluid the team coordination process is; and how cooperation is provided by external stakeholders to aid the team in completion of their goals. Cooperation is the individual difference factor explaining team relations. Chatman and Barsade (1995) found that cooperative individuals in collectivistic cultures were reported to work with the greatest number of people, and had the strongest preferences for evaluating work performance on the basis of contributions to teams rather than individual achievement.

COMMONALITY

The term "team mental model" does not refer to multiple levels or sets of shared knowledge, nor is it simply an aggregate of the mental models of individual team members. Rather, it refers to some inherent degree of similarity or overlap that exists among the mental models of individual team members. This attribute is implied in that it involves a similarity or commonality in mental models. The attribute of congruence is defined specifically in terms of the relationship between the individual mental model and the degree to which they are similar between individuals in a team. Thus, if individual team members have a similar understanding of the task, a similar understanding of their purpose and role within the organization, and a similar understanding of each other's strengths and weaknesses, the overlap between individual mental models could be described as the TMM. Commonality is theorized to improve team performance by improving coordination or activities and making communication more efficient.

Commonality may also be indicative of the fact that the team has a more accurate mental model. Consensus is generally used as an indication that ideas have been communicated and discussed throughout the team and that there is least some form of rationale for holding them, although this may not always be the case. Implications for inaccuracy of the TMM based on low commonality are dependent on whether team members hold contradicting mental models in a particular domain or whether the mental models are merely more developed in some people than others. For example, someone new to a team may not understand team norms and processes and thus does not share a mental model with the team leader who may have a developed mental model of team processes. The implications of this example might be that the new team member requires team training. This is different from when two team members conflict over how work should be done or how team members should interact with one other. Such differences in commonality require conflict resolution.

This immediately raises issues about how similar the individual mental models need to be in order to be considered the same or strongly similar. It also raises the question of how many individuals need to hold the same understanding before it is deemed representative of the team. One problem with this definition, if taken too literally, is that it can result in a lowest common denominator effect. For example, if one team member out of five does not understand something about the task that the other four do, does that mean that that knowledge does not form part of the TMM? Thus, while congruence is important, it would seem that in order for the TMM concept to have utility, congruence needs to be seen in perspective, while acknowledging the other types of relationships between individual members' mental models that can influence team performance. Cannon-Bowers and Salas (2001) summarized the key questions which need to be answered in relation to shared cognitions: What must be shared? What does shared mean? How should shared be measured? What outcomes do we expect shared cognition to affect? (p. 195).

COMPLEMENTARITY

A third attribute of the TMM construct is that of complementariness. Previously, it was an untested assumption that the greater the degree of overlap in TMMs, all things being equal, the higher the performance of the team. However, from empirical studies that have been conducted, investment in achieving congruence in TMMs may result in a redundancy of learning and a loss of specialization. Research into teams of software engineers (Levesque, Wilson, & Wholey, 2001) showed that contrary to predictions, team members' mental models about the group's work and each other's expertise did not become more similar over time. Structural equation modelling revealed that as role differentiation increased in these teams, it led to a decrease in interaction and a corresponding decline in shared mental models. From this study and others (e.g. Cannon-Bowers & Salas, 2001), it has become apparent that there may be something more important than mental model congruence, especially when the task is one involving role differentiation.

The importance of mental model complementariness to the conceptualizing of TMMs includes the following organizational rationales: teams may attempt to combine the expertise of group members so that the total knowledge is greater than any of the individuals; teams provide an ideal environment to develop new staff by positioning experts with new recruits in order to encourage the transfer of knowledge and skills across the organization; what differentiates a team from a group is the team's capacity to be mutually reliant which often involves role differentiation. Through role differentiation, people are able to specialize their skills to maximize group outcomes.

TEAM TASK CONTEXT

When addressing the question of the relative importance of commonality versus complementarity in TMMs, it is important to identify the contexts and domains when one is more important than another. Context refers to what the team does, whether they are software engineers, manufacturing work teams, or operating room teams. Contexts where complementarity is likely to be important would be when teams require specialized knowledge, there is clear role differentiation, division of labour and structure to team processes, and where creativity and diversity of opinions are important. Commonality is likely to be highly important when the context is in many respects the opposite to that stated for complementarity, including when interaction and communication levels are high, processes are implied, and when the task is unstructured. In addition to context, domains of TMMs vary in requirements for complementarity and commonality. Some domains such as team processes, shared vocabulary, and knowledge of team members' strengths and abilities may require greater commonality to improve team performance.

Clearly both factors are important, but it is likely that in some cases putting resources into complementarity may lead to less commonality. This is the case in cross-disciplinary teams. Such teams have the potential to do improved work because the combined pool of knowledge is greater. However, the challenge that results from less commonality may require work to develop a common language between team members. Teams with a transactional style will benefit more from shared mental models.

From the foregoing, it becomes apparent that the teams' potential to function effectively is not only a function of having a congruent understanding, but also a complementary understanding. Complementariness can be defined as the degree to which individual mental models aid and assist the teams' understanding. Similarly, Klimonski and Mohammed (1994) suggested that in order for shared mental models to exist, two team members not only need to have the same understanding of a particular team domain but also need to be aware that the other person has the same understanding. In this sense the concept of shared understanding also involves sharing the workload or what Klimoski and Mohammed

(1994) have referred to as dividing the mental model (see also Mohammed & Dumville, 2001).

DISTRIBUTED COGNITION

Traditionally in psychology the individual is seen as the unit of analysis for understanding cognitive processes and problem solving. Banks and Millward (2000) suggest that theory normally takes the individual as its unit of analysis. However, the interactions of individual members' mental models may form a phenomenon that has an effect on performance beyond the individual alone. Exploring this concept, Banks and Millward found that cognitive processes used in a team-reasoning task were distributed among the team and with the consequent organization of the sharing having an influence on the problem-solving processes.

If it is accepted that the TMM is in some way related to the teams' capacity to function and is not reliant on absolute congruence for an idea to be considered part of the TMM, there arises a need to understand the distribution of knowledge and power within a team. Constructs from social network analysis might be of benefit here (Langan-Fox et al., 2001; Robins, Pattison, & Langan-Fox, 1995). TMMs can be described in terms of density (i.e. the number of members with a shared understanding), intensity of exchange, and as nodes that are outliers and bridges within various team networks such as power, information exchange, and task execution. Such a conceptualization of the TMM construct moves beyond an understanding where a TMM either does or does not exist, to one where the level of complementarity and congruence can be seen as an indicator of the type and sophistication of the TMM, providing greater utility as a diagnostic tool in setting out how teams can improve their coordination of activities and highlight what knowledge or information needs to be exchanged to improve team functioning.

THEORETICAL CHALLENGES

Representations of TMMs

While the TMM construct provides insight into team processes and assists in developing teams' potential, several challenges exist which serve to confuse discussion, stultify theory development, and limit industry applicability (Canon-Bowers & Salas, 2001; Klimoski & Mohammed, 1994; Mohammed & Dumville, 2001). However, some inroads have been made in the area of measurement.

MEASUREMENT

Measurement of TMMs is a major problem for the TMM construct. Current measures are generally time and labour intensive and may fail to tap into the desired construct (see Langan-Fox, Code, & Langfield-Smith, 2000; Mohammed, Klimoski, & Rentsch, 2000, for reviews of methodologies and analytic techniques). One problem is that the measurement tool can define the construct. However, the paradox is that until the construct is defined, it is very difficult to design measures for it. It would appear, also, that some of the measures are quite computationally intensive, suggesting that as the cost decreases and power of computers increases over time, more powerful measures will be available. There is a need for greater comparisons of measures so that the value of the different measures can be ascertained. In addition the predictive and developmental value of the measures needs to be further developed.

MULTIPLE CONSTRUCTS

Klimoski and Mohammed (1994) highlighted the fact that there is a diverse range of constructs related to team and shared mental models with a great deal of commonality between them. Such a multiplicity of constructs can inhibit knowledge exchange across the different disciplines by preventing developments in one construct from filtering through to another. Specific issues that need to be resolved relate to:

(a) whether TMMs should be conceptualized as a single entity or whether a team possesses multiple TMMs;
(b) whether members need to be mutually aware of their shared understanding for that knowledge to contribute to the conception of the team's mental model;
(c) the amount of congruence both in relation to the content of members' understanding and the number of team members, for a set of ideas to be considered part of the TMM;
(d) whether complementariness should form part of the construct of TMMs or whether such an understanding should be considered a separate concept altogether.

Until such theoretical difficulties are resolved, the development of the concept in relation to developing theory, measurement, and a surrounding body of empirical work will be hampered.

MENTAL MODEL OVERLAP

Notwithstanding the benefits of teams developing a TMM, the process of analysing mental model similarity or overlap at the team level has proven to be an obstacle for researchers (Klimoski & Mohammed, 1994). For instance, while a number of techniques have been developed to measure mental model similarity dyadically, the development of techniques to elicit and represent TMMs has been slow (Converse, Cannon-Bowers, & Salas, 1991). Furthermore, the few techniques that have been generated (e.g. Eby et al., 1998; Heffner, Mathieu, & Cannon-Bowers, 1998) are lacking in that they either cannot compare more than two mental models at once, or where more than two mental models can be compared, make assumptions about uniformity or normality which might otherwise be considered inappropriate. The measurement of mental model similarity must be related to some sensible mathematical construct of similarity. It should also be possible to use the measure in some kind of distribution-free statistical analysis that does not rely on random sampling since, particularly in an organizational context, it may be difficult to gain access to participants which would then lead to small, non-random samples (see e.g. Langan-Fox et al., 2001).

DEGREES OF MENTAL MODEL OVERLAP

A problem exists in specifying the optimal degree of overlap among team members. Generally speaking, most researchers agree that a major benefit of teamwork is that team members are able to bring multiple perspectives to bear on the problem at hand. However, a high degree of mental model overlap could be likened to the phenomenon of "groupthink" (Janis, 1972) in which the desire to maintain team cohesion (through unanimity) is awarded priority over the decision-making process, and the evaluation and consideration of divergent viewpoints become neglected. An undesirable degree of overlap could occur if team members refused to abandon inaccurate mental models because the rest of the team held these models to be correct (Cannon-Bowers, Salas, & Converse, 1993). Conversely, too little shared knowledge could lead to poor coordination, thus reducing the team's ability to cope with, and adapt to, changing environmental demands (Cannon-Bowers, Salas, & Converse, 1993). It could be the case that the optimal distribution of knowledge, that is, mental model overlap, varies according to the team task situation (Greene, 1989), or that different kinds of knowledge may be optimally distributed in the team in different ways (Heffner, Mathieu, & Cannon-Bowers, 1998). There is some agreement that broader distributions of knowledge are beneficial to teams that operate in particular environments such as when the jobs of team members are homogeneous rather than divisible and when the status differences between team members are small rather than large (Carley, 1990; Wilkins & Ouchi, 1983). Since poorly coordinated teams would be likely to fail, Cannon-Bowers, Salas, and Converse (1993) have maintained that the simple answer to the question of optimal overlap is that TMMs should be fostered as much as possible. Research is needed into this issue as, unfortunately, little is known about the dynamics of optimally distributed knowledge in teams (Kraiger & Wenzel, 1997).

Thus, there is a certain intangible quality to TMMs which has no doubt led to the multiplicity of construct definitions. Klimoski and Mohammed (1994), when reviewing the literature, examined whether shared mental models were a metaphor or a scientific construct and concluded that it did have the necessary elements and clarity to be a scientific construct. But the very fact that these researchers (Klimoski & Mohammed, 1994) asked this question hints at the abstractness of the construct. Are TMMs something that exist at a social level or are they merely an abstraction from individual mental models? If they do have some tangible quality, how should this be represented and conceptualized?

There is also the issue that TMMs have tended to be used in a prescriptive sense and as synonymous with shared or congruent mental models. But as has previously been discussed, there is some doubt as to whether common understanding is always beneficial to team performance or the best way to conceptualize what occurs in TMMs. In addition TMMs have often been seen as a categorical variable, as either present or not present.

COMPONENTS OF THE TMM

It would seem more beneficial to treat TMMs as something descriptive and occurring on several dimensions. Thus, all teams would be understood to have a TMM, but the nature, quality, and effectiveness of this TMM could be described. Such a description would be explicit to team goals and congruence and mutual awareness would become descriptive dimensions. The concept of complementariness could also be developed further and be defined in prescriptive terms with an explicit applied meaning as the effectiveness to which the interaction of individual member mental models meets team goals.

One important distinction within the TMM construct is between those components pertaining to the team and those to the task. Task mental models are concerned with technical skills and task-relevant knowledge and are closely tied to the individual mental models that team members have that are based on their skills and competencies. At a team level, task mental models represent an aggregation of the task-relevant skills of the team. Team knowledge features suggested by Cooke et al. (2000) include task type and team processes. The aggregation includes lowest common denominator representations, reflecting skills that every member has, and all-encompassing representations reflecting the total amount of knowledge and skills that are present in the team, even if held by only one member. Alternatively, team process mental models are concerned with processes of team interaction, understanding fellow team members' strengths and weaknesses, social and political considerations, and need for certain actions like anticipation of other members' training or information needs. TMMs guide the provision and acceptance of feedback, allocation of roles, and the interactions that occur within the team.

HIERARCHICAL NATURE OF THE TEAM TASK

It is possible to link the concept of TMMs in a hierarchical fashion. In such a system TMMs are an emergent phenomenon that comes about from the interactions of the individual mental models of the team members in relation to team-based activities. The individual mental models are also made of particular individual mental models that operate for sets of domains. Figure 16.1 displays these relationships, highlighting the multiple levels of analysis that can be used when attempting to understand mental models within a team context. When interpreting the model it should be noted that the individual domains of mental models held by team members cover similar domains, and in the sense that there is a shared mental model between members there will be cross-over in perspective and content.

For the purpose of identifying elements of the task in which team interaction occurs, an analysis of the task can be performed. Hierarchical task analysis (HTA) was developed by Annett and Duncan (1967) and has been further elaborated by Shepard (1985) and Patrick (1992). It is a means of analysing and breaking a task down into its constituent component tasks. The four main features of HTA are hierarchical breakdown, operations, criterion for stopping analysis, and plans. Hierarchical breakdown is the process of taking a general task and progressively breaking it down into an exhaustive set of constituent subtasks, which are in turn broken down into finer-grained distinctions. Operations are the unit of analysis and are "any unit of behaviour, no matter how long or short its duration and no matter how simple or complex its structure which can be defined in terms of its objective" (Annett et al., 1971). Criterion for stopping analysis is a heuristic for determining how many levels of subtasks are required for functional purposes and is defined as the combination of the probability that without training inadequate performance will occur and the cost to the system of inadequate performance. Finally, the plan integrates these tasks into a procedure or strategy that guides when and in what order an individual will carry out component tasks.

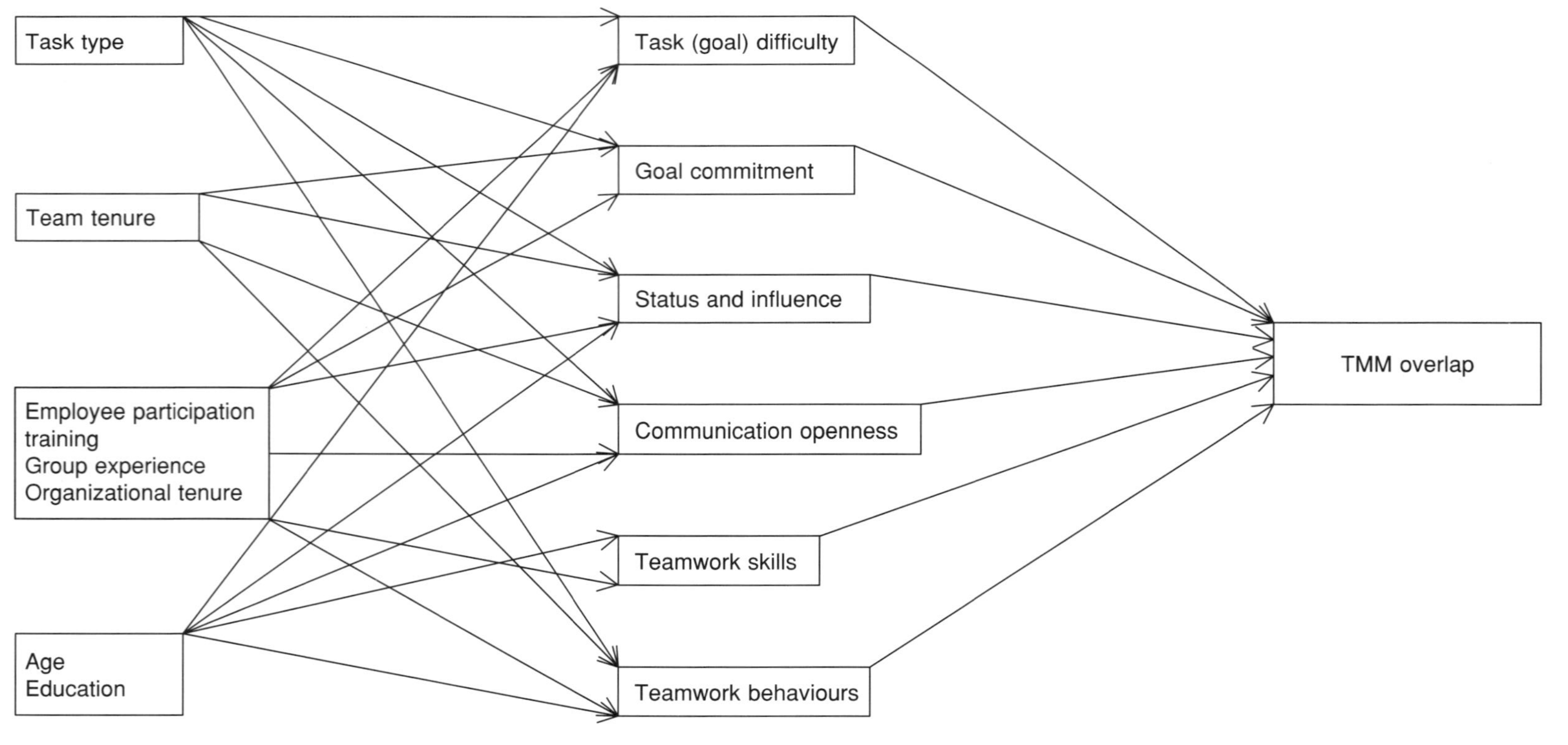

Figure 16.1 Relationship between individual and TMMs

HTA TO TMMs

Benefits of this approach include the fact that it is flexible in analysis requirements, has broad applicability, facilitates translation of tasks into training objectives, and is logically exhaustive. Disadvantages are that it is difficult and is strongly based on the ability of the analyst to exhaust and understand the domain. Other approaches include critical incident technique (Flanagan, 1954) which involves observing and recording either extremely good or poor examples of task behaviour and proceeding through a process of categorization, interpretation, and reporting with the aim of identifying task components and training needs. Task inventories involve getting lists of tasks rated across a range of measures, such as applicability, time spent, difficulty, etc., on a particular job.

Several elements of the task then can be isolated and an attempt made to ascertain those points of the task where there is mental model overlap. It may be useful to distinguish between the concept of shared mental models to describe overlap and the concept of complementary mental model as synonymous with TMMs. The TMM reflects what the team is capable of. The TMM reflects its potential to solve problems, predict outcomes, and perform tasks. Just as individual mental models map closely with the understanding that an individual has of the environment, systems, and task and relates to their performance potential, the TMM should relate to the teams' understanding of environment/system/task. Mohammed and Dumville (2001) suggest that there is a need to qualify the knowledge similarity concept. Overlapping knowledge in teams with distinct roles may be inefficient, create a redundancy of effort, and contribute to a less than optimal use of resources. Therefore, rather than measuring similarity globally and assuming that all team members need to have common knowledge in all domains, future research should work towards specifying the domains and conditions under which distributed and common knowledge will aid or hinder team performance.

The working definition of TMMs used in this chapter involves TMMs being the team level phenomena that are involved in team task completion. TMMs are emergent phenomena that come out of the interactions of the individual mental models. These individual mental models may involve common features or may complement each other through skill differentiation. Mutual recognition is not at the essence of TMMs but merely represents one form of a more cohesive TMM. TMMs cover various domains, including the task itself and the social and interactional team processes.

TMMs AND SKILL ACQUISITION

In the foregoing discussion, the nature of the mental model and TMM concepts, and problems of shared understandings about team tasks and issues of measurement, have been explored. Further, issues of training have been highlighted; how some workers may not have the various skills and abilities necessary for teamwork, and how this issue draws attention to the utility of the TMM concept. We turn now to how a team member might acquire a TMM. Figure 16.2 presents the proposed components of a three-phase theory of TMM acquisition, from the initial novice phase to the high performance or expert team. It also draws out causal factors such as individual differences and accelerators, and performance-related outcome factors.

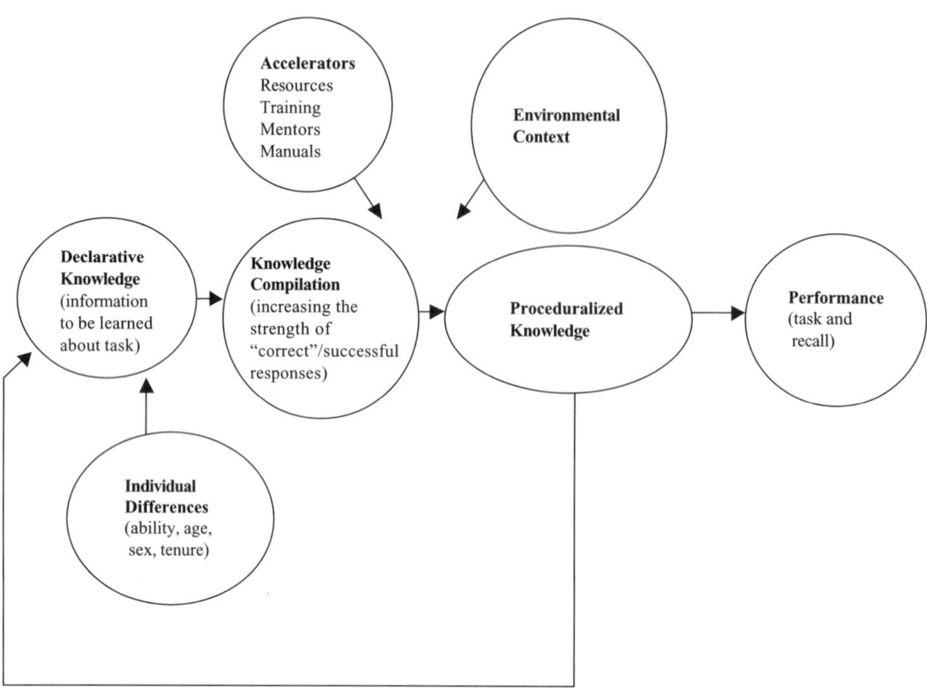

Figure 16.2 Acquisition and development of a mental model of team functioning

It can be concluded that team behaviour in organizations is affected by a combination of individual and team characteristics as well as the conditions of the overall organizational system. Although there are a number of taxonomies in the area of TMMs, progress towards a TMM theory has not been forthcoming (Klein, 1997). To this end, there is theoretical gain to be made in paralleling the acquisition and development of a TMM as comparable to skill acquisition phases. Research into skill acquisition and expert/novice differences illustrate the way in which knowledge is acquired, structured, and represented (Anderson, 1982, 1987; Langan-Fox et al., 2002a; Langan-Fox, Waycott, & Galna, 1997). The new integration called acquisition and development of team mental models (ADTMM) will draw upon the formative work of early theorists in skill acquisition, mental models, and other empirical work in the area of teams and processes.

The acquisition and development of a mental model are ongoing and changing, and cannot be well catered for by lock-step linear models represented by input–process–output research designs. There is no simple "end-product". Our model is therefore a process model that may describe, at one point in time, the shared understanding of the team about the team, task, and the team context. Thus our framework of mental models of team functioning also represents an attempt at identifying the important variables which would influence the ebb and flow of interactions in the organizational context, is strongly ecological, and somewhat phenomenological. At the same time, the model should provide the researcher with features of TMM acquisition and development that can be generalized beyond teams in particular organizations.

The development of TMMs can be described as a process consisting of three learning phases as identified by Anderson's ACT* cognitive skill acquisition model, that is, the declarative, knowledge compilation, and procedural phases (Anderson, 1982, 1987). In organizations, the phases of skill acquisition can be described in terms of team member challenges and experiences and how learners may be affected while completing the team task. Figure 16.2 could loosely be described as one simple example of how the individual and/or team acquires a mental model and the various stages involved in becoming an expert, from an initial stage of acquiring facts about the task, to a final stage when they have successfully completed the task. It is proposed that, secondly, as novices learn about teamwork, they progress through these phases and continue to engage in a learning phase that is typical of the feedback cycles found in cybernetic models. Models of self-regulation are instructive in illustrating the importance of feedback systems which operate through self-monitoring and salient reference values or standards (Carver & Scheier, 1982). Model features are described in more detail below. The Appendix gives some tentative propositions which could be tested by researchers in investigating the dynamics of the acquisition and development of TMMs. First, we describe the acquisition and development of a TMM as it relates to cognitive skill acquisition.

Phase 1: Declarative Phase

THE TEAM MEMBERS

Kay and Black (1990) presented a model of the acquisition of expertise which could be extended to describe the acquisition of any skill. According to this model, the team member builds complex knowledge representations by acquiring knowledge during different learning phases. The first stage is the building of preconceptions—the team member might have preconceptions about the team, the team task, and the organization, based on prior knowledge. Schumacher and Czerwinski's (1992) three-phase description of mental model development reflects cyclic changes in memory retrieval. This framework is based on the assumption that novices initially rely on the superficial features of a domain but with increasing expertise come to rely on the structural or causal features of it. So for novices, first impressions would help to determine initial knowledge of teamwork. These first impressions could be formed on the basis of team composition variables, for instance easily recognizable characteristics of individuals such as their age, sex, education, years of training, tenure, organizational experience, and other variables which we understand to be typically available from organizational records. In the pre-theoretic stage of the model, an individual's understanding is also based on similar instances in memory (analogies), that is, the similarities of the current system or domain, with other more familiar systems. Perhaps experience in groups or other teams might have influence at this stage. Additionally, it may be based on, or interpreted by, analogies with other teams with which the person is familiar. For example, individuals may perceive teamwork in an organization as analogous to playing in a football team. These analogies might be useful for initial understanding of teamwork and teamwork functions. The development of a mental model, then, could rely on collections of experiences that are retrieved from memory based on similarities to prior events.

Also, we know that the first stage of skill acquisition is based on declarative knowledge, that is, knowledge about teamwork which may be provided to learners in the form of instructions. During this stage, interactions that the person has with teamwork may be highly dependent upon rules (Blessing & Anderson, 1996). For example, Blessing and Anderson found that, initially, learners of simple algebra-type problems were heavily reliant upon given rules and examples, but with practice they learned to skip steps and to adapt their behaviour to complete tasks more quickly. Similarly, Norman (1983) observed that people often do extra physical operations rather than the mental planning that would allow them to avoid these actions. This is especially true where the extra actions allow one simplified rule to apply to a variety of situations, thus minimizing the chance of confusion. Presumably, this is how people initially understand a new set of interactions—in terms of broad rules that can be applied with the avoidance of confusion. Thus, learners' initial mental models are composed of declarative, rule-based knowledge that incorporates analogies with other familiar teamwork experiences and organizational systems.

Diversity

In the early stages of acquiring skill about working in teams, easily recognizable characteristics of individuals such as age, sex, education, years of training, tenure, organizational experience and the like, and other team composition variables would affect the new team members' perceptions of each other and also their expectations of each other's future team performance. The issue of diversity of team characteristics is an important early team formation variable, and there have been questions as to whether it is advantageous to have teams that are homogeneous or heterogeneous with respect to team member characteristics (Campion, Medsker, & Higgs, 1993; Guzzo & Dickson, 1996; Jackson, 1992, 1996; Maznevski, 1994; Tziner & Eden, 1985; West, 1997). Diversity can be measured along a number of different dimensions, but most researchers have focused on task-oriented attributes (e.g. specialized knowledge, skills, and abilities), and person-oriented attributes (those inherent to the individual, e.g. age, gender, ethnicity, seniority, personality) (Maznevski, 1994). It is well established at least for tasks that are truly interdependent that it is the level of task-oriented attributes in the team, not homogeneity, that is the crucial factor. For example, high-ability homogeneous teams outperform low-ability homogeneous teams (Tziner & Eden, 1985). However, since heterogeneity automatically implies that each team member will contribute a different set of knowledge and skills to the problem (a necessary ingredient for creative solutions), it should lead to superior performance on complex tasks (see e.g. Campion, Medsker, & Higgs, 1993; Guzzo & Dickson, 1996). In addition, there is some evidence to suggest that teams composed of combinations of person-oriented attributes (e.g. personality traits) perform better on particular tasks (see e.g. Driskell, Hogan, & Salas, 1987). Orpen (1987) refers to "an appropriate" mix of skills and traits and clearly takes the view that homogeneity is not desirable.

On the other hand, diversity can trigger stereotypes and prejudice which in turn (via group conflict) can affect team processes and outcomes (Jackson, 1996; Pfeffer, 1981). The theoretical descriptions that have guided much of the research on diversity in person-oriented attributes include the attraction–selection–attrition model (Schneider, 1987), similarity-attraction theory (Byrne, 1971), and self-categorization theory (Turner et al., 1987). A basic premise of these theories is that we are attracted to those who are similar to ourselves and repelled by those who are dissimilar. Indeed, there is considerable evidence to suggest that demographic characteristics such as age, sex, and education predict conflict, employee turnover, social integration, communication patterns, employee satisfaction, supervisor–subordinate relationships, absenteeism, and organizational commitment (see Mowday &

Sutton, 1993; O'Reilly, Caldwell, & Barnett, 1989; O'Reilly & Flatt, 1989; O'Reilly & Roberts, 1977).

A form of person-oriented diversity that has received particular attention is organizational tenure (Argote & McGrath, 1993). Katz (1982) found that the average group tenure in research and development teams was related to performance in the form of an inverted-U function: increases in group tenure or longevity were associated with increases in performance until about the two- to four-year mark and thereafter were associated with decreases in performance. O'Reilly and Flatt (1989) reported a negative relationship between tenure, diversity, and social integration which was in turn associated with higher turnover rates. The importance of affect and friendship ties, as a product of similarity of values, interests, and the like, has also been emphasized (George, 1989, 1990, 1995; Ibarra, 1992; Robins, Pattison, & Langan-Fox, 1995). George (1990) found that negative affect teams tended to be more rigid in their decision making than positive affect teams, an effect that he attributed to differences in TMM development. It seems, then, that one difficulty in TMM development could be the issue of diversity.

Status characteristics

Besides helping to determine preconceptions about team members, one of the most important aspects of team composition "diversity" is the affect it exerts on status and influence processes. These processes can be captured very well by network and process variables as in the proposed model. The fact that diversity of team member attributes has been linked to attitudes and behaviours in organizational teams (e.g. Pfeffer, 1981) suggests that workers must process and evaluate the characteristics of their workmates in some way. Status characteristics (SC) theoreticians describe how knowledge and attitudes about teammate characteristics are translated into beliefs about the relative status of individuals in the team. Status characteristics theory (SCT) suggests that the order of influence in small groups can be attributed to expectations about performance activated by status characteristics: "... any characteristic that has differentially evaluated states that are associated directly or indirectly with expectation states" (Berger et al., 1977, p. 35). Status characteristics may be external to the team or emerge during the course of interaction (Umberson & Hughes, 1987). The significance of external (or diffuse) status characteristics is defined in the larger social context, prior to and outside the task situation. Examples include gender, education level, seniority in the organization, and whether or not an individual is formally designated as group leader. In contrast, the expectations associated with an internal (or specific) status characteristic are limited to a particular task or situation, e.g. "most valuable team member" or "most helpful technical adviser" (see e.g. Cohen & Zhou, 1991). Since interacting on a collective task requires individuals to estimate the abilities of themselves and others, they will use status characteristics in that estimation, unless there are specific barriers to such use (Cohen & Zhou, 1991). On any given task, the high status affiliates of a status characteristic will automatically be perceived as more competent than the low status affiliates unless there is specific information to suggest otherwise and is typically known as the "burden of proof principle" (see e.g. Cohen & Zhou, 1991). Where individuals possess more than one distinguishing status characteristic, this information will be combined to produce an aggregate status level. The more direct the linkage, or the shorter the path of task relevance between a differentiating status characteristic and a task outcome, the greater the strength of the bond between them and the differentiating effect of the characteristic. This has typically been known as the "path of relevance principle" (see e.g. Berger et al., 1977). As a result of such processes, a schema for the relative influence of each team member is formed in which some degree of consensus and predictability in the team context is granted (Riley & Burke, 1995).

The expectations derived from status characteristics will powerfully determine the prestige order in the team and be manifest in inequalities in interaction. Specifically, distributions of participation level, influence attempts and acceptances, and evaluations, correspond to this power and prestige order (Cohen & Zhou, 1991). Shetzer (1993), while ignoring the importance of task and environment/context models, argued that individuals classify task situations in terms of the relative influence of actors along a "relative equality" to "extreme inequality" continuum and that team interaction can only proceed efficiently when team members share the same action-related knowledge.

THE TEAM TASK

Besides encountering each other as described in the foregoing, the task itself dominates the thinking of individual members. A task is the piece of work to be accomplished and it is possible for the completion of the task to be a goal. In most goal-setting studies, however, the term "goal" refers to attaining a specific standard of proficiency of a given task usually within a specified time limit (Locke & Latham, 1990). A goal is most likely to be achieved when it is in a moderate range of difficulty and there are no constraints to block goal attainment (Locke & Latham, 1990). If a goal is not set within an appropriate range of difficulty for the individual (i.e. if it is perceived as too difficult or too complex) then it will not be attained (Bandura, 1986). Similarly, if goal attainment is blocked by constraints in the environment, the person is less likely to attain the goal (Locke & Latham, 1990). Also tasks that are ill structured or ambiguous may hold an added dimension of difficulty and complexity for team members which may block performance. For instance, teams often develop poor strategies for task completion when faced with difficult goals and tasks of moderate to high complexity particularly when they are unfamiliar with the task (Earley, Lee, & Hanson, 1990). A further complication is a decline in goal commitment. A number of studies have shown that as goal difficulty increases and/or the person's perceived chances of reaching the goal decline, commitment to that goal decreases (see e.g. Erez & Zidon, 1984). These influences presumably take place through the effects of goal difficulty on expectancy and self-efficacy (Locke & Latham, 1990). Poor goal (or task) commitment in a team may present itself as a malaise or illness that begins to grow evident in team processes and performance. Evidence for a positive relationship between goal commitment and performance has been demonstrated in several studies (see e.g. Allscheid & Cellar, 1996; Klein & Kim, 1998; Klein & Wright, 1994; Martin & Manning, 1995; Theodorakis, 1996).

Planning

One tool that can be used to combat difficult and complex tasks is planning. Generally speaking, there are two types of planning: pre-planning which is planning that takes place prior to the onset of task performance, and in-process planning, planning that takes place during task performance (Weingart, 1992). In-process planning reduces uncertainty in unfamiliar task situations because information gained while working on the task can be integrated into the plan as the task progresses. Weingart (1992) found that the quality of the planning process mediated the relationship between the amount of planning and team performance in problem-solving teams. However, only planning about resources and team member roles were important to performance. In-process planning appeared to be central in the planning process and constituted a larger percentage of total planning in the teams than did pre-planning. In addition, there is evidence to suggest setting goals at both the individual and the team level leads to higher goal commitment (see e.g. Bandura, 1986; Brickner & Bukatko, 1987).

Task type difficulty

Although a task can be considered in one sense a goal, we think that the variable of "task type" has substantial implications for the team and its potential success in the sense that more difficult tasks will preoccupy and test the skills of the team than more simple tasks. The influence of task design on team performance has been well documented (Campion, Medsker, & Higgs, 1993; Campion, Papper, & Medsker, 1996; Cohen, Ledford, & Spreitzer, 1994; Drory & Shamir, 1988; Gladstein, 1984; Goodman, 1986; Steiner, 1972). Interest in task design can be traced back to an early study by Kent and McGrath (1969) who found that task characteristics accounted for 87.9 per cent of the variance in group performance. Subsequent research has resulted in a number of task classification schemes. American researchers in the field of task design have tended to classify tasks at a global level such that each task is assigned to one category (West, Borrill, & Unsworth, 1998). For example, Steiner (1972) distinguished between unitary, maximizing, optimizing, conjunctive, disjunctive, and additive tasks. McGrath's (1984) Group Task Circumplex classified task design according to four different performance functions: generating, choosing, resolving, and executing. In contrast, European researchers have tended to classify team tasks in terms of their hierarchical (goals and subgoals), sequential (the order in which different parts of the task are carried out), and cyclical process requirements (e.g. generating goals, planning, decision making, executing behaviour, and reviewing performance for each element of the task) (see West, Borrill, & Unsworth, 1998, for a complete description). One dimension of task design that is highly relevant in the complex setting of an organization is task ambiguity. Grummon (1997) argued that tasks range in their level of ambiguity from well structured to ill structured or ambiguous. The most well-structured tasks are ones with a single "right" answer or solution or a particular performance target (e.g. productivity). Somewhat more ambiguous are tasks requiring teams to generate one or more solutions to problems that have vague boundaries. The most ambiguous or ill-structured tasks are ones where there are numerous solutions and often few criteria for deciding what represents an acceptable solution. Examples of "real world", ill-structured, ambiguous tasks include, for instance, the design and installation of new machinery or setting up a career structure for part-time workers. Complex tasks such as these are tied to the broader organizational context of the team and require deliberation not only within the team itself, but also with key stakeholders in the organizational environment external to the team.

Teams having well-structured tasks may interact in ways that differ from teams with ambiguous tasks (Grummon, 1997). For example, since there are unlikely to be more than a few ways of achieving the goal of well-structured tasks, team members could be likely to simply turn to the team member perceived as the most competent or knowledgeable for the solution. This approach tends to focus team discussion on existing expertise and may result in limited interaction among team members through, say, less contention about what should be done. As a result, status differentials may become particularly salient, with members simply following the dictates of various experts within the team and where perhaps less effort is required of the team (e.g. discussion and problem solving). In contrast, tasks with greater ambiguity may encourage a broader range of team member participation by virtue of the fact that the endpoint of the task has yet to be defined and many subtasks exist for reaching the final goal. Ambiguous problems and difficult–complex tasks, then, could have the effect of reducing status differentials and increase the need for teamwork in completing the team task.

THE ORGANIZATIONAL CONTEXT

Although modest in volume compared to the more traditional areas of team research, the impact of the organizational environment or context on individual and team behaviour has become an important area of investigation (O'Reilly, 1991). Few precise definitions of the organizational context are evident in the literature; however, reviews by Campelli and Sherer (1993) and Cummings (1981) suggest that it encompasses the environment external to the individual and/or team, and phenomena that surround and thus exist within the environment external to the individual and/or team. A person's location within the social context of the organization—the people, jobs, tools, organizational change, and the organization as a whole—influences his/her experience of organizational life.

In the past 20 years, the contextual factors thought to be important to team functioning have grown from a few selected "inputs" to a long list of factors that have been examined both theoretically and empirically, and a number of models of organizational context have been proposed. Sundstrom, DeMuese, and Futrell (1990) argued for an eight-factor model of organizational context: organizational culture, technology, task design, mission clarity, autonomy, rewards, performance feedback, training, consultation, and the physical environment. In contrast, Hackman (1990) suggested reward, educational, and information systems are important features of the organizational context, and there is some support for the effects of reward systems (e.g. Hackman, 1983; Steiner, 1972) and feedback on team effectiveness (e.g. Locke & Latham, 1990). Tannenbaum, Beard, and Salas (1992) proposed that there are eight key aspects of the organizational context: reward systems, resource scarcity, management control, level of organizational stress, organizational climate, competition, inter-group relations within the organization, and environmental uncertainty. However, West, Borrill, and Unsworth (1998) argued that while these factors have high face validity in models of work group functioning there is little evidence of their effects on work group effectiveness. More recently, Cohen and Bailey (1997) pointed to customer expectations and the diffusion of work practices as important features of the organizational context. They described "organizational context design variables", features that can be directly manipulated by managers to create conditions for effective performance and which included rewards, supervision, training, and resources.

Physical context

A large part of the work environment consists of workspace characteristics, such as room darkness, interpersonal distance, and social density (Oldham & Fried, 1987). Steele (1986) provided examples of the effects of physical setting features (furniture arrangements, trafficways, aisles, lighting, design of entrances) on organizational behaviour (breaks in concentration, fatigue, stress, stimulation of thought and action). Features such as job differentiation, density of people in the work area, and proximity of other workers have been linked to processes such as communication and attitude formation (Monge, Edwards, & Kirste, 1983; Rice & Ayden, 1991). For instance, Rice and Ayden (1991) reported that employees' attitudes towards a new data processing system were similar to those of their supervisor and others with whom they interacted on a regular basis at work. These effects of "proximal information systems" were found even after controlling for the effects of system usage, occupational characteristics, and attitude levels in employee work teams.

Cultural context

A recent shift in the team processes literature has been to consider the cultural context of teams (West, Borrill, & Unsworth 1998). Hofstede (1980) distinguished four different cultural dimensions across which teams may vary. Smith and Noakes (1996) argued that variation in these dimensions is likely to be related to team processes. Individualistic cultures, for example, may view a team as a set of individuals who are each responsible for a specific part of the task, while a collectivist culture may define a team as a set of individuals who share responsibility for all aspects of the task.

Phase 2: Knowledge Compilation

At the experiential stage of Schumacher and Czerwinski (1992) and Kay and Black's (1990) second stage of skill acquisition, the goal of initial learning is that the team member overcomes the prior knowledge bias and an understanding of causal relationships emerges. In the model being outlined, it is difficult to state when this second phase would occur. Indeed in the skill acquisition literature there is no way of accurately determining when learning passes from one phase to another (see Ackerman, 1988; Langan-Fox, Waycott, & Galna, 1997). But one example might be through the actions of individual members, say a leader, who makes various initiatives, which are then taken up by the team. Once individuals have acquired basic knowledge, they learn the combinations of requirements that are often used together to accomplish goals. The novice is able to increase expertise: users combine simple plans into more compound plans to accomplish major goals and develop rules for selecting the best plan to achieve a given goal in a particular situation. There is also a reorganization of the knowledge that results in the development of new links between the components of the representation.

In this phase as the learner gains some experience and involvement in the team, procedures specific to the task develop that do not require the active maintenance of declarative knowledge about how to be involved in teamwork, and how to do the team task. That is, the learner gradually constructs (compiles) a set of skill-specific productions that directly incorporate the relevant declarative knowledge (Charney & Reder, 1987). As Blessing and Anderson (1996) have shown, for some tasks, learners may be able to skip steps thus performing the team task in less time. They suggest that initially learners are unable to do this because they follow the given rules. However, with practice they pick up short cuts and begin to apply them, for instance, they get to know "how things get done around here", making the problems easier to solve in one step. Kay and Black (1990) also suggested that during their "plan development" stage (which can be likened to the knowledge compilation stage of the ACT model), individuals begin to realize certain mistakes they have made. This realization leads to a reorganization of the knowledge representation to accommodate the command sequences or plans that are used to accomplish goals. That is, team members learn that there are combinations of rules (norms, values of the team and others in the organization), which are often used together to accomplish goals, so they are able to form plans by combining the actions that were previously represented separately. Similarly, Roschelle (1996) found that when students encounter a new system they initially construct knowledge that is sufficient for solving most tasks but bears little similarity to scientific knowledge. With practice, the students encountered problems and in their attempt to resolve these problematic experiences they transformed their mental models dramatically, bringing them closer to an expert's model.

During phase 2 the role of self-correction becomes more refined. Self-correction is a process carried out by effective teams and involves reviewing events, correcting errors, discussing strategies, and planning for future events (Blickensderfer, Cannon-Bowers, & Salas, 1997). Blickensderfer, Cannon-Bowers, and Salas (1997) argue that effective teams have a natural tendency to self-correct their team cognitions, attitudes, and behaviours without an outside intervention. The key requirement for such behaviour to be facilitated is opportunities for communication.

It is proposed that after people have some experience at working as a team, going through a trial-and-error process of discovering inadequacies in their existing knowledge and possible short cuts that they could use, their mental models develop to incorporate production rules which are constructed and compiled. Therefore, knowledge comes to involve greater understanding of the connections among features and functions of the team, teamwork, and the organization, and relies less upon analogies to other familiar groups and teams.

THE TEAM, TASK, AND ENVIRONMENTAL CONTEXT

Internal and external team relations

One of the ways in which learning how to make "short cuts" would highly benefit the team as it makes its progress towards achieving its task is in the way the team negotiates the relations internal to the team and relations external to it. This aspect of teamwork may provide the strongest test of team members' skills.

Traditional models of team processes tend to treat teams as closed systems or settings that shape individual attitudes, attributions, and decisions, with the major focus being on interaction among team members (Ancona, 1990). Such models hypothesize that a team will perform well to the extent that it manages its internal processes. In reality, however, such a view is much too simple. Crucial to the success of an organizational team is its ability to negotiate and navigate its way in and around the sociocultural, organizational environment. Teams need to interact with individuals and groups outside the team in order to acquire resources, gain legitimacy, manipulate systems (including politics), understand and meet their performance requirements, coordinate their activities with other teams (e.g. union), and so forth (Argote & McGrath, 1993; Campelli & Sherer, 1991). Thus, in studying organizational teams, it is important to extend the theoretical lens from the team boundary outwards, such that the focus shifts to a team in its context, which has an existence and purpose beyond the individuals composing it. We use the term "external relations" (Ancona, 1990; Ancona & Caldwell, 1989, 1992) to refer to the collection of strategies the team uses in interacting with the sociocultural environment, including management, co-workers, outside agencies, unions, shift groups, organizational committees, and others who have the potential to affect the team task.

Research interest in external relations can be traced to a study of 100 sales teams in the telecommunications industry (Gladstein, 1984) which found that while internal relations activity predicted team member satisfaction and ratings of team performance, only external relations activity predicted an objective, external measure of performance, sales revenue. Gladstein (1984) concluded that external relations which had been virtually ignored in the literature previously affected organizational team performance in ways that internal relations did not. Ancona and Caldwell (1992) reported that a key difference between teams with high and low levels of external relations was the team task. For example, a higher degree of external relations was found in teams where the team task was of high priority or importance and required innovation, flexibility, and imagination. Ancona and Caldwell (1992) suggested that the high level of external relations exhibited by these teams was possibly due to a greater pressure to obtain input from other parts of the organization. Team-level antecedents of external relations were specialized roles, experience, skills, and personality: team leaders engaged in more external relations in general and more upward relations (as opposed to lateral) than team members; team members with prior team experience were more likely to engage in external relations than team members with no prior team experience; and those who engaged in external relations were often those with the most technical knowledge, although these individuals often lacked the interpersonal skills to promote the team and negotiate with outsiders.

Achieving a balance between internal and external demands may be one of the most difficult tasks faced by organizational teams. In order to perform successfully, the team must satisfy the requirements of the broader organizational system yet at the same time maintain enough independence to perform its own specialized functions. It will be recalled that earlier in this chapter it was argued that there is probably a skill shortfall in team training. It is in managing the demands of internal and external relations where this shortfall may be most apparent. High external relations activity may have long-term costs for the cohesiveness of the team: team members may have the external knowledge they need but lack the cohesion to pool their perspectives due to substantial investments of time being lost to external activity (Ancona, 1990). Therefore, external relations may present the most challenging aspect of the team's overall activity to complete their task.

On the basis of recent research with teams (Langan-Fox, Code, & Langfield-Smith, 2000; Langan-Fox et al., 2001), six forms of external relations are proposed:

1. Obtaining information: identifying outsiders who can supply task-related and political information and ideas;
2. Obtaining resources: obtaining support, materials, and assistance;
3. Threat evaluation: interpreting, signalling, and gauging individuals who may be a threat to the team;
4. Moulding opinion: influencing and persuading those who are important to the team task;
5. Coordination: coordinating the team's activity with other individuals or groups;
6. Performance monitoring: gaining information about the likelihood of meeting performance requirements.

Another factor that has been linked with external relations is the physical proximity of key individuals and groups in the environment external to the team. Ivancevich (1972, 1974) argued for the importance of frequent team–manager interaction. The manager, responsible for the distribution information to suppliers, workers, and customers, provides a key channel through which the team can achieve two-way, upward, downward, horizontal communication throughout the organization. The capacity for external relations activity may also depend on the extent to which informal, face-to-face interaction is fostered by the shop floor and designated meeting places (Miller, 1959; Sundstrom, 1986).

Phase 3: Proceduralized Knowledge

In phase 2, knowledge compilation included the beginnings of a set of skills in that a person knows how to perform. During the third or procedural phase, performance is thought to become relatively automatic but we suggest continues to improve through refinement of the production rules—the "how to" rules. In an organization, this would consist of negotiating the various routes and gates that would apply to knowing "how things get done around here". The so-called "expert" stage is reached when the individual is able to make abstractions across various representations. Novices have superficial understandings of central terms and concepts whereas experts' knowledge is more structured and interconnected (Glaser, 1989). Experts use knowledge more efficiently (Ericsson & Staszewski, 1989), have the ability to see what is relevant when faced with a problem, and can easily access relevant knowledge (Hollnagel, Hoc, & Cacciabue, 1995). At this stage, the individual team member should be able to recognize systemic patterns of behaviour and retrieve old system knowledge and might also be able to make predictions and outcomes of the work of the team. That is, he/she is able to "run" a mental model of the team task (Cannon-Bowers et al., 1995) and visualize the problem, solution, and outcome.

FLUENT OR OVERLAPPING UNDERSTANDING

Team member–supervisor (expert) relations

The level of shared understanding between the team and their supervisor or manager is equally as important as shared understandings between team members. The team's manager represents a resource controller, judge, evaluator, and performance assessor. Thus, it could be hypothesized that in order to work together effectively, managers and teams need to share an understanding of the problem at hand and to develop the capacity to perceive, encode, store, and retrieve team-related information in a parallel manner (Cannon-Bowers & Salas, 1990; Converse, Cannon-Bowers, & Salas, 1991; Kleinman & Serfaty, 1989; Rouse, Cannon-Bowers, & Salas, 1992).

Does the mental model of the manager and the team need to be congruent? This may depend on the particular task or situation, but some diagnosis is going to be helpful in determining whether there is a misconception about the nature of the team task (the goal) or the manager or the team have "inaccurate" task mental models. Alternatively, different understandings by the manager and team could be naturally occurring and appropriate given that such differences of the team task could merely be representative of their different roles and responsibilities. Differing models would provide a complement to the potentially "total" mental model which comprises the task at hand. However, there may be some aspects of the various mental models which must be congruent and these would need to be identified, for instance the method/s techniques to be used by the team to achieve their goal. It must be remembered that the team's activities draw upon the resources of the organization, that they will be accountable for these, and that the adoption of efficient methods and approaches intrinsic to the team's task would need to be reflected in the degree of mental model overlap between manager and team. Thus, team and manager mental models can be used not only to determine distance and similarity in mental model overlap, but as a diagnostic tool to ascertain a "state of affairs", to log progress, and as a monitoring check of procedures which need to be incorporated in the "working mental model" of the team and the manager. "Working mental model" represents perhaps only a momentary picture of the complete current mental model, an abbreviation in other words, and is analogous to Markus and Nurius's notion of a "working self-concept" (Markus & Nurius, 1991).

In many situations in organizations we might want to regard the team's manager and supervisor as the "expert", in which case the expert mental model would be the one from which some sort of gap or audit analysis would be conducted to ascertain the degree of difference between the expert and any novice TMM. The gap would then be identified and rectified through training. This situation could arise where no alternative mental model to the expert mental model would exist, perhaps in cases of nuclear power plants or an oil rig installation.

HIGH PERFORMANCE TEAMS (EXPERT TMMs)

There has been much written about high performance teams and it is one of the aims of this chapter to assist in developing a theory that could facilitate the development of such teams. Some of the features suggested by Blinn (1996) to characterize high performance include having a common focus, clearly defined team member roles, utilizing internal and external resources, being supportive of diversity and having good conflict resolution mechanisms, effectively using feedback, and successfully managing time and meetings.

FLUENT, EXPERT TEAMS

Expert teams should have greater output, higher performance, smooth operation, with team members comfortable in their roles. They should understand each other's strengths, weaknesses, and role within the team; they should waste less resources and be better coordinated with a high degree of complementarity and cross-transfer of knowledge and skills. They may also be able to predict the actions of other team members.

APPLIED CONSIDERATIONS

General Utility of Framework and Bottom-line Improvements

TMMs have the potential to make communication and coordination more efficient by requiring less communication for the same result (i.e. by using a common language). They should make mutual team member learning more rapid, improve the allocation of tasks and decision control through awareness of team member strengths and weaknesses. There is a need to know how dimensions of TMMs and the notion of expert TMMs relate to enhanced performance by elucidating causal pathways.

The concept of TMMs serves as an organizing framework within which successful teamwork can be understood and specific predictions about team performance generated (Cannon-Bowers, Salas, & Converse, 1993; Cannon-Bowers et al., 1995). Given the complex nature of teamwork in organizations, the cognitive structure (the mental model) that team members use to organize information about team functioning is extremely important. TMMs provide team members with a set of organized expectations for team performance from which timely and accurate predictions about team member behaviour can be drawn (Converse, Cannon-Bowers, & Salas, 1991). Such knowledge forms the basis of team functioning by providing an understanding of global teamwork concepts (i.e. the team goal) and specific aspects of team performance (i.e. knowledge of special skills of team members). This suggests that team members must hold knowledge structures about the task and the team that are compatible with those held by fellow team members. Indirect evidence for a positive relationship between TMMs and performance has been reported by several authors (Foushee et al., 1986; Kleinman & Serfaty, 1989; Orasanu, 1990; Orasanu & Salas, 1993). Furthermore, there is evidence from the work of Walsh, Henderson, and Deighton (1988) to suggest that TMMs play an important role in aspects of team decision making and shared information processes, for instance problem definition, speed and flexibility, alternative evaluation, and implementation.

Acquiring and Training an Expert TMM

The process of ensuring the acquisition of a TMM would involve a TMM developmental programme whereby at regular meetings, teams would regularly check the accuracy and timeliness of their joint understandings of their task, of each other, and their working context. This could be done by a facilitator or supervisor, who would also note any shortfalls. The measurement issue in the applied context could be problematic and this issue remains a difficult one, with more research yet to be achieved.

With a better understanding of mental models for team functioning, organizations might be able to develop training programmes to foster an understanding of the core dimensions of teamwork (see e.g. Stevens & Campion, 1994), and help to develop "accurate" or expert mental models which must be shared among the team and other important people related to the team task. The goal of training would be to enable the development of relevant and accurate mental models that allow for greater understanding of the system and effective performance. With respect to teamwork, it is hoped that participants develop elaborate mental models of team functioning that incorporate all of the structures and processes inherent in team functioning, how they are related, and their purposes. Thus, users should develop mental models that integrate declarative and procedural knowledge in such a way as to allow a full understanding of the team and effective teamwork.

Research has shown that the format of instructions presented during learning affects performance and the mental models that learners develop (e.g. Eylon & Reif, 1984; Hegarty & Just, 1993; Hong & O'Neil, 1992; Kieras & Bovair, 1984; Mayer, 1989a; Zeitz & Spoehr, 1989). For instance, it has been shown that breadth-first, hierarchically organized information is a more effective instructional technique than the use of depth-first or linear representations of knowledge (Eylon & Reif, 1984; Zeitz & Spoehr, 1989). Zeitz and Spoehr defined depth-first knowledge as understanding that is built up from explanations of each of the lowest level elements in the domain. Breadth-first knowledge, on the other hand, involves generating an explanation at the highest level of the domain, then recursively decomposing the representation one level at a time. It has been found that experts tend to use top-down breadth-first strategies when faced with a problem-solving task, whereas novices do not (e.g. Jeffries et al., 1981, cited in Anderson, 1993). Based on the idea that experts organize their knowledge hierarchically, Zeitz and Spoehr predicted that hierarchically organized instructional materials would facilitate learning and that it would be possible to accelerate students' acquisition of procedural expertise by manipulating the organization with which the domain knowledge is presented. The results of their study supported this prediction, with subjects who were given breadth-first knowledge displaying superior performance than depth-first subjects at all phases of the experiment. Similarly, in a series of studies, Mayer (1989a) showed that the provision of an overall conceptual model prior to the presentation of normal instructional material had substantial positive learning effects.

Since it is possible that mental models are likely to be influenced by idiosyncratic experience, attitudes, and beliefs, Converse, Cannon-Bowers, and Salas (1991) argued that there are features of team functioning which may only be weakly impacted by idiosyncrasies and that it should be possible to train shared mental models of the team goal, the overall team task, individual tasks, and procedures. Rouse, Cannon-Bowers, and Salas (1992) suggested that "the emphasis (should be) on training that provides the mechanisms... knowledge structures... that enable formation of accurate and useful expectations and explanations" (p. 1303). However, the determination of the types of mental models that it is possible to train should not serve as the only selection criterion in training content. Rather, what is required is an analysis of the types of mental models that will enhance teamwork (Rouse, Cannon-Bowers, and Salas, 1992). Some concerted effort needs to be undertaken to ascertain whether faulty mental models do exist, perhaps through weekly team meetings, but also, diagnosis and analysis of mental models can be facilitated by team discussion and quantitative information obtained through techniques mentioned elsewhere (see e.g. Langan-Fox, Code, & Langfield-Smith, 2000; Langan-Fox et al., 2002b). In cases where individuals hold faulty or inaccurate mental models in important team task areas, it may be necessary to alter the structure and content of some members' models. Thus, the establishment of methods to train or manipulate mental models is essential. Research to date suggests that fostering or changing mental models is not simply a process of providing information about the general principles of a system or task, but rather giving instruction about the various components of teamwork and the relationships between them. Kieras and Bovair (1984) found that the explicit instruction of mental models through training could be used to manipulate the speed and course of TMM development. Much of what we have learned about mental models has come from human factors or aviation research and, consequently, has examined task-specific mental models as opposed to process-oriented (e.g. teamwork) ones. Research to date on this issue is encouraging (Azar, 1997).

Obviously in occupations where mistakes in the task can be expensive and/or highly undesirable, for instance in cockpit crews, ambulance teams, and the like, the risk of having inaccurate mental models needs to be minimized. But one could argue just as strongly that on the shop floor, production runs, placement of equipment on the factory floor, etc., can involve just as much risk and danger when knowledge is not mutually shared among a team. Therefore, training could provide the platform for achieving accuracy and refinement of individual and TMMs to eliminate those instances where it is undesirable to have "faulty" mental models.

Challenges of Teams in 21st Century and TMM Consequences

Technology is enabling new measurement possibilities. IT will influence TMMs through the creation of intranets and groupware. Knowledge management systems are facilitating communication and knowledge sharing. Knowledge sharing, communication, and working together is at the heart of developing TMMs.

The TMM framework varies from past frameworks in a number of crucial ways. First, it not only emphasizes models of internal team interaction or team context/environmental influence, but models the interplay between the team and its context. Such a perspective focuses on the processes that influence and are influenced by people in the environment as opposed to, say, internal processes in isolation. Second, it emphasizes that external team relations may play a crucial role in the development of the TMM. External relations have been neglected in past frameworks, possibly as a result of being developed on the basis of theory or in closed-environment teams (e.g. cockpit crews), rather than in collaboration with actual organizational teams. Third, the framework was developed from experiences of actual organizational teams in industry and has good ecological validity. Fourth, a dynamic multidimensional interactive approach is taken with a number of variables involved: team composition, task type, organizational context, internal and external team relations, task characteristics, and the development of mental models of team functioning incorporating these factors. Unlike past frameworks, the current one imposes no constraints on the relative importance of these variables. The extent to which each set of factors will be present in a given TMM will vary, depending on which set of variables is most salient for that particular team. Fifth, it is theoretically dynamic, being a new integration drawing upon theories in cognitive and social psychology and human factors. Finally, the model is developmental in the sense that it assumes a degree of noviceness associated with being an organizational team member and that this is a skill acquisition process involved in becoming a team member expert. However, further work is needed to establish the predictive validity of the framework across organizational teams. For instance, predictive validity could be determined by testing the relationship between within-team mental model overlap or team member–manager mental model overlap and performance (e.g. productivity).

Depending on how the TMM construct is measured (there is no established measure as such), the degree of generalizability of the framework will be limited because of the different measures that will be used, especially in the case of using elicited constructs of TMMs. TMMs can be a precursor to performance so the model could be adapted as a model of team performance. Thus, it has a number of potentials, not least of which would be identifying the appropriate content of team member training, the skill acquisition phase of that content, and the processes involved in the team member novice–expert transition.

FUTURE RESEARCH/DEVELOPMENT

TMM research is at a formative stage. The extension of cognition (i.e. shared and TMMs) appears to be a useful heuristic for interpreting the complexity of team functioning in the hurly-burly of modern-day organizations (see e.g. Langan-Fox et al., 2002b). However, there is little theoretical or empirical work (Klimoski & Mohammed, 1994), and there is little research on shared cognition in shop floor teams or between shop floor teams and their managers.

Given these issues, crucial research questions are: Do teams and managers hold similar mental models of team functioning? What should be the degree of overlap between members of a team and between a team and their manager? How do team member characteristics, task characteristics, and internal and external team relations influence the development of a TMM? Propositions for research are given in the Appendix. Figure 16.2 shows a graphical illustration of the framework and the factors that may influence the development and content of mental models of team functioning in an organizational setting. The dynamics of this framework have implications for the formation of shared mental models, between a team and their manager, and for the formation of a TMM. The framework developed with a focus on team processes and in particular the variables that predict a "mental model of team functioning" as opposed to team performance, of which it is a precursor. This variable could be added as a further phase in the model by a researcher. It should be noted that the framework does not claim to represent the complete content of a mental model for any particular individual or team but rather a cross-section or "slice" of what are likely to be the most salient aspects. Considering the complex and dynamic nature of cognitive processes, it would be difficult to obtain a "complete" mental model in the true sense. This concurs with descriptions of the nature of mental models given above.

The framework could be used to elicit individual mental models of important aspects of team functioning and how these are interrelated. Individual (team member) mental models could then be compared for their similarity or "overlap" to derive the TMM (for further information on the elicitation and representation of a TMM, see Langan-Fox et al., 2000). Team member mental models could also be compared for their similarity to the manager's or supervisor's mental model.

Research Needs

INTEGRATED APPLICATION SYSTEMS AND FACILITATING TMMs

New tools could aid in the use of the TMM construct. Such a system would incorporate measurement, analysis, and recommendations or would allow for easy interpretation. There is a need for recommendations to be clearly and validly linked to organizational needs. Technological improvements (e.g. software programs such as Groupware) facilitating teams such as expert identification systems could create teams with the ideal set of members.

TMM ideas need to be oriented towards organizational needs. This could be done by relating TMMs more to performance goals and by defining TMMs in relation to complementary individual mental models, and not necessarily absolutely shared individual mental models. TMMs could be seen as a tool for organizations, not an abstract theoretical construct. Thus, there is also a need for a better understanding of what complementariness means, and how it varies across tasks and organizational contexts.

ACKNOWLEDGEMENTS

Grateful thanks are given to Sharon Code and Jeromy Anglim for assistance with literature reviews. Financial support for this chapter from the Australian Research Council is acknowledged.

APPENDIX

Propositions

Proposition 1: Team members' mental models of team functioning will overlap more in teams composed of members with similar person-oriented attributes than in teams composed of members with dissimilar person-oriented attributes.

Proposition 2: Team members' mental models of the team will correspond with the power and prestige order of the team as defined by the status characteristics of individual team members.

Proposition 3: There should be more overlap between team members' mental models of the task in structured task teams than in unstructured task teams, since structured tasks are associated with well-defined role responsibilities and there is less room for confusion about the requirements of the task.

Proposition 4: Mental models of team interaction will be more important for unstructured task teams than for structured task teams as unstructured tasks are likely to require higher levels of team interaction.

Proposition 5: Team member–manager mental model similarity will be greater for structured tasks than for unstructured tasks, since there are less possible courses of action for achieving the goal.

Proposition 6: Proximity facilitates interaction and communication among team members, therefore team members' mental models should overlap more when their work stations are located within close proximity to one another.

Proposition 7: Individualistic team members will develop mental models of team functioning specific to their own role in the team as opposed to a more global, collective, or TMM. Thus, there should be more mental model overlap in teams composed of collectivist team members than in teams composed of individualist team members.

Proposition 8: There will be less overlap between the mental models of team members when commitment to the goal is low due to a decline in active participation in the task by team members.

Proposition 9: Team members who engage in in-process task planning will have more similar mental models than team members who engage in pre-planning, as the nature of the task and team (functioning) is likely to change over time.

Proposition 10: Where team members fail to strike a balance between the amount of time devoted to internal team relations and external team relations, the TMM is likely to be weak as a consequence of poor team cohesiveness and communication.

Proposition 11: Structured task teams yield "one-of-a-kind" outputs (i.e. generate the same or similar outputs over and over), require only "one off" instances of synchronization with support staff or competitors, have longer cycles of independent, within-team work, and have low external relations requirements. Unstructured task teams (e.g. employee participation teams) yield unique inputs which impact on stakeholders in the organizational environment, need to gather task-relevant information and support from outside the team, and have high external relations requirements. Thus, external relations should feature more significantly in the mental models of unstructured task team members than structured task team members.

Proposition 12: Team member–manager mental model overlap will be greater when there is frequent interaction between the team and the manager.

BIBLIOGRAPHY

Ackerman, P. L. (1988). Determinants of individual differences during skill acquisition: cognitive abilities and information processing. *Journal of Experimental Psychology: General, 117*, 288–318.

Allscheid, S. P. & Cellar, D. F. (1996). An interactive approach to work motivation: the effects of competition, rewards and goal difficulty on task performance. *Journal of Business and Psychology, 11*(2), 219–237.

Ancona, D. G. (1990). Outward bound: strategies for team survival in an organization. *Academy of Management Journal, 33*, 334–365.

Ancona, D. G. & Caldwell, D. F. (1989). Beyond task and maintenance: defining external functions in teams. *Team and Organization Studies, 13*, 488–494.

Ancona, D. G. & Caldwell, D. F. (1992). Bridging the boundary: external activity and performance in organizational teams. *Administrative Science Quarterly, 37*(4), 634–665.

Anderson, J. (1982). Acquisition of cognitive skill. *Psychological Review, 89*, 369–406.

Anderson, J. R. (1987). Skill acquisition: compilation of weak-method problem solutions. *Psychological Review, 94*, 192–210.

Anderson, J. R. (1993). Problem solving and learning. *American Psychologist, 48*(1), 35–44.

Annett, J. & Duncan, K. D. (1967). Task analysis and training design. *Occupational Psychology, 41*, 211–221.

Annett, J., Duncan, K. D., Stammers, R. B., & Gray, M. J. (1971). Task analysis. *Training Information No. 6*. London: HMSO.

Arad, S., Hanson, N., & Schneider, R. (1991). Organizational context. In N. G. Peterson & M. D. Mumford (eds), *An Occupational Information System for the 21st Century: The Development of ONET* (pp. 147–174). Washington, DC: American Psychological Association.

Argote, L. & McGrath, J. E. (1993). Team processes in organizations: continuity and change. In C. L. Cooper & I. T. Robertson (eds), *International Review of Industrial and Organizational Psychology 1993* (Vol. 8, pp. 333–389). New York: John Wiley & Sons.

Azar, B. (1997). Team building isn't enough: workers need training too. *APA Monitor*, July, 13–14.

Bandura, A. (1986). Differential engagement of self-reactive influences in cognitive motivation. *Organizational Behavior and Decision Processes, 38*, 92–113.

Banks, A. P. & Millward, L. J. (2000). Running shared mental models as a distributed cognitive process. *British Journal of Psychology, 91*(4), 513–531.

Barrick, M. R., Stewart, G. L., Neubert, M. J., & Mount, M. K. (1998). Relating team member ability to work team processes and team effectiveness. *Journal of Applied Psychology, 83*(3), 377–391.

Berger, J. M., Fisek, H., Norman, R. Z., & Zelditch, M., Jr (1977). *Status Characteristics and Social Interaction: An Expectation-States Approach.* New York: Elsevier.

Blessing, S. B. & Anderson, J. R. (1996). How people learn to skip steps. *Journal of Experimental Psychology: Learning, Memory, & Cognition, 22*(3), 576–598.

Blickensderfer, E., Cannon-Bowers, J. A., & Salas, E. (1997). Theoretical bases for team self-corrections: fostering shared mental models. In M. M. Beyerlein & D. A. Johnson (eds), *Advances in Interdisciplinary Studies of Work Teams* (Vol. 4, pp. 249–279). Stamford, Conn.: JAI Press.

Blinn, C. K. (1996, Nov–Dec). Developing high performance teams. *Online, 20, 6*, p. 56(1). Online: http://www.coachcarla.com/articles.html

Brannick, M. T., Prince, A., Prince, C., & Salas, E. (1995). The measurement of team process. *Human Factors, 37*(3), 641–651.

Brickner, M. A. & Bukatko, P. A. (1987). Locked into performance: goal setting as a moderator of social loafing affect. University of Ackron, unpublished manuscript.

Bruning, N. S. & Liverpool, P. R. (1993). Membership in quality circles and participation in decision making. *The Journal of Applied Behavioral Science, 29*, 76–95.

Byrne, D. (1971). *The Attraction Paradigm.* New York: Academic Press.

Campelli, P. & Sherer, P. D. (1993). The missing role of context in OB: the need for a meso-level approach. *Research in Organizational Behavior, 13*, 55–110.

Campion, M. A., Medsker, G. J., & Higgs, A. C. (1993). Relations between work group characteristics and effectiveness: implications for designing effective work groups. *Personnel Psychology, 46*, 823–850.

Campion, M. A., Papper, E. M., & Medsker, G. J. (1996). Relationships between work team characteristics and effectiveness: a replication and extension. *Personnel Psychology, 49*, 429–452.

Cannon-Bowers, J. A. & Salas, E. (1990). Cognitive psychology and team training: shared mental models in complex systems. *Human Factors Society Bulletin, 33*, 1–4.

Cannon-Bowers, J. A. & Salas, E. (2001). Reflections on shared cognition. *Journal of Organizational Behavior, 22* (Special Issue), 195–202.

Cannon-Bowers, J. A., Salas, E., & Converse, S. (1993). Shared mental models in expert team decision making. In N. J. Castellan, Jr (ed.), *Individual and Team Decision Making* (pp. 221–246). New Jersey: Lawrence Erlbaum Associates.

Cannon-Bowers, J. A. & Tannenbaum, S. I. (1991). Toward an integration of training theory and technique. *Human Factors, 33*(3), 281–292.

Cannon-Bowers, J. A., Tannenbaum, S. I., Salas, E., & Volpe, C. E. (1995). Defining team competencies and establishing training requirements. In R. Guzzo & E. Salas (eds), *Team Effectiveness and Decision Making in Organizations* (pp. 333–380). San Francisco: Jossey-Bass.

Carley, K. M. (1990). Coordinating for success: trading information redundancy for task simplicity. *Proceedings of the 23rd Annual Hawaii International Conference on System Sciences, 3*, 261–270.

Carver, C. S. & Sheier, M. F. (1982). *Attention and Self-regulation: A Control Theory Approach to Human Behavior*. New York: Springer.

Charney, D. A. & Reder, L. M. (1987). Initial skill learning: an analysis of how elaborations facilitate the three components. In P. Morris (ed.), *Modelling Cognition* (pp. 135–165). New York: John Wiley & Sons.

Chatman, J. A. & Barsade, S. G. (1995). Personality, organizational culture, and cooperation: evidence from a business simulation. *Administrative Science Quarterly, 40*(3), 423–443.

Clegg, C. (1994). Psychology and information technology: the study of cognition in organizations. *British Journal of Psychology, 85*(4), 449–477.

Coates, J. (1996). How to improve the quality of our organizations through the use of TQM, continuous improvement strategies. In *The Olympics of Leadership: Overcoming Obstacles, Balancing Skills, and Taking Risks.* Proceedings of the Annual International Conference of the National Community College Chair Academy, Phoenix, Ariz.

Code, S. & Langan-Fox, J. (2001). Motivations, cognitions and traits: predicting occupational health, well being and performance. *Stress and Health, 17*, 159–174.

Cohen, B. P. & Zhou, X. (1991). Status processes in enduring work teams. *American Sociological Review, 56*, 179–188.

Cohen, S. G. & Bailey, D. E. (1997). What makes teams work: group effectiveness research from the shop floor to the executive suite. *Journal of Management, 23*(2), 239–290.

Cohen, S. G., Ledford, G. E., & Spreitzer, G. M. (1994). A predictive model of self-managing work team effectiveness. *Human Relations, 49*(5), 643–676.

Collins, A. M. & Loftus, E. F. (1975). A spreading activation theory of semantic processing. *Psychological Review, 82*, 407–428.

Converse, S. A., Cannon-Bowers, J. A., & Salas, E. (1991). Team member shared mental models: a theory and some methodological issues. *Proceedings of the Human Factors Society 35th Annual Meeting*, 1417–1421.

Cooke, N. J., Salas, E., Cannon-Bowers, J. A., & Stout, R. J. (2000). Measuring team knowledge. *Human Factors, 42*(1), 151–173.

Cummings, L. L. (1981). Organizational behaviour. *Annual Review of Psychology, 33*, 541–579.

Driskell, J. E., Hogan, R., & Salas, E. (1987). Personality and group performance. *Review of Personality and Social Psychology, 9*, 91–112.

Drory, A. & Shamir, B. (1988). Effects of organization and life variables on job satisfaction and burnout. *Group and Organization Studies, 13*(4), 441–455.

Duffy, L. (1992). Team decision making biases: an information processing perspective. In G. A. Klein, J. Orasanu, R. Calderwood, & C. E. Zsambok (eds), *Decision Making in Action: Models and Methods*, (pp. 234–242). Norwood, NJ: Ablex.

Earley, P. C., Lee, C., & Hanson, L. A. (1990). Joint moderating effects of job experience and task component complexity: relations among goal setting, task strategies, and performance. *Journal of Organizational Behavior, 11*, 3–15.

Eby, L. T., Meade, A., Parisi, A. G., Douthitt, S. S., & Midden, P. (1998). Measuring mental models for teamwork at the individual- and team-level. Paper presented at the Annual Meeting of the Society for Industrial and Organizational Psychology, Dallas, Texas.

Encarta (2001). *Cooperation*. Microsoft Corporation. Online: http://encarta.msn.com

Erez, M. & Zidon, I. (1984). Effect of goal acceptance on the relationship of goal difficulty to performance. *Journal of Applied Psychology, 69*, 69–78.

Ericsson, K. A. & Staszewski, J. J. (1989). Skilled memory and expertise: mechanisms of exceptional performance. In D. Klahr & K. Kotovsky (eds), *Complex Information Processing: The Impact of Herbert A. Simon* (pp. 235–267). Hillsdale, NJ: Lawrence Erlbaum Associates.

Eylon, B. & Reif, F. (1984). Effects of knowledge organization on task performance. *Cognition & Instruction, 1*(1), 5–44.

Flanagan, J. C. (1954). The critical incident technique. *Psychological Bulletin, 51*, 327–358.

Foushee, H. C., Lauber, J. K., Baetge, M. M., & Acomb, D. B. (1986). *Crew Factors in Flight Operations III: The Operational Significance of Exposure to Short-haul Air Transport Operations*. Mountain View, Calif.: NASA.

Gentner, D. & Collins, A. (1981). Studies of inference from lack of knowledge. *Memory and Cognition, 9*(4), 434–443.

Gentner, D. & Stevens, D. (1983). *Mental Models*. Hillsdale, NJ: Lawrence Erlbaum Associates.

George, J. M. (1989). Mood and absence. *Journal of Applied Psychology, 74*, 317–324.

George, J. M. (1990). Personality, affect, and behaviour in groups. *Journal of Applied Psychology, 75*, 107–166.

George, J. M. (1995). Leader positive mood and group performance: the case of customer service. *Journal of Applied Social Psychology, 25*, 778–794.

Gladstein, D. (1984). Groups in context: a model of task group effectiveness. *Administrative Science Quarterly, 29*, 210–216.

Glaser, R. (1989). Expertise and learning: how do we think about instructional processes information processing. In D. Klahr & K. Kotovsky (eds), *Complex Information Processing: The Impact of Herbert A. Simon* (pp. 235–267). Hillsdale, NJ: Lawrence Erlbaum Associates.

Glickman, A. S., Zimmer, S., Montero, R. C., Guerette, P. J., Campbell, W. J., Morgan, B. B., & Salas, E. (1987). *The Evolution of Teamwork Skills: An Empirical Assessment with Implications for Training*. Orlando: Naval Training Systems Centre.

Goodman, P. S. (1986). Impact of task and technology and group performance. In P. S. Goodman (ed.), *Designing Effective Work Groups* (pp. 120–167). San Francisco: Jossey-Bass.

Graham, J. W. & Verma, A. (1991). Predictors and moderators of employee responses to employee participation programs. *Human Relations, 44*, 551–568.

Greene, C. N. (1989). Cohesion and productivity in work groups. *Small Group Behavior, 20*(1), 70–86.

Griffin, M. & Mathieu, J. (1997). Modelling organizational processes across hierarchical levels: climate, leadership, and group processes in work groups. *Journal of Organizational Behavior, 18*(6), 731–744.

Grummon, P. T. H. (1997). Assessing teamwork skills for workforce readiness. In H. F. O'Neil (ed.), *Work Readiness: Competencies and Assessment*. Hillsdale, NJ: Lawrence Erlbaum Associates.

Guenther, R. K. (1998). *Human Cognition*. Saddle River, NJ: Prentice-Hall.

Guzzo, R. A. & Dickson, M. W. (1996). Teams in organizations: recent research in performance and effectiveness. *Annual Review of Psychology, 46*, 307–338.

Hackman, J. R. (1983). A normative model of work team effectiveness (Technical Report No. 2). *Research Program on Group Effectiveness*. Yale School of Organization and Management.

Hackman, J. R. (1990). *Groups that Work (and Those that Don't)*. San Francisco: Jossey-Bass.

Heath, C. & Luff, P. (1996). Convergent activities: line control and passenger information on the London underground. In Y. Engestron & D. Middleton (eds), *Cognition and Communication at Work* (pp. 96–129). New York: Cambridge University Press.

Heffner, T. S., Mathieu, J., & Cannon-Bowers, J. A. (1998). The impact of shared mental models on team performance: sharedness, quality or both? Paper presented at the Annual Meeting of the Society for Industrial and Organizational Psychology, Dallas, Texas.

Hegarty, M. & Just, M. A. (1993). Constructing mental models of machines from text and diagrams. *Journal of Memory & Language, 32*(6), 717–742.

Hofstede, G. (1980). *Culture's Consequences: International Differences in Work-related Values*. Beverly Hills, Calif.: Sage.

Hollnagel, E., Hoc, J.-M., & Cacciabue, P. C. (1995). Work with technology: some fundamental issues. In J.-M. Hoc, P. C. Cacciabue, & E. Hollnagel (eds), *Expertise and Technology: Cognition and Human–Computer Cooperation*. New York: Lawrence Erlbaum Associates.

Hong, E. & O'Neil, H. F., Jr (1992). Instructional strategies to help learners build relevant mental models in inferential statistics. *Journal of Educational Psychology, 84*, 150–159.

Hutchins, E. (1991). The social organization of distributed cognition. In L. B. Resnick, J. M. Levine, & S. D. Teasly (eds), *Perspectives on Socially Shared Cognition* (pp. 283–307). Washington, DC: American Psychological Association.

Ibarra, H. (1992). Homophilly and differential returns: sex differences in network structure and access in an advertising firm. *Administrative Science Quarterly, 37*, 422–437.

Ivancevich, J. M. (1972). A longitudinal assessment of management by objectives. *Administrative Science Quarterly, 17*, 126–138.

Ivancevich, J. M. (1974). Changes in performance in a management by objectives program. *Administrative Science Quarterly, 19*, 563–574.

Jackson, S. E. (1992). *Diversity in the Workplace: Human Resources Initiatives*. The Professional Practice series. New York: Guilford Press.

Jackson, S. E. (1996). The consequences of diversity in multidisciplinary work teams. In M. A. West (ed.), *Handbook of Work Group Psychology* (pp. 53–76). Chichester: Wiley.

Jacobs, G. M. & James, J. E. (1994). A comparison of workplace groups with groups in education. *Annual Meeting of Teachers of English to Speakers of Other Languages,* Baltimore, Md.

Janis, I. L. (1972). *Victims of Groupthink*. Boston: Houghton-Mifflin.

Jeffries, R., Turner, A., Polson, P., & Atwood, M. (1981). The processes involved in designing software. In J. R. Anderson (ed.), *Cognitive Skills and Their Acquisition*. Hillsdale, NJ: Lawrence Erlbaum Associates.

Johnson-Laird, P. (1983). *Mental Models*. Cambridge, Mass.: Harvard University Press.

Jones, G. R. & George, J. M. (1998). The experience and evolution of trust: implications for cooperation and teamwork. *Academy of Management Review, 23*(3), 531–546.

Katz, R. (1982). The effects of group longevity on communication and performance. *Administrative Science Quarterly, 27*, 81–104.

Kay, D. S. & Black, J. B. (1990). Knowledge transformations during the acquisition of computer expertise. In S. P. Robertson & W. W. Zachary et al. (eds), *Cognition, Computing, and Cooperation* (pp. 268–303). Norwood, NJ: Ablex.

Kelly, G. A. (1955). *The Psychology of Personal Constructs*. New York: W. W. Norton and Company.

Kent, R. N. & McGrath, J. E. (1969). Task and group characteristics as factors influencing group performance. *Journal of Experimental Social Psychology, 5*, 429–440.

Kieras, D. E. & Bovair, S. (1984). The role of a mental model in learning to operate a device. *Cognitive Science, 8*(3), 255–273.

Klein, G. (1997). An overview of naturalistic decision making applications. In C. E. Zsambok & Gary Klein (eds), *Naturalistic Decision Making. Expertise: Research and Applications* (pp. 49–59). Hillsdale, NJ: Lawrence Erlbaum Associates.

Klein, H. J. & Kim, J. S. (1998). A field study of the influence of situational constraints, leader–member exchange, and goal commitment on performance. *Academy of Management Journal, 41*(1), 88–95.

Klein, H. J. & Wright, P. M. (1994). Antecedents of goal commitment: an empirical examination of personal and situational factors. *Journal of Applied Social Psychology, 24*(2), 95–114.

Kleinman, D. L. & Serfaty, D. (1989). Team performance assessment in distributed decision making. In R. Gibson, J. P. Kincaid, & B. Goldiez (eds), *Proceedings for Interactive Networked Simulation for Training Conference* (pp. 22–27). Orlando: Institute for Simulation and Training.

Klimoski, R. & Mohammed, S. (1994). Team mental model: construct or metaphor? *Journal of Management, 20*, 403–437.

Kozlowski, S. W. (1995). Organizational change, informal learning, and adaptation: emerging trends in training and continuing education. *Journal of Continuing Higher Education, 43*(1), 2–11.

Kraiger, K. & Wenzel, L. H. (1997). Conceptual development and empirical evaluation of measures of shared mental models as indicators of team effectiveness. In M. T. Brannick & E. Salas (eds), *Team Performance Assessment and Measurement: Theory, Methods, and Applications*. Series in applied psychology (pp. 63–84). Mahwah, NJ: Lawrence Erlbaum Associates.

Langan-Fox, J. (2001a). Communication in organizations: speed, diversity, networks and influence on organizational effectiveness, human health and relationships. In N. Anderson, D. S. Ones, H. K. Sinangil, & C. Viswesvaren (eds), *International Handbook of Work and Organizational Psychology* (Vol. 2). London: Sage Publications.

Langan-Fox, J. (2001b). Teamwork in organizations: measurement, methodologies and effectiveness. In M. O'Driscoll, P. Taylor, & T. Kalliath (eds), *Organizational Psychology in Australia and New Zealand*. London: Oxford University Press.

Langan-Fox, J., Armstrong K., Anglim, J., & Balvin, N. (2002a). Process in skill acquisition: motivation, interruptions, memory, affective states and metacognition. *Australian Psychologist, 37*(2), 104–117.

Langan-Fox, J., Code, S., & Edlund, G. (1998). *Team Organizational Mental Models: An Integrative Framework for Research*. Annual Conference of the Ergonomics Society, Cirencester, England, 125 pp. (April). London: Taylor & Francis.

Langan-Fox, J., Code, S., Gray, R., & Langfield-Smith, K. (2002b). Supporting employee participation: attitudes and perceptions in trainees, employees and teams. *Group Processes and Intergroup Relations, 5*(1), 53–82.

Langan-Fox, J., Code, S., & Langfield-Smith, K. (2000). Team mental models: methods, techniques and applications. *Human Factors, 42*(2), 1–30.

Langan-Fox, J. & Grey, R. (1999) Improving shop floor performance through industrial participation training. In J. Langan-Fox & M. Griffin (eds), *Human Performance and the Workplace* (Vol. 1). Melbourne: APS Imprint Books.

Langan-Fox, J., Waycott, J., & Galna, C. (1997). Ability–performance relations during skill acquisition. *Australian Psychologist, 32*(3), 153–158.

Langan-Fox, J., Waycott, J., Morizzi, M., & McDonald, L. (1998). Predictors of participation in performance appraisal: a voluntary system in a blue collar work environment. *International Journal of Selection and Assessment, 6*(4), 249–260.

Langan-Fox, J., Wirth, A., Code, S., Langfield-Smith, K., & Wirth, A. (2000). Analysing mental models of teams, managers and experts. In *Challenges for the New Millenium*. Proceedings of the Human Factors and Ergonomics Annual Conference, San Diego, July, pp. 146–150.

Langan-Fox, J., Wirth, A., Code, S., Langfield-Smith, K., & Wirth, A. (2001). Analyzing shared and team mental models. *International Journal of Industrial Ergonomics, 28*, 99–112.

Levesque, L. L., Wilson, J. M., & Wholey, D. R. (2001). Cognitive divergence and shared mental models in software development project teams. *Journal of Organizational Behavior, 22*(Special Issue), 135–144.

Levine, J. M. & Moreland, R. L. (1991). Culture and socialization in work teams. In L. B. Resnick, J. M. Levine, & S. D. Teasley (eds), *Perspectives on Socially Shared Cognition* (pp. 257–282). Washington, DC: American Psychological Association.

Locke, E. A. & Latham, G. P. (1990). *A Theory of Goal Setting and Task Performance*. Englewood Cliffs, NJ: Prentice-Hall.
McClough, A. C., Rogelberg, S. G., Fisher, G. G., & Bachiochi, P. D. (1998). Cynicism and the quality of an individual's contribution to an organizational diagnostic survey. *Organization Development Journal, 16*(2), 31–41.
McGrath, J. E. (1984). *Groups: Interaction and Performance.* Englewood Cliffs, NJ: Prentice-Hall.
Magney, J. (1995). Teamwork and cooperative learning in technical education. Paper presented at the American Vocational Association Convention, Denver, Colo.
Marchington, M., Wilkinson, A., Ackers, P., & Goodman, J. (1994). Understanding the meaning of participation: views from the workplace. *Human Relations, 47*(8), 867–894.
Markus, H. & Nurius, S. (1991). Possible selves. *American Psychologist, 41*, 249–260.
Martin, B. A. & Manning, D. J. (1995). Combined effects of normative information on task difficulty and the goal commitment–performance relationship. *Journal of Management, 21*(1), 65–80.
Maslow, A. H. (1970). *Motivation and Personality* (2nd edn). New York: Harper and Row.
Mayer, R. E. (1989a). Models for understanding. *Review of Educational Research, 59*(1), 43–64.
Mayer, R. E. (1989b). Teaching for thinking: research on the teachability of thinking skills. In I. S. Cohen (ed.), *The G. Stanley Hall Lecture Series* (Vol. 9, pp. 139–164). Washington, DC: American Psychological Association.
Maznevski, M. L. (1994). Understanding our differences: performance in decision making groups with diverse members. *Human Relations, 47*(5), 531–552.
Miller, E. J. (1959). Technology, territory, and time: the internal differentiation of complex production systems. *Human Relations, 12*, 245–272.
Miller, R. W. & Prichard, F. N. (1992). Factors associated with workers' inclination to participate in an employee involvement program. *Group and Organization Management, 17*(4), 414–430.
Mohammed, S. & Dumville, B. C. (2001). Team mental models in a team knowledge framework: expanding theory and measurement across disciplinary boundaries. *Journal of Organizational Behavior*. Special Issue: *Shared Cognition, 22*, 89–106.
Mohammed, S., Klimoski, R., & Rentsch, J. R. (2000). The measurement of team mental models: we have no shared schema. *Organizational Research Methods, 3*(2), 123–165.
Monge, P. R., Edwards, J. A., & Kirste, K. K. (1983). Determinants of communication network involvement, connectedness, and integration. *Group and Organizational Studies, 8*(1), 83–111.
Morgan, B. B., Glickman, A. S., Woodward, E. A., Blaiwes, A. S., & Salas, E. (1986). *Measurement of Team Behaviours in a Navy Environment* (Tech. Rep. No. TR-86-014). Orlando, Fla: Naval Training Systems Center.
Mowday, R. T. & Sutton, R. I. (1993). Organizational behavior: linking individuals and teams to organizational contexts. *Annual Review of Psychology, 44*, 195–229.
Norman, D. A. (1983). Some observations on mental models. In D. Gentner & L. Stevens (eds), *Mental Models* (pp. 7–14). Hillsdale, NJ: Lawrence Erlbaum Associates.
Oldham, G. R. & Fried, Y. (1987). Employee reactions to workplace characteristics. *Journal of Applied Psychology, 72*(1), 75–80.
Olson, J. R. & Biolsi, K. J. (1991). Techniques for representing expert knowledge. In K. A. Ericsson & J. Smith (eds), *Toward a General Theory of Expertise: Prospects and Limits* (pp. 240–285). New York: Cambridge University Press.
Orasanu, J. (1990). Shared mental models and crew decision making. In *Proceedings of the 12th Annual Conference of the Cognitive Science Society*, Cambridge, Mass.
Orasanu, J. & Salas, E. (1993). Team decision making in complex environments. In G. A. Klein, J. Orasanu, R. Calderwood, & C. E. Zsambok (eds), *Decision Making in Action: Models and Methods* (pp. 327–345). Norwood, NJ: Ablex.
O'Reilly, C. A. (1991). Organizational behaviour: where we've been, where we're going. *Annual Review of Psychology, 42*, 427–458.
O'Reilly, C. A., Caldwell, D. F., & Barnett, W. P. (1989). Work group demography, social integration and turnover. *Administrative Science Quarterly, 34*, 21–37.
O'Reilly, C. A. & Flatt, S. (1989). Executive team demography, organizational innovation, and firm performance (Working Paper). Berkeley, Calif.: University of California.
O'Reilly, C. A. & Roberts, K. H. (1977). Communication and performance in organizations. Paper presented at *Academy of Management annual meeting*, Orlando, Fla.

Orpen, C. (1987). Strategic planning through group decision-making. *Management and Labor Studies, 12*(3), 133–139.

Patrick, J. (1992). *Training: Research and Practice*. London: Academic Press.

Pfeffer, J. (1981). A partial test of the social information model of job attitudes. *Human Relations, 33*, 457–476.

Pfeffer, J. (1986). A resource dependence perspective on inter-corporate relations. In M. S. Mizruchi & M. Schwartz (eds), *Structural Analysis of Business* (pp. 117–132). New York: Academic Press.

Prince, C. & Salas, E. (1989). Air crew performance: coordination and skill development. In D. E. Daniel, E. Salas, & D. M. Kotick (eds), *Independent Research and Independent Exploratory Development Programs: Annual Report for Fiscal Year 1988* (NTSC Tech. Rep. No. 89-009, pp. 45–48). Orlando, Fla: Naval Training Systems Center.

Rice, L. E. & Ayden, C. (1991). Attitudes toward new organizational technology: network proximity as a mechanism for social information processing. *Administrative Science Quarterly, 36*, 219–244.

Riley, A. L. & Burke, P. J. (1995). Identities and self-verification in the small group. *Social Psychology Quarterly, 58*(2), 61–73.

Robins, G., Pattison, P., & Langan-Fox, J. (1995). Group effectiveness: a comparative network analysis of interactional structure and performance in organizational workgroups. *Social Networks Annual Conference*, London, pp. 240–251.

Roschelle, J. (1996). Designing for cognitive communication: epistemic fidelity or mediating collaborative inquiry? In D. L. Day & D. K. Kovacks (eds), *Computers, Communication and Mental Models* (pp. 15–27). Philadelphia, Pa: Taylor & Francis.

Rouse, W. B., Cannon-Bowers, J. A., & Salas, E. (1992). The role of mental models in team performance in complex systems. *IEEE Transactions on Systems, Man, and Cybernetics, 22*(6), 1296–1308.

Rouse, W. B. & Morris, N. M. (1986). On looking into the black box: prospects and limits in the search for mental models. *Psychological Bulletin, 100*, 349–363.

Salomon, G. (1993). *Distributed Cognitions: Psychological and Educational Considerations.* New York: Cambridge University Press.

Schavaneveldt, R. W. (1990). *Pathfinder Associative Networks: Studies in Knowledge Organization.* Norwood, NJ: Albex.

Schneider, B. (1987). The people make the difference. *Personnel Psychology, 40*, 437–453.

Schumacher, R. & Czerwinski, M. (1992). Mental models and the acquisition of expert knowledge. In R. Hoffman (ed.), *The Psychology of Expertise*. New York: Springer-Verlag.

Shepard, A. (1985). An improved tabular format for task analysis. *Journal of Occupational Psychology, 49*, 93–104.

Shetzer, L. (1993). A social information processing model of employee participation. *Organization Science, 4*(2), 252–268.

Smith, E. E., Shoeben, E. J., & Rips, L. J. (1974). Structure and process in semantic memory: a featural model for semantic decisions.*Psychological Review, 81*, 214–241.

Smith, P. B. & Noakes, J. (1996). Cultural differences in group processes. In M. A. West (ed.), *Handbook of Work Group Psychology* (pp. 477–502). Chichester: Wiley.

Steele, F. (1986). *Making and Managing High Quality Workplaces: An Organizational Ecology*. New York: Teachers College Press.

Steiner, I. D. (1972). *Group Processes and Productivity*. New York: Academic Press.

Stevens, M. J. & Campion, M. A. (1994). The knowledge, skill, and ability requirements for teamwork: implications for human resource management. *Journal of Management, 20*, 503–530.

Sundstrom, E. (1986). *Work Places.* New York: Cambridge University Press.

Sundstrom, E., DeMeuse, K. P., & Futrell, D. (1990). Work teams: applications and effectiveness. *American Psychologist, 45*(2), 120–133.

Sweezey, R. W. & Salas, E. (1992). *Teams: Their Training and Performance*. Norwood, NJ: Ablex.

Tang, T. L. P. & Butler, E. A. (1997). Attributions of quality circles' problem-solving failure: differences among managers, supporting staff and quality circle members. *Public Personnel Management, 26*(2), 203–225.

Tannenbaum, S. I., Beard, R. L., & Salas, E. (1992). Team building and its influence on team effectiveness: an examination of conceptual and empirical developments. In K. Kelley (ed.), *Issues, Theory, and Research in Industrial–Organizational Psychology* (pp. 117–153). Amsterdam: Elsevier Science Publishers B. V.

Theodorakis, Y. (1996). The influence of goals, commitment, self-efficacy and self-satisfaction on motor performance. *Journal of Applied Sport Psychology, 8*(2), 171–182.

Turner, J. C., Hogg, M. A., Oakes, P. J., Reicher, S. D., & Wetherell, M. S. (1987). *Rediscovering the Social Group: A Self-categorisation Theory*. New York: Basil Blackwell Inc.

Tziner, A. & Eden, D. (1985). Effects of crew composition on crew performance: does the whole equal the sum of its parts? *Journal of Applied Psychology, 70*(1), 85–93.

Umberson, D. & Hughes, M. (1987). The impact of physical attractiveness on achievement and psychological wellbeing. *Social Psychology Quarterly, 50*(3), 227–236.

Walsh, J. P., Henderson, C. M., & Deighton, J. (1988). Negotiated belief structures and decision performance: an empirical investigation. *Organizational Behavior and Human Decision Processes, 42*(2), 194–216.

Weingart, L. R. (1992). Impact of group goals, task component complexity, effort, and planning on group performance. *Journal of Applied Psychology, 77*(5), 682–693.

West, M. A. (1997). *Developing Creativity in Organizations.* Chichester: Wiley.

West, M. A., Borrill, C. S., & Unsworth, K. L. (1998). Team effectiveness in organizations. *International Review of Industrial and Organizational Psychology, 13*, 1–48.

Wilkins, A. C. & Ouchi, W. G. (1983). Efficient cultures: exploring the relationship between culture and organizational performance. *Administrative Science Quarterly, 28*(3), 468–481.

Zeitz, C. M. & Spoehr, K. T. (1989). Knowledge organization and the acquisition of procedural expertise. *Applied Cognitive Psychology, 3*(4), 313–336.

17

SOCIAL LOAFING IN TEAMS

Christel G. Rutte

Teams are popular in organizations. Only a few decades ago, companies that introduced teams made news, but today organizations that do not use teams are newsworthy. About 80 per cent of US organizations employed teams in 1995 (Robbins, 2001). A recent European survey among 5000 companies revealed that 84 per cent employed teams (Benders et al., 1999). Teams are popular because they are believed to outperform individuals, in particular on tasks requiring multiple skills (Mohrman, Cohen, & Mohrman, 1995; Tjosvold, 1991). Group performance can be high when all team members are cooperative and exert a lot of effort. However, there is a true danger that team members are not cooperative and that working in teams may lead to motivation losses. This phenomenon is also known as social loafing (Latané, Williams, & Harkins, 1979).

Social loafing can be defined as the reduction in individual effort when individuals work on a collective task compared to when they work on an individual or co-action task (Karau & Williams, 1993). In a collective task the individual's own output is combined with the output of other group members. In an individual or co-action task the individual's own output is not combined with the output of others. Erez and Somech (1996) argue on the basis of a study using managers from Israeli kibbutzim and cities working on a simulated judgement task that social loafing is not the rule in groups but the exception. However, Karau and Williams (1993) conducted a meta-analysis of 78 published and unpublished studies and found a reliable social loafing effect across studies: when working on collective tasks people produce less effort than when working on co-action or individual tasks.

Most tasks of organizational teams are collective tasks and therefore social loafing may also occur in organizations. There is evidence that people who work in teams in organizations worry that social loafing in their team may occur. Kirkman et al. (1996) asked 486 employees working in teams, in this case autonomous work teams, what their three most important worries were when they started working as a team. Of 1200 comments that were made, 25 per cent were related to social loafing. Examples of worries were:

> I may have to work harder than others for the same wages. I may have to work harder than others with the same job. I may have to work with slower others and have to pull their weight on top of my own. Maybe other team members will not work as hard as I. Not everybody may

International Handbook of Organizational Teamwork and Cooperative Working. Edited by M. A. West, D. Tjosvold, and K. G. Smith.

do his fair share of the workload. I may become stuck with a bunch of losers who can't pull their own weight (p. 56).

These examples clearly indicate that group members do worry about the possibility that other group members may loaf. In Box 17.1 a case is presented illustrating that social loafing does occur in organizations and what form it may take (Rutte, 1990).

Box 17.1 Case study (Rutte, 1990)

The coding centre of a large Dutch bank employed 118 punch typists. The tasks of the typists were to punch and inspect cheques. The typists worked in pairs: one typist punched, the other inspected. In the morning the supervisor roughly divided the day's work over the pairs. The pairs occupied themselves with the allocated work until lunch. After lunch the supervisor collected all remaining work and redivided it over the pairs. As soon as a pair had finished that work it was free to go home. Thus, the typists functioned as a group in the morning and as individual pairs in the afternoon.

If the total typist group worked hard in the morning, there would have been little work left after lunch to redivide and all typists would have been able to go home early. However, what typically happened in the coding centre was that the typists put in little effort before lunch hoping that the others in the group would work hard. They did exert a lot of effort after lunch on the other hand to be able to go home as early as possible. Because all typists tended to socially loaf before lunch, a lot of work remained and all typists had a lot of work to do in the afternoon. The results were that all went home late, the atmosphere in the coding centre was quarrelsome, and there were frequent accusations of free-riding.

Thus, social loafing is an issue in teams deserving attention. If so many organizations employ teams and social loafing so abounds in collective tasks, then it pays off to understand more about the determinants of social loafing. In this chapter I present a theoretical model that integrates the variables of which research has shown that they influence the tendency to loaf. On the basis of this theoretical model I will present suggestions for interventions to prevent social loafing from occurring.

DETERMINANTS OF SOCIAL LOAFING

The effect that working in teams has on individual motivation and effort has long received attention of social and organizational psychologists. One of the very first experiments dealt with this issue. Ringelmann (1913) compared performance of adults working as a group on a rope-pulling task with performance of adults working individually and noted that performance increasingly deteriorated as group size increased (see, for a recent replication of the Ringelmann effect, Lichacz & Partington, 1997). Ringelmann's results were received with scepticism in the scientific community and dismissed as an artefact: performance decrements were the result of coordination losses between group members and not of motivation losses (Steiner, 1972). Only much later Ingham et al. (1974) convincingly demonstrated that the motivational component of the performance decrement was an important and replicable phenomenon in itself, apart from the coordination problem. This phenomenon was called social loafing (Latané, Williams, & Harkins, 1979).

Since 1974, studies about social loafing have appeared regularly. Most studies are experimental and social psychological in nature, but some of them have been conducted in field settings like the classroom or sports teams (Karau & Williams, 1993). Karau and Williams (2001) found only three studies conducted in business organizations (i.e. Faulkner & Williams, 1996; George, 1992, 1995). Whether studies were conducted in laboratory settings, non-organizational field settings, or organizational field settings, similar results emerged (Karau & Williams, 2001).

Some 10 years ago Shepperd (1993) and Karau and Williams (1993) wrote review articles about the determinants of social loafing. The most important contribution of both these articles was that they aimed, for the first time, to put the various studies in an integrated framework. In both articles the same well-known motivation theory was used for this purpose, Vroom's (1964) expectancy-value theory. I will use the same theory as a starting point in this chapter. Next, I will argue that expectancy-value theory needs to be complemented with insights from Adams's (1965) equity theory. Vroom's theory was developed for individual tasks. When applied to collective tasks, one cannot do without considerations of social comparison of inputs and outcomes of the various group members, for a more complete understanding of the determinants of individual efforts. Adams's equity theory can be of help here. Hereafter a theoretical model will be developed that combines insights from expectancy-value theory with insights from equity theory. But first I will discuss expectancy-value theory.

Expectancy Value

According to Vroom's expectancy-value theory (1964), individual motivation depends on three factors: (a) expectancy, i.e. the expectancy that effort will lead to a certain level of performance, (b) instrumentality, i.e. the extent to which a certain level of performance will lead to an outcome, and (c) value, i.e. the extent to which the outcome is valued. Karau and Williams (1993) develop the collective effort model, extending Vroom's (1964) theory about individual motivation on individual tasks to collective tasks. They argue that instrumentality in particular is more complex for collective tasks than for individual tasks. On individual tasks instrumentality is only determined by the perceived relationship between individual performance and individual outcome. On collective tasks instrumentality is determined by three factors: (a) the perceived relationship between individual performance and group performance, (b) the perceived relationship between group performance and group outcomes, and (c) the perceived relationship between group outcomes and individual outcomes. As a result, working on collective tasks introduces additional contingencies between individual efforts and outcomes.

According to Karau and Williams (1993), individuals will be prepared to exert effort on a collective task if they expect these efforts to be instrumental in acquiring valued outcomes. Several conditions must be fulfilled before individuals deem their efforts to be instrumental. Individual effort must be related to individual performance. Individual performance must be related to group performance. Group performance must lead to a valued group outcome. This valued group outcome must be related to a valued individual outcome. If one or more of these relationships are not present or disturbed, a group member will not deem the exertion of effort instrumental and will not work hard on a task. Likewise group members will not work hard if they do not value the resulting outcomes, irrespective of whether these outcomes are related to individual effort. Valued outcomes can be of a tangible nature, like financial rewards, or intangible, like fun, satisfaction, and feelings of self-esteem or feelings of belonging to the group.

Karau and Williams (1993) predict that, since individual outcomes are less related to individual effort on collective tasks, individuals will generally be inclined to loaf on collective tasks. On the basis of a meta-analysis of a large number of studies, Karau and Williams conclude that this hypothesis is supported. Compared to co-action tasks, individuals tend to reduce their efforts on collective tasks. The extent to which individuals loaf is often not large, but the effect is consistent (in 79 per cent of the compared instances).

The fact that the extent to which individuals loaf is often not large does not imply that it is an unimportant problem. Apparently the phenomenon occurs consistently on collective tasks. Suppose that in most teams in organizations effort reductions of 10 per cent occur, then the phenomenon per team may be limited in scope, but across all teams this may nevertheless constitute a considerable loss for an organization.

Karau and Williams list, on the basis of their meta-analysis, the variables that influence social loafing. These variables are of influence on social loafing because they influence perceived instrumentality or outcome value. Karau and Williams do not detail this any further. The expectancy that individual effort leads to individual performance is a background condition in Karau and Williams's model. If such an expectation does not exist, individuals do not exert effort anyway, whether they work on an individual task or on a collective task. Below, I will further detail the role of the mediating mechanisms of instrumentality and outcome value and formulate specific hypotheses about which variable influences which mediating mechanism. Where relevant I will add selected references that appeared after Karau and Williams wrote their meta-analysis in 1993, to bring their review up to date.

EVALUATION POTENTIAL

Individuals tend to loaf less when their contributions can be evaluated than when they cannot be evaluated (e.g. Gagne & Zuckerman, 1999; George, 1992; Harkins, 1987; Hoeksema-van Orden, Gaillard, & Buunk, 1998; Price, 1987). When the individual contribution of a group member cannot be distinguished from those of others and, as a result, cannot be identified and evaluated, group members can hide in a team. An example of low evaluation potential is a group of service engineers responsible for servicing copy machines for a group of customers. When a copy machine needs repairing each service engineer can put minimal effort into the repair task—just enough to make the copy machine run again—leaving the major repair job for another service engineer next time. The level of effort each service engineer puts into the task cannot be identified and evaluated. This creates the opportunity to blame others if things go wrong ("it was the previous service engineer who did a bad job"). Punishment is less likely and outcomes will be gained despite one's lack of contribution. When group members' contributions are not identifiable and assessable, the tendency to loaf increases, because—in terms of expectancy-value theory—it decreases the instrumentality of contributions. This means that increasing evaluation potential will decrease the tendency to loaf, because it increases instrumentality. Druskatt and Wolff

(1999) studied 44 self-managing undergraduate student groups and 36 self-managing MBA student groups using a repeated measures time-series design. They examined the effect of peer appraisals on social loafing. They found that peer appraisals had a positive impact. The positive effect was not dependent on the ratio of positive to negative feedback, suggesting that being evaluated in itself caused the effect, and not whether the evaluation is positive or negative.

Increased evaluation potential may also lead to increased outcome value. People in general find it pleasing when they are able to evaluate their own performance and see that they performed well. Performing well is a reward in itself, because it increases feelings of self-esteem (Harkins & Szymanski, 1988; Szymanski & Harkins, 1987). Some tasks lend themselves better for evaluation than others. Henningsen, Cruz, and Miller (2000) argued that intellective tasks increase the potential for evaluation when a correct answer is believed to exist. A judgemental task, on the other hand, like jury decision making, has no objective outside standard against which decisions can be evaluated. Henningsen, Cruz, and Miller (2000) therefore predicted and found more social loafing in judgemental than in intellective tasks.

TASK VALUE

Group members tend to loaf less when task value increases (Petty, Cacioppo, & Kasmer, 1985). This implies that intrinsic task motivation, because the task is, for example, important or significant or pleasant, decreases the tendency to loaf. Members of a research and development project team working on an interesting problem, for example, will be less inclined to loaf than members of a team of data typists working away at a pile of data entries, because the first task is intrinsically more motivating than the second. In terms of expectancy-value theory, high task value leads to high outcome value: executing the task is in itself a valuable outcome. George (1992), for example, found in her field study that the extent to which salespeople were intrinsically involved in their task was negatively related to social loafing. Hoeksema-van Orden, Gaillard, and Buunk (1998) had their student participants work on several tasks for 20 hours without sleep in two experiments and found that fatigue increased social loafing. Presumably working on tasks becomes more unpleasant as fatigue increases, thereby reducing intrinsic task motivation. Task motivation may differ for group members. Smith et al. (2001) found that individuals with a high need for cognition are less likely to loaf on cognitively engaging tasks than individuals with a low need for cognition, presumably because individuals with a high need for cognition have higher intrinsic task motivation when the task is cognitively effortful.

GROUP VALUE

Individuals tend to loaf less when group value increases (Hardy & Latané, 1988). This means that high group cohesion or a strong group identity can reduce social loafing. A team consisting of group members who have known each other for some time and who have similar values will have to deal less with social loafing problems than, for example, a team consisting of complete strangers. The effect of group value was indeed found in a study using 59 dyads discussing a controversial issue (Karau & Hart, 1998), and in two experiments using an idea generation task (Karau & Williams, 1997). When group members want to continue their group membership or when their social identity depends to a large extent to membership of the group, they will loaf less. In terms of expectancy-value theory, high group value leads to high perceived outcome value: contributing to the group is a valuable outcome in itself.

REDUNDANCY

The more redundant the contribution of the individual, the more the individual will be inclined to loaf (Harkins & Petty, 1982). This means that having a unique contribution to give to the group reduces the tendency to loaf. In multidisciplinary teams, for example, where all group members have to deliver a specific disciplinary contribution, redundancy will be less of a problem than in monodisciplinary teams where all group members have to deliver the same type of contribution. When group members are interchangeable and somebody else can easily deliver their contribution, group members will be more inclined to reduce their efforts. The upside of this phenomenon is that if somebody else cannot be expected to deliver one's own contribution as well, group members will not be inclined to socially loaf and may even compensate for others' lack of contribution. Karau and Williams (1997, second experiment), for example, found that individuals with a low able co-worker tended to engage in social compensation. Plaks and Higgins (2000) recently found more evidence for this phenomenon in a series of four experiments. In each of the four experiments participants performed worse when there was a good fit between the strengths of their partner and the requirements of the task (making their own contributions redundant), providing evidence for social loafing. To a lesser extent evidence was found for the opposite effect that participants performed better when there was a poor fit between the strengths of their partner and the requirements of the task (making their own contributions non-redundant), providing some evidence for social compensation.

Perceived redundancy may depend on the type of task and on the type of person. Hertel, Kerr, and Messe (2000) had team members with discrepant capabilities work together. They found that motivation gains occurred under conjunctive but not under additive task demands, and suggested that this was due to the fact that increased effort was perceived to be more instrumental in a conjunctive than in an additive task. Huguet, Charbonnier, and Monteil (1999) found that individuals who are high in feelings of self-uniqueness engaged more in social loafing when working on an easy task, and worked harder on a challenging task, compared to individuals low in self-uniqueness. Presumably, individuals high in self-uniqueness believe that their co-workers are less able than themselves to contribute well on a challenging task, and therefore believe their contribution is necessary. The reverse is true when the task is easy (see also Charbonnier et al., 1998). In terms of expectancy-value theory, redundancy of the individual contribution leads to low perceived instrumentality, whereas uniqueness of the individual contribution leads to high perceived instrumentality, thereby influencing the group members' determination of how much effort to expend.

GROUP SIZE

The tendency to loaf is smaller in small groups than in large groups (Latané, Williams, & Harkins, 1979; Petty et al., 1977). This effect was again demonstrated in a recent study investigating whether social loafing occurred in a collaborative educational task in first-year psychology students, comparing groups of three and eight students (North, Linley, & Hargreaves, 2000). Thus, keeping group size limited can reduce social loafing. In terms of expectancy-value theory, a smaller group size leads to higher perceived instrumentality: chances decrease that the valued outcome can be attained without one's own contributions.

COLLECTIVE ORIENTATION

Karau and Williams (1993) note that women compared to men are less inclined to loaf (see, for a recent replication of this finding, Kugihara, 1999). Karau and Williams (1993) also note that Asian cultures compared to Western cultures are less inclined to loaf. Presumably, women compared to men, and Eastern compared to Western cultures, are more collectively oriented. This means that stimulating a prosocial orientation can reduce social loafing. Recently, Duffy and Shaw (2000) investigated the effects of envy in 143 groups over a period of 16 weeks. The occurrence of high levels of envy, or jealousy, in groups can be seen as a sign of lack of collective orientation. The study found that more envy increased social loafing, and reduced group potency, group cohesion, and group performance. In terms of expectancy-value theory, a prosocial orientation leads to higher outcome value: contributing to the group is in itself considered valuable.

EXPECTATIONS ABOUT OTHERS

Individuals are less inclined to loaf when they expect other group members to perform badly (Jackson & Harkins, 1985; Kerr & Bruun, 1981; Williams & Karau, 1991). This means that group members will loaf less when they believe that other group members will contribute insufficiently, for example because of low effort. Williams and Karau (1991) manipulated participants' expectancies about their partners directly, for example by letting the co-worker explicitly announce that "I (don't) think I'm going to work very hard". They found that participants with partners who announced they would work hard socially loafed. Participants with partners who announced they would not work hard socially compensated (see also Williams, Karau, & Bourgeois, 1993; Williams & Sommer, 1997). Hart, Bridgett, and Karau (2001) examined the joint effect of co-worker ability and expected co-worker effort. When co-worker effort was expected to be low, participants socially compensated when they also believed that the partner had low ability. In terms of expectancy-value theory, low expectations about the performance of others lead to high perceived instrumentality: one's own contribution is necessary to attain the valued outcome.

CONTINGENCY BETWEEN INDIVIDUAL AND GROUP PERFORMANCE

Contingency between individual and group performance is not a variable listed in Karau and Williams's (1993) meta-analysis (because it was apparently not investigated until that time), although it is an important variable in their collective effort model. Shepperd and Taylor (1999, experiment 1) directly manipulated this contingency and believed it to influence perceived instrumentality. Their participants were told that the top 10 per cent performing groups on a brainstorm task would receive a prize. Participants in groups who were led to believe that it was very likely that their group would be in the top 10 per cent (high instrumentality) exerted more effort than participants who believed a top 10 per cent position to be highly unlikely (low instrumentality).

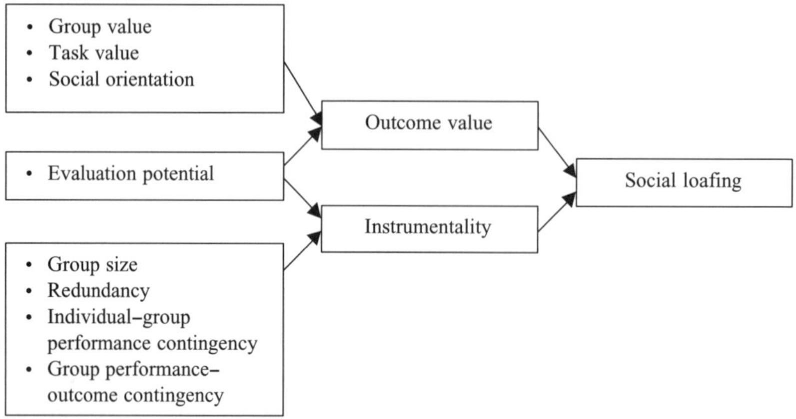

Figure 17.1 Schematic representation of the determinants of social loafing and their mediating variables

CONTINGENCY BETWEEN GROUP PERFORMANCE AND GROUP OUTCOME

Contingency between group performance and group outcome is not a variable listed in Karau and Williams's (1993) meta-analysis (because it was apparently not investigated until that time), although it is again an important variable in their collective effort model. Shepperd and Taylor (1999, experiment 2) directly manipulated this contingency and believed it to influence perceived instrumentality. Half of their participants working on a brainstorm task were led to believe that their group had a 70 per cent chance of winning a prize (high instrumentality), the other half were told their group had only a 1 in 200 chance of winning the prize. Participants in groups who were led to believe that chances to win the prize were high (high instrumentality) exerted more effort than participants who believed those chances to be low (low instrumentality). Thus, the likelihood that a good collective performance will be rewarded reduces social loafing.

Figure 17.1 presents all variables which research has shown to influence social loafing, and the hypothesized relationships with the mediating variables of instrumentality and outcome value. Group size, redundancy, individual–group performance contingency, and group performance–outcome contingency are hypothesized to influence the perceived instrumentality of a contribution and thereby social loafing. Group value, task value, and social orientation are hypothesized to influence the perceived outcome value and thereby social loafing. Evaluation potential is hypothesized to influence social loafing both via outcome value and instrumentality.

Equity

I would like to develop one of the variables that I listed in the previous paragraph a little bit further: expectations about others. According to Karau and Williams (1993), high expectations of others lead to more social loafing than low expectations. I reasoned that this is presumably due to the fact that low expectations of others lead to high perceived instrumentality of one's own contribution. I would like to add that expectations about others may also influence outcome value, albeit outcome value in a different sense than Karau and Williams (1993), Shepperd (1993), and Vroom (1964) use.

The perceived value of an outcome not only depends on the absolute level of the outcome, but also on the point of reference to which the outcome is compared. According to Thibaut and Kelley (1959), outcomes are evaluated by comparing them to a comparison level, an affectively neutral point on a scale of possible outcomes. The comparison level depends among other things on what one knows of the outcomes of others. People compare their own outcomes with those of others and this determines whether their own outcomes are evaluated positively or negatively. Our choice of comparison others is often based on similarity and proximity: we tend to compare ourselves with others who are similar to us or physically close (Festinger, 1954). The point is that team members are likely to not only evaluate the value of their outcomes in an absolute sense, but also relatively. Team members are likely to look at how their own outcomes relate to the outcomes of fellow team members.

Adams (1965) and Walster, Walster, and Berscheid (1978) have extended this reasoning one step further. These authors say that individuals do not only socially compare their outcomes, but also their inputs. Adams (1965) and Walster, Walster, and Berscheid (1978) specifically predict that people strive for equity: the ratio of their own inputs and outcomes should be equal to the ratio of inputs and outcomes of others.

The equity principle is completely non-existent in Vroom's (1964) model. This is understandable considering that Vroom's (1964) model was formulated for individual motivation on individual tasks and not collective tasks. Social comparison is therefore left out of consideration. However, when Vroom's (1964) model is applied to collective tasks, considerations of social comparison of inputs and outcomes cannot be left out of consideration to come to a more complete understanding of the determinants of individual effort.

In a collective task, group members work together to deliver a group performance and, very likely, group members will look at each other and wonder how much each group member contributes. If all group members profit equally from the group's performance, then one may predict on the basis of equity theory that group members will consider it fair that all group members contribute equally. A situation in which contributions are unequal while outcomes are divided equally will be considered unfair. According to equity theory, people are distressed by inequity and they will be inclined to prevent it from occurring, or to seek retribution for it after it has occurred (Greenberg, 1988; Rutte & Messick, 1995; Tyler & Smith, 1998).

Kerr (1983) was one of the first who pointed out the importance of equity in collective tasks. Following Orbell and Dawes (1981), he distinguished two mechanisms that lie at the basis of reduced motivation to contribute in collective tasks. The first is the free-rider mechanism. Free-riders try to take advantage from the fact that the contributions of others may suffice to deliver the required performance and therefore their own efforts are deemed redundant and are withheld. Free-riders profit from the contributions of others without contributing (as much) themselves. The second mechanism is the sucker mechanism. Suckers are those group members who do all or most of the work and do not profit any more than those who did nothing or less. Suckers are those group members on which the free-riders free-ride. The sucker mechanism refers to the phenomenon that people reduce their efforts because they do not want to be a sucker.

Both the free-rider and the sucker mechanism lead, according to Kerr (1983), to a reduction in motivation in group members to contribute to the group. The free-rider mechanism leads to a reduction in motivation because group members perceive their contribution as redundant. This is in agreement with Vroom's (1964) theory in which he deals with perceived instrumentality of contributions. Kerr (1983) points out that if all group members think the same, the required group performance will not be attained. In this sense, working on a collective task has the characteristics of a social dilemma: for each group member it is more rational to defect (i.e. not to contribute) than to cooperate (i.e. to contribute); however, if all group members defect they are all worse off than if all had cooperated (the case in Box 17.1 is a clear example of this).

The sucker mechanism also leads to a reduction in motivation to contribute. People do not like being a sucker. According to Kerr (1983), the equity norm is the most commonly accepted norm for behaviour in work groups. The equity norm makes the sucker role problematic. Why, after all, should one group member contribute more effort than other group members if outcomes are equally divided?

The equity norm also makes the free-rider role problematic, however rational that role may be. Why, after all, should one group member contribute less effort than other group members if outcomes are equally divided? Research has shown that people are more sensitive to inequities when they are to their disadvantage than when they are to their advantage (Walster, Walster, & Berscheid, 1978). Therefore people probably dislike being a sucker more than being a free-rider. But both the free-rider and sucker mechanisms can be active on collective tasks, and both these mechanisms will lead to reductions in motivation and performance.

What is the relevance of all this for expectations about the performance of others? According to Karau and Williams (1993), group members are inclined to increase effort when they expect others to perform badly. This conclusion is at odds with the prediction on the basis of the sucker mechanism. Based on the sucker mechanism, the reverse finding holds: group members are inclined to decrease effort when they expect others to perform badly (Kerr, 1983).

These contradictory findings of expected performance of others on one's own performance can be explained when legitimacy of bad performance is taken into consideration. Some conditions may justify that some group members contribute more to the group's performance than others, for example differences in ability. High able group members have to put in less effort to perform well than low able group members. Because high able group members need to invest less effort for the same performance, it may be justifiable that these group members perform better than low able group members. Under those circumstances a low expectation of the performance of others may lead to an increase in one's own performance. That this reasoning holds has been demonstrated by Kerr and Bruun (1981).

Another condition that may legitimize that some group members perform better than others can be the fact that group members differ in perceived outcome value. Some group members may for instance like the task better. Working on a nice task is a positive outcome value in itself. Because these group members have in this sense more outcomes than group members who do not like the task, it is justifiable that they perform better. Looking at it this way, all variables influencing perceived outcome value (see Figure 17.1) can change the equity judgement.

If there is no legitimization for differences in contributions between group members, group members will avoid becoming a sucker by reducing their contributions. In that case low expectations about performance of others may lead to a reduction in their own

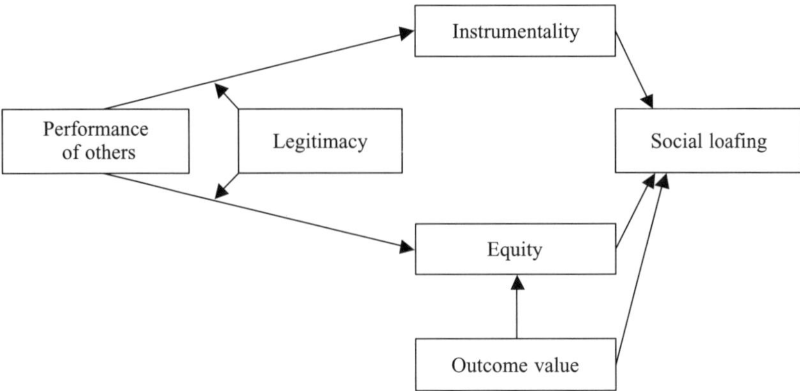

Figure 17.2 Schematic representation of the effect of the expectation about performance of others on social loafing

performance, so that the contributions of the other group members are matched and the situation is fair.

All in all, one may hypothesize that group members have judgements about the fairness of each group member's inputs and outcomes. Perceived unfairness will influence the tendency to loaf. If, for no good reason, other group members are expected to perform badly, then the situation is unfair. Under those circumstances group members will try to reduce unfairness by lowering their own performance and match that of the other group members. Figure 17.2 depicts this reasoning schematically.

Figure 17.2 shows that expectations about the performance of others influence the tendency to loaf, on the one hand via perceived equity and on the other via perceived instrumentality. The weight of each path depends on the perceived legitimacy of the level of performance invested by each group member. The equity judgements about the level of performance invested by each group member are influenced by the perceived outcome value for each group member.

Wilke, Rutte, and van Knippenberg (2000) provide some evidence for the importance of fairness feelings about social loafing in groups. They conducted a field study among 127 members of semi-autonomous teams and found that performance differences between team members led to increased feelings of unfairness. They also found some evidence for our legitimacy hypothesis. They hypothesized that suckers, i.e. team members with relatively high performances, would feel less unfairness when they felt highly rewarded for their efforts. In particular high social rewards and (when the task was unpleasant) high financial rewards appeared to moderate the relationship between performance differences and unfairness feelings for suckers, i.e. for suckers with high rewards performance differences were to a lesser extent associated with feelings of unfairness.

Hart, Bridgett, and Karau (2001) also provide some evidence for our legitimacy hypothesis. They examined the joint effects of expected co-worker effort and co-worker ability. They found that group members who expected co-worker effort to be low, socially loafed when they believed that their partner had high ability, and socially compensated when they believed their partner had low ability. Being a sucker is apparently less problematic with a low than with a high able partner.

Roy, Gauvin, and Limayem (1996) showed that social matching may occur in groups. Undergraduate business school students participated in electronic brainstorming. In one of their experimental conditions, throughout the task, the ideas generated by group members appeared on a public screen. In that condition social matching occurred, i.e. group members adjusted their level of effort to that of the group. All these studies provide some preliminary confirmation for our reasoning that equity plays a role in groups working on collective tasks.

SOLUTIONS

On the basis of the model developed in the previous paragraphs, it is possible to systematically derive possible remedies against social loafing. The mediating mechanisms of instrumentality, outcome value, and equity can be used, alone or in combination, to reduce social loafing.

Outcome Value

When contributions are not rewarded, the outcome value is low and the tendency to contribute diminishes. This suggests one obvious solution: make contributing rewarding. Shepperd (1993) distinguishes four types of rewards: external individual rewards, internal individual rewards, external collective rewards, and internal collective rewards.

Organizations could reward each group member individually. External individual rewards can be financial or social in nature. To reward group members individually, it is necessary to make their individual contributions identifiable and assessable. Each individual's contribution is next linked to an external financial or social reward, e.g. a compliment.

There are internal individual rewards, when an individual judges intrinsic rewards for performing on the task to be present. This is for example the case, according to Shepperd (1993), when individuals have a clear norm or standard against which they can evaluate their performance and find living up to standard performance on the task in itself valuable. Thus, organizations could formulate specific performance goals. There are also individual internal rewards when the group members find the task intrinsically interesting. Organizations could strive therefore to create meaningful or pleasant tasks for their employees.

Organizations could also reward group members collectively. Collective external rewards, i.e. rewarding the group as a group financially or socially, could be such a form of reward. After all, rewarding individual contributions presupposes that individual contributions can be identified and assessed. In real life this will often be difficult, if not impossible. Collective rewards are then an alternative solution. Karau and Williams (1993), however, maintain that collective external rewards will only be effective when there is a direct relationship between the collectively received reward and the individually received reward.

According to Shepperd (1993), there is one final form of reward left: collective internal rewards, such as when individuals identify with, are proud of, or feel obligated towards their group. This will be the case in cohesive groups. When groups are cohesive, individuals value the success of their group as their own success, and this is intrinsically rewarding. This means that organizations could try to increase group cohesiveness, e.g. through careful team composition, to attempt to reduce the tendency to loaf. Karau, Markus, and Williams (2000) suggest that some personality factors may be relevant here. People high in collectivism, need for affiliation, need to belong, and protestant work ethic have the tendency to value collective outcomes and contribute to collective efforts. Having teams composed of members with these characteristics should therefore reduce social loafing.

Instrumentality

Instrumentality refers to the relationship between performance and the acquisition of a valued outcome. Making individuals' contributions indispensable can strengthen this relationship. When individuals' contributions are indispensable they must perform, otherwise the valued outcome cannot be attained. According to Shepperd (1993), there are three ways to convince team members that their contributions are necessary for a sufficient collective performance, i.e. make contributing difficult, unique, or essential.

When contributing is difficult, individuals may become convinced that the task is so complex or difficult that it is unlikely that other group members will duplicate their contributions. As a result, on difficult tasks, group members will loaf less than on simple tasks. Organizations could, thus, increase task difficulty to reduce social loafing, for example by making tasks more complex or by increasing time pressure.

Group members can also be convinced of the necessity of their contribution when their contribution is unique. Organizations could distribute team tasks in such a way to individual group members that they do not overlap, and each group member has a unique contribution to make to the collective performance. As a result, the tendency to loaf will decrease.

Finally, group members can be convinced of the necessity of their contribution by increasing their belief that an adequate collective performance depends on their personal contribution. If, for example, a team leader can make clear to the group that group members differ in ability, then team members who consider themselves able will feel that their contributions are essential. This will decrease the tendency to loaf.

Reducing group size is another possibility organizations can turn to, to increase instrumentality and to reduce social loafing (Karau, Markus, & Williams, 2000). The smaller the group, the less likely each group member's contribution is redundant.

Equity

One can influence perceived equity by making changes in the outcomes of group members, in the inputs, and in the relationship between inputs and outcomes. Organizations can positively influence perceived outcomes by making the task intrinsically motivating, increasing the group's cohesiveness, and giving positive feedback about individual performance. Perceived inputs are influenced by explaining that some group members have, for example, to put in more effort for the same level of performance as others, thereby pointing out that it is legitimate that the performance of some group members is lower than that of others. Organizations can influence the relationship between inputs and outcomes by letting group members know that those who contributed less will be rewarded less or even be punished. All these measures will reduce the tendency to loaf.

CONCLUSION

When individuals work in teams, they all must cooperate for the team to be effective. Group performance can only be high when all team members are cooperative and exert a lot of effort. However, there is a danger that teamwork may lead to motivation losses. In this chapter I presented a framework to organize the results of research on motivation losses in groups. The framework combines insights from Vroom's expectancy-value theory (1964) with insights from Adams's equity theory (1965). Vroom's (1964) theory was developed for individual motivation on individual tasks. On individual tasks, according to Vroom, outcome value and instrumentality determine motivation. Karau and Williams (1993) have argued that working on group tasks negatively influences outcome value and instrumentality, because the link between (group) performance and (individual) outcome is more indirect and because there is potential redundancy of each group member's contribution. In general, working in teams will therefore negatively influence motivation to perform. However, this conclusion of Karau and Williams deserves some comments.

The first is that when one applies Vroom's (1964) theory to collective tasks, amendments from equity theory are necessary for a more complete understanding of the dynamics of individual motivation. Individuals working on collective tasks do not judge their contributions to the collective performance irrespective of the contributions of others. Group members strive for justice. If all receive equal outcomes, contributions should be equal as well. If the ratio of inputs and outcomes is not in balance and is judged unfair by group members, they will influence their own contribution to the collective performance. Working in teams makes free-riding possible. People do not like to be confronted with the free-rider behaviour of others, particularly when there is no legitimization for such behaviour. They will try to avoid being a sucker and reduce their own efforts. When group members start to loaf because they do not want to be a sucker, a downward spiral may be the result: all group members will work increasingly less hard. On the other hand, considerations of fairness may also be a reason for group members to contribute to the group, even if there is no incentive for it in terms of instrumentality and outcome value. In other words, following Vroom (1964) it may be *rational* to loaf, but following Adams (1965) it may be *moral* not to loaf.

A second comment is that Karau and Williams (1993) use Vroom's theory (1964) to organize the determinants of social loafing as they appeared in the literature. Very often, the relevance of these determinants has been demonstrated in experimental laboratory studies. Their conclusion is that working on individual tasks leads to higher productivity than working on collective tasks. This conclusion is at odds with insights from the organizational psychological literature that individual tasks are often more narrow and isolated than group tasks which create their own problems. In a classically structured organization, with individual tasks as building blocks instead of group tasks, several variables presented in the model may be influenced negatively. Evaluation potential, prosocial orientation, group value, task value, perceived redundancy, and perceived contributions of others, all these variables may be negatively influenced when tasks are individual and not collective. In this sense, individual tasks may very well have negative effects on individual performance compared to collective tasks. This chapter is, thus, not a plea against teamwork, but a warning that working in teams is not a panacea, because compared to individual tasks, collective tasks can lead to motivation losses as a result of equity, instrumentality, or outcome considerations. Understanding which variables influence social loafing can help to optimize individual motivation on collective tasks.

Much of the research on social loafing so far has studied small, randomly assembled, ad hoc groups, under controlled experimental conditions, while performing one simple task. Anderson, Lindsay, and Bushman (1999) compared correspondence between laboratory and field study results across a broad range of phenomena, including social loafing. They found considerable correspondence between effect sizes and conclude that laboratory studies may not be as problematic in external validity as often thought. Nevertheless, laboratory groups only exist for a limited time, they have no past and no future and are isolated from the environment instead of being embedded in larger organizations (McGrath, 1991). The nature of this research is reflected in limited theories about groups. Real-world groups, however, often do not have one simple task but need to execute several. Many groups have a past and expect a future. Groups do not exist in isolation, but are embedded in an organization. Group members are not only oriented towards their task, but also towards their individual interest and the maintenance of interpersonal relationships. These circumstances that are normal for many real-life groups are virtually ignored in group research (McGrath, 1991). Relevant research questions in this context are: How do group members deal with social loafing when working on multiple tasks? Is it permissible to loaf on one task if one compensates on another? Are group members equally inclined to loaf when there is a future with the group compared to when there is not? Is it permissible for a group member to loaf on a current task and make up for it on a future task? Is it permissible for a group member to loaf on the present task, because he or she has to work on other tasks with higher priority elsewhere in the organization? Do group members accept social loafing of a co-worker more easily when this co-worker fulfils maintenance or interpersonal roles in the group to compensate?

Erez and Somech (1996) also plead for research using real interactive groups. They are critical about the fact that in most of the research on social loafing participants acted in pseudo-groups, were not allowed to communicate, and did not have specific goals or rewards for performance. In an effort to create more real-life situations, these scholars conducted a study of social loafing in 16 conditions representing four experimental factors: with or without specific goals, with or without communication, with or without rewards, and with or without collectivist values. In all conditions, participants had co-workers they had known for at least six months. Social loafing was found in only one of the 16 conditions. Erez and Somech (1996) conclude that their results demonstrate that social loafing is the exception rather than the rule. It may be concluded that field research on real interactive groups in organizations is necessary, or else laboratory research using more realistic simulations. Comprehensive theoretical models to guide such research are needed. In this chapter I presented a model that will hopefully fulfil a fruitful role in this respect. The model addresses the determinants and dynamics of social loafing. Instrumentality, outcome value, and equity are posed as central mediating mechanisms. The model also offers many starting-points to counter social loafing in practice.

REFERENCES

Adams, J. S. (1965). Inequity in social exchange. In L. Berkowitz (ed.), *Advances in Experimental Social Psychology* (Vol. 2). New York: Academic Press.

Anderson, C. A., Lindsay, J. J., & Bushman, B. J. (1999). Research in the psychological laboratory: truth or triviality? *Current Directions in Psychological Science, 8*(1), 3–9.

Benders, J., Huijgen, F., Pekruhl, U., & O'Kelly, K. P. (1999). *Useful But Unused—Group Work in Europe*. Luxembourg: Office for Official Publications of the European Communities.

Charbonnier, E., Huguet, P., Brauer, M., & Monteil, J. M. (1998). Social loafing and self-beliefs: people's collective effort depends on the extent to which they distinguish themselves as better than others. *Social Behavior and Personality, 26*(4), 329–340.

Druskat, V. U. & Wolff, S. B. (1999). Effects and timing of developmental peer appraisals in self-managing work groups. *Journal of Applied Psychology, 84*(1), 58–74.

Duffy, M. K. & Shaw, J. D. (2000). The Saliery syndrome: consequences of envy in groups. *Small Group Research, 31*(1), 3–23.
Erez, M. & Somech, A. (1996). Is group productivity loss the rule or the exception? Effects of culture and group-based motivation. *Academy of Management Journal, 39*(6), 1513–1537.
Faulkner, S. L. & Williams, K. D. (1996). A study of social loafing in industry. Paper presented at the annual meeting of the Midwestern Psychological Association, Chicago.
Festinger, L. (1954). A theory of social comparison. *Human Relations, 7*, 117–140.
Gagne, M. & Zuckerman, M. (1999). Performance and learning goal orientations as moderators of social loafing and social facilitation. *Small Group Research, 30*(5), 524–541.
George, J. M. (1992). Extrinsic and intrinsic origins of perceived social loafing in organizations. *Academy of Management Journal, 35*, 191–202.
George, J. M. (1995). Asymmetrical effects of rewards and punishments: the case of social loafing. *Journal of Occupational and Organizational Psychology, 68*, 327–338.
Greenberg, J. (1988). Equity and workplace status: a field-experiment. *Journal of Applied Psychology, 73*, 606–613.
Hardy, C. I. & Latané, B. (1988). Social loafing in cheerleaders: effects of teammembership and competition. *Journal of Sport and Exercise Psychology, 10*, 109–114.
Harkins, S. G. (1987). Social loafing and social facilitation. *Journal of Experimental Social Psychology, 11*, 575–584.
Harkins, S. G. & Petty, R. E. (1982). Effects of task difficulty and task uniqueness on social loafing. *Journal of Personality and Social Psychology, 43*, 1214–1229.
Harkins, S. G. & Szymanski, K. (1988). Social loafing and self-evaluation with an objective standard. *Journal of Experimental Social Psychology, 24*, 354–365.
Hart, J. W., Bridgett, D. J., & Karau, S. J. (2001). Coworker ability and effort as determinants of individual effort on a collective task. *Group Dynamics, 5*(3), 181–190.
Henningsen, D. D., Cruz, M. G., & Miller, M. L. (2000). Role of social loafing in predeliberation decision making. *Group Dynamics: Theory, Research, and Practice, 4*(2), 168–175.
Hertel, G., Kerr, N. L., & Messé, L. (2000). Motivation gains in performance groups: paradigmatic and theoretical developments on the Köhler effect. *Journal of Personality and Social Psychology, 79*(4), 580–601.
Hoeksema-van Orden, C. Y. D., Gaillard, A. W. K., & Buunk, B. P. (1998). Social loafing under fatigue. *Journal of Personality and Social Psychology, 75*(5), 1179–1190.
Huguet, P., Charbonnier, E., & Monteil J. M. (1999). Productivity loss in performance groups: people who see themselves as average do not engage in social loafing. *Group Dynamics: Theory, Research, and Practice, 3*(2), 118–131.
Ingham, A. G., Levinger, G., Graves, J., & Peckham, V. (1974). The Ringelmann effect: studies of group size and group performance. *Journal of Experimental Social Psychology, 10*, 371–384.
Jackson, J. M. & Harkins, S. G. (1985). Equity in effort: an explanation of the social loafing effect. *Journal of Personality and Social Psychology, 49*, 1199–1206.
Karau S. J. & Hart, J. W. (1998). Group cohesiveness and social loafing: effects of a social interaction manipulation on individual motivation within groups. *Group Dynamics, 2*(3), 185–191.
Karau, S. J., Markus, M. J., & Williams, K. D. (2000). On the elusive search for motivation gains in groups: insights from the Collective Effort Model. *Zeitschrift für Sozialpsychologie, 31*(4), 179–190.
Karau, S. J. & Williams, K. D. (1993). Social loafing: a meta-analytic review and theoretical integration. *Journal of Personality and Social Psychology, 65*, 681–706.
Karau, S. J. & Williams, K. D. (1997). The effects of group cohesiveness on social loafing and social compensation. *Group Dynamics: Theory, Research, and Practice, 1*(2), 156–168.
Karau, S. J. & Williams, K. D. (2001). Understanding individual motivation in groups: the Collective Effort Model. In M. E. Turner (ed.), *Groups at Work: Theory and Research. Applied Social Research* (pp. 113–141). Mahwah, NJ: Lawrence Erlbaum.
Kerr, N. L. (1983). Motivation losses in small groups: a social dilemma analysis. *Journal of Personality and Social Psychology, 45*, 819–828.
Kerr, N. L. & Bruun, S. E. (1981). Ringelmann revisited: alternative explanations for the social loafing effect. *Personality and Social Psychology Bulletin, 7*, 224–231.

Kirkman, B. L., Shapiro, D. L., Novelli, L., & Brett, J. M. (1996). Employee concerns regarding self-managing work teams: a multidimensional justice perspective. *Social Justice Research, 9*(1), 49–67.

Kugihara, N. (1999). Gender and social loafing in Japan. *Journal of Social Psychology, 139*(4), 516–526.

Latané, B., Williams, K., & Harkins, S. (1979). Many hands make light the work: the causes and consequences of social loafing. *Journal of Personality and Social Psychology, 37*, 822–832.

Lichacz, F. M. & Partington, J. T. (1997). Collective efficacy and true group performance. *International Journal of Sport Psychology, 27*(2), 146–158.

McGrath, J. E. (1991). Time, interaction and performance: a theory of groups. *Small Group Research, 22*, 147–174.

Mohrman, S. A., Cohen, S. G., & Mohrman, A. M. (1995). *Designing Team-based Organizations*. San Francisco: Jossey-Bass.

North, A. C., Linley, A., & Hargreaves, D. J. (2000). Social loafing in a cooperative classroom task. *Educational Psychology, 20*, 389–392.

Orbell, J. & Dawes, R. (1981). Social dilemmas. In G. Stephenson & J. H. Davis (eds), *Progress in Applied Social Psychology* (Vol. 1). Chichester: Wiley.

Petty, R. E., Cacioppo, J. T., & Kasmer, J. A. (1985). Individual differences in social loafing on cognitive tasks. Paper presented at the annual meeting of the Midwestern Psychological Association, Chicago.

Petty, R. E., Harkins, S. G., Williams, K., & Latané, B. (1977). The effects of group size on cognitive effort and evaluation. *Personality and Social Psychology Bulletin, 3*, 579–582.

Plaks, J. E. & Higgins, E. T. (2000). Pragmatic use of stereotyping in teamwork: social loafing and compensation as a function of inferred partner–situation fit. *Journal of Personality and Social Psychology, 79*(6), 962–974.

Price, K. H. (1987). Decision responsibility, task responsibility, identifiability, and social loafing. *Organizational Behaviour and Human Decision Processes, 40*, 330–345.

Ringelmann, M. (1913). Recherches sur les moteurs animés: travail de l'homme. *Annales de l'Institut National Agronomique, 2*(12), 1–40.

Robbins, S. P. (2001). *Organizational Behavior*. Upper Saddle River, NJ: Prentice-Hall.

Roy, M. C., Gauvin, S., & Limayem, M. (1996). Electronic group brainstorming: the role of feedback on productivity. *Small Group Research, 27*(2), 215–247.

Rutte, C. G. (1990). Social dilemmas in organizations. *Social Behaviour: An International Journal of Applied Social Psychology, 5*(4), 285–294.

Rutte, C. G. & Messick, D. M. (1995). An integrated model of perceived unfairness in organizations. *Social Justice Research, 8*(3), 239–261.

Shepperd, J. A. (1993). Productivity loss in performance groups: a motivation analysis. *Psychological Bulletin, 113*, 67–81.

Shepperd, J. A. & Taylor, K. M. (1999). Social loafing and expectancy-value theory. *Personality and Social Psychology Bulletin, 25*(9), 1147–1158.

Smith, B. N., Kerr, N. A., Markus, M. J., & Stasson, M. F. (2001). Individual differences in social loafing: need for cognition as a motivator in collective performance. *Group Dynamics: Theory, Research, and Practice, 5*(2), 150–158.

Steiner, I. (1972). *Group Processes and Productivity*. San Diego, Calif.: Academic Press.

Szymanski, K. & Harkins, S. G. (1987). Social loafing and self-evaluation with a social standard. *Journal of Personality and Social Psychology, 53*, 891–897.

Thibaut, J. W. & Kelley, H. H. (1959). *Interpersonal Relations*. New York: Wiley.

Tjosvold, D. (1991). *Team Organization: An Enduring Competitive Advantage*. Chichester: Wiley.

Tyler, T. R. & Smith, H. J. (1998). Social justice and social movements. In D. T. Gilbert, S. T. Fiske, & G. Lindzey (eds), *The Handbook of Social Psychology* (pp. 595–632). Boston, Mass.: McGraw-Hill.

Vroom, V. H. (1964). *Work and Motivation*. New York: Wiley.

Walster, E., Walster, G. W., & Berscheid, E. (1978). *Equity: Theory and Research*. Boston: Allyn Bacon.

Wilke, M., Rutte, C. G., & Knippenberg, A. van (2000). The resentful sucker: do rewards ease the pain? *European Journal of Work and Organizational Psychology, 9*(3), 307–320.

Williams, K. D. & Karau, S. J. (1991). Social loafing and social compensation: the effects of expectations of co-worker performance. *Journal of Personality and Social Psychology, 61*, 570–581.
Williams, K., Karau, S., & Bourgeois, M. (1993). Working on collective tasks: social loafing and social compensation. In M. A. Hogg & D. Abrams (eds), *Group Motivation: Social Psychological Perspectives* (pp. 130–148). New York: Harvester-Wheatsheaf.
Williams, K. D. & Sommer, K. L. (1997). Social ostracism by coworkers: does rejection lead to loafing or compensation? *Personality and Social Psychology Bulletin, 7*, 693–706.

Section IV

INTEGRATED ORGANIZATIONS

18

INTERGROUP RELATIONS IN ORGANIZATIONS

Daan van Knippenberg

Work groups and teams are the building blocks of organizations. Not surprisingly, then, considerable research attention in the organizational sciences is devoted to the study of the functioning and performance of work groups and teams—this very handbook testifies to the burgeoning of this field. For obvious reasons, key questions in this research area focus on intragroup processes: How may group performance be enhanced? (e.g. Guzzo & Shea, 1992); How can cooperation and coordination between team members be optimized? (e.g. Saavedra, Earley, & van Dyne, 1993); How may interpersonal conflict be managed so that it is constructive rather than detrimental to group functioning? (e.g. Tjosvold, 1998). There is no doubt that the reality of today's organizations justifies this attention for these intragroup processes. However, what tends to attract far less attention than perhaps it should is the fact that each organizational group functions in a network of organizational groups, and that for effective functioning organizations not only rely on cooperation and good social relationships *within* groups, but also on cooperation and good relationships *between* groups. These intergroup relations between organizational groups are the focus of this chapter.

In the following sections, I first discuss what intergroup relations are and why they should be of concern to organizational scientists. Then, I address the main theories of intergroup relations. The final sections are devoted to discussion of the implications for organizational practice and directions for future research. A first thing to note, however, is what this chapter is *not* about. It is not about issues of organizational diversity (i.e. the relationships of members of different demographic and functional groups *within* organizational groups). Organizational diversity is covered elsewhere in this handbook. Moreover, the key questions in diversity research concern *intra*group process. Even though these are often studied from the perspective of theories of intergroup relations (e.g. van Knippenberg & Haslam, in press; Williams & O'Reilly, 1998), these lie outside the focus of the present chapter. The chapter also does not concern relations between unions and management. These typically cross-cut organizations, both in the sense that not all workers are union members and in the sense that union–management relationships often encompass whole sectors rather than a single

International Handbook of Organizational Teamwork and Cooperative Working. Edited by M. A. West, D. Tjosvold, and K. G. Smith.

organization, and therefore do not represent the within-organization intergroup relations that are the focus of the present chapter.

WHAT ARE "INTERGROUP RELATIONS", AND WHY SHOULD WE CARE?

Teams and work groups do not operate in a vacuum, they function in a context of interdependent relationships with other organizational groups. Just like team members need to coordinate their efforts for the team to function effectively, organizational groups fulfill a role as players in the team that is the organization. Organizational groups are, for instance, typically interdependent for their task performance. They need other groups to provide them with necessary information, products, or services. They also rely on other groups to take their interests into account and resolve potential conflicts of interest in a constructive manner. A sales department may, for instance, depend on production to make good on its sales, whereas the production department is dependent on sales for, on the one hand, enough orders to make good on its capacity and, on the other hand, moderation in orders (both in terms of volume and of deadline) to keep work load within limits and deadlines realistic. This interdependence requires groups to coordinate their efforts and to try to accommodate not only their but also the other group's needs. Even when groups function relatively independently where their task performance is concerned, they may be interdependent for important organizational outcomes. Groups may compete for scarce resources within the organization, such as office space, lab time, personnel, or organizational rewards (e.g. Pfeffer & Salancik, 1977; Pondy, 1967). Such situations are potentially inviting of intergroup conflict and may therefore be detrimental to intergroup relations. This may pose a threat to organizational functioning for at least two reasons. First, competitive orientations between groups may stand in the way of more constructive solutions for conflicts of interests, which are more likely when groups have a more cooperative orientation toward each other (cf. Pruitt & Carnevale, 1993). Second, competitive or disrupted intergroup relations invited by conflicting interests may spill over into other areas on intergroup interaction, such as the need to coordinate task efforts, or may feed into intragroup processes when different groups collaborate in cross-functional teams (e.g. project teams, management teams).

This is not to say that intergroup competition is necessarily bad for organizations. Erev, Bornstein, and Galili (1993; Bornstein & Erev, 1994), for instance, argue that intergroup competition may promote intragroup cooperation and performance. In a field experiment with orange-picking teams, they showed that under conditions of intergroup competition with a reward for the best team, teams performed better than under conditions of collective rewards without the element of competition. It should be noted, however, that for this particular task there was no need for intergroup cooperation, or indeed even intergroup interaction (i.e. each team worked independently), and we may raise doubts about whether the benefits of intergroup competition would generalize to situations where there is a need for intergroup cooperation. Moreover, even in the absence of the need for intergroup collaboration or interaction, a cooperative orientation toward other teams may be desirable, for instance because teams working shifts may rely on other teams to leave the workplace clean and tidy. Thus, whereas intergroup competition is not necessarily bad for organizational functioning, even under conditions of intergroup competition organizations need a climate of "friendly" competition and good sportsmanship, that is good intergroup relations. As a case in point, consider this illustrative anecdote. In the harbor of Rotterdam, the Netherlands, a container terminal switched to the use of self-managed teams to load and unload cargo ships. Although these teams were not interdependent for their task performance, competition between teams was said to be so fierce that at a certain point one team returned to the harbor after work hours to *sabotage* another team's outfit—at the obvious expense of overall organizational performance.

Even in the absence of fierce competition or strong task interdependence, organizations are likely to function more effectively when groups have a cooperative orientation toward each other. As Katz (1964) argued, organizations rely on acts of voluntary and proactive cooperation for their effective functioning (see also Organ, 1988). The argument put forward by Katz seemed to be targeted primarily at interpersonal or intragroup behavior, but we may safely assume that it extends to intergroup behavior. As with interpersonal and intragroup citizenship behavior and other prosocial behavior, acts of intergroup cooperation and good intergroup relations may be modest in nature, and "merely" involve being responsive to another group's needs or taking the other group's interests into account when planning their own course of action. Echoing Katz's argument, then, we may propose that such everyday displays of good intergroup relations are crucial for an organization's functioning, and that the very nature of organizations requires that organizational groups not only coordinate their efforts and interests, and resolve potential conflicts that may be invited by their interdependent relationships (cf. Mohrman, Cohen, & Mohrman, 1995), but more generally take a cooperative orientation in their interaction with each other.

A fact that is typically overlooked is that intergroup relations not only concern the relationship between different organizational groups, but also reflect upon the relationship between organizational groups and the organization as a whole. Tensions between organizational groups may focus the individual on his/her own group and turn attention away from the organization as a whole, to the detriment of organizational identification and the willingness to exert oneself in the organization's interest (Kramer, 1991). Thus, from the perspective of employees' relationships with the organization as a whole too, intergroup relations are a core concern.

Importantly, this argument about the value of good intergroup relations in organizations is not just academic. Management theorists have argued that intergroup relations in organizations hold great potential for conflict when groups are interdependent for task completion and need to rely on the specific skills and expertise of the different groups (Brett & Rognes, 1986; cf. Blake, Shepard, & Mouton, 1964). Indeed, empirical and anecdotal evidence suggests that intergroup tensions are typical of many, if not all, organizations (e.g. Alderfer, 1987; Blake, Shepard, & Mouton, 1964; Kramer, 1991), and some researchers have argued that intergroup relations are more important for organizational functioning than individual behavior (Alderfer, 1987). Intergroup relations therefore are, or should be, a core concern for organizations.

Ultimately, then, organizational effectiveness is contingent on the ability to manage intergroup relations. Managing intergroup relations is by no means just a matter of a set of rules or procedures that describe how these relationships should be managed. First, managing such a complex set of relationships between the host of organizational groups that are present in even a modest-sized organization through formal procedures would require such an elaborate bureaucracy that it would most likely be to the detriment of the organization's functioning. Second, many contingencies are unforeseeable, and cannot easily be captured by formal procedures. Moreover, as many organizations adopt more flexible, less bureaucratic structures, the behavior of organizational groups becomes more discretionary. Organizational groups thus often will have substantial leeway in how they act in their relationships with other groups. This makes the study of intergroup relations in organizations very much the study of the perceptions, attitudes, and motivations that underlie the behavior toward other groups, and the question of how to manage intergroup relations very much the question of how to manage the perceptions, attitudes, and motivations of organizational members. Indeed, in recognition of the fact that intergroup relations are ultimately a matter of human agency rather than rules and regulations, the study of intergroup relations places a strong emphasis on the psychological (i.e. cognitive–motivational) component of intergroup relations. What, then, have we learned about the psychology of intergroup relations in organizations? This question is addressed in the next section.

THEORIES OF INTERGROUP RELATIONS IN ORGANIZATIONS

Traditionally, the study of intergroup relations has been the domain of disciplines with a societal focus such as social psychology, sociology, and anthropology, and the study of intergroup relations has accordingly focused primarily on the relationship between societal groups such as ethnic groups rather than on organizational groups. As a consequence, there is relatively little research in intergroup relations in organizations, even though there is a massive body of research in intergroup relations. In accordance with the cognitive–motivational underpinnings of intergroup behavior (Brewer, 1979; Messick & Mackie, 1989; Turner et al., 1987), in the psychological literature "intergroup relations" is taken to refer to "any aspect of thought, feeling, or action that occurs because of group membership" (Mackie & Smith, 1998, p. 499). Perceptions of other groups (e.g. stereotypes) and attitudes toward other groups thus also fall within the domain of intergroup relations. Moreover, not only is the study of intergroup relations not limited to the study of behavior, it also is not limited to the thoughts, feelings, or actions of entire groups. Interpersonal attitudes and behavior too may be understood as a product of intergroup relations to the extent that the individuals in question approach self and other in terms of their group memberships (Sherif, 1966; Tajfel & Turner, 1986; Turner et al., 1987). In the following sections, I review the main theories and developments in the study of intergroup relations as they are applied, or are relevant, to intergroup relations in organizations.

Realistic Group Conflict Theory

An obvious starting point for analyzing problematic intergroup relations is to look for conflicting interests or goals that may explain intergroup tensions. Such was the gist of theories surveyed by Campbell (1965), and this led him to coin the label realistic group conflict theory for this approach to the study of intergroup relations. Central to realistic group conflict theory, also encountered under the label realistic conflict theory (RCT) is the proposition that intergroup behavior reflects group interests. Accordingly, the quality of intergroup relations is proposed to be critically dependent on the relationship between the groups' interests. When group interests are incompatible (e.g. when groups compete for scarce resources), this may elicit a range of negative responses, such as prejudiced attitudes, hostility, and discrimination. When group interests are compatible (e.g. when groups work toward a collaborative goal), in contrast, reactions to the other group will be more positive and intergroup relations will be more harmonious.

RCT is best known as expressed in the work of Sherif (e.g. Sherif, 1966). In a series of experiments in the context of a boys' summer camp, Sherif showed that relationships between two groups of boys deteriorated in the context of competition (i.e. conflicting group interests), whereas they became more amicable in the context of intergroup cooperation toward shared superordinate goals (i.e. converging group interests). Importantly, Sherif was able to demonstrate that introducing a shared superordinate goal worked as an intervention to improve intergroup relations that had suffered as a consequence of intergroup competition. More tightly controlled laboratory experiments have confirmed these basic findings (e.g. Gaertner et al., 1990).

In the context of organizations RCT has also proven itself as an explanatory framework. Blake, Shepard, and Mouton (1964) in particular have demonstrated that the favorability on intergroup attitudes in organizations is related to the perceived compatibility of group interests (see also Brown & Williams, 1984). Importantly too, whereas the basic tenet of RCT seems to concern the objective (i.e. "realistic") degree of compatibility between group interests, work by Blake, Shepard, and Mouton (1964) and others (e.g. Brown et al., 1986) shows that the *perception* of conflicting interest rather than objective conflict of interest per se may drive negative intergroup attitudes. This finding is important, because the conflict literature shows that people often perceive a larger conflict of interest than in reality exists (e.g. Pruitt & Carnevale, 1993). Moreover, this seems to be especially true for groups. Fiske and Ruscher (1993), for instance, suggested that the assumption of negative interdependence is the default condition in intergroup interaction, and Schopler and Insko (1992) demonstrated that groups approach the exact same interdependence situation more competitively than individuals. To a certain extent, then, groups may often create the conditions for intergroup conflict and poor intergroup relations by perceiving group interests as incompatible, even when in fact no such incompatibility exists. Managing intergroup relations from an RCT perspective would thus not only involve managing the "objective" relationship between group goals and interests, but also the subjective perception of these relationships.

RCT is not without its criticism. As Turner (1981) noted, there are a number of theoretical and empirical problems with RCT. It holds that (perceived) compatibility of interests is the key factor in determining intergroup relations, and thus by implication that intergroup relations should deteriorate if conditions of competition are created whereas they should improve if cooperative conditions are created. A number of empirical studies, however, raise doubts about this conclusion. Some studies suggest that competition is only to the detriment of intergroup relations when group members identify strongly with their group, whereas others show that intergroup biases may not disappear when cooperative goals are introduced (Brewer & Brown, 1998). Moreover, studies in the so-called *minimal group paradigm* (e.g. Tajfel et al., 1971), in which there is no interdependence between groups, showed that negative intergroup attitudes and behavior may emerge even in the absence of conflicting interests (for reviews, see Brewer, 1979; Tajfel, 1982). These findings suggest that RCT cannot account for all aspects of intergroup relations, or at the very least that we need a more complex account of the relationship between group interests and intergroup behavior than provided by RCT.

Notwithstanding the criticism of RCT, there is reason to believe that studies of the role of the compatibility of group interests in intergroup relations may often underestimate the importance of this factor. Studies of intergroup relations in organizations typically take place within one single organization (e.g. Brown et al., 1986; Hennessy & West, 1999). Although the compatibility of group interests may vary across groups within a single organization, variations *between* organizations are likely to be much larger, for instance because these may encompass groups that compete for bonuses versus groups that do not and semi-autonomous teams that work independently versus teams that work in strong interdependence with each other. Studying this greater variation in compatibility of group goals and interests is likely to yield a clearer picture of the role of conflicts of interests and interdependence in intergroup relations. Moreover, following the same logic, single organization studies may have to rely more on variations in individual *perceptions* of compatibility of interest and less on actual, objective, variations in compatibility than studies that would encompass several different organizations. Multiple-organization studies of the role of conflicts of interest should therefore be more likely to yield a clear picture of the role of the compatibility of group goals and interests.

Social Categorization/Social Identity Theories

Whereas RCT places the emphasis on the compatibility of interests, social categorization theories of intergroup relations emphasize the role of categorization into groups per se. The most prominent and most fully developed of these theories are social identity theory (Hogg & Abrams, 1988; Tajfel, 1978; Tajfel & Turner, 1986) and self-categorization theory (Turner et al., 1987). Although there are some differences between social identity theory (SIT) and self-categorization theory (SCT) as originally formulated (e.g. SCT provides a further conceptual development of the cognitive underpinnings of the social identity processes described in SIT, and places more emphasis on cognitive processes and less on motivational and affective processes than SIT), developments in SCT fed back into SIT and currently it may be more appropriate to view SIT and SCT as part of one social identity approach (e.g. Haslam, 2001; van Knippenberg, 2000). At the core of SIT/SCT lies the notion that individuals perceive others as well as themselves in terms of their membership of social groups, and that the most fundamental distinction made is between membership of ingroups, groups in which the individual is a member and that have significance for the individual, and outgroups, groups in which the individual is not a member and that are a relevant comparison group for the ingroup. Because these categorizations not only involve others, but also the self, they reflect on the individual's self-concept. *Social identity* is that part of the self-concept that is based on individuals' memberships of social groups. Individuals have multiple group memberships, however, and not all group memberships reflect equally on the self-concept. *Social identification* reflects the extent to which a given group membership is self-definitional in a particular situation (i.e. social identification may change across time and situations). The more an individual identifies with a group or organization, the more the individual's self-image incorporates characteristics associated with the group or organization, and the more likely the individual is to think and act in accordance with the group or organizational identity.

SIT/SCT analyses have been applied to a broad range of intragroup and intergroup processes (e.g. Abrams & Hogg, 1999; Haslam et al., in press; Hogg & Abrams, 1988;

Hogg & Terry, 2001), but SIT was originally developed as a theory of intergroup relations (e.g. Tajfel, 1978; Tajfel & Turner, 1986). At the core of the original SIT analysis of intergroup relations lies the notion that group membership reflects on the self and that therefore the standing or status of the ingroup also reflects on the self. Just as individual status and performance may be determined by interpersonal social comparison, the status of the ingroup is determined by social comparison with outgroups. When the ingroup has higher status than the outgroup, for instance because it performs better, holds a more powerful position, or fulfills a task with greater organizational prestige, this reflects positively on the group members' social identity. Because people are assumed to value feeling good about the self, SIT proposed that individuals will strive for a positive social identity, which may be achieved by becoming and staying a member of high status groups and by achieving positive distinctiveness as a group. The former in part explains social mobility between groups, the latter may directly reflect on intergroup relations because it may invite what Turner (1975) called *social competition* between groups. Even when there does not seem to be an "objective" reason for groups to compete (cf. RCT), groups may compete for social status, because positive social identity is derived from the group's standing relative to other groups. This may lead groups to try to outperform other groups (which could be to an organization's benefit), but may also engender biased intergroup attitudes and behavior which may range from more favorable evaluations of, and attitudes toward, ingroup members, via greater trust in ingroup members and greater willingness to cooperate with ingroup members, to discrimination of, and hostile behavior toward, outgroup members (cf. the incident of sabotage in Rotterdam harbor). Moreover, it may give rise to group-serving attributions and attitudes that legitimize this ingroup favoritism (for reviews, see Brewer, 1979; Tajfel, 1982).

Whereas SIT initially advanced the search for positive social identity or self-esteem as the motive driving intergroup behavior (Abrams & Hogg, 1988), later developments have questioned esteem needs as the primary motive underlying group behavior, and have advanced other motives for intergroup biases (for a review, see e.g. Brewer & Brown, 1998). Primary among these is the desire to maintain group distinctiveness. Group members are argued to value a distinct identity that clearly differentiates the group from other groups (Brewer, 1991; Hewstone & Brown, 1986; Tajfel, 1978). When this distinctiveness is threatened, for instance by an overly strong emphasis on the larger whole that denies intergroup differences (Hornsey & Hogg, 2000) or by the (anticipated) removal of intergroup boundaries (as in a merger; van Leeuwen & van Knippenberg, in press), groups may resort to biased intergroup behavior to maintain or restore their distinctiveness. The notion of distinctiveness threat is of critical importance to our understanding of intergroup relations, because common sense and scientific theory alike have often assumed that problematic intergroup behavior originates in intergroup differences, and that therefore heightening and emphasizing intergroup similarities are a remedy for troublesome intergroup relations. This may be true in some circumstances, and when certain preconditions are met (elaborated in the following), but is not necessarily true in all situations.

In an important deviation from RCT, SIT/SCT, through its emphasis on the social identity implications of group membership and intergroup comparison, is able to account for problematic intergroup relations in the absence of "realistic" intergroup conflict. This should, however, not be misread as saying that SIT/SCT predicts that individuals are always biased toward the members of other groups, or that SIT/SCT assumes that intergroup relations are always competitive, or that SIT/SCT denies the role of the compatibility of group interests. SIT/SCT identifies a number of important contingencies for ingroup-favoring or outgroup-derogating attitudes and behavior to arise. For one, not all groups in which individuals are a member are relevant to the individual, and would thus inspire intergroup biases. Identification with a group thus is an important precondition for intergroup biases. Brown et al. (1986), for instance, found that work group identification was predictive of intergroup biases between departments in a paper factory (see also Brown & Williams, 1984; Hennessy & West, 1999). Even if an individual identifies with a group, however, this group membership is not always salient (salience may, for instance, be induced by identity threats or intergroup competition for organizational outcomes; Kramer, 1991) and social identities are only expected to guide behavior when they are salient (Turner et al., 1987). Social identity salience thus is another important precondition for intergroup biases to occur (Mullen, Brown, & Smith, 1992). Also, not all groups in which the individual is *not* a member are salient as outgroups or pose a threat to group distinctiveness (e.g. a production team is likely to be more motivated to compare favorably to another production team than to personnel administration), and accordingly not all nonmembership groups invite intergroup bias in all situations. For example, Terry and Callan (1998) found in a study of intergroup perceptions in a merger of two hospitals that the threat associated with the merger accentuated intergroup biases toward the merger partner among employees of the lower-status partner. Another important contingency that is especially relevant to organizational contexts is that if group boundaries are permeable, that is, if individuals may move from one group to another, the anticipation of becoming a member of another group may substantially attenuate biases toward that group (Tajfel, 1978). One would, for instance, expect management trainees, who may expect to become part of management, to have a more positive attitude toward the organization's management than employees on the work floor, who have far smaller, if any, chances of becoming part of the organization's management. The nature of the interdependence between groups (cf. RCT) has also been shown to reflect on intergroup relations in research in the social identity tradition. Competitive intergroup relations typically accentuate intergroup biases, whereas cooperative relations may attenuate them (e.g. Gaertner et al., 1990)—although, as noted before, this is no simple one-on-one relationship.

SIT/SCT originates in the study of intergroup relations in nonorganizational contexts, but is now well established as a theory of social identity processes in organizations as well (e.g. Ashforth & Mael, 1989; Haslam et al., in press; Hogg & Terry, 2000, 2001; van Knippenberg & Hogg, 2001, in press). Despite the fact that SIT/SCT provides a well-articulated theoretical framework for the study of intergroup relations in organizations, however, SIT/SCT research on intergroup relations in organizations has remained sparse. Just as SIT was originally developed as a theory of intergroup relations, the first applications of SIT to organizational contexts also focused on intergroup relations (e.g. Brown, 1978). More recent applications, however, have largely focused on organizational identifications and intragroup processes (for examples, see Haslam et al., in press; Hogg & Terry, 2001), or on intergroup relations in the context of organizational diversity (e.g. van Knippenberg & Haslam, in press; Williams & O'Reilly, 1998) rather than on the intergroup relations between formal organizational groups that are the focus of the present discussion (for exceptions, see e.g. Hennessy & West, 1999; Nauta, de Vries, & Wijngaard, 2001). Accordingly, many of the more recent developments in the SIT/SCT analysis of intergroup relations remain yet to be tested in the context of relationships between organizational groups.

Embedded Intergroup Relations Theory

Embedded intergroup relations theory (EIRT) advanced by Alderfer (1987; Alderfer & Smith, 1982) proposes a distinction between formal organizational groups and identity groups, groups based on characteristics that individuals have before they enter the organization and will retain once they leave (e.g. gender, ethnicity). Both organizational and identity group memberships are argued to play a role in intergroup relations in organizations. In its applications, however, the theory seems to have been mainly applied to race relations in organizations (e.g. Alderfer & Tucker, 1996) and not to the relationships between organizational groups that are the focus of this chapter.

EIRT is to a certain extent also a social categorization/social identity theory in that it applies insights from these approaches. In an important deviation from this perspective, however, it is also very much a theory of research and intervention methodology. At the core of EIRT lies the notion that the very act of studying intergroup relations in organizations will inevitably affect the intergroup relations studied. Therefore, Alderfer argues, researchers may, and should, combine research and intervention in what is called *action research*. Action research (as proposed by Alderfer) combines the studying of intergroup relations in something akin to focus groups with the search for ways to improve intergroup relations. Action research requires intensive interaction between researcher and organization and may result in intimate subjective knowledge of the organization for the researcher, but, as critics would argue, at the expense of such key characteristics of scientific research as replicability. This is not the place for the discussion of research methodology, however, and I will leave it at the observation that Alderfer's approach represents a minority position in organizational behavior research in general as well as more specifically in intergroup relations research.

A Social Identity–Social Dilemma Perspective

Social categorization/social identity theories represent the dominant perspective in intergroup relations theory and research, with a huge body of empirical evidence in support of their basic tenets. Arguably, however, even though social categorization/social identity theories typically recognize that intergroup cooperation versus competition may attenuate versus accentuate intergroup tensions, the approach may be criticized for paying less attention to the role of compatibility of interests than perhaps is justified—especially from the perspective of intergroup relations in organizations. In this respect, a theoretical analysis by Kramer (1991) is extremely relevant. Kramer integrates the interdependence/conflict of interest approach and the social categorization/social identity approach. In an important deviation from RCT, however, Kramer emphasizes that conflicts of interest between organizational groups typically have a *mixed-motive* character in that they are usually played out against the backdrop of organizational interests that are shared by the different organizational groups. The use of organizational resources and contributions to organizational goals thus often has a *social dilemma* character, where solely serving group interests is to the detriment of the organization as a whole, and thus ultimately to the detriment of the groups constituting the organization. As an example, Kramer quotes the way in which budgets are allocated in many organizations. Clearly, the organization as a whole is better off when groups only consume the budget they actually need. Often, however, future budgets are contingent on prior budgets, so there is a strong incentive for each group to claim in excess of actual needs. If all groups engage in this behavior, which would appear to serve group interests, however, organizational resources may be depleted and future budgets will drop dramatically, at the expense of all groups. Alternatively, if budgets are restricted to a sustainable level, budgets may be assigned on the basis of power differentials or negotiations skills rather than on the basis of actual group needs, again ultimately at the expense of effective organizational functioning.

Kramer's analysis in terms of social dilemmas suggests that rather than viewing intergroup relations simply in terms of conflicting group interests, it might be better to consider them in terms of the weight assigned to group versus organizational interests and in terms of the willingness to cooperate with other groups to serve the organization's interests. The social dilemma research discussed by Kramer suggests that social categorization/social identity processes may play an important role in both the former and the latter. When the intergroup nature of the situation is salient, groups will be motivated to compete for organizational resources rather than to cooperate for the organizational interest (cf. Turner, 1975). In contrast, when the organizational identity is salient, groups will both value the organizational interests more (cf. Ashforth & Mael, 1989; van Knippenberg, 2000) and be more motivated to cooperate with other groups, because they are seen as part of a larger ingroup (cf. Gaertner et al., 1993).

Kramer's analysis thus points to the interplay of social categorization/social identity processes and the mixed-motive character of many aspects of intergroup relations in organizations as potential causes of intergroup conflict and competition. Accordingly, his proposed strategies to improve intergroup relations focus on social categorization strategies that aim to direct attention away from intergroup categorizations (elaborated in the following) as well as on structural solutions to social dilemmas that change the payoff structure of the situation to remove, or attenuate, the social dilemma character of the situation (cf. Messick & Brewer, 1983).

Intergroup Relations and the Group–Organization Relationship

An issue that is often overlooked when discussing intergroup relations in organizations is that intergroup relations reflect on the group's relationship with the organization as a whole (cf. Kramer, 1991). Social categorization/social identity theories and especially SCT's analysis of the relationship between different levels of self-categorization (Turner et al., 1987) are pertinent to this issue. SCT predicts that categorization at a given level leads individuals to accentuate intergroup differences and intragroup similarities. Not only may this exacerbate intergroup frictions, it may also stand in the way of organizational identification and pro-organizational behavior, because the accentuation of within-organization intergroup differences may distract from the superordinate categorization in terms of organizational membership (Kramer, 1991). Studies of the multiple identifications employees may have (e.g. with their own work group, with the organization as a whole) suggest that this is a major concern for organizations, because the work group is the primary focus of identification in most organizations (Ashforth & Johnson, 2001; Kramer, 1991; van Knippenberg & van Schie, 2000). Managing intergroup relations is thus also important for managing desirable organizational behavior outside of the specific context of the relationship between two organizational groups. Unfortunately, empirical studies of intergroup relations typically do not go beyond studying the intergroup relations themselves.

An exception is recent studies in social identity processes in mergers and acquisition, which have also focused on the implications of intergroup processes for organizational attitudes and behavior. Intergroup relations between the merger partners are a major concern in mergers and acquisitions (e.g. Blake & Mouton, 1985) and not only raise the question of how the merger partners get along, but also of how these intergroup dynamics affect organizational functioning. In recognition of this fact, van Knippenberg et al. (2002; see also van Knippenberg & van Leeuwen, 2001; van Leeuwen & van Knippenberg, in press) studied post-merger organizational identification from an intergroup perspective and found that intergroup power differentials both affected organizational identification directly (i.e. higher identification among members of the dominant partner) and moderated the impact of perceived interorganizational differences on identification (i.e. higher perceived differences were associated with lower identification among members of the dominated partner, but were unrelated to organizational identification among members of the dominant partner). In similar vein, Terry and colleagues (Terry & Callan, 1998; Terry, Carey, & Callan, 2001) showed that status differences between the merger partners in conjunction with permeability of group boundaries affected identification with the organization as well as intergroup biases. There thus is some evidence that intergroup relations affect attitudes and behavior toward the organization as a whole, but more research is clearly needed.

INTERVENTION STRATEGIES

The nature of intergroup relations is an important concern inside and outside of organizations. It is not surprising, then, that research in intergroup relations has not only been concerned with understanding and explaining intergroup relations, but also with ways to improve intergroup relations. In this section, I review and evaluate intervention strategies as proposed by the different theoretical perspectives.

For RCT, the ultimate cause of intergroup conflict is incompatibility of group interests. The obvious intervention to improve intergroup relations, then, is to change the interdependence structure so that the goals and interests of different groups become more aligned. This could, for instance, entail changing the incentive system of the organization. Analogous to the wisdom that it may be better to reward the group rather than the individual if one wishes to promote teamwork, it might be better to reward at the intergroup level rather than at the group level if one desires to engender intergroup cooperation (i.e. reward all groups involved in a certain project, production process, or service collectively rather than judge each group separately or in comparison to each other). In similar vein, the RCT perspective would favor working with goal-setting at the intergroup level rather than at the group level.

Social categorization theories of intergroup relations (i.e. such as SIT/SCT) see social categorization per se rather than the "objective" conflicts of interest identified by RCT as the root cause of intergroup tensions. Accordingly, the interventions to improve intergroup relations proposed by social categorization theorists usually focus on breaking down intergroup categorizations. These may take three basic forms: *de*categorization, *re*categorization, and *cross*-categorization. A decategorization strategy aims to break down ingroup–outgroup categorization by focusing individuals on categorization of the members of ingroup and outgroup as separate individuals (Brewer & Miller, 1984), for instance by creating conditions for interpersonal interaction between members of different groups. Although decategorization has been shown to reduce intergroup biases (e.g. Gaertner et al., 1989), this strategy may be criticized because good interpersonal relationships not necessarily generalize to relationships between groups (Hewstone & Brown, 1986) and because depersonalization may lower identification with the group and the organization and thus be detrimental to employees' willingness to exert themselves on behalf of the group and the organization (cf. Ashforth & Mael, 1989; van Knippenberg, 2000) and may effectively counteract any "team-building" attempts. Also, in organizational contexts depersonalization may not be a feasible strategy, because individuals need to interact as representatives of their groups, thus automatically turning the situation into an intergroup encounter.

Cross-categorization builds on the fact that individuals are members of multiple groups and social categories. When the categorization into organizational groups converges with other bases of categorization, for instance when women and members of ethnic minorities are overrepresented in lower-level positions while white males are overrepresented in higher-level positions, this may render the categorization in terms of organizational groups more salient and exacerbate intergroup tensions (Alderfer, 1987). When, in contrast, two or more categories cut across one another, for instance when both lower- and higher-level positions are held equally by men and women and by individuals with different ethnic backgrounds, this may break down ingroup–outgroup categorizations because individuals who are outgroup members on one dimension are ingroup members on another (e.g. Deschamps & Doise, 1978; Marcus-Newhall et al., 1993). To a certain extent, cross-categorization is a decategorization strategy, because it will render any given categorization less salient. In contrast to decategorization, however, which focuses attention on the individual qua individual, cross-categorization recognizes the different group memberships, but aims to cross-cut these so there are no "real" outgroup members. Cross-categorization as an intervention strategy would entail composing organizational groups so that organizational groupings cross-cut rather than converge with other potential bases of categorization (e.g. demography). If possible, it could, for instance, be desirable to work with cross-functional project teams so that outgroup members from the perspective of functional groups are ingroup members from the perspective of the project teams. Another way of cross-cutting organizational groups is to work with a system of job rotation. If employees spend at least part of their time as a member of other organizational groups, these may become ingroups of sorts (i.e. former or anticipated ingroups; cf. permeability), and accordingly attenuate intergroup biases.

Recategorization, championed by Gaertner and colleagues in their common ingroup identity model (Gaertner & Dovidio, 2000; Gaertner et al., 1993), entails focusing individuals on the fact that ingroup and outgroup share a common identity as part of a larger superordinate group. If a perceptual shift is established from seeing the members of the other group as an outgroup (e.g. the sales department) to seeing the members of the other group as part of a larger, superordinate ingroup (i.e. the organization), the positive regard for ingroup members will extend to members of the other group, and the willingness to cooperate with the other group is enhanced. For two reasons, creating and emphasizing shared organizational goals and rewards are important in this respect. First, cooperative goals are a means to establish a perceptual shift from the group to the organizational level (cf. Gaertner et al., 1990). Second, cooperative goals are also an important precondition for interventions that aim to establish recategorization to be effective (Gaertner & Dovidio, 2000; Gaertner et al., 1993). Even under cooperative goal conditions, however, it seems important to stress the common goals, mission, and culture of the organization to emphasize the higher-order identity. Theories of charismatic and transformational leadership suggest that organizational leaders may fulfill an important function in this respect. Charismatic/transformational leadership is proposed to be an especially effective style of leadership in part because it focuses attention on the organization's mission and the shared organizational identity (Bass, 1985; De Cremer & van Knippenberg, 2002; Shamir, House, & Arthur, 1993). An integration of these insights and the proposed beneficial effects of interventions aimed at recategorization suggests that charismatic/transformational leadership may also be an important factor in attenuating intergroup tensions and promoting intergroup cooperation.

There are limits to the benefits of recategorization, however. A strong emphasis on the superordinate group may be a threat to group distinctiveness (Hewstone & Brown, 1986; Hornsey & Hogg, 2000; van Leeuwen & van Knippenberg, in press). Therefore, a number of theorists have suggested that intergroup relations benefit most if a balance is struck between the emphasis on the common ingroup identity and the distinct subgroup identity. There is evidence from both field research and laboratory experiments (Gaertner & Dovidio, 2000; Hornsey & Hogg, 2000; van Leeuwen & van Knippenberg, in press) that this is a very viable perspective, but to my knowledge it has yet to be applied to the relationship between organizational groups in empirical research. From this perspective, organizations should create intergroup cooperative goal structures and emphasize the shared organizational identity, but at the same time assign groups distinctive roles and recognize the unique contributions of each organizational group to the organization's functioning. Balancing the emphasis on organizational and work group identity is quite a challenge for management, and something that has received hardly any attention in research in intergroup relations.

Allen's (1996) discussion of management practices to increase work groups' sense of fit within the organization as a whole is highly relevant here. Allen argues that for organizations it is very important that employees are not just focused on their membership in their work group, but are also attuned to the needs and interests of the organization as a whole, and to the work group's place within this whole. Allen suggests that to achieve this organizations need to adopt human resource practices that take the position of the work group into account (e.g. letting the work group participate in staffing decisions). Also, they should develop a program of organizational communication and mentoring that educates group members in the role of their group, and that of other groups, within the organization. In addition, they should create opportunities to learn about the role of different organizational groups for the organization's functioning by experience, for instance through job rotation programs or boundary-spanning activities. Finally, Allen argues that there is an important role for group leaders to represent the organization as a whole and not just their own group vis-à-vis other groups. Although Allen did not analyze these practices from a social categorization perspective, these interventions align very well with the interventions discussed here. Highlighting the role of their own group as well as of other groups in relationship to organizational goals would work to both emphasize the organizational identity and the distinct identity of the group within the larger whole. Also, it would point to the cooperative interdependence between groups. In addition, job rotation and boundary-spanning activities would not only educate group members about the role of organizational groups within the organization, but would also create a network of relationships that cross-cut organizational groups and that would thus counter intergroup biases. As cases in point, Campion, Cheraskin, and Stevens (1994) found that job rotation yielded more integrative views of the organization, and Nelson (1989) found that organizations in which there were relatively many intergroup ties had lower levels of intergroup conflict. Finally, the role Allen envisioned for organizational leaders aligns well with my earlier suggestion that leaders may through charismatic/transformational leadership attentuate intergroup tensions and promote intergroup cooperation by focusing group members on collective goals and identity.

To summarize, then, social categorization/social identity research has shown that problematic intergroup relations may arise in the absence of conflicting interests, and that, accordingly, creating cooperative goals (cf. RCT) is not enough to manage intergroup relations. Both Kramer's (1991) social identity–social dilemma perspective and Gaertner and Dovidio's (2000) common ingroup identity model, however, suggest that interventions to manage social categorization processes may be ineffective if conditions of more cooperative interdependence are not created as well. Fortunately, interventions to achieve these ends may reinforce each other. Cooperative/superordinate goals increase the salience of the membership in the organization as a whole (cf. recategorization) and, conversely, an emphasis on the common ingroup identity as members of the organization will increase trust in other group members' cooperative intentions. Importantly, however, research on group distinctiveness threats suggests that the emphasis on the larger whole needs to be balanced with recognition and preservation of distinct group identities. This is a huge challenge, but a number of strategies suggested by Allen (1996) to increase group–organization fit may come quite a way to achieving this end.

DIRECTIONS FOR RESEARCH

As noted on a number of occasions in this chapter, although the body of literature on intergroup relations is huge, research on intergroup relations in organizations is scarce and there remains as yet much to be learned about intergroup relations in organizational contexts. In this section, I discuss a number of areas where there is a clear need for more research. First, I address a number of issues that have come up throughout this chapter. Then, I focus on an issue where research has been conspicuously absent: the nature of the interaction between groups.

RCT's view of the role of the compatibility of group interests may be too simple, but more recent work by Kramer (1991) and Gaertner and colleagues (Gaertner & Dovidio, 2000; Gaertner et al., 1993) suggests that the nature of intergroup interdependence nevertheless plays an important role in intergroup relations. As noted in the discussion of RCT, reliance on single-organization studies may have led us to underestimate this role. Accordingly, our understanding of the role of intergroup interdependence in intergroup relations would greatly benefit from multiorganization studies that are better able to capture the influence of actual variation in cooperative and competitive interdependence between organizational groups. In this respect, the social dilemma nature of intergroup interdependence (cf. Kramer, 1991) especially warrants empirical attention, both because conceptualizing intergroup relations in mixed-motive terms seems to offer a more accurate reflection of intergroup interdependence in organizations and because this conceptualization has received less attention in organizational research.

The most recent insights in the management of intergroup relations suggest that organizations need to balance an emphasis on the collective organizational identity with a recognition of the distinct roles and identities of each organizational group. This is an area that has as yet hardly been addressed in organizational research. Accordingly, future research should determine whether intergroup relations in organizations indeed benefit from a balance between group distinctiveness and organizational identity. Related to this is the question of if, and under what conditions, groups are able to incorporate their relationship with other groups into their identities, thus maintaining their distinctiveness but recognizing their relationships as part of a larger whole. Research on interpersonal relationships has shown that individuals may incorporate their relationships with significant others into their self-definition (i.e. the *relational self*; Brewer & Gardner, 1996) and recently organizational scientists have started to explore the possibility that intragroup diversity may be incorporated as an aspect of the self (Brickson, 2000; van Knippenberg & Haslam, in press). Accordingly, research could address the question of whether organizational groups may through similar processes balance organizational identity and group distinctiveness. In addition, research should aim to identify viable ways of establishing and maintaining group distinctiveness in organizational practice, while at the same time establishing a clear focus on the organizational interests. Allen's (1996) suggestions seem to offer important guidelines here, but the effectiveness of the managerial practices suggested by Allen for managing intergroup relations need yet to be established in empirical research. Among others, this would include attention on the role of leadership in managing intergroup relations. The consequences of intergroup relations for attitudes and behavior toward the organization as a whole also deserve more attention than they have received to date, if only to identify the conditions under which intergroup tensions spill over to situations outside the specific intergroup relationship itself.

Research on intergroup relations in organizations has to a substantial degree focused on the way intergroup processes may shape perceptions of, and attitudes toward, other organizational groups. This leaves the question of what organizational groups actually do in intergroup interaction unanswered. For at least two reasons, this is a serious gap in our knowledge of intergroup relations in organizations. First, although perceptions, beliefs, and attitudes may feed into behavior, they do not do so by definition, and ultimately it is intergroup behavior rather than intergroup perceptions and attitudes that affects organizational functioning. Second, research on conflict management suggests that conflict in itself is not necessarily problematic. Rather, the way in which conflict is handled may determine to a substantial extent whether conflict has negative, or indeed positive, consequences (e.g. Pruitt & Carnevale, 1993; Tjosvold, 1998). Thus, identifying the conditions under which and the processes through which intergroup tensions may arise is one thing, but identifying the way these processes shape intergroup conflict behavior is yet another. Both these considerations therefore suggest that we need to know more about actual intergroup *behavior* in organizations, and that for a proper understanding of intergroup relations in organizations we cannot rely on studies of intergroup perceptions and attitudes alone.

Nauta and colleagues (Nauta, De Dreu, & van der Vaart, 2002; Nauta, de Vries, & Wijngaard, 2001) have made a tentative first step in this direction in studies of interdepartmental negotiation behavior. Nauta, de Vries, and Wijngaard (2001) studied how intergroup power differences affect perceptions of one's own and others' negotiation behavior, and Nauta, De Dreu, and van der Vaart (2002) studied the relationship between inter-individual differences in concern for self and others, organizational goal concerns, and problem-solving behavior of individuals engaged in interdepartmental negotiation. These studies are of interest because they demonstrate how intergroup behavior in organizations may be studied. Unfortunately, they fall short of actually addressing intergroup behavior, because they rely on self-reports analyzed at the individual level, thus turning them ultimately into studies of subjective perceptions of behavior (i.e. as was the aim of Nauta, de Vries, & Wijngaard, 2001) rather than actual behavior, and because they do not incorporate measures that tie negotiation behavior to intergroup processes (e.g. group identification, group membership salience, intergroup perceptions) and thus leave open the possibility that results were attributable to purely interpersonal processes, or indeed intrapersonal processes (i.e. Nauta, De Dreu, & van der Vaart, 2002, focused on the role of an individual difference variable).

In conclusion, then, it may be noted that there still is much work to be done in research in intergroup relations in organizations. In view of the potential for intergroup conflict inherent in all organizations and the potentially high costs to organizations associated with intergroup conflicts, undertaking these research efforts seems a highly worthwhile endeavor.

REFERENCES

Abrams, D. & Hogg, M. A. (1988). Comments on the motivational status of self-esteem in social identity and intergroup discrimination. *European Journal of Social Psychology, 18*, 317–334.

Abrams, D. & Hogg, M. A. (1999). *Social Identity and Social Cognition*. Oxford, UK: Blackwell.

Alderfer, C. P. (1987). An intergroup perspective on group dynamics. In J. Lorsch (ed.), *Handbook of Organizational Behavior* (pp. 190–222). Englewood Cliffs, NJ: Prentice-Hall.

Alderfer, C. P. & Smith, K. K. (1982). Studying intergroup relations embedded in organizations. *Administrative Science Quarterly, 27*, 35–65.

Alderfer, C. P. & Tucker, R. C. (1996). A field experiment for studying race relations in embedded organizations. *Journal of Organizational Behavior, 17*, 43–57.

Allen, N. J. (1996). Affective reactions to the group and the organization. In M. A. West (ed.), *Handbook of Work Group Psychology* (pp. 371–396). Chichester, UK: Wiley.

Ashforth, B. E. & Johnson, S. A. (2001). Which hat to wear? The relative salience of multiple identities in organizational contexts. In M. A. Hogg & D. J. Terry (eds), *Social Identity Processes in Organizational Contexts* (pp. 249–264). Philadelphia, Pa: Psychology Press.

Ashforth, B. E. & Mael, F. (1989). Social identity theory and the organization. *Academy of Management Review, 14*, 20–39.

Bass, B. M. (1985). *Leadership and Performance beyond Expectations*. New York: Free Press.

Blake, R. R. & Mouton, J. S. (1985). How to achieve integration on the human side of the merger. *Organizational Dynamics, 13*, 20–39.

Blake, R. P., Shepard, H. A., & Mouton, J. S. (1964). *Managing Intergroup Conflict in Industry*. Houston: Gulf.

Bornstein, G. & Erev, I. (1994). The enhancing effect of intergroup competition on group performance. *International Journal of Conflict Management, 5*, 271–283.

Brett, J. M. & Rognes, J. K. (1986). Intergroup relations in organizations. In P. S. Goodman (ed.), *Designing Effective Work Groups*. San Francisco: Jossey-Bass.

Brewer, M. B. (1979). In-group bias in the minimal intergroup situation: a cognitive–motivational analysis. *Psychological Bulletin, 86*, 307–324.

Brewer, M. B. (1991). The social self: on being the same and different at the same time. *Personality and Social Psychology Bulletin, 17*, 475–482.

Brewer, M. B. & Brown, R. J. (1998). Intergroup relations. In D. T. Gilbert, S. T. Fiske, & G. Lindzey (eds), *Handbook of Social Psychology* (4th edn, pp. 554–594). Boston, Mass.: McGraw-Hill.

Brewer, M. B. & Gardner, W. (1996). Who is this "we"?: levels of collective identity and self-representations. *Journal of Personality and Social Psychology, 71*, 83–93.

Brewer, M. B. & Miller, N. (1984). Beyond the contact hypothesis: theoretical perspectives on desegregation. In N. Miller & M. B. Brewer (eds), *Groups in Contact: The Psychology of Desegregation* (pp. 281–302). Orlando, Fla: Academic Press.

Brickson, S. (2000). The impact of identity orientation on individual and organizational outcomes in demographically diverse settings. *Academy of Management Review, 25*, 82–101.
Brown, R. J. (1978). Divided we fall: an analysis of relations between sections of a factory workforce. In H. Tajfel (ed.), *Differentiation between Social Groups: Studies in the Social Psychology of Intergroup Relations*. London: Academic Press.
Brown, R., Condor, S., Mathews, A., Wade, G., & Williams, J. (1986). Explaining intergroup differentiation in an industrial organization. *Journal of Occupational Psychology, 59*, 273–286.
Brown, R. J. & Williams, J. A. (1984). Group identification: the same thing to all people? *Human Relations, 37*, 547–564.
Campbell, D. T. (1965). Ethnocentric and other altruistic motives. In D. Levine (ed.), *Nebraska Symposium on Motivation* (pp. 283–311). Lincoln: University of Nebraska Press.
Campion, M. A., Cheraskin, L., & Stevens, M. J. (1994). Career-related antecedents and outcomes of job rotation. *Academy of Management Journal, 37*, 1518–1542.
De Cremer, D. & van Knippenberg, D. (2002). How do leaders promote cooperation? The effects of charisma and procedural fairness. *Journal of Applied Psychology, 87*, 858–866.
Deschamps, J. C. & Doise, W. (1978). Crossed category membership in intergroup relations. In H. Tajfel (ed.), *Differentiation between Social Groups: Studies in the Social Psychology of Intergroup Relations* (pp. 141–158). New York: Academic Press.
Erev, I., Bornstein, G., & Galili, R. (1993). Constructive intergroup competition as a solution to the free rider problem: a field experiment. *Journal of Experimental Social Psychology, 29*, 463–478.
Fiske, S. T. & Ruscher, J. R. (1993). Negative interdependence and prejudice: whence the affect? In D. Mackie & D. Hamilton (eds), *Affect, Cognition, and Stereotyping* (pp. 239–268). San Diego, Calif.: Academic Press.
Gaertner, S. L. & Dovidio, J. F. (2000). *Reducing Intergroup Bias. The Common Ingroup Identity Model*. Philadelphia, Pa: Psychology Press.
Gaertner, S. L., Dovidio, J. F., Anastasio, P. A., Bachman, B. A., & Rust, M. C. (1993). The common ingroup identity model: recategorization and the reduction of intergroup bias. In W. Stroebe & M. Hewstone (eds), *European Review of Social Psychology* (Vol. 4, pp. 1–26). London, UK: Wiley.
Gaertner, S. L., Mann, J., Murrell, A., & Dovidio, J. F. (1989). Reducing intergroup bias: the benefits of recategorization. *Journal of Personality and Social Psychology, 57*, 239–249.
Gaertner, S. L., Mann, J. A., Murrell, A. J., Dovidio, J. F., & Pomare, M. (1990). How does cooperation reduce intergroup bias? *Journal of Personality and Social Psychology, 59*, 692–704.
Guzzo, R. A. & Shea, G. P. (1992). Group performance and intergroup relations in organizations. In M. D. Dunnette & L. M. Hough (eds), *Handbook of Industrial and Organizational Psychology* (Vol. 3, pp. 269–313). Palo Alto, Calif.: Consulting Psychologists Press.
Haslam, S. A. (2001). *Psychology in Organizations: The Social Identity Approach*. London & Newbury Park, Calif.: Sage.
Haslam, S. A., van Knippenberg, D., Platow, M. J., & Ellemers, N. (eds) (in press). *Social Identity at Work: Developing Theory for Organizational Practice*. Philadelphia, Pa: Psychology Press.
Hennessy, J. & West, M. A. (1999). Intergroup behavior in organizations: a field study of social identity theory. *Small Group Research, 30*, 361–382.
Hewstone, M. & Brown, R. J. (1986). Contact is not enough: an intergroup perspective on the "contact hypothesis". In M. Hewstone & R. J. Brown (eds), *Contact and Conflict in Intergroup Encounters*. Oxford, UK: Blackwell.
Hogg, M. A. & Abrams, D. (1988). *Social Identifications: A Social Psychology of Intergroup Relations and Group Processes*. London, UK: Routledge.
Hogg, M. A. & Terry, D. J. (2000). Social identity and self-categorization processes in organizational contexts. *Academy of Management Review, 25*, 121–140.
Hogg, M. A. & Terry, D. J. (2001). *Social Identity Processes in Organizational Contexts*. Philadelphia, Pa: Psychology Press.
Hornsey, M. J. & Hogg, M. A. (2000). Assimilation and diversity: an integrative model of subgroup relations. *Personality and Social Psychology Review, 4*, 143–156.
Katz, D. (1964). The motivational basis of organizational behavior. *Behavioral Science, 9*, 131–146.
Kramer, R. (1991). Intergroup relations and organizational dilemmas. *Research in Organizational Behavior, 13*, 191–228.

Mackie, D. M. & Smith, E. R. (1998). Intergroup relations: insights from a theoretically integrative approach. *Psychological Review, 105*, 499–529.

Marcus-Newhall, A., Miller, N., Holtz, R., & Brewer, M. B. (1993). Cross-cutting category membership with role assignment: a means of reducing intergroup bias. *British Journal of Social Psychology, 32*, 125–146.

Messick, D. M. & Brewer, M. B. (1983). Solving social dilemmas. In L. Wheeler & P. R. Shaver (eds), *Review of Personality and Social Psychology* (Vol. 4, pp. 11–44). Beverly Hills: Sage.

Messick, D. M. & Mackie, D. M. (1989). Intergroup relations. *Annual Review of Psychology, 40*, 45–81.

Mohrman, S. A., Cohen, S. G., & Mohrman, A. M. (1995). *Designing Team-based Organizations: New Forms for Knowledge Work.* San Francisco: Jossey-Bass.

Mullen, B., Brown, R., & Smith, C. (1992). Ingroup bias as a function of salience, relevance, and status: an integration. *European Journal of Social Psychology, 22*, 103–122.

Nauta, A., De Dreu, C. K. W., & van der Vaart, T. (2002). Social value orientation, organizational goal concerns and interdepartmental problem-solving behavior. *Journal of Organizational Behavior, 23*, 199–213.

Nauta, A., de Vries, J., & Wijngaard, J. J. (2001). Power and biased perceptions of interdepartmental negotiation behavior. *Group Processes & Intergroup Relations, 4*, 263–270.

Nelson, R. E. (1989). The strength of strong ties: social networks and intergroup conflict in organizations. *Academy of Management Journal, 32*, 377–401.

Organ, D. W. (1988). *Organizational Citizenship Behavior: The Good Soldier Syndrome*. Lexington, Mass.: Lexington Books.

Pfeffer, J. & Salancik, G. R. (1977). Organization design: the case for a coalitional model of organizations. *Organizational Dynamics, 6*, 15–29.

Pondy, L. R. (1967). Organizational conflict: concepts and models. *Administrative Science Quarterly, 12*, 296–320.

Pruitt, D. G. & Carnevale, P. J. (1993). *Negotiation in Social Conflict.* Pacific Grove, Calif.: Brooks/Cole.

Saavedra, R., Earley, P. C., & van Dyne, L. (1993). Complex interdependence in task performing groups. *Journal of Applied Psychology, 78*, 61–72.

Schopler, J. & Insko, C. (1992). The discontinuity effect in interpersonal and intergroup relations: generality and mediation. In W. Stroebe & M. Hewstone (eds), *European Review of Social Psychology* (Vol. 3, pp. 121–152). Chichester, UK: Wiley.

Shamir, B., House, R., & Arthur, M. B. (1993). The motivational effects of charismatic leadership: a self-concept based theory. *Organization Science, 4*, 577–594.

Sherif, M. (1966). *Group Conflict and Co-operation: Their Social Psychology*. London: Routledge & Kegan Paul.

Tajfel, H. (1978). *Differentiation between Social Groups: Studies in the Social Psychology of Intergroup Relations*. New York: Academic Press.

Tajfel, H. (1982). Social psychology of intergroup relations. *Annual Review of Psychology, 33*, 1–39.

Tajfel, H., Billig, M., Bundy, R. P., & Flament, C. (1971). Social categorization and intergroup behaviour. *European Journal of Social Psychology, 1*, 149–177.

Tajfel, H. & Turner, J. C. (1986). The social identity theory of intergroup behaviour. In S. Worchel & W. G. Austin (eds), *Psychology of Intergroup Relations* (2nd edn, pp. 7–24). Chicago: Nelson-Hall.

Terry, D. J. & Callan, V. J. (1998). In-group bias in response to an organizational merger. *Group Dynamics, 2*, 67–81.

Terry, D. J., Carey, C. J., & Callan, V. J. (2001). Employee adjustment to an organizational merger: an intergroup perspective. *Personality and Social Psychology Bulletin, 27*, 267–280.

Tjosvold, D. (1998). Cooperative and competitive goal approach to conflict: accomplishments and challenges. *Applied Psychology: An International Review, 47*, 285–342.

Turner, J. C. (1975). Social comparison and social identity: some prospects for intergroup behaviour. *European Journal of Social Psychology, 5*, 5–34.

Turner, J. C. (1981). The experimental social psychology of intergroup behaviour. In J. C. Turner & H. Giles (eds), *Intergroup Behaviour* (pp. 66–101). Oxford: Blackwell.

Turner, J. C., Hogg, M. A., Oakes, P. J., Reicher, S. D., & Wetherell, M. S. (1987). *Rediscovering the Social Group. A Self-categorization Theory*. Oxford, UK: Blackwell.

Van Knippenberg, D. (2000). Work motivation and performance: a social identity perspective. *Applied Psychology: An International Review, 49*, 357–371.

Van Knippenberg, D. & Haslam, S. A. (in press). Realizing the diversity dividend: exploring the subtle interplay between identity, ideology, and reality. In S. A. Haslam, D. van Knippenberg, M. J. Platow, & N. Ellemers (eds), *Social Identity at Work: Developing Theory for Organizational Practice*. Philadelphia, Pa: Psychology Press.

Van Knippenberg, D. & Hogg, M. A. (eds) (2001). *Social Identity Processes in Organizations* (*Special issue of Group Processes and Intergroup Relations, 4*). London: Sage.

Van Knippenberg, D. & Hogg, M. A. (in press). *Leadership, and Power: Identity Processes in Groups and Organizations*. London: Sage.

Van Knippenberg, D., van Knippenberg, B., Monden, L., & de Lima, F. (2002). Organizational identification after a merger: a social identity perspective. *British Journal of Social Psychology, 41*, 233–252.

Van Knippenberg, D. & van Leeuwen, E. (2001). Organizational identity after a merger: sense of continuity as the key to post-merger identification. In M. A. Hogg & D. J. Terry (eds), *Social Identity Processes in Organizational Contexts* (pp. 249–264). Philadelphia, Pa: Psychology Press.

Van Knippenberg, D. & van Schie, E. C. M. (2000). Foci and correlates of organizational identification. *Journal of Occupational and Organizational Psychology, 73*, 137–147.

Van Leeuwen, E. & van Knippenberg, D. (in press). Organizational identification following a merger: the importance of agreeing to differ. In S. A. Haslam, D. van Knippenberg, M. J. Platow, & N. Ellemers (eds), *Social Identity at Work: Developing Theory for Organizational Practice*. Philadelphia, Pa: Psychology Press.

Williams, K. Y. & O'Reilly, C. A. (1998). Demography and diversity in organizations: a review of 40 years of research. *Research in Organizational Behavior, 20*, 77–140.

19

DIFFICULTIES FOSTERING COOPERATIVE AGREEMENTS IN MULTIPARTY NEGOTIATIONS

COGNITIVE, PROCEDURAL, STRUCTURAL, AND SOCIAL

Barbara Gray and Dana R. Clyman

I INTRODUCTION

While multiparty negotiations have long been the focus of political and international scholars, they are also increasingly commonplace in the business arena as firms negotiate complex business-to-business transactions, strategic alliances, and joint ventures. A rising number of cross-sectoral problems (among businesses, governments, NGOs, and communities) require multiparty negotiation (Gray, 1989; Hardy & Phillips, 1998; Huxham, 1996; Wondolleck & Yaffee, 2000). Yet, with a few exceptions (see Brett, 1991; Kramer, 1991; Thompson, 2001), remarkably little analysis has been conducted concerning the difficulties fostering cooperative agreements in multiparty negotiations in general, and even less advice has been offered to managers who are increasingly facing such problems and attempting to overcome them.

There are many reasons why multiparty negotiating environments pose problems for the negotiators who must contend with them. These difficulties include everything from the complexity derived from the sheer numbers of participants to the many devilish negotiating structures that characterize multiparty situations, such as two-table problems where one has to simultaneously manage the negotiations at the table and the negotiations with constituents back home (Ancona, Freidman, & Kolb, 1991), the paradox of the chair and other voting dilemmas (Brams, 1990), problems of the commons and social dilemmas (Axelrod, 1984; Hardin, 1968; Murnighan, 1991, 1992; Young, 1994), intergenerational dynamics (Wade-Benzoni, Tenbrunsel, & Bazerman, 1997), and frame discrepancies (Gray, 1997; Lewicki, Gray, & Elliott, 2002), to name but a few.

This chapter attempts to create the foundations of a taxonomy of the complexities in creating lasting cooperative multiparty agreements by focusing on four main categories and offering some insights and examples in each one. These four categories are cognitive,

International Handbook of Organizational Teamwork and Cooperative Working. Edited by M. A. West, D. Tjosvold, and K. G. Smith.

procedural, structural, and social, and are the topics of Sections II–V of this chapter respectively. Along each of these four dimensions, we summarize key insights into what makes multiparty negotiations difficult. So, for instance, along the cognitive dimension, we focus on the computational complexity that arises from the growing number of negotiators. Along the procedural dimension, the topics we explore include showing that rules to simplify the process do not always accomplish their intended purpose.

Along the structural dimension we discuss three broad areas. First, we demonstrate just how complex multiparty negotiations can become in even the simplest of structures by offering an example known as the paradox of the chair (Brams, 1990). Second, we explore social dilemmas—multiparty (multiperiod) prisoner dilemmas. Third, we introduce the idea of incomplete integration, a problem that arises when subgroups make trades that are integrative for the subgroup but not for the whole. Just as individuals caught in a social dilemma can take individually optimal actions that lead to a diminishing of the utility of all, subgroups involved in incomplete integration can make myopically integrative agreements that can lead to a diminishing of the utility of all.

Along the social dimension, we explore framing effects, focusing our examples primarily on issues surrounding identity and power asymmetries. Frame discrepancies refer to differences in the interpretations that negotiators use to make sense of the situation. Frames influence what the parties believe is at stake in the dispute and limit how parties define what the dispute is about and the acceptable responses (Neale & Bazerman, 1991; Tversky & Kahneman, 1981). Frames also shape parties' beliefs about how a dispute should be settled (Gray & Hanke, 2001; Merry & Silbey, 1984; Pinkley & Northcraft, 1994; Sheppard, Blumenfeld-Jones, & Roth, 1989) and what actions parties should take during the negotiations (De Dreu et al., 1994). These frames also influence whether negotiations take place and the outcomes that result from them (Donnellon & Gray, 1989; Gray, 1997; Lewicki, Gray, & Elliott, 2002; Mather & Yngvesson, 1980–81; Pinkley & Northcraft, 1994).

Following these discussions of the types of obstacles to multiparty negotiations, in Section VI we offer a brief discussion of means for overcoming them, along with our conclusions and a call for further research to flesh out the taxonomy and begin the process of untangling the difficulties. The ultimate goal of this research is a collection of strategies that will help managers cope with the many complexities we describe.

II COGNITIVE COMPLEXITY

Increasing the number of players involved in a negotiation dramatically increases the cognitive complexity. Focusing first on just information and computation, note how very quickly the number of pairs grows, as the number of parties increases, and the obvious impact that has on informational and computational complexity when trying to understand and integrate diverse interests. With 3 parties, there are 3 pairs that need to interact—3 separate conversations that might occur. With 4 parties there are 6. With 10 parties, there are 45, and with 100 parties (the size of the US Senate, excluding staff), there are 4950. Now consider the House of Representatives or the United Nations—the numbers grow geometrically. [The formula is $(n)(n-1)/2$, where n is the number of parties, which grows like n^2.]

And if keeping track of all parties' interests is not difficult enough, trying to map all the common and complementary interests of the parties in pairs is even more difficult. Now overlay the fact it is insufficient to look only at pairs. We must track this information across all possible subgroups. So, consider tracking triplets—groups of three parties to see how their interests might overlap. This number grows even faster, with the cube of the numbers of parties involved [e.g. the number is $(n)(n-1)(n-2)/(2)(3)$]. Similarly, the number of groups of quartets grows like n^4 and so on. Thus, the mapping and computational complexity in multiparty negotiations quickly become enormous and threaten even the most capable negotiator's cognitive capacities.

But the computational complexity does not stop there. If one now tries to track all of the possible subgroups—all the possible coalitions—the growth in computational complexity truly becomes exponential. It turns out that the number of all subgroups of a set of n people (if you count the subgroup of all people and the empty subgroup of no people) is exactly equal to 2^n. This means that the total number of possible coalitions grows exponentially, and thus, so does the computational complexity of the situation.

Attempts to manage this level of complexity often lead parties to seek simplifying structures and processes to keep the negotiations tractable. For instance, large governing bodies, like a Parliament or Senate, have voting and other procedural rules, which are often designed to facilitate management of the process and simplify the cognitive complexity. If a majority can reach agreement, the rule says this is a sufficient basis for making a decision (recognizing that obtaining unanimity is virtually impossible). But all such rules have consequences: some for the better, some for the worse. In the voting example, for the sake of reaching agreement, the views of the minority are left out of the decision. In general, multiparty negotiations take longer than bilateral ones (Sebenius, 1996). In addition to the sheer number of parties, there is an increased tendency for parties to assume hard bargaining stances and to try to dominate the process (Bazerman, Mannix, & Thompson, 1988). This cognitive response is particularly likely when audience dynamics are salient (Thompson, 2001) because parties are trying to curry favor with a wider coalition and establish discursive legitimacy for their views (Hardy & Phillips, 1998). And to complicate matters, such tactics lead to other natural cognitive responses from other parties at the table, such as increased use of escalatory behavior and tactics, which in turn cause negotiations to become increasingly intractable and possibly spiral out of control (Raiffa, 1982; Rubin, Pruitt, & Kim, 1994).

Furthermore, any procedural rule designed to slow or delay the negotiations to enable the parties to deal more effectively with these cognitive issues must, by its very nature, lengthen the negotiations and the time needed to come to resolution. This, too, can produce unintended negative consequences. For example, when parties grow impatient with these size of the table discussions, they may fall prey to fundamental attribution error (Heider, 1958) and begin to make negative attributions about the other parties—concluding that others are purposefully stalling—rather than form negative conclusions about the process itself—that it is complex and tedious. When people are blamed personally for dynamics over which they have little control, they often respond in kind, with more blaming. These cycles of blaming escalate the conflict and cause some parties to threaten to resort to their BATNAs or best alternatives to a negotiated agreement (Fisher & Ury, 1983). In the midst of an escalatory process, such threats fuel further escalation and positional bargaining and increase the possibility that the negotiations will be sabotaged.

Finally, the desire to seek simpler or more manageable discussions often leads to coalition dynamics as individuals seek out smaller subgroups with common or complementary interests. However, such subgrouping paradoxically increases the computational complexity by increasing the numbers of parties (e.g. the subgroups whose interests must be considered), as described above. Other efforts to reduce unruly cognitive complexity include simplifying processes like voting rules or Roberts's rules of order. But as is evident to anyone who watches Congressional procedural battles, such efforts to reduce the cognitive complexity through the adoption of procedural rules, voting rules, and other "simplifying" rules of that ilk, increase the possibility of suboptimal results—a topic addressed further in the next section.

III PROCEDURAL COMPLEXITY

As just noted, cognitive complexity often leads negotiators to seek simplifying procedural rules to make the negotiations more tractable. A common way to manage the complexity is to simplify the mechanisms that determine how agreements will be reached. One simple solution is to anoint a single decision maker or "dictator." This solution is often adopted (subject to a variety of checks and balances) in organizations. The solution at the other extreme is to insist upon unanimity or consensus (we must all agree or at least not disagree), a solution often adopted in international framework conventions. Finally, a third solution, often adopted among groups in Western democracies, is majority rule.

Each of these has implications for the processes that will ensue, and the range of outcomes that may be feasible. While procedures themselves are not deleterious (and, in fact, can be beneficial if accepted and carefully managed), failure to anticipate and correct for the potentially negative consequences of any procedure all too often produces negative consequences.

Procedures Can Limit Learning and Integrative Potential

Some procedural rules affect—indeed, because they are designed to help manage complexity, they often reduce—the parties' abilities to learn about each other and craft integrative solutions. If a majority can force its agenda on a minority, it has far less need to integrate the minority's interests into any final solution. Similarly, processes that lead negotiators to limit who may talk with whom, follow fixed agendas, resolve issues sequentially, or follow any of a number of other social and group norms all have a variety of competing potentials. These steps may limit procedural and social dynamics. They may reduce informational and computational overload. They may even increase the chance of reaching agreement. All of which may be seen as beneficial. But by adding constraints to the system, they all also tend to reduce the potential for reaching lasting integrative solutions. The only one of these that may not generate such adverse results is consensus, presuming that the parties are able to consider the inherent complexities in their preferences and possible opportunities for reframing (as discussed below). But be warned, achieving consensus generally requires a willingness to accept and manage the full complexity of the system.

Other Consequences of Voting Rules

In essence, the desire to simplify the overwhelming complexity often leads groups to adopt procedural rules that simplify the calculus too much. Take, for example, voting schema. If everyone understands that a simple majority will carry the day, rather than tracking every combination of common and complementary interests, one need only count votes, a far simpler undertaking. Additionally, while the full complexity of putting together the majority coalition still exists, if one only needs to worry about half the players, then one has only approximately one-fourth the number of pairs of interactions to be concerned with [approximately $(\frac{1}{2}n)^2$ compared with n^2], making it a far simpler process. Similarly, if one considers the full complexity of managing all the possible subgroup coalitions of the majority rather than all the subgroups of the group at large, then the reduction in complexity is even more dramatic as $2^{n/2}$ is equal to the square root of 2^n. But the bounded rationality of limiting one's attention to the issues and interests of the majority subgroup leaves out critical details, information, and interests that might have been used to discover other beneficial trade-offs and craft more integrative solutions. As a result, all such simplifications (though intended to reduce complexity) have the potential of leading to suboptimal results.

Process choices leading to voting rules can also have other undesirable and sometimes surprising implications. Voting has a variety of well-known consequences, and two others bear special mention. First, any time there is a rule that enables one subgroup to enforce its wishes on another group, we have a situation where a minority group may become disenfranchised. Disenfranchisement often leads to undesirable behaviors designed to block the formation of agreements or to "overthrow" existing agreements (Smith, 1982). Second, voting rules are not generally transitive, and hence the sequence in which issues are undertaken matters. For example, suppose in any two-way vote, issue A can beat issue B, which can beat issue C, which in turn can beat issue A. If B is presented first against C, and the winner is presented against A, then A wins. But if A is presented first against B and the winner against C, then C wins, and so on. Parties who understand these possibilities may structure the voting to their advantage if others are not aware of the dynamics of sequencing.

Sequencing of Interactions

Whenever there are multiple parties to a negotiation, sequencing of interactions also becomes an issue (Sebenius, 1996). Thus, this simple example raises another host of questions that must be addressed in multiparty negotiations. Should you speak with the other parties individually or collectively? And if not collectively, to whom (or to which other subgroup) should you speak first, second, etc.?

Speaking to groups collectively enables several positive benefits. These include the parties' discovery of their interdependence (Gray, 1989), the ability to frame the negotiation in terms of a superordinate goal (Sherif, 1958), exertion of collective influence on a grand scale, exertion of facilitating the possibility of building a collective commitment to collaborate (Gray, 1989), and facilitating the widespread sharing of information that can possibly lead to the discovery of joint gains. It also has several possible negative effects. These include allowing opponents the potential to frame the negotiation in their favor, making the process far more difficult to control, and, perhaps most importantly, enabling the potential blockers of a collaborative agreement to discover they are not alone and to build blocking coalitions through the process of public sharing of information.

In trying to determine an acceptable approach to sequencing, the recommended advice is to try to determine the best way to get from where you are to your ultimate goal, and to create a sustainable winning coalition that will support an agreement you favor. This requires a process of backward induction (Sebenius, 1996). Envision whom you need in your coalition. Then determine how to win over the last person. Consider who you cannot get on board without the support of the others, and work backwards. Bill Daley, President Clinton's key strategist for securing Congressional approval of the controversial North American Free Trade Agreement (NAFTA), used to say, "Can we find the guy who can deliver the guy? We have to call the guy who calls the guy who calls the guy" (Sebenius, 1996).

Shifting Contextual Problems

Still another process complication that, while not unique to multiparty negotiations, may produce more dramatic consequences in multiparty settings is the dynamic nature of the economic, political, social, and natural context in which the negotiation is being staged. Changes precipitated by weather conditions, political upheaval, economic downturn, or technological advances can radically alter the shape of the table and who is claiming a seat. And while this is most likely to have detrimental effects on the process, it can occasionally be positive as well:

> Shifts in the policy context may trigger controversy but may also help to create conditions favorable to its pragmatic resolution—for example, by promoting a change in the identity or power relationships of actors in the arena, or by fostering new alliances, changing the availability of resources, or creating a sense of crisis that overrides preexisting disputes (Schon & Rein, 1994, p. 90).

Thus, unanticipated changes in the process due to the dynamic nature of the negotiations can have a positive impact. But more generally, negotiators' well-calculated plans are likely to run amuck when the context shifts. And, as noted above, situational factors may be misattributed as due to the intentional efforts by other parties to garner personal advantage from or to sabotage the negotiations.

In summary, procedural rules are generally designed to overcome difficulties resulting from the complexity of the negotiations and to facilitate the formation of agreements. But in doing so, they constrain the system and thereby limit the negotiators' ability to craft lasting integrative solutions.

IV STRUCTURAL COMPLEXITY

Thompson (2001) describes six levels of analysis that capture much of the variation in multiparty structures. These are: multiparty (many players around a table), coalitions, principal–agent, constituencies, teams, and intergroup. Each of these structures raises a host of predictable behavioral responses and complexities (see Kramer, 1991; Thompson, 2001).

To explore structural complexity, we offer several examples of multiparty situations. We begin by exploring the paradox of the chair: a simple three-party situation where any two of the parties can dictate terms to the third. We then examine social dilemmas, which may be described as multiparty and multiperiod prisoners' dilemma structures. In these situations, the result of individuals acting in their own self-interest can be agreements that destroy value for all. Finally, we explore incomplete integration which can result in any multiparty negotiation structure where subgroups can create agreements that are integrative for them at the expense of others. Similar to social dilemmas, here we will discover that the result of subgroups acting in their own best interest can be agreements that decrease the welfare of all.

Paradox of the Chair

To see just how analytically complex multiparty negotiations can become as a result of coalition dynamics, we offer a simple example with just three parties in a situation known as the paradox of the chair (Brams, 1990). This is an example of a situation with no stable coalition, which Nobel laureate Kenneth Arrow called problems with an empty core.

When there is no stable coalition, parties leave coalitions to join other coalitions that allow them to improve their payoffs (Mannix & Lowenstein, 1993). To see the potential complexity, consider the following very simple three-party negotiation with three possible agreements. We label the parties A, B, and C, and the potential agreements 1, 2, and 3. To complete the definition of the structure of the situation, we need only define each party's preferences for the agreements. To wit:

- A prefers agreement 1 to 2 to 3.
- B prefers agreement 2 to 3 to 1.
- C prefers agreement 3 to 1 to 2.

It is because of this circular structure of preferences that there is no stable resolution. To see that there is no stable agreement, note that given any agreement, one of the parties is left getting his last choice. For instance, if the parties agree to settle on #2, then C would be better off with any alternative agreement. Furthermore, in any such agreement, one of the parties is getting his second choice. In this case A, as A prefers #1 to #2. Therefore, the left-out party (in this case C) can offer the party getting her second choice (A), her first choice (in this case #1), which must, by definition, also be better for C. And so, the original agreement on #2 unravels.

Since this unraveling is possible given any potential agreement, there is no stable solution (see chart below).

Potential agreement	Unravels because
#1	B offers C #3
#3	A offers B #2
#2	C offers A #1
#1	etc.

Now add one more slight additional complication to the structure. We make A the chair of the decision-making body or "committee," if you will. By chair we mean specifically that in a deadlock (as we have here), A has the right to cast the deciding vote ending the cycle. Thus, should there be a deadlock, A will choose #1 and that will be the agreement.

What would be your prediction of the outcome of this situation? Intuitively, one might predict that A would get her first choice, #1. After all, there is no stable solution, and so A decides. However, if everyone understands the true structure of the preferences, it has been argued that the final resolution will be #3, A's last choice, not #1, A's first choice (Brams, 1990).

The reason is straightforward. If B knows that deadlock will cause the chair A to choose resolution #1 (B's last choice), then it is in B's self-interest to offer resolution #3 to C. This gives B her second choice and C her first. What's more, knowing that any future unraveling of the agreement will result in deadlock and hence in agreement #1 should be sufficient to make a strategically insightful B impervious to A's "offers" of settlement #2. And if B becomes impervious to this offer, the cycle ends. Thus, paradoxically, a more sophisticated prediction would be that being in position to cast the deciding vote is detrimental rather than beneficial since the other negotiators will conspire against the chair. Thus, a more sophisticated prediction is settlement #3, A's last choice, rather than its first choice.

But while this ends the cycle, the complexity of the situation does not end here, and nor should the analysis. If A also knows that full disclosure of everyone's preferences will lead to an agreement at her last choice, A has an incentive to change the very nature of the game in an attempt to preempt that resolution from occurring. And a strategic mechanism by which A can do this is to change the game through misrepresentation of her preferences. Thus, a strategically insightful A acts to avoid her worst alternative rather than continuing to try to realize her best alternative by misleading the others as to her true preferences (Brams, 1990).

In other words, A announces that s/he prefers #2 to #1 to #3. This makes #2 the preferred agreement for both A and B, and, if A holds to her "announced" preferences, it makes #2 the adopted resolution. In essence, if A knows that full disclosure will lead to her last choice, s/he has an incentive to misrepresent her preferences in order to achieve her second choice—that is A should change her goal from trying to achieve her first choice, to trying to avoid her last. And this, in turn, leads to a strategy of deception.

This is not a hypothetical example, nor is it the entire analysis—there is more. Brams (1990) argued that this is exactly the situation President Eisenhower and Secretary of State John Foster Dulles found themselves in during the Geneva Conference of 1954, which was about helping the French to exit Vietnam. And one version of history suggests that this is exactly the strategy that Eisenhower and Dulles adopted, when they announced that they were amenable to a settlement based on a demarcation of the country into northern and southern zones of influence (their second choice) rather than a continuation of the war, which was the choice they had first espoused. Note the US reportedly preferred the continuation of the war to a division of the country into northern and southern spheres of influence, which in turn they preferred to free elections because they feared the North would win these elections. Thus, the US was in the role of the chair: if no agreement was reached the war would continue and the US, Eisenhower, and Dulles would get their way. (For a teaching case and teaching note that illustrates this scenario, see Clyman & Kane, 1996b, The Geneva Conference.)

> The Indochina talks concluded in July 1954 with the creation of two major treaties. The first, a cease-fire agreement was signed by the French and the Democratic Republic of Vietnam. This document established a demilitarized zone on both sides of the seventeenth parallel, arranged for the regroupment of military forces into their appropriate territories, and created an international commission to oversee compliance with the terms of the treaty. The second treaty focused on long-term goals: it forbade foreign troops from entering any state in Indochina and, more importantly, set the terms for all-Vietnamese elections to take place two years later.

> Although this final declaration of the conference was accepted by all conference participants other than the United States, it was signed by none, and, as a result, failed to stand up (from Clyman & Kane, 1996b, based on Irving, 1975; Randle, 1969; Wintle, 1991).

By announcing that they preferred demarcation to war, and by dragging their feet and refusing to sign the treaty, the parties got demarcation for a time, and ultimately resumed the war they wanted to fight. So, in essence, the US got its first choice after all.

The critical point of all this is that the complexity of the problem required sophisticated analyses. The naïve analysis says the solution should be A's first choice. A more insightful analysis, based on the presumption that the others understand the situation, suggests that the agreement should resolve around A's last choice. But a super-rational analysis, based on the presumption that A also understood the situation and can predict the others' behavior, leads to a strategy of deception and a resolution around A's second choice. Further, the super-rational account may not be sufficient to capture the complexity, as the quote above suggests. A may agree to choice #2 (its second choice) and still achieve its first choice through foot dragging and other actions at and away from the table all designed to avoid a final agreement. And all this complexity occurs with just three parties and three possible solutions—no agents, no constituencies, no audiences.

Social Dilemmas

Another diabolically difficult problem that often stymies multiparty negotiators is the social dilemma. At the simplest level, social dilemmas occur when it is in each parties' interest to make an individual choice that increases one's own utility at the expense of others. When everyone makes this myopically optimal choice, the negative impacts of each party's actions overwhelm the positive impact of one's own action, and everyone is worse off.

Examples of social dilemma structures abound, starting with the most famous, "The Tragedy of the Commons" (Hardin, 1968). But there is a host of other examples from the simple to the hugely complex, from abstract to real-world situations that are extremely important for the well-being of the planet:

- One simple example of a social dilemma occurs when drivers slow down to view a roadside accident. In essence this is a silent negotiation among many drivers, all of whom would be better off collectively if traffic did not slow, but each of whom is individually better off if they can satisfy their curiosity by slowing to peek. Of course, like all economic externalities, what is good for one is good for all, but if all slow to peek, traffic backs up and all are worse off.
- Another simple example of a multiparty social dilemma is that of competing radios at the beach. As each radio is turned up to drown out the others, everyone suffers.
- On a far more important note, there is the practice of doctors prescribing unnecessary antibiotics so parents can treat their children's minor colds and ailments. As antibiotics are prescribed, these minor ailments become ever so slightly easier to suffer through (psychologically if not physically). In the long run, however, the bacteria develop resistance and we increase our collective risk of returning to a world where many diseases cannot be treated. (For an excellent description of this problem, see Lauerman, 1997.)
- On a similar or perhaps even more important note, the framework negotiations over the control of greenhouse gas emissions also represent a social dilemma. Individual country

economies can grow faster and individuals within those countries can have higher per capita consumption levels (considered a good outcome) if companies and individuals are allowed to emit carbon dioxide and other greenhouse gases freely. However, as worldwide emission levels increase, the general and economic well-being of the world's population at large declines due to warming and the many other environmental catastrophes that may ensue.
- A favorite example of ours as professors at business schools is the MBA game we call, get as many job offers as you can. The more job offers individuals collect, the better they feel; the more stature they accrue among their classmates. But the consequences to the collective are enormous. Not only are there fewer offers available for their classmates this year, but future classes suffer as well because the recruiters' yields drop (the percentage of offers accepted). And when yields drop far enough, it becomes less cost effective to recruit at that institution. So they stop coming, and next year's class and all future classes suffer.

Other examples abound. Here are a few more.

- Running for the exits when someone yells fire.
- Not voting because what's one more vote (ask a Floridian).
- Not conserving water, energy, or any other scarce resource.
- Commuting to work alone.
- Helping your country to obtain nuclear weapons.
- Getting away with cheating on your taxes.

Overcoming social dilemma structures and fostering cooperative agreements are exceedingly difficult. Moreover, much of the advice learned from Axelrod's (1984) computer tournaments for two-party prisoners' dilemmas does not easily apply to real-world multiparty settings.

Axelrod ran a series of tournaments pitting one strategy against another in a multiperiod prisoners' dilemma game. To everyone's surprise, a very simple strategy, called tit for tat, won the tournament. This was surprising because tit-for-tat was functionally unable to win a single game. The best it could do was tie. But though it never won, on average it scored better than any other strategy in the tournament. From this a variety of conclusions were drawn concerning how to promote cooperation in prisoners' dilemma structures.

But these recommendations are very difficult to apply in multiparty environments. For instance, the notion that one should not be envious but rather should be concerned only with how well one does oneself is exceedingly difficult to apply when there are many people around you doing better. When there are lots of examples all around you of others gaining from acting in their own myopic self-interest, strong social pressures are created to behave similarly. If lots of people get away with cheating on their taxes, pretty soon you too will be tempted to cheat. By the very nature of the social dilemma, there are often powerful special interest groups jockeying for special treatment, and it is in their own best interest to defect.

Similarly, Axelrod's advice to increase recognition capability comes apart when there are too many players to recognize. Likewise, Axelrod's advice about reciprocity, that rewards and punishments should be swift and certain, is problematic in multiparty situations. Reciprocate with whom? Who should do the rewarding? The punishing? What governing body has jurisdiction? Often none exist (Gray, 1999). It is often unclear how broadly the definition of "society" has to be, and when it is broadly defined, there is often no body with the requisite authority to act (Gray, 1999). For instance, should the US alone take action to prevent doctors from overprescribing antibiotics. Of course it can, and while it might slow the development of antibiotic-resistant strains of bacteria, it cannot successfully remedy the problem as it is worldwide in nature. Should the industrial world alone act to control the emissions of carbon dioxide or other gases? Even if the industrial nations were to agree, what international body would have jurisdiction over conflicts of interpretation or enforcement. And even when there are "global" organizations that exist such as the World Health Organization, these organizations often have recommendatory status at best.

Incomplete Integration

In two-party environments, the basic advice is to look for integrative settlements and push the search process to find agreements that are better for both. We say that an agreement is integrative if it satisfies the interests of both parties, making it better for both relative to some starting point. We say a settlement is "efficient" or on the "Pareto frontier" if it is impossible to find another agreement better for both parties (or at least better for one and not worse for the other). Because of the large number of participants, it is very difficult in multiparty negotiations to construct Pareto-improving alternatives. Mixed-motive negotiations abound, but because of the dimensionality (which is equal to the number of participants) of the utility space in which Pareto dominance is examined, it is extremely difficult to find solutions that are dominating on all axes. When one looks at two-party mixed-motive negotiations, the utility space (or Pareto space, if you prefer) has two dimensions—how I value the deal and how you value it (e.g. my utility and yours). With three parties, we have to worry about how all three of us think about it. It is therefore much harder to construct something that appeals to us all.

This affects the fundamental advice for forming Pareto-improving alternatives with two parties—make simple trades of low priorities for high ones. With only two parties this must create value for us both. If I give up a low priority (something not that important to me) for a high priority (something of great importance to me), and you do the same, then we must both be better off. But when there are more than two traders, there is the possibility that these Pareto-improving two-party trades may decrease the utility of the other nontrading parties (and hence, the value of the resulting agreement to those parties). For example, with just three parties, there can be three pairs of two-party traders, each of whom can make Pareto-improving trades. But if each of those trades causes more harm to the third, left-out party than it helps the parties to the trade, the ultimate result may be a diminishing of utility for all.

Just as social dilemmas come about because individuals act myopically to enhance their own utility at the expense of others, it is possible for pairs (or larger subgroups) to act myopically by executing incompletely integrating trades—trades that are Pareto-improving for the subgroup, but not for others. If enough such trades are executed, the utility of each party may be diminished and social welfare destroyed.

Thus, this notion of incomplete integration causing a worsening of the utility for all as a result of a series of Pareto-improving agreements among subgroups is an extension of the idea of social dilemmas, which result in a worsening of the utility for all as a result of the myopic actions of individuals. It is also an extension of the idea of parasitic integration (Bazerman & Gillespie, 1997) in which parties to a deal may reach an integrative,

Pareto-improving agreement for themselves at the expense of other parties generally not part of, or integral to, the agreement. The classic example offered by Bazerman and Gillespie of parasitic integration is the Camp David Accords. This has been widely viewed as an integrative settlement between Egypt and Israel. And from their perspective, it probably was. But if we broaden the perspective to include the US, perhaps the agreement was not integrative for all, as much of the benefit accrued to Egypt and Israel, and much of the cost was borne by the US in the form of security guarantees, foreign aid payments, and so forth. Furthermore, if you broaden the perspective further to consider others not at the table, like the Palestinians and nearby Arab nations, some of whom may have found no agreement preferable to any agreement, it becomes hard to think of the Accord as an integrative agreement from this broadened perspective.

Within multiparty groups, incomplete integration is both natural and dangerous, for not only can it harm (lead to a diminishing of utility) the left-out parties, but in some circumstances it can lead to a diminishing of utility for all. As noted, even though mixed-motive negotiations abound, simply because of the dimensionality of the Pareto space in which agreements are measured, it is difficult to achieve agreements that are Pareto-improving for all. And therefore, whenever subagreements are reached, they are likely to be incompletely integrative. Finally, when the incompletely integrative agreements that are reached cause harm to the left-out parties, it is possible that the collection of agreements can lead to a diminishing of the utility for every party and therefore the social welfare of the entire system. (See Brams, 1990, for a game-theoretic discussion, and Clyman & Kane, 1996a, for a teaching case, Oxenfeld College, that illustrates exactly this situation. In Oxenfeld, three pairs of parties each make a Pareto-improving trade. Yet the resulting settlement is worse for each of the three parties individually than had none of the trades been made. And because it is worse for every party, it must therefore be worse for the entire collective.) Note once again that we have illustrated the potential for this structural difficulty with just three parties. When a fourth player is added, there are six pairs and four triads that can make incompletely integrative agreements, and each of these myopically optimal trades can make the other parties worse off, increasing the potential and likelihood of a worsening of the utility of all.

V SOCIAL COMPLEXITY

In addition to the cognitive, procedural, and structural features that render multiparty negotiations difficult to resolve, social and psychological processes also intensify the dynamics (Kramer, 1991). One important social process that contributes to intractability in these settings is framing (Gray, 1997; Lewicki, Gray, & Elliott, 2002). Through framing, negotiators focus their attention on some aspects of the conflict and not on others, highlighting selected issues while ignoring or giving short shrift to others. Frames refer to the interpretations that negotiators use to make sense of the situation. Frames influence what the parties believe is at stake in the dispute by helping parties define what they believe a dispute is about and what their preferences are (Neale & Bazerman, 1991; Tversky & Kahneman, 1981). Frames also shape parties' beliefs about how a dispute should be settled (Gray & Hanke, 2001; Merry & Silbey, 1984; Sheppard, Blumenfeld-Jones, & Roth, 1989) and what actions parties should take during the negotiations (De Dreu et al., 1994). These earlier frames, in turn, influence whether negotiations take place and the outcomes that result from them (Donnellon &

Gray, 1989; Gray, 1997; Lewicki, Gray, & Elliott, 2002; Mather & Yngvesson, 1980–81; Pinkley & Northcraft, 1994). An example of differential framing can be found between technical experts and lay people who are assessing environmental risk. While technical experts often calculate risk based on probabilities of a catastrophic event occurring, lay people focus on the risk associated with extreme cases because they do not trust the effectiveness of detection and mitigation systems (Elliott, 1992).

As the sociolinguist Gumperz (1982, pp. 21–22) notes,

> Frames convey what is meant at any one point in a conversation.... Frames enable us to distinguish among permissible interpretive options. Among other things they also help in identifying overall themes, in deciding what weight to assign to a particular message segment and in distinguishing key points from subsidiary or qualifying information.

While frames help to focus our attention, in multiparty negotiations, building a common frame within which to negotiate can become especially difficult. For example, if negotiators frame the stakes in the dispute as allocations over water rights, the outcome may be different than if they frame the stakes in terms of tribal (or national) sovereignty—the latter evokes much deeper and more fundamental issues related to identity and well-being and is likely to promote nonnegotiable stances and escalatory behavior (Gray & Hanke, 2001; Rothman, 1997). The presence of two kinds of frames, in particular, can impose serious limitations on multiparty negotiations. These are identity frames and asymmetric power frames.

Identity Frames

Identity frames embody core aspects of a negotiator's self-concept (Lewicki, Gray, & Elliott, 2002) and portray how they understand themselves (or their group) to be (Hoare, 1994; Hogg, Terry, & White, 1995). Identities are usually developed through social category membership (Tajfel & Turner, 1985)—that is, we think of who we are in terms of our membership in social groups. Identity framing is not inherently problematic; in fact, identifying with specific social groups provides, among other things, a sense of belonging and well-being for group members (Cox, 1993; Hoare, 1994). However, in negotiations, identity frames can be invoked when a negotiator perceives threats to his/her identity from the stance that other negotiators take (Rothman, 1997). Conflicts often occur over the underlying beliefs and values that challenge people's valued identities (Wade-Benzoni et al., 2002). When this happens, a strong defensive stance, designed to protect our identities from challenge, is mounted. This type of conflict can be particularly difficult to overcome as the participants to the conflict feel that what is at stake is their individual or their group's integrity or viability. Thus, compromising on these issues is not feasible. When these core value-based issues are invoked, negotiators have more difficulty imagining or accepting integrative trade-offs (Tetlock et al., 2000). For example, in disputes between farmers, ranchers, and Native Americans over water rights, the stakes can be framed in terms of property rights or in terms of tribal sovereignty and survivability. These two frames raise very different specters and responses. Property rights only go so far. Sovereignty and survivability are the stuff that wars are made of. Without water, Native American tribes, as peoples, cannot survive. The latter framing evokes much deeper and more fundamental issues related to identity and well-being and, as such, is likely to promote nonnegotiable stances and escalatory behavior (Gray & Hanke, 2001; Rothman, 1997; Tetlock et al., 2000).

Identity frames also surface when judgments about the fairness of potential outcomes are being made. For example, disputes over environmental hazards can be framed solely in terms of the health risks they pose to a particular community (e.g. one adjacent to the hazard) or to health effects they may cause for future, unborn generations (Wade-Benzoni, 1996). These potential intergenerational effects make negotiation dynamics far more complex by raising identity frames about who speaks for the unborn and how their interests are to be protected. Identity issues also surface in environmental injustice cases (Bullard, 1990). For environmental justice advocates, the salient identity that gets framed is that of "victims" who have been put at risk from environmental hazards while others, more economically advantaged or racially distinct, were not (Taylor, 2000). For example, Bullard and his colleagues (Bullard, 1990) have raised the prospect that it is no accident that African-American communities are victims of a disproportionate amount of exposure to toxic materials, and they have used this argument to raise the stakes and demand solutions that address both the health and the ethical issues associated with these situations.

Identity framing can also offer a potential basis for reconciling differences. Since parties usually have more than one salient identity, it may be possible to find identities that they hold in common. For example, a bitter environmental dispute over logging in the Plumas National Forest shifted dramatically when some disputants on each side began to highlight their common identity as residents of the small town of Quincy, California (which was suffering economically from a reduction in logging), rather than their competing identities as loggers and environmentalists (Bryan & Wondolleck, 2002). This shift from a focus on interest-based identities to place-based identities enabled them to find common ground on an environmentally sustainable plan for timber harvesting.

The Effect of Power Differences on Framing

We can further understand the complications injected into multiparty negotiations by framing when we consider that both judgments about stakes and about fairness are affected by the power distribution of the parties. Smith (1982) provided a compelling explanation of the role of power in framing of the stakes of conflicts. He has argued that the lens or frame that disputants adopt depends on the power they hold in the situation. Powerful parties tend to frame the stakes in terms of preserving the status quo (which includes preserving the power they enjoy and their entitlement to it). In contrast, less powerful parties frame their reality as the need to tear down and replace the status quo—for them the stakes involve destroying rather than preserving what currently exists (Smith, 1982) and, presumably replacing it with a more equitable distribution of resources or one that compensates the less powerful for their pain and suffering. Such differential framing makes the convening of collaborative negotiations exceedingly difficult because the parties cannot even reach a preliminary agreement on a common definition of the problem or who should be seated at the table (Gray, 1989).

Power differences also shape fairness perceptions. When parties are of differential power, the typical axioms for what constitutes a "fair" allocation no longer apply (Allisson & Messick, 1990)—that is, parties do not agree that equal division of a resource is the fairest allocation. According to Wade-Benzoni, Tenbrunsel, and Bazerman (1997, p. 191), asymmetries in power "create uncertainty with respect to what constitutes a fair solution" and encourage parties to employ an egocentric bias in judging what is fair. Egocentric biases favor the decision maker over others who are not privy to the decision (Walster, Walster, & Berscheid, 1978).

Such biases and their attendant fairness judgments are particularly common in disputes over environmental issues (Wade-Benzoni, Tenbrunsel, & Bazerman, 1997; Wade-Benzoni et al., 2002). These kinds of disputes typically involve many parties, involve issues that are fraught with uncertainty, and often bridge substantial power differences. Differential framing with respect to fairness and stakes as well as where and how the issues should be resolved often prevent these kinds of disputes from reaching easy resolution and lock them into protracted stalemates (Lewicki, Gray & Elliott, 2002).

If we examine the complexity in current multiparty negotiations over environmental issues such as global warming, the depletion of the ozone layer, pollution of the oceans, and destruction of biological diversity, we often find these framing issues coupled with the structural issues we raised earlier. For example, the problems addressed in the United Nations Conference on the United Nations Framework Convention on Climate Change in Kyoto, Japan, in 1997 and the United Nations Conference on Environment and Development in Rio de Janeiro in June 1992 both have complex social dilemma structures. Not only does defection by large numbers of parties lead to dire consequences for all, but also the problem is complicated because the different parties have very different notions of fairness. Furthermore, one of those fairness notions is that the solution should not be strictly integrative but rather incompletely integrative. In other words, the developing world tends to believe that the only fair solutions require the industrial world to bear the brunt of the cost so that the developing world can catch up. They want to change the underlying distribution of power and allow the developing countries a chance to build their economic base while the developed world pays for having polluted over the last 100 or more years. A similar framing occurs in discussions about reparations to descendants of slaves in the US or to victims of the holocaust in Germany. Depending on which frame you adopt, the stakes in the negotiation dramatically shift.

VI OVERCOMING OBSTACLES TO MULTIPARTY NEGOTIATIONS, CONCLUSIONS, AND FUTURE RESEARCH

Designing Collaborative Multiparty Processes

Perhaps the most promising approaches to overcoming obstacles to multiparty negotiations are those based on some form of societal action: regulation, legislation, building acceptance of social norms, etc. Within the US the use of third-party mediators to bring disputing parties to a common table to explore joint solutions to environmental and other community problems has received considerable success over the last 20 years (Bingham, 1986; Crowfoot & Wondolleck, 1990; Gray, 1989; Susskind, McKearnan, & Thomas-Larmer, 1999; Wondolleck & Yaffee, 2000). Such efforts are commonly referred to as alternative dispute resolution (ADR) because they offer alternatives to more common litigious approaches to resolving these disputes. While initially ad hoc and experimental, over the years ADR has gained a quasi-institutional status (Purdy & Gray, 1998) through the backing of powerful institutional actors such as the judiciary (who refer cases to mediation), the American Bar Association (that has an ADR division and has promoted ADR training within law school curriculums), and the US Congress (who passed the Administrative Procedures Act that established standards for the use of ADR by federal agencies). In addition, in the last 15 years, over 30 states have created statewide offices of dispute resolution that are frequently linked to other powerful institutional actors such as the courts, administrative agencies, or universities (Purdy & Gray, 1998). Through these avenues, ADR has begun to establish itself as a legitimate means of addressing local, regional, and national-level multiparty disputes. While by no means a panacea, ADR approaches have generated lasting agreements to disputes that appeared to be or had been intractable (Bingham, 1986; Susskind, McKearnan, & Thomas-Larmer, 1999).

At an international or global level, attempting to use similar collaborative processes poses what often appear to be insurmountable obstacles. Negotiation of international environmental issues is especially difficult because of complex linkages with underlying economic, political, and social issues; scientific uncertainties; and solutions that require the participation of many nations, as well as agreement and implementation of differential and symmetrical obligations. These issues require commitments that affect the way sovereign states use their own natural resources, affect neighboring country resources, and the international commons (Scott & Trolldalen, 1993, p. 45).

Efforts to construct international or global cooperation are referred to as "regimes" (Young, 1994). Regimes involve negotiations among the stakeholders to establish a system of norms and rules that govern stakeholders' behavior in the future with respect to a particular issue (Young, 1994). Historically, regimes have been enacted at two levels: framework conventions and protocols. These differ in the extent to which they impose binding obligations on the signatories (protocols) or are enforced through voluntary cooperation (framework conventions). The fundamental problems associated with regime formation have been conceptualized as "organizing in the absence of authority" (Gray, 1999) or "how to govern without government" (Young, 1994), since there are few formal auspices through which these regimes can be legitimately constructed. Despite this, some examples of successful international partnerships and global regimes can be identified. One such agreement is the Montreal Protocol agreed to in March 1988 to limit the production and use of chlorofluorocarbons that destroy the protective ozone layer. Another is the London Dumping Convention that limits dumping of hazardous wastes in the oceans and empowers coastal states to impose sanctions on violators. Time is an important consideration in the development of such agreements that may take shape gradually over many years. Spector, Sjostedt, and Zartman (1994, p. 3) highlight the importance of regimes in regulating the participating parties during these processes:

> During the formative and operative stages of agreement implementation, regime mechanisms are needed to foster a sense of cohesiveness, common purpose, and continuity among a set of nations that have agreed to abide by common objectives and standards.

Challenges Posed by Collaborative Processes

Overall, the construction of such transnational norms and agreements is still extremely difficult to achieve for several reasons. First, it is not always clear who should be at the table. In some global environmental negotiations, NGOs have been excluded from voting memberships despite the fact that they often have important knowledge about, and experience with, the problems under consideration and the means to work integratively across national borders (Susskind, 1994). Representational issues of how many and which voices should be at the table are thorny questions that plague domestic as well as international collaboration efforts. In negotiations with the World Bank over large construction projects, for example, low-power stakeholders' efforts to be recognized as legitimate players at the table have often been challenged (Brown & Ashman, 1997). Second, even when parties agree to convene around an issue and to voluntarily submit to a negotiated accord, issues of shirking, reneging, and punishment for noncooperators loom large. By the very nature of those issues with social dilemma structures, there are often powerful special interest groups jockeying for special treatment and it is in their own best interest to defect. Third, as noted earlier, it is often not clear how broadly the definition of "society" has to be, and when it is broadly defined, there is often no body with the requisite authority to act (Gray, 1999).

In general, negotiators trapped in these dilemmas often seek to extract themselves through incomplete integration. If subgroups can argue for or otherwise insist upon agreements that are integrative for them but not for all, incompletely integrative agreements may be reached. The attempted agreement defined by the Kyoto Accords is an example in point. The reason this agreement was recently rejected by the Bush administration was because it saw the US (and other industrial nations) bearing the costs to curtail emissions while the developing world had no similarly agreed-upon emission limits. Similarly, the resolution of budget disputes through deficit spending is another example, as it is often easy for parties today to agree to spend but not tax, when they bear the fruits of that agreement, while others, future generations not party to the agreement, bear the costs. But by their very nature, incompletely integrative solutions are insufficiently satisfying for all.

In summary, multiparty negotiations have amazing complexity. The complexity arises from numerous sources including cognitive, procedural, structural, and social. Even the move to three players is sufficient to create enormous additional complexity, as demonstrated by the creation of such possibilities as incomplete integration and the paradox of the chair, neither of which is possible with only two parties. Indeed, it is much like abstract mathematical theories of geometry and topology. There are whole collections of theorems that are true in worlds of two dimensions that are no longer true in worlds of higher dimension, and similarly there are whole hosts of theorems true when the dimensionality is greater than or equal to three that are simply not true when the dimensionality is equal to two.

Future Directions

This chapter has taken a small step toward identifying some of these added complexities and beginning the process of codifying and categorizing them. It is our view, still to be borne out by further research, that the key is to accept the full complexity of multiparty negotiations and engage it. Attempts to mitigate that complexity by overlaying rules, procedures, and structures all tend to add constraints that lead to suboptimal results. Thus, for example, if you are in a situation where the paradox of the chair can come into play, the only possible answer is to incorporate the fullness of the complexity into a super-rational analysis. Anything less is insufficient.

Far more research is necessary to completely categorize the full complexity of higher-dimensional negotiations and to begin the process of identifying ways and means of dealing with these obstacles to successful multiparty negotiations. We have argued that ADR approaches offer some promise for coping with the pitfalls identified here. They do so for several reasons. First, someone (a neutral third party) is attending to the process issues (such as incomplete integration) that can thwart creating suboptimal results for all. Shifting some of the process concerns to a third party reduces, at least somewhat, the burden of cognitive complexity that disputants must bear. Second, ADR processes at least temporarily level the playing field among the parties, thereby ameliorating problems associated with asymmetric power dynamics. Third, they can include all parties, even those not really there, like future generations, through the appointment of individuals to represent their interests. And finally, because all parties can be represented at the table, problems associated with voting and incomplete integration can also be averted using consensus as the decision rule. In consensus processes, all parties must at least agree that they can live with the solution (even if it is not their most preferred outcome).

As Gray (1989) has noted, however, ADR processes are not a panacea. Efforts to systematically evaluate the successes and limitations of ADR approaches are being proposed (Innis, 1999; O'Leary & Bingham, 2003). Such efforts would be aided by systematic research on a number of multiparty negotiation topics. A few suggestions illustrate fruitful areas for future research:

- What process designs could overcome the paradox of the chair?
- Can disputant knowledge of the current limitations associated with multiparty negotiations empower negotiations to avoid these pitfalls?
- Can the use of web-based technologies for negotiations help to overcome problems of power asymmetry, representativeness, and cognitive complexity and possibly encourage creative new options for global regimes?
- How can new dispute resolution approaches designed for identity-based conflicts reduce negative attributions and defensiveness and promote constructive solutions that affirm, rather than challenge, core identities?

As the examples in this chapter have aptly demonstrated, the importance of this work cannot be underestimated. As a global society we need to understand how best to navigate within these complex dynamics since, in many cases, the very future of the planet may be at stake.

REFERENCES

Allisson, S. T. & Messick, D. M. (1990). Social decision heuristics in the use of shared resources. *Journal of Behavioral Decision Making, 3*, 195–204.

Ancona, D. G., Freidman, R. A., & Kolb, D. M. (1991). The group and what happens on the way to "yes." *Negotiation Journal, 2*, 155–173.

Axelrod, R. (1984). *The Evolution of Cooperation*. New York: Basic Books.

Bazerman, M. H. & Gillespie, J. (1997). Parasitic integration. *Negotiation Journal: On the Process of Dispute Settlement, 13*, 271–282.

Bazerman, M. H., Mannix, E., & Thompson, L. (1988). Groups as mixed-motive negotiations. In E. J. Lawyer & B. Markovsky (eds), *Advances in Group Process: Theory and Research* (Vol. 5). Greenwich, Conn.: JAI Press.

Bingham, G. (1986). *Resolving Complex Environmental Disputes*. Washington, DC: The Conservation Foundation.

Brams, S. (1990). *Negotiation Games: Applying Game Theory to Bargaining and Arbitration*. New York: Routledge, Chapman and Hall.

Brett, J. (1991). Negotiating group decisions. *Negotiation Journal, 7*, 291–310.

Brown, L. D. & Ashman, D. (1997). Social capital, mutual influence, and social learning in intersectoral problem solving in Africa and Asia. In D. Cooperider & J. Dutton (eds), *Organizational Dimensions of Global Change: No Limits to Cooperation* (pp. 139–167). Thousand Oaks, Calif.: Sage.

Bryan, T. & Wondolleck, J. M. (2002). When irresolvable becomes resolvable: what the language of the Quincy Library Group conflict reveals about framing and intractability. In R. Lewicki, B. Gray, & M. Elliott (eds), *Making Sense of Intractable Environmental Conflicts: Concepts and Cases*. Washington, DC: Island Press.

Bullard, R. (1990). *Dumping in Dixie: Race, Class and Environmental Quality.* Boulder, Colo.: Westview.

Clyman, D. & Kane, J. (1996a). Oxenfeld College: Caroline Wilcox; Oxenfeld College: Arthur Vescio; and Oxenfeld College: Jack Tully, UVA-QA-0506, 0507, and 0508, The Darden School Foundation.

Clyman, D. & Kane, J. (1996b). The Geneva Conference on Indochina: Western Alliance; The Geneva Conference on Indochina: Sino-Soviet Bloc; The Geneva Conference on Indochina: Democratic Republic of Vietnam (Vietminh); UVA-QA-0503, 0504, and 0505, The Darden School Foundation.

Cox, T. (1993). *Cultural Diversity in Organizations: Theory, Research and Practice.* San Francisco: Berrett-Koehler.

Crowfoot, J. E. & Wondolleck, J. M. (1990). *Environmental Disputes: Community Involvement in Conflict Resolution.* Washington, DC: Island Press.

De Dreu, C. K. W., Carnevale, P. J. D., Emans, B. J. M., & van de Vliert, E. (1994). Effects of gain–loss frames in negotiation: loss aversion, mismatching, and frame adoption. *Organizational Behavior and Human Decision Processes, 60*, 90–107.

Donnellon, A. & Gray, B. (1989). An interactive theory of reframing in negotiation. Working paper, Pennsylvania State University, Center for Research in Conflict and Negotiation.

Elliott, M. P. (1992). The effect of differing assessments of risk in hazardous waste facility siting negotiations. In G. Bingham & T. Mealey (eds), *Negotiating Hazardous Waste Facility Siting and Permitting Agreements.* Washington, DC: Conservation Foundation.

Fisher, R. & Ury, W. (1983). *Getting to Yes: Negotiating Agreement without Giving In.* New York: Penguin Books.

Gray, B. (1989). *Collaborating: Finding Common Ground for Multiparty Problems.* San Francisco: Jossey-Bass.

Gray, B. (1997). Framing and reframing of intractable environmental disputes. In R. Lewicki, R. Bies, & B. Sheppard (eds), *Research on Negotiation in Organizations* (Vol. 6, pp. 163–188). Greenwich, Conn.: JAI Press.

Gray, B. (1999). The development of global environmental regimes: organizing in the absence of authority. In D. Cooperider & J. Dutton (eds), *Organizational Dimensions of Global Change: No Limits to Cooperation* (pp. 185–209). Thousand Oaks, Calif.: Sage.

Gray, B. & Hanke, R. (2001). Frame repertoires and non-collaborative behavior in an intractable environmental dispute. Working paper, Center for Research in Conflict and Negotiation, Pennsylvania State University.

Gumperz, J. J. (1982). *Discourse Strategies*. Cambridge, England: Cambridge University Press.

Hardin, G. (1968). The tragedy of the commons. *Science, 162*, 1243–1248.

Hardy, C. & Phillips, N. (1998). Strategies of engagement: lessons from the critical examination of collaboration and conflict in interoganizational domains. *Organization Science, 9*, 217–230.

Heider, F. (1958). *The Psychology of Interpersonal Relations.* New York: Wiley.

Hoare, C. H. (1994). Psychosocial identity development in United States society: its role in fostering exclusion of other cultures. In E. P. Salett & D. R. Koslow (eds), *Race, Ethnicity, and Self: Identity in Multicultural Perspective* (pp. 24–41). Washington, DC: National Multicultural Institute.

Hogg, M. A., Terry, D. J., & White, K. M. (1995). A tale of two theories: a critical comparison of identity theory with social identity theory. *Social Psychology Quarterly, 58*, 255–269.

Huxham, C. (1996). *Creating Collaborative Advantage.* London: Sage.

Innis, J. (1999). Evaluating consensus building. In L. Susskind, S, McKearnan, & J. Thomas-Larmer (eds), *The Consensus Building Handbook* (pp. 631–671). Thousand Oaks, Calif.: Sage.

Irving, R. E. M. (1975). *The First Indochina War: French and American Policy 1945–54.* London: Croom Helm.

Kramer, R. M. (1991). The more the merrier? Social psychological aspects of multiparty negotiations in organizations. In M. H. Bazerman, R. J. Lewicki, & B. H. Sheppard (eds), *Research on Negotiation in Organizations: Handbook of Negotiation Research* (Vol. 3, pp. 307–322). Greenwich, Conn.: JAI Press.

Lauerman, J. F. (1997). Homicidal cultures: they're gaining on us. *Harvard Magazine*, March–April, 18–21.

Lewicki, R., Gray, B., & Elliott, M. (2002). *Making Sense of Intractable Environmental Conflicts: Concepts and Cases.* Washington, DC: Island Press.

Mannix, E. & Lowenstein, G. (1993). Management time horizons and inter-firm mobility: an experimental investigation. *Organizational Behavior and Human Decision Processes, 56*, 266–284.

Mather, L. & Yngvesson, B. (1980–81). Language, audience, and the transformation of disputes. *Law and Society Review, 15*, 775–821.

Merry, S. E. & Silbey, S. (1984). What do plaintiffs want? Reexamining the concept of dispute. *Justice System Journal, 9*, 151–177.

Murnighan, J. K. (1991). *The Dynamics of Bargaining Games.* Englewood Cliffs, NJ: Prentice-Hall.

Murnighan, J. K. (1992). *Bargaining Games.* New York: William Morrow and Company, Inc.

Neale, M. A. & Bazerman, M. H. (1991). *Cognition and Rationality in Negotiation.* New York: The Free Press.

O'Leary, R. & Bingham, L. (eds) (2003). *Evaluating Environmental and Public Policy Conflict Resolution Programs and Policies.* Washington, DC: Resources for the Future or Rowan & Littlefield Publishers.

Pinkley, R. L. & Northcraft, G. B. (1994). Conflict frames of reference: implications for dispute processes and outcomes. *Academy of Management Journal, 37*(1), 193–205.

Purdy, J. & Gray, B. (1998). The role of organizational agency in early institutionalization processes. Working Paper, Center for Research in Conflict and Negotiation, Pennsylvania State University.

Raiffa, Howard (1982). *The Art and Science of Negotiation.* Cambridge, Mass.: Harvard University Press.

Randle, Robert (1969). *Geneva 1954: The Settlement of the Indochina War.* Princeton: Princeton University Press.

Rothman, J. (1997). *Resolving Identity-based Conflict in Nations, Organizations, and Communities.* San Francisco: Jossey-Bass.

Rubin, J. Z., Pruitt, D. G., & Kim, S. H. (1994). *Social Conflict: Escalation, Stalemate, and Settlement* (2nd edn). New York: McGraw-Hill.

Schon, D. A. & Rein, M. (1994). *Frame Reflection: Toward the Resolution of Intractable Policy Controversies.* New York: Basic Books.

Scott, P. T. & Trolldalen, J. M. (1993). International environmental conflict resolution: moving beyond Rio. *NIDR Forum*, Winter, 44–51.

Sebenius, James K. (1996). Sequencing to build coalitions: with whom should I talk first? In Richard Zeckhauser, Ralph Keeney, & James K. Sebenius (eds), *Wise Decisions* (pp. 324–348). Boston, Mass.: Harvard Business School Press.

Sheppard, B. H., Blumenfeld-Jones, K., & Roth, J. (1989). Informal thirdpartyship: studies of everyday conflict intervention. In K. Kressel, D. G. Pruitt, & associates (eds), *Mediation Research* (pp. 166–189). San Francisco: Jossey-Bass.

Sherif, M. (1958). Superordinate goals in the reduction of intergroup conflicts. *American Journal of Sociology, 63*, 349–358.

Smith, K. (1982). *Conflict in Organizations: Prisons in Disguise.* Dubuque, Iowa: Kendall Hunt.

Spector, B. I., Sjostedt, G., & Zartman, I. W. (1994). The dynamics of regime-building negotiations. In B. I. Spector, G. Sjostedt, & I. W. Zartman (eds), *Negotiating International Regimes* (pp. 3–8). London: Graham & Trotman/Martinus Nijhoff.

Susskind, L. E. (1994). What will it take to ensure effective global environmental management? A reassessment of regime-building accomplishments. In B. I. Spector, G. Sjostedt, & I. W. Zartman (eds), *Negotiating International Regimes* (pp. 221–232). London: Graham & Trotman/Martinus Nijhoff.

Susskind, L., McKearnan, S., & Thomas-Larmer, J. (1999). *The Consensus Building Handbook.* Thousand Oaks, Calif.: Sage.

Tajfel, H. & Turner, J. C. (1985). The social identity theory of intergroup behavior. In S. Worchel & W. G. Austin (eds), *Psychology of Intergroup Relations* (pp. 7–24). Chicago, Ill.: Nelson Hall Publishers.

Taylor, D. (2000). Advances in environmental justice: research, theory and methodology. *American Behavioral Scientist, 43*(4), 504–580.

Tetlock, P. E., Kristel, O. V., Elson, S. B., Green, M. C., & Lerner, J. S. (2000). The psychology of the unthinkable: taboo trade-offs, forbidden base rates, and heretical counterfactuals. *Journal of Personality and Social Psychology, 78*, 853–870.

Thompson, L. (2001). *The Mind and Heart of the Negotiator*. Englewood Cliffs, NJ: Prentice-Hall.

Tversky, A. & Kahneman, D. (1981). The framing of decision and the psychology of choice. *Science, 211*, 453–458.

Wade-Benzoni, K. A. (1996). Integenerational justice: discounting, reciprocity and fairness as factors that influence how resources are allocated across generations. Unpublished dissertation, Northwestern University, Evanston, Ill.

Wade-Benzoni, K. A., Hoffman, A. J., Thompson, L. T., Moore, D. A., Gillespie, J. J., & Bazerman, M. H. (2002). Barriers to resolution in ideologically based negotiations: the role of values and institutions. *Academy of Management Review, 27*(1), 41–57.

Wade-Benzoni, K., Tenbrunsel, A. E., & Bazerman, M. H. (1997). Egocentric interpretations of fairness as an obstacle to the resolution of environmental conflict. In R. Lewicki, R. Bies, & B. Sheppard (eds), *Research on Negotiation in Organizations* (Vol. 6, pp. 189–206). Greenwich, Conn.: JAI Press.

Walster, E., Walster, G. W., & Berscheid, E. (1978). *Equity: Theory and Research.* Boston: Allyn & Bacon.

Wintle, Justin (1991). *The Viet Nam Wars*. Wars of the Modern Era Series. New York: St Martin's Press.

Wondolleck, J. M. & Yaffee, S. L. (2000). *Making Collaboration Work: Lessons from Innovation in Natural Resource Management*. Washington, DC: Island Press.

Young, O. R. (1994). *International Governance: Protecting the Environmental in a Stateless Society*. Ithaca, NY: Cornell University Press.

20

NETWORK STRUCTURES AND TEAMWORK

Kevin D. Clark

INTRODUCTION

Teamwork is about getting things done. Inherent in the notion of teams is the belief that, at least in some task environments, the pooling of individual efforts may lead to outcomes individuals alone could not achieve. Whereas teamwork and cooperative working are covered extensively in this volume, the emphasis here will be on defining another organizational phenomenon, social networks, and linking research and concepts from social network theory to research on teamwork and group process. I begin with a very brief review of group research.

Teamwork research focuses on the interaction between individuals who are members of a collective, typically a small group. Various constructs have been developed to describe the types of interaction patterns present in such groups, including cohesiveness, consensus, and conflict. Other constructs describe the tenor of relations, or understandings, within the group rather than interactions per se. Trust and norms of reciprocity are good examples.

Group functioning depends not only on the interactions and intentions, but also on the composition of members of the group. The knowledge, skills, and abilities (KSAs) of group members have been shown to impact group outcomes independent of group process (Smith et al., 1994). Although direct measurement of KSAs is possible, much of the research on groups utilizes demographic proxies like age, functional background, etc. In short, the research on groups has largely dealt with questions of who is on the group (demography) and how group members interact (group process).

The use of demographic proxies has been controversial (Lawrence, 1997; Smith et al., 1994), and yet the links between composition and outcomes has been robust in the literature. The main criticisms of demographic research are: (1) "black box" concerns (that unmeasured constructs may account for additional variance in dependent variables); and (2) conflicting results across studies. Still, demographic research continues to be published and constitutes an important part of the body of knowledge on groups.

Whereas there has developed a rather large and growing literature on who is in the group and how group members interact, very little research has examined the importance of who the group members know, how they know them, and what effect these networks have on process and outcomes. This is not to say that there is no research on networks. Structural sociologists

---

International Handbook of Organizational Teamwork and Cooperative Working. Edited by M. A. West, D. Tjosvold, and K. G. Smith.

have developed sophisticated methodologies for the measurement of relationships, and a long-standing body of research has investigated the structure and functioning of networks (Scott, 1991). During the past decade, this research has been utilized to study macro-organizational phenomena like interorganizational alliances (Gulati, 1995) and board of director interlocks (Haunschild & Beckman, 1998; Westphal & Zajac, 1997). Network approaches have also been used to study the diffusion of innovations in industry segments (Abrahamson & Rosenkopf, 1997; Powell, Koput, & Smith-Doerr, 1996). Most recently, organizational researchers have demonstrated great interest in the concept of social capital, with debate raging as to whether social capital inheres in the structure of networks or in the tenor of relationships, also called content (see Adler & Kwon, 2002, for an excellent review). Concepts of trust, norms of reciprocity, and a circumscribed group membership (similar to identity) from the content school of social capital (Coleman, 1988) will sound very familiar to group process researchers. The focus of this chapter is on the structural school of social network theory (Burt, 1982, 1992). In some ways the social capital debate between structuralists and content theorists is analogous to our purpose here. Content theorists are, perhaps unknowingly, bridging a gap between the structuralists and behavioral theorists. By bringing in concepts of content and emotion of relationships, they begin to add context to the structure of networks.

This chapter begins to address three primary questions:

1. To what extent are the two research traditions on small groups and network structure complements vs alternatives?
2. What is the impact of networks on group process?
3. Does the study of networks add to our understanding of how groups function?

We begin with a review of the core concepts from structural network theory. Next, network concepts are compared to concepts from group process theory with some hypotheses developed. Correlational analysis is used to investigate, in an exploratory and preliminary way, associations between network and group process concepts. The chapter concludes with a discussion of the results, and suggestions for future research.

NETWORK CONCEPTS

Structural network analysis is an active area of research within sociology with roots going back over 50 years. It is also prone to the same parochialism found in most fields of study, where separate "schools" have developed constructs and operationalization of said constructs sometimes in isolation from each other. As Burt (1982, p. 20) recalls from the work of Barnes (1972), the network literature can be likened to "a terminological jungle in which any newcomer may plant a tree." Simply put, network analysis is a very large and complex field the complete coverage of which is beyond the scope of this chapter.[1] What follows is an introduction to the main constructs within network analysis and the generally agreed-upon conclusions as to the structure and functioning of networks. I begin with a definition of the term "social network," and will use the example of a top management team of a company to demonstrate network concepts.

[1] Burt (1982) offers a sophisticated introduction to network analysis including the main concepts and "schools." Wasserman and Faust (1994) offer a comprehensive volume on network measurement and methods.

Although definitions abound, in this chapter we will consider the social network of an individual (or actor) to be comprised of the relationships that actor has to other actors in a social system. Although these relationships might include personal friends and family members, organizational research is typically interested only in relationships that can be used to achieve, or that affect, organizational outcomes. Thus the "social" in social network analysis refers to the interaction between people (as distinct from other sorts of technical networks), rather than connoting any sort of personal, emotional, or kinship element to the network.

Individuals have relationships with others within the group, as well as links to actors outside of the group and organization. Just as individuals may belong to multiple groups, they may also hold positions in multiple network systems. For example, a company's VP of marketing may belong to several networks: the top management team; the marketing department; a professional association; the alumni association of his/her undergraduate and graduate schools; the network of employees and former employees of his/her previous employer; a local chamber of commerce, etc. Importantly, some of these networks overlap, some are directly relevant to work, and others become relevant only occasionally as conditions change and opportunities arise. In addition, the types of relationships existing within each of these networks may be expected to differ. In short, there are many types of networks to which an individual may belong, and which may be important to individual, group, and organizational functioning and outcomes. Network analysis provides a methodology for studying the structure and functioning of these networks.

There is some preliminary evidence that networks have the property of both individuals and groups. Regardless of which approach researchers adopt, whether individuals agree to share their networks with others in the group should be associated with group process. For example, one would expect that cohesive groups in which members trust each other and share a common set of objectives would experience a large degree of network sharing such that the contacts of each member become available to others in the group. In groups with shifting membership, conflict, and multiple goals individual group members may choose to restrict access to their networks. Generally, groups who experience a degree of teamwork would also tend to view the individual networks of members as the group network. Indeed, the sharing of the benefits of networks among group members is a form of teamwork. In this chapter, I treat the sum of individual networks as the group network.[2]

The Use of Network Ties

Social network research has focused on two benefits of network ties: information and influence. The relationships an actor has to others present opportunities to access information not already held by the actor. As will be discussed below, the structure of the network as well as the type of linkage present affect the quantity and quality of the information available to the actor. Relationships can also be used to influence the other party. For example, a person may ask a favor of a friend and that friend is likely to oblige by virtue of the presence and tenor of the relationship. A person may ask a favor of a stranger, but is less certain that the favor will be granted since no prior relationship exists. So, relationships obligate actors to one another as well as creating a linkage through which information can flow. The

[2] Examination of ANOVAs, ICC1, and ICC2 for the data used in this research provides support for aggregation of internal but not external networks.

structure and type of relationships present in an actor's network determine the information and influencing benefits that can be extracted.

Characteristics of Networks

Though not exhaustive, the following is a description of major concepts within network analysis. Each of these concepts has been operationalized in many ways and sophisticated methodologies and software packages for the analysis of networks have been developed. The purpose here is to introduce group process researchers to another field of study, thus the trade-off between comprehensiveness and simplicity.[3] Most of these constructs have been operationalized at the individual level and then aggregated. The descriptions below follow this convention.

Network Size

One of the major characteristics of an individual's network is the number of contacts the actor has to other actors. In general, the larger the number of contacts, the more value that can be extracted from the network in the form of information and resource access, with some caveats. Extremely large networks may become unwieldy and inefficient to use. This is similar to search and comprehensiveness problems identified in decision-making theory. More directly, relationships require effort and resources to develop and maintain, thus a large network represents a substantial investment of resources that could be used elsewhere. In truth, some relationships require more resources to develop and maintain than others, as is discussed below. For now, it is sufficient to recognize that larger networks tend to be viewed as desirable but at a cost. The most common measure of network size is a simple count of the number of ties an individual has to other actors (Scott, 1991).

Network Range

Network range refers to the level of diversity represented in an actor's network of ties. For example, if our VP of marketing only had ties to actors with a similar functional background, the network would have low range. Importantly, the focus here is on how many *different* types of contacts are present in the network rather than the *number* of contacts. While large networks contain the potential for diversity, size does not equal diversity. The importance of network range lies in the potential of the network to provide novel information to the actor. Thus, an actor may be able to access a variety of information through the development of a diverse network without investing in network size. Network range has been operationalized as the number of different status groups accessed (Wasserman & Faust, 1994), where a status group represents contacts who are similar to one another but different from other status groups along some dimension deemed important to outcomes (e.g. functional background, organization type, control of a particular class of resources).

[3] The interested reader is directed to the journal *Social Networks*.

Centrality

Actors are considered central when they are visible to many other actors by virtue of their position in the network (Knoke & Burt, 1983). Visibility, or prominence, is enhanced when an actor holds ties to many other actors either directly, or through intermediaries. The diagrams below are adapted from Leavitt (1951) and show different structures of relationships the focal actor (A) could have with others in a network.

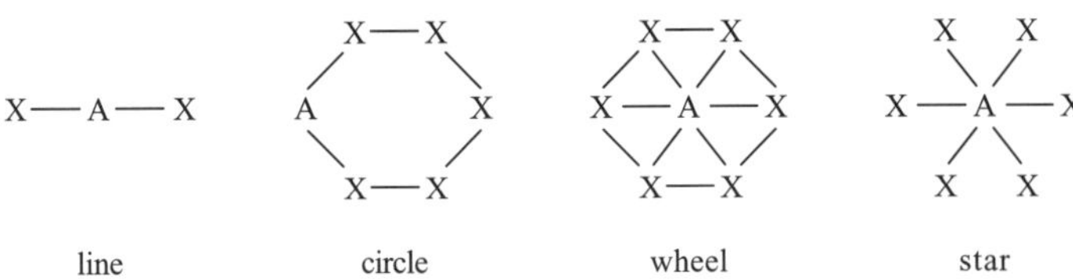

The concept of network centrality should be easily digested by those familiar with communication theory (Freeman, 1979; Shaw, 1981). The key benefits to centrality are the opportunity to broker information and control the flow of resources between parties (Knoke & Burt, 1983). The actor in the star diagram is positioned to control flows between all other actors in the network and may accumulate power and status by virtue of position centrality. This is true to a lesser extent in the wheel diagram since some actors can access others without relying on the focal actor. Other actors in the star and wheel networks are dependent on the central actor for need resources and information (Pfeffer & Salancik, 1978).

In a special case of centrality, Burt's (1992) concept of the structural hole refers to the condition in a network whereby two networks of actors who would benefit by interacting have no linkage. Being positioned as a bridge between two such networks of actors confers power and resources on an actor. The brokerage opportunity represented by the spanning of a structural hole is similar to the benefits an actor receives by virtue of being central in a network. The difference is that centrality refers to the number of contacts, whereas the bridge requires only that the actor be positioned between the two groups, even if only by virtue of being connected to one actor in each network. In the wheel network the actor is central but is not a bridge (that is, others are also directly connected to each other), whereas in the star network the actor is both central and spans a structural hole. Unfortunately, due to the open nature of the network data used in this research centrality and structural holes are not possible to measure.

Strength of Ties

Tie strength refers to the nature of the relationships found in a network. Strong ties are those that are long-standing, frequently exercised, and that have an emotional intensity (Granovetter, 1973). At first glance, one might consider strong ties to be superior to weaker relationships. Certainly strong ties might be functional in difficult situations where trust and familiarity are needed. However, strong ties are also expensive ties. Effort and resources used to develop and maintain strong ties cannot be used elsewhere, and thus are the crux of the problem: the development of strong ties limits the size of the network that can be developed given limited resources and time. Several theorists have touted the "strength of weak ties" (Burt, 1992; Granovetter, 1973), the argument being that a large and diverse network of weak ties, particularly if configured to exploit structural holes, may confer information and brokerage opportunities not available in a strong ties network. The debate rages as other theorists (Hansen, 1999; Krackhardt, 1992) suggest that certain resources and knowledge may only be available by virtue of a strong tie network. Social capital theorists (Coleman, 1988) tend to follow this view. Although tie strength can be measured separately as duration, frequency, and emotional intensity, additive indexes have also been used.

Density

Network density refers to the overall level of connectedness in a network (Wasserman & Faust, 1994). In every network there is a maximum number of possible relationships that could be present (for example, a network of 5 actors contains 10 possible links). Density refers to the proportion of links that exist to the total possible. Thus, a network where each actor knows every other actor would have a density of 1. Network density is considered inefficient by structural theorists, as links are viewed as redundant and less able to provide new information or resources (Burt, 1992). By contrast, social capital theorists (Coleman, 1988) consider the redundancy of dense networks to be functional because such networks may aid in the development of trust and norms. In this research, density is measured as the redundancy, or overlap, of group members' networks.

NETWORKS AND GROUP PROCESS

One goal of this chapter is to identify the similarities and differences between group process and network approaches to the study of groups. As discussed above, network analysis is concerned with describing the network structures that provide information opportunities and influence to actors. Group process research is similarly focused on communication processes within and between groups and behaviors including cooperation, power, decision making, and teamwork. Thus, both theoretical traditions appear to be assessing similar phenomena only using a different lens. This sort of thing has happened before in group research.

Group process researchers will be familiar with the large body of demographic research on top management teams that accelerated after the publication of Hambrick and Mason's (1984) upper echelons theory. Briefly, upper echelons theory proposed that demographic proxies could be used to infer unmeasured team process. Because demographic data were easier to access than direct measurement of process, scores of articles soon appeared in major management journals theorizing about the impacts of top management team process but measuring only demography. The results were robust, but were sometimes in conflict (Finkelstein & Hambrick, 1996; West & Schwenk, 1996). Smith et al. (1994) measured both demography and process and determined that process added explained variance to demographic models of group and organizational performance. Thus, while group demography seems to impact process the value of demography as proxies for process is questionable (Lawrence, 1997; Smith et al., 1994). Researchers have begun to respond to these critiques by seeking to include both demographic and process measures when investigating group phenomena (Keck, 1997; Smith et al., 1994).

THE INTRA-GROUP NETWORK AND GROUP PROCESS

As explained above, group members belong to multiple networks. The intra-group network would appear to most directly impact group process and teamwork. Indeed, measurement of the structure of relationships between group members may be an alternative methodological approach to measurement of group process. Nohria (1992, p. 6) suggests that networks may be more effective than demography in explaining behavior: "... variations in the actions of actors (and the success or failure of these actions) can be better explained by knowing the position of actors relative to others in various networks of relationships, than by knowing how their attributes differ from one another."

Because membership in a group is usually constrained to a relatively small number of people who can reasonably be expected to know one another, network concepts of range, centrality, and density do not apply. The tenor of the relationships between group members, however, can be expected to vary. Strength of ties refers to how well two actors in a network know each other. The components of tie strength are duration, frequency, and emotional intensity. In the network literature, strong ties generate trust and reciprocity between actors as well as familiarity (Krackhardt, 1992). Social capital theorists (Coleman, 1988; Leana & van Buren, 1999) view strong ties in a similar way, yielding benefits of cooperation and trust. Even ardent structuralists like Burt (1992) consider the importance of strong ties is providing for "structural cohesion," a condition in which an individual can access third parties who are strongly linked to actors they know.

Tie Strength and Cohesion

Krackhardt (1992) has developed the concept of *philos* to describe the cohesiveness and cooperative characteristics of strong ties. The key dimensions of tie strength that seem to drive *philos* are the duration of the tie and the emotional bond that results. Certainly frequency of interaction can be important for developing familiarity and trust; however, there are reasons for frequent interaction other than *philos*. So-called "fire-fighting" behaviors and problematic relations can lead to a need for frequent interaction, even though *philos* may never develop between the actors. Thus:

H1: Groups whose intra-group ties are of long duration will experience greater cohesion.
H2: Groups whose intra-group ties are of greater emotional intensity will experience greater cohesion.
H3: There will be no relationship between intra-group tie frequency and group cohesion.

Tie Strength and Trust

The concept of trust has become the focus of a great deal of group and teamwork research of late. Although there are many definitions of trust, Boon and Holmes (1991) developed an intuitive description of trust as "a state involving confident positive expectations about another's motives with respect to oneself in situations entailing risk" (p. 194). Lewicki and Bunker (1996) observe that trust theorists have focused on individuals' psychological predisposition to trust, contextual factors surrounding trust, and relationship characteristics that affect trust. This chapter focuses on the association between relationship, or network tie, characteristics, and trust.

Lewicki and Bunker (1996) explain three forms of trust that occur, sometimes in phase order, beginning with trust based on enforceable sanctions for violation of expected behavior. This sort of trust is also a centerpiece of Coleman's (1988) theory of social capital. A second form of trust stems from familiarity or knowledge of the other. Knowledge-based trust develops as a result of interaction between the parties over a period of time. Finally, identification-based trust is more akin to a deep mutual understanding of the needs and desires of each party. According to Lewicki and Bunker (1996), identification-based trust is critical for cooperative behavior because each party begins to understand "when to lead and follow, each knows how to play off the others to maximize their strengths, compensate for the others' weaknesses, and create a joint product that is much greater than the sum of its parts" (p. 124). In short, identification-based trust is a crucial ingredient of teamwork.

Sanction-based trust is a product of behavioral norms and monitoring and thus is not reliant on relationship per se. Knowledge-based and identification-based trust both result from the tenor of network ties within the group. Knowledge-based trust is developed as actors interact over time and is cumulative. The more interactions we have, the more opportunities to learn about the other's trustworthiness. Each time expectations of behavior are met, knowledge-based trust increases. Thus, the duration and frequency of intra-group network ties should be related to knowledge-based trust. Identification-based trust is deeper. Parties come to understand the drivers of others' behavior and to anticipate how the other will behave and why. This deeper mutual understanding implies a level of emotional intensity not necessary for other forms of trust, and yet it is precisely the sort of trust that underlies the superior performance of the best teams. In addition to duration and frequency of ties, the emotional intensity component of tie strength is necessary for the development of this deeper form of trust.

H4: Groups whose intra-group ties are of long duration will experience greater trust.

H5: Groups whose intra-group ties are of greater emotional intensity will experience greater trust.

H6: Groups whose members interact more frequently will experience greater trust.

Group Process and Network Usage

One outcome of group cohesion is added reliance of group members on each other. Indeed, a key feature of well performing teams is the high degree of coordination between interdependent team members. In the extreme, teams that experience groupthink may come to rely almost solely on the advice of group members, becoming increasingly isolated from outside sources of information (Janis, 1972). The trust that develops in cohesive groups may be one cause for group members' increased reliance on internal contacts for information. Because intra-group contacts may be more readily available than external sources of information, group consensus may be easier to achieve.

Network ties are also used to influence the behavior of the other party. In order to exert influence it is necessary for the actor to have power over the party to be influenced. This power may originate from formal position, expertise, personal qualities, or a host of other attributes (French & Raven, 1959). In the context of this research, power stems from the relationship between actors in the group. Members of cohesive groups have formed bonds that enable such influencing attempts. Members of cohesive groups wish to remain members, and are willing to obligate one another. Thus, the relational power that exists in cohesive groups allows members to influence the behavior of others in the group. When original positions on an issue differ, the ability of group members to influence each other may also lead to greater capacity for consensus.

H7: Cohesive groups will use intra-group ties for information.
H8: Cohesive groups will use intra-group ties for influence.
H9: Groups who use intra-group ties for information will experience greater consensus.
H10: Groups who use intra-group ties for influencing will experience greater consensus.

Cohesion and Internal Network Locus

Cohesion is hypothesized to be related to greater use by group members of the intra-group network for both information and influence. Increased utilization of the intra-group network is also hypothesized to be functional in terms of easing consensus. Groups that experience increased consensus may come to rely more and more on the internal network, and may become reluctant to expend energy and resources necessary for external network development.[4] As a result, the locus of the group network becomes skewed to internal contacts.

H11: Cohesive groups will have an internal network locus.

EXTRA-GROUP NETWORKS AND GROUP PROCESS

Group members also have relationships with those outside of the group, including other organizational members and actors in other organizations. Because individuals may belong to many groups, these extra-team contacts may mitigate the team effect and thus impact the team's process. Evidence for this proposition can be found in the work of Schein (1985) and in the social capital literature (Coleman, 1988). In his work on acculturation, Schein details the importance of indoctrination and isolation practices for the establishment of strong culture with social collectives. Likewise, Coleman suggests that it is the strong attraction of group membership and the sanctions for defection from group norms that allow for the development of robust group norms of behavior, which he suggests is the basis for social capital. Certainly, the relationships of team members with those outside of the team help shape members' perspectives on group membership and their willingness to develop and adhere to group norms. Identification of members with the group is important to teamwork and group cohesion (Kramer, 1993).

Drawing on the socialization, social capital, and group identity literatures, the amount of interaction group members have among themselves serves to define and strengthen the meaning of group membership. Experiences group members have with outsiders, particularly where these relationships are valued, may serve to decrease the attractiveness of group membership. Groups that interact more with group members than with outsiders should be more cohesive than those who spend a great deal of time outside of the group.

[4] This may be one mechanism by which Janis's groupthink teams become isolated from external influences.

Thus, while cohesion may predispose group members to building internal networks, exposure to external contacts (in number and strength) may adversely affect group process.

H12: Groups with externally focused networks will be less cohesive.
H13: Groups with strong ties to external actors will be less cohesive.

Demographic research has established that groups whose members are homogeneous are more cohesive than heterogeneous groups (Finkelstein & Hambrick, 1996). Similarity in background leads to easy communication, less conflict, and greater affect. One reason for this smooth process in homogeneous groups is the similarity of information and approach held by group members (Pfeffer, 1983). Individual networks within a group may also be either similar or heterogeneous. Structural network theorists have pointed out the inefficiency of redundant (similar) networks from an information search perspective (Burt, 1982). Social capital theorists (Coleman, 1988) suggest that network redundancy in a group serves to increase group identity and social capital. Group members with similar networks are likely to access similar information and to develop similar world views. Much like demographic similarity, network similarity should serve to increase group cohesion and consensus as well as the confidence necessary to motivate the group to work in a cooperative fashion.

H14: Groups whose individual networks are redundant social networks will be more cohesive.
H15: Groups whose individual networks are redundant will have greater consensus.
H16: Groups whose individual networks are redundant will experience less conflict.

NETWORKS AND GROUP EFFECTIVENESS

There are many measures of group effectiveness, perhaps the most fundamental of which is decision making. The comprehensiveness and pace of decision making are two commonly utilized measures of decision effectiveness (Eisenhardt, 1989; Fredrickson, 1986). In addition to various team processes, the structure of the intra-team network should be related to team decision-making effectiveness. Teams whose relationships are long-lasting and close should be in a position to accelerate the decision process. Teams that use their relationships for information, rather than influence, should experience more comprehensive and perhaps more rapid decision making.

Tie Strength and Decision Making

Groups with intra-group network ties of long duration may generate the trust and familiarity necessary to allow for frank discussion of alternatives. The cognitive conflict (Amason, 1996) necessary for full development and evaluation of potential solutions is possible in such groups because of the familiarity and long experience group members have with one another. Although it is possible that tie duration, if isolated from outside contacts, could lead to groupthink or decision rigidity, the trust and comfort long-standing relationships within the group allow for disagreements of fact to occur and to be resolved.

Groups whose members have known each other for long periods of time may have generated effective communication and interaction routines. Such routines help these groups to overcome group process losses and to get on with the work of making decisions. Clearly, groups who have experience with one another should be more efficient in their interactions than others.

H17: Groups with intra-group networks of long duration will perceive decisions to be comprehensive.
H18: Groups with intra-group networks of long duration will make faster decisions.

Groups whose members interact frequently should be able to exchange information easily and in real time. Frequent briefings should allow for timely discussion of relevant factors, and facilitate requests for additional information needed to fully evaluate an issue. Frequent interaction should also speed the decision process by providing ample opportunities for discussion and resolution of differences.

H19: Groups with frequent intra-group interaction will perceive decisions to be comprehensive.
H20: Groups with frequent intra-group interaction will make faster decisions.

Emotional intensity among group members should affect the decision process in much the same way as tie duration. As hypothesized above, emotionally close group members are likely to develop a level of trust and familiarity with one another. As such they are likely to rely on information provided by group members as thorough. The trust developed by such groups is also likely to lubricate the decision process.

H21: Groups with close intra-group ties will perceive decisions to be comprehensive.
H22: Groups with close intra-group ties will make faster decisions.

Networks that are used for information should directly impact the decision process. Group members that gain information from their counterparts are likely to value this information and to trust that it is reliable. The trading of information between group members may also lead to confirmation of felt beliefs, in that it is consistent with and supports information the group member is likely to already hold. Under such confirmatory circumstances, group members are likely to feel that their decision process has been comprehensive.

Because group members are relatively proximate (as compared to other external sources of information), reliance on intra-group contacts for information should speed the decision process. In addition, confidence in the information provided by insiders may help group members overcome the need to seek additional information.

H23: Groups who use intra-group networks for information will perceive decisions to be comprehensive.
H24: Groups who use intra-group networks for information will make faster decisions.

Extra-group Networks and Decision Making

Group members also have links to those outside of the group. The structure of these extra-group networks is important to the quality and speed of decision making. The capacity of the network to provide relevant information to the decision process may be critical for issue identification, alternative generation, and decision choice.

Groups whose members have similar or overlapping networks will access similar information. Discussions with such a group are likely to yield similar viewpoints and this confirmation process will lead to a perception of decision comprehensiveness among group members.

The similarity of viewpoint and of information that is likely to exist in such groups may also lead to a restriction of alternatives and a sense of reliability of information that alleviates conflict. This lack of conflict and a lowered need for information seeking outside of the group should speed decision processes.

H25: Groups with redundant extra-group networks will perceive decisions to be comprehensive.
H26: Groups with redundant extra-group networks will make faster decisions.

Groups with large networks can potentially access more information that those with smaller sets of contacts. Certainly, those who have extensive networks of contacts may feel that they are able to access a larger set of information with which to make good decisions. Network size may have a downside, however. The task of navigating a large network in order to locate the best source for information, and the potential for multiple sources to offer conflicting information, may slow the decision process.

H27: Groups with large extra-group networks will perceive decisions to be comprehensive.
H28: Groups with large extra-group networks will make slower decisions.

In addition to network size, the diversity (range) of contacts is an important indicator of the information capacity of a network. Groups whose networks access a diverse set of actors are able to draw on many novel perspectives and should be able to generate many and novel alternatives. These groups should perceive the decision process to be comprehensive. Diversity also presents the group with the problem of deciding which contacts to access. Moreover, diverse sets of actors are very likely to generate multiple and conflicting views that the group will have to sort through.

H29: Groups with diverse extra-group networks will perceive decisions to be comprehensive.
H30: Groups with diverse extra-group networks will make slower decisions.

EMPIRICAL ANALYSIS AND RESULTS

Data on social networks and group process were collected from 73 top management groups (TMG) of technology firms in the Mid-Atlantic region of the United States. During on-site interviews at each firm, TMG membership was defined by the CEO, and all TMG members (including the CEO) were asked by the CEO to complete questionnaires. Overall response rate for the study was 40 percent and tests for nonresponse bias were negative. The intra-team response rate was almost 60 percent, or three of the five members of the average-sized TMG. The results below are bivariate correlations between the hypothesized network and group process constructs. The purpose here is to demonstrate associations between relational and process constructs rather than to suggest, or test, causal links. Further, because the data were collected from a relatively small sample of American technology firms, the analysis should be interpreted as preliminary. The intended use of these results is as an aid to the future development of more sophisticated studies.

Networks and Cohesion

Hypotheses 1 through 3 concerned the association between the components of intra-group network strength and group cohesion. Hypothesis 1 proposed a positive relationship between tie duration and group cohesion. The correlation was significant and in the predicted direction ($r = 0.252$, $p = 0.018$). Hypothesis 2 proposed a positive relationship between the emotional intensity of intra-group ties and group cohesion and was also supported ($r = 0.375$, $p < 0.01$). Intra-group frequency of interaction was not associated with group cohesion as predicted ($r = -0.021$, $p = 0.430$). Thus, two of the three components of network tie strength were significantly associated with group cohesiveness.

Networks and Trust

Hypotheses 4 through 6 concerned the association between components of intra-group network tie strength and group trust. Trust was measured as an index of 12 items representing competence trust, benevolence trust, and integrity trust. Hypothesis 4 proposed a positive relationship between tie duration and trust and was supported ($r = 0.318$, $p = 0.004$). Hypothesis 5 proposed a positive relationship between the emotional intensity of intra-group network ties and group trust and was also supported ($r = 0.419$, $p < 0.001$). Hypothesis 6, proposing a positive relationship between tie frequency and group trust, was not supported ($r = -0.079$, $p = 0.259$).[5] In general, the results suggest that strong network ties are associated with increased trust.

Group Process and Network Usage

Hypotheses 7 and 8 suggested that cohesive groups will use their intra-group network ties for information and for influence. Both hypotheses are supported ($r = 0.443$, $p < 0.001$; $r = 0.253$, $p = 0.018$), suggesting that cohesive groups rely on each other for information as well as using influence to induce action.

Hypotheses 9 and 10 proposed that the use of groups of their intra-group networks for information and influence will be associated with increased consensus ability. The results show that increased use of intra-group contacts for information is associated with increased consensus ($r = 0.224$, $p < 0.05$). Hypothesis 10 was not supported.

Group Process and Network Development

Hypothesis 11 suggested that cohesive groups will focus on building internal network linkages rather than relationships to outsiders. While in the hypothesized direction, the correlation was not statistically significant.

External Networks and Group Process

Research suggests that groups whose members have extensive and strong ties to outsiders may suffer from lower group identity and a consequent loss of cohesion. Hypothesis 12

[5] Correlations between tie frequency and each of the components of trust were all nonsignificant.

suggested that those groups that focused on internal ties over external ties would be more cohesive. The result was in the predicted direction, but was not statistically significant ($r = 0.108$, $p = 0.186$). Hypothesis 13 proposed that groups with strong ties to external actors would experience lower group cohesion. The result was not statistically significant ($r = 0.143$, $p = 0.117$). Thus, I find no support for the idea that insulation of the group from external contacts leads to greater cohesiveness. This research did not, however, measure whether external contacts were considered superior or inferior to intra-group contacts.

Networks Similarity and Group Process

Hypothesis 14 suggested that groups whose individual networks were redundant (similar) would be more cohesive. The correlation was significant and in the predicted direction ($r = 0.348$, $p < 0.001$). Hypothesis 15 suggested that network redundancy would also be associated with greater group consensus. Marginal support for this relationship was found ($r = 0.172$, $p < 0.077$). Hypothesis 16 suggested that network redundancy would be associated with decreased group conflict and was supported ($r = 0.318$, $p = 0.003$). Thus, network similarity appears to relate to smooth group process in much the same way as demographic similarity.

Intra-group Networks and Group Decision Making

Hypotheses 17 through 22 concerned the association between components of intra-group tie strength and decision-making comprehensiveness and speed. Hypotheses 17 and 18, proposing that tie duration is associated with increased comprehensiveness and speed of decision making, were both supported ($r = 0.321$, $p = 0.004$; $r = 0.259$, $p = 0.016$). Hypotheses 19 and 20, proposing that tie frequency is associated with decision-making comprehensiveness and speed, were not supported ($r = -0.183$, $p = 0.066$; $r = -0.118$, $p = 0.167$). As previously explained, in some firms tie frequency may be resultant from crisis situations or a "firefighting" approach to problem solving. Hypotheses 21 and 22, proposing that the emotional intensity of intra-group networks is associated with increased decision-making comprehensiveness and speed, were both supported ($r = 0.276$, $p = 0.011$; $r = 0.361$, $p < 0.01$). Thus, strong ties appear to be associated with positive group outcomes in the form of comprehensive and speedy decision making.

The use of intra-group network ties for information was hypothesized to be associated with increased decision comprehensiveness (H23) and increased decision speed (H24). Both hypotheses were supported ($r = 0.298$, $p = 0.007$; $r = 0.399$, $p < 0.001$). Thus, reliance by group members on each other for information leads both to an increased perception of comprehensiveness and to the generation of quick decisions. Importantly, the mere presence of network ties is not sufficient for performance; it is the way those ties are utilized that matters.

Extra-group Networks and Group Decision Making

The links group members have to those outside of the group are proposed to impact group decision-making comprehensiveness and speed. Hypotheses 25 and 26 proposed associations between network redundancy and decision making. Redundancy and comprehensiveness are related ($r = 0.230$, $p = 0.028$), as are redundancy and decision speed ($r = 0.297$,

Table 20.1 Summary of hypotheses and results of correlational analysis.

	Group construct	Network construct	Direction	Found
H1	Cohesion	Intra-group tie duration	Positive	X
H2	Cohesion	Intra-group tie intensity	Positive	X
H3	Cohesion	Intra-group tie frequency	No relationship	X
H4	Trust	Intra-group tie duration	Positive	X
H5	Trust	Intra-group tie intensity	Positive	X
H6	Trust	Intra-group tie frequency	Positive	
H7	Cohesion	Tie information use	Positive	X
H8	Cohesion	Tie influence use	Positive	X
H9	Consensus	Tie information use	Positive	X
H10	Consensus	Tie influence use	Positive	
H11	Cohesion	Internal network locus	Positive	
H12	Cohesion	External network locus	Negative	
H13	Cohesion	Strong external ties	Negative	
H14	Cohesion	Redundant networks	Positive	X
H15	Consensus	Redundant networks	Positive	X
H16	Conflict	Redundant networks	Negative	X
H17	DM comprehensiveness	Intra-group tie duration	Positive	X
H18	DM speed	Intra-group tie duration	Positive	X
H19	DM comprehensiveness	Intra-group tie frequency	Positive	
H20	DM speed	Intra-group tie frequency	Positive	
H21	DM comprehensiveness	Intra-group tie intensity	Positive	X
H22	DM speed	Intra-group tie intensity	Positive	X
H23	DM comprehensiveness	Intra-group tie information use	Positive	X
H24	DM speed	Intra-group tie information use	Positive	X
H25	DM comprehensiveness	Extra-group tie redundancy	Positive	X
H26	DM speed	Extra-group tie redundancy	Positive	X
H27	DM comprehensiveness	Extra-group network size	Positive	
H28	DM speed	Extra-group network size	Negative	
H29	DM comprehensiveness	Extra-group network range	Positive	
H30	DM speed	Extra-group network range	Negative	

$p = 0.006$). Thus, similarity of group members' networks appears to speed up decision making and group members perceive their search to be more comprehensive.

The size of extra-group networks was hypothesized to increase perceived decision comprehensiveness (H29), but to slow decision making (H28). Neither hypothesis was supported by the data ($r = -0.014$, $p = 0.444$; $r = -0.107$, $p = 0.189$). It seems likely that given extreme growth, networks might become cumbersome. Perhaps the networks studied here have not reached that threshold size, or that individuals with very large networks somehow prioritize or organize their network search processes to deal with the complexity of a large network.

The range or diversity of group network ties was proposed to increase decision comprehensiveness (H29), but at a cost to decision speed (H30). Neither hypothesis was supported by the data ($r = 0.108$, $p = 0.187$; $r = 0.013$, $p = 0.458$). This research did not measure specific search methods utilized by the teams. Perhaps some teams were able to leverage network diversity while others were not.

As Table 20.1 demonstrates, substantial support for the hypotheses was found. Of the 30 proposed relationships, 19 were supported by statistically significant bivariate correlations in the predicted direction. The implications of these findings are discussed below.

CONCLUSIONS AND DIRECTIONS FOR FUTURE RESEARCH

Teamwork refers to the processes of interaction present in a group of individuals who have come together for some purpose. In the context of a task-oriented group, processes such as cohesiveness, consensus, conflict, and formality have been demonstrated to affect the effectiveness of the group with regards to achieving satisfactory task outcomes. The literature on the process–performance link is robust and is discussed elsewhere in this volume. A separate sociological stream of research has measured the tenor of relationships between members of task-oriented groups as well. The focus of this research has been on the frequency of interaction, duration and stability of relationships, the emotional component of relationships, and on whether the relationships are used for the transfer of information or for influencing. Though some of these concepts (e.g. emotional component and cohesiveness) appear to be quite similar, there have been no attempts to integrate the two streams. This preliminary analysis of these concepts suggests that the two streams are connected and may together help to more fully explain the functioning of teams. For example, the emotional closeness and duration of intra-team relationships are strongly correlated with cohesiveness. Moreover, the use of network links for information is positively related to cohesion and negatively related to conflict. Finally, the use of relationships for influencing is also positively related to cohesion, but not to conflict. Thus, it appears that network structures and team process are related in complex ways.

This chapter has demonstrated, in a preliminary way, links between two distinct methodological approaches to the study of groups. Group process researchers have measured process directly by asking group members about the characteristics of their interactions, while network theorists have measured these links structurally. Debate continues to rage within network analysis as to the effectiveness of structural as opposed to more content-oriented approaches to networks. The goal of this chapter was not to resolve this debate, rather to introduce network concepts to group process researchers and to ask fundamental questions concerning the value (or redundancy) of network analysis as a tool for the study of group functioning and outcomes. A review of the literature shows a striking lack of cooperation between these two sets of theorists, and yet the empirical analysis shown here suggests very strongly the utility of integrating the two.

Of the 30 hypothesized relationships between group process and network constructs, 19 were supported in the empirical study. However, network concepts do not appear to be alternatives to group process methods. None of the correlations between network and process constructs were above 0.5. Thus, while network and behavioral theorists are studying related phenomena, their methods are not substitutes, rather they are complementary. Network constructs do appear to be associated with group process constructs in most cases and in some predictable ways. It makes a great deal of sense for group process researchers to begin to incorporate network measures into their analysis. For example, the link between demographic heterogeneity and positive outcome of comprehensiveness of decision making (as opposed to conflict) may work through the structure of links between diverse actors and the cohesiveness strong ties provide. Only by including all of these constructs in the same analysis can we iron out the causal logic of these "black box" relationships.

Strong ties, particularly duration and emotional intensity, appear to be functional in providing a foundation for smooth group process and for important group outcomes like decision making. Are there contexts where strong ties are not so valuable? Do strong ties improve other group performance measures such as innovation and creativity, or is there a dark side to tie strength akin to the groupthink (Janis, 1972) phenomenon?

There are many more plausible relationships between network structure and group process that the present study was not able to assess. For example, how does the centrality of a group in organization-wide networks affect the way members feel about belonging to the group? The combination of network methods with group identification research would seem a fruitful line of inquiry.

How do differences in the centrality of group members in outside networks affect group process? Do more central group members behave differently than their counterparts, and do these behavioral differences affect the smoothness of group process? Under what conditions will well-connected group members attempt to appropriate the value of their networks, to the detriment of the group? What action can group members or leaders take to preserve group process when differences in network or relational power exist among group members?

One likely candidate for helping groups to counter the destabilizing potential of network differences is the evolution of trust and reciprocity. However, does group trust develop from network structure or does trust affect the way networks develop? Are there techniques groups can use to develop trust when individual networks differ so widely?

Though strong support for associations between networks and group process was found, 11 of the hypothesized relationships were not supported. In particular, network size, range, and the frequency of interaction component of tie strength did not relate to decision-making comprehensiveness and speed. Given the rather large theoretical and empirical literatures on the importance of search and information exchange on both decision speed and comprehensiveness (see Fredrickson, 1986, and Eisenhardt, 1989, for examples), it is difficult to believe that these links do not exist. One possible explanation for the nonfinding is that the relationship is nonlinear. In the case of network size and range, extremely large and diverse networks may prove ineffective as an information-gathering mechanism because the sheer complexity of the network overwhelms the cognitive capacity of the individual. Moreover, there is some evidence that the weak ties likely to be present in such networks are not optimal for the transfer of certain types of information (Hansen, 1999). Thus, there may be a curvilinear relationship between these two indicators of a network's capacity to provide information and the achieved information benefits of cognitively limited individuals. The incrementalism school of decision making supports this view (March & Simon, 1958). Similarly, interaction frequency may be functional only up to the point needed to effect the transfer of needed information, after which additional interaction becomes redundant (nothing new is learned). In the extreme, such interaction may begin to focus more on group maintenance or personal issues, detracting from the ability of the group to make decisions in a timely fashion. Again, a curvilinear relationship is plausible.

A clear weakness of this research was the inability to get at causation. An avenue for future research is to better specify the directionality of the relationships between process and networks, and to use longitudinal or experimental design to test these linkages. It seems, as well, that in many cases the relationships may be mutually reinforcing. One approach that may offer promise is the inclusion of group process as mediators of network effects.

This research relied on data from a relatively small sample of top management groups of technology-sector firms. Clearly, more research in other settings must be performed to determine the generalizability of the findings. Work groups may also utilize networks, but in very different ways. Moreover, the possible range of contacts of company executives may far outstrip that of core employees. Issues of centrality may be more, or less, visible in such circumstances. Finally, the meaning of teamwork may vary by task setting, and thus implications for the impact of networks on process and vice versa need to be interpreted to account for such differences.

Another avenue of research concerns the role individual traits may play in network development. Just as personality plays a role in the formation of group process, so might individual differences affect the types and structure of individual networks, and the ability (willingness?) of group members to share their networks with others. Research that identifies links between personality and network development would be important for recruitment and selection. Training programs could be tailored to leverage (or counteract) the interaction between individual traits and predispositions toward network building.

To date, the group literature has focused attention on the impact of individual differences on group process. Group research has conceptualized differences in terms of attributes rather than other ways in which individuals vary. Certainly the number, types, and tenor of individual networks is a salient factor for such research. Indeed, in a period of increased employee transience the ability of groups and organizations to acquire not only human capital, but also relational capital, becomes a critical performance factor. Once individual networks are acquired (though hiring or development), the task becomes how best to leverage these contacts for group performance. The impacts of group process on networks (and vice versa) appear a compelling agenda for researchers.

REFERENCES

Abrahamson, E. & Rosenkopf, L. (1997). Social network effects on the extent of innovation diffusion: a computer simulation. *Organization Science, 8*, 289–309.

Adler, P. S. & Kwon, S. (2002). Social capital: prospects for a new concept. *Academy of Management Review, 27*, 17–40.

Amason, A. C. (1996). Distinguishing the effects of functional and dysfunctional conflict on strategic decision-making: resolving a paradox for top management teams. *Academy of Management Journal, 39*, 123–149.

Barnes, J. A. (1972). *Social Networks*. Addison-Wesley Modular Publication: *26*, 1–29.

Boon, S. D. & Holmes, J. G. (1991). The dynamics of interpersonal trust: resolving uncertainty in the face of risk. In R. A. Hinde & J. Groebel (eds), *Cooperation and Pro-social Behavior* (pp. 190–211). Cambridge, UK: Cambridge University Press.

Burt, R. S. (1982). *Towards a Structural Theory of Action*. New York: Academic Press.

Burt, R. S. (1992). *Structural Holes: The Social Structure of Competition*. Cambridge, Mass.: Harvard University Press.

Coleman, J. S. (1988). Social capital in the creation of human capital. *American Journal of Sociology, 94*(Supplement), S95–S120.

Eisenhardt, K. M. (1989). Making fast strategic decisions in high velocity environments. *Academy of Management Journal, 32*, 543–576.

Finkelstein, S. & Hambrick, D. C. (1996). *Strategic Leadership: Top Executives and Their Effects on Organizations*. St Paul, Minn.: West.

Fredrickson, J. (1986). The strategic decision processes and organizational outcomes: the moderating role of managerial discretion. *Academy of Management Review, 11*, 280–287.

Freeman, L. C. (1979). Centrality in social networks: conceptual clarification. *Social Networks, 1*, 215–239.

French, J. R. P. & Raven, B. (1959). The bases of social power. In D. Cartwright (ed.), *Studies in Social Power*. Ann Arbor: University of Michigan, Institute for Social Research.

Granovetter, M. (1973). The strength of weak ties. *American Journal of Sociology, 78*, 1360–1380.

Gulati, R. (1995). Does familiarity breed trust? The implications of repeated ties for contractual choice in alliances. *Academy of Management Journal, 38*, 85–112.

Hambrick, D. C. & Mason, P. A. (1984). Upper echelons: the organization as a reflection of its top managers. *Academy of Management Review, 9*, 193–206.

Hansen, M. (1999). The search-transfer problem: the role of weak ties in sharing knowledge across organizational subunits. *Administrative Science Quarterly, 44*, 82–111.

Haunschild, P. R. & Beckman, C. M. (1998). When do interlocks matter? Alternate sources of information and interlock influence. *Administrative Science Quarterly, 43*, 815–844.

Janis, I. (1972). *Victims of Groupthink.* Boston: Houghton-Mifflin.

Keck, S. (1997). Top management team structure: differential effects by environmental context. *Organization Science, 8*, 143–156.

Knoke, D. & Burt, R. S. (1983). Prominence. In R. S. Burt & M. J. Minor (eds), *Applied Network Analysis: A Methodological Introduction* (pp. 195–222). Beverly Hills, Calif.: Sage.

Krackhardt, D. (1992). The strength of strong ties: the importance of philos in organizations. In N. Nohria & R. Eccles (eds), *Networks and Organizations: Structure, Form, and Action* (pp. 216–239). Cambridge, Mass.: Harvard University Press.

Kramer, R. M. (1993). Cooperation and organizational identification. In K. Murnighan (ed.), *Social Psychology in Organizations: Advances in Theory and Research* (pp. 244–268). Englewood Cliffs, NJ: Prentice-Hall.

Lawrence, B. S. (1997). The black box of organizational demography. *Organization Science, 8*, 1–22.

Leana, C. R. & van Buren, H. J., III (1999). Organizational social capital and employment practices. *Academy of Management Review, 24*, 538–555.

Leavitt, H. J. (1951). Some effects of communication patterns on group performances. *Journal of Abnormal and Social Psychology, 46*, 38–50.

Lewicki, R. J. & Bunker, B. B. (1996). Developing and maintaining trust in work relationships. In R. M. Kramer & T. R. Tyler (eds), *Trust in Organizations: Frontiers of Theory and Research* (pp. 114–139). London: Sage.

March, J. G. & Simon, H. A. (1958). *Organizations.* New York: Wiley.

Nohria, N. (1992). Introduction: is a network perspective a useful way of studying organizations? In N. Nohria & R. Eccles (eds), *Networks and Organizations: Structure, Form, and Action* (pp. 1–22). Cambridge, Mass.: Harvard University Press.

Pfeffer, J. (1983). Organizational demography. In L. L. Cummings & B. M. Staw (eds), *Research in Organizational Behavior* (Vol. 5, pp. 299–357). Greenwich, Conn.: JAI Press.

Pfeffer, J. & Salancik, G. R. (1978). *The External Control of Organizations.* New York: Harper & Row.

Powell, W. W., Koput, K. W., & Smith-Doerr, L. (1996). Interorganizational collaboration and the locus of innovation: networks of learning in biotechnology. *Administrative Science Quarterly, 41*, 116–145.

Schein, E. (1985). *Organizational Culture and Leadership.* San Francisco: Jossey-Bass.

Scott, J. (1991). *Social Network Analysis: A Handbook.* London: Sage.

Shaw, M. E. (1981). *Group Dynamics: The Psychology of Small Group Behavior* (3rd edn). New York: McGraw-Hill.

Smith, K. G., Olian, J., Sims, H. P., Jr, Scully, J., Smith, K. A., & O'Bannon, D. (1994). Top management team demography and process: the role of social integration and communication. *Administrative Science Quarterly, 39*, 412–438.

Wasserman, S. & Faust, K. (1994). *Social Network Analysis: Methods and Applications.* Cambridge, UK: Cambridge University Press.

West, C. T., Jr & Schwenk, C. R. (1996). Top management team strategic consensus, demographic homogeneity, and firm performance: a report of resounding non-findings. *Strategic Management Journal, 17*, 571–576.

Westphal, J. D. & Zajac, E. J. (1997). Defections from the inner circle: social exchange, reciprocity, and the diffusion of board independence in US corporations. *Administrative Science Quarterly, 42*, 161–183.

21

TEAMWORK IN THE NETCENTRIC ORGANIZATION

Ritu Agarwal

> To help cut international travel costs for its growing global organization, Dow Chemical Co. in Midland, Mich., last fall decided to bring together teams of its workers via real-time data sharing and collaboration. As a result, workers in virtual teams have reduced the number of trips they expected to take on projects, and shortened by 15% the time it takes to edit and pass on conventional electronic-mail documents to other members of the team, Dow officials said. (Hamblen, 1998)

INTRODUCTION

Netcentricity, or the power of digital networks to distribute information instantly and on a global scale (University of Maryland, 1999), has fundamentally transformed traditional notions of an "organization." Fueled by rapid developments in the range and sophistication in information and communications technologies (ICTs), organizations today are experiencing a paradigm shift in the nature and organization of work. Scholars and management consultants use a variety of metaphors to describe the new work, ranging from the boundaryless organization (Ashkenas et al., 1995), the virtual corporation (Davidow & Malone, 1992), the e-lance economy (Malone & Laubacher, 1998), the e-business community (Tapscott, 1996), the agora (Tapscott, Ticoll, & Lowy, 2000), and the value net (Bovet & Martha, 2000). A central and recurrent theme in these metaphors is the idea that increasingly, organizational work crosses traditional boundaries of time, space, and geography. We add the notion of a "netcentric" organization to these metaphors.

There are several compelling motivations and business drivers underlying the emergence of new work forms. In general, the motivations stem from two concurrent developments: (1) the increasing complexity and turbulence of business environments in the wake of the information economy, which have given rise to hypercompetition and intensification of competitive rivalry (D'Aveni, 1995), and (2) the recognition that, often, an organization does not possess all the intellectual capital required to accomplish organizational work.

International Handbook of Organizational Teamwork and Cooperative Working. Edited by M. A. West, D. Tjosvold, and K. G. Smith.

Coupled with business globalization and the availability of ICTs that transcend location and time barriers by supporting seamless communication and coordination, the possibility that individuals outside an organization's formal boundary can contribute effectively to organizational work has moved from a theoretical abstraction to a pragmatic reality.

Examples of firms using ICTs to leverage human capital outside firm boundaries abound. For instance, the increasing prevalence of offshore sourcing of information technology work is, to a large extent, enabled by electronic communication technologies (Carmel & Agarwal, 2000). Orchestrating offshore alliances permits organizations to reap not only the advantages of lower-cost labor, but also provides access to world-class knowledge and skills. IBM's global software factory, constructed around a sophisticated collaborative technology infrastructure, allowed the company to leverage unique talents across multiple continents (Carmel, 1999), reduced product development costs, and considerably accelerated time to market for new products. Haywood (1998) reports that Hewlett-Packard used a virtual project team to develop a product information management system, and in NCR Corporation, the WorldMark team developed a new product together with members located in three different countries.

Recently, Cascio (2000) summarized the business drivers underlying the move to virtual forms of work. He attributes several advantages to virtual workplaces, including reduced real estate expenses, increased productivity and profits, improved customer service, access to global markets, and environmental benefits attributable to telecommuting. When other rewards such as increased flexibility (Mowshowitz, 1994), quicker time to market, and exploitation of location-specific characteristics such as relative labor costs are added to these advantages (Carmel & Agarwal, 2000), it is not surprising that managers are actively seeking ways to incorporate the notion of virtuality in organizational work.

One particular form of virtual work that has generated considerable interest among researchers and practitioners alike is that of the virtual team. While teams as a form of work organization have a long-standing tradition in the organizational science literature (e.g. Mohrman, Cohen, & Mohrman, 1995), the concept of a virtual team is still fairly new. Numerous definitions of such teams have been offered in the literature, although there is no widely agreed-upon conceptualization. In general, researchers agree that virtual teams are task-oriented groups working across geographical, departmental, and sometimes organizational boundaries (Kristof et al., 1995; Lipnack & Stamps, 2000). Some researchers (e.g. Lipnack & Stamps, 2000) include the use of electronic technologies as a primary means of communication as part of the definition of virtual teams, while others assert that fluid membership is a defining character of virtual teams, with members joining and exiting at different points in time depending on the needs of the team (Kristof et al., 1995).

For the purposes of this chapter, we adopt a working definition provided by Townsend, DeMarie, and Hendrickson (1998, p. 18) as it encompasses all of the above characteristics. They define a virtual team as "geographically and/or organizationally dispersed coworkers that are assembled using a combination of telecommunications and information technologies to accomplish an organizational task." This definition encompasses several team structures, including virtual teams whose members seldom meet face to face, yet are able to work together on cross-functional activities, to those who frequently meet face to face but depend on e-mail to facilitate communication between these face-to-face meetings. Hence, "virtuality" can exist in the team along a continuum from low to high.

Although virtual teams offer the promise of unfettered, flexible, uncircumscribed, and productive organizational work, they are not without challenges. Scholars have focused attention on the multitude of problems that could arise in the context of virtual teams, including performance losses due to feelings of isolation and a lack of trust (Cascio, 2000), threats to identity (Wiesenfeld, Raghuram, & Garud, 1999b), low commitment (O'Hara-Devereaux & Johansen, 1994), and a disruption of work–life balance (Hill et al., 1998). The goal of this chapter is to explore the virtual team as a new form of organizational work enabled by ICTs.

The chapter begins with a discussion of empirical findings and highlights from prior work examining the effects of digital technologies on group and team processes. Next, it focuses on the essential differences between collocated and virtual teams. The performance outcomes and, indeed, the success of virtual teams are profoundly influenced by the nature of collaboration and cooperation that occurs. The impediments and facilitators of collaboration and cooperation are presented. The chapter concludes with a discussion of dysfunctional and unintended consequences of virtual teamwork, identifies areas for fruitful future research, and presents organizational imperatives for managing virtual teams.

DIGITAL TECHNOLOGIES: THE ENABLERS OF VIRTUAL TEAMS

In general, ICTs support the work of virtual teams in two ways: (1) through the provision of technologies that allow distributed members to communicate with each other, and (2) through decision aids such as information bases and models that provide access to the resources necessary to accomplish the team's goal. To understand the range of technologies and systems involved, it is instructive to turn to the group decision support system (GDSS) literature, which provides early examples of how digital technologies could be used to support a variety of group processes and outcomes (DeSanctis & Gallupe, 1987).

Although the notion of virtuality was not explicitly discussed by early GDSS researchers, their work nonetheless acknowledged that ICTs could potentially support group work that was asynchronous and distributed (Williams & Wilson, 1997), two essential characteristics of virtual work. Several extensive reviews of the nature and impacts of group technologies in general and GDSS in particular are available (e.g. Benbasat & Lim, 1993; Kraemer & Pinsonneault, 1990; McGrath & Hollingshead, 1994) and are, therefore, not repeated here. It is useful, however, to draw attention to two aspects of this corpus of work: (1) the fact that there is an ever-burgeoning range of ICTs being applied to the group process, and (2) in spite of some conflicting empirical evidence, there appears to be a consistent set of factors that are posited by scholars as being key determinants of the outcomes of technology-supported group processes.

Based on a review of the early GDSS literature, Kraemer and Pinsonneault (1990) distinguish two broad types of technological support for groups: group communication support systems (GCSS), and group decision support systems. The former category of support is viewed as focusing primarily on alleviating communications barriers within groups and includes technologies such as teleconferencing, electronic mail, electronic boardrooms, and video-conferencing. In contrast, GDSS technologies assume a more proactive role in structuring group decision-making processes through the provision of decision models and tools to support the emergence of consensus such as automated Delphi and nominal group methods.

In later work McGrath and Hollingshead (1994) present a classification of electronic systems that support group work based on the functional role played by the technology in the work group. Their taxonomy, then, draws a distinction between four categories of technological support: internal communication support systems, information support systems, external communication support systems, and performance support systems. Embedded within each category is a range of technologies. For example, communication support systems include distal and synchronous forms of communication such as teleconferences and distal and asynchronous support such as that provided by voice messaging technology.

Today, the emergence of the Internet infrastructure as a ubiquitous, always available, and low-cost global platform for communication, and the development of a plethora of tools for collaboration using this infrastructure, have considerably expanded the scope of team support through technology. Consider the following examples. Organizations routinely use intranets for internal information sharing and dissemination systems. 3Com has its 3Community site that allows professionals to access training courses and material on their own time (Parker, 1998), and consultants at KPMG share knowledge and insights gained through client engagements on the firm's intranet. Personal digital assistants support distributed and asynchronous communication on a continual basis, sophisticated management and versioning systems allow for concurrency control so that distributed members all "see" the same data, and low-cost desktop video-conferencing systems permit employees from all over the world to participate in face-to-face meetings. The possibilities are constantly expanding, and with a consistent decline in the price of technology, they appear seemingly limitless.

Besides the technology, which mediates team processes and activities, what determines the outcomes of a technology-supported team? In other words, what antecedents influence, either directly or indirectly, what a technology-supported team accomplishes? Generally researchers have distinguished between two categories of outcomes that are of interest: process- or group-related outcomes that assess the extent to which attitudes such as satisfaction with the group are affected, and task-related outcomes, which focus on outcome dimensions such as quality of the decision and the attitudes of group members toward the decision. For their review of the GDSS and GCSS literature Kramer and Pinsonneault (1990) developed a three-level framework, arguing that contextual variables influenced group processes, which in turn influenced both task-related and group-related outcomes. Task-related outcomes were further posited to affect group-related outcomes. Contextual variables included personal factors, situational factors, group structure, technological support, and task characteristics, while group process factors focused on the characteristics of the decision, the communication, interpersonal characteristics, and the structure imposed by the technology.

In a similar spirit, McGrath and Hollingshead's (1994) conceptual framework for studying the impact of technology on groups proposed a nomological net of four sets of salient factors:

1. Input factors such as member attributes, technology, and context factors;
2. Organizing concepts which focus on the metaphors to be used for the group activity such as "groups as consensus generating systems" and "groups as information processing systems";
3. Process variables, that capture the patterns that emerge during group activity, including information processing and consensus generating;
4. Outcome factors, encompassing task performance effectiveness, user reactions, and member relations.

McGrath and Hollingshead argued that this framework helps bring coherence to the multitude of factors that could potentially influence the performance, behavior, and attitudes of groups, and, as such, provides a useful foundation for future work. More recently, Maznevski and Chudoba (2000) reviewed published studies since 1990 on technology-mediated group work and concluded that, on the basis of these studies, it appears that effective use of communication technology (and, by implication, effective performance) is dependent on the team's task and its context.

Extensive reviews and syntheses of empirical studies are available in the works cited above. Looking across this literature, it is clear that scholars have studied the phenomenon of technology-mediated teams from a plurality of perspectives and have developed rich conceptual frameworks for examining the performance of such teams. Implicit in the literature is a normative view that virtual teams are, in some ways, *useful* and *effective* new organizational forms. The notion of usefulness is self-evident: to the extent that virtual teams enable organizations to pull together geographically distributed talents and competencies and apply them to organizational problems, the utility of virtualization is incontrovertible. However, utility notwithstanding, what is less clear are the conditions under which virtual teams can be most effective. Our understanding of the contingencies that influence the outcomes and performance of teams whose predominant, perhaps only, mode of communication is via technology is limited.

CHARACTERIZING VIRTUAL TEAMS

There is little doubt that virtual teams differ from the conventional notion of teams in profound ways. But what exactly are these differences? Much has been written about the broader context, i.e. the virtual organization, of which virtual teams may be a part. It is important to point out, however, that virtual teams could also exist in organizations that do not satisfy all the requirements of virtuality, i.e. the virtual team, as a structural form, can be observed in traditional organizations as well.

Adopting an organization design perspective, DeSanctis, Staudenmayer, and Wong (1999) argue that traditional organizations are different from virtual organizations along four distinct design dimensions: space, time, culture, and boundary. The space and time dimensions speak to increasing distribution and asynchronicity in teamwork, while culture and boundary recognize that, increasingly, virtual organizations are multicultural, and their form extends beyond what we typically understand as the traditional boundaries of the organization. In subsequent work DeSanctis and Monge (1999) point out the building blocks of a virtual organization are geographically distributed, electronically linked, functionally or culturally diverse, and laterally connected. This, they suggest, facilitates designs such as dynamic processes, permeable boundaries, and reconfigurable structures.

Virtual Team Varieties

Not all virtual teams are identical; indeed, scholars acknowledge that they can exist in many forms. Jarvenpaa and Leidner (1999) characterize teams in general along three dimensions:

1. Context, addressing similarities in culture and geography;
2. Interaction mode, ranging from face-to-face to electronically mediated;
3. Type of group, including permanent groups with a common history and future to temporary groups who do not share a common history nor a common future.

Table 21.1 Characterizing virtual teams

Interdependencies	Virtual teams have more external interdependencies
	Virtual teams have more dynamic interdependencies
	Virtual team interdependencies exhibit more variety
	Virtual team interdependencies are more visible inside the team, but hidden interdependence also increases
Communication	Virtual teams use fewer paraverbal and nonverbal cues
	Virtual teams communicate less rich information
	Virtual teams communicate less efficiently
	Virtual teams exchange more task-oriented rather than socio-emotional information
	Virtual teams experience fewer social inhibitions in communication

Adapted from DeSanctis, Staudenmayer, and Wong (1999); Kiesler and Sproull (1992); Warkentin, Sayeed, and Hightower (1997).

The incidence of virtuality changes from one cell of the framework to another: the most virtual of these teams is the one where members come from a diverse culture and geography, where the primary (and perhaps only) mode of communication is electronic, and where the team itself is transient in nature: assembled to accomplish a specific task and disbanded at task completion.

An alternative classification of virtual teams is presented by Fisher and Fisher (2001), who describe a three-dimensional space bounded by space, time, and culture continua. Each dimension of this classification ranges from "same" to "different," yielding eight possible types of teams. Fisher and Fisher suggest that two types of teams, same space, time, and culture, and same space and time but different culture, really do not qualify as virtual teams. Hence, the defining dimensions in this framework are space and time, yielding a typology of virtual teams that contains six distinct types.

Based on the underlying themes of these conceptualizations, that virtual teams are characterized by physical and temporal (and, perhaps, cultural) distribution, how do their structures and behaviors differ from traditional teams? Table 21.1 summarizes the differences between traditional and virtual teams as presented in the recent literature. Traditional teams are viewed as differing from virtual teams along the core structural dimension of interdependencies and behavioral dimension of communication. Interdependencies describe the nature of the social exchange (Granovetter, 1985) that takes place among team members, and as such capture the extent and manner in which members are reliant upon each other to accomplish team goals (DeSanctis, Staudenmayer, & Wong, 1999).

DeSanctis, Staudenmayer, and Wong (1999) use interdependencies as the conceptual lens for understanding how virtual teams will differ from traditional ones. Their predictions are summarized in Table 21.1—virtual teams, by the very nature, are seen as exhibiting greater links with external actors. Their interdependencies are viewed as morphing and shifting over time, as roles and responsibilities of team members change. For teams that are responsible for multiple tasks, the interdependencies are likely to exhibit greater variety, as the team decides how best to accomplish the requirements of each task. Finally, there is a paradox inherent in the visibility of dependencies in virtual teams. On one hand, dependencies become overt and ostensible as the team uses electronic repositories to document information exchanges.

On the other, because the functioning of the team is in essence decentralized and dynamic, it is possible that certain types of dependence among members may remain hidden from the larger team.

By contrast, the behavioral dimension of communication addresses the limitations imposed by the inherent characteristics of the electronic communication mode: thus, virtual teams are seen as communicating in a less rich and efficient manner, and focusing more on instrumental rather than emotional information exchanges. Additionally, the lack of face-to-face communication is viewed as reducing social hierarchies and status differences that are likely to be prevalent in traditional teams.

In summary, prior research has argued that virtual teams are different from collocated ones across multiple dimensions. Looking across the dimensions proposed by scholars, three distinctions emerge as particularly salient: (1) the richness of the communication that occurs, (2) the synchronicity of work, and (3) the development of relational capital. The first distinction is a direct outcome of the platform used by a virtual team to orchestrate its work. It is widely held that, *ceteris paribus*, ICTs promote less rich communication than does face-to-face dialog. For instance, even though it has been suggested that e-mail is being increasingly "enriched" through the use of multiple cues (Hiltz & Turoff, 1993), it is still a relatively lean medium. Furthermore, although some ICTs such as video-conferencing eliminate the limitation of disembodiment in communication, nevertheless a major component of the value proposition of virtual teams is the notion that they transcend time and geography barriers. Thus, to the extent that members of a virtual team will work on team-related activities in different temporal planes, much of the team's interaction is likely to occur through the mediation of technology.

A second distinction, the synchronicity of the team's work, again follows directly from the idea that virtual teams are distributed across time and geography. Finally, because of limited, and in the extreme case, no, face-to-face contact, virtual teams face challenges in regard to the development of relational ties and the organizational capital that flows from such relational ties. Team members may never develop the empathy and emotional ties that bind coworkers together in a traditional work setting where multiple opportunities for unstructured and nonwork-related interaction arise as a natural course of sharing the same physical space.

COLLABORATION AND COOPERATION IN VIRTUAL TEAMS

Scholars have acknowledged that cooperation is an important outcome associated with any team process (Tuckman, 1965). Indeed, cooperation could be argued to be a proximal antecedent of desired team effects such as member attitudes, task performance, etc.: it appears self-evident that teams where members are unwilling to collaborate with each other are unlikely to engage in actions that would result in task accomplishment. Cooperation implies a willingness to exchange information, a desire to engage in pro-social behaviors, and the conveyance of messages suggesting that individual members are willing to contribute to the overall well-being of the team. Cooperation helps develop a team climate where individuals view each other as supporting the team effort. In essence, then, cooperation represents a crucial outcome for the study of virtual teams, as it is a direct correlate of team effectiveness. What are the drivers of cooperative behavior? What impedes cooperation within teams? These questions are examined next.

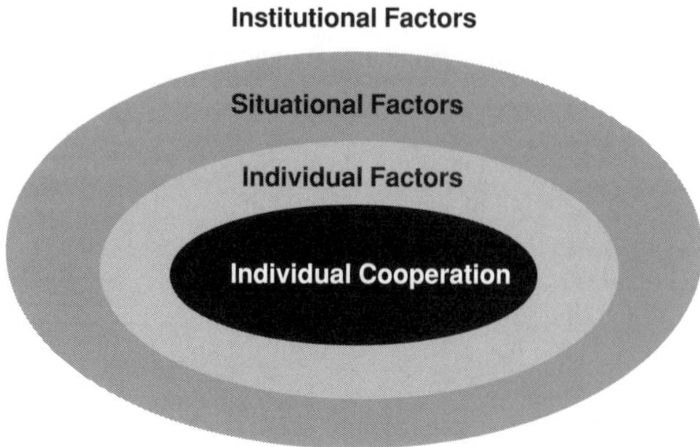

Figure 21.1 Spheres of influence on cooperative behavior in virtual teams

The Drivers of Cooperative Behavior

To help conceptualize the impediments and facilitators of cooperative behavior in virtual teams, we propose the concentric spheres of influence model shown in Figure 21.1. As suggested there, the behavior of cooperation is viewed as being predicated upon three sets of factors existing at micro, meso, and macro levels. First, a set of factors inherent in the individual team member is posited to drive cooperation. Next, factors more distal from the individual that exist within the context of the collective, i.e. the team, influence individual cooperation, but their effects are seen as being mediated by individual-level factors. Finally, influences arising from the institutional environment within which the virtual team exists have an effect on cooperation. As before, these effects are more distal and less potent than those arising from the individual or the team context. Researchers in organizational behavior have contributed much to extending our understanding of cooperative behavior in general, and this chapter will not attempt to synthesize the extensive literature on predictors of cooperation. Rather, the focus will be on the specific context, that of virtual teams, and the drivers of cooperation within this context.

It is important to point out that at a meta level, this conceptualization is not new. Indeed, Lewis, Agarwal, and Sambamurthy (2001) use the idea of concentric spheres to characterize influences on information-technology-use cognitions. Likewise, Cohen and Mankin (1999), in their examination of collaboration within a virtual organization, propose a "rings of collaboration" framework for the outcomes, enablers, and process of collaboration.

Individual Factors

Individual-level factors represent the characteristics and dispositions that each team member carries into the group process. They are what McGrath and Hollingshead (1994) refer to as member attributes: "cognitive, affective, conative, and demographic" characteristics of team members (p. 105). Among the multitude of factors that could be included in this category, we focus on four constructs that we believe are likely to be highly salient to the virtual team context: disposition to trust, remote-work self-efficacy (Staples, Hulland, & Higgins, 1999), technology self-efficacy (Marakas, Yi, & Johnson, 1998), and personal innovativeness with information technology (Agarwal & Prasad, 1998).

The importance of dispositions in general has a long-standing tradition in personality research. Dispositions are those enduring and persistent aspects of personality that are relatively immune to situational influences (Fridhandler, 1986). Some dispositions are more malleable than others; less malleable dispositions are called traits (House, Shane, & Herold, 1996). Dispositions constitute a central component of psychological trait theory. In essence, trait theory argues that predispositions and propensities cause individuals to exhibit predictable behaviors in, and responses to, certain situations (Aiken, 1993). Thus, to the extent that individual behavior can be predicted in part by innate dispositions, these attributes provide managers with levers to utilize in recruitment, selection, and assignment decisions.

For instance, assigning individuals with high disposition to trust to critical but ambiguous organizational projects might result in greater cooperation, information sharing, and other citizenship behaviors. Similarly, assigning individuals with high remote-work self-efficacy to virtual teams is likely to lead to desirable outcomes since these individuals typically have confidence in their ability to contribute from a distance. Likewise, high-technology self-efficacy and personal innovativeness with technology are associated with greater use of technology (Marakas, Yi, & Johnson, 1998) and, to the extent that technology use is a critical requirement in a virtual team, those with more confidence in their ability to use the technology are likely to also engage in more extensive communication. As cogently noted by Buss and Craik (1985), a crucial task confronting social and behavioral researchers is to identify a parsimonious set of traits that are worthy of theoretical and empirical attention by virtue of their unambiguous association with desirable behaviors.

McKnight and Agarwal (2000) define *disposition to trust* as a tendency to be willing to depend on others generally. In a series of empirical studies they found that this disposition related both directly and indirectly to trust-related behaviors such as cooperation and information sharing. This relatively stable personality trait, therefore, is important to extending our understanding of which individuals are likely to be assets to a virtual team.

Emerging from a rich theoretical background in social learning and social cognition, self-efficacy refers to individuals' beliefs about their ability and motivation to perform specific tasks (Bandura, 1977, 1986). The concept of self-efficacy owes much of its conceptual development and empirical refinement to over two decades of research by Bandura and his colleagues. Bandura (1997, p. 79) postulates that self-efficacy beliefs are developed through four primary sources of information: "enactive mastery experiences that serve as indicators of capability; vicarious experiences that alter efficacy beliefs through transmission of competencies and comparisons with the attainments of others; verbal persuasion and allied types of social influence that one possesses certain capabilities; and physiological and affective states from which people judge their capableness, strength, and vulnerability to dysfunction." Of these, enactive mastery experiences, i.e. experiences gained through progressive trials (either success or failure) in a task domain, are considered to be the most potent and salient source of efficacy information. Central to Bandura's notion of self-efficacy is the idea that this personal belief is a major basis of action.

The posited relationship between self-efficacy and behavior has been empirically validated in diverse domains such as education, health, and organizational life (see Bandura, 1997). In the domain of information technology in particular, studies of the effects of self-efficacy collectively point to its crucial role in determining individual behavior toward and performance using information technologies (Compeau & Higgins, 1995; Gist, Schwoerer, & Rosen, 1989).

Staples, Hulland, and Higgins (1999) suggest that the notion of self-efficacy is critical to understanding the behavior of remote workers such as those in virtual organizations. They further describe the concept of remote-work self-efficacy, or the confidence that employees have in their ability to work in a remote environment: one that is facilitated by technology and characterized by limited face-to-face interaction. Remote-work self-efficacy is seen as being influenced by, among other variables, technology self-efficacy, and is theorized to lead to several useful outcomes such as work performance and job satisfaction. In a field study of remote workers across multiple organizations and industries, they found empirical support for these assertions. Therefore, we include these two types of self-efficacy as important individual-level determinants of cooperation in virtual teams.

Finally, personal innovativeness in the domain of information technology (PIIT) is defined as the "willingness of an individual to try out any new information technology" (Agarwal & Prasad, 1998). As a relatively stable descriptor of individuals over time, this trait captures the risk-taking propensity of an individual with regard to information technology. Agarwal and Prasad argued that PIIT was an important construct in studying individual behavior toward information technologies: an assertion that has been empirically validated in a number of research studies (Agarwal, Sambamurthy, & Stair, 2000; Limayen, Khalifa, & Frini, 2000). The effect of PIIT on cooperative behavior in teams is expected to manifest itself because PIIT results in greater technology-use behaviors. As with technology self-efficacy, higher PIIT should lead to greater use of the communication platforms that underlie the work of virtual teams, thereby resulting in more collaboration among team members.

Situational and Social Factors

The second sphere of influence relates to situational and social factors. Here, we move beyond the individual level of analysis to consider influences on individual cooperation arising from the team level of analysis. Two factors are included at this level: these include the range of technologies available for the team to accomplish its goals, and the level of trust existing among the members of the virtual team.

Technologies (in essence, communication channels) differ in their ability to facilitate communication. Daft and Lengel's (1984) media richness theory (MRT) informs much of the research on the differential capacities of alternate communication channels. Daft and Lengel situated media along a richness continuum, with face-to-face exchanges at one end and formal, written documents at the other. They argued that rich media were more effective in reducing uncertainty and equivocality in the communication episode between the sender and the receiver. MRT predicts that a closer match between the content of a message and the richness of the channel used to communicate the message will result in more effective communication. Empirical investigations of MRT have provided mixed support for its conceptualization. Subsequent extensions of MRT (Trevino, Daft, & Lengel, 1990) suggest that media choices are determined not only by message content, but also by contextual determinants such as distance, time pressure, and accessibility.

In contrast to rational explanations, social theories such as social influence models (Fulk, Schmitz, & Steinfeld, 1990) and critical mass theory (Markus, 1990) argue persuasively that media choices are significantly influenced by the social environment within which the communication event takes place, i.e. media perceptions are "subjective and socially constructed" (Fulk, Schmitz, & Steinfeld, 1990, p. 121). For example, the media behavior of coworkers or peer expectations are expected to influence an individual's choice of medium. Citing evidence from a multi-method investigation of managerial media choices in a large organization, Markus (1994) suggests that it is perhaps simplistic to assume that media behavior will be invariant across social settings (an implicit assumption underlying MRT) and driven by overtly "sensible" choices. Rather, it is the social and cultural norms that determine and circumscribe media choice behavior.

Webster and Trevino (1995) argue for treating rational and social theories as complementary, rather than rival, plausible explanations. The former are expected to prove more powerful for explaining behavior related to "traditional" media such as face-to-face meetings and written memos because the use of such media has been institutionalized, resulting in a consistent and widely shared social definition. In contrast, social explanations are expected to dominate as explanatory theories for individual choice of new media because of the lack of routinization and standardization associated with these media. Webster and Trevino (1995) present evidence for these predictions from two empirical studies, and conclude that an integration of rational and social explanations offers considerable promise. They also note that future media choice research should examine multiple media choices and multiple influence factors rather than focusing on a unitary, and perhaps inadequate, explanation.

From these studies it is evident that media choices play a crucial role in determining the effectiveness of a virtual team. However, a proximal determinant of media choice in a virtual team is the range of technologies available to the team to accomplish its work. The greater this range, the more likely that a team member is able to "match the medium to the message," thereby facilitating a common understanding of the message. Indeed, as noted by Ancona and Caldwell (1990), different tasks require different patterns of interaction, and, given the diversity of tasks that a typical virtual team would likely be required to perform, a wide range of technologies is essential. In essence, this gives team members the flexibility to match the medium to the message. Greater understanding and shared mental models, in turn, should result in a greater motivation among team members to engage in cooperative behavior. Technology here plays the crucial role of the communicator of social norms and expectations, and helps ensure that all members of the team share a common view of the task ahead of them.

By definition, virtual teams are interdependent forms of work organization in that the success of the collective is intimately linked to the behaviors of others comprising the collective. In such situations, trust has been shown to be an important antecedent of cooperative behavior (Krackhardt & Stern, 1988). Trust exists when members believe that others will (a) make good-faith efforts to behave in accordance with any commitments, explicit or implicit, (b) be honest in whatever negotiations precede such commitments, and (c) will not take advantage of another member even when the opportunity is available (Cummings & Bromiley, 1996). Because virtual teams may never have an opportunity to engage in the development of relational capital that typically occurs during the early stages of team formation through face-to-face exchanges, trust is all the more pivotal to the outcomes of the team process.

Empirical studies of trust in virtual teams support its salience for team outcomes. Jarvenpaa and Leidner (1999) examined the existence and evolution of trust in global, virtual teams spanning diverse cultural contexts. Their results point to the emergence of "swift" trust as an outcome of the communication behaviors of team members. However, as the authors note, such trust is likely to be short-lived and fragile. In conclusion, Jarvenpaa and Leidner observe: "... systematic research is needed on the virtual team member profile, task requirements, technology capabilities, and other environmental circumstances that allow the team members to react in such a manner as to thicken rather than enervate the team in the face of the inevitable crises that occur in global settings" (p. 813).

At the organization level, trust is seen as vital in managing virtual organizations (e.g. Sparrow & Daniels, 1999) and for effectively responding to crises (Mishra, 1996). In their conceptual examination of processes contributing to high performance in virtual organizations, Grabowski and Roberts (1999) identify trust as a crucial process, noting that in the presence of trust, synergistic efforts in interorganizational missions are more likely. For virtual teams these findings collectively suggest that trust has a direct influence on the level of cooperation that occurs among team members. The more individual members trust each other, the greater their willingness to rely on others and share information.

Institutional Factors

The outermost sphere of influence embodies the constraints and facilitators embedded in the institutional environment within which the virtual team operates. Much has been said about the effects of the broader institutional context on individual behavior. Institutional theory provides the conceptual underpinnings of how and why the thoughts and actions of individuals within organizations are significantly influenced by the prevailing organizational norms, values, culture, and history. Scott (1995; see also Orlikowski, 1992) identifies three ways in which the institutional milieu influences individual cognition and subsequently behavior: through processes of signification, legitimization, and domination.

Signification implies that individuals use information from the institutional milieu to understand how they should form their beliefs about new work processes that are introduced into the organization. Legitimization is suggestive of the validation of specific beliefs and actions of individuals: messages emanating from top management are used as normative templates to reassure oneself about the organizational legitimacy of beliefs and actions. Finally, domination reflects the notion that the institutional milieu regulates individual beliefs. To the extent that organizational workers seek to comply with organizational directives, they will develop behaviors that are consistent with the institutional context. *Ceteris paribus*, an institutional environment that provides the appropriate signals and messages, as well as the infrastructure in support of virtual work, is likely to result in greater cooperation among team members.

Three distinct yet interrelated factors are theorized as belonging to the institutional sphere of influence: work culture and norms, governance structures, and reward mechanisms. Work culture and norms represent a shared set of behavioral expectations that individuals possess (e.g. Schein, 1985). Several decades ago Barnard (1968) noted that that the defining element of any organization (i.e. group) is the necessity of individuals to subordinate, to an extent, their own desires to the collective will of the organization. At the overall firm level, the work group (and individual) is also part of the larger organization. When the organization has existed for a lengthy period of time, basic assumptions and beliefs about how members of the organization respond to certain situations develop (Schein, 1985). New members of the organization, through a process of socialization, internalize these expectations and adjust and modify personal behaviors so that they are consistent with prevailing norms. A work culture that values team work and places a high premium on information sharing and cooperation drives individuals to exhibit behavioral tendencies that support virtual team effectiveness.

Governance structures refer to institutional arrangements that circumscribe how important decision-making and operational processes are executed. Fundamentally, governance structures capture notions of accountability, decision authority, reporting relationships, and how work gets accomplished within the organization. Mohrman (1999) suggests that team dysfunction arises when organizations are structured using a hierarchical, functional logic. To the extent that virtual teams are often groups of cross-functional, perhaps even cross-organizational members, the hierarchical logic is antithetical to a fundamental tenet of the virtual team, that of lateral relationships. A hierarchical organizational structure inhibits individual cooperation within virtual teams because members perceive that lateral decision making is not the "way things are done around here," and hence, the virtual team, as a form of work organization, is not perceived as being endorsed by the elite core of the organization.

Finally, reward mechanisms capture the incentive structures embedded within the organization that signal organizational members about what behaviors have legitimacy within the institutional context. Reward mechanisms also embody structures of domination in that particular behaviors may result in organizational sanctions and are therefore viewed as being less desirable. We characterize reward mechanisms as reflecting the extent to which team performance measures are included in the performance appraisal processes of organizational members.

It is widely accepted that individuals respond to incentives (e.g. Kerr, 1975). Traditionally, performance measurement systems have been designed to assess the extent to which an individual meets stated performance expectations in terms of individual contributions to the workplace and the organization. Recent thinking in performance measurement systems suggests that as organizational work is increasingly performed in teams, elements of team effectiveness need to be incorporated within measures of individual contribution (Ghorpade, Chen, & Caggiano, 1995). When virtual team members see team effectiveness being rewarded, and as they acknowledge their personal behaviors of cooperation as causal mechanisms underlying team effectiveness, not surprisingly, they are likely to be motivated to exhibit greater levels of cooperation.

In summary, then, Figure 21.1 captures the posited influences on the behavior of individual cooperation in virtual teams. Although prior work has suggested multiple additional predictors of cooperation, the choice of the drivers included in the model is strongly influenced by the specific context examined here: that of geographically dispersed, technology-mediated work. As suggested earlier, cooperation is important to focus on because of its expected proximal effects on other important virtual team outcomes such as member satisfaction with the team process, quality of the team's output, and member commitment to the team effort.

SOME (UNINTENDED) CONSEQUENCES OF VIRTUAL TEAMWORK

Although it is patently evident that virtual teams offer organizations the promise of improved flexibility and responsiveness to environmental demands, there is some concern that the effects of participating in virtual teams are not uniformly positive for the individual. Such negative effects are likely to be of interest to managers as well: when individuals suffer unintended consequences, it is possible that these consequences will eventually result in undesirable outcomes for the organization. We briefly discuss the potential damaging effects of virtual teams next.

The fact that members of a virtual team have fewer opportunities to meet with coworkers in social settings where rich, face-to-face interactions abound can potentially lead to feelings of isolation (Cascio, 2000). This negative consequence is likely to be most potent for individuals whose primary mode of contribution to the organization is as a member of perhaps multiple virtual teams. Weisenfeld, Raghuram, and Garud (1999a) argue that traditional organizations rely on multiple social cues and artifacts to establish linkages between the individual and the organization, such as shared behavioral norms, dress codes, expected patterns of interaction, and so forth. This process of organizational identification is important because it has a profound effect on employee expectations, motivations, and behaviors. Virtual teams offer limited opportunities for organizational identification because of the geographical dispersion of members and their reliance on technology as the primary means of communication. The feelings of isolation arising from participation in virtual teams are likely to further exacerbate low organizational identification, undermining the psychological link between the individual and the organization.

In the context of managers specifically, Weisenfeld, Raghuram, and Garud (1999b) observe that virtual work is likely to erode managers' sense of esteem and control. Whereas esteem refers to the individual's positive self-concept, a sense of control captures the notion that an individual seeks to believe that he/she has control over the immediate environment and is capable of influencing the course of events. Threats to esteem arise because the decentralized and self-managed nature of virtual teams renders the importance of the manager as the supervisor of work as less consequential. Additionally, the nature of managerial work shifts: practices that were hitherto effective in traditional contexts such as contacting subordinates to determine progress and overseeing their work might be viewed by virtual team members as meddlesome (Weisenfeld, Raghuram, & Garud, 1999b). Collectively these changes threaten the managers' positive self-concept by questioning the fundamental need for a traditional managerial role.

Likewise, managers' sense of control is diminished in a virtual context because of a variety of reasons. For example, in their study of managing offshore IT development projects, Carmel and Agarwal (2000) found that managers worry about having to manage resources over which they have limited control, and yet the performance of these resources will drive their own evaluations. Weisenfeld, Raghuram, and Garud (1999b) note that in a virtual organization, traditional techniques that managers use to evaluate subordinate performance might be inadequate, further amplifying a perceived lack of control.

Virtual team members are often, although not always, unfettered by the traditional confines of a physical office environment. Assisted by technology, they may choose to work from home, or telecommute. Much has been written about the expected positive outcomes of telecommuting, such as improved morale, productivity, and work–life balance (e.g. Hequet, 1996; Shellenbarger, 1997). Yet, the empirical evidence does not fully support the claims made in these works. In a rigorous examination of the effects of telework among a sample of professional employees, Hill et al. (1998) debunk the traditional argument that virtual work results in uniformly positive outcomes. Their results showed that although telecommuting improves perceived productivity and flexibility, it has a negative effect on work–life balance. Virtual workers reported experiencing difficulty in clearly delineating the boundary between "work" time and "personal" time and found that work encroached into areas otherwise reserved for nonwork-related activities. The net result of declining work–life balance is greater propensity to experience burnout and stress.

Townsend, DeMarie, and Hendrickson (1998) also allude to this negative outcome in their analysis of virtual teams. Technology lengthens the workday and blurs boundaries between work and life. Although not conclusive, evidence suggests that virtual team members who rely on technology to accomplish work are more likely to discover that they work longer hours than their traditional counterparts, experience greater job demands and more role conflict (Sparrow & Daniels, 1999), and lower psychological well-being.

Finally, it is worth drawing attention to a set of dysfunctional behaviors that can potentially arise among members of a virtual team. Because of their dispersed character and reliance on technology as the primary means of communication, virtual teams offer limited opportunities for monitoring individual behaviors and imposing social pressure to contribute to the group effort. In traditional face-to-face team contexts, the mere fact of having to "face" team members induces greater accountability in individuals. The principal–agent problem intensifies in the context of the virtual team: if we treat the organization as the principal and the entire team as the agent responsible for executing the principal's tasks, difficulties in evaluating the relative contribution of individual members to the group effort are significant. As a consequence, virtual team members may be more prone to social loafing, free-riding, and absenteeism (O'Hara-Devereaux & Johansen, 1994). Although such problems can exist in traditional team contexts as well, they are arguably likely to be more prevalent in virtual team situations where behaviors are less observable.

SUMMARY AND CONCLUSION

There is little doubt that the use of the virtual team as a new form of work organization is likely to intensify into the future. Increased organizational dependence on ICTs for strategic and operational purposes, greater socialization of the workforce with the use of technology, and the accelerating pace of competition in business environments that demands increasingly rapid responses to strategic and technological discontinuities, are collectively fueling the search for flexible organizational forms. As with any innovation in organizational work, virtual teams simultaneously offer significant promise and pose challenging dilemmas. Practitioners struggle to incorporate these new forms within existing organizational constraints and researchers seek to develop more powerful explanatory models that help illuminate what determines the success or failure of these forms, the contingencies that should drive their selection, and their effects on individual motivations, attitudes, and behaviors. This chapter provided a broad overview of the virtual team concept, discussed the role of information and communications technologies in facilitating virtualization, distinguished virtual teams from traditional collocated teams, and developed a model proposing three sets of factors as antecedents of the important outcome of individual cooperation in a virtual team. Finally, it focused on some negative consequences associated with participation in virtual teams.

Responding to the ubiquity of virtual teams, the practitioner press offers many prescriptions regarding their effective management and the organizational imperatives for managers of virtual teams (e.g. Fisher & Fisher, 2001; Haywood, 1998). However, the relative infancy of the virtual team phenomenon presents exciting opportunities for scholarly research to address gaps in understanding of the precise psychological and social forces underlying the performance of such teams. Several areas for fruitful future research remain. A few promising avenues are identified next.

Information and communications technologies are pivotal to virtual teams. Over two decades of research in technology-mediated group work has extended our understanding of what technologies work under what circumstances. Researchers have addressed issues related to task–technology fit in the context of media richness and associated theories. Yet, the pace of technological development constantly challenges researchers by providing increasingly more sophisticated platforms upon which to orchestrate virtual work. For example, the emergence of the Internet as a platform for global collaboration calls for a fresh look at the conformance between the various tasks that a virtual team is required to perform and the range of collaborative technologies that could be applied to each task. Developing a shared context among virtual team members might require the use of synchronous communications technologies that display multiple social cues, such as desktop video-conferencing, while sharing interim work products may be more effectively accomplished through an Internet-based knowledge repository. Developing and testing a rich and extensive theory of task–technology fit that incorporates dimensions of the new media and tools would be invaluable for both researchers and practitioners. And, because members of a virtual team need to make choices about what particular communication medium to use, such a normative theory would help virtual team members choose communication technologies more effectively.

Although a model of the antecedents of individual cooperation in a virtual team was described, the relationships implicit in the model are in need of further elaboration and refinement. Several interesting and significant research questions can be raised in the context of the spheres of influence conceptualization. The goal in specifying the model was to be parsimonious; therefore, the model only includes factors that have been identified in prior research as being important to the study of virtual teams. The most obvious question to ask is if there are other factors that should be included at the individual, social, and institutional levels of analysis. More subtle questions relate to the precise nature of the relationships. We implied mediation by suggesting that the intervening spheres mediate the effects of the outer spheres of influence. This assertion is in need of empirical verification. It is also possible that factors existing at one level are related to each other through causal pathways. It may well be the case, for example, that the range of technologies available to the virtual team influences the development of trust: "richer" technologies could allow for a greater wealth of social information to be exchanged, thereby developing greater trust.

Additionally, no moderating influences on the posited relationships were proposed. It is plausible that trust moderates the relationship between institutional factors and individual cooperation: low levels of trust imply that individuals rely on messages from the institutional context to form behavioral expectations, whereas high levels of trust may render the influence of the institutional context insignificant. Finally, the logic underlying the specific relationships embedded in the model, and the causal mechanisms underlying the relationships, are in need of further theoretical development.

The centrality of trust to the performance of virtual teams is beginning to be acknowledged as axiomatic. Yet, empirical studies of trust in virtual team settings are extremely limited. The challenges of conducting such fieldwork notwithstanding, there is an urgent need to better understand the fundamental role that trust plays in the performance of virtual teams. The studies by Jarvenpaa and her colleagues provide a good conceptual basis for launching large-scale examinations of trust development. Several interesting questions can be posed. Consider, for example, an organizational situation where an individual employee is a member of multiple virtual teams: a scenario possible, among other situations, in organizations where telecommuting is prevalent. How fungible is trust? Does a high level of trust in one virtual team transfer to other teams to which this team's members also belong? Does a high level of trust in one virtual team predispose an individual to trust others in the next virtual team encounter? How does experience in working with virtual teams influence the *a priori* level of trust that an individual brings to a virtual team?

Finally, we presented examples of dysfunctional behaviors that may arise in virtual team contexts. This begs the question: what causes such dysfunctional behaviors and how might they be avoided? Are social loafing and free-riding innate propensities of the individual that need to be ascertained prior to their assignment to a virtual team, because the low behavior observability that characterizes virtual teams brings such dysfunction to the fore? Or, are they a more subtle psychological reaction to feelings of isolation and weakened organizational identity that lower individuals' commitment to the team effort? Specific theoretical arguments and empirical support for either relationship would yield a different set of mechanisms that need to be utilized to overcome dysfunction. For example, support for the former hypothesis would argue for greater attention and focus on selection processes surrounding team creation. By contrast, support for the latter would suggest that mechanisms that strengthen feelings of community and organizational identification, such as occasional face-to-face encounters in organizational space, are likely to be effective in eliminating the dysfunction.

The evolutionary process governing structural forms for organizing work exhibits elements of natural selection: forms that prove their value in meeting new organizational demands will survive, while others will die a natural death. Following this logic, virtual teams are likely to survive because of the many reasons enumerated in this chapter. Most importantly, virtual teams will prosper because of the essential flexibility of the form: unlike a U-form organization or an M-form organization, a virtual team can, chameleon like, assume the structure that best matches the requirements of the task at hand.

REFERENCES

Agarwal, R. & Prasad, J. (1998). A conceptual and operational definition of personal innovativeness in the domain of information technology. *Information Systems Research, 9*(2), 204–215.

Agarwal, R., Sambamurthy, V., & Stair, R. (2000). The evolving relationship between general and specific computer self-efficacy: an empirical assessment. *Information Systems Research, 11*(4), 418–430.

Aiken, L. R. (1993). *Personality: Theories, Research and Applications.* Englewood Cliffs, NJ: Prentice-Hall.

Ancona, D. G. & Caldwell, D. F. (1990). Information technology and work groups: the case of new product teams. In J. Galegher, R. Kraut, & C. Egido (eds), *Intellectual Teamwork: Social and Technological Foundations of Cooperative Work* (pp. 173–190). Hillsdale, NJ: Erlbaum.

Ashkenas, R., Ulrich, D., Jick, T., & Kerr, S. (1995). *The Boundaryless Organization.* San Francisco: Jossey-Bass.

Bandura, A. (1977). Self-efficacy: toward a unifying theory of behavioral change. *Psychological Review, 84*(2), 191–215.

Bandura, A. (1986). *Social Foundations of Thought and Action: A Social Cognitive Theory.* Englewood Cliffs, NJ: Prentice-Hall.

Bandura, A. (1997). *Self-efficacy: The Exercise of Control.* New York: W. H. Freeman.

Barnard, C. I. (1968). *The Functions of the Executive.* Cambridge, Mass.: Harvard University Press.

Benbasat, I. & Lim, L. (1993). The effects of group, task, context, and technology variables on usefulness of group support systems: a meta-analysis of experimental studies. *Small Group Research, 24*(4), 430–462.

Bovet, D. & Martha, J. (2000). *Value Nets: Breaking the Supply Chain to Unlock Hidden Profits*. New York: John Wiley & Sons.

Buss, D. M. & Craik, K. H. (1985). Why not measure *that* trait? Alternative criteria for identifying important dispositions. *Journal of Personality and Social Psychology, 48*, 934–986.

Carmel, E. (1999). *Global Software Teams*. Englewood Cliffs, NJ: Prentice-Hall.

Carmel, E. & Agarwal, R. (2000). *Offshore Sourcing of Information Technology Work by America's Largest Firms*, Technical Report, Kogod School of Business, American University, Washington, DC.

Cascio, W. F. (2000). Managing a virtual workplace. *The Academy of Management Executive, 14*(3), 81–90.

Cohen, Susan G. & Mankin, Don (1999). Collaboration in the virtual organization. In Cary L. Cooper & D. M. Rousseau (eds), *Trends in Organizational Behavior*, Vol. 6: *The Virtual Organization* (pp. 105–120); Chichester, UK: John Wiley & Sons.

Compeau, D. R. & Higgins, C. A. (1995). Application of social cognitive theory to training for computer skills. *Information Systems Research, 6*(2), 118–143.

Cummings, L. L. & Bromiley, P. (1996). The organizational trust inventory (OTI). In R. M. Kramer & T. R. Tyler (eds), *Trust in Organizations: Frontiers of Theory and Research* (pp. 302–330). Thousand Oaks, Calif.: Sage.

Daft, R. & Lengel, R. (1984). Information richness: a new approach to managerial behavior and organizational design. In L. Cummings & B. Staw (eds), *Research in Organizational Behavior* (Vol. 6, pp. 191–233). Homewood, Ill.: JAI Press.

D'Aveni, R. A. (1995). *Hypercompetitive Rivalries: Competing in Highly Dynamic Environments*. New York: Free Press.

Davidow, W. H. & Malone, M. S. (1992). *The Virtual Corporation: Structuring and Revitalizing the Corporation for the 21st Century*. New York: HarperCollins.

DeSanctis, G. & Gallupe, R. B. (1987). A foundation for the study of group decision support systems. *Management Science, 33*, 589–609.

DeSanctis, G. & Monge, P. (1999). Introduction to the special issues: communication processes for virtual organizations. *Organization Science, 10*(6), 693–703.

DeSanctis, G., Staudenmayer, N., & Wong, S. S. (1999). Interdependence in virtual organizations. In Cary L. Cooper & D. M. Rousseau (eds), *Trends in Organizational Behavior*, Vol. 6: *The Virtual Organization* (pp. 81–104). Chichester, UK: John Wiley & Sons.

Fisher, K. & Fisher, M. D. (2001). *The Distance Manager*. New York: McGraw-Hill.

Fridhandler, B. M. (1986). Conceptual note on state, trait, and the state–trait distinction. *Journal of Personality and Social Psychology, 50*, 169–174.

Fulk, J., Schmitz, J., & Steinfeld, C. W. (1990). A social influence model of technology use. In J. Fulk & C. Steinfield (eds), *Organizations and Communication Technology* (pp. 117–141). Newbury Park, Calif.: Sage.

Ghorpade, J., Chen, M. M., & Caggiano, J. (1995). Creating quality-driven performance appraisal systems. *The Academy of Management Executive, 9*(1), 32–39.

Gist, M., Schwoerer, C., & Rosen, B. (1989). Effects of alternative training methods on self-efficacy and performance in computer software training. *Journal of Applied Psychology, 74*(6), 884–891.

Grabowski, M. & Roberts, K. H. (1999). Risk mitigation in virtual organizations. *Organization Science, 10*(6), 704–721.

Granovetter, M. (1985). Economic action and social structure: the problem of embeddedness. *American Journal of Sociology, 91*(3), 481–510.

Hamblen, M. (1998). NetMeeting cuts Dow travel expenses. *Computerworld*, March 9.

Haywood, M. (1998). *Managing Virtual Teams: Practical Techniques for High-technology Project Managers*. Boston: Artech House.

Hequet, M. (1996). Working virtually: dispatches from the home front. *Training, 33*(9), 29–35.

Hill, J. E., Miller, B. C., Weiner, S. P., & Colihan, J. (1998). Influences of the virtual office on aspects of work and work/life balance. *Personnel Psychology, 51*(3), 667–683.

Hiltz, S. R. & Turoff, M. (1993). *The Network Nation: Human Communication via Computer*. Cambridge, Mass.: MIT Press.

House, R. J., Shane, S. A., & Herold, D. M. (1996). Rumors of the death of dispositional research are vastly exaggerated. *Academy of Management Review, 21*, 203–224.

Jarvenpaa, S. L. & Leidner, D. E. (1999). Communication and trust in global virtual teams. *Organization Science, 10*(6), 791–815.

Kerr, S. (1975). On the folly of rewarding A, while hoping for B. *Academy of Management Journal, 18*, 769–783.

Kiesler, S. & Sproull, L. (1992). Group decision making and communication technology. *Organizational Behavior and Human Decision Processes, 52*(1), 96–123.

Krackhardt, D. & Stern, R. N. (1988). Informal networks and organizational crises: an experimental simulation. *Social Psychology Quarterly, 51*, 123–140.

Kraemer, K. L. & Pinsonneault, A. (1990). Technology and groups: assessment of the empirical research. In J. Galegher, R. Kraut, & C. Egido (eds), *Intellectual Teamwork: Social and Technological Foundations of Cooperative Work* (pp. 375–405). Hillsdale, NJ: Erlbaum.

Kristof, A. L., Brown, K. G., Sims, H. P., Jr, & Smith, K. A. (1995). The virtual team: a case study and inductive model. In M. M. Beyerlein, D. A. Johnson, & S. T. Beyerlein (eds), *Advances in Interdisciplinary Studies of Work Teams: Knowledge Work in Teams* (Vol. 2). Greenwich, Conn.: JAI Press.

Lewis, W., Agarwal, R., & Sambamurthy, S. (2001). Spheres of influence and cognitive interpretations of information technology: an empirical study of knowledge workers. Working paper, Terry College of Business, University of Georgia.

Limayen, M., Khalifa, M., & Frini, A. (2000). What makes consumers buy from the Internet? A longitudinal study of online shopping. *IEEE Transactions on Systems, Man, and Cybernetics, 30*(4), 421–432.

Lipnack, J. & Stamps, J. (2000). *Virtual Teams: Reaching across Space, Time, and Organizations with Technology*. New York: John Wiley & Sons.

McGrath, J. E. & Hollingshead, A. B. (1994). *Groups Interacting with Technology*. Thousand Oaks, Calif.: Sage.

McKnight, D. H. & Agarwal, R. (2000). How disposition to trust affects trust-related behavior: reason to resuscitate a construct. Working paper, Michigan State University.

Malone, T. W. & Laubacher, R. J. (1998). The E-lance economy. *Harvard Business Review*, September–October, 145–152.

Marakas, G., Yi, M., & Johnson, R. (1998). The multilevel and multifaceted character of computer self-efficacy: toward clarification of the construct and an integrative framework for research. *Information Systems Research, 9*(2), 126–163.

Markus, M. L. (1990). Toward a critical mass theory of interactive media. In J. Fulk & C. Steinfield (eds), *Organizations and Communication Technology* (pp. 194–218). Newbury Park, Calif.: Sage.

Markus, M. L. (1994). Electronic mail as the medium of managerial choice. *Organization Science, 5*(4), 502–527.

Maznevski, M. L. & Chudoba, K. M. (2000). Bridging space over time: global virtual team dynamics and effectiveness. *Organization Science, 11*(5), 473–492.

Mishra, A. K. (1996). Organizational responses to crisis: the centrality of trust. In R. M. Kramer & T. R. Tyler (eds), *Trust in Organizations: Frontiers of Theory and Research* (pp. 261–287). Thousand Oaks, Calif.: Sage.

Mohrman, S. A. (1999). The context for geographically dispersed teams and networks. In Cary L. Cooper & D. M. Rousseau (eds), *Trends in Organizational Behavior*, Vol. 6: *The Virtual Organization* (pp. 63–80). Chichester, UK: John Wiley & Sons.

Mohrman, S. A., Cohen, S. G., & Mohrman, A. M. (1995). *Designing Team-based Organizations*. San Francisco: Jossey-Bass.

Mowshowitz, A. (1994). Virtual organization: a vision of management in the information age. *The Information Society, 10*, 267–288.

O'Hara-Devereaux, M. & Johansen, R. (1994). *Global Work: Bridging Distance, Culture, and Time*. San Francisco: Jossey-Bass.

Orlikowski, W. J. (1992). The duality of technology: rethinking the concept of technology in organizations. *Organization Science, 3*(3).

Parker, E. A. (1998). Distance learning. *Computerworld*, March 25.
Schein, E. H. (1985). *Organizational Culture and Leadership*. San Francisco: Jossey-Bass.
Scott, W. R. (1995). *Institutions and Organizations*. Thousand Oaks, Calif.: Sage.
Shellenbarger, S. (1997). Madison Avenue may need to alter image of 90s telecommuter. *The Wall Street Journal*, B1.
Sparrow, P. R. & Daniels, K. D. (1999). Human resource management and the virtual organization: mapping the future research issues. In Cary L. Cooper & D. M. Rousseau (eds), *Trends in Organizational Behavior*, Vol. 6: *The Virtual Organization* (pp. 45–61). Chichester, UK: John Wiley & Sons.
Staples, D. S., Hulland, J. S., & Higgins, C. A. (1999). A self-efficacy theory explanation for the management of remote workers in virtual organizations. *Organization Science, 10*(6), 758–776.
Tapscott, D. (1996). *The Digital Economy: Promise and Peril in the Age of Networked Intelligence*. New York: McGraw-Hill.
Tapscott, D., Ticoll, D., & Lowy, A. (2000). *Digital Capital: Harnessing the Power of Business Webs*, Cambridge, Mass.: Harvard Business School Press.
Townsend, A. M., DeMarie, S., & Hendrickson, A. R. (1998). Virtual teams: technology and the workplace of the future. *Academy of Management Executive, 12*(3), 17–28.
Trevino, L. K., Daft, R. L., & Lengel, R. H. (1990). Understanding managers' media choices: a symbolic interactionist perspective. In J. Fulk & C. Steinfield (eds), *Organizations and Communication Technology* (pp. 71–94). Newbury Park, Calif.: Sage.
Tuckman, B. W. (1965). Developmental sequence in small groups. *Psychological Bulletin, 63*(5), 384–399.
University of Maryland, R. H. Smith School of Business (1999). Harnessing the power of netcentricity: a national research agenda, sponsored by DARPA, study conducted by R. H. Smith School of Business, University of Maryland.
Warkentin, M. E., Sayeed, L., & Hightower, R. (1997). Virtual teams versus face-to-face teams: an exploratory study of a web-based conference system. *Decision Sciences, 28*(4), 975–996.
Webster, J. & Trevino, L. K. (1995). Rational and social theories as complementary explanations of communication media choices: two policy capturing studies. *Academy of Management Journal, 38*, 1544–1572.
Weisenfeld, B. M., Raghuram, S., & Garud, R. (1999a). Communication patterns as determinants of organizational identification in a virtual organization. *Organization Science, 10*(6), 777–790.
Weisenfeld, B. M., Raghuram, S., & Garud, R. (1999b). Managers in a virtual context: the experience of self-threat and its effects on virtual work organizations. In Cary L. Cooper & D. M. Rousseau (eds), *Trends in Organizational Behavior*, Vol. 6: *The Virtual Organization* (pp. 31–44). Chichester, UK: John Wiley & Sons.
Williams, S. R. & Wilson, R. L. (1997). Group support systems, power, and influence in an organization: a field study. *Decision Sciences, 28*(4), 911–937.

22

DESIGNING ORGANIZATIONS FOR LARGE-SCALE PRODUCT DEVELOPMENT

THE ROLE OF COOPERATIVE WORK TEAMS

Robert Drazin, Robert K. Kazanjian, and Maureen Blyler

The focus of theories of innovation, for the most part, emphasizes either individuals or small groups, with little or no recognition of task interdependencies between units or within the broad organizational system. Exceptions to this rule acknowledge that innovation must be coordinated and integrated across functional areas, and usually suggest matrix management or heavyweight project teams (Clark & Fujimoto, 1991) as a way of organizing disparate knowledge development. Researchers have focused primarily on examining innovation at more micro-levels of analysis (i.e. for individuals, work units, or small project teams), and modeling this as a discrete task largely isolated from broader organizational and operational pressures (Souder, 1987). Such studies investigate innovation in situations where an individual or small team is assigned a narrow, bounded design task or problem and seem most relevant to small team-based new product development in companies such as 3M, Sony, or Thermos (Dumaine, 1993; Peters, 1988).

For example, consider Rubbermaid's successful approach to innovation in plastics. Multi-function groups are organized around a related set of product extensions. Creative individuals from all functions develop ideas and then integrate those ideas in the context of small to moderate-sized teams. Leadership, strategy, and resources are applied to the teams to develop a conducive context for generating ideas and then sharing those ideas across functions. The barriers that traditionally exist between functions are broken down when the multi-function team identifies with the broader problem of innovating and not with the functional area. Thus, innovation and creativity have been related to constructs as varied as: team cohesiveness, diversity, tenure, and degree of cooperation among group members (Andrews, 1979; Drazin & Schoonhoven, 1996; King & Anderson, 1990; Payne, 1990); job design (Amabile, 1988; Kanter, 1988), supervisory style (Stahl & Koser, 1978; West, 1989); and the provision of performance feedback (Carson & Carson, 1993).

The contribution of such research notwithstanding, most models of innovation tend to be less applicable to some newly emerging contexts (Dougherty, 2001). Innovative products,

International Handbook of Organizational Teamwork and Cooperative Working. Edited by M. A. West, D. Tjosvold, and K. G. Smith.

marked by high task interdependence, long duration, and large scale have become increasingly common in practice (DeMaio, Verganti, & Corso, 1994). Examples include development of a new aircraft (Horwitch, 1982; Sabbagh, 1996), new automobiles (Clark & Fujimoto, 1991; Quinn & Pacquette, 1988), space projects at NASA (Sayles & Chandler, 1971) and defense contracting (Scudder et al., 1989). Although such venues provide a very challenging environment for the pursuit of creative design outputs, they have been largely overlooked in the research on product innovation.

One of the most detailed examples of a single, highly complex organizational new product effort is described in Sabbagh's (1996) account of the development of the new Boeing 777 aircraft. By any standard the project was large and lengthy; the 777 ultimately contained over 4 million discrete components, was priced at more than $100 million per aircraft, and took $5^1/_2$ years to complete. Other examples of large complex, innovative, projects include the development of the B-2 "Stealth" bomber (Argyres, 1999), or the development of enterprise-wide software conversions by firms such as SAP and PeopleSoft. In projects such as these, innovation is critical to the success of the effort, yet the context is quite different from that modeled in traditional literature.

Whether implemented at the level of the small multifunctional teams, or in more complex settings involving a large number of teams, the problem of product innovation is always one of creating a division of labor and then integrating the knowledge developed (Burns & Stalker, 1961; Lawrence & Lorsch, 1967). The individuals or teams assigned to the task of designing such new products break down the overall product design into a series of discrete design problems. Analysis of these design problems demonstrates gaps where existing technologies, established design standards, and accepted approaches are inadequate. Through processes of experiential learning, including problem reframing, brainstorming, hypotheses generation, and trial and error testing, creative solutions emerge to fill the gaps; thus, existing technical knowledge is extended and new technical knowledge is developed within the organization. This process, which institutionalizes such new technological knowledge into organizational routines that become embodied in products and processes, constitutes technological learning (Leonard-Barton, 1992). All of this knowledge development occurs among groups that are separated into a division of labor around the innovation process. The innovation process is thus cast as a problem of developing knowledge in multiple domains and then integrating that knowledge together into a cohesive whole in the form of a viable product or service.

In this chapter, our purpose is to investigate how complex product innovation is related to complex organizational architectures. In particular, we are concerned with how innovation unfolds over time across multiple teams, and how it is influenced by a fluid, highly complex organizational architecture characterized by high degrees of interdependence and integration. In the next section, we discuss the problems of organizing very large, complex projects into organizational architectures composed of multiple, multifunctional teams, drawing heavily on the work of Alexander (1964). In the second section, we describe three levels of interdependence embedded in the architectures of large, complex projects. These interdependencies have the potential to generate inconsistencies, problems, and, at times, crises within the design process, all of which have the potential to enhance or hamper the innovation process. In the final section, we discuss the implications of our model for theory development and empirical research on organization design theory and perspectives on new product development.

ORGANIZATIONAL ARCHITECTURES FOR COMPLEX PROJECTS

Much of the literature on large, complex projects is grounded in research related to innovation and, more particularly, new product development. One common theme in this literature is the central role of organizational design to new product development success (Brown & Eisenhardt, 1995; Slappendel, 1996; Verona, 1999). As Gerwin and Moffat (1997) and Loch and Terwiesch (1998) note, concurrent engineering has emerged as an organizing scheme for new product initiatives. Historically, in many organizations, functional design tasks such as product design, manufacturing process design, and procurement were conducted sequentially. Concurrent engineering is the process of pursuing these tasks simultaneously. It integrates new product development by allowing participants making upstream decisions (e.g. product design) to consider the downstream (e.g. manufacturing process design, procurement) implications (Gerwin & Moffat, 1997). This process is typically facilitated through the extensive use of information technology tools such as computer-aided design and computer-aided manufacturing (Argyres, 1999; Cordero, 1991). Associated benefits include reduced time to market, reduced development costs, and the development of more competitive products (Imai, Nonaka, & Takeuchi, 1985; Liker & Hull, 1993).

Innovation is central to the tasks associated with new product development. Product design engineers must deconstruct the product into major subsystems and then into components. A new leading edge product may specify components that must be more durable, but also lighter than components of earlier products. Similarly, manufacturing process engineers may be presented with specifications that call for faster manufacturing cycles for a product that may be more complex than previous products. In both cases, existing knowledge may be inadequate to satisfy the new specifications, requiring designers to engage in creative behaviors such as brainstorming, searching for insights from seemingly unrelated contexts, and experimenting with emerging but unproven approaches.

The critical role of teams in fostering creativity and innovation has long been established. Bennis and Biederman (1997) richly describe the "creative genius" of team efforts within firms such as Disney, Lockheed, Xerox, and Apple. However, the question of how to configure such groups is a critical problem of any new product development effort. A central component of the implementation of concurrent engineering is the deployment of multi-functional teams (MFTs) (Clark & Fujimoto, 1991; Takeuchi and Nonaka, 1986). Clark, Chew, and Fujimoto (1987), Gupta and Wilema (1990), and Womack, Jones, and Roos (1990) have all argued that the use of MFTs creates clear benefits. Clark and Fujimoto (1991), in their global study of product development practices in the auto industry, found that the use of MFTs was a critical factor influencing success. Similarly, Eisenhardt and Tabrizi (1995) also found that the use of MFTs shortened development cycles in their study of new product development in the global computer industry. Although evidence clearly supports the use of MFTs, there is little in this literature which captures the central role of organizational configuration, or what Kusunoki, Nonaka, and Nagata (1998) term "architectural capabilities," in large, highly complex initiatives which might be composed of *multiple, interdependent* MFTs.

In considering how to design organizations for large-scale product development, we draw on the work of Christopher Alexander (1964). Alexander is an architect who became interested in complex design because he saw most architects or designers as returning to "arbitrarily chosen formal orders" (1964, p. 1) when unable to resolve design challenges. His work is centered on how design occurs, in particular when the complexity of the product design outstrips the ability of classic organizations design. Alexander argued that many designers employ established, uninnovative designs that have been demonstrated in practice, rather than innovative forms, due to the demanding requirements presented to them. Increasingly, designers are faced with requirements of "insoluble levels of complexity" (1964, p. 1) characterized by a tremendous number of requirements or factors that need to be taken into account for the resulting design, form, or structure to function.

The "Requirements–Design" Problem

Requirements refer to those fundamentally instrumental criteria that must be met in the creation of a new product or service. Unlike "contingencies" that represent exogenous pressures or factors with which the design shares a close relationship, connection, or affinity, requirements are factors whose very demands must be met to even achieve a design. Requirements are not simple environmental pressures that must be considered; requirements are necessities that must be met literally in the ultimate design of the product. For example, requirement in the design of a watch might include: battery life, readability, fashion, and longevity, stated as specifications. Insoluble complexity is another way of saying that the requirements of today's modern designs are well beyond the cognitive grasp of a single individual or team. Large-scale product development epitomizes insoluble complexity.

Alexander believed that the many requirements of modern designs impose both direct and indirect pressures on the designer. Designers must take each requirement into account. The total of a product's design criteria may be enormous. Further, these requirements also interact with other requirements to yield new requirements. Designers must take such indirect affects into account as well. Figure 22.1 represents these direct and indirect effects: points A, B, C, and D represent single requirements that are essential for the design. Yet the black lines connecting them (e.g. C to A and A to B) are also essential for the design.

For example, municipal planning is an example of the insoluble levels of complexity facing designers. Alexander (a regional planner as well as architect) identified over 100 discrete, significant requirements that a city or urban planner would need to take into account when designing a village in India. From religious or caste rules to water and sanitation needs, Alexander detailed the overwhelming requirements Indian planners would need to

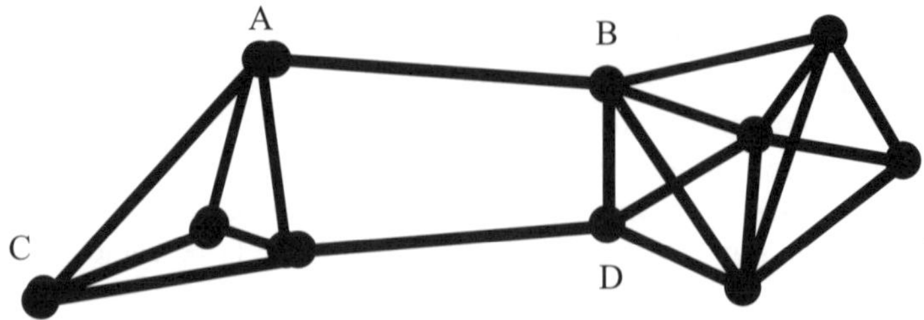

Figure 22.1 Requirements and their interactions: sources of direct and indirect affects on design

meet when structurally organizing a village. These requirements are like points A, B, C, and D. They represent direct effects. Yet again, more requirements resulted once designers started to account for how some of the requirements impacted or interacted with others. For example, some of the villagers' needs for material welfare interact with the dictates of other areas such as social forces and agricultural realities. Thus, while the village's structure would need to ensure sufficient space for housing and commerce, the structure would also have to allow sufficient grazing space for sacred cattle and farmers' cultivation of land. Similarly, while planners would need to ensure access to public or social services for all, planners would have to do so in a way that does not impede the maintenance of caste divisions. Certain castes would not want to interact with other castes in public spaces. Finally, the provision of space for community activities would have to take into account norms requiring marriage to outsiders and the need to often welcome suitors from outside the village to the space.

Indeed, Alexander believed that much of the challenge with design resulted from the subsequent, additional requirements that flowed from the interactions of initial requirements. Alexander also offered the analogy of designing a kettle. At issue with the kettle is a simple design problem of heating water. The kettle itself is not the issue. Rather, the designer faces requirements imposed by the need for, or problem of, heating water until boiling. Solution of the design problem thus demands meeting requirements from a clean pour to a high-temperature threshold to an easy assemble to the ability to contain water to a comfortable hold. Alexander's insight was that while the aforementioned requirements represent challenges to the designer, their interactions pose even greater threats to the designer's creation of an appropriate form. For example, being able to hold the kettle comfortably would prove particularly difficult given the requirement of construction materials that allow for heating of water at high temperatures.

Alexander also noted how not all requirements are apparent or known to the designer from the outset. This imperfect information further contributes to the insoluble complexity of a design, making the design process all the more difficult. Alexander reported that: "What makes design a problem in real world cases is that we are trying to make a diagram for forces whose field we do not understand" (1964, p. 21). As a result, designers must often design iteratively as the form's requirements are only parsimoniously revealed over time.

Alexander offered the concept of *ensemble* to help us understand this point. Alexander likened ensemble to the relationship between a design and the broad context surrounding it. The ensemble thus represents both the known *and* unknown requirements and their interactions with each other that ultimately must be met in the design or form. For example, a biological ensemble equals a natural organism and its physical environment. Ensemble captures the notion that there must be coherence or fit between all of the direct and indirect requirements and the ultimate design. Alexander's notion of ensemble also allows us to recognize the origins of some design's elegance. Indeed, the concept of ensemble suggests that when there is close to total coherence or fit between a design and its requirements, the design will necessarily be elegant—or simply function.

Given the known, unknown, and interactive aspects of design requirements, Alexander proposed that design or the process of achieving good fit between a design and its context is necessarily "a negative process of neutralizing the incongruities, or irritants, or forces which cause misfit" (1964, p. 24). In other words, understanding design means we must understand how the evolving ensemble does or *does not* meet the multitude of requirements at hand. When the ensemble does not meet one or more of the many requirements, then

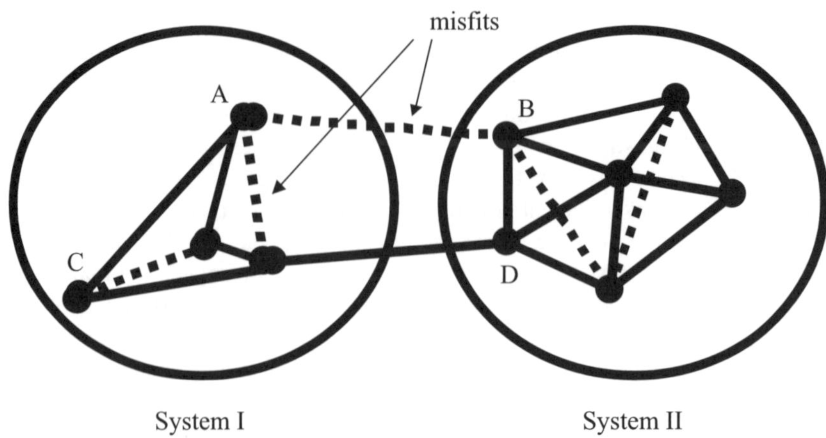

Figure 22.2 Requirements and subsets of requirements: examples of possible misfits with and between systems

misfits result, meaning that there is not coherence or a total level of fit. For example, does the creation of a housing sector within the village under construction in India negatively impact the space made available for cattle grazing and movement or the space available for farmers' cultivation? Or, does the use of one type of material for making the kettle able to boil water and appear aesthetically pleasing prohibit easy assemble? Alexander proposed that designers must attend to the incongruities because the list of possibilities to include when considering the ensemble's fit is infinite. That is, because the list of requirements and their possible interactions number so many, designers must address ensembles' misfits *as they become apparent*. The dotted lines in Figure 22.2 represent possible misfits or some sort of design deviation that must be corrected.

Figure 22.2 depicts two important points. First, the misfits stem from incongruities between single requirements. That is, while the design needs to meet all of the individual requirements (e.g. A, B, C, D, and the other black dots), the design must also accommodate requirements' effects on each other. And because addressing the entire design and its requirements all together at once is cognitively impossible, designers must attend to misfits sequentially, as they arise. Addressing specific instances where disconnects or misfits between the design and requirements are evident is more manageable than attempting to address the ensemble, meaning the design and its entire context. Examining a cluster of misfits is mentally more tractable than trying to understand the fit of the ensemble as a whole.

Moreover, some of the requirements in Figure 22.2 experience misfit with others close by as well as others further away. This is the same as saying some requirements experience disconnect with similar others as well as different others. There can thus be misfit with requirements near and far—or across levels. Incongruities may occur between requirements in immediate spaces as well as between requirements of more distant spaces. Figure 22.3 shows this—that some of the requirements interact more than others.

We can distinguish how some of the requirements interact with some of the other requirements, but not with all of the requirements. For example, points A and C interact more with other requirements nearby than with points B and D. Similarly, points B and D interact more with requirements other than those interacting with A and C. The circles in

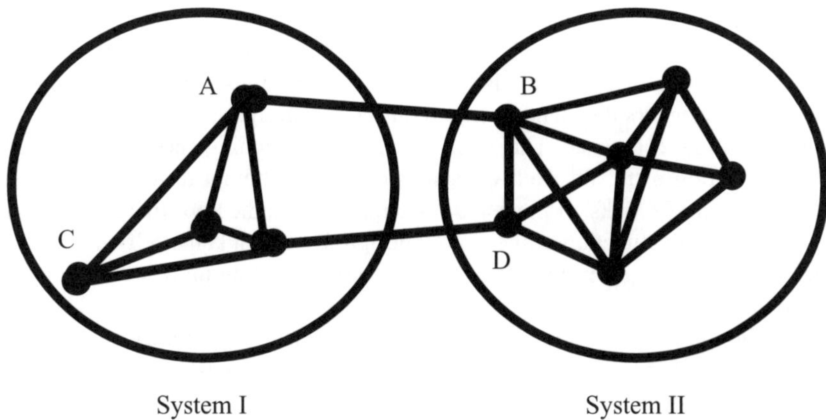

Figure 22.3 Requirements and subsets of requirements: their interactions at multiple levels

Figure 22.3 can thus be seen as representing systems within the ensemble. Points A and B thus indicate a misfit between system I and system II, while points A and C and B and D indicate misfits within systems I and II respectively. In terms of organizational design, multilevel interactions and misfits can be seen in terms of within-group and between-group production challenges. For example, while engineers designing one specific system for a large-scale product may experience disconnect with their individual contributions within that system, engineers generally designing that system may experience disconnect with personnel addressing an entirely different system's requirements.

In considering the design process itself, Alexander distinguished between two camps of designers—whom he labeled the unselfconscious and the self-conscious. We review the unselfconscious and the self-conscious camps here as idealized types at opposite ends of a spectrum in order to better understand how we might best approach the design of organizations responsible for large-scale product development.

The unselfconscious is the camp that thinks little about the design process—they just design. For the unselfconscious, "form-making is learned informally" (Alexander, 1964, p. 36). An artifact of his era, Alexander overemphasized the unselfconscious as "primitive"—form-making by simple imitation and correction based on tradition (e.g. myth, culture). Gradual adaptation is what marks the unselfconscious camp's design processes. As issues and challenges arise that threaten the fit between the requirements and the form, the unselfconscious camp works to adapt or incrementally modify the design: "There is not deliberation in between the recognition of a failure and the reaction to it" (Alexander, 1964, p. 50). Unselfconscious designers recognize misfits and act on them precisely because they focus on the immediate and evident rather than the whole. Reaction is immediate and automatic, natural or primordial. Alexander argued that the unselfconscious camp has a homeostatic or self-organizing structure. In its equilibrium, the unselfconscious is auto-correcting. Missing from the unselfconscious design, however, is a quest for elegance or total fit between the design and its requirements. Unselfconscious design is implicitly resigned to the perennial nature of misfits. They always crop up. Unselfconscious designers take misfits as a given.

In contrast, the self-conscious camp designs deliberately and methodically—aiming for elegance from the outset. Self-conscious form-making follows explicit guidelines. Formal rationality marks self-conscious design. Written or stylized rules govern the design processes and grand attempts are made to anticipate and head off requirement–form misfits. There is nothing automatic or impulsive to the self-conscious approach's form-making. Self-conscious designers thus tend to face requirement–design issues holistically, with an eye toward absolute coherence. That is, self-conscious designing encourages the simultaneous consideration of misfits. Self-conscious designers attempt to resolve misfits all at once, often looking for links within and among misfits with the hope that single pieces are responsible for the dysfunction of the overall design. Design, à la the self-conscious, often becomes like completing a puzzle. If only that magical missing piece were to appear, the design would be complete.

What unifies the unselfconscious and the self-conscious is the presence of misfits in both systems' making of forms or designs. This point is important because misfits do not typically auto-correct or adjust independently. Action is needed. In the case of the unselfconscious, the action is immediate and reflexive albeit incremental. Failure and correction go hand in hand. In the case of the self-conscious, the action is slow-going yet thorough.

In terms of large-scale product development, unselfconscious mechanisms for overcoming misfits may suffice in some situations. Engineers working within a specific system may be able to get rid of incongruities via mutual adjustment or naturally occurring, incremental adaptation. Such engineers may be able to readily and easily adjust to each other's individual contributions to achieve fit within their system.

Conversely, engineers working among different systems may need to overcome misfits via periodic assessments. Differences in time, space, and types of inputs may dictate that they are unable to unselfconsciously overcome misfits. Rather, multilevel misfits may require deliberate, periodic assessments. The entire organization or a significant part of the organization developing a large-scale product may need to periodically stop and take stock of how various systems or groups of requirements are or are not coming together. And again, because of the sheer scale and scope of the endeavor, unselfconscious designing may not be possible. Auto-correction of misfits is more likely to mark within group or system interactions than between groups or system interactions.

Thus, in reviewing the unselfconscious design process, Alexander offered a foil so that we can better understand the challenges facing the self-conscious designer. While both types of design systems ultimately gain more control over the requirement–design fit with time, Alexander implicitly argued that self-conscious designers face greater challenges than the unselfconscious in designing because they approach the misfits holistically, all at the same time. In fact, in doing so, the self-conscious designers work from images or pictures of the relationships between requirements and context.

Constructive diagrams are what Alexander labeled the nascent, rudimentary forms that self-conscious designers often make from the pictures. Alexander offered intersection traffic patterns as an example of a constructive diagram. That is, a form emerges from the drawing of the traffic patterns. For Alexander, these tangible representations of the issues or patterns designers see or view in their heads between requirements and context hold promise for design. How so? Constructive diagrams, if done well, meaning that they take into account the entire ensemble, or the requirements and context as an inseparable couple, can help designers chisel away misfits. Constructive diagrams can provide maps to enable self-conscious designers to more iteratively overcome requirement–design misfits, and in doing so, design in a fashion akin to the unselfconscious.

Complex Architectures for Complex Products

Alexander's perspective on the "requirements–design" problem has application to the organization of highly complex projects. Ordinarily, design or developmental work is organized to reflect the underlying nature of the design requirements (Funk, 1997). Where the products being developed are relatively simple, such as air conditioners or cell phones, this design problem may be quite apparent and easy to organize within a single MFT (Eppinger, 1994; Fujimoto, 1991). In such settings, it is probably the case that the choice of organizing in an MFT is reflective of an unselfconscious organizational design process, with the choice of organizational form the product of tradition and experience.

However, projects that are large and complex present significant and unique organizational design challenges. For instance, the organization design used to complete the Boeing 777 (Sabbagh, 1996) required a hierarchy of over 250 MFTs, embedded in an equally complex project management structure. Although every team had its own area of responsibility, when design changes were needed by one team (as many as 13 000 were forecast at the outset of the process), there were significant implications for many other teams. With the development of the Ford Taurus (Quinn & Pacquette, 1988), a nested hierarchy with a large number of interdependent teams pursued the design in parallel.

It is apparent at Boeing and Ford that the product design problems lie beyond the integrative grasp of a single individual or even that of a small to moderate-sized single group (Alexander, 1964). The corresponding problem of organizing the hundreds or even thousands of individuals assigned to the project is equally complex. Such a unique organizational design problem requires a self-conscious design process where the original conception of the product serves as a "constructive diagram" facilitating the development of a comprehensive and holistic organizational form. The organizational architectures adopted at Boeing and Ford essentially mapped the product design (including systems and subsystems) onto the project organization. Note the parallel correspondence between product design and the design of the organizational architecture to implement that product. So, at Boeing, for instance, the division of teams paralleled the design of the aircraft itself, with teams for each of the major systems such as wings, fuselage, cockpit, etc.

Of course, this initial conception of the product is at best only a fuzzy vision of what the ultimate product will become (despite clearly stated objectives regarding overall product performance, cost, and schedule). The initial organizational configuration is a simplification of the reality of the design process. In simplifying the design of a product, which is itself complex, individual tasks are assigned around some logic of specialization. For example, individuals are often assigned jobs based upon functional tasks to be completed, or a subsystem or component of the product.

Specialization at the individual and group level creates boundaries associated with shared tasks, orientations, and practices, or what Dougherty (1992) calls thought worlds. These boundaries are necessary to avoiding cognitive overload, which might be experienced by individuals working on the project. However, these boundaries then impose interdependencies, which then generate misfits as the design process unfolds, and which must be managed for the design process to progress effectively. Task interdependence exists when the task of one individual or group depends upon the completion of other work by another individual or group (Thompson, 1967; van de Ven, Delbecq, & Koenig, 1976). Interdependence is the main reason groups are formed (van der Vegt, Emans, & van de Vliert, 1998).

The final design of such a creative product cannot be known completely at the outset because it is novel and unique; the design is the result of trial-and-error learning over the course of product development, and from the misfits that emerge from interdependencies across the functions and subsystems. As a result, the corresponding organizational architecture is modified accordingly as the project and its underlying design unfold.

In this chapter, we are interested in understanding interdependent, team-based architectures as contexts for new product development. As Alexander (1964) and others have argued, project architectures for complex design projects create interdependencies at the boundaries of specialized individuals and subgroups. These interdependencies have the potential to generate misfits (i.e. problems and, at times, crises) within the development process which must be reconciled if the new product is to meet its objectives.

ORGANIZATIONAL ARCHITECTURE, INTERDEPENDENCE, AND THE ROLE OF MISFITS

Embedded within the highly differentiated organizational architectures composed of multiple MFTs, such as those described above, are three levels of task interdependence. These are: (1) within-team cross-functional interdependencies, (2) across-team interdependencies, and (3) system-level interdependencies. Although the first of these has been widely discussed in the literature, the latter two have received scant attention. Given the character and degree of interdependence inherent in a complex organizational architecture, as the design process unfolds, misfits occur. These misfits, or design problems, play a central role in the adaptation of the organization design to the product development process.

Within-team Cross-functional Interdependencies

Either implicitly or explicitly, the literatures on project management (Frame, 1994; Larsen & Gobelli, 1988), new product development (Imai, Nonaka, & Takeuchi, 1985; Wheelwright & Clark, 1995), and innovation (Pelz & Andrews, 1976; Tushman & Nadler, 1986) all reinforce the notion that MFTs are preferable to allowing functional units (or subunits) to pursue their tasks in isolation from each other. By creating MFTs, an organization can collect the required skills, experience bases, and functional subspecialties in a setting that allows for greater integration and boundary spanning. Multifunctional teams therefore represent the potential for an integrated definition and solution to problems associated with the development of innovative products and services (Uhl-Bien & Graen, 1998).

The design work of a complex product such as an automobile or aircraft is typically organized around the components of the product itself. As with Boeing's organization of the 777 project team described earlier, each of the major systems of the product might have a dedicated team. Each of these teams was then broken down into smaller sets of MFTs for each subsystem. So, at their core, such projects are composed of small MFTs of specialists (product engineers, manufacturing engineers, software engineers, financial analysts, procurement specialists, etc.) who concentrated their efforts on a subsystem or component of the product.

Inherent in the design of such teams is a degree of task interdependence across team members within the MFTs. Several studies have investigated the effect of task interdependence on individuals within groups and have found a relationship to levels of motivation, responsibility, and satisfaction (Brass, 1985; Hirst, 1988; Kiggundu, 1983). Additionally, several studies have found a relationship of task interdependence to group effectiveness (Saavedra, Earley, & van Dyne, 1993).

The inherent interdependencies existing across the functions *within an individual MFT* often surface misfits that emerge as a constraint in the design process, limiting the field of options to product designers. For example, a product engineer may initially design a component that assumes manufacturing capabilities that are not available, or design a component without knowing its cost implications. By placing different functional specialists in close physical proximity, each can understand the constraints imposed by the requirements of the other functions whose tasks might be positioned earlier in the development process. The MFT setting provides a clear and specific understanding of the true scope of cross-functional complexity, and the opportunity to refine ideas as they are tested with specialists from other functions in a mode of mutual accommodation. Such integration, much of it through face-to-face communication, but increasingly supported by information technology, has multiple benefits (Gerwin & Moffat, 1997; Katz & Allen, 1985). An autonomous MFT facilitates the exercise of technical expertise and creativity (Imai, Nonaka, & Takeuchi, 1985), and speeds the development process (Clark & Fujimoto, 1991). Further, as Sutton and Hargadon (1996) found, face-to-face interactions can affect outcomes positively.

As team members work in an MFT setting, they can develop a better understanding of the capabilities as well as constraints of other functions, and can incorporate that knowledge into the planning and initial designs, making the process of mutual accommodation more efficient over time. After a period of time, team members can develop specific knowledge of the tasks and constraints of their functional peers as well as an understanding of the specific capabilities of each member. Cross-functional interdependence surfaces misfits that constitute constraints on the design process. However, those constraints might actually increase a team's effectiveness, because the team provides a setting that allows for considerable cross-functional integration, coordination, and accommodation.

Across-team Interdependencies

In large-scale project settings, work is often organized across multiple units or teams, potentially numbering into hundreds of MFTs, each working on a component of the overall design. Each team must coordinate and reconcile their own innovation tasks with those of others (Gresov, 1989). Such coordination might be either sequential or reciprocal (Thompson, 1967). In our discussion of MFTs, we noted that teams can be effective in the resolution of misfits resulting from cross-functional interdependencies and hence in the reduction of barriers between functions within teams. As Loch and Terwiesch (1998) discovered in their modeling of concurrent engineering, needs for coordination and information processing are directly related to the number of changes in proposed design, the degree of uncertainty associated with the technology, and the degree of interdependence across groups. Further as Ancona and Caldwell (1992) note, the boundary-spanning literature shows positive relationships between the frequency of lateral communication and performance. However, as MFTs concentrate on their individually assigned tasks, the barriers between teams may be strengthened and the ability to integrate across MFTs proportionally reduced. This cross-team barrier impedes coordination around interdependencies among subsystems of the product being developed.

Misfits in design across MFTs may result as each group optimizes its own component design, but suboptimizes the design of the overall product. In pursuing the maximization of subsystem or component functionality, MFTs encounter circumstances when the design they develop negatively affects the functionality of another MFT working on an interfacing subsystem. An innovative design by one MFT must not only satisfy the goals and assigned specifications of that team, but their design must also fit within a broader system of other components and subsystems which are being developed by other MFTs. Each MFT, therefore, must integrate their decisions with those of other MFTs through a process of mutual adjustment; the adaptation of each team presents problems to the adaptation of other teams (Gresov & Stephens, 1993).

Another cross-team interdependency relates to multiple teams working in similar or related areas. In these cases, a technology or design adopted by one team may be less directly interdependent with that of another team, but each team might learn from each other's successes and failures, realizing some measure of technological synergy (Garud & Nayyar, 1994; Kazanjian & Nayyar, 1994). Further, there may be more direct interdependencies at the system level if serviceability, manufacturability, and maintenance are enhanced by more common use of technologies and components across the product. Interdependencies across MFTs therefore create constraints on the design process, which can only be addressed with high levels of cross-team coordination (Loch & Terwiesch, 1998). As cross-team interdependence increases, so does the amount of coordination and information processing required to resolve the associated design misfits.

System-level Interdependencies

MFTs within large, complex projects pursue their tasks not in isolation, or even in dyadic relation to single teams, but rather within a web of interdependencies with a number of other teams. The organization chart of any project organized into multiple MFTs simply indicates a defined task specialization for each MFT; it does not (and cannot) reflect the interdependencies associated with the tasks of other MFTs. In practice, however, subsystem MFTs must conduct their design tasks within the constraints imposed by these interdependencies. A more accurate depiction of the project organization, which captures these interdependencies, is presented in Figure 22.3, where the nodal points in the diagram represent subsystem MFTs. Clearly, some of the subsystem MFTs face high degrees of interdependence with multiple other teams; they cannot adjust their activities with these other teams without extensive coordination. Alternatively, some subsystem teams may face lower interdependencies and be able to function rather independently. "We may therefore picture the process of [design] as a series of subsystems, all interlinked, yet sufficiently free of one another to adjust independently in a feasible amount of time" (Alexander, 1964, p. 43).

This third type of interdependence, then, which is rarely discussed in the literature, is imposed on MFTs by system-level requirements that cannot be traced back to localized specific source points or teams. Typically, one of the first steps in any product development process is the establishment of product specifications and associated performance capabilities. This is usually accompanied by the development of a general prototype outline of the product.

The design of the product also faces time constraints. Across industries, firms are emphasizing cycle time reduction as a basis of competitive advantage (Stalk & Hout, 1990). Gillette, Intel, HP, and Merck have been offered as examples of firms that gain strategic position based on the cycle time and pace of new production introduction (Brown & Eisenhardt, 1998). Further, as Vesey (1991) found in his study of high-technology product development, products that were six months late in entering the market but were within budget earned one-third less over five years than they would have if they were introduced on time. This places additional stress on all parties to manage to schedule as well as specifications.

Teams are also pressured to reconsider their designs when, at the system level, specifications are not being met. This might be the result of an additive phenomenon across teams, indicating evidence of what Alexander termed a misfit. As some individual MFTs fail to meet their assigned design specifications, and as other MFTs have theirs altered or amended, the design of the overall product might then be imperiled. Even teams which are meeting their assigned design specifications may be asked to search for new approaches which might enhance the design further. Therefore, system-level interdependencies generate misfits that can only be resolved with considerable coordination and redirection of project activities.

Complex projects require a degree of organizational differentiation that matches the character of the product being developed, increasingly incorporating a hierarchy of multiple MFTs. That differentiation creates task interdependence at three levels, each of which generates requirements–design misfits as the design process unfolds. Individual teams create an environment where individuals feel comfortable and motivated to engage in the creative development process, and have access to the skills and resources to pursue creative approaches and designs. In such settings, within-team interdependencies are highlighted quickly due to the inherent task conflicts between product designers and manufacturing engineers, for example.

Across-team and system-level interdependencies, which require coordination and integration with a few or all MFTs, have the potential to generate their own misfits. These may require considerable coordination and integration, if not organizational redesign, to resolve.

The Role of Requirements–Design Misfits in Organizational Redesign

As the development process unfolds, misfits between the current design of the product and the product requirements or specifications become apparent. These may present themselves as local misfits at the within- or across-team level. Alternatively, they may emerge at the project level occasionally, constituting what the organization experiences as a crisis. The more extreme misfits can potentially alter the configuration of the project architecture. The effect of these extreme misfits is informed by research related to the effect of crises on organizations. As Tjosvold (1984, p. 130) states, "crises occur when the decision makers perceive that valued interests are seriously threatened, feel uncertain that a practical response will definitely protect these interests, and believe that a quick response is needed." This is consistent with Habermas (1975), who argues that a crisis occurs when the structure of a social system allows for fewer possibilities for problem solving than are necessary for the continued existence of the system. In settings of highly complex projects, we define a crisis as occurring when a project performance is noted to be seriously below plan, or when conditions require that the project plan be significantly altered in the short term.

Extreme misfits, that might constitute a crisis for an organization, can potentially result from the task complexity and interdependence associated with designing large systems. The misfit, endogenous to the project itself, emanates from the "... structurally inherent system-imperatives that are incompatible and cannot be integrated" (Habermas, 1975, p. 2). For example, system-level interdependencies may be seen to place one or more of the project's objectives related to specifications, budget, or schedule at risk.

At the outset of the project, the overall organizational architecture must be viewed as an initial conceptual map of the design of the product. At that point, MFTs are assigned certain objectives, allocated resources, and are delegated the authority to make design decisions. This is necessary to reduce the complexity and uncertainty inherent in the development process, and to establish an initial allocation of responsibilities, authorities, and resources. However, this architecture is neither a perfect nor comprehensive map of the product itself, but rather is a simplification of the design process (Alexander, 1964). Given the uncertainty and complexity of the development process, the decision-making roles must be viewed as permeable, ambiguous, and likely to change over time. Roles and responsibilities cannot always be preset through bureaucratic rules; it is not possible to set each individual team's autonomy at the start of the project and assume that it will stay fixed. The initial allocation of team-level authority and autonomy must change to reflect the emergence of the final design (Gerwin & Moffat, 1997). We suggest that the emergence of a crisis will potentially alter the configuration of the project architecture.

Hirschhorn (1988) and Hackman (1990) have argued that managers are generally delegative toward their work teams until problems emerge, at which point their mode of interaction may change and they may intervene directly in internal group decisions. So, when a project experiences an event significant enough to be labeled a crisis, the discretion allowed teams to pursue their tasks autonomously may change. Both Kahn and Kram (1994) and Gerwin and Moffat (1997) have discussed the authorizing/reauthorizing of discretion in team settings. For example, teams may be authorized greater decision-making latitude, allowing them to pursue emergent but uncertain solutions which might also be riskier and costlier. Alternatively, they might be constrained in the type and character of decisions they are allowed to make or project managers might review their work more closely.

The effect of such a crisis will be to shift the allocation of responsibility, authority, and resources across MFTs to those capable of solving the crisis (Pfeffer & Salancik, 1978). This may alter the role and autonomy of those MFTs that are determined by senior management to have offered solutions that may significantly alleviate the problem. The result would be a greater delegation of authority and allocation of resources to the designated MFTs, which would allow that team(s) to assert their priorities as primary. In other words, the selected MFTs would immediately face less cross-team and system-level interdependencies. Correspondingly, this would require other teams to be deauthorized and, as such, constrained in their technical approaches or in the resources made available to them.

DISCUSSION

This chapter suggests that the reality of product development is not accounted for in the literature on teams and organization design. To date, most of the extant literature has made a set of assumptions regarding the context in which innovation occurs. Perhaps first and foremost among these assumptions is that the products (or services) being developed are discrete, small to moderate in size, and of limited time duration. The assumptions about products lead to assumptions about organization design. Because products are small and hence cognitively manageable, and because they occur over a bounded period of time, usually coinciding with knowable or predictable outcomes, they are thus manageable by a single MFT. These assumptions are useful for a high percentage of design situations, but they fall short of an accurate description of large, exceedingly complex products whose design unfolds over the course of many years. We have argued that different metaphors are needed to adequately understand this type of product and organization design.

However, much as we believe that the context is different for products of massive complexity, we still see two building blocks in common with our model and models appropriate for smaller, less complex products. At the heart of both product development efforts are MFTs and the need for integration. However, the integration we propose occurs not only within the MFT but also across MFTs and at a broader level of systems coherence. While current literature can guide managers to understand how to better understand what is going on inside the team, it does not deal with what goes on across teams. Here, we argue that misfits across MFTs are what should drive the entire design. According to Alexander, whom we draw on substantially, good design equates to a process that reduces misfits in the most effective and most efficient manner.

We further argued that crises are inevitable in large-scaled complex projects as the organizational architecture, developed to *initially* deal with the complexity of the project, can never anticipate all the design issues that will emerge. When MFTs are created to deal with portions of the product's design, they focus solely on the part of the design for which they are responsible. However, design changes in one part of the project can ripple throughout the entire organization, with a solution from one team creating a constraint on others. In this way, both cross-team and system-level interdependencies begin to manifest themselves within the project. Eventually, the entire system can no longer handle the ensuing design problem and a crisis emerges.

Crises have a positive function in that they provide for periodic opportunities to engage in system-wide learning if creative solutions are put forward which allow the crisis to be resolved. Crises can affect both the allocation of resources and the delegation of authority to MFTs to pursue more novel approaches. The role of critical problems or crises emerges from this study as central to the process of creativity and organizational learning (Normann, 1977; Rhenman, 1973). Miles (1982) argued that organizational learning occurs in response to immediate problems, imbalances, difficulties, or performance gaps. The intra-organizational conflicts and tensions created by these immediate problems serve a constructive function in stimulating search behaviors that lead to creative solutions. Crises require that the organization allocate additional resources to develop new knowledge, acquire existing knowledge from outside sources (which may be new to the firm), and integrate these into unique solutions. It is important to note that the origins of such crises are grounded in the organizational architecture's failure to adequately handle the scope and complexity of cross-team and system-level interdependencies. Such failures are functional in that they identify interdependencies that must be addressed in the design process, and correspondingly they create opportunities for creativity necessary to solve design problems.

While crises may occur naturally in the progress of a project, they may also be staged intentionally from within the firm to suit the purposes of an individual or group. A created sense of crisis among MFTs may intensify their effort level and expedite learning. The proactive "construction" of crises within new product development projects has been identified by Nonaka (1994) in his discussion of Canon, by Prahalad and Hamel (1994) in their discussion of Komatsu, and by Kim (1998) in a discussion of designing automobiles at Hyundai.

The leader of an MFT might time the introduction of a preferred design approach with a crisis that might favor its acceptance. For example, in a study of internal corporate venturing, Burgelman and Sayles (1986) describe the case of a research scientist who had been developing new, innovative types of products, but was having difficulty securing corporate funding. With a dramatic shift in market conditions, the company faced a crisis in new product growth opportunities. The scientist used these events as an opportunity to reintroduce his proposal, which was accepted.

Future Research

Crises may be only one way to surface misfits. Other, more rational and planned approaches may be less traumatic to the organization, but we do expect to see both types of mechanism at work. One avenue for both normative and descriptive research would be on how firms do and should surface misfits.

Our suggestions in this area are based on a model of misfits we have been developing. We hypothesize that there are several forms of misfits. First are those misfits that are in potentia. That is that they exist, but only in the minds and plans of designers, and are not yet explicit. For example, as designers in individual MFTs develop and test creative solutions to the components they have been assigned, they exist only cognitively. A designer may create a new interface for a component that would affect not only the team working on the other side of the interface, but other teams as well. The interface might change to assist the focal team to meet its objectives, but put another team at a disadvantage. At this point in experimentation and testing, the focal team may be exploring several options and not wish to involve downstream teams until the design is solidified. The misfit lives in potentia because there is some probability that the new interface will be put into the final product design.

Other forms of misfit are tangible. Components take shape in physical form, most likely in prototypes, where the design misfit is easily identified. It is here that spillover effects are most likely to be recognized. A new interface may require not only physical and mechanical matching, but also changes in electrical or other requirements. While the physical interface problem is solvable among two teams, spillover misfits may involve multiple teams and the interactions may require multiple teams to coordinate their efforts.

One solution to the misfit problem may be to simulate the design through computer programs. CAD/CAM systems have been designed to highlight common forms of misfit. The designers of electricity plants face a complex problem of laying out the myriad of pipes and cables that run under a plant in such a way that they do not interfere with each other. Waiting for the physical plant to be built before detecting the misfits would be expensive and time consuming. Thus, plant engineers have designed "interference" programs that take the design inputs of multiple teams and model the designs to highlight where pipes and cabling interfere with each other. In this way, the most common forms of misfits can be identified before the plant is built.

Misfits that affect system-wide design parameters can also be surfaced in a periodic manner. Critical performance criteria for a product can be assessed through simulation or prototype testing. For example, an automobile or plane may have requirement of weight, cost, and performance. While these are overall performance metrics for the entire product, they can be used to pinpoint misfits occurring within teams or across teams. If a new automobile exceeds its required weight it will point to areas of component design that need to be addressed.

Other mechanisms might be used to identify misfits. Individuals who are members of functional areas comprise the basic element of all the MFTs. These individuals could be assigned on a rotating basis to adjoining teams. In this manner, misfits that exist only in the minds of designers could be circulated among potentially affected teams. Other human resource practices could assist in integrating MFTs. Reward systems could be introduced that require team members to excel not only in the design of their own teams' components, but also to excel in the design of related teams' components. That is, reward for the early surface of misfits.

Most complex projects are composed of layers of components. An automobile engine is usually associated with a set of related components called the power train. This involves the transaxle, the fuel delivery system, and the exhaust system. Thus, the power train comprises an intermediate, highly interdependent set of components. Periodic reviews of misfits may be possible at the level of these intermediate systems. They are cognitively less complex than the entire ensemble and likely to be managed within the same hierarchy of project managers. Periodic reviews within these intermediate subsystems would serve to reduce misfits that usually surface later in the project life cycle.

One path for additional study involves how large, project-based new-product development efforts change their structures over time. A major premise throughout this chapter has been that the initial design of the organization matches the early, fuzzy vision of product. This initial organization design attempts to map out the interdependencies of the initial product onto the organization. That is, it is management's first attempt to capture the complexity of the product in the array of MFTs it creates. We also noted that as the product is developed it will take paths unforeseen at the outset. The product design may be altered due to changes in customer requirements, the surfacing of major misfits, or creative developments that improve the performance of the product. All of these change possibilities suggest that the original organizational design will no longer match the original product design and that organizational changes will be inevitable. We expect that these changes will primarily show up in shifts in the number, composition, and reporting relationships of MFTs. Such organizational changes will be attempts to remap the changed product design onto a new organization that will reflect new interdependencies between MFTs. Researchers could investigate both the antecedents and consequences of these changes. Consequences of the changes could include the surfacing of new misfits as new teams or transformed teams attempt integration where none had been before.

REFERENCES

Alexander, C. (1964). *Notes on the Synthesis of Form*. Cambridge, Mass.: Harvard University Press.

Amabile, T. M. (1988). A model of creativity and innovation in organizations. In B. M. Staw & L. L. Cummings (eds), *Research in Organizational Behavior* (Vol. 10, pp. 123–167). Greenwich, Conn.: JAI Press.

Ancona, D. & Caldwell, D. (1992). Bridging the boundary: external activity and performance in organizational teams. *Administrative Science Quarterly, 37*, 634–665.

Andrews, F. M. (1979). *Scientific Productivity*. Cambridge, UK: Cambridge University Press.

Argyres, N. S. (1999). The impact of information technology on coordination: evidence from the B-2 "stealth" bomber. *Organization Science, 10*, 162–180.

Bennis, W. & Biederman, P. W. (1997). *Organizing Genius: The Secrets of Creative Collaboration.* Reading, Mass.: Addison-Wesley.

Brass, D. J. (1985). Technology and the structuring of jobs: employee satisfaction, performance and influence. *Organization Behavior and Human Decision Processes, 35*, 216–240.

Brown, S. L. & Eisenhardt K. M. (1995). Product development: past research, present findings, and future directions. *Academy of Management Review, 20*, 343–378.

Brown, S. L. & Eisenhardt K. M. (1998). *Competing on the Edge: Strategy as Structured Chaos.* Boston, Mass.: Harvard Business School Press.

Burgelman, R. A. & Sayles, L. R. (1986). *Inside Corporate Innovation: Strategy, Structure and Managerial Skills.* New York: The Free Press.

Burns, T. & Stalker, G. M. (1961). *The Management of Innovation.* London: Tavistock.

Carson, P. P. & Carson, K. D. (1993). Managing creativity enhancement through goal setting and feedback. *Journal of Creative Behavior, 27*, 36–45.

Clark, K. B., Chew, W. B., & Fujimoto, T. (1987). Product development in the world auto industry. *Brookings Papers on Economic Activity* (Vol. 3, pp. 729–781). New York: Brookings Institution.

Clark, K. B. & Fujimoto, T. (1991). *Product Development Performance: Strategy, Organization and Management in the World Auto Industry.* Boston, Mass.: Harvard Business School Press.

Cordero, R. (1991). Managing for speed to avoid product obsolescence: a survey of techniques. *Journal of Product Innovation Management, 8*, 283–294.

DeMaio, A., Verganti, R., & Corso, M. (1994). A multi-project framework for new product development. *European Journal of Operational Research, 78*, 178–191.

Dougherty, Deborah (1992). Interpretive barriers to successful product innovation in large firms. *Organizational Science, 3*, 179–203.

Dougherty, Deborah (2001). Reimaging the differentiation and integration of work for sustained product innovation. *Organization Science, 5*, 612–631.

Drazin, R. & Schoonhoven, C. B. (1996). Community, population, and organization effects on innovation: a multilevel perspective. *Academy of Management Journal, 39*(5), 1065–1083.

Dumaine, B. (1993). Payoff from the new management. *Fortune*, December 13, 103–110.

Eisenhardt, K. M. & Tabrizi, B. N. (1995). Accelerating adaptive processes: product innovation in the global computer industry. *Administrative Science Quarterly, 40*, 84–110.

Eppinger, S. (1994). A model-based method for organizing tasks in product development. *Research and Engineering Design, 6*, 27–39.

Frame, J. D. (1994). *The New Project Management.* San Francisco: Jossey-Bass.

Fujimoto, T. (1991). Product integrity and the role of the designer as integrator. *Design Management Journal, 2*, 29–34.

Funk, J. L. (1997). Concurrent engineering and the underlying structure of the design problem. *IEEE Transactions on Engineering Management, 44*, 305–315.

Garud, R. & Nayyar, P. R. (1994). Transformative capacity: continual structuring by intertemporal technology transfer. *Strategic Management Journal, 15*, 365–386.

Gerwin, D. & Moffat, L. (1997). Withdrawal of team autonomy during concurrent engineering. *Management Science, 43*, 1275–1287.

Gresov, C. (1989). Exploring fit and misfit with multiple contingencies. *Administrative Science Quarterly, 34*, 431–453.

Gresov, C. & Stephens, C. (1993). The context of interunit influence attempts. *Administrative Science Quarterly, 38*, 252–271.

Gupta, A. K. & Wilemon, D. L. (1990). Accelerating the development of technology-based new products. *California Management Review, 32*(2), 24–44.

Habermas, J. (1975). *Legitimation Crisis.* Boston: Beacon Press.

Hackman, J. R. (1990). Creating more effective workgroups in organizations. In J. R. Hackman (ed.), *Groups That Work (and Those That Don't)* (pp. 479–504). San Francisco: Jossey-Bass.

Hirschhorn, L. (1988). *The Workplace Within.* Cambridge, Mass.: MIT Press.

Hirst, M. K. (1988). Intrinsic motivation as influenced by task interdependence and goal setting. *Journal of Applied Psychology, 73*(1), 96–101.

Horwitch, M. (1982). *Clipped Wings: The American SST Conflict*. Cambridge, Mass.: MIT Press.
Imai, K., Nonaka, I., & Takeuchi, H. (1985). Managing the new product development process: how Japanese companies learn and unlearn. In K. Clark, R. Hayes, & C. Lorenz (eds), *The Uneasy Alliance* (pp. 553–561). Boston: Harvard Business School Press.
Kahn, W. A. & Kram, K. (1994). Authority at work: internal models and their organizational consequences. *Academy of Management Review, 19*, 17–50.
Kanter, R. M. (1988). When a thousand flowers bloom: structural, collective, and social conditions for innovation in organization. In B. M. Staw & L. L. Cummings (eds), *Research in Organization Behavior* (Vol. 10, pp. 169–211). Greenwich, Conn.: JAI Press.
Katz, R. & Allen, T. (1985). Project performance and the locus of influence in the R&D matrix. *Academy of Management Journal, 28*, 67–87.
Kazanjian, R. K. & Nayyar, P. R. (1994). Attaining technological synergies in diversified firms. In M. W. Lawless & L. R. Gomez-Mejia (eds), *Advances in Global High-technology Management* (Vol. 4, pp. 121–138). Greenwich, Conn.: JAI Press.
Kiggundu, M. N. (1983). Task interdependence and job design: test of a theory. *Organization Behavior and Human Performance, 31*, 145–172.
Kim, L. (1998). Crisis construction and organizational learning: capacity building in catching-up at Hyundai Motor. *Organization Science, 9*, 506–521.
King, N. & Anderson, N. (1990). Innovation in working groups. In M. A. West & J. L. Farr (eds), *Innovation and Creativity at Work* (pp. 81–100). Chichester, UK: Wiley.
Kusunoki, K., Nonaka, I., & Nagata, A. (1998). Organizational capabilities in product development of Japanese firms: a conceptual framework and empirical findings. *Organization Science, 9*, 699–718.
Larson, E. W. & Gobelli, D. H. (1988). Matrix management: contradictions and insights. *California Management Review, 29*(4), 126–138.
Lawrence, P. W. & Lorsch, J. W. (1967). *Organization and Environment: Managing Differentiation and Integration.* Boston: Harvard.
Leonard-Barton, D. (1992). Core capabilities and core rigidities: a paradox in managing new product development. *Strategic Management Journal, 13*, 111–126.
Liker, J. K. & Hull, P. (1993). What works in concurrent engineering? Sorting through the barrage of practices. Paper presented at the Academy of Management Conference, Atlanta, Ga.
Loch, C. H. & Terwiesch, C. (1998). Communication and uncertainty in concurrent engineering. *Management Science, 44*, 1032–1048.
Miles, R. H. (1982). *Coffin Nails and Corporate Strategies*. Englewood Cliffs, NJ: Prentice-Hall.
Nonaka, I. (1994). A dynamic theory of organizational knowledge creation. *Organization Science, 5*, 14–37.
Normann, R. (1977). *Management for Growth*. New York: Wiley.
Payne, R. (1990). The effectiveness of research teams: a review. In M. A. West & J. L. Farr (eds), *Innovation and Creativity at Work* (pp. 101–122). Chichester, UK: Wiley.
Pelz, D. C. & Andrews, F. M. (1976). *Scientists in Organizations: Productive Climates for Research and Development*. Ann Arbor, Mich.: Institute for Social Research.
Peters, T. (1988). The mythology of innovation, or a skunkworks tale, part II. In M. L. Tushman & W. L. Moore (eds), *Readings in the Management of Innovation* (pp. 138–147). Cambridge, Mass.: Ballinger Publishing Co.
Pfeffer, J. & Salancik, G. R. (1978). *The External Control of Organizations: A Resource Dependence Perspective*. New York: Harper & Row.
Prahalad, C. K. & Hamel, G. (1994). *Competing for the Future*. Boston: Harvard Business School Press.
Quinn, J. B. & Pacquette, P. (1988). Ford: Team Taurus, Amos Tuck School, Dartmouth College.
Rhenman, E. (1973). *Organization Theory for Long Range Planning*. London: Wiley.
Saavedra, R., Earley, P. C., & van Dyne, L. (1993). Complex interdependence in task performing groups. *Journal of Applied Psychology, 78*, 61–72.
Sabbagh, K. (1996). *Twenty-first-century Jet: The Making and Marketing of the Boeing 777*. New York: Scribner.
Sayles, L. R. & Chandler, M. K. (1971). *Managing Large Systems: Organizations of the Future*. New York: Harper & Row.

Scudder, G., Schroeder, R., van de Ven, A., Seilor, G., & Wiseman, R. M. (1989). Managing complex innovation: the case of defense contracting. In A. van de Ven, H. Angle, & M. S. Poole (eds), *Research on the Management of Innovation: The Minnesota Studies* (Ch. 12, pp. 401–438). New York: Ballinger.

Slappendel, C. (1996). Perspectives on innovation in organizations. *Organization Studies, 17*, 107–124.

Souder, W. (1987). *Managing New Product Innovation*. Lexington, Mass.: Lexington Books.

Stahl, M. J. & Koser, M. C. (1978). Weighted productivity in R&D: some associated individual and organizational variables. *IEEE Transactions on Engineering Management, EM-25*, 20–24.

Stalk, G. & Hout, T. M. (1990). *Competing against Time: How Time-based Competition is Reshaping Global Markets*. New York: Free Press.

Sutton, R. I. & Hargadon, A. (1996). Brainstorming groups in context: effectiveness in a product design firm. *Administrative Science Quarterly, 41*, 685–718.

Takeuchi, H. & Nonaka, I. (1986). The new product development game. *Harvard Business Review, 64*(1), 137–146.

Thompson, J. D. (1967). *Organizations in Action*. New York: McGraw-Hill.

Tjosvold, D. (1984). Effects of crisis orientation on managers' approach to controversy in decision making. *Academy of Management Journal, 27*, 130–138.

Tushman, M. L. & Nadler, D. A. (1986). Organizing for innovation. *California Management Review, 28*(2), 74–92.

Uhl-Bien, M. & Graen, G. B. (1998). Individual self-management: analysis of professionals' self-managing activities in functional and cross-functional work teams. *Academy of Management Journal, 41*, 340–350.

Van de Ven, A. H., Delbecq, A. L., & Koenig, R. (1976). Determinants of coordination modes within organizations. *American Sociological Review, 41*, 322–338.

Van der Vegt, G., Emans, B., & van de Vliert, E. (1998). Motivating effects of task and outcome interdependence in work teams. *Group & Organization Management, 23*, 124–143.

Verona, G. (1999). A resource-based view of product development. *Academy of Management Review, 24*, 132–142.

Vesey, J. T. (1991). The new competitors: they think in terms of speed to market. *Academy of Management Executive, 5*(2), 23–33.

West, M. A. (1989). Innovation amongst healthcare professionals. *Social Behavior, 4*, 173–184.

Wheelwright, S. C. & Clark, K. B. (1995). *Leading Product Development: The Senior Manager's Guide to Creating and Shaping the Enterprise*. New York: Free Press.

Womack, J. P., Jones, D. T., & Roos, D. R. (1990). *The Machine that Changed the World: The Story of Lean Production*. New York: Harper Perennial.

23

TEAMWORK AS COMPETITIVE ADVANTAGE

Russell W. Coff

Resource-based theory suggests that sustainable competitive advantage stems from unique "bundles" of resources that rivals cannot imitate (Barney, 1991; Wernerfelt, 1984). Following this, prescriptive advice revolves around identifying and acquiring critical resources. Here, Barney (1991, p. 110) noted, "physical technology, whether it takes the form of machine tools or robotics in factories or complex information management systems, is by itself typically imitable." In contrast, human assets are often hard to imitate due to scarcity, specialization, and tacit knowledge (Grant, 1996; Hall, 1993; Teece, 1982).

In this context, teams are often cited as a source of competitive advantage in literatures ranging from organizational behavior to strategic management (Barney, 1991; Pfeffer, 1994). While the importance of teamwork extends back to the early roots of organizational theory (Barnard, 1968 [1938]), few firms seem able to take advantage of teams as a source of competitive advantage—it is not as easy as it sounds.

This chapter will focus on the strategic management literature to identify how and why team-based capabilities may lead to a competitive advantage. I then turn to the question of management dilemmas created by this type of resource, along with the types of solutions that may help firms cope with or mitigate these dilemmas. The final moderating dimension I discuss is the impact of team-based resources on the rent appropriation process. This determines how much of the rent will be observable in typical organization-level performance measures.

TEAMS AS A SOURCE OF COMPETITIVE ADVANTAGE

In focusing on competitive advantage, it is important first to acknowledge that the outcome of interest is firm-level performance. As such, when referring to a competitive advantage, I am not comparing effective teams to ineffective teams within a firm, but rather a system comprised of teams in one firm to systems of teams in rival firms. This cross-firm comparison differs from much of the organizational behavior literature which examines factors that lead to team performance relative to other teams in the firm.

Perhaps the biggest difference is the need to view the system of teams as a component of a rent-generating capability. This means that the concept of teams must be extended

International Handbook of Organizational Teamwork and Cooperative Working. Edited by M. A. West, D. Tjosvold, and K. G. Smith.

to include social capital as a mechanism for inter-team coordination. Portes defines social capital as "the ability of actors to secure benefits by virtue of membership in social networks or other social structures" (Portes, 1998, p. 6). In this case, actors use their social networks to secure resources for their team that enhance productivity and coordination across teams.

In order for this type of capability to be valuable, it must enable the firm to either deliver its products or services at a lower cost than rivals, or it must enable the firm to deliver unique products and services that command a price premium (Porter, 1980). Furthermore, there must be something about this system of teams that prevents rival firms from acquiring or developing a comparable capability—it must be inimitable, nonsubstitutable, and unavailable in factor markets (Barney, 1991). In the remainder of this section, I turn to the role of teams in generating and sustaining a competitive advantage.

Teams as a Source of Cost and Differentiation Advantages

There is considerable evidence suggesting that teams may enable firms to reduce costs and/or increase productivity. For example, partnerships of mutual consultation helped cut search costs that federal law enforcement agents incurred when seeking case solutions (Blau, 1969). Social capital was shown to facilitate the inter-unit resource exchange essential for reducing product innovation costs within some firms (Tsai & Ghoshal, 1998). A corporate law firm was also shown to have reduced the costs related to contracting for labor and business development by utilizing social relationships (Lazega, 1999).

Furthermore, evidence suggests that teams may help firms to differentiate. For example, brainstorming among teams of engineers with unique backgrounds was crucial to the technology brokering behind IDEO's premium-commanding product designs (Hargadon & Sutton, 1997; Sutton & Hargadon, 1996). Indeed, in some cases, clients paid for IDEO's team-based capability directly, paying per brainstorm. Moreover, they called attention to the role of social capital in distinguishing engineers.

Accordingly, team production requires a social capital-rich environment to facilitate within- and across-team coordination (Hargadon & Sutton, 1997). Social capital, in turn, has been identified as a source of capabilities such as building intellectual capital and knowledge creation (Grant, 1996; Nahapiet & Ghoshal, 1998). Accordingly, the root of most team-based capabilities may be an enhanced ability to integrate and transfer knowledge (Grant, 1996). As such, teams should not be viewed as isolated units but rather as part of a complex system of knowledge integration.

Teams as a Source of Inimitability

Given that team-based capabilities may lead to either a cost or differentiation advantage, the next question is how sustainable would such an advantage be? As posited in the broader resource-based literature, an advantage may be sustainable if the underlying capability is unavailable to rivals. In general, this suggests that imitation is hindered by social complexity, causal ambiguity, and/or asset specificity (Barney, 1991). Team-based capabilities may be linked to each of these attributes. First, and most obviously, teams necessarily rely on complex human relations and are therefore most closely associated with social complexity.

Second, it can be argued that a complex social network such as that embedded within and across teams may make it hard to identify the contributions of individual resources. For example, the team production problems Alchian and Demsetz (1972) identified stem from a form of social complexity. While they described how ambiguity about individual inputs might cause spot labor markets to fail, this same ambiguity may prevent rivals from acquiring or developing an essential rent-generating resource. As such, it may also be associated with causal ambiguity, which is the degree to which the firm's performance can be linked to the specific capability (Barney, 1991).

Finally, social ties are often firm-specific in that they cannot be easily redeployed in a different firm. In some cases, firms have hired and transferred intact teams. However, this is likely to be the exception rather than the rule because teams often do not work in isolation from other teams. As such, removing a single team will extract it from the network and will often reduce its effectiveness. This is especially the case when viewing capabilities as a complex network of teams.

INFORMATION ASYMMETRIES AND MANAGEMENT DILEMMAS

Despite the promise for a competitive advantage described up to this point, team-based capabilities also lead to serious information dilemmas that may impede an advantage (Coff, 1997). Again, these are closely related to the classic dilemmas inherent in team production described by Alchian and Demsetz (1972)—individual contributions are unobservable. They argue that the information problems are more hazardous in markets and that hierarchies are therefore more efficient at governing teams. However, while hierarchies may be preferred over markets for team production, asymmetric information also poses governance problems within firms.

Accordingly, team-based capabilities are associated with information dilemmas including adverse selection, moral hazard, and bounded rationality in decision making. Firms must cope with or mitigate these problem in order to realize a competitive advantage.

Hiring Dilemmas: Adverse Selection and Fit

Adverse selection is caused by asymmetric information in labor markets. Specialized or tacit knowledge is not observable and may lead to a "market for lemons" problem (Akerlof, 1970). This means that the labor market would harbor a disproportionate number of low-quality workers. This occurs if employers offer lower wages to hedge their risk of hiring a "lemon." High-quality workers might then be reluctant to change jobs—perpetuating the problems.

Causal ambiguity can further exacerbate this problem. Applicants may misrepresent themselves by taking credit for the success of their former employers. Causal ambiguity will thwart efforts to verify such claims. Employers may then discount information that cannot be verified and offer even lower starting wages.

In the context of teams, this effect is complicated by the need for fit with the rest of the team. That is, the hiring process cannot focus only on finding the needed skills, but must also address how candidates would fit with the existing team. Candidates, in turn, may present themselves in such a way that they emphasize how they would fit and play down aspects suggesting that they would not fit. Employers may respond similarly to the other quality issues explored above by lowering the initial wages to transfer some of the cost of hiring a "lemon" to the job candidate. This, in turn, may exacerbate the problem that high-quality individuals are reluctant to change jobs.

Motivation Dilemmas: Moral Hazard and Information Asymmetries

Moral hazard refers to shirking, motivation problems, or even the subversion that can occur in team production when individual contributions are difficult to observe. While these problems are the focus of agency theory (Jensen & Meckling, 1976), the motivation literature also documents reduced effort in some team settings (Kidwell & Bennett, 1993). When individual contributions are intertwined, employees may be uncertain about whether their effort will impact performance (e.g. expectancy). In addition, the firm cannot easily provide performance-based rewards (e.g. instrumentality).[1] If both expectancy and instrumentality are low, it will be difficult to motivate employees (Vroom, 1964).

Causal ambiguity also paves the way for problems of moral hazard. People often take credit for successes and assign external attributions for failures when it is difficult to observe causality. Attribution theory refers to this as the "self-serving bias" (Ross, 1977). Since causality cannot be established, organizations may inadvertently reward or punish employees for events that are beyond their control or influence (Kerr, 1975).

Bounded Rationality and Distributed Knowledge

Finally, even in the absence of opportunism, asymmetric information is a hazard for decision makers. Since managers are boundedly rational, they may not know to ask for required information and employees may not know what to provide (Simon, 1976). While this lack of information can lead to serious errors in decision making, the problem is not driven by opportunism.

Causal ambiguity is especially hazardous in this respect. Not only do managers lack information required to make decisions, the information is not readily available from *any* source. Ouchi (1980) suggests that such extreme uncertainty can cause hierarchies, as a transaction governance mechanism, to break down.

In a team setting, knowledge is created within the team and transferred to other teams typically through informal networks or linkages. Again, at IDEO, creative product development was facilitated through brainstorming at the group level as well as links to other project groups based on social ties developed from past projects (Hargadon & Sutton, 1997). From a management standpoint, this means that formal hierarchies are bypassed for much of the most important information exchanges and managers may lack information to make sound decisions or to evaluate individual team members.

In sum, adverse selection, moral hazard, and bounded rationality may be formidable challenges arising from information asymmetries when managing team-based strategic capabilities. While hierarchies may be more efficient than markets, they also fail under conditions of asymmetric information (Grossman & Hart, 1986; Ouchi, 1980). Thus, in order to generate a sustainable advantage, firms must either find ways to obtain scarce information or learn to cope in the absence of information.

---

[1] Interestingly, while the economics and organizational behavior literatures describe essentially the same problem, they differ somewhat in their attributions of the root cause. The economics literature tends to focus on opportunistic or lazy agents while the organizational behavior literature focuses on the perverse incentives and poor direction provided by the organization. These are two sides of the same coin.

MANAGEMENT PRACTICES FOR REALIZING TEAM-BASED ADVANTAGES

Since team-based capabilities are typically associated with information dilemmas, the overarching proposition here is that firms must develop coping mechanisms in order to achieve an advantage. Absent mechanisms to cope with hiring, motivation, and decision-making dilemmas, firms will be unable to organize, coordinate, and motivate teams to generate a competitive advantage.

This section explores policies that may help firms cope with the dilemmas. These fall into three categories: (1) rent-sharing strategies, (2) organizational design strategies, and (3) information strategies. Rent-sharing strategies explicitly allocate a portion of the rent to provide incentives that align employee and firm goals. Organizational design strategies involve manipulating the organization's governance, structure, and culture to cope with dilemmas. Finally, information strategies entail obtaining and analyzing unique sources of information to gain an information advantage.

Table 23.1 lists three case studies that will be used to illustrate this framework: (1) a management training seminar company, (2) a consumer magazine, and (3) a public accounting firm. These vignettes were developed through semi-structured interviews with managers regarding the nature and management of their human assets. These data are not presented to test hypotheses. Rather, the examples serve to illustrate how different remedies might be employed depending on the management dilemmas.

Rent Sharing

Rent-sharing strategies help to align goals and cope with agency and motivation problems in the absence of information. As examined earlier, asymmetric information creates a risk that employees will use the information imbalance to exploit the firm. The classic remedy in agency theory is to align individual and organizational objectives through rent sharing or *residual claimancy* (Barzel, 1989; Chi, 1994). Thus, by making employees' earnings contingent on profitability or performance, the firm need not incur high monitoring costs to cope with the dilemma.

In this context, it is important to note the level at which the residual is observable. Given that this chapter is focused on team-based capabilities, it is unlikely that individual-level contributions are observable. However, it may be possible to observe residuals (contributions) at the organization or team level. Rent-sharing strategies should generally focus on the lowest level at which residuals can be observed (Zenger & Marshall, 1995).

ORGANIZATION-LEVEL RENT SHARING

Stock ownership and profit sharing are classic solutions to agency problems (Jensen & Meckling, 1976). When employees are owners, their rewards depend on organizational outcomes. Ownership should align employee goals with those of the firm even if the stock does not grant employees control because they would still have something at stake. However, a number of factors limit the effectiveness of organization-level rent sharing: (1) the amount of rent shared may be insignificant to influence behavior; (2) employees may not have an

Table 23.1 Examples of organizational coping strategies

	1 Technology-oriented investment bank (Teams delivering M&A advisory services)	2 Consumer magazine (The editor who turned the publication around)	3 Public accounting firm (Partners who cooperate to bring in business)
Management dilemmas	Highly networked ad hoc teams are hard to monitor; hard to observe contributions	It is hard to evaluate what makes such a publication successful	Information is limited by team production and external client networks
Coping strategies			
Rent sharing	*Profit sharing:* Individuals get a share of the fees from the services they help to deliver	*Profit sharing:* The editor gets a sizable bonus based on the publication's performance	*Profit sharing:* The bonus is based on total revenue to promote cooperation in the business development process
Organizational design	*Participation:* Egalitarian management style *Shared norms:* High tech culture promotes common goals	*Participation:* The editor has considerable professional autonomy	*Participation:* Partners share in firm governance *Shared norms:* Firm has a strong culture and promotes from within
Information	*External sources:* Customer-based performance appraisals	*External sources:* Ad revenue is a leading indicator *Labor hoarding:* Firm retains editors to avoid adverse selection	*Internal sources:* The up or out position limits the risk of adverse selection—people are observed over time prior to promotion

Source: Adapted from Coff (1997).

opportunity for voice; and (3) some employees may cash the stock in nullifying its binding properties (Lawler & Jenkins, 1990).

Nevertheless, there are a number of successful high-profile employee-owned firms that suggest that these problems can be resolved. Organization-level rent sharing, such as long-term incentives (Balkin & Gomez-Mejia, 1986) and profit sharing (Smith, 1988), is especially common in high-technology firms. Similarly, the consumer magazine (firm 2 in Table 23.1) used firm-level incentives to align goals on the editorial team. These encouraged them to adopt a scope beyond their specific function and even to cooperate with other publications that the firm held.

TEAM-LEVEL RENT SHARING

In team-based production, it may be possible to share gains at the team level (Lawler & Jenkins, 1990). Team-level performance measurement and incentives can increase productivity (Pritchard et al., 1988). Similarly, Zenger and Marshall (1995) found group incentives were especially effective when applied to the smallest possible group.

The public accounting firm (firm 3 in Table 23.1) uses rent-sharing strategies to address the problem of cooperation in the business development process. Partner bonuses are not determined solely from the revenue generated from their specific clients (even though this is easily measured). That is, all partners share the incoming revenue. This is because efforts to track different roles in the business development process tend to discourage cooperation. Individual incentives would require identifying roles such as referring the client to another partner; establishing a rapport; conceptualizing the product; writing the proposal; selling the product; and closing the deal. More importantly, each of these interdependent roles would have to be valued.

Organizational Design

Organizational design strategies involve managing or influencing elements of the structure and culture to align individual goals with those of the organization in the absence of information. Within the domain of design strategies, there are three types of mechanisms: shared governance, organic structure, and culture. Each of these, in turn, has the potential to help the firm cope with the hazards of asymmetric information.

SHARED GOVERNANCE

Shared governance is similar to the concept of participation in decision making. However, much of the organizational behavior research examines interventions at the lower levels in the organization, such as quality circles or participation in individual goal setting (Wagner & Gooding, 1987). While these shop-floor interventions can be valuable, shared governance is intended to include a broader scope of issues and a more serious commitment to "symbolic egalitarianism" (Pfeffer, 1994).

Such participation can also help managers to make decisions when there is asymmetric information. Thus, the availability of information is one of the primary situational factors in Vroom and Yetton's (1973) normative model of participation in decision making. Similarly, quality interventions (e.g. quality circles, TQM, reengineering) assume that management has incomplete information and must seek input from employees, customers, and competitors (Deming, 1989).

Participation also plays a fundamental role in higher-level strategic decisions. For example, Mintzberg (1987) suggests that "grass roots strategy-making" is critical for the process of crafting a business strategy. Similarly, Eisenhardt (1989) and Dean and Sharfman (1996) found that the decision process was an important determinant of decision quality. Eisenhardt (1989) found that the best decision makers used "consensus with qualification" and relied on input from others in the firm (e.g. real-time information about the firm's operations). The group process and involvement of others outside the executive team allowed them to make faster, higher-quality, decisions. The accounting firm and the consumer magazine (firms 2 and 3 in Table 23.1) granted significant authority and autonomy to managers. Asymmetric information and uncertainty demand that these professionals be involved in "crafting" the strategy for the firm as a whole.

ORGANIC STRUCTURE

Mechanistic structures have clearly specified routines and a clear line of authority (Burns & Stalker, 1961). However, such systems may break down if there is asymmetric information (Ouchi, 1980). The alternative is a more organic or flexible structure. Organic structures are flatter with more lateral and face-to-face communication. Tasks and roles also tend to be loosely defined. Put another way, organic structures are designed to accommodate social complexity (e.g. team production). This link is supported by Snell's (1992) finding that work-flow integration is negatively associated with output and behavior control. In other words, when there is greater interdependence (e.g. reliance on networks), firms are less likely to rely on formal controls.

CORPORATE CULTURE

Culture refers to common values, beliefs, and norms held within a firm. A strong culture is one that is widely shared in the organization (Schein, 1985). Like the other design strategies, a strong culture may help a firm cope with information dilemmas. Ouchi (1980) suggests that a strong culture (e.g. clan control) may substitute for other types of control that do not function well under conditions of asymmetric information. That is, employees may choose to adhere to the firm's informal norms and not act opportunistically, even if the firm cannot monitor them.

Therefore, organizational design strategies in the form of shared governance, organic structures, and culture management may help firms to address information dilemmas without directly allocating rent. This may help to explain why design strategies are featured in many of the "emergent" organizational forms (horizontal, networked, boundaryless, upside down, etc.).

Information Enhancement

As discussed above, asymmetric information can lead to agency problems, and even in the absence of opportunism, poor decisions. Thus, information is a valuable commodity, and firms have strong incentives to seek better information sources.[2] If a firm is able to obtain scarce information, this, in itself, may be an important part of gaining a sustainable advantage. Firms must seek distinct types of information to mitigate the problems of moral hazard and adverse selection.

INFORMATION SOURCES TO COPE WITH MORAL HAZARD

Firms may seek information about current workers through supervisory monitoring, peer and subordinate feedback, or external information sources. In general, as will be explored below, the first alternative may not be viable for managing human assets.

Supervisory monitoring

Agency theory suggests that a common way of responding to problems of moral hazard is increased supervisory monitoring. This assertion is supported by empirical findings that bureaucratic controls are associated with firm-specific skills and technological change (Baron, Davis-Blake, & Bielby, 1986; Pfeffer & Cohen, 1984). Similarly, DiPrete (1987) attributed internal hiring patterns in a government agency to asymmetric information and task idiosyncrasy. Since firm specificity is associated with causal ambiguity and social complexity, these may represent attempts to cope with information problems.

Nevertheless, monitoring can be very costly and ineffective, especially if it lowers morale. Health maintenance organizations (HMOs) monitor doctors to help mitigate problems of asymmetric information. That is, while the firm cannot monitor each decision, it does track and analyze data on doctors' decisions over time. The firm then uses the possibility of dropping doctors from the network to influence decisions (*Wall Street Journal*, 1993). Of course, doctors do not relish having the firm "looking over their shoulder." Morale and organizational commitment tend to suffer.

Peer/subordinate feedback

Common sources of internal information include peer and subordinate appraisal. Used in concert, these may provide better information in a team context without the hazard of lowering morale. Firms often collect such information as part of management development efforts. Managers then use these multiple perspectives to improve their skills (Smither et al., 1995). Some firms also use peer and subordinate evaluations as part of the formal appraisal system (London & Smither, 1995). Since management is a tacit skill (Castanias & Helfat, 1991), these additional information sources can be critical.

Pritchard et al. (1988) found that in a team production context, group feedback may improve performance substantially. A group may be able to disentangle differences in performance and effort that a manager might find difficult to observe. Also, they found that the focus on performance feedback helps groups to establish strong performance norms.

[2] Note that this opportunity is not available under conditions of extreme uncertainty because information is not available from any source. In contrast, asymmetric information implies that the information does exist.

External information sources for evaluating employees

Firms may also seek external information from customers, external peers, or suppliers to evaluate employees. This information, in turn, may be used for traditional promotion and reward allocation decisions. The consumer magazine (firm 2 in Table 23.1) collected extensive information from advertisers because they are "leading indicators" of how subscribers will receive a new editor's vision. Similarly, the investment bank (firm 1 in Table 23.1) tracked customer comments to evaluate the effectiveness of individuals and teams. This type of customer-based performance measurement is often a central component of TQM initiatives (Deming, 1989).

In the case of professionals, the external network of peers can help the firm evaluate performance. Zucker (1991) describes how universities often lack expertise in specific fields to evaluate academic excellence. Consequently, they use external networks to mitigate asymmetric information. Similarly, Henderson and Cockburn (1994) found that pharmaceutical companies rely on external recognition, in the form of publications, to reward top performers. Strong professional norms driven by an external knowledge base and network may augment or even substitute for internal control mechanisms (Scheid-Cook, 1990).

INFORMATION SOURCES TO COPE WITH ADVERSE SELECTION

The problem of adverse selection requires that firms be able to assess labor market data to evaluate tacit knowledge. Firms often rely on crude signals, such as the educational level achieved, even though wide variations in productivity remain (Spence, 1973). This is part of the reason why adverse selection might keep high performers out of the labor market (Akerlof, 1970). The ability to identify exceptional people who will fit into a team using incomplete information may even be central to gaining a sustainable advantage. This mastery may take the form of limiting exposure to the external labor market, a competency in interpreting tacit labor market signals, or the ability to identify talent in the absence of information. In the case of teams, this may take the form of utilizing social networks to identify individuals who would fit and thereby overcome problems of adverse selection.

Limiting exposure to the labor market

One way to avoid adverse selection is to limit the firm's exposure to external labor markets. Firms may hoard human capital or promote from within right to the very highest levels to avoid adverse selection (Dalton & Kesner, 1985). Hoarding involves retaining workers during economic downturns so that the firm need not hire people of uncertain quality at the crest of each business cycle. The consumer magazine (firm 2 in Table 23.1) sometimes employed mediocre editors for extended periods of time because it would take up to three years to know whether a replacement was any better. In contrast, the accounting firm (firm 3 in Table 23.1) used an up or out position in their hierarchy to promote only those employees that they had observed for a time.

Competency in interpreting labor market signals

An alternative to avoiding the labor market is to develop sophisticated ways of gathering and interpreting information. For example, as knowledge about productivity has increasing strategic value, employment information from competitors takes on strategic significance (Waldman, 1990). Thus, senior management at the consumer magazine (firm 2 in Table 23.1) monitored departmental editors' performance at competing publications to help identify talented junior editors. Often, these promising junior editors become part of the applicant pool for senior editor positions.

Competency in identifying talent without labor market signals

In some cases the competency may require decision making in the absence of labor market signals. Poppo and Weigelt (2001) present a reputational model of competitive advantage in labor market transactions. In studying the market for free agents in baseball, they find that owners are able to exploit the lag between performance and recognition in the market. Teams take advantage of asymmetric information about free agent performance in the early years of players' careers and base compensation more on the owner's perceptions of the player than on actual performance. Because the owner has better information, his/her perception can precede the player's development of a reputation and the owner can realize rent from the information imbalance. Later, as players approach retirement, owners place more emphasis on actual performance (lagged) and less on their perception because the player's reputation is established and there is less asymmetric information.

In sum, firms may be able to overcome some information problems by obtaining better information or by honing their ability to interpret tacit information. Problems of moral hazard require that these efforts be focused on existing employees, while adverse selection indicates that effort should be focused on the labor market. In either case, human assets would generally demand astute information management.

RENT APPROPRIATION FROM TEAM-BASED ADVANTAGES

There is a strong need for research exploring the rent appropriation process (Barney, 2001; Coff, 1999). Indeed, there may be reasons to believe that a large portion of the rent from knowledge-based capabilities may be appropriated internally since the primary rent-generating resources may not be owned by the firm (Coff, 1999). This is a final moderating aspect of a team-based advantage that should also be explored. On one level, one might assume that rent appropriation follows from the ability to hold up the rent-generation process. In this sense, the inability to measure and identify the top performers accurately would seem to be a barrier to their appropriating rent. That might suggest that internal stakeholders would have difficulty appropriating rent and that more of the rent would be observable in measures of organizational residuals (like profitability).

However, two factors should be considered here. First, just because it may be hard to know exactly who the critical contributors are does not mean that individuals will not make claims as though they have the ability to hold up the firm. Second, in the context of information asymmetries, bargaining power is not predicated on the actual ability to hold up the firm but the perceived ability to do so. Can an individual or team make a credible claim that rent production would cease without them? Lazega (1999, p. 242) even noted that individuals may intentionally blur evidence of their contributions to make bigger claims about their roles: "members can make their relative contribution to firm performance unmeasurable—for example by bringing more resources into exchanges—which is made possible precisely by the existence of multiplex and generalized exchange system."

Having already identified that team-based capabilities require a social capital-rich environment, it is worth exploring the role of social capital in rent appropriation. Again, drawing on Portes's (1998, p. 6) definition of social capital as the ability of actors to "secure benefits" through social networks, it should not be surprising that individuals may deploy their social capital to make credible claims of their role in rent generation.

When individual contributions are unclear, opportunistic claims to rent are made easier. If the allocation of credit is difficult, then the "fair" allocation of compensation is also likely to be difficult. Here I draw support from organizational behavioralists' conceptions of bounded rationality (Simon, 1976). Accordingly, opportunistic claims might be made and met because of owners' and managers' limited rationality.

Again, IDEO might be an example of a setting in which individual contributions are obscured. An engineer noted, "This technical hierarchy was so dominant that managers sometimes complained they didn't get enough credit" (Sutton & Hargadon, 1996, p. 705). However, this does not mean that credit was not assigned. Rather, engineers' contribution to brainstorming created a "status auction" and contributed to the firm's "peer-oriented meritocracy." This sort of credit allocation system operates in lieu of sound information about individual contributions. Furthermore, this allocated credit can allow individuals and teams to make credible claims of their critical roles even without more solid evidence. The only way their claims could be fully verified is by "calling their bluff" and letting them leave the firm. However, if they are correct about their role, the cost of this verification may be quite high.

In sum, it is the social capital underlying team-based capabilities that makes rent generation susceptible to appropriation. By definition, social capital allows actors to secure benefits from social ties as they contribute to social capital.

CONCLUSION

Resource-based theory stresses the role of teams in achieving a sustainable advantage. However, as indicated here, teams engender major management challenges that must be overcome to achieve an advantage. In order to move forward, resource-based theory requires a keen understanding of the problems introduced by such resources. While this chapter has explored some of these dilemmas, its most significant contribution is to raise new research questions. The overarching premise is that team-based resources must be coupled with appropriate coping mechanisms to yield a sustained competitive advantage (see Figure 23.1).

Directions for Research

While the essential dilemma examined here is linked to resource-based theory, the discussion has also drawn on a variety of other literatures. That is, the problem arises within the strategic management literature, but the solutions must span disciplinary boundaries. As such, the directions for future research begin in the strategy literature but extend well beyond that domain.

STRATEGIC MANAGEMENT

The framework set forth here suggests two major areas for future research in strategic management: (1) research should examine the organizational capabilities required to generate

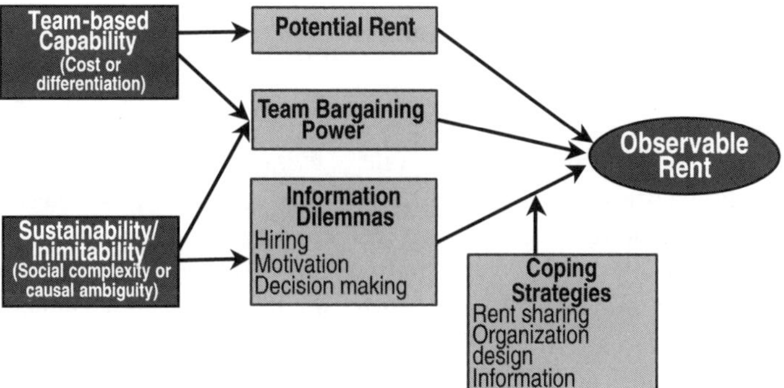

Figure 23.1 From team-based capabilities to organizational performance

a sustainable advantage; and (2) research should identify different configurations or types of human assets.

First, this chapter questions what resources really have the potential to generate a sustainable advantage. Considering the obstacles described here, it might be argued that teams alone cannot be the source of a sustainable advantage. Rather, firms can only generate rent if they also have systems to cope with the associated dilemmas. These systems may represent inimitable capabilities since they reflect the idiosyncratic nature of the teams. Research that expands and integrates organizational learning with the resource-based view would help us to understand these capabilities (Lant & Mezias, 1990; Williams, 1992).

In addition, Figure 23.1 helps to highlight that observed organizational performance is a function of team-based capabilities, bargaining power, information dilemmas, and the associated coping mechanisms. It is important to understand each of these elements in order to develop a complete theory of competitive advantage through teams.

HUMAN RESOURCE MANAGEMENT AND ORGANIZATIONAL BEHAVIOR

In addition, this chapter highlights a need for studies that explore how firms resolve these dilemmas. Here, coping strategies were presented with a mixture of anecdotal and existing empirical evidence. Subsequent research should identify the strategies and assess their relative effectiveness in dealing with the various challenges.

Furthermore, this discussion has not explored interdependencies among coping strategies—some strategies may be linked or even causally dependent upon others. For example, culture management entails influencing elements of satisfaction such as supervision, coworkers, promotion criteria, and rewards (Schein, 1985). There is also a chronological link between hiring, motivating, and retaining. While these activities are ongoing and concurrent, they must be compatible as employees proceed from one process to the next.

Exploration of the coping strategies requires strategy-driven studies that integrate the organizational behavior, human resource management, and organizational theory literatures. For example, the information strategies especially require extensions of existing human resource strategy research. Rent sharing has been examined in the strategic compensation literature (Ehrenberg & Milkovich, 1987; Lawler & Jenkins, 1990). However, this literature has not examined how strategic compensation practices should vary with the type of team.

That is, rent-sharing strategies might be effective with some types of teams and not with others. Similarly, information strategies are drawn from the appraisal and selection literatures. While these areas are well developed, there has been relatively little work examining how such policies should vary with the type of human assets. These inquiries are important for a research agenda that is linked to the strategy literature.

The organizational design strategies are drawn, to an extent, from structural contingency theory. While this literature is very mature (Miller et al., 1991), the more flexible, innovative designs are closely linked to the study of emergent organizational forms (Daft & Lewin, 1993). Neither of these literatures has been integrated with resource-based theory. Future studies might correlate different configurations of human assets with various design strategies. What dilemmas do the emergent forms help to resolve?

These questions are central to the applicability of resource-based theory. Without answers, we cannot hope to understand the link between merely having resources and achieving a sustainable advantage from them. Again, the framework presented here suggests that firms must have both the human assets and the organizational capabilities to manage them. Each element may be necessary, but neither may be sufficient to bring about a sustainable advantage.

Implications for Managers

Numerous authors offer prescriptions for how to achieve a sustainable competitive advantage (e.g. Peters & Waterman, 1982; Pfeffer, 1994). While these suggestions are often based on observations of actual firms, they are not generally drawn from theory. Likewise, managers adopt some of the policies implemented by successful firms without the benefit of a theory explaining exactly what the policies accomplish.

For example, Pfeffer (1994) outlines employment practices, such as symbolic egalitarianism, overarching philosophies, and cross-utilization, that successful firms consistently employ. While this enumeration is useful, it does not focus on the role that these practices play in generating an advantage. Specifically, these practices should help to resolve the problems discussed earlier. Interestingly, almost all of the practices that Pfeffer describes are either organizational design or rent-sharing strategies. In other words, they should help firms cope with both the threat of turnover and information problems. It may be useful for firms implementing "excellent practices" to understand how these steps should be paired with team-based capabilities to mitigate specific management dilemmas.

REFERENCES

Akerlof, G. A. (1970). The market for "lemons": quality uncertainty and the market mechanism. *Quarterly Journal of Economics, 84*, 488–500.

Alchian, A. A. & Demsetz, H. (1972). Production, information costs, and economic organization. *American Economic Review, 62*, 777–795.

Balkin, D. B. & Gomez-Mejia, L. (1986). Compensation practices in high technology industry. *Personnel Administrator, 30*, 111–123.

Barnard, C. I. (1968) [1938]. *The Functions of the Executive*. Cambridge, Mass.: Harvard University Press.

Barney, J. B. (1991). Firm resources and sustained competitive advantage. *Journal of Management, 17*, 99–120.

Barney, J. B. (2001). Is the resource based "view" a useful perspective for strategic management research? Yes. *Academy of Management Review, 26*, 41–56.

Baron, J., Davis-Blake, A., & Bielby, W. (1986). The structure of opportunity: how promotion ladders vary within and among organizations. *Administrative Science Quarterly, 31*, 248–273.

Barzel, Y. (1989). *Economic Analysis of Property Rights*. Cambridge, UK: Cambridge University Press.

Blau, P. (1969). *The Dynamics of Bureaucracy: A Study of Interpersonal Relations in Two Government Agencies*. Chicago: University of Chicago Press.

Burns, T. & Stalker, G. M. (1961). *The Management of Innovation*. London: Tavistock.

Castanias, R. & Helfat, C. (1991). Managerial resources and rents. *Journal of Management, 17*(1), 155–171.

Chi, T. (1994). Trading in strategic resources: necessary conditions, transaction cost problems, and choice of exchange structure. *Strategic Management Journal, 15*(4), 271–290.

Coff, R. W. (1997). Human assets and management dilemmas: coping with hazards on the road to resource-based theory. *Academy of Management Review, 22*(2), 374–402.

Coff, R. W. (1999). When competitive advantage doesn't lead to performance: the resource-based view and stakeholder bargaining power. *Organization Science, 10*(2), 119–133.

Daft, R. L. & Lewin, A. Y. (1993). Where are the theories for the "new" organizational forms? An editorial essay. *Organization Science, 4*(4), 513–528.

Dalton, D. R. & Kesner, I. F. (1985). Organizational performance as an antecedent of inside/outside chief executive succession: an empirical assessment. *Academy of Management Journal, 28*(4), 749–762.

Dean, J. W. & Sharfman, M. P. (1996). Does decision process matter? A study of strategic decision-making effectiveness. *Academy of Management Journal, 39*(2), 368–396.

Deming, W. E. (1989). *Out of Crisis*. Cambridge, Mass.: MIT Press.

DiPrete, T. (1987). Horizontal and vertical mobility in organizations. *Administrative Science Quarterly, 32*, 422–444.

Ehrenberg, R. G. & Milkovich, G. T. (1987). Compensation and firm performance. In M. M. Kleiner, R. N. Block, M. Roomkin, & S. W. Salsburg (eds), *Human Resources and the Performance of the Firm*. Madison, Wis.: Industrial Relations Research Association.

Eisenhardt, K. M. (1989). Making fast strategic decisions in high velocity environments. *Academy of Management Journal, 32*(3), 543–576.

Grant, R. M. (1996). Prospering in dynamically-competitive environments: organizational capability as knowledge integration. *Organization Science, 7*(4), 375–387.

Grossman, S. J. & Hart, O. D. (1986). The costs and benefits of ownership: a theory of vertical and lateral integration. *Journal of Political Economy, 94*(4), 691–719.

Hall, R. (1993). A framework linking intangible resources and capabilities to sustainable competitive advantage. *Strategic Management Journal, 14*(8), 607–619.

Hargadon, A. & Sutton, R. I. (1997). Technology brokering and innovation in a product development firm. *Administrative Science Quarterly, 42*, 716–749.

Henderson, R. & Cockburn, I. (1994). Measuring competence? Exploring firm effects in pharmaceutical research. *Strategic Management Journal, 15*(S2), 63–84.

Jensen, M. C. & Meckling, W. H. (1976). Theory of the firm: managerial behavior, agency costs and ownership structure. *Journal of Financial Economics, 3*, 305–360.

Kerr, S. (1975). On the folly of rewarding A while hoping for B. *Academy of Management Journal, 18*(4), 769–782.

Kidwell, R. E. & Bennett, N. (1993). Employee propensity to withhold effort: a conceptual model to intersect three avenues of research. *Academy of Management Review, 18*(2), 429–456.

Lant, T. K. & Mezias, S. J. (1990). Managing discontinuous change: a simulation study of organizational learning and entrepreneurship. *Strategic Management Journal, 11*, 147–179.

Lawler, E. E. & Jenkins, G. D. (1990). Strategic reward systems. In M. Dunnette & L. Hough (eds), *Handbook of Industrial and Organizational Psychology*. Palo Alto, Calif.: Consulting Psychologists Press, Inc.

Lazega, E. (1999). Generalized exchange and economic performance: social embeddedness of labor contracts in a corporate law partnership. In R. T. A. J. Leenders & S. M. Gabbay (eds), *Corporate Social Capital and Liability* (pp. 237–265). Boston: Kluwer.

London, M. & Smither, J. W. (1995). Can multi-source feedback change perceptions of goal accomplishment, self-evaluations, and performance-related outcomes? Theory-based applications and directions for research. *Personnel Psychology, 48*(4), 803–839.

Miller, C. C., Glick, W. H., Wang, Y., & Huber, G. P. (1991). Understanding technology–structure relationships: theory development and meta-analytic theory testing. *Academy of Management Journal, 34*(2), 370–399.

Mintzberg, H. (1987). Crafting strategy. *Harvard Business Review*, July–August.

Nahapiet, J. & Ghosal, S. (1998). Social capital, intellectual capital and the organizational advantage. *Academy of Management Review, 23*(2), 242–266.

Ouchi, W. G. (1980). Markets, bureaucracies, and clans. *Administrative Science Quarterly, 25*, 129–141.

Peters, T. & Waterman, R. (1982). *In Search of Excellence: Lessons from America's Best-run Companies*. New York: Harper & Row.

Pfeffer, J. (1994). *Competitive Advantage through People: Unleashing the Power of the Work Force*. Boston, Mass.: Harvard Business School Press.

Pfeffer, J. & Cohen, Y. (1984). Determinants of internal labor markets in organizations. *Administrative Science Quarterly, 29*, 550–572.

Poppo, L. & Weigelt, K. (2001). A test of the resource-based model using baseball free agents. *Journal of Economics and Management Strategy, 9*(4), 585–614.

Porter, M. E. (1980). *Competitive Strategy: Techniques for Analyzing Industries and Competitors*. New York: The Free Press.

Portes, A. (1998). Social capital: its origins and applications in modern sociology. *Annual Review of Sociology, 24*, 1–24.

Pritchard, R. D., Jones, S. D., Roth, P. L., Stuebing, K. K., & Ekeberg, S. E. (1988). Effects of group feedback, goal setting, and incentives on organizational productivity. *Journal of Applied Psychology, 73*(2), 337–358.

Ross, L. (1977). The intuitive psychologist and his shortcomings: distortions in the attribution process. In L. Berkowitz (ed.), *Advances in Experimental Social Psychology*. New York: Academic Press.

Scheid-Cook, T. L. (1990). Ritual conformity and organizational control: loose coupling or professionalization. *Journal of Applied Behavioral Science, 26*(2), 183–199.

Schein, E. H. (1985). *Organizational Culture and Leadership*. San Francisco: Jossey-Bass.

Simon, H. A. (1976). *Administrative Behavior: A Study of Decision-making Processes in Administrative Organization*. New York: The Free Press.

Smith, S. C. (1988). On the incidence of profit and equity sharing: theory and an application to the high tech sector. *Journal of Economic Behavior, 9*(1), 45–58.

Smither, J. W., London, M., Reilly, R., & Millsap, R. E. (1995). An examination of the effects of an upward feedback program over time. *Personnel Psychology, 48*(1), 1–34.

Snell, S. A. (1992). Control theory in strategic human resource management: the mediating effect of administrative information. *Academy of Management Journal, 35*(2), 292–327.

Spence, M. (1973). Job market signaling. *Quarterly Journal of Economics, 87*, 355–374.

Sutton, R. I. & Hargadon, A. (1996). Brainstorming groups in context: effectiveness in a product design firm. *Administrative Science Quarterly, 41*, 685–718.

Teece, D. (1982). Towards an economic theory of the multiproduct firm. *Journal of Economic Behavior and Organization, 3*(1), 38–63.

Tsai, W. & Ghoshal, S. (1998). Social capital and value creation: the role of intrafirm networks. *Academy of Management Journal, 41*(4), 464–476.

Vroom, V. H. (1964). *Work and Motivation*. New York: Wiley.

Vroom, V. H. & Yetton, P. W. (1973). *Leadership and Decision-making*. Pittsburgh: University of Pittsburgh Press.

Wagner, J. A. & Gooding, R. Z. (1987). Shared influence and organizational behavior: a meta-analysis of situational variables expected to moderate participation–outcome relationships. *Academy of Management Journal, 30*(3), 524–541.

Waldman, M. (1990). Up-or-out contracts: a signaling perspective. *Journal of Labor Economics, 8*(2), 230–250.

Wall Street Journal (1993). Physicians fight back as insurers cut them from health networks. December 30, A1.

Wernerfelt, B. (1984). A resource-based view of the firm. *Strategic Management Journal, 5*, 171–180.

Williams, J. R. (1992). How sustainable is your competitive advantage? *California Management Review, 34*(3), 29–51.

Zenger, T. & Marshall, C. R. (1995). Group-based pay plans: an empirical test of the relationships among size, incentive intensity, and performance. *Academy of Management Best Papers Proceedings*, 161–165.

Zucker, L. (1991). Markets for bureaucratic authority and control: information quality in professions and services. In S. Barley & P. Tolbert (eds), *Research in the Sociology of Organizations: Organizations and the Professions*. Greenwich, Conn.: JAI Press.

24

A STRATEGIC HR PERSPECTIVE ON TOP EXECUTIVES

Cynthia Kay Stevens

A STRATEGIC HR PERSPECTIVE ON TOP EXECUTIVES

The rise of global corporations and their impact on the international economy has renewed interest in factors that affect the quality of firms' strategic and operational decision making. Recognizing the importance of this topic, strategic management researchers have long sought to understand the management practices that promote prudent decision making by senior executives. With conceptual roots deriving largely from agency and institutional theory, this research on corporate governance has identified a host of economic and political factors associated with CEO selection and compensation that show relationships with firm performance (e.g. Zajac, 1990). The implication of this work is that corporate boards can, through careful design of such practices, ensure that senior executives' decisions will optimize firm performance.

Despite gains in understanding how management practices foster improved decisions among senior executives, two omissions in this work are notable. One is a tendency to focus on individual practices, such as contingent compensation, without regard for the impact of the larger system of human resource (HR) practices. A growing literature in the area of strategic human resource management (SHRM; e.g. Arthur, 1994; Huselid, 1995) suggests that the impact of individual practices, such as incentive plans, should be considered in the context of other HR practices, such as selection, performance management, and development initiatives. Although SHRM research has concentrated exclusively on lower-level employees, it is conceivable that the assumptions and frameworks underlying this area of study may generalize to senior executives.

A second omission is the absence of work focused on the full top management team. Clearly, the CEO is a critical decision maker and some CEOs may effectively strip their top management teams of any real decision power (e.g. Pitcher & Smith, 2001). Yet, a growing body of work suggests that top management team cognitive diversity, through its impact on internal debate, shows significant relationships with firm performance (e.g. Simons, Pelled, & Smith, 1999). Thus, expanding the scope of research on senior executives'

International Handbook of Organizational Teamwork and Cooperative Working. Edited by M. A. West, D. Tjosvold, and K. G. Smith.

management practices to include those pertaining to the top management team may yield greater explanatory and predictive power in clarifying the impact of such practices on firm performance.

The purpose of this chapter is to explore how the inclusion of an SHRM perspective and consideration of the entire top management team might benefit strategic management research on corporate governance. My goal is not to provide an exhaustive review of these literatures, but rather to identify promising points of integration among them. Toward this end, the chapter first describes the SHRM perspective, highlighting implications for senior management. Then it briefly reviews the findings for CEOs and considers how broadening the focus to include the full senior management team might yield interesting insights.

A STRATEGIC APPROACH TO UNDERSTANDING GOVERNANCE ISSUES

The field of HR encompasses a wide range of practices and policies pertaining to managing people, including (but not limited to) such diverse issues as drug testing, union relations, worker health and safety, and workplace privacy. The core areas across different types of jobs and organizational levels, however, include recruitment and selection, compensation, performance evaluation, training and development, and termination (see Tichy, Fombrun, & Devanna, 1982). Traditionally, HR researchers examined the influence of design changes in individual practices on a limited range of outcomes, such as differences in interview formats on interview validity coefficients. This shifted in the 1980s when HR researchers began to consider the effects of collections of practices (e.g. structured interviews, biodata, cognitive tests, and recruitment source studies) on business unit or firm-level outcomes (e.g. Terpstra & Rozell, 1993). Among some HR researchers, the idea took hold that the impact of HR practices may best be understood from a systems perspective.

Consistent with the corporate governance literature, the primary thrust of SHRM research is on identifying optimal designs in HR systems for achieving superior organizational performance or competitive advantage. Most work has examined sets of existing HR practices for their concurrent or delayed effects on aggregate performance measures such as turnover rates, productivity levels, or financial performance (although for data on the impact of changes in existing HR practices, see Banker et al., 1996). Findings suggest that, both across and within industries, small but financially significant, positive relationships exist between sets of company-wide HR practices and firm-level outcomes (Arthur, 1994; Delery & Doty, 1996; Huselid, 1995; Youndt et al., 1996).

Several important assumptions undergird this work. One such assumption is that systems of HR practices affect unit competency levels or workforce behaviors—or both—which in turn yield higher-quality products or services, reduced waste, or greater productivity (Becker & Gerhart, 1996). Although much remains unknown, recent studies examining the intervening mechanisms through which HR systems influence firm-level outcomes (e.g. Collins, Smith, & Stevens, 2001) have yielded results consistent with these explanations. A second assumption is that HR practices may be substitutable or interactive in their impact on competency levels or workforce behaviors (Lado & Wilson, 1994). For example, a given firm may achieve requisite employee skill levels through either its recruitment and selection system or its training and development programs; alternatively, inclusion of both elements might foster increased employee commitment that results in greater long-term retention and productivity gains than would be achieved by either approach alone. Although this argument has not yet been subjected to rigorous empirical testing, it has largely been accepted on logical grounds.

Both of these assumptions might usefully be generalized to the corporate governance context. For example, it seems likely that senior executives need both considerable job-related capabilities and the motivation to behave in ways that promote strong firm performance. As Henderson and Frederickson (1996) have noted, such a human capital perspective has been largely absent in the governance literature. Similarly, there may be equifinalities and interactive effects in the management practices used to identify, develop, compensate, evaluate, and terminate senior executives. To the extent that researchers overlook or misspecify such effects, they may generate incomplete or inaccurate models of the relationships between management practices and firm performance.

In addition to these implications, the SHRM literature has grappled with several conceptual and methodological issues relevant to corporate governance research (e.g. Becker & Gerhart, 1996; Wright & McMahan, 1992). Conceptually, both literatures provide uncertain answers regarding whether a universal set of best practices exists or if the "best" practices depend on firms' competitive landscapes and strategies. Becker and Gerhart (1996) have suggested that, depending on the level of abstraction with which HR practices are defined and measured, it is possible that both conceptualizations are valid. This approach may prove helpful in guiding research in both areas. Methodologically, both SHRM and corporate governance researchers have measured different sets of practices, and even within similar sets (e.g. contingent compensation plans) have defined specific practices differently. Moreover, both groups of researchers frequently examine reports of company policies without considering meaningful differences in how such policies are implemented. As such, each literature may benefit from measurement innovations achieved by the other.

Given the similarities in their research foci and challenges, the SHRM and corporate governance literatures may provide useful cross-fertilization of ideas. The next section considers the implications of the SHRM perspective for research on CEOs and top management teams.

HR PRACTICES AMONG TOP EXECUTIVES

In contrast to the relatively recent attention given to firm-level effects of company-wide HR practices, strategic management researchers have long been interested in the relationship between firm performance and how top executives are managed (e.g. Grusky, 1963). Two distinct conceptual approaches have dominated this literature. The first derives from agency theory and related economic views of management. Philosophically compatible with the SHRM literature, this approach predicts that practices that align top executives' interests with those of shareholders will be related to improved firm performance (e.g. Jensen & Meckling, 1976). Institutional theory, in conjunction with related social psychological and sociopolitical theories, forms the basis for the other approach, which predicts that the structure and content of top executives' HR practices are subject to influence and negotiation by those managed under them (e.g. Westphal, 1998). Several studies have sought to pit divergent predictions from these perspectives against each other; however, neither has emerged as the clear "winner."

Existing research focuses nearly exclusively on practices used to manage CEOs, particularly in the areas of selection and compensation. Nonetheless, there are several reasons to expect that HR practices for the full top management team—of which the CEO is a member—may better inform thinking on corporate governance. As noted earlier, considerable research on top management teams indicates that cognitive diversity within this group (for which demographic characteristics provide a proxy measure) is linked to improved firm performance (e.g. Kilduff, Angelmar, & Mehra, 2000; Pitcher & Smith, 2001; Simons, Pelled, & Smith, 1999; Smith et al., 1994). Thus, one extension of this work is that top management team practices may be linked with firm performance through their effects on the team's cognitive diversity.

Similarly, several studies suggest that the development of constructive task-related debate among diverse top management team members and the inhibition of destructive emotional conflict are necessary to facilitate effective strategic decision making (e.g. Amason, 1996; Simons & Peterson, 2000). The development of constructive interaction patterns and resulting trust levels among members are likely affected both by the top management team's composition (e.g. respectable credentials, interpersonal similarities) as well as by relative internal comparisons deriving from reward systems (Henderson & Frederickson, 2001). Thus, the larger system of HR practices as applied to the top management team may influence interaction norms and conflict patterns, which in turn affect strategic decision quality and firm performance.

The next sections review factors in CEO governance that affect firm performance. For each set of findings, I consider how broadening the analysis to include an SHRM perspective and the full top management team might yield a richer understanding of corporate governance effects.

CEO Succession and Selection

The selection of a new CEO has significant consequences for firms, in that it may signal changes in the power structure or strategic direction. These symbolic aspects provide corporate boards with strong incentives to manage the process carefully (Ocasio & Kim, 1999). Several features of CEO selection processes have been studied, including factors that affect the desirability of candidate attributes (e.g. insider/outsider status with respect to the firm, age, functional background), the role played by the preceding CEO, and organizational precedents.

Existing data indicate an overwhelming preference for insider candidates, especially when current firm performance is strong (Zajac, 1990). This supports agency predictions that boards will prefer candidates for whom solid, reliable information is available. Consistent with the political–behavioral perspective, however, there is a strong precedent effect in which prior selection of an outsider candidate increases the odds that a subsequent outsider will be chosen (Ocasio, 1999). Moreover, Cannella and Lubatkin (1993) found that poor firm performance prompted choice of outsider candidates only when incumbent CEOs had low power relative to their boards of directors. Yet, a subsequent study (Cannella & Shen, 2001) showed that powerful CEOs in high-performing firms often delayed their departures and thus stymied promotion of their internal heirs apparent, suggesting complex relationships among candidate insider/outsider status, CEO power, and firm performance.

With regard to candidates' functional backgrounds, firm strategy has been shown to exert significant moderating effects on the choice of successors. For example, differentiation strategies increase the attractiveness of candidates with output (i.e. sales and marketing) backgrounds (Guthrie & Datta, 1997), high R&D intensity increases desirability of candidates with technical backgrounds (Datta & Guthrie, 1994), and US multinationals perform better with CEOs who have had international experience (Carpenter, Sanders, & Gregersen, 2001). Moreover, the research on CEO and candidate functional backgrounds indicates strong links between incumbent CEOs' backgrounds and firm strategy and between existing firm strategy and successors' functional backgrounds (Smith & White, 1987). This suggests that agency and human capital factors may be offset at earlier or later points in time by political–behavioral considerations.

IMPLICATIONS OF THE SHRM PERSPECTIVE AND EXTENSION TO TOP MANAGEMENT TEAMS

Although the empirical findings provide a coherent picture of CEO succession dynamics, integration of the SHRM perspective would offer additional insights. For example, selection researchers typically advocate collection of extensive information on candidates' competencies and validation of these through subsequent performance data. To date, only one study (Russell, 2001) has empirically examined measures of executive competencies and their relationship to job performance. This study found that general managers' resource problem-solving competencies predicted initial job performance following promotion, whereas people-oriented competencies predicted performance after several years on the job. Although this study involved executives at the general manager level, it does suggest that the corporate governance literature might benefit from more precise competency measures as well as use of individual performance as an explanatory variable in predicting firm performance.

With regard to selecting top management team members, a fruitful avenue for research would be to identify practices (e.g. tournaments, succession planning) that promote optimal compositions of the team. For instance, Barsade et al. (2000) found that top management team homogeneity on trait-positive affectivity was associated with greater cooperation, more use of participative decision making by the CEO, and improved firm financial performance. To the extent that succession planning permits better identification of team members with compatible levels of positive affectivity, its use may be associated with better firm performance than tournament approaches to team selection. Similarly, Chattopadhyay et al. (1999) reported that executives' beliefs were more strongly influenced by similar others on the top management team than they were by their own functional backgrounds or current positions. This suggests that cognitive diversity of the top management team may be a moving target and that executive development efforts might prove better in maintaining debate. As researchers identify additional member characteristics linked with optimal firm performance, analysis of how various selection practices promote or hinder the creation of top management teams with these characteristics may yield improved explanatory and predictive power.

CEO Compensation

Most corporate governance research has concentrated on CEO compensation as a primary determinant of firm performance. Early work in this area was stimulated by agency theory predictions that CEOs whose personal wealth was aligned with firm wealth would work to make firms more profitable. However, existing studies suggest that this relationship is more complicated. Kerr and Bettis (1987) found no evidence of a relationship between stock performance and changes in CEOs' salaries or bonuses in either bull or bear markets. In contrast, Barkema and Pennings (1998) reported a relationship between CEO bonuses and firm performance, and Gibbons and Murphy (1990), using a sample of over 1000 firms, showed that CEO pay revisions were positively linked to firm performance but negatively related to industry and market performance. Zajac (1990) found that, while CEO satisfaction with their pay was unrelated to firm performance, CEOs' *perceptions* that their pay depended on firm performance was positively associated with profitability.

Several other studies suggest that the CEO-pay–firm-performance relationship is moderated by factors such as CEO tenure, industry, and prior firm performance. For example, Hill and Phan (1991) showed that this relationship declined with longer CEO tenure. Balkin, Markman, and Gomez-Mejia (2000) found that industry influenced the relationship between CEO pay and an alternative performance measure—the capacity to innovate. CEOs in high-technology firms showed significant relationships between their short- and long-term pay and firm capacity to innovate (i.e. R&D investment and patents), whereas CEOs in non-high-technology firms showed no such relationships. Finally, some data indicate that the relationship may be pronounced in distressed firms for which the CEO is held responsible. Gilson and Vetsuypens (1993) reported that new CEOs with ties to the prior regime were paid 35 percent less than the prior CEO, but those without such ties were paid 36 percent more than the prior CEO.

Researchers relying on the political–behavioral perspective have sought evidence that pay policies vary more with CEO power and influence than they do with "rational" criteria such as firm performance. A wide variety of studies support this proposition. For example, Staw and Epstein (2000) showed that CEOs whose firms implemented popular management fads had higher pay, but that such fads were unrelated to overall firm performance. Westphal and Zajac (1994) found that early adopters for long-term incentive plans for CEOs did so in ways that aligned CEO incentive pay with shareholders' interests, but that later adopters (who may use such plans to signal their legitimacy) often advertised such plans without actually implementing them. Zajac and Westphal (1995) also reported that explanations to shareholders in proxy statements that described such plans were tailored to appear rational given current levels of firm performance. When performance was good, statements emphasized the need to retain strong talent; however, when performance was poor, statements emphasized the need to align CEO interests with those of shareholders. Finally, Porac, Wade, and Pollock (1999) reported evidence that boards of directors selectively expanded their definitions of comparable "peer firms" beyond industry boundaries when: (a) their firms were performing poorly, (b) their industries were performing poorly, (c) their CEOs were highly paid, and (d) their shareholders were powerful and active.

A variety of studies have also shown that CEO pay varies with the level of CEO power, especially relative to structural indicators of board independence. Barkema and Pennings (1998) found that greater CEO power (i.e. as a result of equity holdings) was associated with larger CEO pay. Similarly, Wade, O'Reilly, and Chandratat (1990) showed that although "golden parachutes" in CEOs' contracts were more prevalent in firms for which takeovers might be in shareholders' best interests, the incidence of these contracts was also greater when CEOs and board members were similar demographically. This is consistent with Westphal and Zajac's (1995) findings that greater demographic similarity between board members and CEOs was linked to more generous CEO compensation packages. Finally, Westphal (1998) reported compelling evidence that CEOs used more ingratiation and persuasion when their boards of directors were more structurally independent (e.g. contained fewer outsiders); moreover, a higher rate of CEO ingratiation and persuasion was associated with later board compliance on firm strategy and CEOs' compensation policies.

IMPLICATIONS OF THE SHRM PERSPECTIVE AND EXTENSION TO TOP MANAGEMENT TEAMS

Research into the economic and political factors influencing CEO compensation has yielded a fascinating body of research. Expanding the paradigm to incorporate human capital factors may add further to the richness of this debate. Indeed, recent studies have moved in this direction. Carpenter, Sanders, and Gregersen (2001) showed that CEOs with past international assignment experience received higher compensation than those without such experience. Similarly, Henderson and Fredrickson (2001) found evidence that CEO pay was related to the level of information-processing demands inherent in their jobs, as assessed by the presence of a diversification strategy, technology-intensive industries, and larger top management teams. Such findings are consistent with Barkema and Pennings's (1998) contention that the salary component of CEO pay compensates executives for job complexity, whereas bonuses reward them for performance. Although studies that include economic, political, and human capital variables may confront increased complexity, it is possible that such factors are not mutually exclusive in their impact, especially over time. Moreover, fuller incorporation of human capital factors may help researchers move productively beyond the current economics versus politics debate.

A limited number of studies have also examined the effect of pay policies within the top management team on firm performance. For example, Conyon, Peck, and Sadler (2001) used tournament theory to predict that larger pay gaps between the CEO and board executives would create a competition for which the reward would be eventual promotion to CEO. They demonstrated that, for a sample of UK firms, large pay gaps did exist, particularly when the number of board executives was large. However, they found no relationship between the existence of such gaps and firm financial performance. One possible explanation for this is that the competition for limited financial rewards may reduce executives' willingness to coordinate their efforts. Testing this hypothesis, Henderson and Fredrickson (2001) found that larger pay gaps were positively related to firm performance when there were more vice presidents and business units were in related industries, both of which may reduce coordination needs. However, the relationship to firm performance was negative when the number of business units was larger or the firm had a higher level of capital investment, which they argued increased coordination needs.

In the SHRM literature, compensation is viewed primarily as a motivational tool and secondarily as a recruitment/retention device. It may be helpful for researchers to broaden the focus to include both aspects when considering how compensation affects top management teams. Thus, in addition to studies on how pay differentials affect cooperation and conflict, researchers might also consider the impact of within-industry pay levels on top management team stability. Moreover, it would be instructive to consider how a larger variety of incentive plans (e.g. contingent pay; individual, unit, and organizational incentives) affects team processes and performance.

Other HR Practices

Although most corporate governance research has focused on selection and compensation, several studies have explored other HR practices such as performance evaluations and dismissals. Dismissing the CEO provides a strong statement regarding a board's dissatisfaction with CEO performance. Fredrickson, Hambrick, and Baumrin (1988) proposed that while firm performance would be a factor in CEO dismissals, the board's expectations and attributions about CEO performance, allegiances with the CEO, and the availability of attractive alternative candidates for the position would play a larger role. Some research supports these contentions. Puffer and Weintrop (1991) found that boards develop expectations for firm performance that are used to evaluate CEO performance: CEO turnover occurred when annual earnings per share fell short of board expectations. However, other data suggest that CEOs' power reduces the likelihood of dismissal. Boeker (1992) reported that poorly performing organizations with powerful CEOs were less likely to experience CEO dismissals, but more likely to have top managers reporting to CEOs replaced (Boeker, 1992). Similarly, Phan and Lee (1998) found that CEOs' social network ties with the board reduced the rate of CEO dismissals.

However, little empirical data exist regarding performance evaluations that do not result in dismissals or how these influence executive development efforts. Gioia and Longenecker (1994) provide qualitative data suggesting that executive performance management efforts are highly politicized and affected by factors extraneous to executives' actual performance, such as their position within the firm's political climate. They found that top executives are unlikely to receive regular feedback about their job performance, in part due to assumptions that the nature of their work (e.g. profit/loss responsibility) yields sufficient information (Longenecker & Gioia, 1992). To the extent that people-related competencies are strongly related to longer-term performance (Russell, 2001), this assumption may not be warranted.

With the exception of Boeker's (1992) study, virtually no research has examined performance or dismissals within top management teams. Given that data on team member demographics and dismissals in publicly traded firms are readily available, this oversight is puzzling. Schneider (1987) proposed the ASA framework, which predicts that organizations tend to attract and select individuals similar to the founder, and to promote attrition among any nonsimilar individuals inadvertently selected. To the extent that this principle holds in top management teams, it suggests that extremely heterogeneous teams would not long endure. Research testing this hypothesis could provide an interesting counterbalance to existing work on top management team heterogeneity.

STRATEGIC HR AND THE TOP MANAGEMENT TEAM

As the foregoing discussion suggests, an integration of research on corporate governance, SHRM, and top management teams offers several exciting avenues for research. In addition to the extensions noted above with regard to specific management practices, several general observations are in order.

First, corporate governance research would benefit from recent prescriptions in the SHRM literature to articulate more precisely the mechanisms through which agency, institutional, and even human capital factors should influence senior executives and firm performance, as well as when these factors should be operative. As one example of this, consider the proposed but inconsistent relationship between CEO pay and firm performance. Agency theory predicts that aligning executives' financial incentives with those of shareholders will improve firm performance. Yet, SHRM researchers routinely conceptualize individual performance as resulting from an interaction of motivation (i.e. incentives) and ability, with the potential for external factors beyond individual control to suppress observed relationships. The omission of executive ability from the equation may hamper researchers' ability to find motivational effects of aligned incentive plans without disproving the underlying agency-theory prediction. Similarly, data regarding the ongoing influence process between boards and CEOs (Westphal, 1998) suggest that agency or human capital factors will be salient early in such relationships and decline as CEOs gain power. Thus, specifying which factors are operative at which points in time can provide a clearer picture of proposed relationships.

A second suggestion from the SHRM literature would be to consider larger sets of HR practices when testing for effects. The existing data suggest, for example, that the conditions under which CEO successors assume power (e.g. insider/outsider status, firm performance, and strategy) may give CEOs more or less power relative to the board or other top management team members, which in turn may influence their ability to obtain more generous compensation packages. It also provides a context that may influence board performance expectations and subsequent actions in the face of met or unmet expectations. Clearly the relationships are potentially complex, but the point is that HR practices are experienced in concert with one another, and focusing on a single practice may yield a misleading view of their impact on executive or firm performance. Use of HR indices, which capture multiple practices, may provide a method through which to model such effects.

With regard to top management teams, initial investigations into the impact of compensation plans illustrate both the difficulties and potential gains. The inclusion of multiple individuals per firm as well as their unique employment terms adds complexity; issues such as the mean level and differences among members in employment terms require more sophisticated conceptual development and analytic techniques. Yet an exclusive focus on the CEO hardly seems justified, especially among large diversified corporations where decision making is often decentralized. The larger executive team provides an important context for understanding both how CEOs view the practices used to manage them as well as how political dynamics influence compensation, succession, and dismissals. Given that the majority of CEOs were, at an earlier point, company insiders (Zajac, 1990), the top management team can be viewed as a mechanism for developing CEO talent. As such, the practices used to staff, incentivize, and evaluate top management teams deserve greater scrutiny.

Summary

The different foci and research traditions within the fields of corporate governance, SHRM, and top management teams have yielded divergent approaches for examining the relationship between firms' governance practices, decision processes, and performance. Each area contributes unique insights into the factors that influence these complex relationships. With greater cross-fertilization of concepts and methods across these disciplines, a more comprehensive picture may yet emerge regarding how to design HR systems for optimal senior executive decision making in the new century.

REFERENCES

Amason, A. C. (1996). Distinguishing the effects of functional and dysfunctional conflict on strategic decision making: resolving a paradox for top management teams. *Academy of Management Journal, 39*, 123–148.

Arthur, J. B. (1994). Effects of human resource systems on manufacturing performance and turnover. *Academy of Management Journal, 37*, 670–687.

Balkin, D. B., Markman, G. D., & Gomez-Mejia, L. R. (2000). Is CEO pay in high-technology firms related to innovation? *Academy of Management Journal, 43*, 1118–1129.

Banker, R. D., Field, J. M., Schroeder, R. G., & Sinha, K. K. (1996). Impact of work teams on manufacturing performance: a longitudinal field study. *Academy of Management Journal, 39*, 867–890.

Barkema, H. G. & Pennings, J. M. (1998). Top management pay: impact of overt and covert power. *Organization Studies, 19*, 975–1003.

Barsade, S. G., Ward, A. J., Turner, J. D. F., & Sonnenfeld, J. A. (2000). To your heart's content: a model of affective diversity in top management teams. *Administrative Science Quarterly, 45*, 802–836.

Becker, B. & Gerhart, B. (1996). The impact of human resource management on organizational performance: progress and prospects. *Academy of Management Journal, 39*, 779–801.

Boeker, W. (1992). Power and managerial dismissal: scapegoating at the top. *Administrative Science Quarterly, 37*, 400–421.

Cannella, A. A., Jr & Lubatkin, M. (1993). Succession as a sociopolitical process: internal impediments to outsider selection. *Academy of Management Journal, 36*, 763–793.

Cannella, A. A., Jr & Shen, W. (2001). So close and yet so far: promotion versus exit for CEO heirs apparent. *Academy of Management Journal, 44*, 252–270.

Carpenter, M. A., Sanders, W. G., & Gregersen, H. B. (2001). Bundling human capital with organizational context: the impact of international assignment experience on multinational firm performance and CEO pay. *Academy of Management Journal, 44*, 493–511.

Chattopadhyay, P., Glick, W. H., Miller, C. C., & Huber, G. P. (1999). Determinants of executive beliefs: comparing functional conditioning and social influence. *Strategic Management Journal, 20*, 763–789.

Collins, C. J., Smith, K. G., & Stevens, C. K. (2001). Human resource practices, knowledge-creation capability, and performance in high technology firms. Unpublished manuscript.

Conyon, M. J., Peck, S. I., & Sadler, G. V. (2001). Corporate tournaments and executive compensation: evidence from the UK. *Strategic Management Journal, 22*, 805–815.

Datta, D. K. & Guthrie, J. P. (1994). Executive succession: organizational antecedents of CEO characteristics. *Strategic Management Journal, 15*, 569–577.

Delery, J. E. & Doty, D. H. (1996). Modes of theorizing in strategic human resource management: tests of universalistic, contingency, and configurational performance predictions. *Academy of Management Journal, 39*, 802–835.

Frederickson, J. W., Hambrick, D. C., & Baumrin, S. (1988). A model of CEO dismissal. *Academy of Management Review, 13*, 255–270.

Gibbons, R. & Murphy, K. J. (1990). Relative performance evaluation for chief executive officers. *Industrial and Labor Relations Review, 43*, 30–51.

Gilson, S. C. & Vetsuypens, M. R. (1993). CEO compensation in financially distressed firms: an empirical analysis. *The Journal of Finance, XLVIII*, 425–458.

Gioia, D. A. & Longenecker, C. O. (1994). Delving into the dark side: the politics of executive appraisal. *Organizational Dynamics, 22*, 47–58.

Grusky, O. (1963). Managerial succession and organizational effectiveness. *American Journal of Sociology, 69*, 21–31.

Guthrie, J. P. & Datta, D. K. (1997). Contextual influences on executive selection: firm characteristics and CEO experience. *Journal of Management Studies, 34*, 537–560.

Henderson, A. D. & Frederickson, J. W. (1996). Information processing demands as a determinant of CEO compensation. *Academy of Management Journal, 39*, 575–606.

Henderson, A. D. & Frederickson, J. W. (2001). Top management team coordination needs and the CEO pay gap: a competitive test of economic and behavioral views. *Academy of Management Journal, 44*, 96–117.
Hill, C. W. L. & Phan, P. (1991). CEO tenure as a determinant of CEO pay. *Academy of Management Journal, 34*, 707–717.
Huselid, M. A. (1995). The impact of human resource management practices on turnover, productivity, and corporate financial performance. *Academy of Management Journal, 38*, 635–672.
Jensen, M. C. & Meckling, W. H. (1976). Theory of the firm: managerial behavior, agency costs, and ownership structure. *Journal of Financial Economics, 3*, 305–360.
Kilduff, M., Angelmar, R., & Mehra, A. (2000). Top management-team diversity and firm performance: examining the role of cognitions. *Organization Science, 11*, 21–34.
Kerr, J. L. & Bettis, R. A. (1987). Boards of directors, top management compensation, and shareholder returns. *Academy of Management Journal, 30*, 645–664.
Lado, A. A. & Wilson, M. C. (1994). Human resource systems and sustained competitive advantage: a competency-based perspective. *Academy of Management Review, 19*, 699–727.
Longenecker, C. O. & Gioia, D. A. (1992). The executive appraisal paradox. *Academy of Management Executive, 6*, 18–28.
Ocasio, W. (1999). Institutionalized action and corporate governance: the reliance on rules of CEO succession. *Administrative Science Quarterly, 44*, 384–416.
Ocasio, W. & Kim, H. (1999). The circulation of corporate control: selection of functional backgrounds of new CEOs in large US manufacturing firms, 1981–1992. *Administrative Science Quarterly, 44*, 522–562.
Phan, P. H. & Lee, S. H. (1998). Human capital or social networks: what constrains CEO dismissals? *Academy of Management Best Papers Proceedings*, 37–41.
Pitcher, P. & Smith, A. D. (2001). Top management team heterogeneity: personality, power and proxies. *Organization Science, 12*, 1–18.
Porac, J. F., Wade, J. B., & Pollock, T. G. (1999). Industry categories and the politics of the comparable firm in CEO compensation. *Administrative Science Quarterly, 44*, 112–144.
Puffer, S. M. & Weintrop, J. B. (1991). Corporate performance and CEO turnover: the role of performance expectations. *Administrative Science Quarterly, 36*, 1–19.
Russell, C. J. (2001). A longitudinal study of top-level executive performance. *Journal of Applied Psychology, 86*, 560–573.
Schneider, Benjamin (1987). The people make the place. *Personnel Psychology, 40*(3), 437–454.
Simons, T., Pelled, L. H., & Smith, K. A. (1999). Making use of difference: diversity, debate, and decision comprehensiveness in top management teams. *Academy of Management Journal, 42*, 662–673.
Simons, T. L. & Peterson, R. S. (2000). Task conflict and relationship conflict in top management teams: the pivotal role of intragroup trust. *Journal of Applied Psychology, 85*, 102–111.
Smith, K. G., Smith, K. A., Olian, J. D., Sims, J. P., Jr, O'Bannon, D. P., & Scully, J. A. (1994). Top management team demography and process: the role of social integration and communication. *Administrative Science Quarterly, 39*, 412–438.
Smith, M. & White, M. C. (1987). Strategy, CEO specialization, and succession. *Administrative Science Quarterly, 32*, 263–280.
Staw, B. M. & Epstein, L. D. (2000). What bandwagons bring: effects of popular management techniques on corporate performance, reputation, and CEO pay. *Administrative Science Quarterly, 45*, 523–556.
Terpstra, D. E. & Rozell, E. J. (1993). The relationship of staffing practices to organizational level measures of performance. *Personnel Psychology, 46*, 27–48.
Tichy, N. M., Fombrun, C. J., & Devanna, M. A. (1982). Strategic human resource management. *Sloan Management Review, 23*, 47–61.
Wade, J. B., O'Reilly, C. A., & Chandratat, I. (1990). Golden parachutes: CEOs and the exercise of social influence. *Administrative Science Quarterly, 35*, 587–603.
Westphal, J. D. (1998). Board games: how CEOs adapt to increases in structural board independence from management. *Administrative Science Quarterly, 43*, 511–537.

Westphal, J. D. & Zajac, E. J. (1994). Substance and symbolism in CEOs' long-term incentive plans. *Administrative Science Quarterly, 39*, 367–390.

Westphal, J. D. & Zajac, E. J. (1995). Who shall govern? CEO/board power, demographic similarity, and new director selection. *Administrative Science Quarterly, 40*, 60–83.

Wright, P. M. & McMahan, G. C. (1992). Theoretical perspectives for strategic human resource management. *Journal of Management, 18*, 295–320.

Youndt, M. A., Snell, S. A., Dean, J. W., Jr, & Lepak, D. P. (1996). Human resource management, manufacturing strategy, and firm performance. *Academy of Management Journal, 39*, 836–866.

Zajac, E. J. (1990). CEO selection, succession, compensation, and firm performance: a theoretical integration and empirical analysis. *Strategic Management Journal, 11*, 217–230.

Zajac, E. J. & Westphal, J. D. (1995). Accounting for the explanations of CEO compensation: substance and symbolism. *Administrative Science Quarterly, 40*, 283–308.

Section V

ALLIANCES BETWEEN ORGANIZATIONS

25

TEAMWORK IN RELATIONSHIP MARKETING

Peter A. Dunne and James G. Barnes

WHY A RELATIONSHIP PERSPECTIVE?

Despite much recent attention in the ranks of management and in the academic and popular press, the principles of relationship marketing are not new. In fact, the foundations of such an approach to marketing represent the historical essence of the discipline with its focus on concepts such as trust and commitment. These are concepts also fundamental to any discussion of cooperation or teamwork.

A relationship requires some level of satisfaction with the interactions/transactions that take place between parties. Reflection upon these exchanges determines whether or not that relationship will continue and thrive. Contemplation determines how the parties feel about the relationship and the other members that are involved. Members must decide that some acceptable level of satisfaction exists or the relationship will not continue. If it should continue without mutual satisfaction, perhaps out of necessity for one or both sides, it may not be a positive experience for at least one of the parties.

How do these relationship variables mediate each other within the context of business relationships? Business is built upon the principles of exchange: between management and employees, between different employees and departments, and between employees (the firm) and clients.

If we accept that the ultimate goal of marketing is the creation of long-term customer satisfaction and that such satisfaction is created through the delivery of value to the customer, we must determine what it is that allows us to deliver maximum value to existing and prospective customers. We must re-evaluate the relationships we have with clients and employees. These groups must be conceptualized as different consumer groups whose needs must be considered. Mutually beneficial relationships with these groups must be encouraged through reconsideration of the value proposition each is being offered. Each group represents a valuable stakeholder, responsible for the ultimate success of the organization.

The utility of relationship marketing within the organization is demonstrated to foster/enhance the development of a team culture within the firm, creating a beneficial environment

International Handbook of Organizational Teamwork and Cooperative Working. Edited by M. A. West, D. Tjosvold, and K. G. Smith.

for employees (internal customers) and clients (external customers), ultimately benefiting the firm. Often cooperation is difficult to achieve within the firm owing to the traditional adversarial nature of the employee–employer relationship, and as a result of interdepartmental rivalries and/or conflicting departmental goals. Frequently, these rivalries result from a lack of understanding or effective communication across the firm.

Delivering poor service to customers will result in low satisfaction and increased turnover within both customer and employee groups. Such turnover is very costly. These groups should be considered long-term assets of the firm. It is posited that reduction in rates of turnover is achieved through the development of enduring positive-affect relationships that enhance cooperation and lead to long-term mutually beneficial bonds.

Marketing planners must now pay explicit attention to the design of a thoroughly integrated boundary-spanning marketing programme. They must make internal customers one of their priorities. This focus on the human resources of the firm as a vital link in the firm's success raises questions as to whether the marketing function can capture the full potential of this opportunity independently. As such, more than ever before, marketing must not be relegated to the status of a department, but developed as an organizational objective and an influence on corporate culture. The breakdown of the traditional adversarial management model in the face of increasingly fierce competitive pressures makes this necessary. Management must work with the employees that make up the firm. It is perhaps this organizational resource that represents the greatest potential for competitive advantage in our evolving service economies. It has become recognized by both manufacturing and service industries that employees are ultimately responsible for the efficient and tailored customer service that is needed to remain competitive in business today (Grönroos, 1990).

Do the principles that underscore personal relationships have the same relevance in the world of business? Solomon (1993) concluded that the basic virtues conceptualized for business do include many of the concepts fundamental in interpersonal relationships, such as trust, fairness, and often commitment.

Fairness, or the perception of such, is not so much an ideal in business as a basic expectation. It has to do with honesty, dependability, and trust, insofar as mutual agreement is, in business, the hallmark of fairness (Solomon, 1993). It also has to do with the notion of equivalence or "equity", the equal value of what is exchanged, whether it is goods, work, or wages. Reflected in business vernacular are terms such as "fair price", "reasonable return", and "fair wage". This brings us back to the ideal of mutual agreement, which, writ large, is what we call "market value". This sense of market has historically been, and still often is, resisted—nowhere more so than within the firm. And nowhere more than within the firm (by employees) is this sense of market required.

Although not often vocalized, perhaps not even at the employees' level of awareness, equity and fairness of treatment and conditions are being assessed on a regular basis. This influences, perhaps unconsciously, the employee's level of performance and commitment to the task, and to the organization as a whole. This influences the productivity and quality of the products and services produced and, of course, the morale of the firm. This has a series of implications for the future of the organization.

Thus the connection between the employee and the long-term viability and success of the firm is established. Relationship thinking is very much in vogue in the modern firm, although it tends to be most often focused outwardly at the establishment of some form of relationship with external customers. The case must be made that customer relationships have their origin in the connection between external customers and the employees of the firm, whether or not those employees ever come into direct contact with their customers. The most lasting and successful of customer relationships are grounded in the way employees regard and treat customers, a situation very much influenced by how those employees are themselves treated by their employer. The employee relationship becomes a precursor to and a predictor of the customer relationship.

CUSTOMER RELATIONSHIP MANAGEMENT

A customer "relationship" requires more than a series of interactions or exchanges over time. Something more must exist and it must be recognized by both parties—in other words, it must be mutual. Customer relationships do not exist because customers hold a loyalty programme card in their wallets, or because their addresses and buying history are recorded in a database—this is not a relationship, this is simply database marketing. This is not to suggest that such programmes are inappropriate, or that such "membership" excludes the possibility of relationship development. But this is not what makes a relationship.

Relationship marketing's most fundamental component is a focus on customer retention—but not because the firm has promised every tenth purchase free or offers "points" leading to rewards! Genuine customer relationships focus on the client's long-term satisfaction, going far beyond individual transactions. It is not database marketing or a frequent-shopper programme, or the establishment of "barriers to exit" such as locking the customer in through agreements, service contracts, or by putting in place prohibitive switching costs.

It begins with an internal environment that has a focus beyond the current transaction. The customer must be recognized by all in the firm as a potential stream of revenue and long-term earnings for the company. The objective of developing genuine relationships with customers is long-term satisfaction that causes them to return voluntarily time and time again. It is mutually perceived to exist, having a "special status" beyond just occasional contact. Such a status is difficult to define but partners recognize when it exists—clearly relationships can, and usually do, involve more than these things, but without these it cannot be said that a true relationship exists.

It is about producing or delivering value for the customer—this does not simply mean the promised product at the agreed-upon price. While price and its connection to the product or service delivered are a meaningful understanding of value, the firm must look beyond this simple equation. Quality in relation to price is commonly understood to represent value, but today a "fair" or competitive price does not always translate into value in the consumer's perception. It is often not enough.

Today, value is created when, in consumers' minds, they have received more than they expected or had to be given. According to Barnes (2001), value creation occurs when customers receive something more from the person serving them, when they are made to feel important, respected, and appreciated. Often this results from seemingly small gestures, the perceived attitude in the communication, a willingness to communicate, or the impression of trying to be helpful, etc. All employees must understand value creation and the value of long-term customer relationships.

What Drives Customer Satisfaction?

Genuine customer relationships result from the development over time of an emotional connection between customers and the firm (or its employees) and likewise within the organization between employees and the firm. Both groups develop a certain comfort level resulting from ongoing and sustained satisfaction of their needs, both functional and emotional. Such satisfaction creates loyalty—and loyalty means that they remain with the firm.

The objectives of many tactics intended to create higher levels of customer loyalty are behavioural, while what we really wish to address is emotional in nature—establishing a "bond" that the client can, upon reflection, recognize as existing. The goal is to have the client feel that such a bond exists—feeling means emotion. Emotion is a social construct, constructed as part of a developing relationship emerging from real-time encounters with people (Elliot, 1998). Emotional response is a function of shared expectations regarding appropriate behaviour and most often arises in response to events that are important to an individual's goals, motives, or concerns. The law of emotion underpins the consumer's involvement and thus drives many consumption decisions. Of course, many consumers will not identify or acknowledge these bonds as a "relationship"—that term is usually reserved for family and close friends. But with a little prompting clients will use terms such as "trust" or "rely" or "count on" when referring to a regular service provider and often use the possessive "my ——" when referring to that provider; as in "my hairdresser", "my dry cleaner", or "my broker".

And what about the "relationship" the employee has with the firm? Employees must deal with the organization, and each other, every working day. To be certain, stronger impacts and reactions must result in this context. Do they perceive a choice exists or that they are free to leave the firm? Do they enjoy coming to work? Do they feel loyal to the firm, each other, or to clients after 10 or 15 years in the organization? If not, what are the potential impacts on the organization and its success?

Satisfied Employees, Satisfied Customers

Clearly, employees are ultimately responsible for the products and services that customers buy and consume. This contribution may be as part of a manufacturing line or in the service component of selling or delivering that same tangible product. Alternatively, it may be the employee's responsibility to wholly deliver an intangible product—a service. The point to bear in mind is that all employees have some responsibility for the overall quality, efficiency, and reliability of what the firm does. Therefore, all employees bear some responsibility for the ultimate satisfaction of the customer upon whom they may never set eyes. This responsibility is, perhaps, most critical in the service component of the offer where the greatest opportunity usually lies to add value—or lose it!

How can we best understand the relationship that exists between employee contribution and value creation? The relationship is clearly expressed in the notion of the service–profit chain (Heskett et al., 1994), illustrating how the value added by each employee creates satisfaction, leading to increased retention and thus profitability. This model is important because it acknowledges that quality of service provided to a customer is a function of the satisfaction level of the employees responsible for service provision. Applying this proposition throughout the organization to include all employees illustrates a much longer chain with value potential in each successive link.

The service–profit chain depicts a series of effects within the employee group that parallels similar effects among customers. Satisfied employees are more likely to provide superior levels of service. They stay longer with the firm and have a greater sense of commitment to the firm and all its customers. This often translates into better relations among employees and between employees and management. The implications for employee and customer retention are obvious.

Delivering superior customer service starts by focusing on the quality of service within the organization. This, in large part, determines the satisfaction and loyalty of employees. It plays a significant role in the degree of gratification they receive in their positions, thereby shaping their attitudes and the behaviours that result.

As with any other customer group, the firm must look at the value being delivered to employees—what is the value proposition being offered to them? What represents value to the employee in this business exchange? Value in the employee context, like price to consumers, goes far beyond monetary considerations; in this case, wages (although these must be fair and competitive). We are talking about internal service quality, communication, and the treatment of employees as individuals. Employees are making investments—with psychological costs—and they need to perceive there is at least an equitable return on this investment for a mutually beneficial arrangement to continue. Management is also typically looking for an increase in their investment in the firm (diligence, quality, productivity, commitment, loyalty, etc.). This parallels the external customer relationship and the exchanges sought there.

A review of the research evaluating the roles of trust, commitment, loyalty, and satisfaction in employee and buyer intentions indicates that trust is a strong predictor of loyalty, and trust, commitment, and satisfaction are each strong predictors of future buying intentions (Ben-Rechav, 2001; Garbarino & Johnson, 1999). Trust is positively related with perceived task performance, team satisfaction, and relationship commitment and negatively related to stress in a teamworking environment, while satisfaction with coworkers is strongly related to team commitment (Bishop & Dow, 2000; Costa, Roe, & Taillieu, 2001).

Increased levels of communication in the firm enhance the quality of organizational relationships and perceived organizational influence, thereby increasing employee satisfaction. In turn, this influences profitability and customer satisfaction (Avtgis, 2000; Koys, 2001).

Tepper, Lockhart, and Hoobler (2001) found that employees differ in how they define the place of organizational citizenship behaviour (OCB) in their job roles. Two effects have been found to exist. There are those who believe that OCBs are a part of their job—this is the role enlargement effect. There are also those who believe such behaviours are discretional—the role discretion effect. Employees with more favourable work attitudes define OCB as in-role behaviour resulting in greater demonstration of citizenship behaviours such as interpersonal helping and altruistic behaviour.

Relationships as Assets—Customer Relationship Management as an Investment

When we talk about assets, we generally think of those elements within the organization that require a cash investment and can be assigned a monetary value by the accounting department. This is not so easy to do with some of a firm's most valuable assets. Long-term customers, human resources (not just the department), and the organizational culture—these can be very valuable assets. They are often not recognized as such. It is easy to appreciate how money can be invested in these areas, but valuation of the resultant output is another story. Such intangibles are becoming increasingly recognized as a source of potential competitive advantage (Rowe & Barnes, 1998).

There is payback from this investment. Meaningful results include repeat business or larger share of wallet. Satisfied customers become easier to serve because of the greater knowledge the firm has about them, but also because they are more cooperative and understanding. They also make referrals (sphere of influence), and the ripple effect results in an enhanced image and reputation attracting a greater pool of potential customers and employees. With fewer turnovers in each group, there are reduced recruitment costs. The result is higher revenues and lower servicing costs; it makes economic sense. The result of relationship building has similar streams of effects in both customer groups.

It is important to demonstrate to all members of the firm a genuine focus on the long-term value of the external customer—not simply provide lip service to the ideals. Internal and external customers must perceive, or feel, that the organization has a genuine commitment to developing real relationships. Only through systematic and dedicated application of relationship principles will genuine buy-in from relationship members result. Only through an appropriate corporate culture led by a CEO or MD who understands these principles can genuine employee and customer relationships be created and sustained.

The greatest potential from a relationship strategy can be realized through also treating the employee group as a customer group with whom the firm wishes to have a meaningful and mutually beneficial relationship. In turn, employees come to see a similar relationship existing between themselves and other departments of the firm. This develops the needed building blocks to a different organizational culture.

Grönroos (1995) notes that relationship strategies should be conceptualized as a continuum to be implemented according to the appropriateness of the industry and marketplace specifics. At one end of the continuum are predominantly transaction-oriented strategies, and at the other genuine relationship orientations. The marketing implications of occupying various positions along such a continuum are understandably different. What might be considered possible and appropriate in the financial services industry, for example, differs from that in grocery retailing or airlines. Likewise, what may be successful with full-time staff may not be effective with part-time employees.

Expectations and Needs

Entering into the exchanges currently being discussed with different customer groups (whether external or internal) brings with it expectations and needs as would be expected of any exchange. There are implicit expectations of fairness and equity in the transaction, or "relationship" if you will, that must be satisfied for a mutually beneficial outcome to occur and for the potential to exist for future positive exchanges. The perception of this potential must be fostered and protected. As is the case with many areas of marketing, such conditions are necessary but may not be sufficient predictors of future outcomes.

As discussed, both external and internal customer groups make investments in these exchanges. What must be addressed are the psychic/psychological costs or investments that are put into these "relationships". These are the time, energy, effort, commitment, and even the anxiety or aggravation that may be involved for these groups. What the firm offers has to balance or counteract these variables. Ideally, customers should feel their costs have been more than compensated for in the exchange.

These basic expectations will generally only attract attention, and a response, when outcomes fall below or exceed a tolerable level in the customer's view. The restaurant service was rushed and my group did not enjoy the dining experience; therefore, my patronage is not appreciated. Employees become dissatisfied with their jobs because the physical environment in which they must work is dirty, cluttered, and not maintained—therefore, management does not respect its employees. Such interpretations are often expressed in emotion-laden terms, indicating the level of importance they can reach for those involved.

Emotional involvement can invoke strong responses. Of course, what we are looking for are strong positive responses. In creating relationships it is hoped that emotions will be invoked, as this is how a bond develops. The goal is to elicit emotions such as commitment and loyalty. Quite often, it is surprise that produces a customer's emotional response—either expectations have been dashed or have been exceeded. What is desired is the stimulation of emotion through the creation of a pleasant surprise—expectations have been exceeded and value has been created—the "wow" factor.

Borrowed from social psychology, the term "emotional tone" refers here to the frequency with which clients feel certain positive and negative emotions through their dealings with the firm. Research conducted by Barnes (1997) throughout that author's professional experience has "revealed quite conclusively that the satisfaction that a customer feels when dealing with any business is very much influenced by the emotional tone of the interaction". The best predictors of a customer's overall satisfaction in dealing with a business is the extent to which that company succeeds in creating positive as opposed to negative emotions for that customer. The employment relationship can also be seen as a balance of positive and negative outcomes that will be evaluated by individual employees.

Broadening the Focus

Marketing in today's environment requires that we broaden our definition of what constitutes marketing and whose responsibility it is. Marketing today is all about increasing customer satisfaction through creating value for customer groups—it is more than deciding the right marketing mix (Barnes, 2001).

The task of relationship building is too important and complex in the current environment to be left to the marketing department alone. It must become the responsibility of everyone in the organization. Every employee has the potential to influence customer satisfaction directly or indirectly. With such an orientation, marketing is not so much a department as it is a state of mind—a pervasive cultural influence. This is not to suggest that specific marketing functions do not still exist or that there is not still a well-defined role for such a department. Instead it is suggested that the organization as a whole, beginning at top management levels, must work to fulfil this role and the potential of the firm. MacKenzie, Podsakoff, and Rich (2001) have found that leadership style can influence sales performance and OCB. Transformational leadership has been found to influence personnel to perform "above and beyond the call of duty". Such an influence would create the necessary change environment.

It is essential that employees be on-side to present a consistent face to customer groups. Perhaps more importantly, they must "feel" it—actually believe it! They must internalize the idea that they are all in marketing—or experience the culture that makes them feel as we want the customer to feel—how they should be treated.

The shift from a transaction-based to a relationship-based marketing practice obviously has implications for the entire firm. There must be a shift in focus to include *both* customer acquisition and customer retention. This retention is achieved through long-term customer satisfaction—this is based on creating value for the customer. If customers perceive that they receive value through their dealings with a firm, they will likely "reward" that firm with their loyalty—hopefully even referral business. A very simple model, indeed. With all else equal, how customers are treated—how they felt before, during, and after the transaction—determines if they will return. According to Barnes (2001), "whether a customer comes back to deal with a company again often has absolutely nothing to do with what we sell or even what we charge for the product or service".

STRATEGIC, HUMAN RESOURCES, OR MARKETING PERSPECTIVE?

Just about every sector of the marketplace today contains, or relies to varying degrees upon, a service element. But, service also exists within each organization—employees and departments provide services and products to each other. In addition, efficiency and the quality of physical product produced depend upon the level of internal service quality. Under such circumstances, employees become a critical resource with a vital role in long-term success. As the global economy moves toward reliance upon innovation-based organization and knowledge-based workers, firms will be left with no other choice but to reflect inwardly for potential sources of meaningful competitive advantage (Dunne & Barnes, 2000). In this current environment of change, the only competitive weapon remaining may well be that of organization (Ulrich, 1998). Employees are the organization and therefore represent the basis upon which to begin the development of sustainable firm competencies.

We know that firms want to develop sources of competitive advantage. They want to develop relationships inside and outside the boundary of the firm as well as throughout the distribution channel. But whose responsibility is this development? Marketing, promotion, and the development of a differential advantage, of course, most often fall under the responsibility of the marketing department. On the other hand, the development of people, the firm's human resources, falls under what else?—the human resource (HR) department. Then again, as with any strategic objective or undertaking of an organization, both customer development and employee development become the ultimate responsibility of top management. This is, not unlike any strategic initiative, where buy-in begins and the initiative toward an integrated approach to relationship thinking must be mandated—insisted upon. The recognition of the most constant and fundamental component of the firm—its employees—as a "marketing" resource only solidifies this assertion—marketing, defined as having a customer or relationships focus, is an organizational goal. To achieve such a goal requires an integrated view of how the marketing and HR departments must work together as co-equal partners on the team.

When we talk of internal marketing in this context we are taking the theoretical underpinnings of "traditional" marketing and applying them to a market of customers within the firm.

What must be recognized is that doing this demonstrates common roots or philosophy with the intended role of HR departments. This convergence must be recognized and acknowledged, as in many organizations the HR function has come to revolve around administrative tasks, focusing more on developing paperwork and procedures than the human resource.

The Role of Human Resources

As the functional unit within an organization responsible for the recruitment, selection, and retention of employees, it must be seen that this implicitly proposes a "marketing" role be established within or assigned to the HR department, particularly in service organizations where interaction between customers and employees is at its greatest. In this sense, HR is an integral component of the firm's promotional mix in the broadest sense. Its function is to recruit desirable candidates, to prepare employees for life in the firm, to become a part of the culture, to be productive and contributing members, and to positively evaluate the firm.

The HR function has perhaps never been more necessary than it is in today's turbulent environment. Unfortunately, this is at a time when some believe HR to be often ineffective and costly (Ulrich, 1998). The HR function has generally not evolved in many firms to meet changes in the marketplace. Today's organization requires more innovative and creative HR processes through shifting from traditional activities such as staffing, compensation, policy policing, and the role of regulatory watchdog toward more outcome-based activities. HR should be defined not by what it does but what it delivers. These "deliverables" should be results that enrich the organization's value to customers, investors, and employees. In envisioning the future of HR, Ulrich (1998) believes organizational excellence can be pursued in the following ways, by HR becoming:

1. A partner in strategy execution; helping to move planning into the marketplace;
2. An expert in how work is organized;
3. A champion for employees, representing their concerns while working to increase employee contribution and commitment;
4. An agent of continuous transformation, shaping processes and a culture that improves the organization's capacity for change.

A cooperative programme is required to initiate change. Tasks such as shaping the vision, leading the change, creating and communicating a shared need, and mobilizing commitment are all very strongly marketing-oriented tasks. At the least, they can be appreciated for the benefits achievable by undertaking a marketing perspective in their design and implementation. Change is often resisted and threatens employees and management, as recent capricious times have taught employees to be wary. The development of a marketing-oriented initiative that delivers a relevant value proposition will help reduce such apprehension and replace resistance with resolve, commitment, greater loyalty, and understanding.

Employees? Customers?

Employees as customers? What does this mean exactly? As with the identification and selection of any customer segment—the firm must decide whom it wants as customers and to whom it will sell. How can their needs be addressed? The answer, of course, is the same for these internal customers as for any other customer group—value creation.

Because this customer group is also the personnel of the firm, it should make sense that the HR department should support or even lead this "marketing" programme. It is an invaluable resource in furthering these initiatives and ultimately making the company more customer and relationships focused. Indeed, these are the functions that the department was created to serve.

Needs that must be met for the employee group deal with issues such as compensation, benefits, working conditions, training (orientation, preparation, initiation), development opportunities, involvement, autonomy, meaning, participation, "control", socialization, camaraderie, and environmental conditions around elements such as morale, trust, and reliability, and support of fellow workers. If provided to employees, these will improve the value proposition offered by the "seller". There is payback for the firm. Really, it is no different from the revenue provided by the external customer. In many ways, this HR/marketing collaboration directly influences the firm's flow of earnings.

By offering greater work–life benefits (value) to the internal customer the firm is increasing the employee's level of satisfaction. As this increased satisfaction results in increased patronage and loyalty of the external customer it likewise increases the commitment and productivity of the employee. Other elements affected include quality, efficiency—all increasing the level of service to the external customer. Faster, defect-free, and pleasantly delivered products and services should result.

In addition, as the "customer-relationship" view develops within the firm, loyalty increases—employees stay! That is the whole idea—employee retention. This reduces the cost and downtime of always bringing in new employees. The employees are more experienced and have developed contacts within and outside the firm in their role. This increases the intellectual capital and organizational memory of the organization. This further enhances external satisfaction with the firm.

With the passage of time, a culture develops within and around the firm—attracting potential internal and external customers. Attitudes toward the firm and the work become more positive in effect. The social context between employees increases and is enriched and a more cohesive group emerges. Cooperation and teamwork can easily be fostered within such an environment. The image and reputation of the firm have been enhanced. The employees become marketers for the organization. This ability to attract larger pools of employee candidates affords the opportunity to choose a higher quality of employee. This also feeds into this positive affect loop.

The Tools of Cooperation

Tools are usually collected in a toolbox—our toolbox is the organization, or rather our toolbox is organization. More specifically, it is the corporate culture that will result from appropriate design and arrangements of the elements.

What is required is participation and support from all departments, a redefined role for the HR department working with the marketing department to create an appropriate internal marketing mix that can be applied throughout the firm and span the boundary between customer groups. This is in strategic combination with the development of relationships (and mixes) throughout the channel and with external customers. What is required within the firm is a transformation from the often strained and adversarial employee–management model to a cooperative model where these two parties work together—a culture of teamwork and employee participation.

And what of the tools, or elements, that are intended to facilitate this cultural makeover? There is trust, loyalty, commitment, satisfaction, empowerment, cooperation, collaboration, teamwork, organizational citizenship behaviours, and external customer satisfaction and cooperation. A review of the literature would illustrate that these variables cannot, in fact, be discussed in isolation from each other. The relationships or mediating roles that exist between these render the following discussion somewhat arbitrary in its organization.

Staff Empowerment

Empowerment is generally defined in terms of how much discretion and autonomy personnel are given within their workplace context. Research has found fully empowered employees are more likely to produce the most satisfied customers, but only when the employees engaged in accommodating styles of communication. No meaningful distinctions were found among less empowered workers with regard to their style of communication (Bradley & Sparks, 2000; Sparks, Bradley, & Callan, 1997).

The service encounter, and the service provider's behaviour within it, have become recognized as powerful sources of customer satisfaction or dissatisfaction. This encounter can include experiences as varied as simple speed of order delivery of a physical product to the interactions that occur in an extended personal exchange during the delivery of a wholly intangible service. Given an appropriate corporate culture, staff empowerment should result in high levels of staff commitment to on-the-spot decision making for the benefit of others. Empowerment is considered linked to service quality, as employees are rated as more professional and concerned in their roles. Further, customers report the perception of receiving individualized service attention.

Full empowerment provides employees "creative discretion"—allowing them to solve problems flexibly, independently, and efficiently. It should keep the decision close to the customer—seemingly less arbitrary and removed (Sparks, Bradley, & Callan, 1997). Empowerment has the potential to provide meaningful interactions between employees and clients, while affording each group respect.

Interpersonal communication style used by empowered employees is important. They have been provided with discretion, but may not be empathetic or effectively communicating the exchange process to the client. Effort and cooperation are ongoing discretionary decisions of degree for each individual employee. It differs from mere mandated politeness. Accommodating communication styles (and a willingness to communicate) have been found to consistently produce higher satisfaction ratings among clients.

What are the internal effects of such an approach to treating customers and employees as decision makers? Employees are given responsibility and "power"—they are working with management and shaping what happens each day. Employees' opinions begin to matter—employees want to feel valued—valuable in their role—to be involved in their jobs, and proud of their work. Ironically, managers and employees actually do want very compatible outcomes—those associated with empowerment. These include ownership, responsibility, and involvement. These values encourage working with others, sharing outcomes, and commitment. This reflects a different model of management than is traditionally considered—one that is less hierarchical and where managers and employees jointly define performance goals. Such change is not easy to implement—particularly in an environment as turbulent as the corporation throughout the 1990s (Randolph, 2000). People do not change easily—why should I give up control? Why should I take on more responsibility? Maybe it is just another trend that will pass soon! People have information and personal concerns. But it is more than sharing information that is required. The firm must replace the old hierarchy with self-directed teams.

Siegall and Gardner (2000) examined the four contextual factors related to empowerment (communication with supervisor, general relations with company, teamwork, and concern for performance), and four components of psychological empowerment (meaning, impact, self-determination, and competence). The contextual factors were found to be differentially associated with the elements of psychological empowerment. Communication with supervisor and relations with the company were significantly related to the empowerment facets of meaning, self-determination, and impact. Teamwork was related to meaning and impact. These associations also found to vary according to type of job.

In studying service workers, Corsun and Enz (1999) found psychological empowerment was generally higher among workers when positive and supportive relationships existed with peers who are helpful and customers who are concerned. In short, if organizations are to be truly customer focused, a sense of a team atmosphere must be created.

Empowerment has been found to increase employee productivity and proactive behaviours. Likewise, it has been found to increase job satisfaction, and organizational and team commitment (Kirkman & Rosen, 1999; Liden, Wayne, & Sparrowe, 2000).

Collaboration, Cooperation, Teamwork

Cooperative work environments enhance employee communications, performance, and job satisfaction (Cosier & Dalton, 1988). Cooperation includes the day-to-day pro-social gestures of individual accommodations to the work needs of others. Such citizenship behaviours include altruism, or helping specific persons, and generalized compliance, or following the rules of the system. Such findings are consistent with research on altruism, suggesting a link between positive mood state and altruistic behaviour. It appears that people who value helping behaviour may work better in a cooperative environment with regard to their pay outcomes and, in turn, may not work well if forced to compete for outcomes.

Increasingly, rewarding and mutually beneficial work exchanges and relationships increase willingness to communicate—to cooperate. It follows that this would lead to increased quality and productivity within the firm, leading to better results for the customer. But, the effect would be twofold in that it could be anticipated that greater willingness to communicate and to cooperate would carry over the firm's boundaries and result in better exchanges between the firm and its customers.

Implications exist for human resource selection. LePine and van Dyne (2001) found conscientiousness, extraversion, and agreeableness to be strongly related to voice and cooperative behaviour, while Sonnentag (2000) found that when workers described "excellent" performers in their organizations the most frequently mentioned competencies were cooperation and communication.

Much of the research on the value of collaborative environments has been done in the areas of education and medical care, where the rate of burnout is quite high. Weiss (1999) studied perceived workplace conditions and morale, career choice commitment, and planned retention for first-year teachers. It was found that a school culture that supports collaboration and teacher participation in decision making was most strongly related to higher morale, stronger commitment to teaching, and intentions to remain in the profession. Particularly important during the formalized induction year were opportunities to socialize teachers into a collaborative and participatory work ethic that sustains commitment.

Customer Cooperation

Quite often the quality and effectiveness of an exchange are not only the result of employee effort. Many areas—especially within the service industry—require, or at least benefit from, the cooperation of the customer. According to Bettencourt (1997), customers contribute to service quality through their roles as promoters of the firm (part-time marketers for the cause), as co-producers of the firm's service, and as "consultants" to the organization. Referred to as customer voluntary performance (CVP), these behaviours are helpful and discretionary customer behaviours that support the ability of the firm to deliver service quality. Three types of behaviours are suggested—loyalty (encourage others to patronize firm), cooperation (follow policies and cooperate with staff), and participation (constructive suggestions, as well as reporting complaints or service excellence).

INTERNAL MARKETING—RELATIONSHIPS AND VALUE CREATION

More than ever before, marketing planners must pay careful attention to the design of an integrated *internal* marketing programme. Increased attention toward the internal market (i.e. employees) is warranted because of the challenge facing organizations in today's increasingly competitive global climate. Business has evolved such that both manufacturing and service industries are realizing the importance of a genuine customer focus as a source of competitive advantage in today's economy (Grönroos, 1990).

A recent issue of *Personnel Review* (MCB University Press, 2000), focusing on new employee development, reported that the focus on costs that characterized organizations in the 1980s and early 1990s is being replaced by interest in the concept of value. Many firms are recognizing that it is the "intangible assets" of an organization that are *potentially* worth a great deal more than historically measured tangible ones. This is a challenge for traditional accounting approaches. These assets, however, must be identified and understood for their contribution to the firm. "Human capital" can be logically argued to be the ultimate driver of all value growth. The key variables suggested for growth are individual capability, individual motivation, leadership, organizational climate, and workgroup effectiveness. Further, it is suggested that the key driver of value growth in any organization is the continuing generation and exchange of knowledge and experience resulting from cooperation and teamwork.

As the global economy moves toward increased reliance upon innovation-based organizations and knowledge-based workers, firms will have to look internally for sources of competitive advantage. Amidst the current environment of change, the only competitive weapon remaining *is* organization (Ulrich, 1998). In an environment of great flux where profound changes occur, it is perhaps *only* this resource that the firm can depend upon as possessing ongoing potential for sustainable competitive advantage. The employees represent the most constant and fundamental component of the organization as they, in fact, *are* the organization and are the basis upon which to begin the development of sustainable firm competencies. The development of a "human resource as customer" initiative would best be served through the contributions of both the marketing and HR functions as it reflects the common roots of both disciplines within psychological theory.

Background of Internal Marketing

Although the term "internal marketing" (IM) has been employed in the marketing and HR literature for over 20 years, there still remains an ambiguous cloud around how it is conceptualized, and the extent to which a shared definition exists among researchers and practitioners. Effective IM practices develop effective internal exchanges between the organization and its employee groups as a prerequisite for successful exchanges in external markets.

Gilmore and Carson (1995) describe the range of IM activities as including:

1. The internal and external marketing interface;
2. The application of the marketing mix to internal customers;
3. The use of marketing training and internal communication methods to *sell* the staff on their role within the organization;
4. The involvement and empowering of staff to allow them to make decisions in relation to dealing with customers;
5. The development of managers' and employees' role responsibility and cross-functional participation;
6. The functional responsibility of the organization for internal marketing integration.

Evidence suggests that success in the marketplace is predicated upon successful integration *within* the organization. The literature portrays IM as having two primary focuses. It is designed to complement external strategic marketing efforts through the facilitation of personal interactions between staff and "clients". These interactions are seen to be instrumental in encouraging customer attraction and satisfaction. Secondly, and more fundamentally, it serves to develop and maintain a motivated and satisfied workforce that contributes to the organization's external and strategic marketing objectives, as well as to quality, productivity, and efficiency (Congram, Czepiel, & Shanahan, 1987; MacStravic, 1985). As such, a successful IM initiative would serve both the organization and the individual employee.

Cultural Initiative

An IM programme should be envisioned as a culture change initiative in that it transforms the orientation of the organization such that it is focused upon a customer service orientation. Such a culture demonstrates an appreciation of *all* customers. The firm grows to value its employees through greater employee focus, employees treat their internal customers similarly (cooperation and teamwork), which is carried through to the external customer. A service- and customer-oriented culture should come to dominate most of the functioning of the firm. Such a culture can be expected to create parallel streams of value for the internal and external customer groups.

Hogg, Carter, and Dunne (1998) believe that enlightened employers communicate the business aims, values, and performance of their organization, in order to encourage employees to participate actively in the success of the business. Despite this, resistance to cultural change on the part of employees will persist. The internal social psychological environment of the organization is an important element, and like the culture is related to the influences and perceptions of the values and behaviour of the participants of the organization in relation to their environment. Employee development such as this will be an effective means to evolving organizational culture, provided it is a long-term commitment of the organization.

Efforts to produce external customer value should include parallel development of inward functions aimed at creating value for the internal client as a means of leveraging all other marketing, promotional, and service-quality initiatives: Such efforts would address factors such as internal communications, workplace design, job design, employee selection and development, employee reward/remuneration and recognition, as well as the tools and technology utilized. Such a culture would focus not only upon internal administration and functioning, but would place great emphasis on the "softer" components of the organization and on functioning at the interpersonal level. As such, great value and importance would be placed not only upon the customer, but also upon the employee as a valuable resource of the firm.

The Role of Employees

Customer satisfaction, loyalty, efficient service provision, and the firm image must become the joint responsibility of management, support, and contact employees. This responsibility can only be successfully distributed if the cooperation of all involved is sought and nurtured. It is important that employees have a sense that their role is recognized and valued by management.

Employee involvement and commitment are obtained through the creation of "ownership" of the responsibility for quality service delivery within and outside the firm. Such ownership cannot be dictated. In one respect, the employee can be seen as holding the power to control successful service delivery (Mills, 1986). Also, over time employees increase in value to the firm as they develop an organizational memory. They have developed skills, contacts, associations, and affiliations that enhance their organizational contribution. If such employees feel that the firm is not fulfilling its obligation as an employer to the internal market, and/or its role as a service provider to the external market, employees may decrease the commitment they show to the firm, or even sabotage the process. Through a failure to develop such "faith" in the employer, or in losing the respect of employees, the organization will miss out on the full potential of employees through their conscious or unconscious reactions. Employee reaction may not be evident, as it can manifest itself through a simple reduction in the expenditure of effort, their consideration for others in the firm, or concern for outcomes of their job actions.

Within the service organization, HR can be seen and utilized as a marketing resource. As such, HR can provide a potential competitive advantage through the development of integrated HR/personnel and marketing plans. Social complexity provides a formidable barrier to competition, thereby serving as a sustainable source of competitive advantage in a service economy. Social complexity is a function of the degree of integration and complexity of social and communicative functions within the firm. The greater the complexity, the lower the likelihood of successful imitation by competitors. Integration between functional units improves communication and understanding with regard to the desired goals. This can range from informal consultation and information to hierarchical, multi-point structures (Lewis & Varey, 1999). Integration between these units creates synergies that may not otherwise be achieved and further enhances potential competitive advantage.

SUMMARY

This chapter has provided an overview of the role of organizational teamwork in the creation of an environment that is conducive to the development and maintenance of genuine relationships with external customers—a growing field often referred to as "relationship marketing". It advocates the cultivation of relationships *within* the firm, with employees playing the role of *internal* customers. This is not a new view, as the importance of employees as boundary-spanning representatives of the firm—playing roles as both representatives of the firm to the outside world and as internal customers of other divisions and of management—has long been acknowledged.

The perspective presented here is different in that it stresses an expanded and cooperative role for both the HR and marketing functions within the firm to establish an environment conducive to the creation of a relationships focus. Teamwork is required that sees HR and marketing operating in a seamless manner, with the single goal of cultivating genuine, lasting relationships with external customers. To do so will require an acceptance of the fact that both departments and others are responsible for creating such an environment and that interaction with external customers cannot be seen to be the sole or even principal responsibility of marketing.

Not addressed in this chapter, although implied, is the fact that membership on the "relationship creation team" should not be limited to the obvious HR and marketing departments. In fact, if the establishment and nurturing of genuine relationships with customers and other stakeholder groups are to be accepted as the organizational goal and responsibility of the firm, then it demands an organization-wide commitment to the task. This requires that literally all components of the firm be on the team. For example, communications, both internal and external, are an essential component of relationship building. Although a communications function might be found within the marketing department, it is generally focused on the development of advertising, public relations, and other forms of communications with customers and other external groups. Internal communications with employees are also an essential component of a relationship-building strategy, as it is critically important that employees are provided with the information they need to perform in accordance with the goals of the relationship-focused firm.

Similarly, individuals within the firm who are responsible for operations, information technology, and systems are equally important to relationship building. It should be obvious that various systems and processes that exist within all organizations often get in the way of establishing lasting relationships with external customers. The same is true of the internal relationship-building function. Providing employees with the tools they need to do the job, with information systems, and with seamless technology is important to enabling them to behave in a manner that encourages them to build relationships with customers, as is the elimination of rules and processes that create frustrations and impediments to relationship building.

In short, the practice of "relationship marketing" demands an organizational commitment to teamwork. It requires that all departments of a firm are members of the team and not just those who have an obvious responsibility for customer interaction. Those who are responsible for the management of the HR of the firm, and those who develop, install, and manage systems, processes, and technology, are all valuable members of the team.

REFERENCES

Avtgis, T. A. (2000). Unwillingness to communicate and satisfaction in organizational relationships. *Psychological Reports, 87*, 82–84.

Barnes, J. G. (1997). Closeness, strength, and satisfaction: examining the nature of relationships between providers of financial services and their retail customers. *Psychology and Marketing, 14*, 765–790.

Barnes, J. G. (2001). *Secrets of Customer Relationship Management: It's All About How You Make Them Feel*. New York: McGraw-Hill.

Ben-Rachev, G. G. (2001). Relationship selling and trust: antecedents and outcomes. *Dissertations Abstracts International Section A: Humanities and Social Sciences, 61*(9-A), April 2001, 3658.

Bettencourt, L. A. (1997). Customer voluntary performance: customers as partners in service delivery. *Journal of Retailing, Special Issue: Service Marketing, 73*(3), 383–406.

Bishop, J. W. & Dow, S. K. (2000). An examination of organizational and team commitment in a self-directed team environment. *Journal of Applied Psychology, 85*(3), 439–450.

Bradley, G. L. & Sparks, B. A. (2000). Customer reactions to staff empowerment: mediators and moderators. *Journal of Applied Psychology, 30*(5), 991–1012.

Congram, C., Czepiel, J., & Shanahan, J. (1987). Achieving internal integration in service organizations: five propositions. In J. Czepiel, C. Congram, & J. Shanahan (eds), *The Services Challenge: Integrating for Competitive Advantage*. Chicago: AMA Proceedings Series.

Corsun, D. L. & Enz, C. A. (1999). Predicting psychological empowerment among service workers: the effect of support-based relationships. *Human Relations, 52*(2), 205–224.

Cosier, R. A. & Dalton, D. R. (1988). Competition and cooperation: effects of value dissensus and predisposition to help. *Human Relations, 41*(11), 823–839.

Costa, A. C., Roe, R. A., & Taillieu, T. (2001). Trust within teams: the relation with performance effectiveness. *European Journal of Work and Organizational Psychology, 10*(3), 225–244.

Dunne, P. A. & Barnes, J. G. (2000). Internal marketing: a relationships and value-creation view. In R. J. Varey & B. R. Lewis (eds), *Internal Marketing: Directions for Management* (pp. 192–220). New York: Routledge.

Elliot, R. (1998). A model of emotion-driven choice. *Journal of Marketing Management, 14*, 95–108.

Garbarino, E. & Johnson, M. S. (1999). The different roles of satisfaction, trust, and commitment in customer relationships. *Journal of Marketing, 63*(2), 70–87.

Gilmore, A. & Carson, D. (1995). Managing and marketing to internal customers. In W. J. Glynn & J. G. Barnes (eds), *Understanding Services Management*, Chichester: John Wiley & Sons.

Grönroos, C. (1990). *Service Management and Marketing: Managing the Moments of Truth in Service Competition*. Lexington, Mass.: Lexington Books.

Grönroos, C. (1995). Relationship marketing: the strategy continuum. *Journal of the Academy of Marketing Science, 23*(4), 252–254.

Heskett, J., Jones, T., Loveman, G., Sasser, W., & Schlesinger, L. (1994). Putting the service–profit chain to work. *Harvard Business Review, 72*(2), 164–174.

Hogg, G., Carter, S., & Dunne, A. (1998). Investing in people: internal marketing and corporate culture. *Journal of Marketing Management, 14*, 879–895.

Kirkman, B. L. & Rosen, B. (1999). Beyond self-management: antecedents and consequences of team empowerment. *Academy of Management Journal, 42*(1), 58–74.

Koys, Daniel J. (2001). The effects of employee satisfaction, organizational behavior, and employee turnover on organizational effectiveness: a unit-level, longitudinal study. *Personnel Psychology, 54*(1), 101–114.

LePine, J. A. & van Dyne, L. (2001). Voice and cooperative behavior as contrasting forms of contextual performance: evidence of differential relationships with big five personality characteristics and cognitive ability. *Journal of Applied Psychology, 86*(2), 326–336.
Lewis, B. & Varey, R. (1999). Beyond the popular conception of internal marketing. Presented at the 1999 SERVSIG Services Research Conference of the American Marketing Association, "Jazzing into the New Millennium", April 10–13, New Orleans, La.
Liden, R. C., Wayne, S. J., & Sparrowe, R. T. (2000). An examination of the role of psychological empowerment on the relations between the job, interpersonal relationships, and work outcomes. *Journal of Applied Psychology, 85*(3), 407–416.
MacKenzie, S., Podsakoff, P., & Rich, G. (2001). Transformational and transactional leadership and salesperson performance. *Journal of the Academy of Marketing Science, 29*(2), 115–134.
MacStravic, R. S. (1985). Internal marketing for hospitals. *Health Marketing Quarterly, 3*(2/3), 47–54.
MCB University Press North America (2000). New employee development: successful innovations or token gestures? *Personnel Review: Special Issue, 29*(4), 521–533.
Mills, P. (1986). *Managing Service Industries*. Cambridge, Mass.: Ballinger Publishing Company.
Randolph, W. A. (2000). Re-thinking empowerment: why is it so hard to achieve? *Organizational Dynamics, 29*(2), 94–107.
Rowe, G. W. & Barnes, J. G. (1998). Relationship marketing and sustained competitive advantage. *Journal of Market Focused Management, 2*, 281–297.
Siegall, M. & Gardner, S. (2000). Contextual factors of psychological empowerment. *Personnel Review, 29*(5/6), 703–722.
Solomon, R. C. (1993). *Ethics and Excellence*. New York: Oxford University Press.
Sonnentag, S. (2000). Excellent performance: the role of communication and cooperation processes. *Applied Psychology: An International Review. Special Issue: Work Motivation: Theory, Research and Practice, 49*(3), 483–497.
Sparks, B. A., Bradley, G. L., & Callan, V. J. (1997). The impact of staff empowerment and communication style on customer evaluations: the special case of service failure. *Psychology and Marketing, 14*(5), 475–493.
Tepper, B. J., Lockhart, D., & Hoobler, J. (2001). Justice, citizenship, and role definition effects. *Journal of Applied Psychology, 86*(4), 789–796.
Ulrich, D. (1998). A new mandate for human resources. *Harvard Business Review, 76*(1), 124–134.
Weiss, E. M. (1999). Perceived workplace conditions and first-year teachers' morale, career choice commitment and planned retention: a secondary analysis. *Teaching and Teacher Education, 15*(8), 861–879.

26

STRATEGIC ALLIANCES AND THE EVOLUTION OF TRUST ACROSS ORGANIZATIONAL LEVELS

Steven C. Currall and Andrew C. Inkpen*

There is an extensive literature examining the role of trust as a central issue for successful management of strategic alliances. Many researchers have argued that alliances should be based on trust (e.g. Buckley & Casson, 1988; Child, 2001; Das & Teng, 1998; Gulati, 1995; Harrigan, 1986; Inkpen & Currall, 1998; Madhok, 1995; Park & Ungson, 1997; Parkhe, 1993; Saxton, 1997; Yan & Gray, 1994). Practitioners echo this perspective, frequently citing trust as essential to successful alliances. In this chapter we summarize the antecedents and consequences of trust in alliances. We then examine trust at multiple organizational levels. For example, trust may exist between the individual managers assigned to the alliance by the respective alliance partners. Or, trust may exist at an organizational level because of extensive interfirm collaboration prior to the formation of the focal alliance. In some cases, alliance-based trust may be present at one level and absent at another. More specifically, we are interested in the question of how trust at one organizational level shapes and influences trust at another level. To do this, we develop the metaphor of trust traveling across organizational levels. The question of how trust travels has important implications for the successful formation and implementation of strategic alliances. As Doz (1996) pointed out, negotiating and forming an alliance initiates a dynamic relationship that, to be successful, will have to go through a series of evolutionary transitions. We believe that the evolution of trust, as well as the movement of trust across levels, plays a central role in these transitions.

The chapter is organized as follows. We begin by providing some definitional background material on alliances and trust, which is followed by a discussion of the antecedents and consequences of alliance trust. We also explain how trust can be conceptualized at different organizational levels. We then consider the factors that facilitate trust traveling

* The authors contributed equally to this chapter.

International Handbook of Organizational Teamwork and Cooperative Working. Edited by M. A. West, D. Tjosvold, and K. G. Smith.

across organizational levels (e.g. from person level to organization level), as well as factors that block trust from traveling across levels. Finally, we discuss research and managerial implications and directions for future research.

DEFINITIONAL BACKGROUND

Strategic alliances have three important characteristics. First, the two (or more) firms partnering remain as independent firms subsequent to the formation of the alliance. Second, alliances possess the feature of ongoing mutual interdependence, in which one party is vulnerable to the other (Parkhe, 1993). Mutual interdependence leads to shared control and management, which contributes to the complexity of alliance management and often creates significant administrative and coordination costs. Third, because the partners remain independent, there is uncertainty as to what one party is counting on the other party to do (Powell, 1996). As a result, alliances are frequently described as difficult to manage and highly unstable.

Alliance Trust

We define alliance trust as the decision to rely on another alliance party (i.e. person, group, or firm) under a condition of risk. Reliance is action by one party that allows that party's fate to be determined by the other party (Zand, 1972). Risk means that a party would experience potentially negative outcomes, i.e. injury or loss (March & Shapira, 1987; Sitkin & Pablo, 1992), from the untrustworthiness of the other party. Thus, under a condition of risk, a party's trust is signified by a decision to take action that puts its fate in the hands of the other party (Currall & Inkpen, 2002; Currall & Judge, 1995; Inkpen & Currall, 1998). Trust is based on assessments of the level of risk associated with the alliance as well as on the extent to which the other party is likely to be trustworthy. At the person level, these perceptions are formed and held by a single individual. At the group or firm level, these perceptions are formed and held by a collectivity of individuals.

Risk is a precondition for the existence of trust, and the trustor must be cognizant of risk (Mayer, Davis, & Schoorman 1995; Sitkin & Pablo, 1992). The risk of negative outcomes must be present for trust to operate. In the absence of risk, trust is irrelevant because there is no vulnerability. There are several sources of risk in alliances. For example, an alliance will often involve the exposure of key knowledge and technology resources to a partner. In this situation, there is risk that a partner will appropriate the resources as the basis for eliminating partner dependence and making the alliance bargain obsolete. A second type of risk is associated with the resources and efforts devoted to building a cooperative relationship. These resources and efforts probably have no external financial value and cannot be recovered if the alliance terminates due to the untrustworthiness of the partner firm (Smith & Barclay, 1997). A third type of risk involves the inability of a partner firm to execute its share of the alliance bargain. When an alliance is formed, the partners must decide how tasks will jointly be performed. Before the partners have worked together, they have little information about each other's skills. If one firm misleads the other into believing it can perform certain tasks when it cannot, it may be impossible to achieve the objectives set out by the alliance agreement.

ANTECEDENTS AND CONSEQUENCES OF ALLIANCE TRUST

Antecedents of Alliance Trust

When a new alliance is created, the partners may have initial uncertainties about working together, particularly if they have had no prior cooperative relationship (Inkpen & Currall, 1998). On the other hand, alliances that start with an existing stock of "relationship assets" may begin with a honeymoon period that effectively buffers the firm from early dissolution (Fichman & Levinthal, 1991). Previous cooperative ties between alliance partners can generate an initial base of interpartner trust and also shape the form of subsequent alliances (Gulati, 1995). If firms have worked together in the past, they will have basic understandings about each other's skills and capabilities (Heide & Miner, 1992). A history of relations between firms can shape the context for new exchange by reducing uncertainty. Based on their findings from a study of 186 international JVs, Park and Ungson (1997) observed that prior cooperative experiences promoted alliance longevity. Park and Ungson inferred that prior experiences contributed to a trusting relationship.

A second antecedent of alliance trust is habitualization, which is the familiarity and mutual understanding that develop through interactions based on social exchange (Nooteboom, Berger, & Noorderhaven, 1997). The key elements in habitualization are repeated interactions and the length of time the parties have worked together. In contrast with the prior relationships variable, which deals with interactions that occurred before alliance formation, habitualization reflects the ongoing and continuing relationships associated with the *current* alliance. Several theories suggest that cooperative behavior between firms increases with the length of the relationship. Interaction over time may lead to commitment (Deutsch, 1962) and to the development of relationship-specific assets such as a partner's knowledge of the other's procedures and values (Fichman & Levinthal, 1988). This implies that when firms repeat transactions with partners over time, as they will in a typical alliance, an opportunity is created for the development of interpartner trust. Ring and van de Ven (1994, p. 489) argued that emphasis on trust by organizations can be expected to emerge between business partners when they have successfully completed transactions in the past and they perceive one another as complying with norms of equity.

Another antecedent, individual attachment, reflects socialization by individuals during their involvement in exchange activities. Personal relationships between alliance managers can then serve to shape and modify the evolving structure of interorganizational relationships (Jarillo, 1988; Ring & van de Ven, 1994) and should be viewed as critical to the establishment of trust between partner firms (Yoshino & Rangan, 1995). According to John Browne, CEO of British Petroleum, "you never build a relationship between your organization and a company.... You build it between individuals" (Prokesch, 1997, p. 155). Alliance managers, responsible for the day-to-day operations of relationships between the alliance partners, foster trust by building one-on-one relationships with partner managers and by developing a familiarity with the partner's strategy, organization, and culture.

Ring and van de Ven (1994) suggested that personal bonds of friendship can lead to norms of group inclusion and such bonds enhance the commitment by parties to a cooperative relationship. They proposed that over time, the likelihood of termination of interorganizational relationships decreased because economic exchanges become transformed into socially embedded relationships. A potential problem associated with attachment is that when alliances depend on trust based on personal bonding, problems may arise if personal loyalties deviate from organizational interest (Nooteboom, Berger, & Noorderhaven, 1997). This can occur because as Ring and van de Ven (1994) noted, alliance relationships at the person level, such as personal ties and friendships, may differ from interpersonal relations that are based on work roles alone.

Organization fit as an antecedent is based on the argument that similarities between the partner organizations help establish trust and enhance the appropriability of knowledge necessary to form the basis for a common frame of reference (Saxton, 1997). In turn, learning can help offset cultural differences (Barkema, Bell, & Pennings, 1996) that often exist in international alliances. Inkpen and Crossan (1995) found that a lack of compatibility between international alliance partners, particularly with regard to expectations about venture profitability, frustrated learning processes, which in turn contributed to breakdowns in trust.

Organizational fit and partner compatibility will evolve from a variety of factors, including similar corporate cultures and values, compatible control and decision-making systems, common time horizons for performance assessment, and convergence of strategic goals for the alliance. A problem with the concept of partner compatibility is the difficulty of measurement given the range of factors that determine organizational compatibility (Osborn & Hagedoorn, 1997). Another factor that contributes to organizational fit is the concept of shared fate. In population ecological theory, shared fates indicate interdependence in that the outcome of one party is influenced by the actions of the other (Barnett & Carroll, 1987). The belief by both partners that they share a similar fate may help bind them together.

The final antecedent of trust is assessment of partner competence. Brockner et al. (1997) suggested that because trust is based on the expectation that the trustee will perform certain desired behaviors, the trustor must believe that the trustee has both the desire and ability to perform the behavior in question. Without that belief, trust will be absent. In the alliance context, before a firm decides to rely on another firm to perform critical collaborative tasks, there must be an assessment of that firm's competence and skills. If the firm is viewed as competent, there may be a decision to trust. A firm viewed as incompetent will be too high a risk and, as a result, trust will likely not develop. The assessment of competence is often based on reputation. Although reputation associated with a potential firm's past behaviors is desirable to obtain, frequently this information will not exist in the public domain (Parkhe, 1993) and will be difficult to obtain for international alliances.

Consequences of Alliance Trust

The risk of partner opportunistic behavior plays a pivotal role in all alliances, not because all economic agents behave opportunistically all the time, but because it is difficult to differentiate those that do from those that do not (Parkhe, 1993). The risk stemming from opportunism has two dimensions: the probability that Partner 1 will behave opportunistically and the extent of loss incurred by Partner 2 if Partner 1 does (Nooteboom, Berger, & Noorderhaven, 1997). Firms that refrain from acting opportunistically are said to forbear. In a truly cooperative alliance, mutual forbearance is an essential feature of the relationship. With growth in trust there is an increasing willingness to put oneself at risk and to increase commitment to the alliance.

Trust will impact the nature and form of alliance governance structures as they evolve over time. The level of trust between the partners will influence the choice of governance structures. Noncontractual safeguards are more likely when there is a high level of trust between the partners. Governance costs under conditions of distrust will be greater and procedures will be more formal, such as more detailed contract documentation, more frequent board meetings, and closer scrutiny by lawyers. These procedures will result in additional transaction costs to the alliance partners. Parkhe (1993) found support for the hypothesis that elaborateness of safeguards and the perception of opportunistic behavior are directly related. As the fear of opportunism fades because of the development of mutual trust, there should be a reduction in coordination and monitoring costs and firms may substitute trust for contractual safeguards when they form repeat alliances (Gulati, 1995).

The formation of an alliance requires an investment in relation-specific assets. The risk associated with some alliance assets is that they may have limited alternative uses in the event of alliance termination. Subsequent to the alliance formation, the partners will often be faced with additional investment decisions involving expansion or shifts in strategic direction. We propose that the willingness of alliance partners to make subsequent investments in relation-specific assets will be related to the level of interfirm trust that has developed over the life of the alliance. By the time subsequent relation-specific investments are required, the partners will have worked together and a high or low level of trust will be established. Therefore, subsequent investments will be able to take into account the relationship history.

After start-up, the scope and objectives of alliances often change as strategic priorities shift and as trust between the partners increases. We posit a positive relationship between scope and the development of interpartner trust. Initially, partners may be uncertain about their partner's competence and reputation. As the alliance ages and trust develops, the partners may decide to increase the alliance scope.

ALLIANCE TRUST AT MULTIPLE LEVELS

In this section we continue our examination of alliance trust by examining trust at different organizational levels. As noted by other writers (Currall & Judge, 1995; Kee & Knox, 1970; Mayer, Davis, & Schoorman, 1995; Nooteboom, Berger, & Noorderhaven, 1997), previous definitions of trust have focused upon either trust as an action (e.g. an action that puts one party's fate in the hands of another) or trust as a subjective expectation (e.g. a probability concerning another party's future trustworthiness). Our definition of trust as a decision applies to persons, groups, and organizations because all three are capable of decisions and their observable actions that signify reliance under a condition of risk. For example, an alliance manager may trust by sharing sensitive information with another alliance manager; a group of alliance managers may trust (e.g. based on group decision making such as consensus or majority vote) to open access to facilities and operations; and a firm may trust (e.g. based on corporate board votes and the resultant formal policies) to share intellectual property with partner firms. Because this common conceptual core of trust as a decision applies to the person, group, or firm, our definition of alliance trust may be said to "travel" (Osigweh, 1989) across levels.

A first step in examining trust at different organizational levels is to distinguish the "trustor" (the party that engages in trusting action) from the "trustee" (the target of trust). Specification of the trustor answers the question "Who trusts?" Specification of the trustee answers the question "Who is trusted?" Identification of both trustors and trustees is critical because, as Mayer, Davis, and Schoorman (1995, p. 711) pointed out, failure to do so "encourages the tendency to change referents and even levels of analysis, which obfuscates the nature of the trust relationship." Given the three organizational levels—person, group, or firm—there are several possible combinations of trustor and trustee (Currall & Inkpen, 2000; Currall & Inkpen, 2002). Three of these are "pure" forms in which both the trustor and trustee are at the same level: person to person, group to group, and firm to firm.

At the person level there are two primary types of individuals involved in alliance management: business development executives in the parent firms and managers responsible for the operation of the alliance (Barney & Hansen, 1994). These individuals perform important boundary role functions with respect to communication and monitoring the implementation of alliance arrangements (Aldrich & Herker, 1977; Alter & Hage, 1993) and determining the evolving structure of interfirm collaboration (Jarillo, 1988; Ring & van de Ven, 1994). As Child and Faulkner (1998) argued, because trust between organizations is largely determined by the quality of trust between individuals in the alliance, individual alliance managers should be viewed as trust guardians for interfirm cooperation.

At the person level, alliance managers may engage in various aspects of trust. For example, stronger trust relations may exist between the human resource managers of the two partner firms than between the human resource managers and finance managers within the same partner firm. At the group level, a group is said to engage in trust when, resulting from group decision-making methods such as consensus or majority vote, the group engages in actions that involve reliance on another party (i.e. group members are cognizant that the group has decided to act trustfully). Various groups exist in the alliance context, including the partner representatives on the board of directors (assuming there is a board), groups of operation managers, and groups of parent managers with responsibility for alliance performance. Group decision making evolves through a series of interactions, events, and negotiations (Morgeson & Hofmann, 1999).

At the firm level, a firm is said to trust when it formalizes policies or contracts (i.e. through corporate governance procedures) that involve reliance on another party. Most research in the alliance trust area has used the firm as the level of theory.[1] One manifestation of interfirm trust is when alliance partners use simple contracts with few contingencies. Another manifestation is the nature of technology-sharing arrangements between partners. A willingness to share technology, as in the case in Toyota's willingness to share its manufacturing processes with General Motors via NUMMI, is also evidence of trust at the firm level.

ALLIANCE EVOLUTION AND MOVEMENT OF TRUST ACROSS LEVELS

Over the course of their life, successful alliances will go through a series of transitions. Alliances must evolve if they are to survive and, according to Lorange (1997), can be seen as always in a temporal stage and always on the way to something else. Although there is a dearth of research on the evolution of strategic alliances, the work by Ariño and de la Torre (1998), Doz (1996), and Child and Faulkner (1998) provides some important understanding in this area. Doz (1996) proposed that successful alliances go through an

[1] However, virtually all previous work fails to empirically substantiate that trust existed at the firm level because data were collected only from individual persons as key informants (Currall & Inkpen, 2002).

evolutionary process involving sequential interactive cycles of learning, reevaluation, and readjustment. In contrast, failing projects were highly inertial and characterized by little learning or divergent learning. Child and Faulkner (1998) considered the evolution of trust-based relationships and suggested that trust tends to develop gradually over time as the partners move from one stage to the next.

As we discussed in the previous section, alliance trust can be expressed at the person, group, or firm level. In this section, we consider how trust at one level impacts the development of trust at another level. Specifically, what factors support or block trust from traveling across organizational levels? We focus most of our attention on two levels of analysis: individuals and organizations. Our examination of trust at different levels, absent in prior work, provides deeper insights into how trust changes as alliances move through evolutionary stages.

Three critical alliance life-cycle stages can be identified: (1) negotiation and formation, (2) implementation and operation, and (3) evaluation,[2] with feedback loops from evaluation to operation. In the formation phase, the partners make the decision to collaborate, negotiate shareholder terms, and establish the initial conditions (Doz, 1996) for the alliance. In the implementation and operation stage, the alliance becomes productive and viable. Groups of alliance managers are appointed, systems are established, and operations commenced. In the evaluation phase, partners review the performance of the alliance relative to alliance strategic intent and make decisions as to the future of the relationship. The Fuji–Xerox case (McQuade & Gomes-Cassares, 1991) is an excellent example of how an alliance moves through these phases and illustrates what Ring and van de Ven (1994) referred to as a repetitive sequence of stages, each of which is assessed in terms of efficiency and equity. Both partners were willing to adjust the alliance governance structure in response to changing competitive conditions and with the objective of maximizing mutual value creation.

As an alliance moves through the phases and becomes an operating entity, the partners and partner managers learn about each other and the alliance adapts and evolves. As the alliance evolves, person-level trust may impact the development of trust at the firm level. Or, firm-level trust may travel to a person level. The movement of trust across organizational levels suggests a series of spirals in which trust travels upwards or downwards. The spirals notion is adapted from Nonaka's (1994) notion of knowledge creation as an upward spiral process, starting at the person level, moving up to the group level, and then to the organizational level. Nonaka's model begins at the person level. As individual tacit knowledge is amplified, it spirals up through expanding groups or communities of interaction. Thus, the spiral is the metaphor for the expanding spread of knowledge. We propose that in alliances, the trust spiral also involves a process of traveling and amplification as various individuals, groups, or communities interact. As the trust travels upwards or downwards, a greater number of managers make decisions to trust and trust can be said to be robust. We use the term "robust" to mean that trust does not change dramatically in strength as it travels across organizations. Rather, the spiral involves the dispersion of trust from person-level actions to firm-level expressions of trust, say, in the form of institutionalized structures, processes, or routines. Of course, trust may not travel and may become blocked at the person or firm levels. Trust blockages will be addressed later.

[2] Other researchers have referred to "evolution" as a third phase (e.g. Lorange & Roos, 1992). In the evolution phase, the alliance develops further after it becomes an established entity. We prefer to use the evaluation term because after an alliance is formed, the partners must regularly evaluate the alliance performance and make decisions as to future collaboration. We believe that evaluation captures an alliance's evolutionary aspects and specifically addresses the issue of review and adjustment.

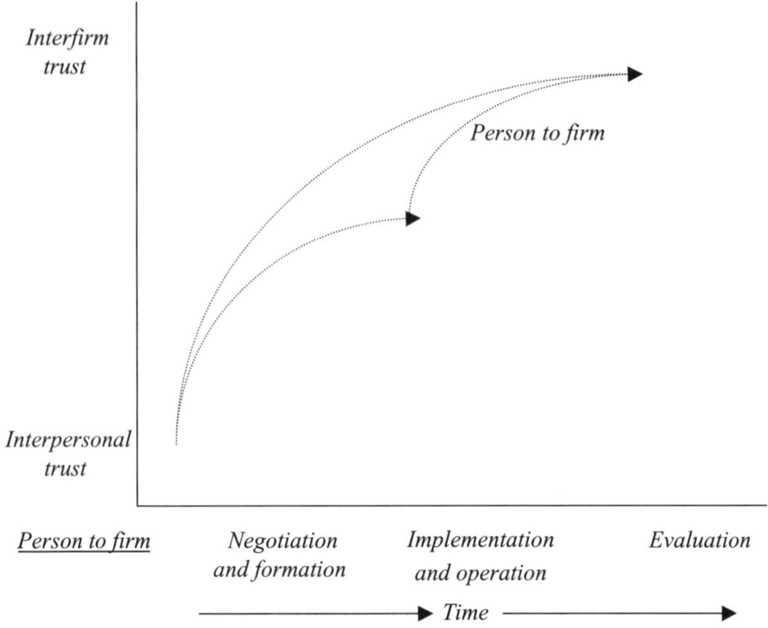

Figure 26.1 Interpersonal trust to interfirm trust

Trust can travel both from the person level to the firm level and from the firm level to the person level. Figures 26.1 and 26.2 illustrate the evolutionary phases, the three organization levels, and the movement of trust. Figure 26.1 shows the movement of trust from person to firm level. As the basis for theory development, we show only two possible initial trust conditions, i.e. alliances that begin their life with either person-level trust or firm-level trust. The reality is more complex. Some alliances may be formed in the absence of any trust. Other alliances may be formed with both firm-level and person-level trust in existence. For example, a manager we interviewed indicated that a new alliance was under discussion because the firms had a strong history of working together and because "we know and trust their people well." In this case, prior relationship between the individual managers created a strong foundation of both firm- and person-level trust. Figure 26.2 illustrates how firm-level trust travels to the person level.

How Alliance Trust at the Firm Level Creates Conditions that Promote Interpersonal Trust

We begin by considering how firm-level trust creates enabling conditions for the development of person-level trust. As we have discussed, relationship assets at the time of alliance formation play a key role in initial trust development. For example, Doz (1996) discussed the successful alliance between GE and SNECMA and the strong firm-level trust that had evolved. If GE and SNECMA were to form a new alliance, this new organization would

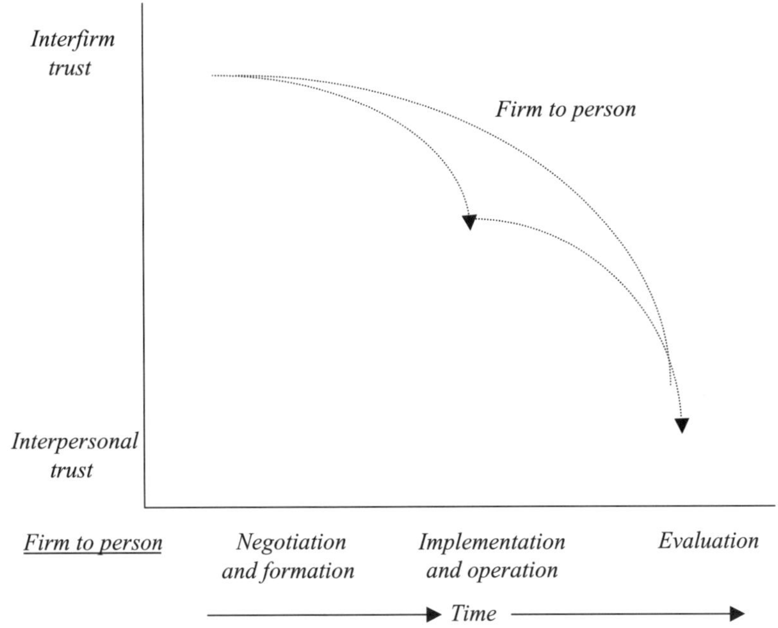

Figure 26.2 Interfirm trust to interpersonal trust

begin its life with a strong base of institutional commitment, positive reputations at the firm level about the respective partner, and expectations of successful performance. Assume that in the new alliance, each partner appoints a manager to represent its interests. Even if these two managers have never personally interacted, a backdrop of strong firm-level trust would characterize the initial conditions in the alliance.

Although relationship assets may exist at the time of alliance formation, a new alliance requires new interactions. In particular, prior relationships may not prepare firms for the complexity of mixed-motive structural forms such as equity JVs (Inkpen, 1995; Powell, Koput, & Smith-Doerr, 1996). Thus, the existence of firm-level relationship assets does not necessarily mean that interpersonal trust will develop. We dispute the argument made by various researchers (e.g. Gulati, 1995) that prior firm relationships can be a valid operational proxy for interpersonal trust or that interpersonal trust is a valid proxy for interfirm trust (Currall & Inkpen, 2002). As we suggested, prior relationships and ties should be viewed as an antecedent of (i.e. it produces) organizational trust, not the interpersonal trust construct itself. An absence of prior relations and ties means that initial firm-level trust will be very tentative because of the absence of direct experience with a successful partnership (Gambetta, 1988).

If prior relationship assets contribute to initial high level of interfirm trust, the prior relationships also will likely be viewed as successful. In this scenario, it is less likely that a negative event will materially reduce the high level of trust that has been created. More importantly, the high level of interfirm trust and the "story" associated with that trust will have a positive effect on individual trustors, even if these individuals have had no prior interactions.

INSTITUTIONAL RESOURCE COMMITMENT

When interfirm trust exists, we propose that institutional resource commitment will play a key role in how trust travels from the firm to the person level (Doz, 1996). Institutional commitment is demonstrated by various firm-level actions associated with the formation of a new venture, such as the willingness of the partners to commit key resources to the alliance, senior management of the partner firms interacting outside the alliance, and structures to promote communication from partner senior executives to alliance managers. Institutional commitment signifies alliance legitimacy and strategic importance in the eyes of the alliance managers. It is a signal and institutional cue to alliance managers that the partner firms are committed to developing an effective relationship. Furthermore, institutional commitment as a signal may negate deficiencies in interpersonal trust that could decrease the likelihood of formation of an alliance. Furthermore, in some cases, top management team members may resist an alliance because of personal reasons. Lorange and Roos (1992, p. 32) observed that "CEOs may be hesitant if they perceive that the prospective alliance might diminish their own discretionary power."

STRUCTURAL ASSURANCE SAFEGUARDS

When a new alliance is formed, information about the other partner and, in particular, information about the managers involved in alliance management will be incomplete. Assume a manager is assigned to the alliance from one of the partners. Although this manager may be aware of prior relationships between the partners and may have been told that "our firm and firm x have a strong relationship," the trust of the manager still may be tentative. Various structural safeguards may reduce uncertainty and encourage the manager to believe that the individuals in the partner firm are trustworthy. These safeguards, referred to by Shapiro (1987, p. 204) as institutional "side bets," include regulations, control mechanisms, and legal recourse. Because the partner institutions involved in the alliance influence the actions of managers, beliefs about the institutions will help form beliefs about the managers involved in the alliance (McKnight, Cummings, & Chervany, 1998). For example, the specific language of the alliance shareholder agreement may provide for legal recourse in the event that the partner violates certain provisions. If an individual manager believes that such legal recourse provides positive assurance about the partner's likely future action, the manager will be more likely to engage in trust of his (her) own.

MANAGEMENT STYLE SIMILARITY

Earlier we suggested that organization fit was an antecedent to trust development. Management style similarity is a component of organization fit that will impact the ability of firms to work together. For example, in a study of synergy realization in mergers and acquisitions, Larsson and Finkelstein (1999) found that management style similarity played a role in determining employee resistance to mergers. Style similarity was defined as the degree to which managers in merging organizations emphasized risk-taking, authority, and structure. Similarly, in alliances, we believe that when alliance managers begin working together, similarity in management style between the partner firms will facilitate the development of interpersonal trust.

How Alliance Trust at the Person Level Creates Conditions that Promote Interfirm Trust

In new alliances where there are no firm-level relationship assets, the partners often have initial uncertainties about working together, particularly if they have had no prior interfirm cooperative relationships. In the absence of interfirm relationship assets at the time of alliance formation, the evolution of alliance trust will begin with interactions between the managers responsible for forming the alliance. Once the alliance is formed, these managers, and possibly other managers, will be in a position to build person-level trust. Once person-level trust is established it may lead to the development of trust at the firm level. Note that, in the absence of a history of interaction, trust development at the person level will begin with the individual's disposition to trust (McKnight, Cummings, & Chervany, 1998) in conjunction with the perceived reputation of the partner firm. As alliance discussions unfold, experiential processes of interactions among partner managers in the alliance will begin to outweigh dispositions or partner firm reputation.

MANAGERIAL CONTINUITY

In the event that trust emerges between individual managers involved in alliance management, we predict that the continuity of these managers will be critical to the development of interfirm trust. For example, consider the case of an equity JV with strong interpersonal trust between the JV president (from Partner A) and the JV general manager (from Partner B). If one of these managers is replaced or there is an expectation of replacement, interpersonal trust may vanish. As Child and Faulkner (1998) pointed out, alliance relationships are fragile. If an important source of trust, such as a specific alliance manager, is withdrawn, the future development of trust may be arrested. On the other hand, if the managers remain with the alliance and have the opportunity to interact with an increasing circle of other managers in the partner's firms, these groups as "guardians of trust" will spread the development of organizational level trust. As this circle of managers increases, trust will be diffused and spiral upwards to the firm level.

MANAGERIAL INCLUSION

Individual managers often have multiple affiliations and connections with other managers in their organizations. These connections and social networks will involve both horizontal and vertical relationships. In the alliance context, managers appointed to an alliance may or may not be well connected with counterpart managers from the partner firm. If a manager appointed to a new alliance is connected with the group that negotiated the alliance or was part of that team, there will likely be a shared understanding between alliance managers and partner managers about alliance goals, partner motives, and so on. On the other hand, if a manager is brought in without having been included in earlier negotiations, this new manager must build a network from scratch and convince the partner managers that he (she) is competent and can be trusted. For example, when LM Ericsson formed a JV with the French firm Matra, the senior manager appointed to the alliance had not been involved in the alliance negotiations (Inkpen, 1998). As a result, this manager was forced to build new connections with board members and other senior Ericsson executives. Additionally, this new manager had to work with a Matra counterpart who had been involved in the earlier negotiations and was well versed in the intricacies of the alliance agreement. In contrast, when General Motors formed its alliance in China with Shanghai Automotive Industry Corp., the two senior members of the partner's negotiating teams became the president and executive vice president of the newly formed JV (Kraar, 1999). These two managers were well connected with different groups in their parent organizations and were in a position to influence managers at higher levels. Using the concept of inclusion (Lindsley, Brass, & Thomas, 1995), we predict that greater inclusion of the alliance managers in the partner organizations will support the movement of interpersonal trust to the firm level.

QUALITY AND QUANTITY OF INFORMATION

During the alliance implementation phase, the partners will have to create new systems for the alliance. Some of these systems will be designed to provide the partners with feedback about the performance of the alliance. If the partners have access to high quality and quantity of information, they will be in a better position to understand alliance performance. This is particularly critical in the early phases of the alliance evolution when partner uncertainty remains high. If performance information about the alliance is of high quality and quantity, as well as relevant to the partner's strategic objectives, there is a greater likelihood that the alliance interpersonal trust will travel to the organizational level. In contrast, if information is not readily forthcoming or is of questionable validity, trust at the partner firm level where the information is received will be less likely to reach the same extent as that at the interpersonal level in the alliance.

Blocked Trust during the Formation and Implementation Phases of an Alliance

Drawing on Doz's (1996) notions of inertia in alliance evolutionary patterns, trust may become blocked at either the person or firm level. In that sense, trust can be seen as fragile because it does not penetrate beyond the point of its initial development. Obviously, the absence of the enabling conditions identified above will limit movement of trust. In addition, several further factors directly contribute to trust blockage.

All alliances involve a cooperative–competitive tension between the partners. In a situation of high competitive overlap between the partners, the firms may be reluctant to share knowledge because of the risk of knowledge spillover. If alliance partner firms are competitors or potential competitors,[3] it seems reasonable to suggest that a firm would have a limited incentive to share its knowledge. In fact, a firm may have little incentive to form alliances, let alone share knowledge that could potentially lead to the creation of a competitor. In addition, the managers in partner firms may remain wary and even suspicious of their respective partners, even when the alliance managers have developed trust-based relationships. In situations of high competitive overlap, trust may be circumscribed, in that firms

[3] One of the costs of alliances is that, in the event of alliance termination, a firm that has acquired alliance knowledge may be in a position to compete with its former partner. For a discussion of this scenario in the context of international joint ventures, see Inkpen and Beamish (1997). Also, it should be noted that in many industries, alliances between competitors have become much more common in recent years.

may take deliberate actions to maintain strict boundaries around the alliance and prevent diffusion of excess trust outside the narrow scope of the alliance.

As discussed previously, the level of interfirm trust at the negotiation and formation phases will influence the choice of alliance control mechanisms. We believe that the fear of opportunism will lower the efficiency of the relationship and block the movement of trust. For example, we have heard alliance managers say that "I trust Joe from Partner A but I don't trust Partner firm A."

Blocked Trust during the Performance Evaluation Phase

The trust–performance relationship has been discussed extensively in the alliance literature. The rationale for the relationship is as follows. Trust ensures a sound and cooperative working relationship between the alliance partners. The higher the trust, the more efficient the alliance will be in transforming an input of cooperation into a collaborative output (Buckley & Casson, 1988). A foundation of trust, although time-consuming and expensive to create, can contribute to the sustained continuation of cooperative relationships (Child, 2001; Madhok, 1995).

Although it has generally been argued that trust leads to performance (e.g. Harrigan, 1986; Saxton, 1997), the argument that performance leads to trust has merit as well. Yan and Gray (1994) suggested that performance may have a feedback effect on trust. Poor performance may cause distrust between the partners, which in turn leads to poor long-term alliance performance (Killing, 1983). A firm's review of past alliance results, in comparison with expectations, can lead to a firm's prediction of the extent to which the partner firm will follow through on its current promises (i.e. is trust in the partner warranted?).

The strongest empirical support for the trust-to-performance relationship in an inter-firm context can be found in the marketing literature on channel relationships (e.g. Aulakh, Kotabe, & Sahay, 1996; Dyer & Chu, 2000; Mohr & Spekman, 1994; Robichaux & Coleman, 1994; Smith & Barclay, 1997). Using perception of opportunistic behavior as a proxy for trust, Parkhe (1993) found a strong relationship between perception of opportunistic behavior and alliance performance. Inkpen and Currall (1997) found support for the argument that trust has an indirect effect on performance mediated by forbearance. In their qualitative study of United States–China JVs, Yan and Gray (1994) identified trust as a mechanism that moderated the relationship between formal management control and alliance performance. Both Park and Ungson (1997) and Saxton (1997) found a positive relationship between antecedents of trust and alliance outcomes.

If alliance performance is worse than expected, alliance partners are likely to question the competence and capabilities of their partners. The level of trust in the relationship may therefore suffer accordingly. In turn, performance may suffer because the alliance managers become embroiled in conflict, resulting in a deviation-amplifying loop where a decrease in alliance performance leads to a decrease in trust, which continues to amplify deficiencies in performance. Thus, when alliance managers say "Our relationship is built on trust," they may mean that, because performance outcomes exceed expectations, neither partner has questioned the motives and actions of the other. As we heard from a manager experienced in alliance management, "Nothing improves an alliance relationship better than making money."

Going one step further, performance should also influence the traveling of trust across organizational level. If an alliance begins with strong firm-level trust and limited interpersonal trust, a positive performance evaluation could strengthen firm commitment to the alliance, which in turn leads to a greater willingness for individual managers to work closely together and trust each other. Similarly, positive performance evaluation will support the movement of trust from the person to firm level in an alliance with limited relationship assets. Positive performance is a signal to parent firm executives that effective interpersonal interactions are occurring with the alliance. When the performance evaluation is negative, trust may be blocked from traveling.

IMPLICATIONS AND CONCLUSION

Although the seed of alliance formation may exist at the interpersonal level between international business development executives, the execution of its operations likely depends on trust between groups of alliance managers, and its long-term financial competitiveness may hinge on interfirm trust expressed as firm-level policies and routines concerning information and technology sharing. Trust can exist at different organizational levels; trust at one level does not necessarily mean that it exists at another. Thus, managers involved in alliances should have two primary objectives: (1) to create the necessary conditions for trust to travel and (2) to remove the factors that block trust from traveling.

As many researchers have argued, a failure to develop trust in an alliance may induce the partners to act opportunistically and defensively (e.g. Kumar & Nti, 1998). Lack of trust may increase the need for control, raising the cost of collaboration and reducing alliance efficiency. In this chapter our view is that if trust cannot travel and is confined to one organizational level, alliance success cannot be assured. Stated simply, if trust is restricted to one organizational level, it is unlikely the alliance relationship will endure.

We explored in detail two scenarios: person-level trust traveling to the firm level and firm-level trust traveling to the person level. Several managerial implications can be identified. Managers responsible for forming and implementing alliance strategies must be cognizant of the factors that impact the movement of trust across levels. As a starting point, firms should seek to leverage existing relationships that create the antecedents for initial firm-level trust. That suggests that firms will enter the negotiation process with substantive knowledge about their potential partners, including why the other firm wants an alliance, the firm's strengths and weaknesses, and the firm's reputation and experience with alliances. Detailed knowledge about the potential partner can help in planning the negotiation strategy and increase the probability of collaborative success. Knowledge about the partner can also be a source of bargaining power in the negotiation process.

Firms also must view manager selection as a key alliance success factor. Managers often lose sight of the reality that partner trust and forbearance are strongly linked to the strength of interpersonal relations. As we have pointed out, the strength of interfirm relationships grows from relationships between individual managers who are involved in the day-to-day alliance management. Given the importance of interpersonal relationships, the individuals who will be involved in the alliance formation phase should be chosen carefully. We strongly suggest that firms involve operational managers in alliance formation, beginning with initiation of potential ventures as well as through the negotiation process. By operational managers, we mean managers from the firm's operational units, not from headquarters staff. Involving operations managers in the negotiations means that deal makers and business development specialists do not drive the process alone.

Conclusion

Scholars studying alliances and trust have tended to focus on firm-level issues, with few studies adopting a multilevel approach to studying trust. Furthermore, in the alliance literature in general, evolutionary perspectives are not common. In our view, a critical issue associated with alliances is how trust evolves over the life of the alliance at different organizational levels. In order to study trust at different organizational levels, researchers must adopt a multilevel approach. A multilevel approach will bring to light the different ways that the alliance trust construct can be measured at the person and firm levels. Measuring trust at multiple levels will also require researchers to develop new measures—most prior trust studies have relied on fairly simplistic key informant methods.

Many interesting and challenging theoretical questions in the alliance area involve considerations of trust at multiple levels. For example, weak interfirm trust between alliance partners and strong interpersonal trust may exist simultaneously and create interesting challenges for alliance managers (Barney & Hansen, 1994). Alliance managers may develop a strong trust-based relationship and still have to deal with partner-imposed control and monitoring driven by a lack of firm-level trust. Alternatively, partner firms may have an extensive history of prior relationships that provides the antecedent for strong firm-level trust. However, a failure to create the necessary conditions for person-level trust to develop could jeopardize the alliance performance.

We believe that as the use of alliances continues to increase, issues involving trust and its development will remain a central concern of alliance researchers. Also, we believe that the evolution of alliances will also emerge as a central research issue. Our proposed framework and relationships facilitate an analysis of trust's role in the evolution of alliances and provide an agenda for future research.

REFERENCES

Aldrich, H. & Herker, D. (1977). Boundary spanning roles and organizational structure. *Academy of Management Review, 2*, 217–230.

Alter, C. & Hage, J. (1993). *Organizations Working Together*. Newbury Park, Calif.: Sage.

Ariño, A. & de la Torre, J. (1998). Learning from failure: towards an evolutionary model of collaborative ventures. *Organization Science, 9*, 306–325.

Aulakh, P. S., Kotabe, M., & Sahay, A. (1996). Trust and performance in cross-border marketing partnerships: a behavioral approach. *Journal of International Business Studies, 27*, 1005–1032.

Barkema, H. G., Bell, J. H. J., & Pennings, J. M. (1996). Foreign entry, cultural barriers, and learning. *Strategic Management Journal, 17*, 151–166.

Barnett, W. P. & Carroll, G. R. (1987). Competition and mutualism among early telephone companies. *Administrative Science Quarterly, 32*, 400–421.

Barney, J. & Hansen, M. H. (1994). Trustworthiness as a source of competitive advantage. *Strategic Management Journal, 15*, 175–190.

Brockner, J., Siegal, P., Daly, J. P., & Martin, C. (1997). When trust matters: the moderating effect of outcome favorability. *Administrative Science Quarterly, 42*, 558–583.

Buckley, P. J. & Casson, M. (1988). A theory of cooperation in international business. In F. Contractor & P. Lorange (eds), *Cooperative Strategies in International Business* (pp. 31–53). Lexington, Mass.: Lexington Books.

Child, J. (2001). Trust—the fundamental bond in global collaboration. *Organizational Dynamics, 29*, 274–288.

Child, J. & Faulkner, D. (1998). *Strategies of Co-operation*. Oxford: Oxford University Press.
Currall, S. C. & Judge, T. A. (1995). Measuring trust between organizational boundary role persons. *Organizational Behavior and Human Decision Processes, 64*, 151–170.
Currall, S. C. & Inkpen, A. C. (2000). Joint venture trust: interpersonal, intergroup, and interfirm levels. In M. de Rond & D. Faulkner (eds), *Cooperative Strategies: Economic, Business and Organizational Issues*. Oxford: Oxford University Press.
Currall, S. C. & Inkpen, A. (2002). A multilevel measurement approach to trust in joint ventures. *Journal of International Business Studies, 33*, 479–495.
Das, T. K. & Teng, B. S. (1998). Between trust and control: developing confidence in partner cooperation in alliances. *Academy of Management Review, 23*, 491–512.
Deutsch, M. (1962). Cooperation and trust: some theoretical notes. In M. R. Jones (ed.), *Nebraska Symposium on Motivation* (pp. 275–320). Lincoln: University of Nebraska Press.
Doz, Y. (1996). The evolution of cooperation in strategic alliances: initial conditions or learning processes? *Strategic Management Journal, 17* (Summer special issue), 55–84.
Dyer, J. & Chu, W. (2000). Determinants of trust in supplier–automaker relationships in the US, Japan, and Korea. *Journal of International Business Studies, 31*, 259–286.
Fichman, M. & Levinthal, D. A. (1991). Honeymoons and the liability of adolescence: a new perspective on duration dependence in social and organizational relationships. *Academy of Management Review, 16*, 442–468.
Gambetta, D. (1988). Can we trust trust? In D. Gambetta (ed.), *Trust: Making and Breaking Cooperative Relations* (pp. 213–237). Oxford: Blackwell.
Gulati, R. (1995). Does familiarity breed trust? The implications of repeated ties for contractual choice in alliances. *Academy of Management Journal, 38*, 85–112.
Harrigan, K. R. (1986). *Managing for Joint Venture Success*. Lexington, Mass.: Lexington Books.
Heide, J. B. & Miner, A. S. (1992). The shadow of the future: effects of anticipated interaction and the frequency of contact on buyer–seller cooperation. *Academy of Management Journal, 35*, 265–291.
Inkpen, A. C. (1998). *Matra-Ericsson Telecommunications 1990*. Case number A07-99-0011 Thunderbird: Glendale, Ariz.
Inkpen, A. C. (1995). *The Management of International Joint Ventures: An Organizational Learning Perspective*. London: Routledge.
Inkpen, A. C. & Beamish, P. W. (1997). Knowledge, bargaining power and international joint venture stability. *Academy of Management Review, 22*, 177–202.
Inkpen, A. C. & Crossan, M. M. (1995). Believing is seeing: joint ventures and organization learning. *Journal of Management Studies, 32*(5), 595–618.
Inkpen, A. C. & Currall, S. (1997). International joint venture trust: an empirical examination. In P. W. Beamish & J. P. Killing (eds), *Cooperative Strategies: North American Perspectives* (pp. 308–334). San Francisco: New Lexington Press.
Inkpen, A. C. & Currall, S. C. (1998). The nature, antecedents and consequences of joint venture trust. *Journal of International Management, 4*, 1–20.
Jarillo, J. C. (1988). On strategic networks. *Strategic Management Journal, 9*, 31–41.
Kee, H. & Knox, R. (1970). Conceptual and methodological considerations in the study of trust. *Journal of Conflict Resolution, 14*, 357–366.
Killing, J. P. (1983). *Strategies for Joint Venture Success*. New York: Praeger.
Kraar, L. (1999). China's car guy: Hu Mao Yuan has skillfully blended GM's best practices into a creaky state industry. *Fortune*, October *11*, 238–246.
Kumar, R. & Nti, K. O. (1998). Differential learning and interaction in alliance dynamics. *Organization Science, 9*, 356–367.
Larsson, R. & Finkelstein, S. (1999). Integrating strategic, organizational, and human resource perspectives on mergers and acquisitions: a case survey of synergy realization. *Organization Science, 10*, 1–26.
Lindsley, D. H., Brass, D. J., & Thomas, J. B. (1995). Efficacy-performance spirals: a multilevel perspective. *Academy of Management Review, 20*, 645–678.
Lorange, P. (1997). Black-box protection of your core competencies in strategic alliances. In P. W. Beamish & J. P. Killing (eds), *Cooperative Strategies: European Perspectives* (pp. 59–73). San Francisco: New Lexington Press.

Lorange, P. & Roos, J. (1992). *Strategic Alliances: Formation, Implementation and Evolution*. Cambridge, Mass.: Blackwell.

McKnight, D. H., Cummings, L. L., & Chervany, N. L. (1998). Initial trust formation in new organizational relationships. *Academy of Management Review, 23*, 473–490.

McQuade, K. & Gomes-Cassares, B. (1991). Xerox and Fuji–Xerox, Case No. 9-391-156. Boston: Harvard Business School.

Madhok, A. (1995). Revisiting multinational firms' tolerance for joint ventures: a trust-based approach. *Journal of International Business Studies, 26*, 117–138.

March, J. G. & Shapira, Z. (1987). Managerial perspectives on risk and risk taking. *Management Science, 33*, 1404–1418.

Mayer, R. C., Davis, J. H., & Schoorman, F. D. (1995). An integrative model of organizational trust. *Academy of Management Review, 20*, 709–734.

Mohr, J. & Spekman, R. (1994). Characteristics of partnership success, partnership attributes, communication behavior, and conflict resolution techniques. *Strategic Management Journal, 15*, 135–152.

Morgeson, F. P. & Hofmann, D. A. (1999). The structure and function of collective constructs: implications for multilevel research and theory development. *Academy of Management Review, 24*, 249–265.

Nonaka, I. (1994). A dynamic theory of organizational knowledge. *Organization Science, 5*, 14–37.

Nooteboom, B., Berger, H., & Noorderhaven, N. G. (1997). Effects of trust and governance on relational risk. *Academy of Management Journal, 40*, 308–338.

Osborn, R. N. & Hagedoorn, J. (1997). The institutionalization and evolutionary dynamics of interorganizational alliances and networks. *Academy of Management Journal, 40*, 261–278.

Osigweh, C. A. (1989). Concept fallibility in organizational science. *Academy of Management Review, 14*, 579–594.

Park, S. H. & Ungson, G. R. (1997). The effect of national culture, organizational complementarity, and economic motivation on joint venture dissolution. *Academy of Management Journal, 40*, 279–307.

Parkhe, A. (1993). Strategic alliance structuring: a game theoretic and transaction cost examination of interfirm cooperation. *Academy of Management Journal, 36*, 794–829.

Powell, W. W. (1996). Trust-based forms of governance. In R. M. Kramer & T. R. Tyler (eds), *Trust in Organizations: Frontiers of Theory and Research* (pp. 51–67). Thousand Oaks, Calif.: Sage.

Powell, W. W., Koput, K. W., & Smith-Doerr, L. (1996). Interorganizational collaboration and the locus of innovation: networks of learning in biotechnology. *Administrative Science Quarterly, 41*, 116–145.

Prokesch, S. E. (1997). Unleashing the power of learning: an interview with British Petroleum's John Browne. *Harvard Business Review, 75*(5), 146–168.

Ring, P. S. & van de Ven, A. H. (1994). Developmental processes of cooperative interorganizational relationships. *Academy of Management Review, 19*, 90–118.

Robichaux, R. A. & Coleman, J. A. (1994). The structure of marketing channel relationships. *Journal of the Academy of Marketing Science, 22*(1), 38–51.

Saxton, T. (1997). The effects of partner and relationship characteristics on alliance outcomes. *Academy of Management Journal, 40*, 443–461.

Shapiro, S. P. (1987). The social control of interpersonal trust. *American Journal of Sociology, 93*, 623–658.

Sitkin, S. B. & Pablo, A. L. (1992). Reconceptualizing the determinants of risk behavior. *Academy of Management Review, 17*, 9–38.

Smith, J. B. & Barclay, D. W. (1997). The effects of organizational differences and trust on the effectiveness of selling partner relationships. *Journal of Marketing, 61* (January), 3–21.

Yan, A. & Gray, B. (1994). Bargaining power, management control, and performance in United States–Chinese joint ventures: a comparative case study. *Academy of Management Journal, 37*, 1478–1517.

Yoshino, M. Y. & Rangan, S. U. (1995). *Strategic Alliances: An Entrepreneurial Approach to Globalization*. Boston: Harvard Business School.

Zand, D. (1972). Trust and managerial problem solving. *Administrative Science Quarterly, 17*, 229–239.

27

WHEN EAST AND WEST MEET

EFFECTIVE TEAMWORK ACROSS CULTURES

Kwok Leung, Lin Lu, and Xiangfen Liang

INTRODUCTION

Asia, especially East Asia, has emerged from poverty and underdevelopment into a symbol of rapid economic development in the last century (Chen, 1995). Accounting for half of the annual growth in world trade, Asia today has become the third largest business partner in the world. Although the Asian economic crisis in 1997–98 put an end to the high-growth era, some countries have restructured their economy successfully and are once again on the path of growth. With China becoming the economic locomotive for the region, East–West encounters and collaborations are bound to increase.

Positive East–West interactions are only a recent phenomenon. Not too long ago, Asia was a land of mystery to Westerners, and Asians saw the West as synonymous with gunboat diplomacy. The mysterious veil of Asia has now been lifted by globalization, and gunboat diplomacy has long been replaced by multilateral dialogues and economic rationality. Nonetheless, deep-seated cultural differences persist, and East–West contact is sometimes marked by frustration and tension. Considerable research has been conducted to examine how teamwork and cooperation can be encouraged in East–West contact (e.g. Baran, Pan, & Kaynak, 1996; Berger, 1996; Dunung, 1998; Hofstede, 1980, 1995; Mo, 1996). In this chapter, a framework based on the notion of cultural tuning will be introduced for understanding and facilitating teamwork between East and West. A review of the cultural and social characteristics of Asian countries is then given to provide the background for the final section, which describes how the cultural tuning framework can be applied to overcome barriers to effective teamwork between Asians and Westerners in the workplace.

East–West Encounters

A myriad of problems can stifle East–West collaboration, and most people find it hard to rely on a set of simple principles to guide their actions in diverse situations. Different East–West encounters seem to involve different problems and call for different solutions. For

International Handbook of Organizational Teamwork and Cooperative Working. Edited by M. A. West, D. Tjosvold, and K. G. Smith.

example, when Sage Publications was planning to operate in India, they faced a wide range of challenges, including the political relationship between the US and India, the instability of the Indian currency, governmental bureaucracy, involvement of unions in resisting some Western management practices, and incongruence in nonverbal communication between Americans and Indians (Whiting & Reardon, 1994). Very different problems surfaced in the case of the Aladdin and Dunes Hotel in Las Vegas, a US–Japan collaboration. Americans found the emphasis on consensus by Japanese too slow and cumbersome in the fast-moving casino environment (Ricks, 1993).

To help practitioners deal with the complexities of cross-cultural encounters, some general guidelines have been proposed. Trompenaars (1993), in the best-seller *Riding the Waves of Culture*, emphasizes three basic principles in handling culture differences: awareness, respect, and taking advantage of cultural differences. On a more practical level, Berger (1996) has proposed five guidelines for intercultural encounters:

1. Be patient and persistent in communicating with speakers using a second language;
2. Recognize cultural differences, but resist stereotypes;
3. Recognize cultural differences in norms about politeness and communication style;
4. Be aware of status differences;
5. Be sensitive about the influence of people's loyalty toward their own cultural group.

CULTURAL TUNING

These types of guidelines are often derived from anecdotes and experiences, and lack a firm conceptual foundation. To overcome these problems, Leung (in press) has recently introduced a framework of cultural tuning for effective intercultural interaction, the essence of which is to facilitate two cultural groups to use the same frame of reference in communication and interaction.

Cultural tuning involves three rules, and the first is the holistic rule. Ashmos and George (1987), in their systems theory, argue for a holistic approach to organizational theory because all elements in the universe are interrelated and interdependent, and they should be studied in the context of their interconnections. In terms of East–West interactions, we also argue that all important elements that are directly or indirectly related to an interaction, such as norms, motives, and cognitive processes, must be considered simultaneously. In fact, cultural psychologists argue that cultural elements cannot be understood in the abstract and in isolation (e.g. Greenfield, 2000), and a holistic perspective is essential to the understanding of another cultural group. The holistic rule avoids the problems of misunderstanding and misinterpretation in intercultural interaction created by a narrow focus. For instance, although cultural differences account for numerous intercultural problems, a given problem may be triggered by socioeconomic differences, and will remain unresolved if both parties only focus on cultural issues.

The second rule in the cultural tuning framework is the synergistic rule, which stipulates that the effort of both cultural groups is necessary for effective collaboration. Unilateral initiatives without a corresponding effort from another cultural group are typically inadequate in sustaining effective cross-cultural interactions. For instance, a key element in the "graduated reciprocation in tension-reduction" (GRIT) proposed by Osgood (1962) for thawing the cold war between the US and USSR is reciprocity. Conciliatory moves, when reciprocated, will lead to a positive spiral toward disarmament and peace. Obviously, for such a scheme to work, joint effort is needed.

The third rule is the learning rule, which stipulates that each intercultural encounter should be viewed as a new learning process. In cross-culture settings, cultural membership is only a fuzzy cue at best for interpreting the behavior of members of other cultural groups because of significant individual variations within a culture. For instance, the fact that a person is from a materialistic culture does not necessarily imply that this person is materialistic. One frequent failure in cross-cultural encounters is the overgeneralization of cultural characteristics. Mechanical applications of cultural knowledge are likely to be misleading, and cultural knowledge should only provide the basis for initial hypotheses, which may be proven wrong by subsequent observations. Also, factors other than culture may also play a significant role in shaping people's behavior. Thus, a learning approach, which involves a careful evaluation and revision of initial hypotheses, is key to veridical judgments.

The cultural tuning framework has not been tested systematically, but some support has been provided by Kelman (1999), who found that intense, interactive problem-solving sessions between Arabs and Jewish Israelis were able to reduce their conflict. In these sessions, the two groups focused on the underlying causes and dynamics of their conflict and were motivated to understand the fears and needs of each other. Kelman (1999) also noted that learning is a major outcome of the interaction and a critical factor for promoting intercultural understanding and accommodation. It is clear that the three cultural tuning rules are observed in these sessions. The two groups were asked to take a holistic view of their conflict from a broad perspective, engage in an open, sincere dialogue, and exchange synergistically to arrive at mutual understanding and accommodation, and learn from the exchange and revise their views and judgments.

To sum it up, the holistic perspective together with the synergistic and learning rules of cultural tuning should give rise to a common frame of reference, which will facilitate constructive dialogue and effective interaction between two cultural groups. A similar notion, "microculture," has been discussed by Kimmel (2000), which arises from mutual adaptation and active engagement by two cultural groups. In the cultural tuning framework, this new culture is labeled as a common *cultural platform*, which serves as the basis for productive intercultural interaction.

Before we discuss how the cultural tuning framework can be applied to improve East–West teamwork, we first provide a brief overview of Asia. The holistic perspective requires a broad understanding of East–West differences in social, cultural, economic, and political domains, which is given below.

AN OVERVIEW OF ASIA

Being the largest continent on Earth, Asia is home to three-fifths of the human population. Very diverse languages, religions, cultures, and socioeconomic–political conditions can be found in this vast continent, which are briefly reviewed below.

East Asia

The major countries in this region are China, Japan, and Korea.

CHINA

China is the most populous country in the world. China's trade has been expanding at a rate double that of world trade, and it is now among the world's top 10 trading nations, accounting for 4 percent of total world trade, compared to 1 percent in 1980. Since China opened up for foreign investments in 1979, it has become a popular destination for foreign direct investment (FDI), second only to the US (Lounsbury & Martin, 1996). Joint ventures have remained the preferred choice of FDI, with the total sales volume of the 500 top Sino-foreign joint ventures rising to US$72 billion in 1998 (Liu & Pak, 1999).

China is certainly on its way to becoming a major global economic player, but its integration into the global economy is not problem-free. Many Western businesses have suffered from clashes with the communist-influenced Chinese business ideology (Tung, 1988), as well as disagreements in how interpersonal relationships should be managed (Hsu, 1970). A prominent Chinese value is *guanxi* or interpersonal connections (Hwang, 1987), which shapes Chinese behaviors in many domains (Osland, 1989). To succeed in a competitive environment, Chinese people believe in the development of *guanxi* to support and protect each other from adversity. With *guanxi*, one becomes an "insider" of a network and cooperation can proceed smoothly (Lee & Lo, 1988; Leung, Bond, & Schwartz, 1995). Lack of an understanding of the *guanxi* dynamics by non-Chinese often leads to intercultural problems. For instance, Chinese often see American businesspersons as insufficiently familiar with Chinese business practices and the *guanxi* dynamics (Brunner, Koh, & Lou, 1992).

JAPAN

Japan has ascended to the second largest economy in the world from a war-torn economy after World War II. However, Japan began to slide into recession in the early 1990s, marked by a sharp drop in stock and estate prices. Japanese workers, known to be disciplined, efficient, and high quality, began to question the grueling, stressful work demand imposed on them.

Japanese people are famous for borrowing or learning from other cultures, but their enthusiasm for borrowing does not mean a constant dilution of the Japanese culture. Gannon (1994, p. 255) noted that Japanese "have always been aware of the difference between things foreign and native, and early on they recognized the value of borrowing from others while maintaining their Japaneseness." For instance, English speakers may recognize many English pronunciations in the Japanese language, but the meaning may be quite different.

Japan is known for its group orientation inherited from its agricultural past when rice farming required routine but diligent and communal work. In fact, even leadership in Japan takes on a collectivistic tone, as Sakaiya (1993, p. 78) noted that "what Japan looked for in its leaders was neither decisiveness nor foresight, but a gentleness that helped rice cultivation proceed smoothly and a spirit of self-sacrifice to take the lead in getting to work."

SOUTH KOREA

South Korea lies on the southern part of the Korean Peninsula and is heavily populated with about 45 million people. Like Japan, Korea is homogeneous in terms of language, culture, and heritage. The Korean War in 1953 separated South Korea from communist North Korea. Soon after the Korean War, the country took off economically, with its manufacturing industries as the spearhead. South Korea was crippled by the financial crisis in 1997 (Dunung, 1998), but it has returned to the road of recovery because of decisive and effective structural reforms.

Koreans are under the influence of Confucianism and Buddhism, but a large percentage of Koreans are now Christians. South Korea is a fast-changing country, and seemingly contradictory behaviors coexist. Examples are harmony vs change, face-saving vs aggressiveness, and emotional community vs impersonal achievement, a pattern described as "dynamic collectivism" (Cho & Park, 1998).

THE CONFUCIAN HERITAGE

Confucianism originates from China, but it is the cultural root of all East Asian countries. Yum (1991) noted that in Korea, Confucianism was adopted as the official philosophy of the Yi dynasty for 500 years, and in Japan, it was adopted by the Tokugawa shogunate for 250 years. To understand East Asian cultures, some knowledge of the Confucian philosophy is essential.

Five principles constitute the foundation of Confucian doctrines: *ren* (benevolence), *yi* (righteousness), *li* (propriety), *zhi* (wisdom), and *xin* (trustworthiness). Confucianism is relationship-oriented, with five central relations: emperor–subject, father–son, brother–brother, husband–wife, and friend–friend, the so-called five cardinal relations (*wu lun*). In essence, Confucianism emphasizes the acceptance of social hierarchies, with an emphasis on deference to authorities, who should show benevolence to their subordinates (Bond & Hwang, 1986). Diligence is emphasized, and so is harmony with nature and other people. In dealing with others, it is important to maintain *ren* (benevolence), *yi* (righteousness), *li* (propriety), and *xin* (trustworthiness).

While Confucianism was often credited for the phenomenal growth prior to the Asian financial crisis, a more balanced view of its effects on economic growth has been promulgated. Alon and Kellerman (1999, p. 7) provide a summary of this position:

> While the Asian ideals of hard work, respect for learning, and collectivism over individualism brought them unparalleled growth, many analysts now believe that these cultural factors led to the abuses of collusion, lack of transparency, poor banking practices, and corruption that precipitated large weaknesses in many of these countries' economies and continue to forestall recovery.

Southeast Asia

Southeast Asia is a complex region, where diversity is wide-ranging. Buddhism, Islam, Christianity, and Hinduism coexist peacefully, and large variations in size, geography, history, language, and economic development can also be found. Four major countries are reviewed below, i.e. Indonesia, Malaysia, the Philippines, and Thailand, all of which are members of the Association of Southeast Asian Nations.

THAILAND

Unlike East Asian countries, Thailand has a heterogeneous population, with 75 percent ethnic Thais and 14 percent Chinese. The dominant religion is Buddhism, with over 95 percent Buddhists in the population. The country has a long history of free trade and private enterprise, and has a diverse industrial base. Before the Asian financial crisis Thailand enjoyed a rather long period of growth, and is now grappling with serious economic, financial, social, and political problems.

The research on the "Nine Thai Values orientation" has shed some light on Thai culture (Komin, 1990, 1995). Two indigenous concepts, *kreng jai* and *jai yen,* are important for understanding the emphasis of Thais on smooth interpersonal relationships. According to Komin (1990, p. 691), *kreng jai* is "to be considerate, to feel reluctant to impose upon another person, to take another person's feelings into account, or to take every measure not to cause discomfort or inconvenience for another person." In contrast, *jai yen* literally means "cool heart," which arises from a Buddhist ideal (Roongrengsuke & Chansuthus, 1998). Both *kreng jai* and *jai yen* practices can be observed in Thais' daily interaction. When disagreement may result in destructive conflict, the concern for *kreng jai*, aided by *jai yen*, often leads to harmonious solutions.

INDONESIA

Indonesia is the world's largest Islamic nation, with approximately 80 percent of the population being Muslims (Kayam, 1996). However, Earl (1994, p. 105) noted its diversity by concluding that "Indonesia is a place of extraordinary contrast, with people being drawn to European fashion houses and car manufacturers as much as traditional *Wayang* puppet theatres."

Indonesia's economic performance in the three decades before the Asian financial crisis was considered among the best in Southeast Asia, with a GDP growth averaging 7 percent annually since 1970 (Harvie, 2000; www.worldbank.com). However, the Asian financial crisis has sent Indonesia into a deep economic, financial, political, and social crisis, from which the country has yet to recover. The pace of the recovery depends very much on whether the nation can achieve the necessary political stability for implementing economic reforms, and whether it will get necessary international financial support (Harvie, 2000).

The culture in Indonesia, like other Southeast Asian countries, emphasizes group harmony, which is best illustrated by the notions of *musyawarah* and *mufakat* in conflict resolution. *Musyawarah* refers to a decision-making process in which opinions from all parties are considered in order to arrive at an agreement (Benton & Setiadi, 1998). Once the results are accepted by all the people involved, *mufakat* (consensus), the final objective of *musyawarah*, is achieved.

MALAYSIA

Malaysia has an ethnically mixed population of around 23 million people with 62 percent Malays and other indigenous groups, 27 percent Chinese, 8 percent Indian, and 3 percent others. Dominant religious beliefs include Islam, Hinduism, Buddhism, and Christianity. Islam is the official religion, but freedom of religion is allowed. Ethnic relationships are generally harmonious. Malaysia made a quick economic recovery from the Asian financial crisis, and most of the capital controls imposed by the government in response to the crisis have been relaxed.

Malays are well known for their modesty, self-effacement, politeness, and courtesy. Historically, Malays lived in a *kampung* (village) with a strong sense of community, where the *adat* (norms) are important. A strong and cohesive community results in a strong emphasis on order and respect for the elders. Malays were governed by a sultanate system, characterized by patronage and feudalistic traditions. Despite the fading out of this system, the value of tolerating authoritarianism, especially when it is accompanied by benevolence, is still prevalent. Another popular attitude among Malays is *tidak apa*, a Malay phrase meaning "it's alright," "never mind," or "don't worry," which aptly describes the easy-going Malays. It is also noted that Malaysians strive to be "honest, generous, respectful, sincere, righteous, and caring" (Mansor, 1998, p. 157).

THE PHILIPPINES

The Philippines consist of a cluster of over 7000 tropical islands, with farming and fishing as the traditional sources of livelihood. Compared to other Southeast Asian countries, the economic development of the Philippines has been slow because of ineffective economic policies and political instability. However, the Philippines are currently pursuing export-led economic growth and the expansion of the private sector. Despite the adverse impact of the Asian financial crisis, structural reforms over the past decade, particularly improved financial market control, have reduced the economic vulnerability of the country.

Spain colonized the Philippines from the 1550s to the 1890s, when they were ceded to the US after the Spanish–American War. The US remained in control until the independence in 1956. Filipinos are of Malay stock, with Islamic, Hindu, Chinese, Spanish, and American influence. Racial relationships in the Philippines are generally harmonious. The Chinese in the Philippines, as elsewhere in Southeast Asia, dominate the economic arena. Filipino society is family-oriented, and Filipino extended families include kinship ties and unrelated others, such as godfathers and wedding sponsors. Smooth interpersonal relationships play a key role in Filipino social life, and sincerity and sensitivity toward others are regarded as important attributes. Considerable gender equality exists in the Philippines, with many women in senior positions in different sectors.

South Asia

South Asia consists of large countries such as India and Pakistan and a few other smaller ones. We provide a brief review of India, the major country in this region.

INDIA

India is the seventh largest in territory and the second most populous country in the world. More than four-fifths of its people are Hindu, and the rest include Muslims, Christians, Sikhs, Buddhists, and Jains. With a vast array of religions and languages and dialects, people are differentiated from each other in terms of their religion and language rather than their ethnic origin. India is a developing country, which constantly struggles with overpopulation, natural disasters, political unrest, and religious tensions. However, the country has survived many crises, and maintained a growth rate ranging from 5 to 6 percent since 1991. India's economy is currently the fifth largest in the world and was designated by the Clinton administration as one of the world's 10 big emerging markets (MacClure, 1995). Its software industry is especially noteworthy, growing at a very high rate.

The *karma* doctrine, i.e. achieving a better afterlife, is central in the Hindu value system. Unlike the Western value system, *karma* stipulates that the "pursuit of economic objectives and involvement with the material world are discouraged as they are considered distractions that could detract an individual from attaining salvation" (Gopalan & Rivera, 1997, p. 163). In addition, the notion of *dharma* (duty) requires people to perform their duties as defined by their particular role in life (Sinha, 1978). *Dharma* is conceptually broader than the Western idea of duty in that it includes the totality of social, ethical, and spiritual harmony. It is generally believed that social conflict, oppression, and unrest originate in nonadherence to *dharma* by those in positions of power, and that it is their actions that have created the cycle of disharmony. Finally, Indian society is hierarchical as reflected in its traditional caste system, in which people are divided into four castes, which will be discussed in detail in a later section.

CULTURAL CHARACTERISTICS OF ASIA

The previous section reviewed the cultural, social, and economic conditions in Asia. In this section, we provide an integrative review of the cultural characteristics of Asians and how East–West differences in these characteristics may strain their collaboration. The first part focuses on cultural values because there are significant East–West differences, and Chen, Bishop, and Scott (2000) note that cultural values will influence the willingness and ability to work in teams. The second part focuses on social–economic conditions that may impact East–West collaborations.

Cultural Values

Despite the diversity in Asia, based on Hofstede's (1980, 1991) framework, two commonalities are obvious in the previous review: Asian cultures are collectivistic and high in power distance.

GROUP ORIENTATION

Collectivism refers to a preference for a tightly knit social network in which individuals can expect their relatives, clan, or other in-group members to look after them in exchange

Table 27.1 Individualism scores

The West	Scores	The East	Scores
USA	91	Hong Kong	25
Great Britain	89	Japan	46
Canada	80	South Korea	18
Netherlands	80	Thailand	20
Italy	76	Indonesia	14
Spain	51	Malaysia	26
Finland	63	The Philippines	32
Germany	67	India	48

Note: Adapted from Hofstede (1980, 1991).

Table 27.2 Power distance scores

The West	Scores	The East	Scores
USA	40	Hong Kong	68
Great Britain	35	Japan	54
Canada	39	South Korea	60
Netherlands	38	Thailand	64
Italy	50	Indonesia	78
Spain	57	Malaysia	104
Finland	33	The Philippines	94
Germany	35	India	77

Note: Adapted from Hofstede (1980, 1991).

for their loyalty and commitment (Hofstede, 1980; Triandis, 1995). Western countries are individualistic, and people live in a loosely knit social network and only take care of themselves and their immediate families. In contrast, Asian countries are collectivistic, a view that is supported by numerous empirical findings (e.g. Boisot & Child, 1996; Triandis, McCusker, & Hui, 1990). For instance, research has shown that the most frequent way of handling problems in Japan was through coworkers' advice, while in Britain and the US it was the reliance on one's own experience and prior training (Luthans, Marsnik, & Luthans, 1997). In the following, several collectivistic attributes that are relevant for East–West collaboration are reviewed.

Relationship networks in Asia

A major feature of Asian collectivism is the ubiquitous relationship networks. It is often argued that the capitalist economies of East and Southeast Asia are organized through business networks, which provide an "institutional medium of economic activity" (Hamilton, 1996). A good interpersonal relationship is viewed as fundamental to success in business, and Asians often go out of their way to maintain extensive interpersonal networks.

Westerners operating in Asia may sometimes be frustrated by the low performance of their suppliers and subordinates, without knowing that perhaps their lack of networks has handicapped their ability to obtain results. Networks operate outside a firm as well, and through stable networks, firms support each other by sharing resources and information, and hedging risk. Examples of such business networks include Japanese *kaisha*, a group of firms functioning in alliance to maximize competitiveness (Woronoff, 1996), Korean *chaebol*, diversified family-owned business groups, and Chinese family businesses (Carney & Gedajlovic, in press).

To illustrate the subtle influence of these networks, take planning in Japan as an example. Firms often draw up 10- or even 20-year plans, but these plans are symbolic, and the main objective is to reassure customers, suppliers, and partners that the firm is committed to long-term relationships with them.

The demarcation between in-groups and out-groups is embedded in Asian relationship networks. In-group members often receive preferential treatment, whereas out-groups are treated with caution, and sometimes even as targets of exploitation. For instance, Indians are sensitive to the in-group–out-group boundary, and people from the family, kinship, the same caste, the same religion, or even the same language group are considered in-groups. Gopalan and Rivera (1997, p. 165) noted that "Attitudes towards members of the out-group range from suspicion to outright hostility, and violent clashes frequently erupt between members of different castes." This type of parochialism often hinders intergroup communication and collaboration, stifling teamwork in culturally mixed groups. For effective teamwork, Westerners cannot ignore the need to develop in-group ties with their Asian coworkers and business partners.

The supremacy of harmony

Westerners are often struck by the extensive effort by Asians to preserve harmony in in-groups. Because of the emphasis on in-group harmony, teamwork and group incentives often work better in Asian countries than in the West (Hofstede, 1980; Luthans, Marsnik, & Luthans, 1997). Take Japan as an example: to arrive at a consensus, decisions are often made with the *ringi* system, which requires all parties affected by a decision to be consulted (Brake et al., 1995). In traditional Indonesian villages, as mentioned before, *musyawarah* is a consultative decision-making process for conflict resolution, in which all voices and opinions are heard (Mulder, 1992). Like the *ringi* system, the objective of *musyawarah* is to achieve *mufakat* (consensus).

One consequence of the emphasis on harmony is the prevalence of conflict avoidance in Asia. Asians are more inclined toward conflict avoidance, whereas Westerners are more inclined toward a competitive conflict style (Morris et al., 1998). Asians are also more in favor of mediation and compromises, whereas Westerners are more in favor of win–lose settlements (Leung, 1997). Leung, Koch, and Lu (2002) argue that Asians' concern for harmony may be driven by instrumental concerns because disharmony may damage one's self-interest. One function of conflict avoidance is to protect the face of other people (Kirkbride, Tang, & Westwood, 1991). An affront may be viewed as an insult, and if done in public, it is a serious challenge to the target's face. In the West, criticizing an idea is common in meetings, but in Asia, criticizing someone publicly, especially a senior person, may result in severe retaliation. The notion of face is often associated with China, but similar concepts can be found in various Asian languages. In South Korea, *inhwa* and *kibun* are used to mean "face," and in Malay, face is referred to as *maruah* and *air muka*. Westerners working in Asia need to be sensitive about maintaining the face of their Asian colleagues for maintaining smooth working relationships.

High-context communication

Effective communication is a key to successful teamwork, and cultural differences in communication present significant challenges to East–West collaboration. Asian cultures are characterized by the high-context communication style, whereas in the West, low-context communication is the norm. Brake, Walker, and Walker (1995) noted that in high-context cultures, a major purpose of communication is for forming and developing relationships rather than for exchanging facts and information. Furthermore, communication in high-context societies goes beyond verbal expressions, and such nonverbal behaviors as eye contact, special gestures, and even silence are important means of information exchange. These nonverbal communicative behaviors present no problem in intracultural communication, but across cultural lines they are likely to be misinterpreted. For instance, silence during negotiation does not signal passivity in Japan (Brake, Walker, & Walker, 1995), and

Westerners often mistake it as a lack of response or an indication of consent (Graham & Sano, 1984). A different type of misunderstanding may arise when Asians misread an American's direct, adversarial arguments as an indication of unreasonableness and lack of respect (Morris et al., 1998).

Another characteristic of high-context communication is indirectness, as a direct expression of disagreement and objection may damage the face of the receiver. In Korea, for example, formal meetings are not regarded as a place for debates, but are instead for expressing group harmony and mutual trust (Cho & Park, 1998). Westerners who are not sensitive to the connotation of indirect messages may find themselves caught in a web of misunderstanding and miscommunication in Asia.

POWER DISTANCE

Asians are high in power distance, which refers to a tendency to accept an uneven distribution of power and status and to regard hierarchical social systems as desirable (Hofstede, 1980). In the organizational context, high power distance fosters a structural hierarchy and centralization, and discourages participation in decision making. In Asia, workers often wait for their bosses to make decisions (Mo, 1996), and delegation or participation is uncommon (Hofstede, 1980, 1991). Several major characteristics of the high power distance in Asia are reviewed below.

Social hierarchies

Social hierarchies are prevalent in Asia. Because East Asian countries are often discussed in the literature, two countries outside of East Asia, India and Thailand, are chosen to illustrate the social hierarchies in Asia.

The Hindu caste system is unique in India, which assigns people into four castes: the *Brahmins* (priests, poets, and intellectuals), the *Kshatriyas* (warriors, rulers, and statesmen), the *Vaishyas* (traders, merchants, bankers, and artisans), and the *Shudras* (laborers and menials). Based on these castes, occupations were hereditary and marriages took place within the same castes. Despite active campaigns against the social hierarchies, many high positions are still held by people from higher castes, while low-level jobs are occupied almost exclusively by people from lower castes.

In Thailand, *Sakdina*, prominent in the Ayudhya period, is probably the origin of social hierarchies in modern Thailand. *Sakdina (sakdi* means power, and *na* means fields) is a system of social stratification that gives each person a rank or "degree of power" and a portion of land based on that rank (Keyes, 1987). In this system, all residents are sorted into a hierarchy and are graded in terms of their bureaucratic distance from the king. Each person within the *Sakdina* hierarchy is expected to respect the dignity of others according to their rank. The influence of *Sakdina* on Thai social and work life is still significant.

A major consequence of social hierarchies in the workplace is the importance given to employee participation in decision making (Newman & Nollen, 1996). In Asia, employees may be unwilling to make decisions without explicit endorsement or direction from their superiors, posing a frequent challenge to East–West collaboration. When Western managers leave initiatives and decision-making authority to Asian employees, it is possible that they may be confused and even doubt the leadership of the Western managers. If Western managers fail to understand the tendency of Asians to look to authorities for support and instructions, they may see the unwillingness of Asians to take charge as an excuse to evade responsibility and to avoid work.

Respect for authority

Respect for seniority and authority is emphasized in Asia. For instance, in traditional Indonesian villages, *musyawarah*, a consultative process for conflict resolution described above, is managed by the village elders. In the workplace, seniority is often used as a criterion in compensations and promotion decisions. Asians' deference to authority figures may seem unnatural to Westerners, but failure to take into account these social dynamics will hinder their collaboration with Asians. Challenging a senior person in public may backfire into a personal dispute, and omission of social practices that respect the seniority and status of others may engender unnecessary ill feelings. In short, egalitarian managerial practices that bring results in the West may not work in an Asian context (Newman & Nollen, 1996).

Leadership

Leadership in Asia shows characteristics of high power distance. Take *Phradetphrakhun*, a traditional Thai leadership style, as an example. *Phradet* (autocratic leadership) calls for a strict leadership style that demands loyalty and service, and provides clear directions and decisions. *Phrakhun* (benevolence) ensures loyalty and commitment by providing desired rewards, protection, and personal care to followers that sometimes extend to their family members (Roongrengsuke & Chansuthus, 1998). A similar style of leadership is also observed in China (Westwood & Chan, 1992). Western managers, who are unfamiliar with this leadership style, may be seen as businesslike and cold by their Asian employees. In a similar vein, Western subordinates may also find their Asian superiors autocratic and unnecessarily inquisitorial about their private life.

Socioeconomic Differences

While collectivism and power distance provide the common thread running through diverse Asian countries, socioeconomic conditions vary drastically throughout the continent, and have significant impact on East–West collaboration. Several major dimensions are reviewed below.

LANGUAGE BARRIERS

English is the lingua franca of the business world, but English proficiency varies in Asia. English is widely used in India, the Philippines, Hong Kong, and Singapore, but rarely used in countries such as Japan and Korea. Although young Asians are learning more English than their parents, the paralyzing effect of language barriers on East–West collaboration cannot be underestimated. The involvement of interpretation complicates intercultural interaction by adding errors to the communication and reducing its fidelity, especially in competitive situations such as in a negotiation. In addition, in intercultural communication, cultural values often tint the decoding of meaning on the part of the receiver (Beamer,

1992), and lead to subtle misrepresentation and misinterpretation. For example, unlike in English, the word "collectivism" (*ji ti zhu yi*) in Chinese connotes unselfishness and noble devotion, while "individualism" (*ge ren zhu yi*) has a negative ring of egoism and selfishness. These subtle differences in meaning may cause difficulties in communication and collaboration.

ECONOMIC DEVELOPMENT

Asia has been a high growth area in the past several decades. Intraregional trade in Asia first surpassed that of US–Asia trade in 1986, and has grown to 43 percent of the total trade in the region in 1992 (Baran, Pan, & Kaynak, 1996). Japan started the trend of high growth, then followed by the dragons and tigers, and currently China is the growth engine of the region. Nevertheless, very diverse economic conditions exist in Asian countries.

DIFFERENTIAL COMPENSATIONS

When Westerners work with locals in developing countries in Asia, the typical arrangement is that Westerners are paid according to their home labor market conditions, whereas locals are paid according to the local labor market. This arrangement is sensible, but creates a huge gap between the pay of Westerners and locals. In fact, it is well documented that local staff are often frustrated by the huge gap between their compensations and those of expatriate managers, resulting in animosity between these two groups (Gladwin & Walter, 1980).

Leung et al. (1996) investigated this phenomenon in international joint ventures in China, and found that comparison with overseas expatriates in terms of compensations did not add to the prediction of the job satisfaction of local staff, whereas comparison with other local employees was able to account for additional variance. Furthermore, locals regarded their pay as fair even in light of the very high salary of the expatriate staff. To explain these results, Leung et al. argued that because Chinese employees were aware of the economic differences between China and developed nations, they would not use expatriate employees as their referent group to assess the fairness of their compensations. However, in a follow-up study three years later, Leung, Wang, and Smith (2001) found that, in sharp contrast to previous results, comparison with expatriates was significant in predicting the job attitudes of locals, and that they also regarded their pay as highly unfair in comparison with that of expatriates. Leung, Wang, and Smith (2001) suggest that this shift is likely to be caused by the familiarity with expatriates and a perception that the gap between the know-how of expatriates and locals is narrowing. They warn that this change in attitudes will pose a serious threat to teamwork between locals and expatriates.

JOINT VENTURES AND TECHNOLOGY TRANSFER

Joint ventures have been a major form of Western investments in developing countries in Asia, such as China and India. On the one hand, joint ventures enhance East–West cooperation and benefit both partners in terms of higher market share and lower costs for the Western partners, and capital injection and technology transfer for the Asian partners. However, the technology gap between Western and local partners often leads to conflict and mistrust. Technology transfer from Western firms can equip the local partners with the know-how for their long-term development and independence. But to avoid local competition, Western firms are keener to transfer production know-how than engineering or innovation capabilities, particularly when the intent of the joint venture is to capture local market share (Kim, 1998). Consequently, issues surrounding technology transfer are often thorny topics in joint venture negotiations. For example, foreign investors invariably find it difficult to persuade Chinese partners to accept many of the typical commercial provisions found in their standard technology transfer contracts used elsewhere, because the Chinese parties prefer their own laws that give them more access to Western technology (Peerenboom, 1998). In fact, because of the long-term implications of technology transfer, some Western investors have shifted their concern from short-term profitability to issues of management control and long-term competitiveness in Asia. Technology transfer may prove to be a structural issue that is hard to be resolved in some East–West collaboration.

THE APPLICATION OF CULTURAL TUNING TO ENHANCING EAST–WEST TEAMWORK

Holistic Perspective

Given that Asian cultural characteristics and socioeconomic conditions deviate drastically from those of the West, teamwork and cooperation between the East and the West are complex. In many cases, it is hard to determine the main cause of a conflict among a myriad of potential causes that span across cultural, economic, and linguistic domains. In fact, a problem may result from the interaction of several factors. It is exactly for this reason that we advocate a holistic perspective in our cultural tuning framework. Take the case of a Western expatriate manager who is sent to a newly established Asian subsidiary, say, in China. Assume that many workers are late for work, and she tries to resolve the problem with a local human resource (HR) manager without success. Her failure may be caused by many reasons. First, the language barrier between the expatriate manager and the local workers may prevent her from understanding the difficulties encountered by local workers as well as communicating her management values to them. Second, the norm against lateness may be weak in this particular setting. In many state-owned enterprises, punctuality is not emphasized. Third, to avoid conflict, the HR manager may not want to punish and reprimand workers who are consistently late. Fourth, the expatriate is soft and polite in her tone, and the HR manager mistakes it as a lack of seriousness of the problem. Finally, unreliable public transport may be the culprit. We can add more potential causes to the list, but the point is obvious that without a holistic perspective, the chance of identifying the major causes of any given problem is limited.

A real case is used to illustrate the holistic rule, which requires consideration of a broad range of issues in approaching an intercultural problem. Electronic Associates, Inc. (EAI), an American developer and manufacturer of computer systems for dedicated and general-purpose simulation applications, were trying to sell their products to Chinese clients in the late 1970s, shortly after China opened its doors to the West. One Chinese client was interested in their products, but demanded frequent presentations and explanations from EAI staff, including even minor technical details. To make things worse, the Chinese client was reluctant to reveal to EAI information about their business activities. The communication process dragged on for a very long period of time, with constant demand for more information from EAI, but without any signal from the Chinese client about a purchase contract. Naturally, EAI staff were frustrated, and many interpretations of the fastidious behavior of the Chinese client are possible. EAI staff may invoke cultural explanations (Chinese are indirect in their communication style, or they are suspicious of out-groups because of their collectivistic orientation), or economic explanations (they are collecting market information to find the best deal). These two interpretations, if endorsed, are likely to result in lukewarm responses to the inquiries of the Chinese client. A holistic perspective, however, demands a comprehensive search for likely interpretations, and a sociological explanation is also possible. The Chinese just started their contact with the West, and because of the lack of experience, they might become extremely cautious. In any event, according to Sanders, EAI's vice president for marketing, they were patient and thorough in their responses to the inquiries of the Chinese client, and eventually their persistence was rewarded by a sizeable contract (see Tung, 1982, for details of this case).

The Synergistic Rule

Once a holistic view is adopted, the next concern is how to manage a culturally diverse team. Three approaches are identified in managing international operations (Taylor, Beechler, & Napier, 1996). The exportive strategy attempts to completely export the management practices of the parent firm to the target country. The adaptive strategy requires the expatriate managers to adapt themselves to the local customs or practices. The integrative strategy orients toward identifying the best practices regardless of their cultural origin. A major problem of this type of framework lies in its unilateral focus. One may try the exportive strategy, only to be charged with chauvinism and imposition. The adaptive strategy is likely to be well received by the locals, but it may not generate desirable behavior. It is easy to adapt to, say, a lack of punctuality by ignoring it, but productivity may suffer. Finally, the integrative strategy sounds excellent in theory but, in practice, it is hard to identify and agree on what the best practices are across cultural groups.

The synergistic rule argues for a joint effort in building a culturally diverse team, because unilateral effort is typically suboptimal. In fact, the integrative strategy discussed above would work best if it is done in a synergistic fashion. A good case to illustrate this point comes from a rare, but increasingly common, case, in which Huali, a Chinese company, purchased an R&D department of Philips (http://www.cctv.com/financial/dialogue). To show concern to the newly acquired team, the president of Huali sent daily e-mails from China to a Canadian who was in charge of a technical project in Vancouver. In China, concern is often expressed by frequent inquiries, and close supervision is less resisted. However, the Canadian, who is from an individualistic and low power distance culture, saw the frequent inquiries as a sign of mistrust and decided to resign. Shocked by this incident, the president learnt about the cultural differences and decided to resolve the problem constructively. He explained his intentions to his Canadian subordinate, and finally they reached an agreement that involved synergistic adjustments from both sides. The president would stop sending frequent e-mails to the Canadian subordinate, and the latter would report to the president regularly about the progress of the project. This case clearly illustrates that a satisfactory resolution of an intercultural problem requires the joint effort of all the cultural groups involved.

The Learning Rule

There is no standard, preset solution to intercultural problems because every problem may be unique in some way, and intracultural variations may be huge and defy the application of cultural generalizations. The learning rule is proposed to take into account the idiosyncrasies of problems in cross-cultural teamwork. Under this rule, each case should be analyzed individually, and the search for an optimal solution should be regarded as a learning process. To illustrate this rule, consider a case described by Roongrengsuke and Chansuthus (1998), in which an American senior manager was trying to set up a management-by-objective (MBO) system in an American–Thai joint venture in Thailand. However, he could not get his Thai production manager, who had worked in the US for 10 years previously, to give him concrete objectives. After failing to deliver the objectives a few times, the production manager finally told his American boss that a lot of people resisted the MBO system and saw it as a way to make them work harder. His advice was to implement the system slowly, and focus on helping the staff understand the benefits of the MBO system to them. The American manager rejected the advice, and in fact, he regarded him as ineffective and uncommitted to his plan.

If we explore this case from the learning perspective, we can see that the American manager had been frustrated by the low priority given to objective results and efficiency in the Thai environment. It is probably true that on the average, factories in Thailand are not as efficient as similar factories in the US. Thus, this American manager developed an expectation that if he cannot improve productivity, the stumbling block must be the lack of a positive attitude toward efficiency and getting results on the part of the Thai employees. However, in this specific situation, the Thai production manager actually supported the MBO system and had positive experience with it when he worked in the US. He just did not believe that a quick implementation would be productive. Instead of putting pressure on the production manager and other local staff, a more productive approach for the American manager to take is to learn more about the resistance and objections of the local staff, and to explore innovative strategies to get results without sacrificing team morale and cohesiveness.

CONCLUSIONS AND DIRECTIONS FOR FUTURE RESEARCH

The review makes it clear that for effective East–West collaboration, a holistic perspective is essential. While previous research typically focuses on one aspect of East–West collaboration, such as the structural conflict triggered by technology transfer from the West to developing countries in Asia, or the behavioral conflict triggered by the different importance attached to face, in real-life settings, however, all hurdles, cultural and socioeconomic as well as structural and behavioral, have to be overcome. Omission of one aspect may nullify all effort that intends to forge effective cross-cultural teamwork. It is in this spirit that the holistic framework of cultural tuning is proposed. Perhaps effective cross-cultural teamwork can be likened to an iron chain, the strength of which is defined by its weakest link. One major lesson made clear by this review is that we cannot ignore any hurdle in East–West collaboration, because every hurdle counts.

Directions for Future Research

While much has been learned about East–West collaboration in the past several decades, this review has also raised a number of important gaps for future research, which are reviewed below.

More Research outside of East Asia

It is clear that research activities are driven by economic prominence, and this is why most research on Asia concentrates in East Asia. For theoretical reasons, research has to branch out to Southeast and South Asia. Such questions as whether power distance may take different forms in South Asia cannot be answered with research on East Asia only. A related issue is that research on East–West collaboration often uses Americans as the Western group, and we know relatively little about how Asians interact with Europeans. Research on East–West collaboration simply has to take on a more global outlook.

The Role of Governments

Most cross-cultural research focuses on elements of subjective culture, such as values and beliefs. However, Asian countries have been a popular destination of Western investment, and complaints are often raised about bureaucratic hurdles and inefficient governments. Lasserre and Probert (1994) surveyed over 800 expatriate managers in the Asia Pacific region about risks of doing business in the region. They noted that the role of government varies and they listed three levels of government in terms of their strategic importance to business interests. Korea, China, Malaysia, and Indonesia are listed at the top for governmental importance; Japan occupies the middle ground together with the Philippines and Thailand; while in Taiwan, Singapore, and Hong Kong the authorities exert negligible influence over business affairs. We do not know much about how government policies and interventions affect East–West collaboration, a topic that deserves serious attention in the future.

More Attention to Context

Throughout the chapter, the diversity of Asia has been repeatedly highlighted. Because of differences in economic development, issues confronting Westerners in China are quite different from those they encounter in Japan, despite the common Confucian heritage of the two countries. Cross-cultural interaction is sensitive to contextual elements, and a full understanding of the dynamics involved cannot be achieved by general knowledge about cultures alone. Furthermore, the fact that Asians are characterized by high sensitivity toward the social context (e.g. Chua & Gudykunst, 1987) adds to the importance of contexts. An obvious area for future research is to examine how culture interacts with contextual factors in influencing cross-cultural teamwork.

Broadening the Conceptual Basis

The theoretical framework guiding research on East–West collaborations owes much to the classic work of Hofstede (1980), which is based on work values. Indeed, Leung et al. (2002) noted that the vast majority of cross-cultural research is guided by value frameworks. For the field to progress, we are in sore need of alternative conceptual tools to inform our empirical work. Leung et al. (2002) have proposed that general beliefs, or social axioms, may provide a new perspective on cultural similarities and differences. While values refer to the importance people attach to a set of goals, social axioms refer to general beliefs about how the social world functions. Leung et al. (2002) identified five social axioms that are generalizable across five cultural groups: Hong Kong, Japan, US, Venezuela, and Germany. For instance, cynicism refers to the belief that the social world is malevolent. Peoples are likely to take advantage of others if they are given the opportunity. In addition to values, cultures also vary systematically along dimensions of social axioms, and it would be interesting to examine the teamwork problems that may occur between two cultural groups that differ in, say, their degree of cynicism. Thus, a productive research avenue would be to explore how East–West differences in social axioms may affect teamwork between these two cultural groups.

REFERENCES

Alon, I. & Kellerman, E. A. (1999). Internal antecedents to the 1997 Asian economic crisis. *Multinational Business Review, 7*, 1–12.

Ashmos, D. P. & George, P. H. (1987). The systems paradigm in organization theory: correcting the record and suggesting the future. *Academy of Management Review, 12*, 607–621.

Baran, R., Pan, Y., & Kaynak, E. (1996). Research on international joint ventures in East Asia: a critical review and future directions. *Journal of Euro-Marketing, 4*, 7–22.

Beamer, L. (1992). Learning intercultural communication competence. *The Journal of Business Communications, 29*, 285–303.

Benton, S. & Setiadi, B. N. (1998). Mediation and conflict management in Indonesia. In K. Leung & D. Tjosvold (eds), *Conflict Management in the Asia Pacific: Assumptions and Approaches in Diverse Cultures* (pp. 223–253). Singapore: John Wiley & Sons (Asia).

Berger, M. (1996). *Cross-cultural Team Building: Guidelines for More Effective Communication and Negotiation*. London: The McGraw-Hill Companies.

Boisot, M. & Child, J. (1996). From fiefs to plans and network capitalism: explaining China's emerging economic order. *Administrative Science Quarterly, 41*, 600–628.

Bond, M. H. & Hwang, K. K. (1986). The social psychology of Chinese people. In M. H. Bond (ed.), *The Psychology of the Chinese People* (pp. 213–266). Hong Kong: Oxford University Press.

Brake, T., Walker, D. M., & Walker, T. (1995). *Doing Business Internationally: The Guide to Cross-cultural Success*. New York: Irwin.

Brunner, J. A., Koh, A., & Lou, X. (1992). Chinese perceptions of issues and obstacles confronting joint ventures. *Journal of Global Marketing, 6*, 97–127.

Carney, M. & Gedajlovic, E. (in press). Context, configuration and capability: organizational design and competitive advantage in Asian firms. In K. Leung & S. White (eds), *Handbook of Asian Management*. New York: Kluwer.

Chen, M. (1995). *Asian Management Systems: Chinese, Japanese and Korean Styles of Business*. London: International Thomson Business Press.

Chen, X. M., Bishop, J. W., & Scott, K. D. (2000). Teamwork in China: where reality challenges theory and practice. In J. T. Li, A. S. Tsui, & E. Weldon (eds), *Management and Organization in the Chinese Context*. New York: Macmillan Press.

Cho, Y. & Park, H. (1998). Conflict management in Korea: the wisdom of dynamic collectivism. In K. Leung & D. Tjosvold (eds), *Conflict Management in the Asia Pacific: Assumptions and Approaches in Diverse Cultures* (pp. 15–48). Singapore: John Wiley & Sons (Asia).

Chua, E. & Gudykunst, W. B. (1987). Conflict resolution styles in low and high context cultures. *Communication Research Reports, 4*, 32–37.

Dunung, S. P. (1998). *Doing Business in Asia: The Complete Guide*. San Francisco: Jossey-Bass.

Earl, G. (1994). Indonesia from strangers to partners. In S. Mills (ed.), *The Australian Financial Review Asian Business Insight*. Sydney: Financial Review Library.

Gannon M. J. (1994). *Understanding Global Cultures: Metaphorical Journeys Through 17 Countries*. London: Sage Publications.

Gladwin, T. N. & Walter, I. (1980). *Multinationals under Fire: Lessons in the Management of Conflict*. New York: John Wiley & Sons.

Gopalan, S. & Rivera J. B. (1997). Gaining a perspective on Indian value orientations: implications for expatriate managers. *The International Journal of Organizational Analysis, 5*, 156–179.

Graham, J. L. & Sano, Y. (1984). *Smart Bargaining: Doing Business with the Japanese*. Cambridge, Mass.: Ballinger.

Greenfield, P. M. (2000). Three approaches to the psychology of culture: where do they come from? Where can they go? *Asian Journal of Social Psychology, 3*, 223–240.

Hamilton, G. G. (1996). *Asian Business Networks*. Berlin: Walter de Gruyter.

Harvie, C. (2000). Indonesia: the road from economic and social collapse. In T. V. Hoa (ed.), *The Asia Crisis: The Cures, Their Effectiveness and the Prospects After* (pp. 110–139). New York: St Martin's Press.

Hofstede, G. (1980). *Culture's Consequences: International Differences in Work Related Values*. Beverly Hills, Calif.: Sage.

Hofstede, G. (1991). *Cultures and Organizations: Software of the Mind*. London: McGraw-Hill.

Hofstede, G. (1995). The cultural relativity of the quality of life concept. In G. Redding (ed.), *International Cultural Differences*. Dartmouth Publishing Company Limited, UK.

Hsu, F. L. K. (1970). *American and Chinese: Passage to Differences* (3rd edn). Honolulu: University Press of Hawaii.

Hwang, K. K. (1987). Face and favor: the Chinese power game. *American Journal of Sociology, 92*, 944–974.

Kayam, U. (1996). On foreign influence: the Indonesia case. *The Indonesian Quarterly, 24*, 214–220.

Kelman, H. C. (1999). Interactive problem solving as a metaphor for international conflict resolution: lessons for the policy process. *Peace and Conflict: Journal of Peace Psychology, 5*, 201–218.

Keyes, C. F. (1987). *Thailand: Buddhist Kingdom as Modern Nation-state*. Boulder, Colo.: Westview Press.

Kim, L. (1998). Technology policies and strategies for developing countries: lessons from the Korean experience. *Technology Analysis and Strategic Management, 10*, 311–323.

Kimmel, P. R. (2000). Culture and conflict. In M. Deutsch & P. T. Coleman (eds), *The Handbook of Conflict Resolution: Theory and Practice* (pp. 453–474). San Francisco: Jossey-Bass.

Kirkbride, P. S., Tang, S. F. Y., & Westwood, R. I. (1991). Chinese conflict preferences and negotiations behavior: cultural and psychological influences. *Organization Studies, 12*, 265–386.

Komin, S. (1990). Culture and work-related values in Thai organizations. *International Journal of Psychology, 25*(4), 681–704.

Komin, S. (1995). Socio-cultural influences in managing for productivity in Thailand. In Kwang-Kuo Hwang (ed.), *Easternization: Socio-cultural Impact on Productivity*. Tokyo: Asian Productivity Organization.

Lasserre, P. & Probert, J. (1994). Competing on the Pacific Rim: high risks and high returns. *Long Range Planning, 27*(2), 12–35.

Lee, K. H. & Lo, T. W. C. (1988). American businesspeople's perception of marketing and negotiating in the People's Republic of China. *International Marketing Review, Summer*, 41–51.

Leung, K. (1997). Negotiation and reward allocations across cultures. In P. C. Earley & M. Erez (eds), *New Perspectives on International Industrial and Organizational Psychology* (pp. 640–675). San Francisco: Jossey-Bass.

Leung, K. (in press). Effective conflict resolution for intercultural disputes. In T. Gärling, G. Backenroth-Ohsako, B. Ekehammar, & L. Jonsson (eds), *Diplomacy and Psychology: Prevention of Armed Conflicts After the Cold War.*

Leung, K., Bond, M. H., Reimel de Carrasquel, S., Muñoz, C., Hernández, M., Murakami, F., Yamaguchi, S., Bierbrauer, G., & Singelis, T. M. (2002). Social axioms: the search for universal dimensions of general beliefs about how the world functions. *Journal of Cross-Cultural Psychology, 33*, 286–302.

Leung, K., Bond, M. H., & Schwartz, S. H. (1995). How to explain cross-cultural differences: values, valences, and expectancies? *Asian Journal of Psychology, 1*, 70–75.

Leung, K., Koch, T. P., & Lu, L. (2002). A dualistic model of harmony and its implications for conflict management in Asia. *Asia Pacific Journal of Management, 19*, 201–220.

Leung, K., Smith, P. B., Wang, Z. M., & Sun, H. F. (1996). Job satisfaction in joint venture hotels in China: an organizational justice analysis. *Journal of International Business Studies, 27*, 947–962.

Leung, K., Wang, Z. M., & Smith, P. B. (2001). Job attitudes and organizational justice in joint venture hotels in China: the role of expatriate managers. *International Journal of Human Resource Management, 12*, 926–945.

Liu, H. & Pak, K. (1999). How important is marketing in China? *European Management Journal, 17*, 546–554.

Lounsbury, P. & Martin, D. (1996). China retains its FDI allure. *China Business Review, 23*, 5.

Luthans, F., Marsnik, P. A., & Luthans, K. W. (1997). A contingency matrix approach to IHRM. *Human Resource Management, 36*, 183–199.

MacClure, J. (1995). India: strong tradition, new frontiers. *Canadian Business Review, 22*, 40–43.

Mansor, N. (1998). Managing conflict in Malaysia: cultural and economic influences. In W. Leung & D. Tjosvold (eds), *Conflict Management in the Asia Pacific: Assumptions and Approaches in Diverse Culture*. Singapore: John Wiley & Sons (Asia).

Mo, Y. H. (1996). Orientation values with eastern ways. *People Management, 2*, 28–31.

Morris, M. W., Williams, K. Y., Leung, K., Larrick, R., Mendoza, M. T., Bhatnagar, D., Li, J. F., Kondo, M., Luo, J. L., & Hu, J. C. (1998). Conflict management style: accounting for cross-national differences. *Journal of International Business Studies, 29*, 729–747.

Mulder, N. (1992). *Individual and Society in Java: A Cultural Analysis* (2nd rev. edn). Yogyakarta: Gajah Mada University Press.

Newman, K. L. & Nollen, S. D. (1996). Culture and congruence: the fit between management practices and national culture. *Journal of International Business Studies, 27*, 753–779.

Osgood, C. E. (1962). *An Alternative to War or Surrender*. Urbana: University of Illinois Press.

Osland, G. (1989). Doing business in China: a framework for cross-cultural understanding. *Marketing Intelligence and Planning, 8*, 4–14.

Peerenboom, R. (1998). China: China's new contract law fails to address concerns of foreign technology providers: a missed opportunity? *East Asian Executive Reports, 20*, 9–16.

Ricks, D. A. (1993). *Blunders in International Business*. Cambridge: Blackwell Business.

Roongrengsuke, S. & Chansuthus, D. (1998). Conflict management in Thailand. In W. Leung & D. Tjosvold (eds), *Conflict Management in the Asia Pacific: Assumptions and Approaches in Diverse Culture* (pp. 167–222). Singapore: John Wiley & Sons (Asia).

Sakaiya, T. (1993). *What is Japan: Contradictions and Transformations*. Translated by S. Karpa. New York: Kodansha International.

Sinha, J. B. P. (1978). Power in superior–subordinate relationships: the Indian case. *Journal of Social and Economic Studies, 6*, 205–218.

Taylor, C., Beechler, S., & Napier, N. (1996). Toward an integrative model of strategic international human resource management. *Academy of Management Review, 21*, 959–985.

Triandis, H. C. (1995). *Individualism and Collectivism*. Boulder, Colo.: Westview Press.

Triandis, H. C., McCusker, C., & Hui, C. H. (1990). Multimethod probes of individualism and collectivism. *Journal of Personality and Social Psychology, 59*, 1006–1021.

Trompenaars, F. (1993). *Riding the Waves of Culture: Understanding Cultural Diversity in Business*. London: Nicholas Brealey.

Tung, R. L. (1982). *US–China Trade Negotiations*. New York: Pergamon Press.

Tung, R. L. (1988). Towards a conceptual paradigm of international business negotiations. In R. D. Famer (ed.), *Advances in International Comparative Management* (Vol. 3, pp. 203–219). Greenwich, Conn.: JAI Press.

Westwood, R. I. & Chan, A. (1992). Headship and leadership. In R. I. Westwood (ed.), *Organisational Behaviour: Southeast Asian Perspectives* (pp. 118–143). Hong Kong: Longman.

Whiting, V. R. & Reardon, K. K. (1994). Strategic alliance in India: Sage Publications. In R. T. Moran, D. O. Braaten, & J. E. Walsh (eds), *International Business Case Studies: For the Multicultural Marketplace*. London: Gulf Publishing Company.

Woronoff, J. (1996). *Japan as Anything but Number One*. Wiltshire: Antony Rowe Ltd.

Yum, J. O. (1991). The impact of Confucianism on interpersonal relationships and communication patterns in East Asia. In L. A. Samovar & R. E. Porter (eds), *Intercultural Communication: A Reader* (6th edn). Belmont, Calif.: Wadsworth.

Section VI

CONCLUSIONS

28

PAST, PRESENT, AND FUTURE PERSPECTIVES ON ORGANIZATIONAL COOPERATION

Michael A. West, Ken G. Smith, and Dean Tjosvold

In this concluding chapter we offer three perspectives on cooperation and teamwork as important overarching themes that deserve sustained development. First, we look back and consider how our emotional reactions to team processes and intergroup relations shape much of our behaviour in organizations. The study of emotions in teams and in intergroup relations has often taken second place to more rational, cognitive, and social perspectives. Understanding some of the determinants of our emotional reactions in these contexts can, we believe, offer a liberating distance from them. In particular, we focus on the strategies suggested by research from social psychology for reducing anxiety and anger that is so often a feature of intergroup relations within and between organizations and, therefore, such a threat to the development of cooperation.

Second, we consider the development of a new phenomenon that offers a sharp contrast with our previous history as a species: integrated organizations embedded in alliances and cultures of cooperation and knowledge generation. Humans are not restricted by the shackles of their evolutionary past, precisely because they can create institutions and organizational forms that offer new freedoms. We argue that organizational theory and strategic management are moving away from perspectives based on economic arguments towards conceptualizations based on organizations viewed as entities engaged in social and cooperative knowledge generation. This is occurring both within and across organizations.

Finally, we examine the implications of the arguments presented in this handbook for our understanding of the future of cooperation in and between organizations. We suggest that research offers the opportunities of freeing us from some of the chronic difficulties of cooperation and teamwork within and between organizations. We identify themes of justice, trust, respect; the compatibility of conflict and cooperation; and the value of diversity in cooperative contexts. Pressing research issues are highlighted including power and hierarchy, leadership in cooperative contexts, organizational justice, and cooperation in cross-cultural contexts. We propose that there is a need for social scientists to come together

International Handbook of Organizational Teamwork and Cooperative Working. Edited by M. A. West, D. Tjosvold, and K. G. Smith.

(as they have in the production of this handbook) to engage with each other's paradigms in order that we can offer theoretically powerful and practically significant ways of developing our understanding of cooperation and teamwork. Our message is unashamedly optimistic.

We begin, however, by examining the experience of emotions within and between teams and the motivational origins of our tendencies to cooperate and build teams to accomplish our shared and individual goals.

EMOTIONS WITHIN AND BETWEEN TEAMS

What are the emotional implications of teamworking and cooperation in organizations? In this section we explore the emotional components of teamworking and suggest that a range of positive and negative emotions are experienced within groups, but that anxiety and anger in particular are evoked by relationships between groups in organizations. This has important implications for our understanding of organizational teamworking and cooperation. While social psychologists have made great headway in understanding intra- and intergroup relations in experimental settings, they have neglected organizations as a context for this research. And yet, we suggest, this is an ideal context in which to explore and understand the anger and anxiety evoked by in-group favouritism, out-group derogation, and intergroup hostility. More importantly, given the threat that intergroup bias has always posed for our species (think of Rwanda, Bosnia, Cambodia, and the Holocaust), it may be that in the relatively constrained environments of organizations that we can begin to discover how to control and channel this otherwise destructive force.

Emotions in Organizational Teams

The fundamental human drive and pervasive motivation to form and maintain lasting, positive, and significant relationships help us to understand the functioning of teams at work, and in particular the emotions manifested in work groups. Satisfying this need to belong, according to Baumeister and Leary (1995), requires that our relationships (and by extension our experiences of teams) are characterized by the following:

- Frequent interaction—we need to meet fellow team members frequently
- Temporal stability and likely continuity—we need to know that the team will be relatively enduring in order to invest sufficiently in the relationships
- Mutual affective concern—team members need to feel that they are cared for and in turn care for fellow team members
- Freedom from destructive conflict—high levels of aversive conflict will undermine the team

Most current research studies and theories about the functioning of teams fail to take account of the fact that the tendency to form strong attachments and, by extension, to live and work in groups has a solid evolutionary basis. Human beings work and live in groups because, in our evolutionary history, they enabled individual survival and reproduction (Ainsworth, 1989; Axelrod & Hamilton, 1981; Barash, 1977; Bowlby, 1969; Buss, 1990, 1991; Hogan, Jones, & Cheek, 1985; Moreland, 1987). By living and working in groups human beings could share food, easily find mates, and care for infants. They could hunt more effectively and defend themselves against their enemies. Individuals who did not readily join groups would be disadvantaged in comparison with group members as a consequence. "Over the course of evolution, the small group became the basic survival strategy developed by the human species" (Barchas, 1986, p. 212). Children who stuck close to adults were more likely to survive to be able to reproduce, because they would be protected from danger, cared for, and provided with food. Adults who formed attachments would be more likely to reproduce and adults who formed long-term relationships would stand a greater chance of producing infants who would grow to reproductive age.

Another perspective argues that there are also costs to cooperation in groups. By living and working in groups, individuals expose themselves to increased competition for resources or mates, and increased likelihood of disease transmission and of parasites. But individuals may benefit from being part of a group since they can then compete with other groups for resources. Thus group membership may be a means to have direct competitive conflict with other groups (see Kurzban & Leary, 2001). This interpretation suggests that stigmatization (of homosexuals, obese people, the mentally ill, and the mentally retarded, for example) is an evolutionary consequence of group membership. Those whose characteristics suggested they would not make an optimum contribution to the group would be stigmatized and rejected via various exclusionary mechanisms.

By recognizing the influence of the need to belong to groups upon the behaviour of individuals in teams we can understand something of the range and underlying causes of emotions in teams. Being accepted, included, and welcomed in the team will lead to feelings of happiness, elation, contentment, and calm. Being rejected, excluded, or ignored will lead to feelings of anxiety, depression, grief, jealousy, or loneliness. Team members' emotional reactions will therefore be stimulated by real, potential, or imagined changes in their belongingness within their work team (see West, 2001, for an extended discussion).

One of the characteristics of a strong sense of belonging is the sense of mutuality in the relationships. So satisfaction in teams is also likely to be a consequence of both the costs as well as the rewards of team membership. People prefer relationships and teams within which all give and take. For example, Hays (1985) examined relationship satisfaction from the perspective of behaviourism, assuming that rewards would determine people's satisfaction. He found instead that satisfaction was predicted by rewards plus costs, apparently because people prefer relationships and groups in which all both give and receive support and care (see also Baumeister, Wotman, & Stillwell, 1993). Within teams, therefore, satisfaction will be highest when the sense of mutuality is strong. Satisfaction will also be higher to the extent that the team members interact frequently, the tenure of the team is perceived to be relatively enduring, the team is a stable entity, and there is not a high level of conflict.

Horney (1945) proposed that our basic anxiety resulted from a feeling of being isolated and helpless in a potentially hostile world. Individual team members may typically experience anxiety at the prospect of the break-up of the team, the impending ending of a long-running team project, or their transfer to another team (Leary, 1990; Leary & Downs, 1995). Group instability (frequent member changes) and threatened dissolution of the team will also cause anxiety. High levels of conflict will also engender anxiety since individuals are likely to develop an anxious watchfulness in anticipation of conflict between team members.

Human beings feel lonely when their needs to belong are insufficiently met. Jones (1981) has shown that this is not simply a result of lack of social contact. The crucial factor appears to be spending time with people with whom one is close. It is social isolation rather than size of network that appears to influence loneliness, along with lack of intimate connection (Williams & Solano, 1983). Those who work in multiple teams on short-lived project teams, or work in different locations and manage their interaction via technology-mediated communication, may feel loneliness nevertheless because they are prevented from developing close social contacts with other team members.

But there is other evidence that simply not belonging may be damaging in itself, regardless of enacted support from those around. Cohen and Wills (1985) report that simply being a part of a supportive social network reduces stress even if those in the network do not provide emotional or practical assistance. Moreover, effects may translate from emotional reactions through to immunological and other physiological functioning, particularly among those working in stressful environments, such as health care workers. Kiecolt-Glaser et al. (1984a, b) found that loneliness was associated with a decrease in immunocompetence, particularly in relation to natural killer cell activity and elevations in levels of cortisol levels.

In summary, the emotional life of teams is rich and complex, and, we suggest, hitherto neglected in organizational research. Even more significant, we propose, is the emotion generated by intergroup relations in organizations. Chronic anger and anxiety are damaging to human health and well-being, and intergroup relations can be a powerful and chronic source of such emotions. We now turn, therefore, to examine the negative emotional concomitants of intergroup relations and how these can be reduced or avoided. We develop themes identified by van Knippenberg (Chapter 18 this volume) since they have, we propose, vital implications for our understanding of teamwork and cooperation in organizations generally.

The Emotional Consequences of Organizational Intergroup Relations

The strengths of teamworking in organizations are the involvement of all in contributing their skills and knowledge, in good collective decision making and innovation. The fundamental weakness is the tendency of team-based organizations to be riven by intergroup competition, hostility, and rivalry with likely consequent negative impacts on organizational performance overall; in short, intergroup bias.

Early research in social psychology, such as the famous Robbers' Cave study, showed how psychological group identification occurs almost immediately when people are randomly assigned to groups, with dramatic behavioural consequences of strong loyalty and in-group favouritism (Sherif et al., 1961). People develop group identification with the most minimal social cues (Billig & Tajfel, 1973; Tajfel, 1970; Tajfel & Billig, 1974). The tendency of people to discriminate in favour of their own group and to discriminate against members of out-groups is pervasive (Turner, 1985). Moreover this in-group favouritism occurs spontaneously and without obvious value to the individual. Research indicates that there is no need for material advantage to the self or inferred similarity to other group members for group identification to occur. However, there is evidence that external threats lead to the creation of firmer bonds within groups (Stein, 1976), while at the same time increasing the threat of rejection to deviants (Lauderdale et al., 1984). Groups clearly seek solidarity when confronted by external threat. An alternative explanation, which we referred to above, is that within-group solidarity occurs in order to create intergroup competition, particularly in situations where there are scarce resources (Kurzban & Leary, 2001).

Intergroup bias therefore refers to our tendency to evaluate our own membership groups ("in-groups") more positively than groups of which we are not members (the "out-group"). Such bias includes attitudes in the form of prejudice ("when an order is not completed properly it's always the result of the salespeople not getting accurate information in the first place, not us in production"), cognitions in the form of stereotyping ("the sales department are all greedy individualists"), and behaviour (refusing to give information to the sales department about the likely date of completion of an order) (Mackie & Smith, 1998). At its most extreme, of course, intergroup bias manifests itself as "ethnic cleansing" and genocide.

Emotions aroused in intergroup contexts can include disgust, contempt, and anger (Smith, 1993). The range of emotions we experience in relation to out-groups and our reactions vary proportionately to the threat they are perceived to present according to social psychologists (see, for example, Mackie, Devos, & Smith, 2000, and Brewer, 2001). An out-group that violates the norms held by an in-group may elicit reactions of disgust from the in-group. For example, a group of ward nurses who see a doctor behaving brusquely and irritably with a patient may react with disgust and avoid the doctor. When an out-group is seen as unfairly winning a large share of scarce resources, the in-group members may feel resentment and try to find ways of reducing the out-group's success. For example, a university department of psychology may feel resentment that another department (of sociology) has been preferred in the allocation of funds for new staff appointments. They may then try to undermine the sociology department in the allocation of library resources. An out-group that is seen as posing a direct threat will elicit fear and hostile actions. This is most plainly seen in a business context in acquisitions and hostile takeovers.

Threats (or perceived threats) by out-groups to in-groups are therefore at the root of much anxiety and anger within and between organizations (see Brewer, 1999; Hagendoorn, Linssen, & Tumanov, 2001). The hierarchy of threat ranges from threats to the in-group's social identity (male managers being threatened by the increase in numbers of female managers in a top management team); through threats to their goals and values (doctors perceiving hospital managers forcing them to consider resources alongside quality of patient care); position in the hierarchy (doctors perceiving managers as threatening their authority); to the group's very existence (doctors seeing nurse practitioners as a threat to their own existence). Such threats can be realistic as in the battle between departments for scarce resources, or symbolic when values or norms are threatened (Esses, Jackson, & Armstrong, 1998).

An insidious and almost invisible source of threat is that of heightened intergroup similarity (Henderson-King et al., 1997). Here the in-group is threatened as the out-group becomes more similar to it, as in the case of the conflict between psychiatrists and psychologists. The in-group, in such circumstances, will work hard to differentiate itself from the out-group (e.g. Jetten, Spears, & Manstead, 1996, 1998; Roccas & Schwartz, 1993).

But this volume is about cooperation and, although intergroup bias is the reverse side of this coin, our focus is on how to reduce such bias. It is to this question that we now therefore turn, revisiting the excellent categorization offered by Hewstone, Rubin, and Willis (2002) to structure our analysis of methods for reducing intergroup bias.

Reducing Intergroup Bias in Organizations

We examine a variety of approaches to reducing intergroup bias. Which method works, in which situations, and with what types of groups is unclear, particularly with groups in organizational settings. Some approaches include confronting individuals' biases and prejudices directly in order to encourage them to change their attitudes and behaviours. Other approaches involve increasing contact with out-group members and encouraging ways of categorizing out-group members other than a simple in-group/out-group dichotomy. However, injustice, unfair distribution of resources, power plays, hostile actions, and real threats are often at the root of intergroup anxiety and anger in organizations. If the difficulties of intergroup relations are to be dealt with effectively, we have to deal with the real threats posed by groups—the hostile takeover that threatens jobs, values, skills, or beloved traditions; the surreptitious politicking in organizations that results in unfair or dysfunctional distribution of resources; the bullying of members of out-groups; or the lack of justice as a result of favouritism shown to particular functional groups over others. If such issues are not dealt with by social scientists in their attempts to ameliorate or exorcize intergroup hostility, their efforts will command little respect.

Moreover, there is a need to attempt to deal with problems of intergroup relations in organizations by directly addressing the issue at a meta level. Rather than simply dealing with conflicts between different professional groups in health care, we should try also to encourage awareness and discussion of the pervasive tendency of humans to discriminate in favour of in-group members and against out-group members. Focusing on the specific intergroup issue may not raise the awareness of those who work in organizations of the deeply entrenched nature of this most destructive aspect of human behaviour. We therefore call for programmes of education of managers to emphasize this area of knowledge and research in particular, and to encourage them to make intergroup cooperation a central part of their managerial philosophy and efforts.

Beyond these strategies of addressing the legitimate grievances of groups in intergroup conflict and raising awareness of the phenomenon of intergroup discrimination in human social behaviour, what strategies does social science offer? We answer this question by building on the approaches to interventions described by van Knippenberg in Chapter 18 in this volume and given below.

1. *Highlighting value–behaviour discrepancies*. One way of reducing intergroup bias is to make individuals aware of discrepancies between their personal values (tolerance, respect for others, equality of treatment) and their behaviour (out-group derogation, discrimination, and stereotyping) (see, for example, Monteith, 1993). This is only likely to be effective with individuals who have relatively low levels of prejudice, but there is some evidence that this can encourage a reduction of bias in relation to multiple groups (in-group members reduce their negativity about customers and suppliers, although the focus of bias-reducing efforts was in relation to customers). So-called "political correctness" in the use of language, when it was first promulgated, made prejudiced people aware that, however apparently mild their prejudice, their expressions reflected a level of prejudice of which they were unaware and that this level of prejudice (however low) as evidenced by their use of language moreover had a destructive effect on members of the out-group.

2. *Suppressing biases*. Another direct approach advocates in-group members deliberately suppressing their biases (for example health care workers suppressing their biases against social workers) (see Macrae & Bodenhausen, 2000; Monteith, Sherman, & Devine, 1998). This can lead to individuals developing an almost automatic response and suppressing their cognitions and verbalizations against out-groups in the process of pursuing the goal of not being biased.

3. *Retraining, raising awareness, and value confrontation*. Individuals can be exposed to explicit retraining (e.g. Kawakami et al., 2001), emphasizing broader, positive ideologies

("we're all in the business of caring for people in the community, whether health care or social worker") (see, for example, Pratto, Tatar, & Conway-Lanz, 1999); emphasizing positive values (e.g. tolerance; Greenberg et al., 1992); confronting individuals with their biases (e.g. confronting health care workers with their extreme statements about the motivations and competence of social workers), and requiring individuals to explain or account for their bias (Dobbs & Crano, 2001).

4. *Empathy training.* Reducing destructive intergroup discrimination in organizations can include training people to develop more empathic responses to out-group members. For example, benefits workers are sometimes trained to be more empathic about the clients they deal with in order to overcome biases that they are simply abusing benefits systems, unmotivated, and not deserving of support. Such training can lead to more generalized positive feelings towards the out-group (Batson et al., 1997; Finlay & Stephan, 2000; Galinsky & Moskowitz, 2000).

5. *Increasing intergroup contact.* A group-level strategy often employed to reduce intergroup bias in organizations is to increase the quantity and quality of intergroup contact, for example by having the conflicting groups meet on a regular basis. However, there is evidence that contact itself can increase bias, unless quality of contact is managed effectively. Experimental research suggests ways to ensure that contact is likely to reduce rather than increase intergroup bias (see Pettigrew, 1998). A key method of improving intergroup contact is to reduce the salience of category distinctions. *Decategorization*, *differentiation*, and *personalization* represent three strategies for reducing the salience of in-group/out-group category distinctions. *Decategorization* involves de-emphasizing in-group/out-group category distinctions, such as bringing together, prior to a merger, personnel from each of the two companies to work on a culture change programme, and forming working groups on the basis of a third category dimension, such as country of birth. *Differentiation* involves emphasizing each out-group member's uniqueness and how this relates to the self: Jeremy (a member of the other company's marketing group) sings in the cathedral choir, he is (like me) a Sheffield Wednesday Football Club supporter, and he is an outstanding statistician. *Personalization* involves making clear distinctions between the out-group members in order to counteract the tendency to treat the out-group as a homogeneous and negative whole. Thus we may emphasize the different qualities, knowledge, skills, and characteristics of each of the out-group members.

Experimental research also suggests that overcoming problems of intergroup bias when groups come into contact is *not* best achieved by having the groups work on a task together, but is better achieved by encouraging them to get to know each other on a personal level. Moreover, these effects tend to generalize to other out-group members (e.g. Bettencourt et al., 1992). In this light it is not surprising that having friends who are members of the out-group also reduces bias (e.g. Pettigrew, 1997; Phinney, Ferguson, & Tate, 1997).

6. *Recategorization.* The most common method of recategorization is termed the "common in-group identity" (CII) model, in which the aim is to replace subordinate ("us" and "them") categories with superordinate ("we") categorizations (Gaertner & Dovidio, 2000). Social and health care workers in a geographical area may be encouraged to identify themselves as common members of the superordinate category of Arcadia Community and Health Action Group rather than the subordinate groups with which they currently identify. Intergroup bias is reduced because former out-group members are now recategorized as in-group members. Moreover, intergroup relations improve because individuals tend to engage in more self-disclosing interactions with, and develop more differentiated representations

of, former out-group members as a consequence of their recategorization (Dovidio et al., 1997; Gaertner & Dovidio, 2000).

Such strategies are not simple fixes where categorizations are of long standing or are based on very strong categorizations such as the long-standing tensions between midwives and junior doctors in hospitals. In that circumstance, appealing to a common superordinate group identity (we are all employees of one hospital) may be ineffective. Similarly, where there is a history of direct antagonism, and where minorities have been dominated by a majority out-group (van Oudenhoven, Prins, & Buunk, 1998), superordinate group identity may constitute a threat (Brewer, 2000; Hornsey & Hogg, 1999). In this case, both decategorization and recategorization models threaten valued social identities in small groups (Brewer, 1999). Members of a small family firm that has produced high-quality craft products for a generation, in competition with larger multinational firms, may find attempts to decategorize and recategorize in a merger immensely threatening. It is to the strategy of maintaining the salience of category distinctions in such circumstances that we now turn.

7. *Maintaining the salience of category distinctions.* Hewstone et al. (2002, p. 591) argue that

> to protect against loss of distinctiveness for groups involved in contact, two factors are important: (1) the salience of group boundaries should be maintained during contact, to promote generalization across members of the target out-group; (2) each group should be distinct in terms of the expertise and experience it brings to the contact situation, resulting in "mutual intergroup differentiation" (MID), where groups recognize and value mutual superiorities and inferiorities.

In such circumstances, groups should be encouraged to recognize and value differences between them. This can be accomplished by ensuring that when two groups cooperate, it is clear that they have separate roles that maintain their positive distinctiveness (e.g. Dovidio, Gaertner, & Validzic, 1998). Encouraging social services and health service workers to cooperate will be more effective if their distinct expertise is acknowledged and applied in interacting but distinct roles.

Research in this field also suggests that when an in-group member has positive contact with an out-group member, this leads to favourable out-group attitudes when the contact is with a "typical" out-group member and/or there is frequent reference to the person's out-group membership (Brown, Vivian, & Hewstone, 1999; Brown et al., 2001). The implication of this is that the person from Company A, who has a positive (perhaps friendly, constructive, and humorous) meeting with someone from Company B with which they are to merge, will have a more favourable view of Company B if that person is seen as a typical employee of Company B (rather than being the CEO, for example).

Thus far we have considered interpersonal and intergroup contact as means of reducing intergroup hostility and increasing intergroup cooperation. These contacts, of course, can reinforce one another, as when we interact with friends who are members of an out-group. However, this effect is most likely to be positive when out-group identity is emphasized during the course of the interaction (Hewstone, Rubin, & Willis, 2002).

8. *Increasing complexity of categorizations.* The "dual identity" model (Dovidio, Gaertner, & Validzic, 1998; Gaertner et al., 1990, 1994, 1999; Gaertner & Dovidio, 2000) ensures the benefits of both CII approaches and MID are achieved. The aim is to reduce bias between subgroups that share a common superordinate identity, rather than consider

themselves as members of separate groups—exactly the circumstances we find in most medium-sized organizations. The sales and marketing department and the production department are separate groups, but they can be encouraged to emphasize both their separate and common superordinate identity (employees of the same company).

Where there is a dominant majority, it will tend to favour assimilation of minority groups (e.g. health care workers often demand that attached social workers do things their way and conform to health care norms and values). Minorities in such situations tend to favour "pluralistic integration" such that they maintain their distinctive subgroup identity while achieving the privileges of being part of the bigger whole. Thus they will tend to have competing preferences about the approach to be adopted. This is particularly characteristic of the problems of mergers or acquisitions in which a dominant or large organization seeks to subsume a smaller or less successful organization (Berry, 1997; Dovidio, Gaertner, & Kafati, 2000; van Oudenhoven, Prins, & Buunk, 1998; Wolsko et al., 2000). Thus a dual identity may reduce bias for the minority, but not the majority (Zagefka & Brown, in press). Mummendey and Wenzel (1999) argue that a superordinate category must be developed that enables the retention of subgroups' distinctive characteristics in the face of the characteristics of the dominant group.

9. *Crossed categorization.* Encouraging in-group members to classify out-group members on multiple dimensions, especially where this involves category membership including overlaps between in- and out-group members, is another effective way of reducing out-group bias: in addition to being a social worker, this person is a Houston Astros fan; she plays the cello; she is a supporter of Amnesty International. Such methods reduce bias because they make the process of categorization more complex and cognitively demanding; they decrease the power and importance of any single category; they push in-group members to be aware that the out-group consists of a number of different subgroups; they ensure out-group members are classified on multiple dimensions, at least some of which are likely to be positive; and they increase the likelihood of trust and contact across boundaries. There is also evidence that emphasizing cross-cutting social identities as part of cooperative contact between groups is particularly effective at reducing intergroup bias. Thus bringing together the two marketing departments to cooperate on a new joint marketing strategy is likely to be especially effective if cross-cutting categorizations are emphasized.

Political scientists argue that such cross-cutting cleavages make for stability of exchanges and, therefore, trust in plural societies. However, they caution that (for example) state encouragement of these cross-cutting categories is often perceived by minority groups as denying fundamental and valued differences. For example, some feminists argue such approaches assume that there is nothing fundamentally different between a man and a woman and that, further, under the guise of equality we ignore the reality of manipulation of power by dominant groups (in this context some men). Thus the strategy could be seen as a subtle ploy to silence a restive minority.[1] Certainly, where there is one overriding category (as when Company A is a small family firm facing a hostile takeover from a large Company B), such a strategy is unlikely to be effective.

Cross-categorizations can be particularly effective when out-group members are simultaneously classified as in-group or out-group members on multiple dimensions. Such overlapping category memberships reduce bias because they make social categorization more complex; decrease the importance of any single in-group/out-group distinction; make

[1] We are grateful to Catherine Fieschi for alerting us to this perspective.

perceivers aware that the out-group consists of different subgroups; ensure out-group members are classified on multiple dimensions; and increase the degree of contact and trust across category boundaries (Brewer, 2000). There is evidence that emphasizing cross-cutting social identities or role assignments during cooperative intergroup contact is especially effective.

All of these approaches to reducing intergroup bias offer strategies that can be employed within and between organizations. The challenge is discovering what works when, for which groups, and in what situations. Some will be effective in managing bias and conflict within organizations and some will clearly be more suitable for managing relations between organizations. Of course, multiple strategies are likely to work together in some situations, rather than single-pill fixes. This presents a challenging but realistic research and intervention agenda for the future.

Immense damage is done to organizational functioning as a result of the problems of intergroup bias. We have used the examples of cooperation between health and social care a number of times, and examples of the conflict between different groups of health care professionals. These problems hinder the provision of the best health and social care in our societies. Overcoming them is a (if not the) key challenge for students of teamworking and cooperation in organizations. We also have to test which strategies are effective in organizational contexts: building trust via encouraging increasing intergroup risk; increasing contact between groups in ways that maximize the likelihood of positive experience and minimize the likelihood of single and negative categorizations; encouraging raised awareness of these issues among managers, employees of organizations, and particularly leaders; teaching leaders to emphasize positive discourse about out-groups and their members that emphasizes complexity of categories and the benefits of engagement. There is, moreover, a need to encourage an understanding of the importance of forgiveness when values or rights appear to have been violated by out-group members.

Examining intra- and intergroup relations in organizations by considering the emotional reactions of people is, we propose, a potentially powerful way in which social scientists can delve more deeply and powerfully into understanding the complexities of the ways we humans interact. Doing so in organizational settings, we believe, may help us to make advances that are denied to those working in more desperate contexts, such as wars, hate crimes, and atrocities. But such advances just may have applications in those contexts as well. But there are other routes to liberation. As Fieschi (Chapter 4 this volume) has suggested, humans also develop by creating new institutions and organizational forms to meet their need. The impact of institutions on human behaviour should not be underestimated and their impact on cooperation promises to be revolutionary (just think of the impact of the Internet on human relationships and knowledge). It is to a consideration of the new integrated organization that we now turn.

THE NEW INTEGRATED ORGANIZATION

Since Ronald Coase's (1937) "The nature of the firm", a long line of research has argued that the existence, boundaries, and internal functioning of a firm can be best understood in terms of economic arguments—profit motive, property rights, incentives, and contracts (Alchian & Demsetz, 1972; Foss, 1996; Williamson, 1985). Despite this tradition, some scholars are beginning to make a case that organizations are more than economic institutions; they are unique for the willingness of individuals in organizations to cooperate with one another to generate new knowledge (Argote, 1999; Moran & Ghoshal, 1999). Dosi, Winter, and Teece (1992) contend that organizations are distinctive because they are able to learn and grow based on the new knowledge their members produce. Kogut and Zander (1992) argue that organizations benefit from their members' ability to cooperate and integrate, leading to the development of new knowledge. Nahapiet and Ghoshal (1998) theorize that organization members create new knowledge through the combination and exchange process. They claim that the organizational capabilities for creating new knowledge is a key social feature of the firm, providing it an organizational advantage over individual and other market arrangements.

At the heart of the knowledge creation process is the willingness of individuals to cooperate for the mutual benefit of the organization. Nahapiet and Ghoshal (1998) argue that for individuals to come together and exchange information and ideas into new knowledge they must have access to one another, perceive value from the knowledge creation process, and have the individual capability to combine information into new knowledge. The value of new knowledge to the organization is that it allows for greater flexibility and adaptability to changing environmental concerns. Indeed, it is in rapidly changing environments that the role of cooperation and a social based view of the firm may provide its greatest insights (see Coff, Chapter 23 this volume).

The recent emphasis on the organizational capabilities for cooperating and creating new knowledge is important because it highlights how firms may grow and develop independent of market and economic conditions. As such, it has the potential to provide a new, and perhaps more encompassing, social explanation of the firm, separate from economic theory (Nahapiet & Ghoshal, 1998). This perspective may also be more appropriate for understanding today's extended organization where boundaries are unclear and constantly changing (see Agarwal, Chapter 21 this volume).

As the chapters in this book suggest, if organizations have social advantages relative to other economic market arrangements, it is because individuals in organizations agree to cooperate to achieve the firm's goal (Young, Chapter 5 this volume). After all, organizations are social entities in which individuals come together and interact to achieve some purpose (Drazin, Kazanjian, & Blyler, Chapter 22 this volume; March & Simon, 1958; Porter, Lawler, & Hackman, 1975). As such, organizations emerge under conditions of shared beliefs, joint effort, and patterned behaviour (Galbraith, 1977; Thompson, 1967). The challenge for organizational designers is to develop the proper systems and incentives to achieve the necessary cooperation and integration.

The concept of organizational design reflects the combination of the definition of the organization as a social and purposeful entity, and the concept of strategic choice, or the proposition that there are choices about how organizational goals are to be achieved (Galbraith, 1977). Indeed, as noted by Drazin, Kazanjian, and Blyler (Chapter 22 this volume), organizational design is the decision process to achieve coherence between goals of the organization and the people who will do the work (Galbraith, 1977). The concept of strategic choice suggests that there are important decisions regarding the alternative organizing modes and how individuals are to behave in order to achieve the organization's goals (Child, 1972).

With regard to organizational design choices, two extreme positions exist in the literature. At one end of the continuum, perhaps representing the economic efficiency interpretations of the firm, is the mechanistic structure (Burns & Stalker, 1961), the differentiated organization (Lawrence & Lorsch, 1967), the machine organization (Mintzberg, 1979), and the defender organization (Miles & Snow, 1978). At the other end of the continuum, conceivably representing more social/cooperative principles, is the organic organization (Burns & Stalker, 1961), the integrated organization (Lawrence & Lorsch, 1967), the innovative organization (Mintzberg, 1979), and the prospector firm (Miles & Snow, 1978). Although these extreme positions differ on many counts, they are most dissimilar in views of human nature. The transactional perspective perceives employees as opportunistic and self-serving, whereas the social viewpoint assumes employees are trusting, seeking cooperative, long-term relationships. We will focus on the design principles reflecting the social/cooperative features of organization. We will first review the literature on how organizations achieve integration. Next we will explore some new principles of organizational design that may be more appropriate in today's changing environments.

Traditional Ways of Achieving Integration

In today's increasing complex turbulent environments, organizations must segment themselves according to the specialized knowledge required in their environments. This structural segmentation is necessary in order to deal with increased environmental uncertainty (Thompson, 1967). The reality is that no single worker or manager is likely to have the necessary knowledge to deal with today's complex environment. Yet, this segmentation of knowledge creates coordination/cooperation problems if the organization is to effectively deal with uncertainty. The concept of integration has been used to explain how firms can achieve the necessary coordination and cooperation. Lawrence and Lorsch (1967, p. 11) defined integration as the quality of the "state of collaboration that exists among departments that are required to achieve unity of effort by the demands of the environment". We broaden this definition of integration for today's extended network organization as the quality of cooperation that exists among different stakeholders and knowledge workers to maintain an ongoing organization/environment fit. We are concerned not only with integration within the organization but across its stakeholders and networks of relationships.

Galbraith (1977) describes how organizations can use lateral forms of communication and joint decision making as an alternative to hierarchy to achieve cooperation and coordination. He identifies four types of lateral relations that can facilitate cooperation: direct contact, liaison roles, task forces, and teams. With good lateral relations, decision makers can achieve cooperation and integration at the appropriate level of knowledge sharing. Thus, they can avoid time-consuming delays in sending the decision to a higher level.

Galbraith (1977) notes that the simplest form of lateral relations is direct contact. With direct contact, individual employees work together to solve the problems where they identify them instead of referring them to upper management. As the volume of information between differentiated knowledge workers grows, it is often necessary to set up liaison integrator roles. Liaison roles involve the specialized task designed to facilitate communication and cooperation between differentiated groups as opposed to sending all information up the hierarchy. Task forces may be useful when the number of contacts necessary to create change increases dramatically. Task forces might be composed of individuals across the various segmented groups. Task forces are specifically formed to solve cooperation and coordination problems that cut across domains of knowledge. As the tasks involved become more unpredictable, cooperation and teamwork can be an effective solution to coordination.

We may think of the four types of lateral relationships as useful depending upon the nature of the coordination/cooperation problem. As the coordination/cooperation problem becomes more complex, we can imagine the type of lateral relations used will move from direct contact to increasing use of formal coordination teams.

Integration in the Extended Organization

As we have described in this book, the boundaries of today's organization are often extended beyond the traditional definitions of the firm, to include networks of suppliers and buyers and even competitors (Agarwal, Chapter 21 this volume). Some of these relationships are formal (e.g. alliances and contracts), yet many are informal and depend on interpersonal relationships (Coff, Chapter 23 this volume). The traditional tools of integration, as described above, do not deal directly with the extended boundaries of the firm or the question of how to achieve cooperation between extended and less directly related and connected knowledge workers.

A key distinction of the extended organization is that knowledge workers will likely be dispersed and under less direct control of managers (Agarwal, Chapter 21 this volume). Thus, the design issues in the extended organization have to do with setting up the parameters and conditions so that knowledge workers can work independently, while also be encouraged to cooperate in the exchange and combination process (Drazin, Kazanjian, and Blyler, Chapter 22 this volume). We are concerned with their capability to cooperate, their motivation to cooperate, and the access they have to other knowledge workers to achieve cooperation (Nahapiet & Ghoshal, 1998). We contend that organizational designers can proactively affect workers' capability, motivation, and access by developing policies and procedures that influence the stocks of knowledge (e.g. individual knowledge through selection and training), the interconnectedness or flows among knowledge workers and stakeholders (e.g. procedures for developing networks), and how this knowledge is integrated (e.g. culture). In proposing an introductory model of cooperative knowledge creation, we aspire to provide a richer and more complete understanding of the social advantages firms have over markets.

Knowledge Stocks and Cooperation

Dierickx and Cool (1989) use the bathtub metaphor to distinguish asset stocks, which for our purposes may reflect the stock of existing knowledge among key knowledge workers, from flows, which reflect the mechanisms by which changes in stocks of knowledge occur. We may think of the stock of knowledge as average knowledge of key knowledge workers and top management team members, defined as the years of education and industry experience and the diversity of information and knowledge this group holds. From a design perspective, organizations can influence the stock of individual knowledge through their human resource selection and development policies (Hayes & Wheelwright, 1984).

Most studies of organizational learning and organizational memory recognize initial knowledge of employees as a key factor in organizational learning, and employees as a primary repository of organizational knowledge (Argote, 1999). Indeed, the natural abilities, intelligence, and skills acquired from informal and formal education and job experience of key employees in the firm reflect the level of the organization's human capital

(Becker, 1964). Cohen and Levinthal (1990) argued that the greater the unique knowledge held by individuals in the firm, the greater the potential for cooperation and new knowledge development. They specifically note how a lack of investment in individual knowledge and expertise can foreclose growth of new knowledge. Hargadon and Sutton (1997) demonstrated that successful cooperation and innovation not only depend on the connections of technological brokers to other brokers but also on the ability of these brokers to store and retrieve knowledge when confronting problems or opportunities. Thus, we predict that employees who possess greater knowledge, skills, and abilities will be more likely and capable of cooperating to exchange and combine knowledge in a desire to learn, grow, and develop (Simon, 1985). In essence, such employees will be more capable of bringing something new to the exchange and combination process.

Human Resource Practices and Cooperation

The strategic human resource (HR) literature, which views HR policies from an organizational design viewpoint (Stevens, Chapter 24 this volume), has made a distinction between transactional or efficiency-based HR policies and more social relational policies (Arthur, 1992; Rousseau, 1995). We propose that the level of cooperation may be affected by two opposing sets of HR practices: high commitment, representing a social design perspective, and transactional, reflecting an efficiency and individualism design perspective (Arthur, 1992; Rousseau, 1995).

High-commitment HR practices are defined as a set of mutually supporting HR policies that manage and motivate employees to cooperate and work together. This set of HR practices may include policies to affect the level of cooperation through performance appraisals that encourage cooperation (Rousseau, 1995), training on cooperative work strategies (e.g. mentoring, job rotation), and compensation systems (e.g. stock ownership, team-based pay) which are designed to increase cooperation and knowledge sharing (Delany & Huselid, 1996). Because high-commitment HR practices demonstrate investment in employees, individual workers are more inclined to contribute their know-how and be motivated to cooperate and learn firm-specific skills and knowledge (Rousseau, 1995). Research suggests that high-commitment HR practices have a particularly positive effect on performance when the business or manufacturing strategy requires cooperation or high levels of discretionary effort on the part of employees (MacDuffie, 1995).

In contrast, transactional practices are expected to limit employee motivation to cooperate beyond their formal agreements (Rousseau, 1995). Transactional practices are defined as that set of policies and procedures that control behaviours through formal work rules, direct monitoring, and rewarding for individual outputs (Arthur, 1994). For example, Tsui et al. (1997) found that some firms attempt to directly control work behaviours and expect employees to perform the tasks directly stipulated in their employment contract. A transactional set of HR practices would include recruitment and selection based on ability to perform a specific job or function, individual-based pay tied to performance, and monitoring performance appraisals (Arthur, 1992). Because this type of system supports an individual employee–organization relationship, employees have little motivation to cooperate more than their employment contracts specifically state. Overall, we predict that high-commitment practices will lead to greater cooperation and thus the greater potential for knowledge exchange and combination. In essence, high-commitment policies enhance the motivation of employees to cooperate, and this will facilitate the exchange and combination process.

Organizational Policies to Connect Knowledge Workers and Cooperation

In the extended organization, we are interested in the extent of interconnectedness of key boundary spanners and knowledge workers to important stakeholders and employees, and the potential knowledge flows that stem from these connections. The extent of interconnectedness is important because it facilitates access to knowledge. Thompson (1967) and Mintzberg (1973) argue that the boundary-spanning role is crucial because it provides a key linking pin role between internal and external constituents that can provide critical information and knowledge. We conceive of interconnectedness in terms of the extent to which boundary spanners are electronically linked to key stakeholders and employees, and the organizational policies that reinforce the development of these networks.

The strategic importance of information systems has increased with advances in computer and Internet technology (Roberts & Grabowski, 1997). As information technology is integrated in the organization, it increases the potential linkages that facilitate effective information exchange and workflow (Agarwal, Chapter 21 this volume). As these technologies become increasingly sophisticated, becoming more intelligent, they have the capability to include more human processing capability, including sophisticated search models for gathering information, decision models for evaluating information, and data-mining models for identifying patterns and opportunities. By increasing the access of knowledge workers, the technology has the potential to increase cooperation. For example, Fulk, Schmitz, and Steinfeld (1990) show how electronic linkages (e.g. e-mail) increase the level of organization communication in an organization. Galbraith (1977) contends that the key challenge of organization design is to be certain that organization decision makers have the key information at the appropriate time. Information technology is ideally suited to such needs (Roberts & Grabowski, 1997).

For many years, Peter Drucker has contended that the most effective organizations establish multidirectional information paths to the knowledge of key stakeholders and employees. Thieraut (1999) claims that the best way to achieve cooperation and knowledge sharing is through an electronic knowledge-sharing system. He notes, “By bringing all sources of information together and providing universal access to decision makers, it is possible to build an integrated knowledge management system environment” (Thieraut, 1999, p. 105). He suggests that by tying employees and stakeholders together, the new knowledge that is developed will be greater than the sum of the parts.

From an organizational design perspective, top managers can also encourage boundary spanners to build their individual networks by providing them time and resources to attend professional meetings and to engage in non-work social activities. For example, by providing key boundary spanners the opportunity to attend professional meetings, the organization may be able to increase the size and range of contacts; by encouraging spanners to participate in non-work activities, such as professional, social, and community associations, these managers may increase the strength of their network ties. Dougherty (1997) argues that organizational designers must create an environment where individuals have the freedom to cooperate, interact, and learn and grow. Policies that encourage employees to attend professional and social meetings outside of the workplace can extend organizational linkages and connections to important knowledge and information. Organizational policies that promote network development can be considered investments in social capital (Burt, 1982) and the benefits that flow from this capital will primarily be in information and knowledge (Nahapiet & Ghoshal, 1998).

Strength of Ties and Cooperation

Strong ties are defined as the closeness of contact and relationship between individuals in a network (Granovetter, 1973). While strong ties may be a natural outcome of continual long-term relationships, organizations can also facilitate the development of strong ties by job assignments, and by supporting network-building activities, for example, membership to social and business organizations. Although weak ties may provide certain efficiency benefits, especially where the meaning of information is not problematic (Granovetter, 1973; Nahapiet & Ghoshal, 1998) or when networks are used for search activities (Hansen, 1999), strong ties will be critical when the information is uncertain and ambiguous, such as in new knowledge generation. There is significant evidence that when ties are strong, individuals will be more trusting and cooperate for mutual benefit (Mishira, 1996). In general, we argue that the individual's strength of ties will impact the level of cooperation and knowledge sharing through the trusting relationships. Knowledge workers with strong ties will be able to access more information and knowledge and be able to transfer more complex knowledge that can be used in the combination and exchange process (Hansen, 1999).

Embedded Culture and Cooperation

Researchers have recently examined the role of embedded culture in generating cooperation and knowledge sharing (Weick & Westley, 1997). Culture generally is considered part of an organization's structure (Argote, 1999; Dougherty, 1997; Galbraith, 1977) and subject to organizational design principles. Levitt and March (1988) contend that the knowledge and procedural information embedded in the organization's culture are important because they serve as an expression of how things in the organization are to be done (cooperate or not). Grant notes that the organizations need mechanisms to integrate the knowledge held by various stakeholders and employees. These mechanisms are necessitated by the differences in knowledge across individuals. He notes that, "The importance of common knowledge is that it permits individuals to share and integrate aspects of knowledge which are not common between them" (Grant, 1996, pp. 115–116).

Culture is defined as the system of values and behavioural norms widely shared by organization members that motivates and controls future behaviour. We suggest both that organizations will vary culturally and that culture can be developed and shaped in a purposeful manner by management (Denison, 1990; Kotter & Heskett, 1992; Tushman & O'Reilly, 1997). One aspect of an organization's culture that is important for cooperation is the extent to which the organization values individual behaviours versus team behaviours. In general, we believe cultures that encourage teamwork and cooperation will facilitate knowledge integration and hence increases in the new knowledge that is developed.

Organizational theory and strategic management are moving away from economic and transaction costs-based arguments for a theory of the firm in favour of social and cooperative knowledge generation viewpoints. The literature on organizational design has emphasized the concept of integration as a way of achieving cooperation and unity of organizational effort. However, this literature has emphasized integration within organization and does not address cooperation in today's extended organization. We have suggested that organizational designers can proactively impact the level of cooperation and new knowledge generation by influencing the stocks of knowledge held by individuals, the access and flows of knowledge through linkages within and among key stakeholders, and knowledge integration through embedded culture. Note that all of these approaches rely on procedures to indirectly affect cooperation by affecting the conditions that should increase the likelihood that new knowledge will be generated. However, as the chapters in this volume indicate, achieving cooperation is complex and in need of much more conceptual and empirical work. This work is necessary if we are to fully understand the social advantages that firms may enjoy over market transactions. Let us finally turn to consider what knowledge we have derived from this extended examination of cooperation offered by this handbook and to gaze into the future of the field.

ENDURING ISSUES AND FUTURE PERSPECTIVES

Cooperative work can help us move away from win–lose thinking to understand how we can integrate our efforts and ideas for mutual benefit. Cooperative work, as the chapters have attested, can pay off for individuals, organizations, and society. But realizing these advantages, especially when change is so rapid and fragmentation so possible, poses significant intellectual and practical obstacles. Cooperative work offers the promise of reconciling the reality of individual self-interest with the essential benefits of groups and organizations. The choice does not need to be between the group and the self. We can move beyond thinking whether action is selfish or altruistic, for the self or for the group. Cooperative work not only allows for, but is based on, the understanding that people are pursuing their individual interests together.

The handbook chapters recognize that, just as every person is unique, every group and organization has its own ways and methods, and every society has its own culture. But differences need not threaten nor divide us. With cooperative work, our diversity becomes a significant advantage as we employ our various abilities and perspectives to improve our common endeavours. Clearly, the prevalence of intergroup hostility and warfare underlies how difficult applying this insight is and how tremendous is the potential payoff.

Progress has been made in our understanding that conflict complements cooperative work. Through conflict within cooperation, group members express their individuality, become known and valued, and problems are solved and implemented. Conflict when handled cooperatively communicates genuine respect for individuals as well as commitment to quality task accomplishment. Strengthening and applying this understanding require persistence and courage.

Much more theorizing and research are needed on power and hierarchy. The choice is not between leadership and teamwork, for groups require a great deal of attention and care by both supervisors and members. High- and low-power people, leaders and employees, value and assist each other to the extent they believe they are cooperatively united. Yet it is clear that significant barriers obstruct strong relationships across hierarchical levels. Managers and employees will continue to experiment with leadership and power—the organizations of the future may well surprise us all.

Justice is the first principle of organizations. Organizations where employees feel unfairly treated are in danger. There are no simple steps to developing an organization where procedures are open and responsive, the distribution of benefits and burdens are accepted, and people feel respected and supported. We have much work to do to ensure leadership styles, labour–management relationships, and HR management practices reinforce fair, cooperative work.

And fairness and respect are as critical for working across organizations and cultures as they are within organizations. Cross-cultural research has focused on identifying value differences among societies that make misunderstandings more likely and cooperative work more difficult. Researchers are beginning to identify how obstacles can be overcome so that diverse people learn about and learn from each other.

We are just beginning to understand how cooperative work is essential for industries, indeed the economy as a whole. While there are important competitive aspects of the market system, we have too glibly extrapolated to assume that competition should dominate relations among organizations and relegated cooperation as relevant only within organizations. Relational marketing, supply chain, and industry research have reaffirmed that organizations are highly interdependent and can often pursue their missions and provide customer value most effectively through cooperative work. Governments are not simply neutral and hands-off institutions, but are essential for providing the education, political leadership, and infrastructure vital to a robust economy. Shaping education systems that build the skills of cooperation and teamwork is a vital task for future governments, but currently much neglected by most Western governments. Supporting the global economy requires new insights into how to foster cooperative work across diverse, geographically distributed organizations.

Competition and cooperation are compatible. There is much discussion about cooperative–competitive mixed situations and combining their value. Organizational research has not, though, much documented the conditions and dynamics by which competition can complement cooperative productive work. This research has the potential to clarify both concepts as well as improve organizational practice.

The various perspectives of social scientists are needed to understand cooperative work. Structure and power, incentives and rewards, cultural values, and justice concerns all impact cooperative work and are in turn affected by it. Cooperative work is part of strategic management, leadership, and most other management fields. But these cooperative research partnerships require researchers to extend their paradigms and reach out to their colleagues. Researchers and practitioners have joined forces in developing cooperative learning for schools and universities (Johnson & Johnson, Chapter 9 this volume). Researchers have shown the conditions under which cooperative groups promote student learning and, together with educators, developed and tested professional procedures to implement cooperative learning appropriately and effectively in the classroom. We need many more such alliances. Unfortunately, researchers tend to be oriented only to other researchers and their journals. Many organizational leaders are under great pressure to find quick fixes and short-term solutions. We need mutual commitment and cooperative relationships across the research–practice boundary to develop valid, applicable knowledge about the antecedents, dynamics, and consequences of cooperative work.

Learning to work together is fundamental because cooperative work stimulates learning. When people work cooperatively, they suggest and advise, question and challenge, and integrate their views to create new understandings. Managers and employees, researchers and practitioners, regulators and the regulated can be cooperatively united behind the common effort to strengthen their relationships and their collaboration. We all have a vested interest in developing and applying knowledge on cooperative work. Building theory, research, and testing practical procedures for cooperative work provide a realistic basis for confidence that we will together prosper and deal with the threats and adversities that threaten to divide us. We hope that this handbook will make an effective contribution to that effort.

REFERENCES

Ainsworth, M. (1989). Attachments beyond infancy. *American Psychologist, 44*, 709–716.

Alchian, A. A. & Demsetz, H. (1972). Production, information, costs, and economic organization. In *Economic Forces at Work: Selected Works by Armen Alchian*. Indianapolis, Ind.: Liberty Press.

Argote, L. (1999). *Organizational Learning: Creating, Retaining and Transferring Knowledge*. Boston: Kluwer Academic Publishers.

Arthur, J. (1992). The links between business strategy and industrial relations systems in American steel minimills. *Industrial and Labor Relations Review, 45*(3), 488–506.

Arthur, J. (1994). Effects of human resource systems on manufacturing performance and turnover. *Academy of Management Journal, 37*, 670–687.

Axelrod, R. & Hamilton, W. D. (1981). The evolution of cooperation. *Science, 211*, 1390–1396.

Barash, D. P. (1977). *Sociobiology and Behavior*. New York: Elsevier.

Barchas, P. (1986). A sociophysiological orientation to small groups. In E. Lawler (ed.), *Advances in Group Processes* (Vol. 3, pp. 209–246). Greenwich, Conn.: JAI Press.

Batson, C. D., Polycarpou, M. P., Harmon-Jones, E., Imhoff, H. J., Mitchener, E. C. et al. (1997). Empathy and attitudes: can feeling for a member of a stigmatized group improve feelings toward the group? *Journal of Personality and Social Psychology, 72*, 105–118.

Baumeister, R. F. & Leary, M. R. (1995). The need to belong: desire for interpersonal attachments as a fundamental human motivation. *Psychological Bulletin, 117*, 497–529.

Baumeister, R. F., Wotman, S. R., & Stillwell, A. M. (1993). Unrequited love: on heartbreak, anger, guilt, scriptlessness, and humiliation. *Journal of Personality and Social Psychology, 64*, 377–394.

Becker, G. S. (1964). *Human Capital*. New York: Columbia University Press.

Berry, J. W. (1997). Immigration, acculturation, and adaptation. *Applied Psychology: An International Review, 46*, 5–68.

Bettencourt, B. A., Brewer, M. B., Rogers-Croak, M., & Miller, N. (1992). Cooperation and the reduction of intergroup bias: the role of reward structure and social orientation. *Journal of Experimental Social Psychology, 28*, 301–319.

Billig, M. & Tajfel, H. (1973). Social categorization and similarity in intergroup behavior. *European Journal of Social Psychology, 3*, 27–51.

Bowlby, J. (1969). *Attachment and Loss*. London: Hogarth.

Brewer, M. B. (1999). The psychology of prejudice: ingroup love or outgroup hate? *Journal of Social Issues, 55*, 429–444.

Brewer, M. B. (2000). Reducing prejudice through cross-categorization: effects of multiple social identities. In S. Oskamp (ed.), *Reducing Prejudice and Discrimination* (pp. 165–184). Mahwah, NJ: Erlbaum.

Brewer, M. B. (2001). Ingroup identification and intergroup conflict: when does ingroup love become outgroup hate? In R. Ashmore, L. Jussim, & D. Wilder (eds), *Social Identity, Intergroup Conflict, and Conflict Reduction*. New York: Oxford University Press.

Brown, R., Maras, P., Masser, B., Vivian, J., & Hewstone, M. (2001). Life on the ocean wave: testing some intergroup hypotheses in a naturalistic setting. *Group Processes and Intergroup Relations, 4*, 81–98.

Brown, R., Vivian, J., & Hewstone, M. (1999). Changing attitudes through intergroup contact: the effects of group membership salience. *European Journal of Social Psychology, 29*, 741–764.

Burns, T. & Stalker, G. M. (1961). *The Management of Innovation*. London: Tavistock.

Burt, R. S. (1982). *Toward a Structural Theory of Action*. New York: Academic Press.
Buss, D. M. (1990). The evolution of anxiety and social exclusion. *Journal of Social and Clinical Psychology, 9*, 196–210.
Buss, D. M. (1991). Evolutionary personality psychology. *Annual Review of Psychology, 42*, 459–491.
Child, J. (1972). Organization structure, environment and performance: the role of strategic choice. *Sociology*, January, 1–22.
Coase, R. H. (1937). The nature of the firm. *Economica, 4*, 386–405.
Cohen, S. & Wills, T. A. (1985). Stress, social support, and the buffering hypothesis. *Psychological Bulletin, 98*, 310–357.
Cohen, W. M. & Levinthal, D. A. (1990). Absorptive capacity: a new perspective in learning and innovation. *Administrative Science Quarterly, 17*, 178–184.
Delaney, J. T. & Huselid, M. (1996). The impact of human resource management practices on perceptions of organizational performance. *Academy of Management Journal, 39*, 949–969.
Denison, D. R. (1990). *Corporate Culture and Organizational Effectiveness*. New York: Wiley.
Dierickx, I. & Cool, K. (1989). Asset stock accumulation and sustainability of competitive advantage. *Management Science, 33*, 1504–1513.
Dobbs, M. & Crano, W. D. (2001). Outgroup accountability in the minimal group paradigm: implications for aversive discrimination and social identity theory. *Personality and Social Psychology Bulletin, 27*, 355–365.
Dosi, G., Winter, S. G., & Teece, D. J. (1992). Towards a theory of corporate coherence. In G. Dosi, R. Giannetti, & P. A. Toninelli (eds), *Technology and Enterprise in Historical Perspective*. Oxford, UK: Clarendon Press.
Dougherty, D. (1997). Organizing for innovation. In S. Clegg, C. Hardy, & W. Nord (eds), *The Handbook of Organizational Design* (pp. 424–439). London: Sage.
Dovidio, J. F., Gaertner, S. L., & Kafati, G. (2000). Group identity and intergroup relations: the common ingroup identity model. In S. Thye, E. J. Lawler, M. Macy, & H. Walker (eds), *Advances in Group Processes* (Vol. 17, pp. 1–35). Stanford, Conn.: JAI Press.
Dovidio, J. F., Gaertner, S. L., & Validzic, A. (1998). Intergroup bias: status, differentiation, and a common in-group identity. *Journal of Personality and Social Psychology, 75*, 109–120.
Dovidio, J., Kawakami, K., Johnson, C., Johnson, B., & Howard, A. (1997). The nature of prejudice: automatic and controlled processes. *Journal of Experimental Social Psychology, 33*, 510–540.
Esses, V. M., Jackson, L. M., & Armstrong, T. L. (1998). Intergroup competition and attitudes toward immigrants and immigration: an instrumental model of group conflict. *Journal of Social Issues, 54*, 699–724.
Finlay, K. & Stephan, W. (2000). Improving intergroup relations: the effects of empathy on racial attitudes. *Journal of Applied Social Psychology, 30*, 1720–1737.
Foss, N. (1996). Knowledge-based approaches to the theory of the firm: some critical comments. *Organization Science, 7*(5), 470–476.
Fulk, J., Schmitz, J., & Steinfeld, C. W. (1990). A social influence model of technology use. In J. Fulk & C. Steinfield (eds), *Organizations and Communication Technology* (pp. 117–141). Newbury Park, Calif.: Sage.
Gaertner, S. L. & Dovidio, J. F. (2000). *Reducing Intergroup Bias: The Common Ingroup Identity Model*. Philadelphia, Pa: Psychology Press.
Gaertner, S. L., Dovidio, J. F., Rust, M. C., Nier, J. A., Banker, B. S. et al. (1999). Reducing intergroup bias: elements of intergroup cooperation. *Journal of Personality and Social Psychology, 76*, 388–402.
Gaertner, S. L., Mann, J. A., Dovidio, J. F., Murrell, A. J., & Pomare, M. (1990). How does cooperation reduce intergroup bias? *Journal of Personality and Social Psychology, 59*, 692–704.
Gaertner, S. L., Rust, M. C., Dovidio, J. F., Bachman, B. A., & Anastasio, P. A. (1994). The contact hypothesis: the role of a common ingroup identity on reducing intergroup bias. *Small Group Research, 25*, 224–249.
Galbraith, J. (1977). *Organization Design*. Reading, Mass.: Addison-Wesley.
Galinsky, A. D. & Moskowitz, G. B. (2000). Perspective-taking: decreasing stereotype expression, stereotype accessibility, and in-group favoritism. *Journal of Personality and Social Psychology, 73*, 708–724.

Granovetter, M. (1973). The strength of weak ties. *American Journal of Sociology, 78*, 1360–1380.

Grant, R. M. (1996). Prospering in dynamically-competitive environments: organizational capability as knowledge integration. *Organization Science, 7*, 375–387.

Greenberg, J., Simon, L., Pyszczynski, T., Solomon, S., & Chatel, D. (1992). Terror management and tolerance: does mortality salience always intensify negative reactions to others who threaten one's worldview? *Journal of Personality and Social Psychology, 63*, 212–220.

Hagendoorn, L., Linssen, H., & Tumanov, S. (2001). Intergroup relations in states of the former Soviet Union: the perception of Russians. *European Monographs in Social Psychology*. Hove East: Psychology Press.

Hansen, M. (1999). The search–transfer problem: the role of weak ties in sharing knowledge across organization subunits. *Administrative Science Quarterly, 44*, 82–111.

Hargadon, A. & Sutton, R. (1997). Technology brokering and innovation in a product development firm. *Administrative Science Quarterly, 42*, 716–749.

Hayes, R. & Wheelwright, S. (1984). *Restoring our Competitive Edge: Competing through Manufacturing*. New York: Wiley.

Hays, R. B. (1985). A longitudinal study of friendship development. *Journal of Personality and Social Psychology, 48*, 909–924.

Henderson-King, E., Henderson-King, D., Zhermer, N., Posokhova, S., & Chitcer, V. (1997). In-group favouritism and perceived similarity: a look at Russians' perceptions in the post-Soviet era. *Personality and Social Psychology Bulletin, 23*, 1013–1021.

Hewstone, M., Rubin, M., & Willis, H. (2002). Intergroup bias. *Annual Reviews of Psychology, 53*, 575–604.

Hogan, R., Jones, W., & Cheek, J. (1985). Socioanalytic theory: an alternative to armadillo psychology. In B. M. Schlenker (ed.), *The Self and Social Life* (pp. 175–198). New York: McGraw-Hill.

Horney, K. (1945). *Our Inner Conflicts*. New York: Norton.

Hornsey, M. J. & Hogg, M. A. (1999). Subgroup differentiation as a response to an overly-inclusive group: a test of optimal distinctiveness theory. *European Journal of Social Psychology, 29*, 543–550.

Jetten, J., Spears, R., & Manstead, A. S. R. (1996). Intergroup norms and intergroup discrimination: distinctive self-categorization and social identity effects. *Journal of Personality and Social Psychology, 71*, 1222–1233.

Jetten, J., Spears, R., & Manstead, A. S. R. (1998). Dimensions of distinctiveness: group variability makes a difference to group differentiation. *Journal of Personality and Social Psychology, 74*, 1481–1492.

Jones, W. H. (1981). Loneliness and social contact. *Journal of Social Psychology, 113*, 295–296.

Kawakami, K., Dovidio, J., Moll, J., Hermsen, S., & Russin, A. (2001). Just say no (to stereotyping): effects of training in trait negation on stereotype activation. *Journal of Personality and Social Psychology* (in press).

Kiecolt-Glaser, J. K., Garner, W., Speicher, C., Penn, G. M., Holliday, J., & Glaser, R. (1984a). Psychosocial modifiers of immunocompetence in medical students. *Psychosomatic Medicine, 46*, 7–14.

Kiecolt-Glaser, J. K., Richer, D., George, J., Messick, G., Speicher, C., Garner, W., & Glaser, R. (1984b). Urinary cortisol levels, cellular immunocompetency and loneliness in psychiatric inpatients. *Psychosomatic Medicine, 46*, 15–23.

Kogut, B. & Zander, U. (1992). Knowledge of the firm, combination capabilities, and the replication of technology. *Organization Science, 3*, 383–397.

Kotter, J. P. & Heskett, J. L. (1992). *Corporate Culture and Performance*. New York: Free Press.

Kurzban, R. & Leary, M. P. (2001). Evolutionary origins of stigmatization: the functions of social exclusion. *Psychological Bulletin, 127*, 187–208.

Lauderdale, P., Smith, C., Parker, J., & Inverarity, J. (1984). External threat and the definition of deviance. *Journal of Personality and Social Psychology, 46*, 1058–1068.

Lawrence, P. & Lorsch, J. (1967). *Organization and Environment*. Boston: Harvard Business School Division of Research.

Leary, M. R. (1990). Impression management: a literature review and two component model. *Psychological Bulletin, 107*, 34–47.

Leary, M. R. & Downs, D. L. (1995). Interpersonal functions of the self-esteem motive: the self-esteem system as a sociometer. In M. H. Kernis (ed.), *Efficacy, Agency, and Self-esteem* (pp. 123–144). New York: Plenum.

Levitt, B. & March, J. (1988). Organizational learning. *Annual Review of Sociology, 14*, 319–340.

MacDuffie, J. (1995). Human resource bundles and manufacturing performance: organizational logic and flexible production systems in the world auto industry. *Industrial and Labor Relations Review, 48*, 197–221.

Mackie, D. M., Devos, T., & Smith, E. R. (2000). Intergroup emotions: explaining offensive action tendencies in an intergroup context. *Journal of Personality and Social Psychology, 79*, 602–616.

Mackie, D. M. & Smith, E. R. (1998). Intergroup relations: insights from a theoretically integrative approach. *Psychological Review, 105*, 499–529.

Macrae, C. N. & Bodenhausen, G. V. (2000). Social cognition: thinking categorically about others. *Annual Reviews of Psychology, 51*, 93–120.

March, J. G. & Simon, H. A. (1958). *Organizations*. New York: Wiley.

Miles, R. & Snow, C. (1978). *Organizational Strategy, Structure, and Process*. New York: McGraw-Hill.

Mintzberg, H. (1973). *The Nature of Managerial Work*. Englewood Cliffs, NJ: Prentice-Hall.

Mintzberg, H. (1979). *The Structuring of Organizations*. New York: Prentice-Hall.

Mishira, A. K. (1996). Organizational responses to crisis. The centrality of trust. In R. M. Kramer & T. M. Tyler (eds), *Trust in Organizations* (pp. 261–287). Thousand Oaks, Calif.: Sage.

Monteith, M. (1993). Self-regulation of stereotypical responses: implications for progress in prejudice reduction. *Journal of Personality and Social Psychology, 65*, 469–485.

Monteith, M., Sherman, J., & Devine, P. (1998). Suppression as a stereotype control strategy. *Personality and Social Psychology Review, 1*, 63–82.

Moran, P. & Ghoshal, S. (1999). Markets, firms, and the process of economic development. *Academy of Management Review, 24*(3), 390–412.

Moreland, J. P. (1987). *Scaling the Secular City*. Grand Rapids: Baker Book House.

Mummendey, A. & Wenzel, M. (1999). Social discrimination and tolerance in intergroup relations: reactions to intergroup difference. *Personality and Social Psychology Review, 3*, 158–174.

Nahapiet, J. & Ghoshal, S. (1998). Social capital, intellectual capital, and the organizational advantage. *Academy of Management Review, 23*, 242–266.

Pettigrew, T. F. (1997). Generalized intergroup contact effects on prejudice. *Personality and Social Psychology Bulletin, 23*, 173–185.

Pettigrew, T. F. (1998). Intergroup contact theory. *Annual Reviews of Psychology, 49*, 65–85.

Phinney, J. S., Ferguson, D. L., & Tate, J. D. (1997). Intergroup attitudes among ethnic minority adolescents. *Child Development, 68*, 955–968.

Porter, L., Lawler E., & Hackman, R. (1975). *Behavior in Organizations*. New York: McGraw-Hill.

Pratto, F., Tatar, D. G., & Conway-Lanz, S. (1999). Who gets what and why: determinants of social allocations. *Political Psychology, 20*, 127–150.

Roberts, K. & Grabowski, M. (1997). Organizations, technology and structuring. In S. Clegg, C. Hardy, & W. Nord (eds), *The Handbook of Organizational Design* (pp. 424–439). London: Sage.

Roccas, S. & Schwartz, S. H. (1993). Effects of intergroup similarity on intergroup relations. *European Journal of Social Psychology, 23*, 581–595.

Rousseau, D. (1995). *Psychological Contracts in Organizations: Understanding Written and Unwritten Agreements.* Thousand Oaks, Calif.: Sage.

Sherif, M., Harvey, O. J., White, B. J., Hood, W. R., & Sherif, C. W. (1961). *Intergroup Conflict and Co-operation: The Robbers' Cave experiment*. Norman, Okla.: Institute of Group Relations.

Simon, H. A. (1985). What we know about the creative process. In R. L. Kuhn (ed.), *Frontiers in Creative and Innovative Management*. Cambridge, Mass.: Ballinger.

Smith, E. R. (1993). Social identity and social emotions: towards new conceptualizations of prejudice. In D. Mackie & D. Hamilton (eds), *Affect, Cognition and Stereotyping* (pp. 297–315). San Diego, Calif.: Academic Press.

Stein, A. A. (1976). Conflict and cohesion: a review of the literature. *Journal of Conflict Resolution, 20*, 143–172.

Tajfel, H. (1970). Experiments in intergroup discrimination. *Scientific American, 223*, 96–102.

Tajfel, H. & Billig, M. (1974). Familiarity and categorization in intergroup behavior. *Journal of Experimental Social Psychology, 10*, 159–170.

Thieraut, R. (1999). *Knowledge Management Systems for Business*. Westport, Conn.: Quorum.

Thompson, J. D. (1967). *Organizations in Action*. Englewood Cliffs, NJ: Prentice-Hall.

Tsui, A., Pearce, J., Porter, L., & Tripoli, A. (1997). Alternative approaches to the employee–organization relationship: does investment in employees pay off? *Academy of Management Journal, 40*, 1089–1121.

Turner, J. C. (1985). Social categorization and the self-concept: a social cognitive theory of group behaviour. In E. J. Lawler (ed.), *Advances in Group Processes: Theory and Research* (Vol. 2, pp. 77–122). Greenwich, Conn.: JAI Press.

Tushman, M. L. & O'Reilly, C. A., III (1997). *Winning through Innovation*. Boston, Mass.: Harvard University Press.

Van Oudenhoven, J. P., Prins, K. S., & Buunk, B. (1998). Attitudes of minority and majority members towards adaptation of immigrants. *European Journal of Social Psychology, 28*, 995–1013.

Weick, K. & Westley, F. (1997). Organizational learning: affirming an oxymoron. In S. Clegg, C. Hardy, & W. Nord (eds), *The Handbook of Organizational Design* (pp. 440–458). London: Sage.

West, M. A. (2001). The human team. In N. Anderson, D. S. Ones, H. Sinangil, & C. Viswesvaran (eds), *Handbook of Industrial, Work & Organizational Psychology*, Vol. 2 *Organizational Psychology* (pp. 270–288). London: Sage.

Williams, J. G. & Solano, C. H. (1983). The social reality of feeling lonely: friendship and reciprocation. *Personality and Social Psychology Bulletin, 9*, 237–242.

Williamson, O. E. (1985). *The Economic Institutions of Capitalism*. New York: Free Press.

Wolsko, C., Park, B., Judd, C. M., & Wittenbrink, B. (2000). Framing interethnic ideology: effects of multicultural and color-blind perspectives on judgments of groups and individuals. *Journal of Personality and Social Psychology, 178*, 635–654.

Zagefka, H. & Brown, R. (in press). The relationship between acculturation strategies, relative fit and intergroup relations: immigrant–majority relations in Germany. *European Journal of Social Psychology*.

AUTHOR INDEX

Note: Page numbers in *italic* indicate where the reference is given in full.

SUBJECT INDEX